HISTORY OF POLAND

HISTORY of POLAND

by

ALEKSANDER GIEYSZTOR
Professor of Warsaw University

STEFAN KIENIEWICZ
Professor of Warsaw University (editor-in-chief)

EMANUEL ROSTWOROWSKI
Professor in the Polish Academy of Sciences

JANUSZ TAZBIR
Pofessor in the Polish Academy of Sciences

HENRYK WERESZYCKI
Professor of Cracow University

2nd edition

PWN—POLISH SCIENTIFIC PUBLISHERS · WARSZAWA, 1979

Acknowledgement

The authors owe a great debt to Professor R. F. LESLIE *of Queen Mary College, University of London, and Doctor* GEORGE SAKWA *of Bristol University, for their invaluable contributions in kindly agreeing to undertake the revision of the English text.*

Translation from the Polish manuscript:

KRYSTYNA CĘKALSKA, ILONA RALF-SUEZ, JANINA RODZIŃSKA
LEON SZWAJCER, ANTONI SZYMANOWSKI

Maps:

JÓZEF HUMNICKI, BOGUSŁAW KACZMARSKI, WANDA LEWANDOWSKA
TADEUSZ ŁADOGÓRSKI, WŁADYSŁAW PAŁUCKI, ZBIGNIEW PUSTUŁA
HENRYK RUTKOWSKI (editor), ANNA ŻABOKLICKA DUNIN-WĄSOWICZ

Diagrams:

IRENA GIEYSZTOR, STEFAN JACKOWSKI

Lay-out:

ZYGMUNT ZIEMKA, WITOLD MOTYL

Editor:

ZUZANNA STEFANIAK

© Copyright by
Państwowe Wydawnictwo Naukowe
PWN—Polish Scientific Publishers
Printed in Poland by DRP

ISBN 83-01-00392-8

CONTENTS

INTRODUCTION 17
by S. Kieniewicz
Translation: K. Cękalska

MEDIEVAL POLAND 23
by A. Gieysztor
Translation: K. Cękalska

Chapter I
BEFORE THE RISE OF THE POLISH STATE 25

Slavic Antiquity 25
The Slavic Wends and the Germans on the Fringes of Roman Influence 28
Slavic Migrations and the Age of Crises (The Fifth to the Seventh Centuries) 31

Chapter II
THE ORIGINS OF POLAND 35

Economic Foundations of Poland in the Eearly Middle Ages 35
The Social Structure and Organization of Regional States 37
The Origins of the Polanes 41
The Spiritual and Mental Culture on the Eve of the Unification of the Polish State 43

Chapter III
THE EARLY YEARS OF THE POLISH STATE 47

The Consolidation of the State and the Christianization of Poland in 966 47
Polish Boundaries Established in the Odra and Vistula Basins 50
The Polish Empire under Bolesław the Brave 52
The Crisis of the First Polish Monarchy 55
Economic and Cultural Achievements of the Architects of the State 57

Chapter IV
THE AGE OF MATURITY OF THE POLISH MONARCHY 65

Struggle for International Position and the Establishment of Royal Authority 65
Feudal Disintegration Gains the Upper Hand (1138–1146) 67

Economic Foundations of the Oligarchy. Village and Town Prior to the Mid-Twelfth Century — 71
Cultural Relations in the Eleventh Century and in the First Half of the Twelfth Century — 76

Chapter V

THE CENTURY OF ECONOMIC GROWTH AND SOCIAL TRANSITION — 80

Evolution of Settlements in the Twelfth and Thirteenth Centuries — 80
Foreign Colonization and the Introduction of German Law in the Thirteenth Century — 84
The Duchies of Poland — 89
The Growing External Danger — 93
Efforts at Unification in the Late Thirteenth and the Early Fourteenth Centuries — 97
Transition of Polish Culture from the Romanesque to the Gothic — 102

Chapter VI

THE *CORONA REGNI POLONIAE* AT THE HEIGHT OF ITS POWER IN THE FOURTEENTH AND THE FIFTEENTH CENTURIES — 107

The State Apparatus Centralized — 107
Political Problems in the Reigns of Władysław the Short and Casimir the Great — 111
The Period of Angevin Rule — 114
The Union of Poland and Lithuania. The Struggle with the Teutonic Order — 114
Poland and Lithuania in the Hussite Period. The Union with Hungary — 117
The Growing Political Role of the Gentry. The Restitution of Crown Lands — 120
Casimir IV's Foreign Policy in the Second Half of His Reign — 121
From Land Diets to a National Parliament — 122
Western Pomerania, Lubusz Land and Silesia in the Fourteenth and the Fifteenth Centuries — 125
Economic Life in the Fourteenth and Fifteenth Centuries — 127
Culture in the Fourteenth and Fifteenth Centuries — 133

THE COMMONWEALTH OF THE GENTRY — 143

by J. Tazbir (VII–IX) and by E. Rostworowski (X–XIII)

Translation: L. Szwajcer and A. Szymanowski

Chapter VII

POLAND'S "GOLDEN AGE" (1492–1586) — 145

General Characteristics of the Period — 145
Between the Habsburgs and Muscovy — 146
The Social and Political Foundations of the "Democracy of the Gentry" — 149
The Movement for the "Execution-of-the-Law" — 154
Sigismund Augustus' Foreign Policy — 156
The Reformation — 158
The First Interregnum and the Period of Elective Kings — 161
The Policy and Wars of Stephen Batory — 167
Batory and the Gentry — 169
Humanism in Poland — 170
The Development of a National Culture — 171
Renaissance Culture and Life — 176

Chapter VIII
THE COMMONWEALTH AT THE TURNING POINT (1586–1648) — 180

- The struggle for power — 180
- The Political Crisis of the Commonwealth — 181
- The Zebrzydowski Rebellion — 184
- Attempts to Check Russia — 186
- The Conflict with Turkey — 188
- The Agrarian Crisis — 190
- The Growing Importance of the Magnates — 192
- The Situation of Towns and Burghers — 196
- The Doctrine of the Counter-Reformation — 197
- The Methods of the Counter-Reformation — 199
- The Election and Reign of Władysław IV — 203
- The Cossack Question — 206

Chapter IX
THE COMMONWEALTH IN THE YEARS OF CRISIS (1648–1696) — 211

- The Main Features of the Period — 211
- The War with the Cossacks — 212
- The Swedish Invasion of 1655 — 214
- The Peace of Oliwa and the Eastern Question — 217
- Attempts to Introduce Reform and the Lubomirski Rebellion — 218
- War with Turkey — 220
- The Anti-Turkish League — 221
- Economic and Political Crisis — 223
- Religious Problems — 225
- Sarmatian Baroque — 226
- Literature and Arts — 229
- Education and Learning — 231

Chapter X
THE CRISIS OF SOVEREIGNTY (1697–1763) — 234

- General View of the Eighteenth Century — 234
- The Personal Union of Saxony and Poland — 235
- The Northern War and the Struggle for the Crown — 237
- The Confederation of Tarnogród and the Arbitration of Peter I — 239
- The Struggle for the Polish Throne — 242
- Demilitarization and Neutralization of the Commonwealth — 245
- The System of "Anarchy" — 247
- Western Pomerania and Silesia under Prussian Rule — 251
- Sarmatian and Catholic Conformism — 253
- Late-Baroque Culture — 256
- The Forces of Progress — 261
- The Political Deadlock — 265

Chapter XI
TENTATIVE REFORMS UNDER RUSSIA'S TUTELAGE (1763–1788) — 267

- The Russo-Prussian Alliance — 267
- The Plans of "The Family" — 268
- The Interregnum (1763–1764) — 270
- The First Years of Stanisław Augustus — 272
- The Confederation of Radom and the Seym of 1767–1768 — 275

The Confederation of Bar (1768–1772)   277
The First Partition   280
Constitutional Transformations (1773–1780)   283
Government by the Permanent Council   285

Chapter XII

THE SOCIETY AND CIVILIZATION OF THE AGE OF ENLIGHTENMENT   288

The Economic Revival   288
The Social Transformation   293
Conflict of Fashions and Ideals   297
The Intellectual Upheaval   300

Chapter XIII

THE STRUGGLE FOR THE INDEPENDENCE AND FOR THE REFORM OF THE COMMONWEALTH (1788–1794)   305

The End of the Guarantee   305
The Seym Control   307
Political Literature   310
The Constitution of 3 May, 1791   315
The Russian Intervention and the Second Partition (1792–1793)   320
The Emigration and the Situation at Home   322
The Insurrection of 1794   325
The Extinction of the Polish State   332

POLAND UNDER FOREIGN RULE 1795–1918   335

by S. Kieniewicz (XIV–XVII) and by H. Wereszycki (XVIII–XXI)
Translation: I. Ralf-Suez and J. Rodzińska

Chapter XIV

THE NAPOLEONIC ERA (1795–1815)   337

The Enfranchisement of the Peasants and the National Uprisings   337
Poland after the Third Partition   338
Attitude of the Population and the Independence Movement   340
The Legions   342
Adam Czartoryski and the Puławy Plan   345
Jena and Tilsit   346
The Constitution of the Duchy of Warsaw   348
Economic and Social Changes Within the Duchy of Warsaw   351
The Year 1809   354
The Downfall of the Duchy of Warsaw   356

Chapter XV

THE KINGDOM OF POLAND AND THE NOVEMBER INSURRECTION (1815–1831)   360

Pesasant Reform in Prussian Poland   360
Establishment of the Congress Kingdom of Poland   363
The Agrarian Question in the Kingdom of Poland   367
The Beginnings of Modern Industry in the Kingdom of Poland   369
Opposition and Conspiracy   373
Neo-Classicism and Romanticism   377
The Origins and the Outbreak of the November Insurrection, 1830   380
The Political Struggle to Control the Insurrection   382

The Polish-Russian War	384
The Revolutionary Left and the Peasant Question	385
The International Situation and the Collapse of the Rising	388

Chapter XVI
ON THE EVE OF AN AGRARIAN REVOLUTION (1832–1849) — 391

Reprisals after the Insurrection	391
Economic Development in the Three Partition Zones	392
The Liberal Camp and "Organic Work"	394
The National Question in Silesia and Pomerania	397
The Great Emigration	398
Conspiracy Within Poland	405
The Disaster of 1846	409
The Poznań Rising of 1848	413
Galicia in 1848	418
Poles in European Revolutionary Movements	420
Polish Culture in the Romantic Period	422

Chapter XVII
THE PERIOD OF THE JANUARY INSURRECTION (1850–1864) — 431

The Revolutionary Situation in Russia and Poland	431
Patriotic Demonstrations	435
The National Organization	438
The Armed Struggle of 1863	441
The Emancipation of the Peasants and the End of the Period of National Risings	445

Chapter XVIII
POSITIVISM AND TRI-LOYALISM. THE BEGINNINGS OF THE WORKING-CLASS MOVEMENT (1864–1885) — 449

The Aftermath of Disaster	449
The Post-1863 Emigration	450
The Russianization Policy in the Kingdom	451
The Polish Provinces of Prussia. The *Kulturkampf* and the National Revival in Silesia	456
The Autonomy of Galicia	458
The Development of Industry in the Congress Kingdom	463
Positivism	465
The Beginings of the Polish Working-Class Movement	473
The "Proletariat"	476
The Beginnings of the Peasant Movement	478
Three Provinces and One Nation	479

Chapter XIX
THE FORMATION OF MASS POLITICAL PARTIES. NATIONALISM AND SOCIALISM (1885–1904) — 482

The Prussian Expulsions. The Colonization Commission	482
The Polish League	484
The Socialist Movement	486
Attempts at Compromise with the German and Russian Governments	489
Polish Nationalism at the Turn of the Century	492
The Peasant Movement in Galicia	493
The Defence of Polish Nationality in the Prussian Area	495

Economic Emigration ... 498
"Young Poland" and the Arts ... 500

Chapter XX

THE PERIOD OF REVOLUTION AND THE APPROACHING EUROPEAN WAR (1904–1914) ... 505

Changes in Russian Economic Policy Towards Poland ... 505
The 1905 Revolution in the Russian Empire and Poland ... 506
The Reorientation of the Policy of the National Democrats ... 513
The Expropriation Decree in Prussian Poland and the National League ... 515
Political Changes in Galicia ... 516
The Debate on Political Attitudes on the Eve of the World War ... 518

Chapter XXI

THE FIRST WORLD WAR AND THE REBUILDING OF THE POLISH STATE (1914–1918) ... 521

Piłsudski and the Legions ... 521
The Austro-German Occupation of the Kingdom ... 525
The Declaration of 5 November, 1916 ... 526
The Downfall of the Tsarist Régime, 1917 ... 528
The Regency Council ... 530
The October Revolution and the Peace Treaty of Brześć Litewski (Brest Litovsk) ... 531
Germany's Defeat. The Declaration of the Powers on the Polish Question, 1918 ... 533
The Liberation of the Austrian Area ... 535
The Świeżyński Government ... 536
The Lublin Government ... 537
Liberated Poland ... 538

POLAND 1918–1939 ... 541

by H. Wereszycki

Translation: J. Rodzińska

Chapter XXII

THE DEMARCATION OF THE FRONTIERS AND THE ENACTMENT OF THE CONSTITUTION (1918–1921) ... 543

The First Moments of Independence ... 543
The Legislative Seym ... 546
The Peace Treaties ... 549
The War with Soviet Russia ... 550
The Demarcation of the Western Frontiers ... 552
The March Constitution, 1921 ... 555

Chapter XXIII

PARLIAMENTARY GOVERNMENT (1922–1926) ... 558

The 1922 Elections ... 558
Władysław Grabski and the Stabilization of the Currency ... 560
The Ukrainian and Byelorussian Questions ... 563
The Communist Movement ... 564
Polish Foreign Policy and Locarno ... 565
Education, Science and Culture ... 567

Chapter XXIV
PROSPERITY AND THE CRISIS: THE STRUGGLE TO LEGALIZE PIŁSUDSKI'S DICTATORSHIP (1926–1931) — 577

The May *coup d'état* — 577
The Social Aspect of Piłsudski's Dictatorship — 579
The Struggle between the Government and the Seym — 580
Gdynia and Mościce — 582
The Centre-Left and the Brześć Affair — 584
The Great Economic Crisis of 1929–1931 — 586

Chapter XXV
TOWARDS TOTAL DICTATORSHIP (1931–1939) — 588

The Foreign Policy of Piłsudski — 588
The Death of Piłsudski. The Conflict in the Ruling Party — 590
The Growth of Opposition — 595
The National Unity Camp — 596
Beck and the Cieszyn Question — 599
Facing German Aggression (1938–1939) — 601

CONCLUSION — 605
by S. Kieniewicz
Translation: K. Cękalska

CHRONOLOGICAL TABLES — 611

BIBLIOGRAPHICAL NOTES — 622

INDEX — 636

PLATES

Ślęża mountain, Wrocław voivodship. *Woman with Fish*	26
Łęg Piekarski, Konin voivodship. Roman imports, 2nd–3rd cent.	27
Proboszczowice, Sieradz voivodship. Stronghold, 9th cent. Photo from a helicopter	39
Leźno, Toruń voivodship. Cult stone, 10th cent.	40
Denarius of Bolesław the Brave "Gnezdun Civitas", c. 1000, National Museum, Cracow	53
Cieszyn. Katowice voivodship. St. Nicholas' Chapel, 11th cent.	54
Włocławek cup, 10th cent. National Museum, Cracow	69
Gniezno Doors, c. 1170–1180. Holy Wirgin Mary's and St. Adalbert's Cathedral	70
Strzelno, Bydgoszcz voivodship. Holy Trinity Church, second half of the 12th cent., detail of a Romanesque column	81
Trzebnica, Wrocław voivodship. Cistercian Nuns Church, c. 1220–1230. Tympanum	82
Wąchock, Kielce voivodship. Cistercian Monastery, 13th cent. Chapterhouse	96
Sulejów, Piotrków Trybunalski voivodship. St. Thomas's Church, first half of the 13th cent. Keystone	97
Cracow, St. Florian's Gate, 14th cent.	109
Cracow, St. Catherine's Church, 14th cent.	110
Cracow, Church of the Virgin Mary, 14th cent.	123
Cracow, Barbican, 1498–1499	124
Nicolaus Copernicus. Portrait by an unknown painter, first quarter of the 16th cent. Regional Museum, Toruń	151
Cracow, Wawel. Envoys Hall. 1529–1535	152
Stanisław Samostrzelnik, *Investing the Szydłowiecki Family with Coat-of-Arms*, 1522. Title page of *Liber geneseos*. National Museum, Poznań (Kórnik branch)	165
Poznań, Town Hall, 1550–1560. Architect: Giovanni Battista Quadro	166
Jan Kochanowski. Tombstone at Zwoleń, Radom voivodship, 1584	177
Thomas Treterus, *Disputation of Cardinal Stanisław Hozjusz with Toruń Protestants*, 16th cent. Drawing from *Theatrum virtutum d Stanislai Hosii*, Pelplin, 1928	178
Portrait of a nobleman, 16th cent. National Museum, Warsaw	193
Krasiczyn, Przemyśl voivodship. Renaissance castle, 1598–1614. Architect: Galeazzo Appiani	194
Kazimierz Dolny, Lublin voivodship. Przybyła House, 1615	205
Powroźnik, Nowy Sącz voivodship. St. James' Orthodox Church, c. 1643	209
Białystok. Palace, rebuilt 1728–1758. Architects: Jan Z. Deybel and Jan H. Klemm	259
Canaletto (Bernardo Belotto), *Election of Stanisław Augustus*, 1778. National Museum, Warsaw	260
Warsaw. Łazienki Park. The Water Palace, 1784–1795. Architect: Dominik Merlini	273
Ignacy Krasicki. Copperplate by Jan Ligber. Adam Mickiewicz Museum, Warsaw	274

Hugo Kołłątaj. Portrait by Józef Peszka, c. 1792. National Museum, Warsaw (Wilanów branch) — 313

Jan Śniadecki in the observatory of Wilno University. Water colour by unknown painter, second half of the 18th cent. Adam Mickiewicz Museum, Warsaw — 314

Tadeusz Kościuszko. Portrait by Karol Schweikart, 1789–1792(?). National Museum, Warsaw (Wilanów branch) — 326

Ożarów, Tarnobrzeg voivodship. Manor House, second half of the 18th cent. State Institute of Art, Warsaw — 329

General Jan Henryk Dąbrowski entering Poznań on November 6, 1806. Gouache by Michał Stachowicz. Polish Army Museum, Warsaw — 347

Sielpia Wielka, Kielce voivodship. Factory shop, first half of the 19th cent. — 365

Stanisław Staszic. Medallion by unknown artist, first half of the 19th cent. National Museum, Warsaw — 371

Warsaw, Polish Bank, 1825. Architect: Antonio Corazzi. Aquatint by Friedrich Christoph Dietrich. Institute of Art, Polish Academy of Sciences, Warsaw — 372

Attack on the Belvedere Palace, November 29, 1830. Aquatint by Friedrich Christoph Dietrich, based on a drawing by Jan Feliks Piwarski. Polish Army Muzeum, Warsaw — 381

Joachim Lelewel. Lithography, probably of a drawing by N. Maurin, c. 1832. Adam Mickiewicz Museum, Warsaw — 403

Poles in Berlin after their Release from the Moabit Prison. From a contemporary drawing published in the "Illustrierte Chronik", Leipzig 1848 — 414

Adam Mickiewicz. Portrait by Aleksander Kamiński, 1850. National Museum, Warsaw — 423

Juliusz Słowacki. Engraving by J. Hopwood, according to a drawing by J. Kurowski from 1838. Adam Mickiewicz Museum, Warsaw — 424

Cyprian Kamil Norwid. Heliography according to a Paris photograph from 1856. Adam Mickiewicz Museum, Warsaw — 427

Fryderyk Chopin. Portrait by Eugène Delacroix — 428

Piotr Michałowski, *Portrait of an Old Peasant*. National Museum, Cracow — 429

Artur Grottger, *Battle* from the series *Lithuania*, 1864–1866. National Museum, Cracow — 442

Jacek Malczewski, *The Last Stage*, 1883. National Museum, Warsaw — 447

Bolesław Prus. Photograph, 1910 — 467

Maria Konopnicka. Photograph, 1910. National Museum, Warsaw — 468

Henryk Sienkiewicz. Portrait by Kazimierz Pochwalski, 1890. National Museum, Warsaw — 469

Jan Matejko, *Stańczyk*, 1862. National Museum, Warsaw — 470

Maria Skłodowska-Curie. Photograph, 1913 — 471

Aleksander Gierymski, *Sand-diggers*, 1887. National Museum, Warsaw — 473

Ludwik Waryński. Photograph — 477

Stanisław Wyspiański, Self-portrait, 1902. National Museum, Warsaw — 501

Leon Wyczółkowski, *Digging Beetroot*, 1892. National Museum — 502

Olga Boznańska, Self-portrait, 1900. National Museum, Warsaw — 503

Stanisław Lentz, *The Strike*, 1910. National Museum, Warsaw — 509

Stanisław Masłowski. *Spring of 1905*, 1906. National Museum, Warsaw — 511

Stefan Żeromski. Photograph, 1924. Property of Monika Żeromska — 569

Tadeusz Żeleński (Boy). Head. Sculpture by Alfons Karny — 572

Xawery Dunikowski, *Bolesław the Bold*. Tombstone, 1916–1917. National Museum, Warsaw (Xawery Dunikowski Museum branch) — 573

Władysław Skoczylas, *Stone Stairs*, s. 1930. National Museum, Warsaw — 574

Henryk Kuna, *Christ*, 1926. Sculpture in wood — 575

Gdynia. Harbour — 583

MAPS IN THE TEXT

Migrations of Slavic tribes, 5th–7th cent. *by H. Rutkowski*	32
Gniezno before the 12th cent. *by J. Humnicki, H. Rutkowski*	61
The separate Polish duchies, 1138 *by A. Gieysztor*	73
The expansion of the Teutonic Order State, 1230–1329 *by H. Rutkowski*	94
The Polish Kingdom, 1320 *by J. Humnicki, H. Rutkowski*	100
Monuments of Romanesque architecture in Poland *by Z. Świechowski*	103
The battle of Grunwald, 1410 *by H. Rutkowski*	118
Cracow, 15th cent. *by J. Humnicki, H. Rutkowski*	130
The dominions of the Jagiellonian dynasty, 15th/16th cent. *by H. Rutkowski*	147
Major centres of the Reformation in Poland, 16th and 17th cent. *by A. Żaboklicka Dunin-Wąsowicz*	162
Jesuits' and Dissenters' schools, 16th–18th cent. *by W. Lewandowska*	201
The Chmielnicki uprising, 1648–1653 *by H. Rutkowski*	207
Main residences of magnates, 17th and 18th cent. *by A. Żaboklicka Dunin-Wąsowicz*	249
Warsaw, second half of the 18th cent. *by J. Humnicki, H. Rutkowski*	291
The school system under the Commission for National Education *by W. Lewandowska, E. Rostworowski*	301
Major military actions during the Kościuszko Insurrection *by H. Rutkowski*	330
The Duchy of Warsaw *by H. Rutkowski*	349
The Congress Kingdom of Poland and the Free State of Cracow, 1815 *by H. Rutkowski*	366
The November Insurrection, 1830/1831 *by H. Rutkowski*	386
Textile inudustry in the Kingdom of Poland, c. 1850 *by A. Żaboklicka Dunin-Wąsowicz*	432
Blast furnaces in the Kingdom of Poland and Silesia, c. 1857 *by B. Kaczmarski*	434
Industry in Poland and neighbouring countries, c. 1910 *by Z. Pustuła, H. Rutkowski*	507
Poland, 1918/1919 *by T. Ładogórski*	544
The Silesian uprisings, 1919–1921 *by T. Ładogórski*	553
Plebiscite areas *by T. Ładogórski*	554
Density of population, 1931 *by H. Rutkowski*	581
Population of Poland according to occupation, 1936 *by W. Lewandowska*	592
Industrial centres in Poland, *1918–1939* *by T. Ładogórski*	594

INSERTED MAPS

Poland, c. 963–1034 by J. Humnicki, H. Rutkowski	48
Poland in the second half of the 12th cent. by J. Humnicki, H. Rutkowski	64
The Polish Kingdom under Casimir the Great, 1370 by H. Rutkowski	112
Poland and Lithuania, 1466 by H. Rutkowski	128
The Polish Commonwealth after the Union of Lublin, 1569 by A. Żaboklicka Dunin-Wąsowicz	160
The Polish Commonwealth during the partitions, 1772–1795 by H. Rutkowski, W. Pałucki	320
Polish participation in the European Revolutions, 1848 by A. Żaboklicka Dunin-Wąsowicz	416
Poland under foreign rule, c. 1870 by H. Rutkowski	464
Poland, 1923 by H. Rutkowski	560
The Polish People's Republic	608

DIAGRAMS

I. Growth of population in central Poland, 1000–1800 and 1800–1914	18
II. Growth of population in Poland, 1900–1940	20
III. Structure of peasant farms in Poland, c. 1900's	497
IV. Emigration from Polish lands, 1870–1914	499
V. Structure of small holdings in Poland, 1921 and 1938	591
VI. Growth of population in Poland, 1000–1975	608

DIAGRAMS

I, II, VI by I. Gieysztor ; III, IV, V by S. Jackowski

Genealogy of the Piasts	138
Genealogy of the Jagiellons and the Vasas	182

INTRODUCTION

Poland is a country which inherited and, at the same time, played her part in the development of European culture. Situated in the heart of the continent, between the Carpathian Mountains and the Baltic Sea, between Germany and Russia, Poland came under the influence in the course of ten centuries of all the major migrations, conflicts and crucial economic and social changes experienced by Europe since the Middle Ages. There were times when Poland was a power of continental dimensions. There were times also when she disappeared from the political map of the world. She enjoyed on occasion great esteem in world opinion but she also sank at times into utter oblivion.

Today Poland is the seventh largest country in Europe in size and the seventh in population. She is a member of the group of socialist countries which is associated with the Soviet Union by ties of alliance and friendship, but she also maintains lively economic and cultural relations with the nations of the West. From being an agricultural country, exporting grain, timber, and later coal to the more prosperous communities of the West, Poland has become an industrial country and an equal partner with them in international trade. The land of Copernicus, Chopin and Maria Skłodowska-Curie, of Kościuszko and Mickiewicz is still contributing its share to common achievements of human thought and creative art.

At different times, according to the current political climate of opinion, Poland's historical role was variously defined as that of the "bulwark of Christianity", of the "Western bastion of the Slavs", or of the "bridge between East and West". Poland's rich and varied past cannot be interpreted and described by any one facile formula. In the course of history, every European country has experienced vicissitudes of fortune. Yet in this part of the world there is probably no country which can claim to have undergone such an erratic development as Poland.

The fully developed Polish State appeared upon the stage of history in the second half of the tenth century. Dominion over the Vistula and Odra

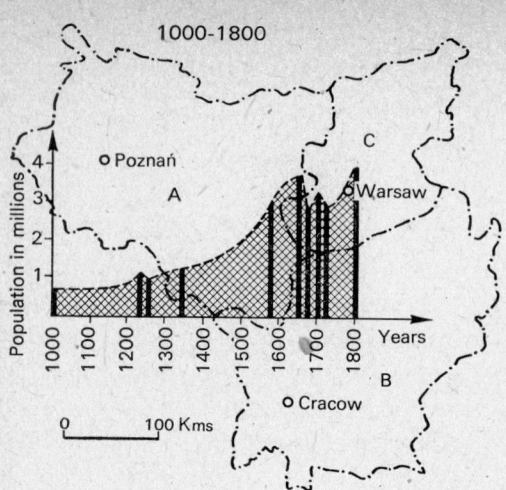

I. Growth of population in central Poland.
The vertical lines indicate the population figures. 1000–1800 according to available estimates on the basis of treasury sources of Great Poland (A), Little Poland (B) and Mazovia (C). 1800–1914 according to the statistics of the Grand Duchy of Poznań (A), Galicia (B) and the Kingdom of Poland (C). Incomplete data for 1800–1820 amended

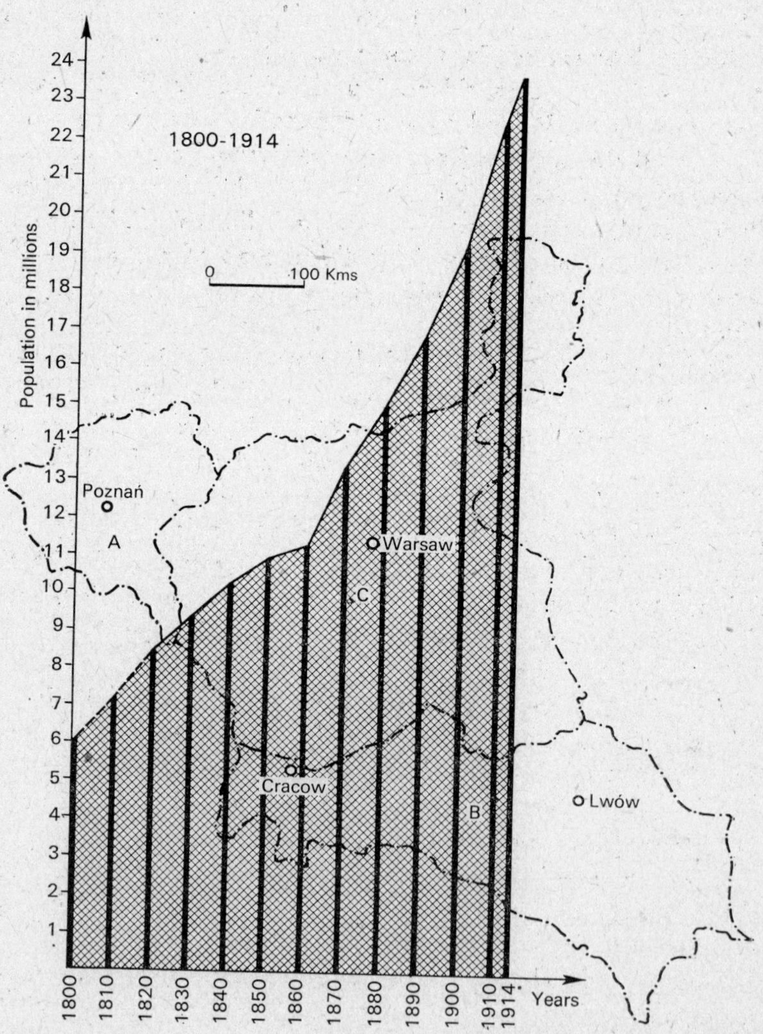

(Oder) valleys was exercised with a firm hand by a hereditary ruler, asserting his sovereignty and taking part successfully in critical political struggles with the Empire, Rome, Kiev and Byzantium. The first monarchy in Poland did not survive long. In the twelfth and the thirteenth centuries we find in Polish territories a score of contending petty duchies, harrased by Tartar raids, threatened by the expansionist policies of German lords marcher and by the peaceful infiltration of German settlers, both burghers and peasants.

In spite of parcellization and weakness Poland's cultural development nevertheless followed the west European model. Settlements spread throughout the country and urban life flourished. The country experienced moreover the growth of constitutional institutions normal in the Middle Ages. Parcellization, however, was succeeded by a fresh consolidation when the last rulers of the Piast dynasty reunited Poland at the dawn of the fourteenth century. Although only a landlocked state pushed back from the Odra river and cut off from the Baltic Sea, Poland nevertheless had a vigorous life of her own and was capable of defending her independence. A political union with the Grand Duchy of Lithuania concluded at the close of the fourteenth century, suddenly extended the frontiers of the Jagiellonian monarchy to the sources of the Dnieper and to the shores of the Black Sea. In this way the country became one of the major powers of Europe. Poland absorbed the learning of the Renaissance and became a wealthy and brilliant community, a granary of Europe and cradle of scholarship providing patronage to artists and a haven of refuge for thinkers who suffered persecution elsewhere.

This golden age of Poland's history was followed by a period of decline. In modern times the development of central Europe followed a course different from that of the leading countries of the West. Polish wheat was shipped to the Low Countries and England while Poland imported industrial products from western Europe. The balance of trade was always unfavourable to the east European States, a fact which had repercussions on the development of the economy in the peculiar growth of demesne farming and the so-called "second serfdom". The carefree and hospitable life of the Polish gentry was accompanied by a decline in the crafts, the stagnation of the towns and the oppression of the peasants. The overwhelming political superiority of the gentry over the townsmen and the peasants destroyed the basis for the rise of an absolute monarchy in Poland. At the close of the sixteenth century the Polish Commonwealth could proudly point to its parliamentary system, to the toleration, equality and freedom enjoyed by the gentry. In the following century however the Commonwealth was transformed into an oligarchy of magnates with a feeble parliament and an administration reduced to impotence. The country, with a wide area open to attack on all sides and torn internally by the uprisings of Ukrainian peasants, was destined to fall victim to the greed of its powerful neighbours. Too late, in the second half of the eighteenth century, Poland began to rise out of her intellectual, economic and political sloth. It was nevertheless precisely her

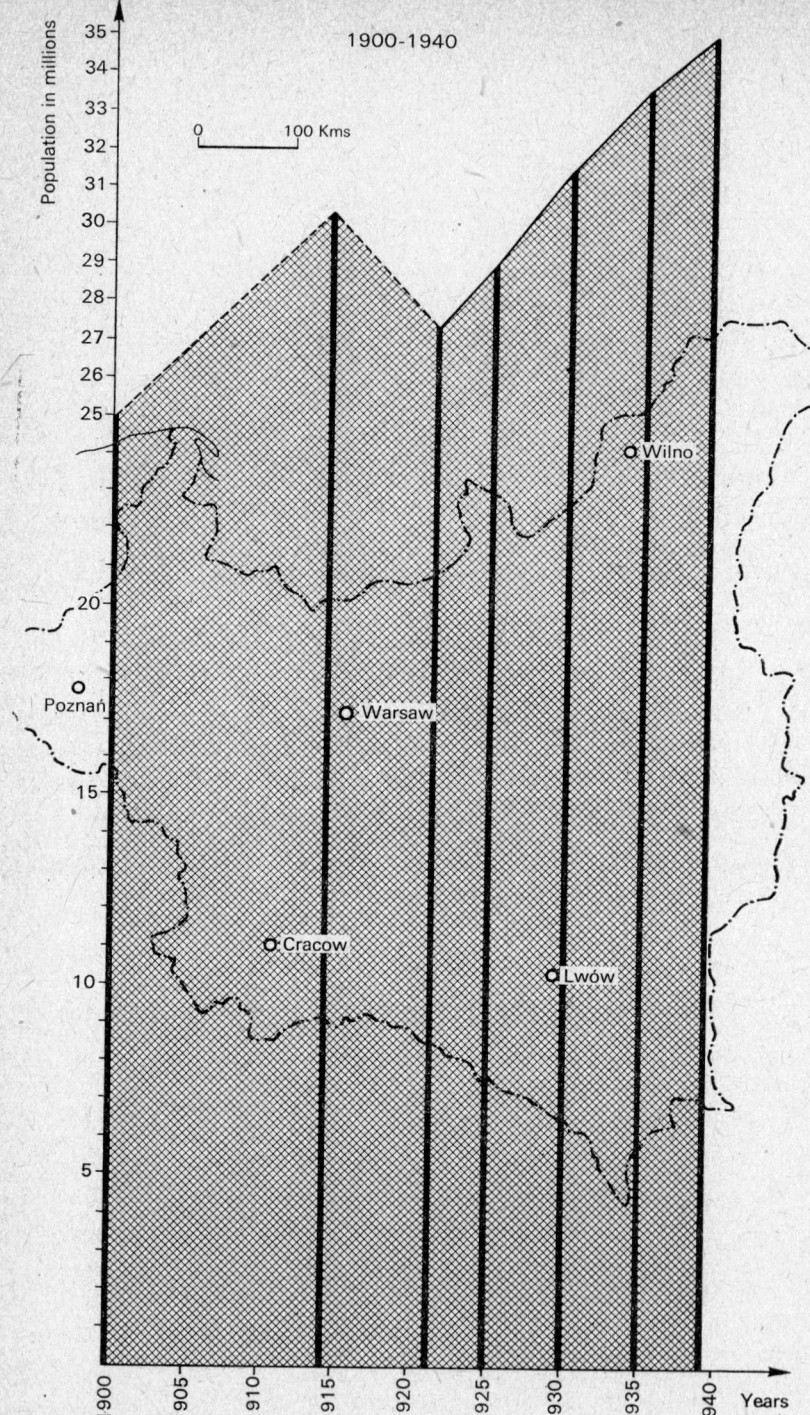

II. Growth of population in Poland

The data for 1900–1914 relate to the territory of Poland within the pre-1939 frontiers

achievements in the field of administration and military reforms which induced Russia, Prussia and Austria to destroy the state which might become an obstacle to their expansion.

There was indeed another paradox. Having lost their own state owing to centuries of misgovernment, the Polish people were to fight with undaunted resolve for the restoration of independence, appealing to the conscience of Europe by their military endeavours, playing upon the antagonisms of rival powers and establishing alliances with the European revolutionary movements. Superficially it appeared that all these efforts were of no avail. One insurrection after another ended in defeat until finally after 1864 nothing was heard of the Polish cause in Europe. The whole of eastern Europe and with it Poland in fact witnessed the destruction of the last vestiges of feudalism and experienced an industrial revolution. As a consequence of the transformation induced by the capitalist era, the population of Poland more than doubled in the second half of the nineteenth century. National consciousness, moreover, reached the mass of the population even in areas like Upper Silesia and Pomerania which seemed near to being completely Germanized. When the three partitioning Powers were brought to defeat and ruin by the First World War, the Polish people were ready and capable of demanding a state of their own.

This awakening of dormant nationalism may be seen in many other European countries in the nineteenth century. Unlike the Czechs and Hungarians and even more unlike the Balkan peoples, Poland had existed as a state up to the close of the eighteenth century and the advent of industrialization. Consequently, Poland had not lost her aristocracy and gentry, but on the contrary had even assimilated the upper classes in the Lithuania and parts of the Ukraine. The society which lost its independence at the beginning of the nineteenth century, a century of growing national awareness, still retained a social structure and a political tradition inherited from the epoch of self-government. This explains the exceptional dynamism of the Polish national struggle and the fact that it was regarded by the leaders of European revolutionary movements as a disruptive element within the Holy Alliance. This fact also explains many peculiar characteristics in the political life of Poland's more recent history. It was the poorer, declassed section of the gentry that fought for independence up to 1863. This element was to transmit its ideals and traditions to the Polish intelligentsia, a large proportion of whom came from the gentry. Here are the sources of the particular role played by the radical representatives of the intelligentsia at the turn of the nineteenth and twentieth centuries. It was they who stimulated the growth of workers' and peasants' movements, though unable to identify themselves entirely with them. This political tradition explains the high-minded ambition of the Polish intelligentsia apparent in the years between the two world wars, their aspiration to play the part of rulers and leaders of the nation. Those singular characteristics which have emerged in the political and social upheaval of the post-war years, and which distinguish Poland from other People's Democracies, may perhaps be traced to this same source.

Poland's history was determined only to a certain degree by her geographical position and her role in Europe's development. Like the rest of the continent, Poland lived through the Middle Ages, participated in the Renaissance and the age of Enlightenment and experienced the consequences of the industrial revolution. Unlike the countries of central and eastern Europe, however, Poland began to suffer, by the eighteenth century, the consequences of an economy which was retarded by comparison with that of the western European countries. In this broad frame of reference this history seeks to analyse the salient features of Polish historical development in both the decline of the Commonwealth and in the national revival after the loss of independence.

At home and abroad widely differing views of the Polish nation's characteristics have been held. Poland "the Christ of nations" and "the conscience of the world", Poland ruined by misgovernment and incapable of throwing off her anarchy, these are the widely disparate judgements. Rejecting these concepts many historians of recent years veer towards an opposite extreme in refusing to admit that Polish history has claims to singular characteristics of its own and in detecting in it only the refllections of universal processes.

The truth lies somewhere between these two points of view. Account ought to be taken both of the European character of Poland's history and of her specific and peculiar contribution to the history of Europe. This short history aims at examining the course of these two themes as they run through Poland's past.

MEDIEVAL POLAND

by Aleksander Gieysztor

Chapter I
BEFORE THE RISE OF THE POLISH STATE

SLAVIC ANTIQUITY

Mention of Poland and the Poles first appears at the close of the tenth century in the pages of foreign chroniclers who had obtained more exact information about this people. This single fact, however, cannot serve as a point of departure for an examination of the evolution of the Poles or Poland. At this early date the names as well as the ideas which these terms represented reveal a centuries-old heritage which remained in constant evidence through the Middle Ages and into the present. The Polish language, the most significant cultural phenomenon in Poland's history, began to emerge in a remote antiquity. Other features of a geographic, historic and ethnographic nature also hark back to the period before the rise of the Polish State.

Most probably, a pronounced language division occurred among the Slavs in the last centuries B.C. The two large groups which emerged from this division were the West Slavs, who occupied an area north of the Carpathian and Sudeten Mountains and east of the Odra river, and the East Slavs whose settlements spread east of Volhynia up to the middle Dnieper.

There was an affinity between the material cultures and the social systems of the early Slavs. The language differences between the two groups were the result of geographic conditions, namely a large expanse of area in which it was impossible to maintain one uniform language despite the common ethnic background designated by the old native term *Slavs*. However, the principal factor was the different historic evolution of each of these groups. Their individual histories were affected by the cultural and political conditions of neighbouring peoples, some of whom were integrated with the Slavs and exerted varying influences on the Slav culture.

The West Slavs emerged in the first centuries B.C. in an area occupied earlier by an older stratum of Indo-European inhabitants, from whom they most probably took the name Wends (Veneti). The subject under consideration is the ethnic affiliation of the people of what the archaeologists call the Lusatian culture. Though it belonged probably to an earlier ethnic stratum

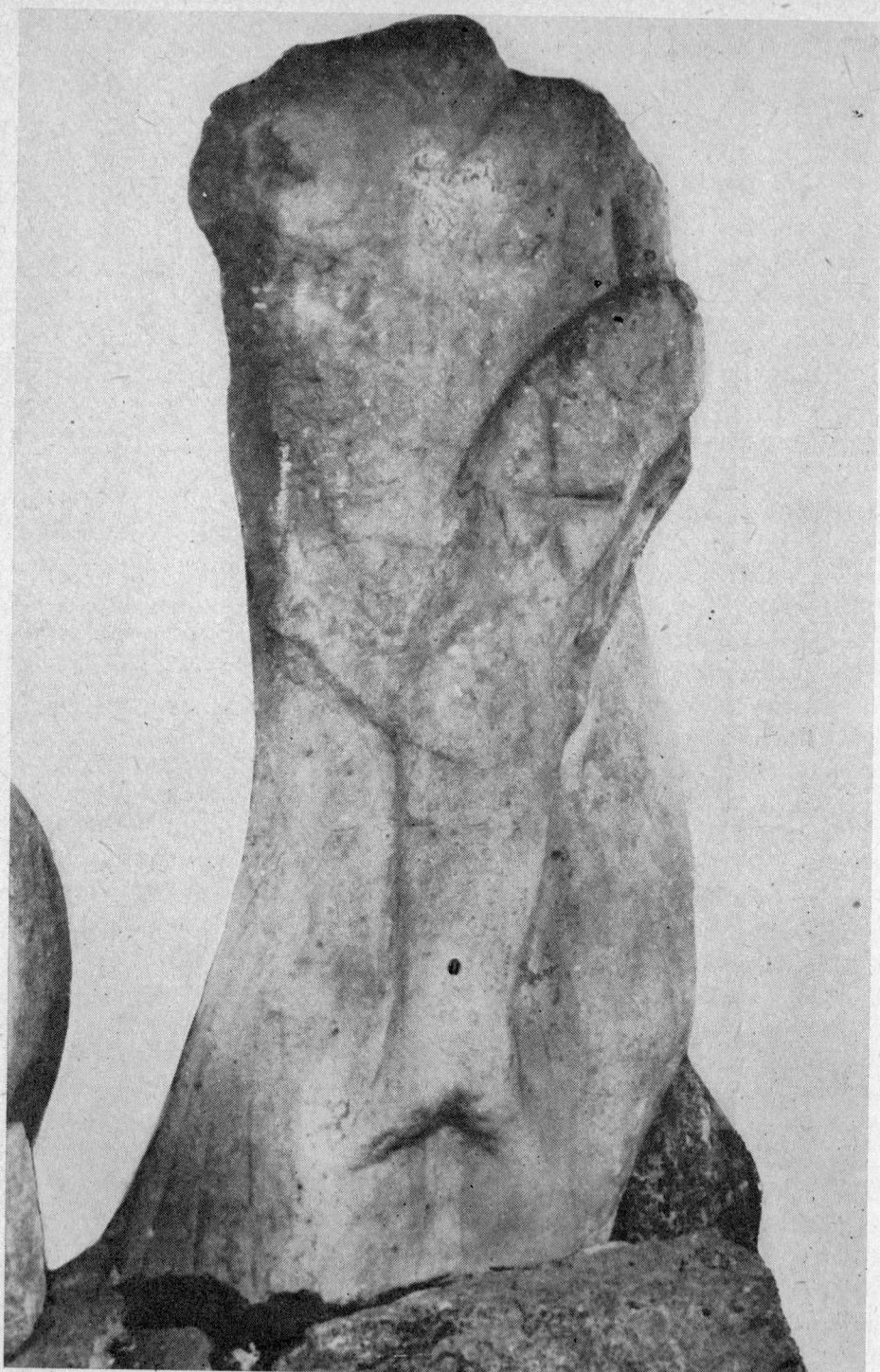

Ślęża mountain. *Woman with Fish*

Łęg Piekarski. Roman imports, 2nd–3rd cent.

than the Slavs, the Lusatian culture was nevertheless absorbed completely by them. The peoples of the Lusatian culture occupied virtually the whole of contemporary Poland and reached far to the west and south west beyond the present Polish frontiers. The long centuries of peaceful development, from about 1300 to 400 B.C., years untroubled, it seems, by alien incursions, promoted a considerable uniformity in the features of the material culture. From these days and up through the Middle Ages and on, the cultural thread in our country remained unbroken, which can be seen in the features of the timber buildings, the settlements and their anthropological substratum. It may be assumed that the Lusatian culture played an important part in the formation of the West Slav culture.

It has been possible to study the cultural achievements of this people in the large fortified settlement of about 400 B.C. which has been excavated at Biskupin in the Bydgoszcz voivodship. The principal features were: primitive farming methods and animal husbandry, a high skill in carpentry and pottery, and the use of iron to forge weapons and some of the tools. A considerable section of the Biskupin settlement has been uncovered on a lake island. The old settlement comprised about 100 houses of the same size lining eleven parallel streets all ending in one street that inscribed a surrounding oval line. A 15 to 19 feet high powerful wooden rampart and a structure that broke the floes and the force of the waves, surrounded the settlement. A large gate opened on the bridge that joined the island with the mainland. It may be assumed that fortified settlements of this type were the seat of the wealthier patriarchal families who protected their growing wealth from greedy neighbours.

The genesis of the West Slavs may be traced to the modification of this Lusatian culture under the influence of the Slavs. It is no accident that this change coincided with economic changes, related on the one hand to the development of iron metallurgy—with the ore mined locally from the second and first centuries B.C.—and on the other to improvements in agriculture. It seems that the proximity of federations of Celtic tribes helped the ancient Slavs to adopt a number of technical innovations. In the late fourth and the early third century B.C. the Celts reached across the lands on the Danube and the territory of Bohemia as far as Silesia where they established a settled community in the region of the Ślęża mountain. The magnificent sculptures ascribed to them which are scattered on the slopes and at the foot of the mount would indicate that this was their chief centre of worship, inherited later by other peoples. Another settlement was established in Upper Silesia while Celtic influence also extended as far as western Little Poland. The assumption is that the tribal name of the Lugii may refer to those Celtic groups. Other scholars, however, place them among Slavic tribes.

THE SLAVIC WENDS AND THE GERMANS ON THE FRINGES OF ROMAN INFLUENCE

Starting with Herodotus (fifth century B.C.) the Slavic peoples were recorded by geographers in the Mediterranean basin under a variety of names. More definitive remarks pertaining especially to the West Slavs appear in the first and second centuries A.D. The later chroniclers speak of the Wends who lived on the Baltic seacoast west of the Vistula, east of the Sudeten Mountains and north of the Carpathians, occupying an area that extended to the river Dnieper. Close study of the records left by Roman writers has led to the conclusion that the Wends are Slavic in character. Approximately at the beginning of the Christian Era, these peoples were threatened by the pressure of Germanic tribes who, in a period of political activity, invaded and settled for varying lengths of time various parts of the Wend lands.

Among these Germanic peoples were the Goths who in the first decades of the Christian Era came to Pomerania from Scandinavia. They remained in a part of Gdańsk-Pomerania until the third century and established trade between the lower Vistula and the Moravian Gate and the Kłodzko Pass.

The name of the Lugii was eventually extended to include all Celtic, Germanic and Slavic tribes which, no matter what their origins, lived in this area. At first the federation of the Lugii showed good will toward the Markomanns (a Germanic tribe) but at the end of the first century concluded an alliance against them with the Roman Empire. The Burgundians, originally from Bornholm and other Scandinavian countries, lived at that time on the lower reaches of the Odra but they were soon to continue their Odyssey towards the west and the south. The Gepidae lived at the mouth of the Vistula. Larger German groups departed from the territories of the Slavic Wends between the second and fourth centuries and moved closer to the Roman frontier. Thus about 250 A.D. the Goths reached the Black Sea. Soon after the Gepidae followed them bringing others in their wake. It may be accepted that in the fourth century the Slavic Wends became again the sole masters of the Polish territories. In the first centuries A.D. the Wends occupied some regions of these original territories side by side with other peoples although they remained the sole inhabitants of the major section of these lands. This period marked also a broad social and economic transformation of the Wends.

Written records contain little information about this. Much more can be gleaned from abundant archaeological evidence which indicates that the Polish territories were on the fringes of the influence of Mediterranean culture. When the Romans crushed the Celtic power in Gaul and in the Alpine countries, they opened trade routes to the north and east of Europe, to lands inhabited by German and Slavic peoples whose elders purchased Roman goods imported from the imperial provinces of the Rhineland, Gaul and the Danube valley. One may conclude that some of these communities knew how to set aside means for the purchase of such luxuries as glassware, vessels which bore the stamp of far-off producers (*terra sigillata*), amphorae filled with wine and bronze and silver vessels.

Some of the graves of that period, called the "princes' graves", contain an astonishing wealth of objects. Valuable Roman imports, bronze vessels, silver goblets, dice and stones used in games and statuettes of Hellenic and Roman gods indicate, that the chiefs adopted a style of life which imitated that of the upper classes in Roman provincial society. The less opulent though more numerous graves of the warriors indicate that members of wealthier families maintained a personal relationship with the leaders.

The luxury trade route from the countries of the Roman Empire ran from the direction of the Rhineland and Aquileia through the Polish territories to the Baltic seaboard. Pliny the Elder wrote of the amber trade which attracted a wealthy Roman trader, who in the days of Nero set out for the Baltic from the Danubian Carnuntum near Vienna. He made such large purchases of amber that the whole Roman amphitheatre could be adorned with it. He was one of the first Romans to explore the trading conditions and routes of this region. However, it seems that go-between agents played the dominant part in this trade. They carried skins, furs, honey, wax, some slaves and, above all, amber to frontier trade outposts in the Roman provinces. Impressive quantities of amber, called "the gold of the north", were exported to the south, especially in the second century A.D. One of the stores discovered at Partynice near Wrocław contained three tons of this valuable material. Roman silver coins made their appearance in the Slavic lands, and were in abundance in the second century, but became increasingly rare from the third century on.

News of distant lands lying north of the Carpathians reached the Mediterranean writers through the traders. Thus in the middle of the second century, Claudius Ptolemy, the Alexandrian geographer, placed on his map the first place name in the Polish territories. Ptolemy's Kalisia, identified with present day Kalisz on the Prosna river, lay on the amber route.

In the southern Polish territories the crafts, practiced in an earlier period to satisfy domestic needs, were taken over later by specialists in some branches of production in certain regions of the territory. The development of iron smelting was based on turf ores mined in strip pits and partly, as in the Świętokrzyskie Mountains, on mined red iron ore or haematite. From the third to the fifth centuries, after the departure of the Germanic tribes who did not engage in smelting, other important smelting centres operated in an area near Cracow where fifteen centuries later there was to be built one of the most powerful metallurgical combines in the country, known as Nowa Huta. A great many primitive smelting furnaces were discovered and studied at the time when Nowa Huta was built. It is assumed that the iron produced here was exported south beyond the Carpathians.

The family community which continued as the basic unit of the social structure was undergoing diversification. Owing to the contact between the Slavic Wends and the martial Celtic and Germanic groups, certain families became engaged in fighting and looting, others in trading or even perhaps in the organization of industrial production on quite a large scale. The system employed in the production of pottery near Cracow in the first centuries A.D., has been compared with that of the Pannonian workshops which employed slave labour.

However, these phenomena were neither permanent nor prevalent. In spite of the activities of these leading families, the Polish territories were still a land of free farmers and cattle breeders who lived on self-sufficient farms. As among all the Slavs, so here too, land was held in common. This organization was based on the principle of military aid and agricultural cooperation among neighbours. The common use of pastures and forests was widespread, though families tilled their own land individually. The existing farm tools enabled some leading families to work the same strips of land continuously. However, new areas of settlement were usually brought under the plough by the majority of farmers by the more primitive burnbeat method of cultivation. A noticeable rise in the number of settlements signified a growth in the population. Archaeologists and historians put the hypothetical density of population in the second century A.D., in the area which corresponds to that of present-day Poland, at about 1.2 to 2 persons per square kilometre, or roughly a population of about 375,000.

The distribution of the settlements and the concentration of Roman imports would indicate several territories which correspond to the later regional division of Medieval Poland. Several groups seemed to have gained considerable importance in the first centuries A.D. They settled in the vicinity of Wrocław, Cracow and Sandomierz. This may have been the beginning of an important political organization in southern Poland, each of which embraced several tribes. In the plains of central Poland, the more significant groups of this type were settled around Poznań, Kruszwica, Łęczyca and Płock. Similar communities were known in Pomerania and in the Baltic region of Pruthenia and Sudovia (Jaćwież). It is not known whether this phenomenon carried the seed of the rise of states on a regional scale. Notwithstanding their political activity, it would seem that these groups never advanced beyond the stage of tribal federations and that the twilight of the Ancient world engulfed in its descending shadows the Polish lands as well, retarding the formation of social classes by a few centuries.

SLAVIC MIGRATIONS AND THE AGE OF CRISES
THE FIFTH TO THE SEVENTH CENTURIES

The tribal federations of Slavs were at the peak of their prosperity in the third and fourth centuries. This fact enabled large groups of Slavs to spill beyond their native area between the Odra and the Vistula and the upper Dniester and middle Dnieper.

Warrior leaders of the tribal federations of Slavs stood at the head of these expeditions which turned, especially in the fifth and sixth centuries, into migrations of large sections of the population. The economic, social and political reasons behind the Slavic migrations are not entirely clear. At any rate, it seems that the Polish lands were experiencing a period of a comparative population growth, because large groups of settlers issued from these regions and, as early as the fifth century, moved south to Bohemia, Moravia and Slovakia, areas which were completely absorbed by the Slavs. In the course of the fifth and sixth centuries they moved westwards to the area between the Odra and the Elbe which for many centuries hence was to be occupied by Slavs, who by their language and customs were most closely related to the Poles.

Conclusive evidence is available regarding the original Veleti settlements in the Polish territories, especially in Pomerania, before this people moved west to the Odra. The Serbs lived here before they moved into the Lusatian

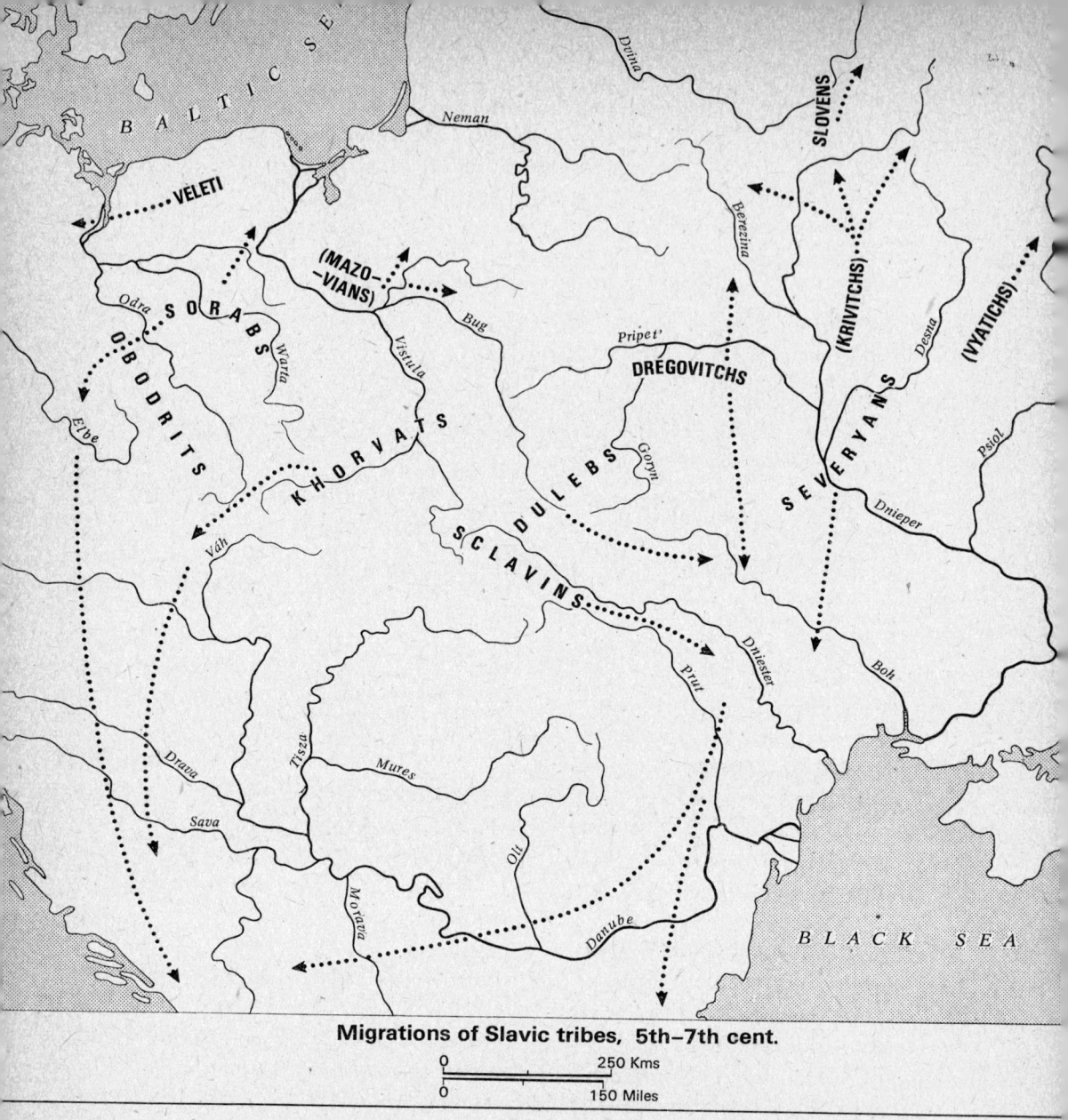

Migrations of Slavic tribes, 5th–7th cent.

area, and south to the Danubian lands. The Obodrits lived on the Odra before they moved to the lower Elbe. The Croats probably inhabited the upper Vistula before they moved off in different directions; their main body was carried to the Sava river. In the age of Slavic migrations, some of these names denoted only enterprising groups of warriors led by princes. The Slavic population subjugated by them in the Balkans came from the great East Slavic language family.

In contrast with the impressive German march across the lands of the Roman Empire and its peripheries, the main feature of Slavic settlement was the complete mastery of the occupied areas by planting settlements and by effecting a permanent slavification, embracing not only the mass of incoming Slavs, but also other ethnic groups which assimilated the Slavic language. This expansion was facilitated by the economic, social and political cataclysm that struck the Roman Empire, and by the migrations of other barbarians across its territories. The westward thrusts of the Huns set off a chain reaction. Numerous German tribes surged in the direction of the Roman Empire and at the end of the fourth century the Slavic peoples moved into the Danubian lands which were left vacant by the departing Germans and Roman garrisons.

It is supposed that in the second quarter of the fifth century during the rule of Attila, the peoples which lived in the Polish territories were subdued by Huns. The signs may be read in the archaeological finds of southern Poland. The graves discovered in Jakuszowice southwest of Cracow have yielded a bow embossed with gold, a symbol of authority among the Huns. Teophylaktos Simokattes, a Byzantine historian, wrote (book VI, chapters 2-4) that at the close of the sixth century an Avar Chagan (khan) sought the aid of Slav chieftains who lived on the Baltic and sent gifts to them. Their strength must have been considerable if the formidable Avars appealed to them for military and political aid against the Byzantines. In 562-567 the Avars probably not without the cooperation of some Slavic tribes, assaulted the Merovingian Kingdom, launching the attack from southern Poland, which may have been under the control of the Avar empire in one way or another. Whatever the dependency it must have been rather loose, for archaeology provides very little evidence of the presence of Avars north of the Carpathians. The Polish word *olbrzym*, which means giant, may have come from the name of the Avars in the same manner, as the old French term *ogre* may be traced to the Hungarian invasions of the tenth century.

No outline shall be given here of the Slavic migrations to the Balkans, particularly in the sixth and seventh centuries, where the East Slavs displayed a greater vigour in establishing their settlements. It is sufficient to say that this period witnessed a regrouping of the Slav peoples. In addition to the East and West Slavs there now emerged a third group, the South Slavs. The main role in the creation of this group was played by the East Slavic elements though not without an admixture of certain West Slavic elements.

Later a further diversification made itself felt among West Slavs, in the form of a split into the Southwest Slavs, the ancestors of the later Czechs and Slovaks, and into the Northwest group, comprised of the Polish and Polabian Slavs.

The material culture of the inhabitants of Poland declined on account of the emigration of large groups of the Slavic population — west beyond the Odra and up to the Elbe, and south across the Sudeten Mountains and the Carpathians, and owing to the severance of trade ties with the now depopulated Roman provinces. There was a pronounced slump in the living standards of the tribal elders as trade with distant lands deteriorated. The descendants of the elders depended more on domestic products than on loot from distant lands and on external trade.

This reversion to primitive culture affected chiefly the leading families. It was, however, not quite as catastrophic as in the case of the downfall of Roman grandeur and the ruin of its high intellectual culture. The Slavic population which continued to live in rural conditions and whose demands or means of satisfying them were not exorbitant, may have breathed more freely when great potteries and metallurgical workshops, which were in no way integrated with their peaceful and easy-going life on territories held in common, were abandoned or destroyed following the nomadic invasions.

The subsequent years did not bring peace. The Roman model was replaced by others. Most significant, however, was the development and expansion of the heritage of the by-gone epoch, that is the cultivation of soil and stock-breeding. Extensive burnbeat cultivation was still prevalent. It led to great mobility of settlement and internal colonization. Although intensive farming with the use of the ard was still limited yet it was common enough in southern Poland as early as the fourth and fifth centuries, as is borne out by the discovery of ploughshares. As the migrations of German tribes and nomads came to a halt, the seventh century ushered in a steady economic expansion which, though modest at first, bore promise of qualitative growth.

Meanwhile, the Slavic peoples in the Polish territories were still organized into territorial tribes living under a democratic system. Byzantine observers reported that all problems whether favourable or not were discussed by the Slavs at assemblies attended by all the people. Here differences among the leaders were brought to light. The assemblies appointed princes whose authority was limited, because the general assembly had the power to vote for or against war and to make grants to the chosen ruler.

In this type of society, conservative as all groups with little internal stratification, there were, however, the seeds of cultural change. Economic progress required time, but the impatience of certain sections of the community speeded development. The impetus came from the narrow group of lords who were eager to turn their influence to profit by the division of labour, the concentration of political power, and an extension of territorial organization. With the dawn of the new age the proto-Polish tribes and peoples stood on a similar culture level to the other Slavic, Baltic and Scandinavian peoples. Their entry into medieval civilization still required a considerable re-structuring of all aspects of their social life.

Chapter II
THE ORIGINS OF POLAND

ECONOMIC FOUNDATIONS OF POLAND IN THE EARLY MIDDLE AGES

The research of the last few years has established the fact that Poland and Polish nationality did not emerge suddenly in the middle of the tenth century, nor did they spring full grown from the head of Mieszko I, son of Siemomysł, the first Polish duke who is better known owing to written records and who was by and large an excellent ruler. The origin of Poland is spread over several centuries. The statesmen of that period remain anonymous. Their activity is but vaguely known while events and details are submerged in oblivion. The period of Poland's origins in these centuries is marked mainly by the daily effort of the people who changed the features of history by clearing primeval forests for arable land, by building settlements and homes and by their concern to transmit to their successors the growing material, social and spiritual heritage.

The period of emergence from obscurity, from the end of the Slavic migrations in the seventh century to the rise of a Polish State in the tenth century, was remarkable for events of special significance and long lasting consequences. The foundations of a new and diverse medieval society following the course of feudal evolution and the development of Polish ethnic traits as distinct from the Slavic family as a whole and the West Slavs in particular, may already be perceived. Modern research has enabled closer study to be made of the economic foundations of the changes that occurred concurrently on many levels of human activity.

The general progress noted in agriculture and stockbreeding before the formation of the State, was a factor in overcoming the social and political crisis, which marked the Slavic migrations. In the early Middle Ages social organizations again began to gain control over their natural surroundings in order to increase the yield of the soil. By the clearing of trees, and the burning of brushwoods, human settlements cut deep swaths into the forests, and with the use of iron ploughshares the lands around the settlements could be cultivated intensively. Grain crops, especially important in view of the growing population, seem to have been produced in larger quantities between the seventh and tenth centuries, a time when the major parts of the Slavic lands adopted the ard and abandoned, except in remote or outlying settlements, the older and more primitive methods of agriculture.

The soil was the chief source of wealth in the Polish land. Its productivity was related directly to the improvement of farming implements. The lighter soil of Great Poland, Pomerania and Mazovia were easy to plough. When ploughshares were armed with iron during the late period of Roman influence, it was possible to till the heavy and fertile soil of Silesia and Little Poland. The prevalence of the ard and the sickle must have effected changes in the quality of Polish agriculture as early as the tenth century. The pursuit of agriculture and cattle farming gave the landscape of early Poland an appearance of uniform husbandry. There were regional differences of lesser importance, resulting from the abundance of wild life or bees' nests in the forests, or from an abundance of fresh water fish. The chief mineral mined in this period was bog iron ore which was found in virtually all Polish territories. In many parts of Poland iron smelting was conducted most probably as a seasonal occupation secondary to farming. Salt was extracted from salt springs by evaporation, principally at Kołobrzeg in Western Pomerania, in the Kujawy region, near Cracow and in other local salt springs. Skills in various crafts spread gradually. Having survived the critical period between the fifth and seventh centuries, such crafts as pottery and metallurgy revived under the influence of new stimuli. Domestic products still fell far short of the luxury handicrafts imported from both near and distant countries to satisfy the needs of the leading social groups.

As the upper ranks of society established their position on the new economic foundations, the severed or tenuous trade ties with other countries were reestablished. Though not numerous, the archaeological sites of the seventh, eighth and ninth centuries indicate that the economy of the Slavic, proto-Polish and Baltic tribal federations, though they still bore the traits of a primitive, natural economy conducted within settled groups, nevertheless had contacts with the external world. The trade of this period involved a small number of goods which were especially attractive to the ruling group. The most important items were weapons which domestic producers could not supply in sufficient quality and number; next came luxury goods, such as gold and other ornaments. It is known, although this information pertains to other Slavic countries, that horses were used in the barter trade.

One of the frontier posts through which goods from and to the West had to pass was Magdeburg on the Elbe, designated by Charlemagne's decree as one of the places to which Frankish merchants, chiefly Jews, could come to trade with the Slavs. In the ninth and tenth centuries, the items exported were principally furs and slaves despatched usually from Mainz, the emporium from which the goods were carried to Gaul, northern Italy and even Islamic Spain, where Slavic slaves were highly valued. In southern

Germany, Ratisbon (Regensburg) was an important market centre of a far-flung trade.

Trade with Ruś (Ruthenia) was established at an early date. One of the routes between Ruthenia and central and western Europe ran through Poland as early as the ninth century. The route led from Kiev to Cracow and thence through Bohemia and Bavaria. Imports of Moravian metallurgy were also known in Polish territories.

Sea commerce on the Baltic with the distant Frisian and the closer Scandinavian ports gains in vigour in the course of the ninth century. Wulfstan, the voyager and informant of King Alfred of Wessex, sailed at the close of the tenth century from Haithabu (Hedeby) at the base of the Jutland peninsula and down the Slavic coast eastwards to the market settlement of Truso-Drużno, an active buying and selling centre lying in the Vistula delta in the Slav-Pruthenian border area, not far from present lake Drużno and Elbląg.

It may be inferred from written evidences supported by archaeological data that in the early Middle Ages the forest frontiers between the lands of the Balts and the Slavs were crossed by both sides. In addition to the sea and coastal routes from the mouth of the Vistula to Sambia, renowned for her amber, the roads between the settlements of Chełmno region and the borders of Pomerania led deep into the Prussian region; an important Mazovian route joined by a southern branch from south Poland ran up the Narew towards Sudovia, a region situated between Poland, Ruthenia, Lithuania and Pruthenia, which was for many centuries a neuralgic cross-road of economic and political interests in this part of eastern Europe.

THE SOCIAL STRUCTURE AND ORGANIZATION OF REGIONAL STATES

The early medieval trade expanded concurrently with the organization of the larger states which were capable of insuring a steady supply of the raw material sought by foreign merchants. The materials were collected from the tributes exacted from the population by their rulers. The rulers also guaranteed a supply of slaves, principally, though not exclusively, war hostages.

In the Polish territories, as among the neighbouring peoples, this trade satisfied the demands of the higher social classes which cut themselves off from the territorial rights held in common. These people accumulated more arable land and more cattle because they worked their farms with slave labour made up of war captives and native serfs. As the accumulated movable wealth was inherited, the lords had a greater opportunity for conducting wars, for pursuing political interests and for leading the free population. Representatives of this group stood at the head of larger territorial federations and compelled the population to make free gifts and imposed tributes for the ducal treasury and for their own political activity. Wars of expansion and loot were conducted by means of a standing group of warriors and also troops raised by levy in the whole of the political organization.

The new type of organization was heralded by the emergence of the castle-town (*gród, castrum*), a fortified settlement raised as a centre of authority by several powerful families whose political influence extended over the surrounding still fairly small territories. The archaeological remains of these wood and earth works are studied today as evidence of Polish history. The oldest, built between the seventh and ninth centuries, are of two types. There are the small forts built as seats of the leaders which were known in Great Poland, Lower Silesia and also in western Mazovia. The second type are the large structures which served as a refuge for the whole population of a given area. We know, however, from Little Poland that the whole of the fortified area was not occupied permanently. Political power vested in the most powerful economic groups tended to concentrate in both types of such castle-towns. The political centres began to show great vigour. This fact may be ascribed to the aspirations of lords who, in the struggle with their rivals and with the population from whom they exacted tribute, created the military and financial foundations of the state structure.

Among the Slavs and the Balts the political struggle for power took place most likely at the general assemblies of freemen called the *wiec*. Here the antagonisms between the interests of the freemen and the ambitions of the notables and between the rival tendencies of individual notables, came to light. Actually, policies of war and peace were resolved by the assembly's body of aldermen drawn from among the notables, who also chose or deposed their leader, the duke (Polish *knędz*, later *ksiądz* and *książę*, latin *dux*).

The dukes were originally, and for a long time, only military commanders, but they strove to increase their wealth and to secure office for life. Later they tried to make this honour hereditary also. The success of their endeavor depended on what interest could be excited among the notables in external expansion. Among the Polish and Russian Slavs, this expansion led to concentration of political power in the course of the ninth and tenth centuries. Among the Balts, this power did not cross the low threshold of territorial and castle-town districts until the emergence of the Lithuanian State in the thirteenth century, their expansion having been checked by powerful Polish and Russian neighbours.

In the early Middle Ages, the duke led a small group of warriors which the Slavs called a *drużyna*. This institution was indispensable to the success of authority, though the warrior group alone did not constitute a state. The state emerged from a struggle waged by the duke, the notables and the warriors on the one hand, against the free members of territorial communes on the other, upon whom they sought to impose heavy burdens to support the treasury and to defray military costs. The enactment of tribute and gifts

Proboszczowice. Stronghold, 9th cent.

signified that a State machinery was in operation. The ruling groups had a share in the income of the treasury and by this fact indentified their interests with the policies of the highest authority, working to strengthen its position internally and externally.

The factors which secured an uneasy balance in this antagonistic social structure are noteworthy. One of these, and not the least important, was the fact that the free population still constituted the overwhelming majority in the expansionary and defensive enterprises undertaken by the political organization, which also offered a chance of development for many of the inhabitants. They were still integrated by a common faith and belief, a common language and culture, a fluidity between the social groups and the way of life of individual groups of the population.

A record written in the eastern part of the Carolingian Empire, most probably immediately after 843, and called the Bavarian Geographer (*Descriptio civitatum ad orientalem plagam Danubii*), gives an account of the organization of the Slavic and Baltic political associations of the ninth century. Several other ninth and tenth century texts fill in the picture and disperse the mists of anonymity surrounding certain phenomena, which at this date had a long history of evolution. Informants of the Carolingian of-

Leźno. Cult stone, 10th cent.

ficials knew comparatively a great deal about the nearest neighbours of the Frankish State; but less was known about the territorial organizations that lay on the trade routes to the east and very little indeed about the political institutions of the lands of the Slavs and the Balts in the remoter areas.

What were the oldest Polish territorial organizations?

In Silesia we find at least five territorial organizations: the Dziadoszanie (Dadodesani), Bobrzanie, Ślęzanie (Sleenzani), Opolanie (Opolini) and Golęszyce (Golensizi). A large group of the Polanie (Polanes) inhabited all of central Poland. Some scholars hold that the term Polanes was preceded by Lędzice (Lendizi) and that this term was extended from central Poland to embrace various other regions as far as the Ruthenian boundary, where the Poles were known as Lachy; they were called by the Baltic peoples the Lenkai and by the Magyars (Hungarians) the Lengyel. It is probable, however, that the term Lędzice was first applied to the south-eastern strip of proto-Polish lands on the forefield of Sandomierz. Written evidence reveals two smaller regions, one of the Wolinianie (Velunzani) and the Pyrzyczanie (Prissani) and of other smaller groups whose names have become extinct. Another large regional group known as the Vislanes (Wiślanie) lived in southern Poland on the upper Vistula and its tributaries.

Virtually nothing is known of the rest of the Polish lands and of their organization. The geographic extent of these groups mentioned above is often an object of scholarly controversy. It is possible to determine the territorial delimitations, bounds with permanent settlement, by the names which these large and small organizations carried, but only in rare instances did the names survive a greater length of time. This is eloquent evidence of the political ferment in which the peoples who bore these names lived. Unrecorded battles and invasions, attempts to consolidate large areas and their subsequent disintegration, was most likely the content of their political history.

Two major centres proved capable of survival. One of these formed around Cracow, the capital of the small State of the Vislanes, and the second rose around Gniezno, the capital of the Polanes.

In the second half of the ninth century the Moravian neighbours considered the Vislanes "very powerful" for having opposed the political expansion and the attempts at conversion to Christianity that came from Moravia. However, this opposition ended in disaster for the duke of the Vislanes and his lands were incorporated into the Moravian State. The Life of Methodius, an apostle from Moravia, gives an account written by a contemporary: "The pagan duke, very powerful among the Vislanes, defied the Christians and caused them harm. Methodius sent to him and said 'My son, it would be well for you to accept baptism of your own free will in your own land, for otherwise, taken captive you will be forced to accept Christianity in a foreign land. Remember my words!' And so it came to pass".

Despite its favourable geographical situation and it would seem a swifter, economic development, southern Poland could no longer fulfil the role of being the nucleus of a growing State, owing to the pressure of more powerful neighbours to the south, Moravia and Bohemia, and later to the influence of the Polanes to the north.

THE ORIGINS OF THE POLANES

The Polanes inhabited a territory on the middle Warta. Their expansion was most fruitful in political consequences. The term Polanes—Polanie is undoubtedly derived from the Slavic *pole*, the word for field. This testifies to the agricultural nature of settlement in an area under permanent cultivation, though surrounded and cut up by forests. Very little is known as yet about the earliest history of this political federation. The large expanse of territory inhabited by the Polanes in the tenth century would indicate that their conquests must have begun at least in the middle of the ninth century. The duke, who ruled in Gniezno, succeeded in uniting in a state of considerable scope the smaller territories around such castle-towns as Poznań, Kruszwica, Ląd and Kalisz and to set it on a course of continued territorial expansion.

Recent archaeological excavations have yielded tangible evidence about the castle-town of Gniezno, which the written records name as the capital of the Polish duke in the tenth century. This well fortified town was founded between the eighth and ninth centuries and expanded later several times. The names of the dynasty to which Mieszko I belonged are known. The name itself testifies to the fact that the ruling house was of native origin. Mieszko I succeeded to a throne upon which not a few predecessors had sat: his father Siemomysł, his grandfather Leszek (also Lestek or Lestko) and great grandfather Siemowit preceded by yet another duke, called Chościszko, a person who cannot be identified with the legendary Piast. There is a vague tradition that this dynasty ascended the throne by an act of violence committed most probably in the second half of the ninth century. Medieval history created the legend that the dynasty was founded by Piast, a peasant of the Duke Popiel from the preceding dynasty. Modern history of the seventeenth and eighteenth centuries bestowed upon the ruling house the dynastic name of Piast, although in the Middle Ages these rulers called themselves "the family of Polish dukes".

The shaping of the Polish State started a hundred, if not more, years earlier than about the year 963 when Mieszko I led Poland onto the stage of European history. Mieszko I and his predecessors expressed the interests of the small group of lords who surrounded them. The organization of a strong Polish State accorded not only with the goals and interests of the centre of authority with its seat at Gniezno and not only did it protect the population from foreign invasion, but also insured a distinct ethnic and cultural evolution to the native elements. The bell of history had sounded for the West Slavs. The fact that the German State had frustrated the political development of the Polabian Slavs, led eventually to their loss of independence and to their gradual, but final disappearance from the map of Europe. After 955, following the twin victory of Otto I over the Hungarians and the Slavs, the Polanes brushed against the mounting influence of large power that was rising in the west.

The leaders of the Polanes showed considerable political sense at this hour of the birth of their State. The prospects awaiting them were clearly extremely attractive unlike those offered to the small Polabian or Pruthenian States. It was incumbent upon them to meet the challenge of history. The prospects were of expansion which promised to strengthen the central organization of the State, which was the repository of every type of revenue, loot and prisoners. One of the consequences in the evolution of an expansionary political organization was the early emergence among the Polanes of the authority of a hereditary duke. However, this did not preclude the fact that the lords had to give their approval to the manner in which the title was transferred to the descendents.

A large area was united in the course of the ninth and tenth centuries. It embraced, even before the reign of Mieszko I, a wide expanse of plain, and therefore all of central Poland, the later Great Poland, the lands of Łęczyca and Sieradz and all of Mazovia. It is quite probable that at this early date the Polanes had already reached across the Land of Chełmno for suzerainty over Gdańsk-Pomerania, which was conveniently connected with central Poland by the course of the lower Vistula and roads alongside both its well populated banks. Apart from this loosely-connected territorial group there was still the northern zone of the lake and coastal countries of Western Pomerania ruled by various dukes and local lords, and the uplands of Silesia and Little Poland, embraced by Bohemian influence.

Most of these territories were drawn together by their similar social evolution. Physical-geographic links between the basins of the Odra and the Vistula, as well as the cultural, ethnical and lauguage similarities, were conducive to unification. These factors were very important to the cohesion of early medieval states, although their architects did not always take them into account, trying instead, with varying success, to extend their rule beyond the related ethnic groups.

THE SPIRITUAL AND MENTAL CULTURE ON THE EVE OF THE UNIFICATION OF THE POLISH STATE

What common cultural heritage could attract to each other the population of the Polish territories in the tenth century? It is not easy to distinguish the features inherited from earlier developments and the flowering of the Slav community, from the changes introduced when the new political system began to emerge.

A most notable feature of the beliefs held by the Slavic peoples is the subservient role of their pagan religions to the needs of the agricultural population. They worshipped fire and the sun, a mysterious power to the people of that age which gave them the means of livelihood, warmth and a good harvest, but one that could show its anger by causing drought, by hurling lightning bolts and wreaking fire. They worshipped the life giving properties of the mother earth. A few relics that survive in folk customs would indicate that there was worship of water, of the springs, rivers and lakes, though this was not as important among the pagan Slavs. Mythical creatures were invoked in forests under trees of venerable age or of unusual appearance, and in enclosures designated as sacred groves. Here the people worshipped. Here auguries were taken and large sacrificial feasts were held with gifts from the first fruits to insure a good harvest for the year.

The most important cult, however, was sun worship, which must have come down from a very remote past as evidenced by the fact, that the chief god heaven and thunder was known by the common name of Perun to many of the Slav peoples. According to ninth century Arabic accounts about the harvest rites practised by the Slavs, a handful of grain was cast upwards to the sky to propitiate the gods. Until the late Middle Ages, the Polish nobility took the oath by raising the hand to the sun.

Inherited from ancient times, this cult of the gods and of the phenomena of nature was practised on a family or local scale. The sacrifices were made by the head of the family or by one of the elders on behalf of the community. There were soothsayers who told fortunes and cast spells, who turned back evil and foretold good luck and who also acted as medicine-men.

There is reason to believe, that as the new society emerged in the Polish lands, attempts were made to extend the scope of some cults and to invest them with political meaning, or at any rate, to bind them to the centre of authority. Among the Polabian Slavs this was accomplished by evolving more elaborate sacrificial rites and by establishing special servants around the personification of the chief god. There are traces of a similar effort in the Polish territories. We know that the Ślęża-Sobótka mountain, whose lone peak looms in the middle of the fertile plain of Lower Silesia was a centre of a pagan cult at the close of the tenth century. "It was greatly honoured by all inhabitants", wrote Thietmar Bishop of Merseburg (lib. VII, c. 59), "owing to its hugeness and purpose, for magic rites were performed here." Archaeological evidence of a ninth century cult centre was discovered on the summit of Mount Łysiec, later called Święty Krzyż (Holy Cross) in the central Polish massif. This was a 1.5 kilometres (about a mile) long stone wall that surrounded the summit of that mount.

The people had stone images and wooden gods. The heads of some of the oak statues have come down to our times. A bearded and moustached head of a natural size (22.5 cm together with the neck) carved in oak with a sure hand was found on a lake island at Jankowo, southeast of Gniezno. The hole at the base of the neck was made for fixing the head on a figure or post. Another head was discovered in the basin of the upper Warta, thereby offering tangible proof of the Old Ruthenian chronicle's story of the eradication of pagan cults, by casting the images into the water. Several large roughly carved stones have been preserved in central and northern Poland. They are anthropomorphic in character as may be seen by the three images on the rock of Leźno in Gdańsk-Pomerania. The Life of St. Adalbert charged that the Slavs worshipped stone and wood instead of god (Vita, I c. 1).

The people worshipped their ancestors by invoking the ghosts of the forefathers. There was a gradual change in the funeral ritual. Owing to the influence that came from the south, from the Christian area of Moravia, cremation was abandoned and the bodies of the dead were buried. The victory of Christianity accelerated this process of change which, however, was completed only as late as in the twelfth century. The Mazovian custom of surrounding and covering the body with rocks has remained to this day as a trace of local beliefs.

Although little is known of the cult and the rites, there is reliable evidence furnished by folklore and ample illustration provided by later day medieval records, regarding the various kinds of magic spells and taboos, which the Christian clergy combated for many centuries.

The general level of intellectual ideas may be assessed by means of linguistic data, and especially the vocabulary, and from the abundant ethnographic evidence common to all the Slavs. On this basis it may be accepted that prior to the ninth and tenth centuries, when new and intensive intellectual and cultural contacts were established with the outside world, all the Slavic peoples, including those in the Polish territories, had a considerably diversified vocabulary. They had words not only to describe ideas relating to concrete objects used in their daily life, to the material culture and technical knowledge and to information about nature, but also words designating quite elaborate abstract ideas, which would testify to a knowledge of the basic phenomena of abstract thought.

The Slavs were broken up into language groups and began to evolve internally along different lines at an early period. The language group that settled the valleys of the Vistula and the Odra was uniform for genetic reasons because for centuries, at least from about 500 B.C., it had lived on the same territories, which may be regarded as the cradle of the Slavs. The vernacular spoken in these lands began to differ in the early Middle Ages from that spoken by the neighbours to the west, the Polabian and Czech Slavs, although the precise chronology of this event is a controversial matter.

Archaeological excavations offer a better view of various aspects of culture among the earliest Poles. The modest finds provide evidence of an art that was as little varied as the society of the early Middle Ages. The need for monuments found expression in the mounds of earth raised as tribute to a great leader, or duke of the regional political organization. Few of the mounds have survived to our times. The most prominent height is the mound, called the tumulus of Krakus, which looms above Cracow on the right bank of the Vistula, a work of the seventh century, which is an impressive technical achievement of a society in which the territorial communities of free farmers were still a dominant feature. The mound is about 17 m (56 feet) high with a diameter of about 61 m (200 feet) and a volume of 16,000 cubic metres (571,000 cubic feet).

Art handicrafts, metal objects, especially weapons and ornaments, were imported from the Rhineland, Scandinavia, the land of the Avars and Moravia. By the early ninth century, Arabic silver coins and objects made by Oriental silversmiths, were brought in by way of the Baltic. Before the middle of the tenth century, the Slavic countries on the Baltic organized their own handicraft industries, imitating the Arabic filigree work, to satisfy the growing demands of their native lords. From Ruthenia there were the weaver's shuttles made of pink Volhynian slate glazed baby rattles.

Pottery used in daily life which appear in great abundance in excavations from before the tenth century represent a definitely native trend in ornamentation. The simple though varied decorative themes could be executed under primitive conditions of production, and it seems highly probable that they were performed by women as a home craft. On the vessels from northern Poland the grouping of all kinds of lines, zigzags, herring bone design and arcs exhausted the decorative possibilities. We may assume that the geometric design was strongly entrenched and had a long history here. In southern Poland the designs were arranged in stripes. This pattern may have resulted from the fact that the pots, or parts of them, were shaped on a potter's wheel. This technique spread across the whole of Polish territory by the tenth century, and the making of pottery became a trade performed by men, who worked in shops that were attached to the castle-towns.

Although the level of the Slavic civilization cannot compare even with the reduced and barbarianized heritage of the Mediterranean culture, and even less with Oriental culture, yet it did not differ from the culture of other Scandinavian and Baltic peoples, who were new members of the large family of European races. The Slavic civilization was based on many centuries of native achievement which survived and defined their distinct character through the ages and to the present day. From earliest times, the Polish people participated in the heritage of the general Slavic traits and made contributions which were distinctly their own. Only later, after the acceptance of Christianity, did they establish cooperation with the more distant German and Latin neighbours, and also with the closer neighbours, Ruthenia and Hungary.

Chapter III
THE EARLY YEARS OF THE POLISH STATE

THE CONSOLIDATION OF THE STATE AND THE CHRISTIANIZATION OF POLAND IN 966

The second half of the tenth century marked the consolidation of the State machinery placing it on firm territorial foundations. Although the Polish State arose from the former state of the Polanes, there are reasons to view the political organization ruled by that energetic Duke Mieszko as in many respects a novel achievement, effected during a turbulent transition to a higher form of organization. Ibrahim ibn-Yaqub, a Jewish traveller from distant Spain, wrote in 966 that the country of Mieszko, the King of the North, was the most extensive of the four known Slav states (the Obodrits—in present day Mecklenburg; the Bohemians; the Bulgars; and the Poles). According to his report, the Polish State had an elaborate fiscal system, with tribute paid to the ducal court which performed the function of the country's central administration. Tribute was used to pay the rank and file of the knights living in the environs of the castle-towns and to maintain a standing and battle seasoned squad (*drużyna*).

Archaeological data reveal that at least a score of castle-towns were rebuilt in the second half of the tenth century or built afresh on new foundations, and that there were important changes in the re-distribution of the castle-towns to locations that suited the needs of a more extensive State. The network of administrative, fiscal, defense and judiciary organs extended to all parts of the land and united the components into a single whole, which was governed personally by the duke and a circle of lords associated with him. The towns enjoyed the services of the peasant population which was compelled to pay tribute and to render services for the benefit of the lords of the castle-town and their garrisons of knights. Almost all these garrisons, whether deep in country or on its borders, were protected by a network of obstacles and fortifications in their approaches. Traces of these constructions remain in contemporary place names such as Zawady (Obstacle), Słupie (Post), Stróże (Guards) and others. The organization of the administration must also have led to the fixing of State boundaries by the annexation of small peripheral territories which, though independent, nevertheless vacillated in their fealty between one more powerful neighbour and another.

Mieszko's personal ability is evident in his initiative and energetic military and diplomatic activity. His vision embraced Europe from Rome to Kiev and from Hungary to Scandinavia. Owing to his great talent he could successfully undertake to carry out tasks which were also supported by his lords. The first task was to buttress the internal structure of a State organization constructed with admirable ingenuity, and then to extend the State's administration over territories which were gravitating towards the Polish State by ethnic kinship, indispensable to a Polish State if it was to emerge safe, and sound from the competition with the states of central and east Europe, which were also consolidating their power in the tenth century. The second of these tasks was completed in the last few years of Mieszko's rule, from 989 to 992. The frontiers of the State were extended to the Baltic coast, from the mouth of the Odra to the mouth of the Vistula, and included all of southern Poland from the western boundaries of Silesia to the upper reaches of the Wieprz river. The success may be ascribed to the pronounced internal cohesion in which a major role was played by the consolidation of the apparatus of authority further strengthened by the acceptance of Christianity in 966.

The consequences of Christianization extended to all aspects of life, though not to all at one and the same time. The introduction of Christianity by the court was in the first place a political act. The conversion of the country was a necessity to the group which was building a powerful new State. Not only in Poland but also in other Slavic and in Scandinavian societies was this group alive to the fact, that a new system of beliefs and views was necessary to consolidate the group itself, and at the same time to exert an influence on the whole of society at large, in order to integrate it with the new State organization. Not without reason did the local Pruthenian leader of the opposition to the Polish mission of Bishop Wojciech (Adalbert) fear the alien Christian law under the cover of which the Poles sought to expand their power over their northern neighbours. In the same manner, the tribal duke, in the borderland town of Sudovia preferred to trust his own gods when he welcomed Brunon of Querfurt.

There was no elaborate hierarchical system in the pagan religion of the Poles. Slavic rulers, who sought to reinforce their new States with a system of ideas, tried occassionally to reorganize and centralize the pagan religions. Tribal beliefs were organized and firmly implanted, as was the case in Kiev, before the Christian religion was ultimately accepted. Elsewhere the hierarchy of the priests of the chief god was raised in status, examples of which may be found among the Polabian Slavs and in Pomerania. At that time Pomerania reverted to pagan beliefs and cast off Polish suzerainty. The most advantageous and effective solution of both the internal and the exter-

Poland, c. 963–1034

Map legend:
- The Polish State in 992
- Conquests of Bolesław the Brave
- Boundaries of the Polish State in 1031
- ✝✝ Archbishoprics, bishoprics
- ✝ Monasteries

PWN Warsaw 1979
Imprint PPWK. Zam. 9074/79-X-30 218-10 285 egz

nal political pressures exerted by the neighbouring Christian countries upon the pagans was to accept Christianity while independence was maintained. This course was followed in the late eighth century by the Slovene and Croat dukes, in the ninth century by the Bulgarian, Moravian, Bohemian and Serb dukes, in the tenth century again by the Bohemian as well as by the Ruthenian and Hungarian dukes; in the north by the Scandinavians.

The Christian Church gave its sanction to the new social structure, lent support to and extended the authority of the duke. It provided models of organization and people well equipped to conduct correspondence and maintain international relations as well as to carry on the internal administration. The Church threw the gates wide open to the cultural heritage of the ancient world and to the achievements of the early Middle Ages by introducing writing, that basic tool of culture, and by establishing contact with more highly developed centres of culture, education and art.

The political conditions attendant upon Poland's conversion were advantageous to the country. Nothing is known of any kind of foreign pressure to christianize Poland. It is clear, however, that the decision to accept Christianity was made in order to strengthen her position with regard to the two Catholic neighbours in the west, Germany and Bohemia. Hence, this decision was justifiable as a measure of political expediency and to insure Poland equal rights in international relations. The choice between the Eastern and Western Church was determined by Poland's proximity to countries that professed the Roman Catholic faith and by the close political ties with Catholic Bohemia. Embers of the Slavic rites, surviving from the Moravian State, still flickered in Bohemia, but the Court and the Church of Bohemia had close ties with the Church organization of Bavaria. There is no conclusive evidence available that the Slavic rite survived the Moravian period in Cracow or that it had been implanted there in the tenth and eleventh centuries.

The baptism of the Polish duke and his courtiers occurred in 966 in an agreement with the Bohemian Premyslids, a dynasty which had a year earlier provided Mieszko with a wife named Dobrava. Emperor Otto I declared his support and confirmed the appointment of the first Polish bishop. The first mission, comprised of churchmen from the Holy Roman Empire, was headed by Bishop Jordan who, it is presumed, came from lower Lorraine, perhaps from Liège or from Italy. Bishop Jordan assumed the government of an embryonic Church organization. There may have been only one diocese extending over the whole of Mieszko's State and directly subordinated to the Apostolic See. The Polish mission's independence of the German Church must be regarded as evidence of the political perspicacity of the Polish ruler as well as evidence of his advantageous position in relation to Otto I who needed the Polish duke's support in his struggle with the more powerful State of the Veleti that lay west of the Odra river. The Christian name of Lambert, which recurs in the ducal family (carried by Prince Lambert, son of Mieszko I, and by his grandson, King Mieszko II Lambert) was the name of the patron saint of the cathedral of Liège. Other western influences noted in the earliest Polish clergy came from Ratisbon (Regensburg) and Augsburg. Mieszko I was known to worship at the grave of St. Udalrich at Augsburg.

Although the Church organization of Poland subsequently reverted to the model established by the Holy Roman Empire, it was nevertheless Bohemia, then still without a bishop of her own, which first helped the Poles adopt the Church terminology through the agency of her clergy and contacts between the Bohemian abbeys and the earliest Church of Poland. In consequence the terminology of the Polish Church is derived from that of Bohemia, Moravia and indirectly of Bavaria. It ought to be remembered that for many years before this, Christianity had exerted an influence on Little Poland, which was not governed by Mieszko I, preparing the ground for the conversion of his country. The Moravian mission which came to the land of the Vislanes at the close of the ninth century did not find the political conditions favourable to its aims, and there is reason to doubt whether the faint traces of a cult of the Moravian saints found in southern Poland can be connected with the mission of Methodius. On the other hand, the Bohemian mission of the tenth century did achieve its aim. For a time the Church of Prague maintained Bohemian influence north of the Carpathians.

POLISH BOUNDARIES ESTABLISHED IN THE ODRA AND VISTULA BASINS

The Polish-Bohemian alliance helped Mieszko I adopt certain elements of State organization which opened the door to foreign cultural influence. In the political sense this alliance covered Mieszko's southern flank during his campaign to conquer Western Pomerania. The country at the mouth of the Odra played an extremely important role in the economy of the ninth and tenth centuries, and the Baltic littoral with some of its ports, such as Wolin and Szczecin on the southern coast, became a powerful factor in the extensive commerce through the northern Ruthenian lands and to the Arab East. Large amounts of silver extant among the great many treasuries of Pomerania, Great Poland and Mazovia came this way from the Near East. In the tenth century, Poland entered the orbit of world commerce and politics via the Baltic. In the course of several decades, Mieszko tried to establish himself on the Baltic seabord from the mouth of the Odra as far as Pruthenia. For a number of reasons Western Pomerania became the most alluring prize.

About 963 Mieszko I, *rex Misaca* as the Saxon chronicler Widukind called him, suffered a defeat at the hands of the Veleti who, living beyond the Odra, also reached out for the whole area at its mouth. Trying to safeguard his position with regard to the Holy Roman Empire by paying tribute for the contested territory, Mieszko arrived at the mouth of the Odra in 967. In 972, he defended his prize by defeating Margrave Hodo, who had been greatly disquieted by Mieszko's progress, at Cedynia at the confluence of the Warta and the Odra. In 979 Mieszko successfully repulsed a German expedition led by Otto II and soon established relations with the regency which ruled the Empire. The Polish State held its boundary on the Baltic and the Odra and also established political relations with Scandinavia. Evidence of these ties is established by the marriage of the daughter of Mieszko I, Świętosława, identified by historians as Sigrid Storrada, first to Eric Segersäller, King of Sweden and Denmark, and then to Sweyn Forkbeard, King of Denmark. She is known as the mother of Canute the Great.

Under Mieszko Poland's main problems came down to matters that were of vital importance to the Polish plans, in short establishing access to the Pomeranian ports and participating in the goods and metal exchange of that time. Apart from the ties with the Bohemians Mieszko allied himself with the Holy Roman Empire to fight the common foe, the federation of the Veleti. This agreement proved valuable when the Poles parted company with Bohemia.

The territory of the Polish State was finally rounded off in the war with Bohemia for Silesia and Cracow, which in 989–992 Mieszko incorporated into his dominions. The order and chronology in which these lands were conquered is still a subject of controversy. The latest historical and archaeological data point to the different characteristics and to the high level of the economy and culture of the Polish highlands. Incorporated in the Piast dominions they immediately began to play a prominent role and drew the country into political problems resulting from the proximity of Bohemia, Hungary and Ruthenia.

Mieszko I took it upon himself to perpetuate his acquisitions in the south and in the north by strengthening the Church. It is likely that he had hoped to achieve what was ultimately accomplished by his son, that is to set up a Church metropolis and a Polish archbishop who was to crown the future sovereigns of Poland. Evidence of these diplomatic moves is provided in a document known by the first two words as *Dagome iudex*. The document contained a description of the Polish boundaries and of the dedication of the capital town of Gniezno and its environs to St. Peter by Mieszko, that meant a submission of Poland to the special protection of the Pope, a religious rather than political tutelage, for Papal power was weak at this time.

Poland, like some of the Scandinavian and Slavic countries and like Hungary, turned away from the archaic phase of development of her own free will. Poland accepted Christianity and by the same token entered the *Christiana respublica*, as this loose cultural federation was called by the contemporaries. Unlike the Polabian Slavs, Poland was not the object of the missionary policies of its Christian neighbours. On the contrary, Poland herself intended to perform a missionary role among her heathen neighbours: the Pomeranians, Pruthenians and Petcheneguians. The architects of the new States were quick to see that the values represented by the Church and the acceptance of its cultural contributions went beyond the core of the policies professed by an Empire which called itself Roman, but which in its essence was Teutonic. The conflict that arose between the ambitions of these rulers and the intentions of the German State with regard to the Church was to be resolved by a test of strength on the diplomatic arena and the battle field.

THE POLISH EMPIRE UNDER BOLESŁAW THE BRAVE

Upon the death of Mieszko I in 992, the majority of the lords declared themselves in favour of maintaining the unity of the State. This attitude enabled Bolesław, eldest son of Mieszko, to drive out his three younger brothers, born to Mieszko's second wife, Oda, daughter of Dietrich, Margrave of the North March. Another ruler endowed with a powerful personality ascended the Polish throne. He gave the country thirty three years of energetic political activity and brilliant military operations as he fought to extend his country's boundaries beyond the territory of the State.

In the first years of his reign, Poland continued the policy of cooperation with the Empire, established by Mieszko in the waning years of his life. The Holy Roman Empire evaluated the events that had come to pass east of the Odra as the birth of a new and vigorous State whose alliance would be of immense value. Interesting prospects of an agreement seemed to have presented themselves during the reign for Otto III, who in the year 1000 came to Gniezno to visit the grave of his friend St. Adalbert who had died a martyr for the Christian faith while conducting a mission to Pruthenia on the instructions of Bolesław. The negotiations at Gniezno were a conspicuous Polish success. Gniezno was established as a metropolis of the Church, new bishoprics were set up in Wrocław, Kołobrzeg and Cracow, and the independence of the Polish duke was recognized. The political programme of Otto III, which proposed to bring Poland into the universal empire as an equal of the German, Italian and Burgundian kingdoms, failed to win the support of the German lords. Under his successor Henry II they launched and continued a long war against Poland.

This meant a reversal of alliances. The pagan Veleti became allies of the Christian King of Germany who also received aid from Bohemia. Poland turned for assistance to Hungary.

Bolesław proved to be a formidable neighbour to the Empire. At the close of the tenth century he strove to extend his rule beyond the ethnic

Bolesław the Brave, c. 1000

boundaries of Polish territories. In 1004, he tried to unite Poland and Bohemia under his way, but was checked by Henry II and by the Bohemian lords. Łużyce (Lusatia) and Milsko (Milzenland), lands of the Polabian Slavs which Bolesław the Brave wished to annex in order to secure the western boundaries of Silesia, became the bone of contention in the subsequent Polish-German conflict. Bolesław managed to hold on to Moravia for several years thus establishing an analogous Polish march in the south.

Bolesław the Brave conducted war with the Holy Roman Empire in three separate stages: from 1004 to 1005, from 1007 to 1013 and from 1015 to 1018. The war was concluded by the peace of Bautzen (Budišyn) which left the controversial territories in Polish hands. The war revealed the military power and the abilities of the Polish commanders as well as the political acumen of Bolesław who used every means to penetrate Germany with the purpose of weakening the opponent. Through the marriage of Mieszko, his

son, with Richeza, the daughter of Herenfried Ezzon, the Palatine of Lorraine, Bolesław allied himself with the lords of the western borders of the Empire who were in opposition to the German King. Bolesław opposed the power of the Empire, superior to that of Poland, with a front that embraced lords, knights and peasants who were roused to take arms in defense against the invader. Despite the heavy burden imposed upon the country, the war was ultimately of benefit to the Polish State. The war led the social forces and more specifically the Polish ruling group to consolidate their ranks.

In 1018 Bolesław led a successful war of intervention in Kiev on behalf of Prince Svatopolk, his son in law, and annexed to Poland the disputed borderland territory on the upper Wieprz and Bug with the principal castle-towns of Czerwień on the Huczwa river and the lands on the upper San including Przemyśl. The Polish ruler stood at the peak of his success. From Kiev he sent triumphant letters to the Byzantine and Roman Emperors.

In 1025, at the very end of his life, Bolesław took advantage of the uneasy internal situation of Germany and assumed the royal crown. His son Mieszko II, who succeeded him that same year, also had himself crowned, emphasizing by this act the rank of the Polish monarch, the indivisibility of the State and the consecrated character of his authority.

THE CRISIS OF THE FIRST POLISH MONARCHY

In the first years of his reign, Mieszko II successfully continued the policies initiated by his father. In 1031, however, he found himself face to face with dire peril both inside the country, where his brothers led a rebellion against him, and outside the country, where he was threatened by a coalition of the Holy Roman Empire and Ruthenia. When the Hungarians abandoned their alliance with him, the Polish King found himself in a hopeless situation and fled the country.

His brother, Bezprym, took over the government but had to give up the royal insignia of his brother and father and to renounce title to their conquests, to Lusatia, Moravia and to the area on the upper Wieprz and Bug. The brief reign of duke Bezprym was filled with terror to which he himself fell victim. Mieszko II returned to the throne but he had to recognize the suzerainty of the emperor and grant to his two brothers a share in the rule of the country. Several months before his death, Mieszko II succeeded in reuniting the country. He died in 1034, leaving nothing but ruins to his son Casimir.

During the crisis, the structure of the State created by the efforts of several preceding generations, showed grave fissures, all the graver because they were internal. Their essence was the trend towards decentralization noted

Cieszyn. St. Nicholas' Chapel, 11th cent.

among the lords who had strengthened their social and economic position in the victorious wars led by Bolesław the Brave, and now looked with less favour upon the machinery of a strong central authority. As in many other countries of Europe so in Poland, the lords sought greater economic autonomy, that is they themselves aspired to the right to exploit the subject population. Some of them even aimed at territorial independence. The incentives for expansion, that were instrumental during the reign of Mieszko I and in the first decades under Bolesław the Brave, were now lacking. The boom of the luxury trade on the Baltic and the influx of silver broke down in the early eleventh century. The economic growth within the country was slow and could not hope to fill the royal coffers left empty when the once vigorous, though actually primitive trade, of the heroic age of the Slavs and Varangians in the ninth and tenth centuries began to wither. Ducal authority was broken in the eyes of the lords.

In 1034 Poland broke up into several regions. Power was seized by various lords and Casimir was driven out into Germany. Only one of these lords is known by name, he was called Miecław or, as some other sources would have it, Mojsław or Masław, cupbearer to Mieszko II. He ruled over Mazovia for ten years and it seems, that he conducted an active policy of alliances with Pruthenia and Sudovia, which was threatened by the expansion of Kievan Ruś (Kiev Ruthenia). There is some speculation whether Miecław intended to expand his rule over other Polish lands. Faced by the danger of peasant revolts, a part of the ruling group hastened to join Miecław's colours.

The crisis of the monarchy released in a section of Polish territories a mass movement against the social order that had been established by the firm hand of the architects of the Polish State. Soon after power had been seized by the impostor dukes, a peasant insurrection broke out and spread quickly to include the population threatened by the yoke of feudalism, the slaves and lesser officials of the State and to the estates of powerful lords. The insurrection turned against the lords secular and spiritual and at the same time took on an aspect of a pagan resurgence. The Church suffered serious losses in some parts of Poland.

Bretislav I, Duke of Bohemia, took advantage of the anarchy that broke out in Poland. He seized Silesia and pillaged and looted the towns of Great Poland. We know of an impressive list of treasures taken from Gniezno at that time. Among them was the reliquary with St. Adalbert's remains, which were a spiritual necessity for the organization of an independent Church of the State, which Bretislav needed, in order to promote his plans of establishing a bishopric in Prague as an independent See.

The Bohemian invasion, and especially the annexation of Silesia, was a warning signal to the German lords. They were not happy to see a strong Bohemia and professed in this respect the principle of an international equilibrium with the participation of Poland. The exiled Casimir, who had powerful relatives on his mother's side, including his uncle the Archbishop of Cologne, was given military assistance. He quickly returned to Poland and mastered the situation by 1040. He also found allies among the Polish lords. For many of them the insurrection of the people was a dire warning. The neighbouring Ruthenian lords also took heed when they experienced similar peasant unrest. Shortly afterwards Casimir concluded an alliance with Ruthenia which was further strengthened by his marriage to Dobronega-Maria, sister of Duke Yaroslav of Kiev. Keeping his own interests in view, Duke Yaroslav helped Casimir in the battle of 1047 waged against Miecław of Mazovia.

Ultimately, the maturing social system emerged victorious from the contest while the monarchy suffered painful setbacks which weakened it considerably. Silesia was regained at the price of tribute and the territories of Poland were again restored to their extent as under Mieszko I, although without Western Pomerania and other lands which had been won by Bolesław the Brave, but it is probable that Gdańsk-Pomerania had to accept Polish suzerainty. Under the pressure of adverse circumstances and surrounded by more powerful neighbours, the weakened state had to renounce any plans of regaining her previous acquisitions. The internal situation had changed from that which had prevailed under the Slavic and Nordic empires of the tenth century and during the first decades of the eleventh century. Significant structural changes became apparent in the situation of the Polish oligarchs. Having blazed a trail to the expansion of their estates by subjugating the free population, they would not countenance a reversion to the old order. The knights who appeared in this period were intent upon exerting an influence on the superior authority. The early medieval monarchy, rebuilt by Casimir the Restorer, entered a period of economic, social and political transformation.

ECONOMIC AND CULTURAL ACHIEVEMENTS OF THE ARCHITECTS OF THE STATE

Before continuing the history of the people and the State from its revival in the middle of the eleventh century, it may prove interesting to survey briefly the principal features of the achievements of Mieszko I, Bolesław the Brave and Mieszko II. The most striking feature was the dynamic growth of the new social system and similar progress in the diversification of the culture. The first castle-towns which arose in the Polish territories were inhabited by a few lordly families and their retainers. The castle-towns built by the centralized State on the other hand were an agglomeration of large groups of lords and strong military garrisons that evinced a growing demand for consumer goods. The demands were satisfied by the extensive luxury trade, but they also stimulated domestic production.

In order to make use of and to spur rural production, a system of services for the castle-towns and ducal courts were set up by the Piast monarchy, according to a carefully conceived plan. The system operated within its fundamental framework from the middle of the tenth century to the end of the eleventh century. Artisans and servants (*ministeriales*) pursued up to forty different crafts; cobblers (*sutores*), shield and bolt makers, bakers (*pistores*), cooks (*coci*), men collecting wild bees' honey (*mellifices*) and beaver hunters (*castorarii*) were still included among the agricultural people. The authorities enforced a division of labour in subsidiary occupations for the performance of special duties or provision of articles produced by the different artisans. In this division only a portion of the output capacity and specialized services were organized and then only where they were indispensable to the functioning of the medieval state. This autarchic method was soon found inefficient. Although place names like Szewce (Cobblers), Kuchary (Cooks), Bobrowniki (Beaver-hunters) and Bartodzieje (Honey-collectors) have survived, indicating the elaborate organization of these services, this type of organization was declining and began to disappear in the second half of the eleventh century. First to go were the craft services, followed much later by these of cattle breeders and hunters. The handicraft industry has arisen independently of this official organization of services. Agricultural surpluses and stocks of cattle increased in the course of the tenth and eleventh centuries; a variety of workshops were set up and a local exchange of products gradually came into being.

The first centre of this economic development was the castle-town (*gród*) and suburbs (*suburbium—podgrodzie*), a situation similar to that of the English towns and boroughs in the early Middle Ages, together constituting the first form of town life in Poland and in the neighbouring countries. At the foot of the castle-town proper (described as the *castrum* or *castellum* in the Latin terminology of that time) there sprang up a suburbium, beneath the castle walls. The suburbs were usually surrounded by a wall of earth and timber like the castle-town itself. Each performed a different social and economic function.

The castle-town enclosed the residence of the ruler ready to receive him at all times, or the seat of his representative in the person of the lord of the town, later called the castellan, entrusted with wide military, administrative, judicial and fiscal powers over the people residing in the neighbourhood. In densely populated areas, the radius of influence of the centre did not exceed 14 km (c. 9 miles), though this could be more on the fringes of the inhabited areas. The suburbs consisted of small built up areas with streets paved with wood, housing a motley population, ranging from members of the ruling group and the rank and file knights of the castle-town, themselves often engaging in foreign trade, to innkeepers, artisans and servants of all kind, as well as fishermen and peasants brought here by the will of the prince, or who settled there of their own accord.

In the eleventh century the castle-towns and suburbs attracted rural artisans and were responsible for the development of the crafts into permanent and distinct trades. Archaeological evidence reveals a beginning of specialization and consequent technical improvement as early as the tenth century in pottery, shoemaking and tanning, in articles made of horn, gold, as well as metalwares. The social conditions of life and work of the artisans are not sufficiently well known to us. It seems that they were dependents of the duke and were compelled to make contributions in kind, both in articles produced by themselves as well as in personal services. Fishermen and ploughmen, for example, were obliged to provide the castle-towns with food the production of which remained the major concern of the entire population.

As centres of growing consumption, castle-towns and suburbs encouraged the expansion and diversification of handicraft production. The margin of economic initiative expanded despite the fact that the craftsmen were burdened with obligations to the State. They could exchange their articles for food and other goods and valuables. Money, or more strictly speaking silver, both in the form of Arab coins as well as ornaments, soon made its appearance among them. In the tenth and eleventh centuries silver was weighed and therefore coins and ornaments had to be cut to make smaller transactions possible. Domestic money coined under Mieszko I was not abundant and was a symbol of ostentation rather than a medium of exchange. Markets were known in Poland already during the reign of Bolesław the Brave as places of public trade and were under the protection of ducal law.

The network of castle-towns and suburbs in the large expanse of Polish territories—250,000 square kilometres—were in direct conjunction with the density of settlements and other factors which encouraged people of principally non-agricultural persuasions to assemble and live together.

On the Baltic littoral most prominent were the early port towns of Western Pomerania, especially those at the mouth of the Odra, like Szczecin, founded as a castle-town at the close of the ninth and the beginning of the tenth century, Wolin, established a whole century earlier and Kamień, founded most likely in the early tenth century, Kołobrzeg was built at the mouth of the Prośnica river; the salt springs and salt works of Kołobrzeg operated as early as the ninth century. All these towns experienced a period of economic prosperity in the tenth and eleventh centuries both because of the Baltic trade and of the domestic production of pottery and metal and amber articles. The lords who lived in these castle-towns conducted an independent policy and successfully opposed Polish overlordship, which established a firm foothold here only during the reigns of Mieszko I and Bolesław the Brave. The independence of the towns was demonstrated by the elaborate pagan cult. The temples of Wolin and Szczecin built in the eleventh century vied with the splendour of the churches raised by the Christian rulers of Poland. Archaeological evidence, however, bears out the fact that the material culture of Pomerania, hence the manner of constructing towns and techniques employed in the crafts, was homogeneous with that of the remaining towns of central Poland. There is also abundant evidence of mutual trade relations between the coastal and the inland towns.

In the central plains, as well as in the southern highlands, the urban centres of this period were identical with the network of early fortified seats of the dukes. It can be estimated that there were about eighty such castle-towns in the Polish territories under Mieszko I, Bolesław the Brave and Mieszko II, Pomerania excepted. These castle-towns were not distributed evenly throughout the country, but were communities separated by large forest areas. Some of the castle-towns rose to prominence from the earliest days of their founding as main capitals of the State, or as significant provincial centres. Contemporary sources endow these centres with the term *civitas*, by which is meant a large community with diverse functions. Among the most prominent were Gniezno, a fortified ducal seat which expanded to one and then three suburbs in the eleventh century; Poznań on the Warta was established as a *gród* at the close of the ninth century and raised to the rank of castle-town of the monarchy in the tenth century with a large suburb from the same period; Kruszwica on the Gopło lake in existence in the ninth century with a suburb dating from the end of the tenth century and expanded later; Włocławek (known as Włodzisław) on the Vistula, an important military camp from the early eleventh century, whose suburb originated also in this period; Płock on the Vistula, founded as a castle-town at the end of the tenth century together with its suburb, was the Piast capital of ancient Mazovia; Sandomierz on the Vistula, whose *gród* and environs lead to the assumption that it was a large community in the tenth and eleventh centuries; Cracow fortified in the course of the tenth century enclosed a *gród* on the Wawel hill and a suburb together with other neighbouring settlements; Wrocław, the castle-town and suburb lying on an island in the middle of the Odra, the most important town centre of Silesia since the end of the tenth century. Finally in the second half of the tenth century, Gdańsk, the castle-town, port and suburb, flourished at the mouth of the Vistula, in that part of Eastern Pomerania, which was more closely bound with the Polish State than Western Pomerania. Several more names may be added to these nine centres which were either temporarily as important, such as Giecz, or but slightly smaller, such as Legnica, Głogów, Opole, Kalisz, Sieradz, Łęczyca or as Wiślica, Lublin, and Przemyśl in the eastern borderlands.

The early Piast castle-town performed a multitude of new functions in the broad areas that surrounded them. They were seats of the State administration, points of armed resistance and military outposts, trade centres for articles and services, religious and cultural centres. The towns were not only related to each other by a common state system, but also, though much more loosely, by trade routes. The routes served more often for the transport of luxury goods designated for the thin upper stratum of society rather than the population at large. The lords of the castle-town eagerly purchased such

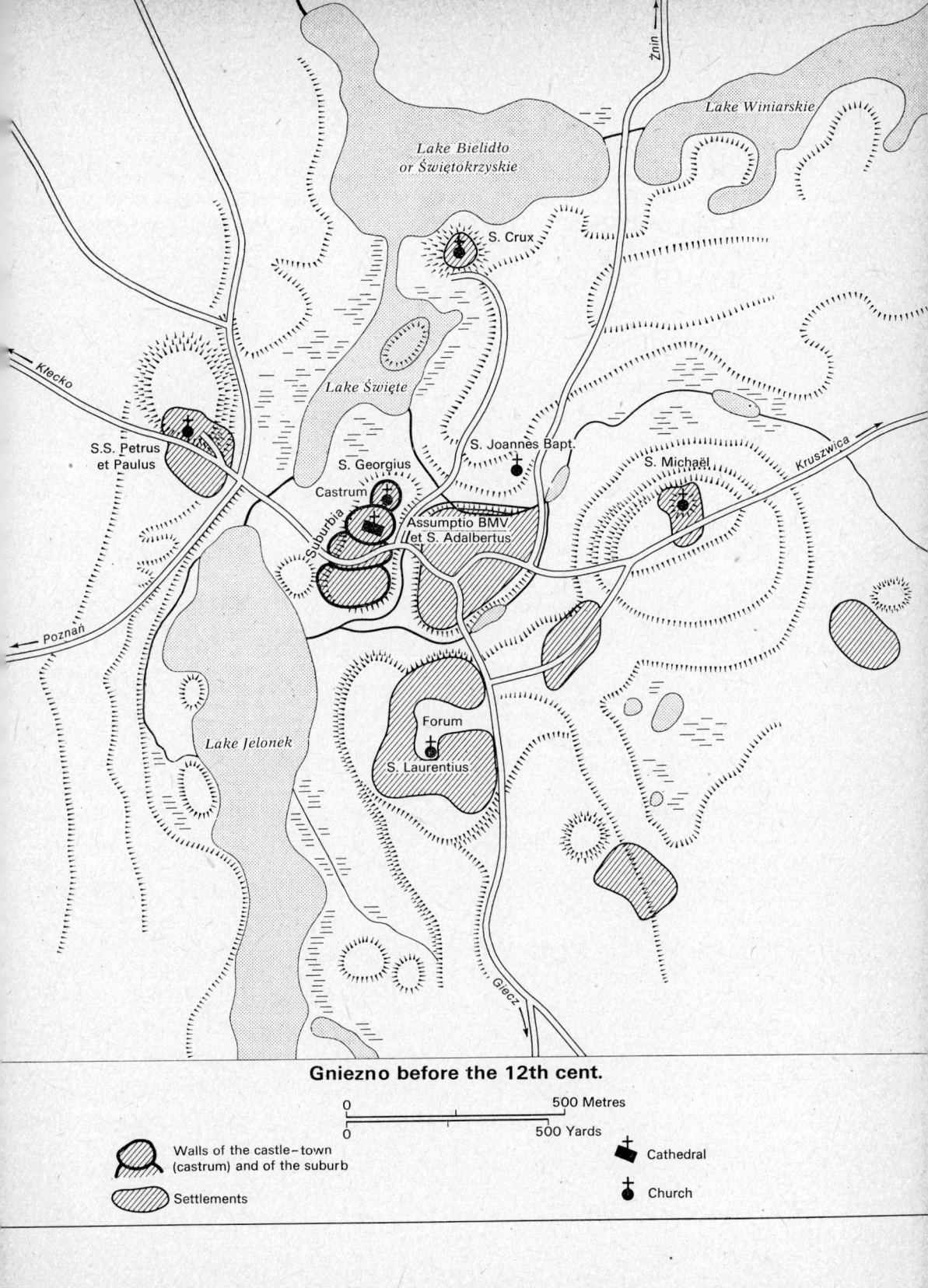

articles, exchanging for them raw materials and slaves which Poland of Mieszko I and of Bolesław the Brave was so capable of providing. The routes travelled by foreign and native traders, served above all as links between the chief castle-towns and between Poland and her neighbours. In addition to the Baltic trade which continued strongly until the first decade of the tenth century, later turning its attention to other commodities than metal from the Orient, one may note the functioning of a whole web of overland routes. They led from Kiev Ruthenia through Mazovia or, crossing the middle Vistula, to Gniezno and other castle-towns in the cradle of the Piast State. The roads continued from here to the mouth of the Odra, or through Lower Silesia and Meissen to Magdeburg and the German countries. Another route from Ruthenia led through Przemyśl, where a colony of Jewish merchants was settled in the first years of the eleventh century, and Sandomierz or along the fringes of the foothills to Cracow, and from there either to Gniezno or Wrocław, and finally through the Moravian Gate to Prague and farther west. Undoubtedly there were also overland routes to Pruthenia which began in Gdańsk-Pomerania and Mazovia and roads to Hungary along the Dunajec and Poprad valleys and perhaps also the Dukla Pass.

This trade flowed in a very narrow channel and trickled to the local markets in a very limited assortment. Although it imparted a certain glory to the early towns, trade by itself was not a decisive factor in their growth.

The lords who lived in the towns benefited from special economic, social and political opportunities which in turn led to distinctions in dress, housing and diet. Here, their mounting demands in the intellectual sphere were readily satisfied. The outstanding feature of these times was the desire of the Court and of the lords to hoard their wealth. That is why treasures of silver bullion money and other objects, which could be readily concealed in a safe place, are being discovered at the present time. They were stored as a reserve to use when luxury goods often haphazard in their appearance might arrive. Stores were the mark, the measure and at times the very foundation of the rank and standing of the lords and the monarch. The written records which describe the magnificence of the Court and of the generosity of the dukes are highly credible, an example of which were the gifts which Mieszko I sent to the German emperors and kings, as well as to the Cathedral of Augsburg, and Bolesław the Brave's rich gifts to Otto III.

In this period the culture of the Polish lands was preponderantly the native product of developing productive forces. The broad masses of the people were both producers and consumers of this culture. Here we also note a mounting demand and an expanding ability to satisfy their needs. The most tangible evidence are the wooden buildings of the tenth and eleventh centuries raised by carpenters whose skill was admired by Ibrahim ibn-Yaqub and the stone structures which appeared with the conversion to Christianity.

The large complex of church buildings in the suburbs of Poznań, consisting of several structures and a three-nave basilica which served as a cathedral, was built according to the findings of modern research immediately after 968, as was also the oldest three-nave church of Gniezno whose original foundations have been preserved. It was reconstructed after the fire of 1018 with a coloured majolica floor added at the same time. More modest structures of the same age are two monastery churches, one in Trzemeszno and the other in Łęczyca. The palatium, the adjacent palace chapel, that echoes the style of northern Italy and the monastery on an island on the Lednica lake near Gniezno, were all constructed at the close of the tenth century. These buildings provide eloquent testimony to the fact, that the Polish monarchs aspired to the level of the neighbouring countries. The palatium is reminiscent of similar, though bigger residences of the German emperors. On the island of the Lednica lake the stone architecture was combined with masterly timber work which provided the palace with fortifications, using up 40,000 cubic metres (1,420,000 cubic feet) of material. The Lednica complex included a harbour and a 700 metre (2295 foot) long road bridge that joined the island town with both shores of the lake. The royal residence of Giecz, also a centre of authority in Great Poland, was never finished. The construction was interrupted by the Bohemian invasion. Traces of eight such residences have been established. The church of the Virgin Mary on Wawel hill at Cracow, built on a complicated four-leaf plan with the addition of a front porch, was also constructed at the close of the tenth and the beginning of the eleventh century. It served as a chapel and stood a little apart from the stone dwelling houses of the castle-town.

Other arts and crafts evolved and improved in skill and technique. From the middle of the tenth century, great improvement was noted in the techniques employed in pottery. Geometric designs were adapted to the shape of the vessels and for the next hundred years the art of pottery was marked by a very ornate style. Silversmiths likewise achieved their own distinct artistic forms. In the tenth and eleventh centuries the silversmiths attained great technical skill thanks to their imitation of Oriental wares. The local style that evolved contained a wide variety of designs. Apart from non-figurative patterns there were noted, in the eleventh century especially, influences of Romanesque art coming from west Europe and Scandinavia and influences from Ruthenia which embraced motifs of the steppe art, and from Byzantium. Iron and nonferrous metal work also offered scope for the art of ornamentation. Articles of horn and bone found in archaeological excavations reveal a complete technical mastery of these materials and the artists who were capable of producing articles of daily use and for decorative purposes. In contrast with the rather rigid and geometric patterns used to ornament metal, horn and bone, soft woods were ornamented with Scandinavian basket-weave motifs. Anthropomorphic and zoomorphic designs came from the outside world, but they found their way into domestic workshops and gave greater flexibility to the strict limitations of non-representational art. There are individual figurines in wood which may have served some magic purpose and figures in stone as, for example, the mysterious stone figure of an ox found near the chapel of the Virgin Mary on the Wawel hill.

Simultaneously an intellectual transformation was taking place among the people. Through contacts with the outside world and as a result of sosial transitions, an incompatibility made itself felt between the archaic form of life of the Slavs and the new feudal system. At the close of the tenth century, Christianity began to make a wider and deeper impact. We know from the records of the times that the daughters and sons of magnates took holy vows. The defenders of Niemcza (1017) raised the cross with pride and at the same time with political shrewdness, against the besieging pagan Veleti whose aid had been enlisted by the Christian emperor. The Polish Court used the martyrdom of St. Adalbert as an argument for establishing an independent Church organization and provided the initiative for the writing of his life. Soon afterwards Bruno of Querfurt composed the life of the Five Brothers, Eremites connected with St. Romuald, who had been killed in Poland in 1003 and whose cult was propagated by the ruler and by the Polish Church. The annals brought to Poland by foreign clergy from other countries were continued at the Polish Court. Noteworthy political and ecclesiastical events were recorded there. The annals open with a description of a dynastic event set down under the year 965 relating to the arrival of the Bohemian Princess Dobrava to Mieszko I. The first version of these accounts was collected by the presbyter Suła, later Bishop of Cracow under Casimir the Restorer. This was the beginning of a literature written in Latin which opened for the upper strata an avenue to cultural contacts with the outside world. It has been established that King Mieszko II knew both Latin and Greek. Contacts with Germany and Ruthenia instructed the Polish Court in a feudal style of life. The foreign clergy played an important role in transmitting it from abroad. Poles may be found among their ranks quite early, for one of the first archbishops of Gniezno had a Polish name : Bossuta-Bożęta.

Besides the distinct culture and political factors which served to create a national Polish community, there were also the conscious attemps to mould a sense of unity among its prominent members. The most tangible evidence is offered by the adoption of one name, both in the native tongue and in the language of the neighbours, to designate the people of this area which was no longer an amorphous grouping of various component parts. This occurred in the lands between the Odra and the Bug rivers at the close of the tenth century when the foreigners began to call these regions by a lasting name of native derivation, a name which was taken from the original core, the small State of the Polanes (Polanie), and extended it to include the whole state. The terms Poland and Poles (Polonia, Poloni), accepted in international usage, reflected the essential fact that the nation and the State had already come into existence. The Latinized form of the country's name was known in Old High German as Polân, in Old French as Polaine, Paulenne, Puille.

History of Poland

Poland in the second half of the 12th cent.

0 — 100 Kms
0 — 50 Miles

- Boundaries of the Polish State and other States
- Boundaries of the Ducal Provinces under Bolesław the Curly
- **POZNAŃ** Capital towns   **CRACOW** Capitals of States
- • Castellaneries
- ✝ Archbishopric, bishoprics
- + Monasteries

PWN Warsaw 1979

Imprint PPWK. Zam. 9074/79-X-30 218-10 285 egz.

Chapter IV
THE AGE OF MATURITY OF THE POLISH MONARCHY

STRUGGLE FOR INTERNATIONAL POSITION
AND THE ESTABLISHMENT OF ROYAL AUTHORITY

The reconstruction of the State machinery, though on a more modest scale than under his predecessors, together with the organization of the Church, was the real achievement of Casimir the Restorer who died in 1058. The centre of gravity of the State shifted after the reconstruction to the south of Poland, to Cracow, which acquired the status of a ducal seat. Thanks to the consolidation of the monarchy, Casimir's oldest son Bolesław II the Bold could pursue the ambitious policy of winning independence from the Holy Roman Empire.

This policy yielded a most impressive result, namely the third coronation of a Polish monarch in the eleventh century. To achieve this end the Polish ruler offered his support to Pope Gregory VII in the conflict with Henry IV. But the most decisive factor was the revival of Poland's military strength in the struggle with Bohemia, to whom Bolesław ceased to pay tribute for Silesia. He also waged wars of intervention against Ruthenia on behalf of his brother-in-law Izaslav, later a protégé of Gregory VII, and against Hungary where Bolesław supported those dukes who were opposed to Germany. The coronation of Bolesław on Christmas Day of 1076 at Gniezno was performed by Archbishop Bogumił assisted by Papal legates, who strengthened the new organization of the Church and reestablished the archbishopric of Gniezno and the bishoprics of Poznań, Cracow, Wrocław and Płock. The coronation was to guarantee the internal consolidation of the monarchy. However, there was not to be another coronation for a few centuries to come. The policy of Bolesław spurred on a mobilization of centrifugal forces among the lords, who organized a conspiracy in which Bishop Stanisław of Cracow and the King's brother, Władysław Herman, took part. The conspiracy was quelled by Bolesław the Bold. The Bishop was sentenced to death and executed. The King failed, however, to gain control over the situation and had to flee to

Hungary (1079) where he was killed. The reign of his successor, Duke Władysław Herman was fraught with conflicting tendencies represented by the powerful lords. In the international arena, Władysław Herman abandoned all independent political plans and surrendered claims to the royal crown. Poland again found herself a part of the imperial sphere of influence. Władysław Herman married Judith, the sister of Henry IV, and again paid tribute for Silesia to Bohemia.

Sieciech (Sethec), a magnate and powerful palatine of the Court, was for a long time the actual ruler of the country, a fact which rallied the magnates in their opposition to the central authority. Taking advantage of the coming of age of the two sons of the old prince, the magnates demanded that the country be divided between him and his sons. The division occurred in 1097. Attempts to reestablish Polish suzerainty over Pomerania were without effect.

The Polish monarchy was given one more chance to rise to power by taking advantage of the social forces favouring a strong central authority. A Polish ruler who wished to maintain a unified state could rely upon the lower ranks of the knights for they counted on benefits arising from political expansion, namely, prisoners, loot and financial assistance from the prince, and they also attached themselves to influential magnates holding office at Court. Bolesław III the Wrymouth, the younger son of Władysław Herman, undertook and successfully completed this political gambit. Upon the death of his father in 1102, he took the field against his elder brother, Duke Zbigniew who ruled in Great Poland and Mazovia. Assisted by the knights, and having finally established an alliance with Hungary and Ruthenia, Bolesław drove his brother out of the country in 1107. In 1109 he repulsed the expedition of intervention led by the German King Henry V which was shattered against the ramparts of Głogów and checked in the forefields of Wrocław. The chronicler speaks of the "resistance of the dogged peasants" who, together with the knights, repelled the German invasion. As a result of this conflict Bolesław won complete independence and in 1114 Bohemia renounced all claim to tribute for Silesia. About 1119 he brought Gdańsk-Pomerania under direct Polish administration.

To a great extent Bolesław the Wrymouth owed his successes to the fact that he offered his knights a noteworthy goal as early as 1102, in the invasion and annexation of Western Pomerania, with its inviting attractive centres of industry and maritime trade such as Kołobrzeg, Kamień, Wolin, Szczecin and Uznam (Usedom). In the period of independence from Poland, Western Pomerania created a state organization which, though unconsolidated internally, was nevertheless aggressive toward her neighbours. The raids of the Pomeranians were a thorn in the side of Great Poland; Zbigniew's attempt to establish an alliance with them compromised him in the eyes even of his followers. On the other hand, Bolesław the Wrymouth's plans to subordinate Pomerania secured him the support of the preponderant majority of the Polish lords and knights. About the year 1122, following several military expeditions, the suzerainty of the Polish duke was imposed upon and tribute was exacted from Warcisław I of Western Pomerania.

Polish arms were followed by missionary activity. The first missions were led by the Spanish missionary Bernard and later with complete success by Bishop Otto of Bamberg. Initially Bishop Otto came to Western Pomerania at the bequest of Poland and with a group of Polish clergy. Later, however, he hoped to subordinate the Church of Pomerania to the influence of the Empire. A new expedition launched by Bolesław the Wrymouth in alliance with Denmark secured Polish rule up to the Odra river by 1129. The bishopric of Lubusz (Lebus) on the left bank of the Odra, founded in 1124, rounded off the territorial organization of the Polish Church in the west, and the Western Pomerania bishopric, established before 1140 (in Uznam and later in Wolin to be finally moved to Kamień), was to bind these acquisitions to the metropolis of Gniezno.

After a period of brilliant successes achieved by the ruling circle, the lords again began to foment discord. The Palatine Skarbimir, the duke's closest collaborator, rose in rebellion in 1117. Thus at the close of his reign, the international position of Bolesław the Wrymouth suffered a painful setback. His intervention in Hungarian affairs on behalf of Boris, the anti-German pretender to the throne, failed and invited several retaliatory raids by Bohemia. Eventually Bolesław the Wrymouth had to submit to the arbitration of Emperor Lothair III and in 1135 paid hommage to the Emperor for the right to Western Pomerania and the island of Rügen on which the Polish duke aimed to establish himself against Danish influence. At this time also the influential Archbishop Norbert of Magdeburg undertook steps to abolish the Polish Church metropolis, but his efforts were successfully checked by the Polish duke and clergy about 1136. The reign of Bolesław the Wrymouth was drawing to a close in comparative stability which guaranteed the economic and social development of the country.

FEUDAL DISINTEGRATION GAINS THE UPPER HAND (1138–1146)

Like some other European countries in the twelfth century, Poland was to enter upon the course of transformation from old ways of life to new and more highly developed forms. The Polish Court was alive to the fact that some old institutions were obsolete. The concentration of State authority in one person was no longer tenable. As we have seen, the monarchy was embroiled in the conflicting aspirations of local oligarchs, who turned the dynastic quarrels, claims and counterclaims of the ducal brothers to their own immediate advantage.

An interesting attempt at compromise with these centrifugal trends was the testament of Bolesław the Wrymouth, drawn up with the agreement of the bishops and lords, which took effect upon his death in 1138. The act accepted the principle that the country could be divided into duchies between the ruler's sons, each composed of several castellanies, which corresponded roughly to the old provinces. Three of the sons received their districts immediately, while the remaining two, who were still minors, had to wait for the lands held for life by Dowager-Duchess Salomea, from the house of the Counts of Berg. The testament ruled that the oldest living brother was to be the Grand Duke and that he would enjoy considerable prerogatives in foreign and military affairs and in ecclesiastical matters relating to the country as a whole. In addition to his hereditary district, the Grand Duke was to be heir to Little Poland and acquire suzerainty over Western and Gdańsk-Pomerania. Every duke who succeeded to these regions gained an economic, military and political advantage over the other Polish dukes.

In 1138 Władysław II, the oldest son of Bolesław the Wrymouth, succeeded to Silesia, whose boundaries embraced the dioceses of Wrocław and Lubusz, and the Grand Duke's dominions of Cracow and Sandomierz, hence the diocese of Cracow; he thus stood at the head of the Polish State. The second son, Bolesław the Curly, held Mazovia and Kujawy, hence the diocese of Płock and a part of the dioceses of Włocławek and Poznań. The third son, Mieszko III, received Great Poland with the Poznań diocese and part of the archbishopric of Gniezno. The remainder of the archdiocese of Gniezno, included in the territory of Sieradz and Łęczyca, fell to the Dowager-Duchess Salomea, who died soon afterwards in 1145. The Grand Duke took possession of her lands and immediately came into conflict with his brothers who hastened to the defense of the expected inheritance of the two youngest dukes, Henry and Casimir.

The first trial of strength demonstrated that neither the compromise devised by Bolesław the Wrymouth nor the restoration of the monarchy were feasible. Władysław II, secure in the feeling that his brother-in-law, the German King Conrad III, would come to his assistance, tried to unify the State at the expense of his brothers. The centrifugal forces reflected a certain course of historical evolution and, as in other eastern and central European countries, led Poland inevitably to feudal disintegration. The powerful magnate Piotr, son of Włost, declared himself against Władysław and was blinded for his insubordination. Archbishop Jakub (James), Palatine Wszebor and other great lords joined the party of the cadet dukes. A unified State in the old political sense was no longer possible.

Having lost the battle of Poznań in 1146, Władysław II, called the Exile from this time onwards, was succeeded by his brother Bolesław the Curly in the Grand Duke's dominions and in Silesia. At the same time Bolesław continued to hold Mazovia creating a separate duchy of Sandomierz which he gave to his brother, Henry. Bolesław the Curly and the other dukes paid a ransom to Conrad, the German King, but established relations with the

Włocławek cup, 10th cent.

opposition inside Germany. Neither the Polish episcopate nor the dukes accepted the excommunication pronounced by the Papal legate nor the interdiction cast upon the country by Pope Eugene III. In consequence of the second German intervention led by Frederick Barbarossa, Bolesław the Curly had to pay another ransom in 1157 and pledge fealty to the Emperor but nothing could bring back Władysław the Exile.

The division into regional duchies was impressed upon the mind of the society and accepted by it. New subdivisions were made by bequest. Upon the death of Henry of Sandomierz in 1166 in an expedition against pagan Pruthenia, part of his dominion reverted to Casimir, the last of the brothers, as the small Duchy of Wiślica. Mieszko the Old, the third Grand Duke, who as the senior of the family ruled from 1173, tried to invest his sovereign

Gniezno Doors, c. 1170-1180

authority over the whole of Poland in the full sense of the term, but his actions spurred an open revolt of the lords temporal and spiritual and led to his expulsion from the capital in Cracow.

Contrary to the principle of seniority, Casimir, called the Just, the youngest son of Bolesław the Wrymouth, was installed on the throne in 1177. In continued conflict the throne of Cracow gradually lost its suzerain status and sank to the rank of the other duchies. Although the authority of the Grand Duke was not formally abrogated, it became extinct however and the Polish State now consisted of a group of independent and sovereign duchies whose numbers continued to grow through the thirteenth century.

ECONOMIC FOUNDATIONS OF THE OLIGARCHY, VILLAGE AND TOWN PRIOR TO THE MID-TWELFTH CENTURY

The old form of the Polish State in the middle of the eleventh century, after its reconstruction, encountered many obstacles and a concerted opposition which it could not surmount. The new social, economic and cultural content of the state aggravated the political difficulties throughout the twelfth century. As early as the eleventh century, large tracts of land were concentrated in the hands of bishops and abbots who were not satisfied with the old method of payments from the duke's treasury and asked for a more permanent material basis in the form of large landed estates.

In this manner by 1136 the archbishop of Gniezno had over 1000 peasant farms with about five thousand subjects. Similarly, though at a slower pace, the foundations of the oligarch's power changed. They tried to create large consolidated estates though most estates still remained dispersed. Family solidarity was cemented by the fact that the estates were hereditary and henceforth Polish law acknowledged the custom of *retrait lignager*, i.e. the right of all kin to the estate of a deceased without issue. At the close of the eleventh and the beginning of the twelfth centuries, there emerged several clans of oligarchs with a decisive voice in the affairs of state. The members of these clans held important offices of Church and State from which they drew sizable benefits for their families.

The estate of a great lord of the eleventh or twelfth century may be estimated at from 200 to 600 chimneys, but many lords enjoyed an additional income in salaries paid for services rendered at Court or as a castellan. The lord's estate was inhabited by peasants who had been free and who in the past had rendered services only to the duke. The peasants now became a mass of dependent subjects exploited mainly by the feudal lords who, enjoying the privilege of immunity, were intent upon restricting the duke's rights upon their estates. After the suppression of the peasant insurrection in the second quarter of the eleventh century, the population did not rise again in mass rebellion. An elaborate system of names was used to designate various degrees of subjection of the peasant population, ranging from the free *rustici ducis* and *heredes* to the non-free *decumi* and *servi*.

The organization of the duke's own estate also was subject to change. The system of villages following particular crafts or rendering specific services, both types ministering to the fortified seat of the duke (*gród*), was mostly abandoned. The dukes created their own *curiae*, expanded the fiscal system and organization of customs and adopted more elaborate monetary and other operations. Although the dukes made land donations to the Church and secular lords, yet it is estimated that in the twelfth century the dukes still held half the land under cultivation in the country.

The rural population sought to alleviate its lot by fleeing to areas that were less developed and where feudal exploitation was not as harsh. Progress in agriculture, resulting from improved farm implements and a rising population, factors also noted in the neighbouring countries, stimulated a lively internal colonization in the border regions of the state and on the fringes of old settled regions, such as the south of Great Poland and the foothills of the Świętokrzyskie Mountains.

There are two ways by which it is possible to designate quite closely the eleventh century date that marked the turning point in the life of the castle-towns and suburbs of Poland. Coins provide evidence that the first abundant supply of metal coins minted in Poland appeared under Bolesław the Bold (before 1079). Silver could not be supplied in unlimited quantities to the mints because the flow of foreign silver from the East had stopped completely, the quantities that arrived from the West were negligible, and the output of domestic silver mines was low. Poland, nevertheless, managed to mint her own coins as an indispensable means of exchange and measure of value, bearing the ducal and royal stamp. Silver treasures, characteristic of the period of the rise of the new society, became rare in the second half of the eleventh century. Crude silver was required as coins of nominal value by the money and commodities market still predominantly local, but money was quickly adopted and became a daily necessity, too valuable to be hoarded. In the event of shortage of coins, payments were made in ermine, martin and fox furs, or in barrels of salt. Metal coins were the prevailing currency as witnessed by the fact that in the twelfth century payment of tribute and customs was made partly or wholly in money. Other evidence is provided by the system introduced in Poland between 1136 and 1146 of frequent and compulsory renewal of coinage, under which old money was called in periodically; the operation was carried under the supervision of the ducal mints and new coins were issued.

Not without significance also is the fact that more numerous documents relating to markets appeared in the second half of the eleventh century. Among them are markets growing up beside the castle-towns and in the suburbs, and those that operated in other localities. In the course of the

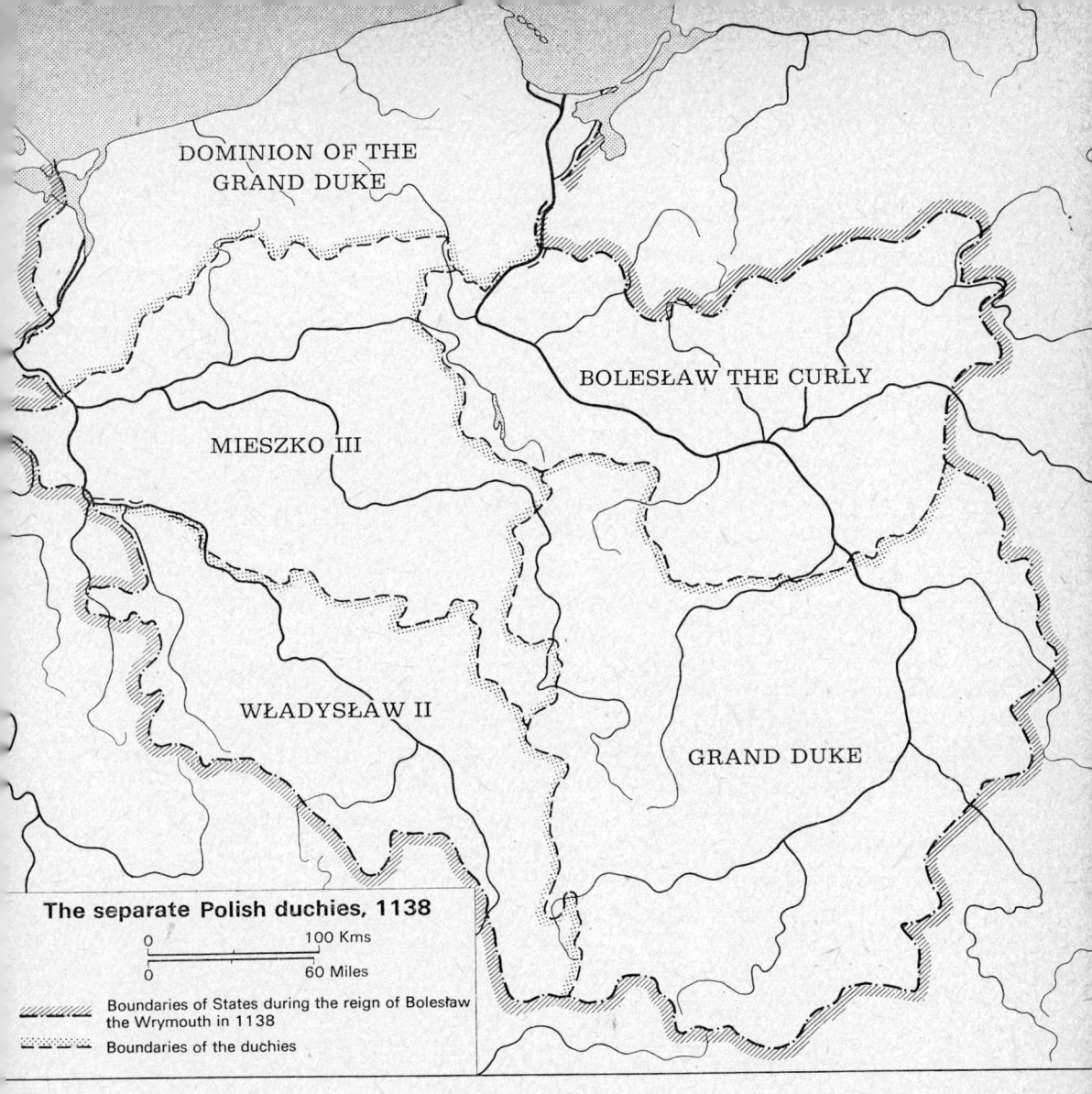

twelfth century, the number of markets rose to total about 250. This figure also includes Western Pomerania which was closely united with Poland in this century.

The number of centres of trade manufactures and services doubled in comparison with the end of the tenth century. This increase may be explained not only by a rise in population figures alone. It it estimated that under Bolesław the Brave, in about 1000, Poland (Silesia, Pomerania, Great Poland, Mazovia and Little Poland) had a population of about 1,250,000. Assuming that the annual population increase of Poland was 0.16 per cent, that is the same as the estimated annual increase for Europe, then it may be reckoned that two hundred years later Poland had a population of about

1,700,000, or an increase of 37 per cent. We see that the expansion of towns and markets is connected not so much with the population increase as with the changes that occurred in the social and economic structure of the population.

The stimulus was provided both by the growing production of urban handicrafts and the rising output of farms which was due in this period principally to the expanding acreage of farmed land and an upward trend in the number of livestock. More noticeable improvement in farming techniques was to occur in the following period.

On the other hand, the list of urban crafts, whose products are found in archaeological excavations, increased markedly in the course of the eleventh and twelfth centuries. While there is evidence of only a few crafts being practiced in the rural areas, and these only as subsidiary occupations, with the exception of metallurgy and mining, about a score of different crafts may be enumerated in the towns. Polish archaeologists have identified over 20 crafts and trades in all: ferrous and non-ferrous metalwork, pottery, tanning, shoemaking, bone and horn work, wheelwrights, shipwrights, glass work, stonecutting and others. The evidence for this is supplied by the traces of workshops, tools, articles of production and waste products, discovered at Gniezno, Gdańsk, Opole and elsewhere. The artisans attained great skill in their trades and produced a wide assortment of articles. Some artisans also combined their crafts with other occupations.

There is more information available about the social conditions among craftsmen. They made articles to order and also produced commodities for direct sale on the market. Sufficient corroboration is provided by the casts for large scale production of metal articles and the large volume of semi-finished products, waste products and raw material found in the excavations as well as written records of "artisans selling their goods" at the market. Less is known of the range of distribution, but it is likely that it varied with each trade and was regulated by the demands of a socially diversified domestic market. The subsistence economy of the Polish rural areas existed side by side for a considerable length of time with the commodity-money economy, to which some of the dependent peasants had only sporadic access, being restricted to the purchase of knives and salt. Part of the rural population as well as the knights and lords made wide and frequent use of the market. From the second half of the eleventh century, the lords began to expand their large land holdings intensively and established residences outside the towns.

At the close of the eleventh century, even the smallest rural centres had their weekly market day which drew off some of the pressure from the town markets. Some of the new market places were called after the days of the week, such as Wtorek (Tuesday), Środa and Śródka (Wednesday), Czwartek (Thursday), Piątek (Friday), Sobótka (Saturday). Others were called by some modified form of the word market (*targ* in Polish). Some of these were Tarczek, Targowisko, Targowa Górka. Others took new names in an attempt to designate their new social and economic role in relation to their former function as exclusively a settlement, took the name of *miejsce—mieście*—which in the Polish of that time is equivalent to the modern *miasto* (*locus* according to the Latin sources). The term *miasto* (town—city) was to become widely used in the Polish, as it did in the Czech language. It soon supplanted the once popular term *gród* (castle-town) in reference to urban centres.

The principal commodities traded at all the markets were articles produced by native artisans in the large and in some small centres. Of some significance also was the import of such mass commodities as western European cloth, which appeared in the excavations of Gdańsk at the close of the eleventh century, Baltic herring salted in Kołobrzeg, salt from Pomerania, Kujawy, Ruthenia and Cracow, iron in bars and in articles, pottery, glassware and other articles produced by goldsmiths and silversmiths. The hour of Polish grain and livestock export through the Baltic ports had not yet struck and, besides a short Arabian and Scandinavian episode in the tenth and eleventh centuries, the country concetrated above all on the development of its local economic possibilities for domestic consumption. In exchange for town produced articles, the markets and towns received farm and forest products, principal among which were honey, wax and furs; the towns were likewise consumers of grain, cattle and pigs. The towns, even the larger ones, were still engaged to some extent in farming, fishing and stock breeding.

Market towns and hamlets, in which the crafts were at an early stage of their development, acted as middlemen in contacts with the larger centres of manufacture, but they rose and were supported not only by commerce. Services, an important component of urban function, developed in these centres. By the eleventh century, inns or taverns appeared in large numbers in large as well as in small centres. Every market had its inn (*forum cum taberna*). The inn served as a place where the people ate, drank beer, caroused and slept and operated on other than market days as well. Customs and import duties, minting, sale of salt and other manufactures—all these were activities carried on in the inns.

Urban and market settlements also offered cultural services to the surrounding villages. Churches, often built near the markets, created a close network of parishes. The rural district was subordinated to the urban church. The ducal administration operating in the towns of the castellan still extended to the peasants, despite the immunity enjoyed by the lords spiritual and temporal, and the market days were the occasion to show the power of the ruler even in the times of Bolesław the Brave. It may be added here that certain urban trades, such as the butcher's and baker's stalls that appeared at the close of this period, provided services that stimulated rural consumption.

The large Polish towns of this period found favour in the eyes of foreign observers who compared them with the towns they knew. The Sicilian geographer, al-Idrisi, wrote about Poland in 1154, in a work based on information gathered over many years from merchants and Jews, that "her (Poland's) towns flourish and the population is numerous"—"Among her towns are Cracow (Kraku). It is a beautiful and large town with a great many houses, inhabitants, markets, vineyards and gardens". He writes in the same manner about Gniezno, Wrocław, Sieradz and Szczecin. It may be averred on the basis of archaeological excavations, traces of town plans, monuments of church architecture and the more abundant written records of this period, that towns of this category could have become large agglomerations in the course of the twelfth century, each with a number of settlements scattered over a fairly wide area. The settlements performed different functions and were held under different titles. The duke's castellan's residential castle-town, played the most important role in the agglomeration. The castle-town frequently had its own chapel and a fortified suburb. As a rule a cathedral or a few churches rose in the provincial or diocesan capitals. From the end of the eleventh century, if not earlier, the population overflowed out of the suburbs and established separate settlements, each with a market, inns and chapels.

The social and legal condition of the people who lived in these centres of urban life was widely differentiated, especially in such large towns as Szczecin and Wrocław, Gniezno or Cracow. All the inhabitants of the towns, as well as the artisans, merchants and buyers (irrespective of their social derivation) who came to the market, were protected by the law called market *mir* (peace) of the duke. The safety of person and goods was guaranteed by the castellan and his deputy. In the twelfth century, if not earlier, the trading centres received a magistrate for the market, who, in addition to this jurisdiction, also performed general administrative duties and acted as an agent of the treasury.

CULTURE IN THE ELEVENTH CENTURY AND IN THE FIRST HALF OF THE TWELFTH CENTURY

It may be assumed from the fairly large number of early Polish towns, with a widely diversified population, that they were centres of culture which gradually grew distinct from the culture of the Polish countryside. There the traditional Slavic way of life persisted, but the towns readily accepted and adapted to local needs the influences of both near and distant neighbours. The regional traits were softened and transmitted into original new forms.

The decline of the early medieval monarchy was marked by the universal acceptance of Christianity. The close network of eight dioceses, with Gniezno as the metropolis, was established for centuries to come during the reign of Bolesław the Wrymouth. The castle-towns each had their own chapel built in the suburbs or in the market place. At the close of the eleventh century secular canons were appointed; this helped reform the cathedral chapters and supplemented them with a network of provosts and prebends. By the middle of the eleventh century Benedictine abbeys connected with the reform movement of Lorraine were set up, among them Tyniec in Little Poland, Lubin in Great Poland and Mogilno in Kujawy. King Bolesław the Bold was most generous in building abbeys. In the second quarter of the twelfth century, the canons regular appeared in Trzemeszno and the Cistercian Order was established between 1140 and 1149.

Diplomatic missions and pilgrimages to St. Gilles-en-Provence, to Rome, to the Imperial Court and to Kiev, sporadic travels to the Holy Land, marriages contracted with the dynasties of Bohemia, Hungary, Ruthenia, Swabia, Lorraine, Austria and of other principalities of the Empire, not excluding ties with the Imperial Court, Denmark and Sweden, all these factors served to broaden the horizons and link the culture of Poland with the cultural centres of the Latin, Germanic, Scandinavian and Ruthenian countries. Poland and Polish affairs made their appearance on the pages of the chronicles and annals of the neighbouring countries. Some echoes may be found in the learned and literary works of western and southern Europe and in the intellectual climate where the *Chanson de Roland* was composed. The Crusading movement, however, never affected the Polish dukes and knights. Only a few rare exceptions, such as Władysław the Exile, or the powerful lord Iaxa, who brought the canons of the Holy Sepulchre to Miechów, were swept up in the Crusades or pilgrimage to the Holy Land. Polish rulers and knights and the Polish Church were busy fighting the pagans in Pomerania, and later in the twelfth century the more troublesome Pruthenians. Poland also remained largely unaffected by the popular heretical movements which did not find a favourable climate in a country where, though the population was Christian, it nevertheless reconciled for many centuries the teachings of the Church with the folklore of its daily life.

There is evidence that cathedral schools were in existence in the eleventh century. A growing number of Poles occupied the bishop's thrones and if the Sees were ceded to strangers then this was done by the dukes for the purpose of maintaining contact with the world and of sheltering them from the influence of the magnates. We know that Casimir the Restorer and Zbigniew were educated in foreign monasteries. Gertrude, the daughter of King Mieszko II and wife of Izaslav of Kiev, wrote Latin prayers and remained faithful to the Roman rite even in Ruthenia. A psalter has been preserved that contains the compositions of this earliest Polish woman writer, set down most probably in her own hand. According to two inventories taken at the beginning of the twelfth century, the library of the Cracow chapter possessed the basic church and secular literature. Polish pupils found their way to leading schools of the West, such as in Laon and Paris. The area of present day Belgium, especially the country on the Meuse produced two outstanding prelates, Alexander and Walter, born in Malonne, who became the Bishops of Płock and Wrocław respectively. Their cultural patronage is commemorated in several outstanding works of art in Poland.

The court annals were continued. Separate excerpts were made for the use of individual bishoprics and abbeys. The transitory supremacy of centralist trends at the Court of Bolesław the Wrymouth yielded a work of exquisite literary elegance which defended with great ardour and zeal the policy of state unity and of the specific role of the ducal dynasty, the *domini naturales* of Poland. This *Cronicae et gesta ducum sive principum Polonorum* was written in 1116–1119 by an unknown foreign Benedictine monk called by historians as Gallus Anonymus. Based upon years sojourn in the country and information furnished by persons from the ruling circle his outline of the heroic deeds of Bolesław the Wrymouth, projected against the background of the history of Poland and of the dynasty, is composed with profound perspicuity and provides evidence of the patriotism of Poles of this age.

In addition to these *Gesta ducum* there were also the *gesta* of the magnates who, as has been pointed out from the example of *Chronicon comitis Petri* constituted a grave danger to the former. Piotr of Silesia, son of Włost was a legendary figure even during his life. Married to a Ruthenian princess, he was reputed to possess a fabulous fortune which he obtained from the ransom paid for a captured Ruthenian prince. He maintained contacts with many monastic centres of the West from where, namely from Arrovaise, he brought monks whom he installed in the monasteries which he founded at the mount Ślęża-Sobótka and Wrocław. Soon after he was blinded and died, he became the hero of a Latin poem, a genuine Polish *chanson de geste* which has come down to our times in several versions of a later date.

A similar social phenomenon may be observed at the close of this period as regards monuments of architecture. Like the dukes before them, the lords now appeared as benefactors endowing building construction.

The earliest Romanesque art of Poland bears an unmistakable mark of the influence derived from the ethnically heterogeneous, but culturally rich archidiocese of Cologne as did the whole Polish Church reconstructed after the cataclysm. The western dioceses of the Cologne archbishopric among which Liège was the foremost again exerted an influence on Poland.

Romanesque cathedrals erected mainly in the suburbs according to the style prevailing in western Europe, though adapted to local needs and possibilities and usually reduced in scale, were raised by the effort of dukes and the resourcefulness of the bishops. The most impressive Romanesque structures are preserved to our day within the precincts of Wawel, the castle and cathedral hill of Cracow where the ducal residence was established. The church of St. Gereon and the cathedral of St. Wenceslaus with the St. Leonard's Crypt and nearby the churches of St. Michael and St. George, were built beside the stone-built town. At the close of the eleventh century, Gniezno, the archbishop's See, was endowed with a new cathedral, built on the classical plan of three naves. The cathedrals of Płock, Włocławek, Poznań and Wrocław received a new form of stone in the twelfth century. The abbey churches of Kruszwica, Mogilno and Tyniec were built earlier in the eleventh century. Other churches like that of Trzemeszno, joined their noble company in the first half of the twelfth century. The wave of Romanesque architecture lapped the shores of less notable towns. Chapels, usually rotundas with a tower or one-nave churches were constructed to take the typical example of the church of St. Nicholas of Cieszyn.

In the middle of the twelfth century, the lords with their growing financial power challenged the supremacy of the dukes. The previously mentioned Piotr, son of Włost, *comes Poloniae,* as he is called in the obituary of the St. Giles abbey, made a truly princely foundation: the St. Vincent abbey at Ołbin in Wrocław. This imposing complex of churches and buildings dominated by the abbey basilica with its granite columns was destroyed in the sixteenth century. Other lords, such as the Odrowąż clan at Prandocin, began with smaller chapels built within their residences, where emphasis was laid on sculptured and painted ornaments.

Very few early paintings survived the holocausts of war. Chapter libraries contain remnants of Romanesque illuminated volumes which had been acquired in the eleventh and twelfth centuries. Notable among these are the magnificent *Sacramentarium* of Tyniec, originally from Cologne, which dates back to the middle of the eleventh century; from the same period is the Pułtusk *Codex aureus* formerly at Płock, written in gold letters on purple. It has been established that one of the codices, namely the Cracow *Pontificale,* was definitely produced in Poland at the close of the eleventh century. Manuscripts of *Musica scolarum* of the eleventh and twelfth centuries were also brought to Poland.

Monumental sculpture was much more modest in scale than that found in Lombardy, its place of origin, or in the country of the Walloons. Examples may be found in the rare surviving capitals, portal jambs and other fragments of architectural ornamentation. This art flickered into a bright flame after the middle of the twelfth century and shines with undimmed brilliance in several peerless and impressive works. In spirit, however, it seems to belong to the succeeding period. The monarchy of the early Polish Middle Ages descended into the grave in a severe garb.

Chapter V
THE CENTURY OF ECONOMIC GROWTH AND SOCIAL TRANSITION

EVOLUTION OF SETTLEMENTS IN THE TWELFTH AND THIRTEENTH CENTURIES

The victory of particularism led to the rejection of an obsolete political order which, in many instances, constituted an impediment to the new social and economic forces. A new century of progress was inaugurated although a high political price was exacted for it. The defensive forces of the state were weakened, external pressure was not always successfully countered, and its true nature not always recognized.

The index of development is the increase of population mentioned in the previous chapter. An accelerated rate of population growth, resulting from improved economic conditions, is observed in the twelfth century. The general proliferation of rural settlements proceeded from the wider use of improved farming tools, most notably the wheeled plough and from the integration of peasant lands within the framework of large estates. In the course of the thirteenth century this second factor made possible the introduction of the three field system, which marked a great step forward in farming efficiency throughout Europe, to replace the old methods whereby the fields were allowed to lie fallow in alternate years. Agricultural improvement was affected in part spontaneously, in part as the result of pressure of the lords, who were interested in a settled farming system which enabled them to exact consistently large contributions. Encouraged by the higher revenues, the lords eagerly supported the planting of settlements in the vast forest areas. On the other hand, the population of the established settlements must likewise have derived certain advantages from this new situation, because only a pronounced improvement in their conditions could have induced them to remain in their old homes.

New settlements were established on the basis of a new Polish law called *mos liberorum hospitum*, or the customary right of free settlers. The earliest settlements were in Silesia, Little Poland and somewhat later in Great Poland. In essence the Polish law superseded the earlier services by strictly defining a rent in kind or money. It corresponded to the trend which prevailed

Strzelno. Holy Trinity Church, second half of the 12th cent., detail of a Romanesque column

Trzebnica. Cistercian Nuns Church, c. 1220–1230. Tympanum

in the eleventh century Europe, namely the freeing of peasants from earlier services rendered to the lord. This measure was combined with an agrarian reform. Analogous to the feudal conditions appearing in other, and especially in western European countries, landed estates grew in size in Poland also, partly at the expense of the once boundless ducal estates and partly by increasing the area of arable soil by moving into uninhabited regions. These lands were acquired by what was called *interdictio* or *inhibitio hereditatis*, that is by occupation with or even without the approval of the duke. The most profitable system both in the old and new settlements was to unite all lands in one area by purchase and getting rid of enclaves. The boundaries of lay and Church estates were staked out by *circumequitatio, circuitio*, a custom whereby the duke himself or his agent rode around and marked out the boundaries of the area. Judicial and economic immunities granted to these estates brought great economic advantages. The estates were granted independence and immunity in varying degrees from the intervention of the duke's officials. The Church as well as larger lay estates, founded their fortunes upon these liberties in the course of the thirteenth century.

This new development promoted a division between the estates of the knights. The position of certain groups of knights who owned more land with a larger dependent population was strengthened while that of the lower ranks of knights was weakened. A contemporary observer notes in the *Liber fundationis claustri Mariae Virginis* in Henryków in Lower Silesia, the wane of small land holdings in the thirteenth century and the rise of large estates in the vicinity of the Cistercian monastery which had itself stripped the lower ranks of knights of their property. As was customary in the West, so in Poland many knights took service with a bishop or a lord. A number of knights survived by virtue of being directly subordinated to the duke. A great many knights of lesser rank, derived from the earlier free population, continued to live in the districts of Mazovia where the growth of large estates was slow. The main reason for their survival was the fact that this duchy was in constant danger of Pruthenian and Lithuanian invasion. Consequently it was necessary to organize a permanent force by calling into service the knights who as a rule did not own serfs.

The growth of the towns was promoted by similar economic incentives. At the close of the twelfth and in the early thirteenth centuries, a small group of wealthy persons may be noted among the urban population, most certainly the merchants, who, on the basis of personal privileges, granted them by the duke or the bishop as overlords of the urban settlement, came to occupy a leading position among the inhabitants. This group corresponds to what were known in other central European towns as the *meliores*, the nucleus and backbone of the community, who organized the towns. In Poland the towns were headed by a *scultetus* and infrequently by a *villicus* or *procurator*, appointed by the duke to what was generally a hereditary office. In the early years of the thirteenth century, the *scultetus* administered the laws on market days and controlled the settlement, but principally he was the chief magistrate of the growing urban community. This community did not embrace all the permanent or temporary residents of the town, but was restricted to citizens (*cives, burgenses*) or denizens (*hospites*) enjoying this privilege in hereditary right. In several known instances these were local men, some of them knights. It comes as no surprise that in seeking the appropriate form of legal privilege, Płock granted its *hospites* the rights of Mazovian knights. From the earliest years of the thirteenth century it is possible to observe the presence of growing numbers of foreign, and especially German merchants. They strengthened the economic and social importance of the burghers of such large townships as Cracow, Wrocław, Poznań and Gdańsk and obtained separate liberties for their language group. Foreign craftsmen also were introduced into the towns. In the twelfth century, Walloon weavers settled in the suburbs of Wrocław and the Italian and German experts who came to Little Poland, enjoyed special mining privileges from about 1220.

At the close of the twelfth century, towns and markets were granted the *forum liberum*, or rights of a free market, in return for a specified rent. Grant of a *forum liberum* meant that all were free to use it and were not liable to ducal taxation or subject to the jurisdiction of the castellans and voivodes. No payments in kind, services or money were made to the ducal treasury or to the ducal officials. The scope of immunities was related to the role of the town. The immunities thus evolved into what became the Polish municipal law. The smaller towns adopted this method of organizing their social and economic life throughout the thirteenth, fourteenth and even the fifteenth centuries, abandoning it quite late in favour of another law, the *ius Teutonicum*, which had been tried and tested by the towns of Silesia since the second decade of the thirteenth century.

FOREIGN COLONIZATION AND THE INTRODUCTION OF GERMAN LAW IN THE THIRTEENTH CENTURY

In order to evaluate correctly the role played by foreigners in releasing the social energy that gave impetus to the transition of the material and social life of Polish towns and villages, it is first essential to grasp the fact that Polish towns had already acquired self-government and that they already had a complicated social and administrative structure before the close of the twelfth and the beginning of the thirteenth centuries. Foreign settlers, principally Germans, but Flemings and Walloons and Jews as well, all contributed in the course of the thirteenth and fourteenth centuries to the acceleration of progress with regard both to the volume of production and to the quality of urban life.

The foreign immigrants were not evenly distributed in the Polish lands. The largest wave of rural and urban colonists swept into Lower Silesia, Western Pomerania and Pruthenia, bringing about in the course of several centuries a linguistic change in these areas, because the ruling class, the courtiers of the dukes and the feudal lords, came under the influence of the German language while German peasant colonists squeezed out the Slavs and Pruthenians and restricted their development. In Upper Silesia, Great Poland, Gdańsk-Pomerania and Little Poland, however, the foreigners left their mark only on a few large towns and only in a very small degree upon the villages. In the majority of cases these foreigners were absorbed into Polish society at the beginning of the modern epoch. In a few important instances, such as Gdańsk and Toruń, they preserved their language within the framework of the then multinational Polish State. In Central Poland, Mazovia and Podlasie, and from the fourteenth century in Ruthenia and the Grand Duchy of Lithuania, the German element was of no numerical significance and was assimilated with the local urban and rural population.

Even in towns ruled by patricians whose language was German and inhabited by German artisans and merchants, the proportion of Poles in crafts and services was quite considerable. The mounting social and political tensions rarely erupted, however, into a conflict of nationalities. Class divisions were very complex, causing plebeians of both language groups to unite against the German patricians. Although there was open conflict between the

German community and the Polish feudal lords, as for example in the revolt of mayor Albert in Cracow in 1311, there were long periods of peaceful cooperation, and many patricians of foreign birth formed the ranks of Polish nobles.

The acceptance of German law by Polish towns was called *locatio civitatis*. It was widely adopted in the first half of the thirteenth century by agency of foreign merchant colonies which enjoyed the protection of Henry the Bearded, the shrewd ruler of Silesia. His urban policy was similar to that pursued by rulers in the neighbouring western states and its aim was to adapt tried legal forms to the country's commodity-money economy. Without doubt Henry the Bearded was guided not only by fiscal considerations, but also by the desire to invigorate the economy by bringing into the area both foreign merchant capital as well as expert artisans and miners. Henry the Bearded by way of experiment restricted this policy to smaller settlements. Before 1211 he granted the *hospites* coming to Złotoryja (in Auro), a famous mining centre of precious ores, the charter given under the law of 1188 to the burghers of Magdeburg by its archbishop. A few years later, but before 1223, a similar charter of a *Novum Forum ducis Henrici* was granted to Silesian Środa, a settlement located in fertile farming country on the important route from Lusatia through Głogów to Wrocław; this was based on Magdeburg law but with elements of the Flemish law. This was adopted without any changes in Nysa in 1221. Other *locationes civitatum* in Silesia kept to the version of the Magdeburg law worked out at Środa and called it the law of Środa—*ius Novi Fori Sredense*. It was later generally applied on the whole of the extensive region of central and southern Poland.

As early as 1237 the German merchant community of Szczecin in Western Pomerania, was exempted from the jurisdiction governing the urban Slav settlement, while in 1243 Duke Barnim I put the town's administration according to the Magdeburg law in the hands of the German community. On the other hand, the initially small German colony in Gdańsk and several other Pomeranian cities that were linked with the Hansa, adopted the Lübeck law. Another centre of municipal reform established by the Teutonic Order in the course of the thirteenth century, had a much profounder influence. In the area of Pruthenia that the Teutonic Knights had conquered, they destroyed the burgeoning Baltic trade and crafts in the markets and suburbs (called *liszki, pilate, palte*). The Polish territory, especially the Chełmno Lands, where a new town rose in 1233 close to the old fortified town of Chełmno, became the springboard of their activity in the economic field as well. The Chełmno charter became the model not only for the towns of the Teutonic Order but also for the towns of all northern Poland, including Mazovia, and was known as the *ius Culmense*.

Despite the wide influence that the administrative system of some towns had upon that of others over the next few centuries, it must not be assumed that the period of the earliest *locatio civitatis*, which ended in southern Poland with the Mongol invasion of 1241, constituted a rigid dividing line between one period and another. The search for the best solution was continuous, though some of the methods devised were a failure, others proved hardly adequate. Occasionally the founding charters were renewed, as in Wrocław in 1242 and 1261. In Cracow evidence of the *locatio* of a settlement near Trinity Church goes back to the reign of Leszek the White, or to be more exact to about 1220; in 1257 Bolesław the Chaste granted a definitive *locatio* for the town. The first founding act provided only for the appointment of a *scultetus* and exempted settlers, usually but not always foreigners from Polish law which remained binding on the native inhabitants of the settlement. The early charters were a far cry from the charters establishing a municipal self-government. The *scultetus* remained an official of the duke and the interference of the duke and his administration though still effective was restricted to matters relating to the market facilities. The original privilege established standards of court and trade law, but did not concern itself, even in the thirteenth and fourteenth centuries, with the political system of the town administration, which was allowed to evolve from local practice that was the outcome of the socio-political power struggle.

In the second period that began in the middle of the thirteenth century, the town charters embraced a broader area of Poland and a greater number of towns, such as Poznań (1253) followed soon by Kalisz (1253–1260), Cracow (1257) and many others. In the thirteenth century 38 towns were reorganized in Great Poland alone. Although privileges under Polish law granted to some inhabitants to the towns are mentioned in the sources still at the end of the thirteenth century, the constant use of identical legal forms led ultimately in the fourteenth century to a situation where the law called German law applied to all the burghers of towns which had been granted the *locatio civitatis*. For this reason the *ius Teutonicum* became synonymous with the *ius civile*, the rights of the citizens of towns. The chief magistrate was the *advocatus*, though still known as the *scultetus* in Gdańsk-Pomerania. This official was responsible to the duke, but his office was hereditary; he was independent of the town community and collected a large revenue from rents and court fees. Pomeranian communities were the first to aspire to free themselves from this subjection by purchasing the office and by establishing a town council. In this respect success was achieved by the town of Tczew as early as 1258. Other towns were less fortunate and had to wait many long decades and even centuries for this privilege.

The transformation of the municipal administration was the result of the economic role of the town, both in the local market and in far-flung commerce. The thirteenth century witnessed changes in rural life (villages founded on the principle of rent law), in consequence of which a considerable part of the peasantry, once they had settled their dues in the form of rents, became valuable trade partners for the burghers. The peasants supplied grain, cattle and pigs and in turn demanded articles produced by the artisans. Such products as cloth and ironware reached even remote villages in Poland over a number of centuries.

The growing commodity and money exchange in the local markets led to the slow formation of economic regions and of a hierarchy of towns, ranging from the regional capital through the smaller townships and market settlements, a growing number of which were granted the German law. The total number of towns did not change, or grew only slightly. Owing to their diverse functions, however, they performed a new economic role. Large towns, like Cracow, Wrocław, Poznań, Toruń and Gdańsk, conducted trade on a local and regional scale and ventured farther afield in their commercial endeavours, attracting goods to their fairs and their markets from the farthest regions of Poland and from abroad. The scope and assortment of luxury goods were extended to include silks and expensive cloth from Flanders and spices. More important were articles of general consumption, such as cheaper cloths, metal goods, precious metals, salt, herrings and beer of a better quality than could be obtained locally. The importance of the Baltic as an area of operation of the Hanseatic towns increased in the second half of the thirteenth century. The town of Lübeck had secured the cooperation of the larger towns on the Vistula which was soon to become the chief waterway of the Polish lands. The Hungarian copper and wine trade, passing through Cracow, Toruń, Gdańsk or Elbląg reached the Baltic. The East–West trade extending from the Black Sea and Ruthenia to the Baltic as well as to Bohemia and Germany carried furs, hides, cattle, silk and spices in one direction and metal goods, haberdashery (called Nuremberg wares) and cloth in the other. Polish towns added their own goods, agricultural produce, mineral salt and lead to the foreign transit trade. The ducal treasury profited from this trade by enforcing the right of way whereby the merchants were allowed to travel along stipulated routes, where they had to pay dues at the numerous land and water customs offices.

The towns sought to obtain a partial or total exemption from custom duties at all the customs houses in the given duchy. Poznań obtained the exemption in 1283, Cracow in 1288–1306. Occasionally, towns like Wrocław managed to buy the customs houses and themselves collected duties from foreign merchants. In the competitive struggle some towns obtained rights of staple (*ius stapulae, depositorii*) which obliged foreign merchants in transit to offer their whole cargo for sale to the local merchants, or to put it on sale for a specified number of days. Wrocław had obtained this privilege in 1274, Szczecin in 1283 and Cracow in 1306.

The changing pattern of urban occupations, the development of crafts and trading, the transformation of the social structure of the burghers and the influence exerted by foreign town charters, brought about a far reaching reform in the lay out of Polish towns. It is noticeable in the large towns but the change was apparent also in the small towns. The fortified castle-town with a suburb and several market settlements, which together formed the twelfth-century Polish town, was replaced in the thirteenth century by closely built up areas, housing the population with streets laid out in a regular plan with a fairly large quadrangular market. The basic element of the town plan was an elongated plot, on whose narrow side contiguous with the square or street, a dwelling with a workshop or merchant shop was built, the rear being occupied by a yard and outbuildings. Despite the striking regularity of the town plans based on central European experience in measuring and city planning, the plots, squares and streets were laid out in diverse patterns and the public buildings, such as the town hall, the public scales, the mercer's hall, meat and bread stalls, the parish church, walls or ramparts and wooden palisades, the gates and fortified towers were located in different ways.

The choice of a site for a new town development was restricted by the property rights of lords and the clergy, or determined by topographical conditions. There were cases, as for example at Trzebnica, where an old settlement was redeveloped within the old boundaries, or where new towns, as in the instance of Gniezno, were located on the site of one of the markets lying close to the castle-town and suburb.

Very often, however, the old town site was abandoned and the new centre was founded by charter some distance, even several kilometres away from the earlier settlement which, though it still bore the name of *stare miasto* (the old town), declined to the level of village or a suburb. This is what happened at Sandomierz, Łęczyca, Radom, Kalisz and a great many other urban centres. Some transfers were fairly complex in nature, as for example in the Sącz valley beneath the point where the Poprad joins the Dunajec and where Podegrodzie (suburb) as well as Stary and Nowy Sącz (Old and New Sącz) are a considerable distance apart (8–12 km). Even when the new chartered towns were located close to the earlier settlement, part of the population left the old town which then became a risidential centre. This may be illustrated by the example of the cathedral or collegiate isles called Ostrów Tumski in Poznań, Wrocław and Głogów. Once a castle-town with its suburb, the Ostrów Tumski now became a religious centre, the residence of the clergy and the servants of the church alone. In some towns there are still fairly distinctive traces of old settlements which have become merged with the planning of the new chartered towns. Grodzka Street in Cracow, for example, was the axis of the old settlement Okół. On the other hand, on the land of Pruthenians the Teutonic Order founded the Prussian towns, in a virgin area, which were notable for their particularly rigid geometric plan, of which one of the finest examples is Reszel.

Occasionally, the new town area failed to accomodate local and foreign trade. This was the case at Toruń. The Teutonic Knights settled in Górsk—Old Toruń in 1231. In 1233 they founded a charter town about 10 kilometres up the Vistula. The town was laid out on an irregular pentagon with the Teutonic castle on its eastern wall. In 1264, the New Town of Toruń, mostly inhabited by artisans and with its own town government, sprang up next to the castle and the Old Town.

As a rule, however, there was adequate room for construction within the early ramparts or later within the town walls, thanks to the ample allowance made in staking out the plots. The walls were built with the aid of the duke. In a great many cases he moved his seat from the old earth and wood castle-town to the stone castle, which was constructed as a part of the new town's defense system. This was the case in Wrocław, Poznań, Łęczyca and many other towns.

THE DUCHIES OF POLAND

There were a great many dukes in thirteenth century Poland. The prolific Piast dynasty divided its heritage among its heirs. The dynasty was split into several lines : the Piasts of Great Poland, Little Poland, Mazovia, Kujawy, Lower and Upper Silesia. The dynasty that ruled Western Pomerania was of local origin and was founded by Warcisław I, who has been mentioned in another connexion, a member of a lordly family and a vassal of Bolesław the Wrymouth. Sobiesław who died about 1178, one of the viceroys of Gdańsk-Pomerania appointed by the supreme duke, founded another dynasty which soon usurped sovereign power in this region.

The last representative of the system established by Bolesław the Wrymouth was Mieszko III the Old who died in 1202. He ascended the throne of Cracow on four different occasions amid the conflicts between various groups of lords. The last demonstration of the Grand Duke's claims was the journey to Gdańsk made in 1227 by Leszek the White, successor of Mieszko III in Cracow and son of Casimir the Just. The journey resulted in the tragic death of the Grand Duke which occurred on his passage home, following the conspiracy of two allied regional rulers, the dukes of Great Poland and Gdańsk. Beginning with 1202, the formed senior duchy of Cracow and Sandomierz was treated as a province subject to the same laws of succession as the other provinces.

We may now turn to consider the salient political events that took place in each of the duchies into which the Polish State had been split.

Upon the death of Leszek the White, power in the Cracow-Sandomierz duchy passed into the hand of the great lords, who during the minority of Bolesław the Chaste, the son of Leszek, placed various princes on the throne. One of them, Władysław Spindleshanks of Great Poland, son of Mieszko the Old, granted the lords in 1228 a privilege at Cienia in which he promised to observe "just and noble laws according to the council of the bishop and the barons". The privilege of Cienia is recognized as the first charter of a general nature granted to the higher nobility. Henry the Bearded and Henry the

Pious, dukes of the Silesian line who for several years were the rulers of Cracow and Sandomierz, tolerated the government of the Palatine Teodor of the Gryf clan, who styled himself "We by the Grace of God Palatine of Cracow". With the aid of the clergy Bolesław the Chaste, faithful servant of the Church, tried to enlist the clergy to weaken some of the lordly families and their retainers, but he met with rebellious opposition as did his successor Leszek the Black (1279-1288), a duke of the line of Kujawy, who died without an heir. Leszek the Black clashed with the Bishop of Cracow, Paweł of Przemankowo, and the Palatine Janusz of the Starża clan. Both in Silesia and in Cracow, the burghers were emerging as a new social force. They defended Cracow from the rebels and upon Leszek's death installed on the throne Henry IV Probus of Wrocław, one of the first champions of the reintegration of Poland.

In 1163 Silesia returned to the sons of Władysław II the Exile with the agreement of Bolesław the Curly, Grand Duke of Poland. They were allowed to inherit the lands of their father. They soon divided the Silesian territories into three provinces which in the course of the thirteenth century disintegrated further into still smaller districts. The swift economic growth of these lands, the leading economic role of the Duchy of Wrocław in particular, enabled Henry the Bearded, who ascended the throne in 1202, to attempt to expand his dominions. He managed to seize different titles of succession from various relatives, or to set himself up as the guardian of the juvenile heirs to the territories of southern Great Poland, most of Silesia and the whole of Little Poland. In 1238, these considerable though still loosely integrated possessions were inherited by his son, Henry the Pious. Upon his death in 1241 his sons' succession was restricted to Lower Silesia which they divided between themselves. Eventually Henry IV Probus reestablished his supremacy over the lords who strove to break his power. Most dangerous was the Bishop of Wrocław, Thomas II, who fought for the *privilegium fori* for the Church lands. Henry IV formulated the programme of the integration of the Polish territories; he seized Little Poland and attempted to revive the royal title, but he did not live to carry out this plan. When he died in 1290 he bequeathed Little Poland to Przemysł II, the energetic Duke of Great Poland, who a few years later was to place the royal crown on his head.

Great Poland entered upon the course of disintegration belatedly and then only for a short period. It was guided for 64 years by the firm hand of Mieszko the Old, the exponent of traditions of the old monarchy. Mieszko assigned to his sons separate provinces only under pressure and then only for a brief period. His successor and son, Władysław Spindleshanks, restricted and later removed his nephew and co-ruler Władysław, son of Odo, who yielded to the bishops and the abbots. Władysław Spindleshanks was a representative of the traditional relations between the duke and the Church; he opposed the Gregorian emancipation of the Church. Hence such measures as the election of bishops by chapters, freedom from taxes and celibacy of the clergy, were delayed in reaching Poland by almost hundred years. The Archbishop of Gniezno, Henryk Kietlicz, won this battle by turning for help to other dukes, who were hostile to Władysław Spindleshanks and his plans for expansion. Two meetings of the dukes, the first in 1210 at Borzykowa and the second in 1215 at Wolborz, laid the foundations for the evolution of the economic and judicial immunity of the Church in Poland. In 1247 Great Poland was finally divided by Bolesław the Pious and Przemysł I, nephews and heirs of Władysław Spindleshanks. When Przemysł I died, shortly afterwards the two areas were merged again. Thus Great Poland formed a solid base for all plans that aimed at the reintegration of the Polish duchies, especially under the rule of Przemysł II (1279–1296), the son of Przemysł I.

In Mazovia and Kujawy, however, the process of disintegration went far deeper. The irresponsible policy of Conrad of Mazovia, the younger brother of Leszek the White, who was established in the duchy from 1202, ultimately failed to deliver into his hands the coveted throne of Cracow. On the contrary, his policy prevented Mazovia from carrying out its principal task, in regard to the rest of the Polish territories, namely to defend them from the raids of the Baltic peoples. Conrad's sons were the founders of two dynastic lines. Casimir I founded the dynasty of Kujawy which produced Władysław the Short, the toughminded ruler who was to unify the Polish Kingdom. He was surrounded by a countless progeny of brothers and nephews whose sway frequently extended over one castellan's district only. The Mazovian line, descendent from Siemowit I, was even more prolific, dividing and subdividing Mazovia and ruling over it until the first quarter of the sixteenth century.

The territories of Pomerania were for years composed of two separate units, Western Pomerania and Gdańsk-Pomerania, each with its separate history. At the close of the twelfth century Gdańsk-Pomerania dissolved its ties with the Grand Duke. The rulers of the country came from a family of court officials and consequently designated themselves until 1227 by the Latin title of *princeps* rather than *dux*, the title used by other Polish rulers. This family also divided the country about 1220 with unreserved support of the lords who were hostile to powerful rulers. The country prospered owing to the grain trade of the Vistula valley and by its water-way, of which there is evidence as early as the thirteenth century. Gdańsk, the capital of the chief duchy in this region, began to play a decisive role by its ties with German ports on the western Baltic coastline through the small colony of Lübeck immigrants who settled among the native population. Gdańsk-Pomerania was a prize coveted from different sides. On the one hand the margraves of Brandenburg, moving through Lubusz (Lebus) Land from the middle of the thirteenth century, drew menacingly close to the Pomeranian duchies; on the other hand, in the east, the Teutonic Order was to become a still more formidable neighbour. Caught between the two, Duke Mestvin II (Mściwój), who succeeded to the whole of Gdańsk-Pomerania after the death of his kinsmen, concluded in 1282 a secret pact with Przemysł II of Great Poland, whom he named heir to the duchy. In the face of this deadly external peril, the lords of Pomerania agreed to the terms of the pact, which became one of the first steps toward the integration and the revival of the Kingdom of Poland.

In the twelfth century, Western Pomerania was divided into the duchies of Wołogoszcz (Wolgast) lying on the left bank of the Odra and Szczecin mostly on the right bank. In 1177 Duke Bogusław I of Szczecin appeared at a meeting held in Gniezno by the Grand Duke Mieszko the Old. In order to escape becoming vassal of the Danes, he paid homage to Frederick Barbarossa in 1181. This fact did not deter Denmark from exacting fealty from Western Pomerania three years later, but as the power of Denmark declined at the beginning of the second quarter of the thirteenth century, Western Pomerania owed fealty to no one for a brief span of time. Despite the opposition of the dukes, the Bishop of Kamień won in the course of the thirteenth century virtual territorial sovereignty for his ecclesiastic estates in the Kołobrzeg region, and strove to create an independent episcopal principality. At the close of the twelfth century he dissolved all ties by which he was bound to the archdiocese of Gniezno and became instead directly subordinated to Rome. The rapid growth of the towns of Pomerania, in which the German element became dominant in the first half of the thirteenth century, led to a close association with the Hanseatic towns. The Court and the nobility succumbed to Germanization in the thirteenth century, the monastic orders as the Cistercians of Kołbacz, brought in German colonists. The Slavic population lost all political influence. The castellan system in Pomerania developed upon the Polish model now decayed and was replaced by town administrations headed by *advocati* and *burgraves*. In 1278, upon the death of Barnim I, the ruler over the whole of Western Pomerania, the territories were again divided into the two duchies of Szczecin and Wołogoszcz. The towns and the lords organized themselves into a state representation and compelled the dukes in 1283 to sign the land peace of Rostock. They acquired thereby a share in the government and the right to resist rulers, who failed to observe the provisions of the pact.

Brandenburg likewise constituted a formidable external threat to Pomerania as well. In the course of the thirteenth century the margraves imposed vassalage upon territories extending as far as Szczecin. For this reason Bogusław I concluded an alliance with Mestvin II of Gdańsk and Przemysł II of Great Poland in 1287. Neither, however, was able to help Western Pomerania. The dukes of Szczecin finally severed their feudal ties with the March of Brandenburg in 1320, and in 1338 became vassals of the Holy Roman Empire. The dukes of Wołogoszcz did not recognize the sovereignty of the Emperor until 1348. One line had its seat after 1340 in Sławno and Słupsk, on the eastern border of Western Pomerania, and was bound politically with the renascent Kingdom of Poland.

THE GROWING EXTERNAL DANGER

The political disintegration of the former monarchy was accompanied by the ambitious plans of its neighbours to expand their power over Polish territories.

The tributary and feudal relations with the Holy Roman Empire established by individual Polish dukes in the course of the twelfth century, the last of these being in 1184 by Casimir the Just, were actually very loose. The decline of the power of the Hohenstaufens frustrated all hope of reestablishing the imperial position. Meanwhile Pope Innocent III at the express wish of several Polish dukes extended his protection to Poland. In the middle of the thirteenth century virtually all the Polish dukes established a feudal relationship with the Papacy for the purpose of neutralizing the claims of William of Holland, King of Germany. This formal dependence did not produce any political effects. Its tangible consequence was the reform of St. Peter's Pence which had been levied upon the population probably since the times of Mieszko I, and in the second half of the thirteenth century the increased activity of Papal legates in matters affecting the Polish Church.

Of real danger was the open or hidden aggression of the German rulers in the west and north, and the destructive Baltic and Mongol invasions from the east. The Tartar armies, as the contemporary European documents called the Mongols, wrought havoc wherever they passed. In 1241 their first invasion swept through the southern and central part of Poland up to Legnica in Lower Silesia. Here the knights of Silesia and Great Poland, the miners of precious ores and the peasants of Silesia, with some detachments of the Templar, Joannite and Teutonic Knights, united under the command of Henry the Pious. The Duke fell in battle and the remainder of his army fled to seek cover at the castle-town of Legnica, which resisted the Tartar onslaught. The nomads turned back and set out for Hungary. From 1240, the year the Mongols overran Ruthenia, Poland found herself on the borders of the powerful Mongol Empire from which further destructive raids were launched. In 1259 Lublin, Sandomierz, Cracow and Bytom were burned down, and in 1287 only the fortified towns of Sandomierz and Cracow could resist the invaders.

The north-eastern frontier lands of Poland were harrassed by the looting and pillaging invasions of the Baltic peoples, Pruthenians, Sudovians and Lithuanians. The attacks grew in intensity as the political organization of these peoples grew in size and permanence. In the thirteenth century the duchies of Mazovia, Cracow and Sandomierz, together with Halicz Ruthenia, opposed Sudovia and Lithuania. Futile attempts were made to convert Sudovia by missions sent from the ephemerial diocese in Łuków (1257), and likewise Lithuania where a Polish Dominican went as a missionary bishop in 1255. The Lithuanian raids repeated at intervals of several years wrought great damage and made incursions into central Poland. In the attack of 1262 the castle-town of Jazdów at an important ford on the Vistula was razed by fire,

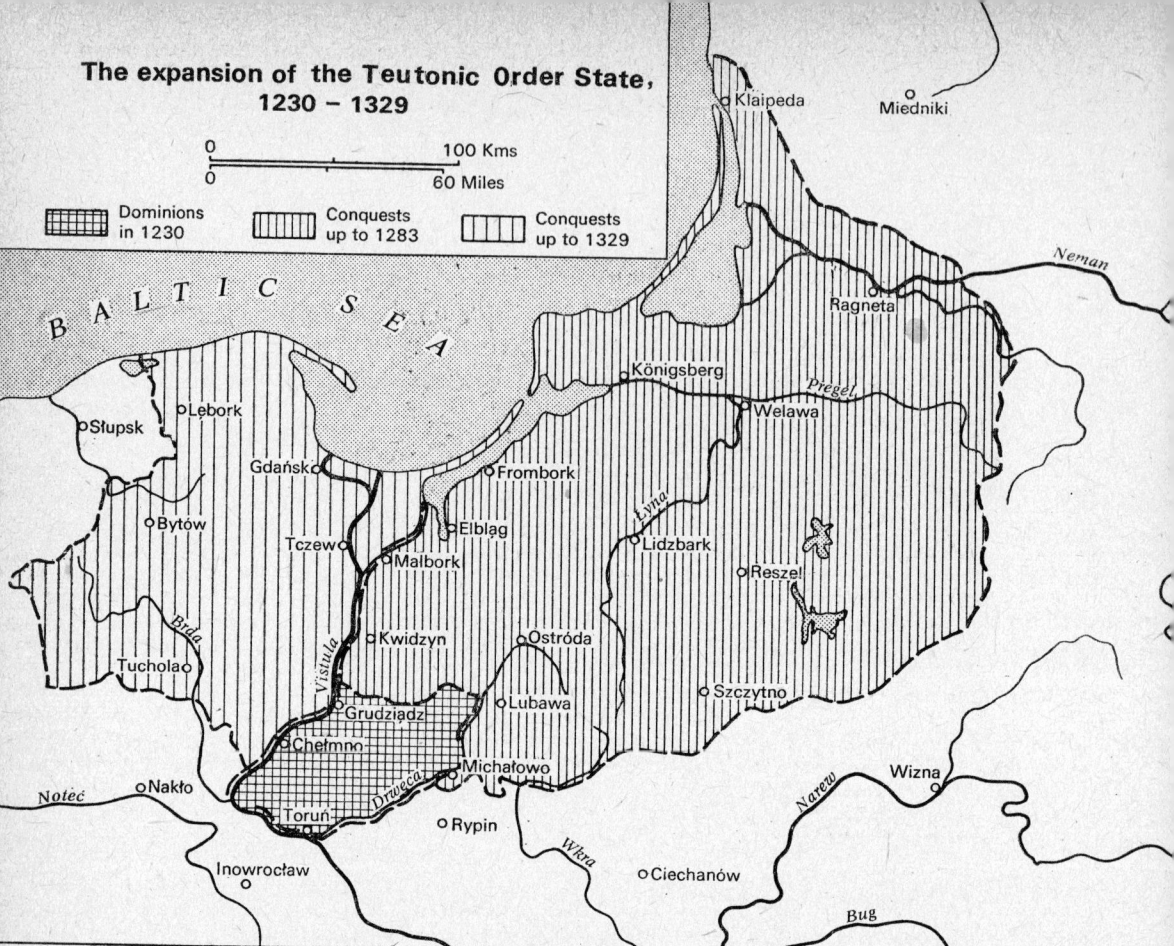

Some thirty years later the town of Warsaw was built a little below Jazdów in order to guard this important route. The raids of the Sudovians ended with the last quarter of the thirteenth century when the power of this people was weakened by a Polish-Ruthenian coalition and afterwards completely crushed by the Teutonic Knights.

The Order emerged as a formidable military force in consequence of the short-sighted policy of Conrad of Mazovia. Despite the many military efforts and attempts at trade and missionary penetration in the twelfth century and the early thirteenth century, a solution of the Pruthenian problem was beyond the strenght of a divided Poland. A Polish bishopric for Pruthenia was created in 1216 and Bishop Christian of the Cistercian Order established himself in the castle-town of Chełmno. Polish dukes organized coalitions against the Pruthenians who replied with renewed attacks against the Chełmno Land, Mazowia and Gdańsk-Pomerania. Other measures were taken to strengthen the defense of the frontiers, in Mazovia with the aid of the small order of the Knights of Christ, called the Dobrzyń friars after the castellanship granted to them, and in Gdańsk-Pomerania with the aid of a small Spanish colony of the Calatrava Order established in Tymawa. These measures proved useless.

Conrad of Mazovia therefore resolved in 1226 to invite the Teutonic Knights to Chełmno for the purpose of organizing its defense and the counter-attack. The German Order of St. Mary, called in Poland the Knights of the Cross, settled on Polish soil when their large convent was banned from Hungary for trying to establish the sovereignty of their lands and to throw off the authority of the Hungarian kings. From the start the Teutonic Knights set out to establish by fire and sword their territorial authority at the expense of their Polish benefactor and patron. Before they had settled in Poland they had received an Imperial golden bull which granted them Pruthenia as a fief. Some years later they also acquired Pruthenia from the Pope as an "estate of St. Peter" and forged a document by which Duke Conrad in 1230 had allegedly made them a gift of the Chełmno Lands and of all of Pruthenia. In 1253 Chełmno and Toruń were granted town charters according to the German law. The Teutonic Knights launched a systematic and cruel campaign of conquest against the pagan population of Pruthenia. For this purpose they brought in reinforcements of western knights and built fortified castles. In 1237 the Livonian Order of the Knights of the Sword joined as a separate branch the Teutonic Order. Despite the resistance of the conquered population, Prussia was subdued by about 1283. Thus a powerful centralized state rose north to Poland, hostile both to Poland and Lithuania. German colonists came in number to a country whose Pruthenian population had been decimated. The new towns organized the exploitation of the country under the watchful eye of the Order and established close contacts with the Hansa through the town of Elbląg, founded in 1237.

Another enemy grew and expanded in the west, namely the March of Brandenburg. It rose in the twelfth century in the territories of the Polabian Slavs and now cast its covetous eye upon Polish lands. The first to fall to the expansionary pressure of Brandenburg was Lubusz (Lebus), a frontier castle-town on the left bank of the Odra which succumbed in the middle of the thirteenth century. From then on the margraves began to drive a wedge up the Warta at the expense of Great Poland and Western Pomerania. The area called New March with its capital in Gorzów (Landsberg) was the springboard for the plans of further conquest in Gdańsk-Pomerania, where the Teutonic Order had similar plans of conquest.

Though these two bases of aggression, the Teutonic Order and the March, foreshadow the dual power of the Prussian state of the modern era, attention must be drawn to the rapid economic expansion of the Polish territories which offered ample opportunities for the settlement of large numbers of German colonists. How dangerous the colonists came to be was soon learned in these parts of Poland which in the last quarter of the thirteenth century made an effort to rebuild a united state. A rebellion of German burghers against the Polish duke occurred in Cracow in 1311 and was put down only with great effort. Western Pomerania dissolved its political ties with the remainder of the Polish territories owing to the influence of the German lords who infiltrated

Wąchock. Cistercian Monastery, 13th cent.

Sulejów. St. Thomas' Church, first half of the 13th cent. Keystone

the feudal class of the province, to the Germanization of the Duke's Court and the Church, as well as to the preponderance of Germans in the towns. The same factors may be noted in Silesia, although German influence was much weaker there and weakest above all in Upper Silesia. The State of Poland, which became reunited in the fourteenth century, recovered only small portions of Silesia and Pomerania.

EFFORTS AT UNIFICATION IN THE LATE THIRTEENTH AND THE EARLY FOURTEENTH CENTURIES

The territorial disintegration did not nullify the previously enumerated factors that kept the State and the people together. The concept of *gens Polonica* survived and acquired added value in a period of external danger and foreign immigrations. Even the fiercely independent Piast dukes who jealously guarded their petty dominions, had a sense of belonging to the *Regnum Poloniae*. In the eyes of her neighbours it continued to exist as a geographic and political concept, further enhanced by the fact that its territories corresponded to one ecclesiastic province with a see established in Gniezno. Occasionally several provinces were united under one sovereign head by family ties between the various lines of the dynasty. In the second half of the thirteenth century a number of contracts for life tenure and bequests were made which played an important role in initiating the process of reunification.

In this period moreover economic and political conditions were conducive to the renewal of the severed ties in order to form a united State. Economic expansion which pressed for large regional markets stood in direct conflict with the political disintegration and feudal anarchy. The Mongol invasion of 1241 brought to naught the attempt of the Silesian Dukes, Henry I the Bearded and his son Henry II the Pious, to unite the whole of southern Poland from Lubusz and Wrocław to Sandomierz and Lublin. Other social forces took over the task of uniting the country at the close of the thirteenth century. The first to declare in favour of the programme of integration were the burghers who were interested in removing the barriers to free commerce. For this reason they supported the dukes who stood for the unity of the State. However, because the German element was strong among them, these burghers preferred to see foreign sovereigns in authority, and consequently they were instrumental in helping the Bohemians to establish a shortlived supremacy over most of the Polish territories.

King Wacław (Venceslaus) II of Bohemia directed the expansion of his powerful state toward Silesia and later the whole of Poland. He claimed the inheritance of Henry IV Probus. Despite other dispositions made by Henry's will, Wacław II seized the territories and in 1291 granted the clergy, towns and knights of Little Poland the privilege of Lutomyśl in which he vowed that he would not impose any new taxes upon them. He occupied Little Poland despite the resistance of Władysław the Short, the pretender to Cracow and Sandomierz and brother of Leszek the Black. Wacław made several of the Silesian duchies his vassals.

Another kind of attempt to integrate the Polish territories came from the feudal classes, the clergy and the broad masses of knights. The increasingly coherent Polish gentry was hostile alike to foreign intervention and to lords descended from powerful old families, the champions of disintegration. That is why this class formulated a programme of national unification. With a flourishing economy, ruled efficiently by its dukes and fully aware of the external dangers, Great Poland was the centre of this integration movement. The metropolis of Gniezno played here an important and positive role. Archbishop Jakub of the Świnka clan elevated Przemysł II of Great Poland and served as his political adviser in the acquisition of Gdańsk-Pomerania.

In 1295 he crowned him King of Poland in Gniezno. The people who strove for unity were proud of the revival of the Kingdom after an interval of so many centuries. Evidence of it may be found in the inscription on the royal seal of Przemysł II: *Reddidit Ipse Potens Victricia Signa Polonis.*

The programme of integration was merely initiated. Polish territory, however, was never restored to the size of the first Polish monarchy and the Polish rulers found it extremely difficult to keep the royal crown on their heads. Przemysł II died in the winter of 1296, treacherously murdered by assassins sent from the March of Brandenburg and cooperating with the native opposition led by two local clans.

Przemysł II bequeathed his kingdom to Henry of Głogów, a Silesian duke whom Wacław barred from his birthright in Wrocław. Henry was a proponent of the Silesian concept of the integration of Poland. The lords of Great Poland resented the fact that Henry surrounded himself with Germans and that he based himself on the German patricians in the towns. They therefore gave their support to Władysław the Short, Duke of Kujawy, who failed however to fulfil their hopes in putting down the anarchy of the knights, in combating highway robbery and other abuses. In consequence of his quarrel with Bishop Andrzej of Poznań the lords deposed Władysław the Short in 1300 and installed Wacław II on the throne of Great Poland. In this year Wacław II was crowned King of Poland at Gniezno and further strengthened his position by marrying Richeza, daughter of King Przemysł II.

The reign of Wacław II (to 1305), and of his son Wacław III (to 1306), demonstrated to Polish political circles the perils that arise when foreigners lay hold of the throne. Both monarchs based their power upon the German patricians and German monasteries. They placed Germans and Bohemians in high posts. Immediately upon his coronation Wacław II accepted Poland as an imperial fief from Albrecht of Habsburg, and concluded alliances with Brandenburg and the Teutonic Order. Wacław III negotiated with the Margrave of Brandenburg an exchange of Gdańsk-Pomerania, which was to go to Brandenburg, for Meissen, which lay closer to Bohemia. The rising opposition in Little Poland found a leader in the undaunted pretender Władysław the Short. He spent his years of exile planning alliances with Pope Boniface VIII, with Charles Robert d'Anjou, King of Hungary, and with Halicz Ruthenia.

Simultaneously a conviction was taking root among the privileged classes of Poland that the State must be united on the principle of self-determination. After the death of Wacław III in 1306, the claims of the successive Kings of Bohemia, Rudolf of Habsburg and John of Luxemburg, to the Polish succession were both rejected. Władysław the Short drove out the Bohemian garrisons and took possession of the province of Cracow–Sandomierz as well as Gdańsk-Pomerania. The lords of Great Poland remained hostile and gave the throne of their province to Henry of Głogów. The path to integration bristled with adversity.

The cause of Władysław the Short was betrayed in Gdańsk-Pomerania by

the powerful Święca clan. They submitted the duchy to the Brandenburgers when they laid siege to Gdańsk in 1308. Bogusza, judge of Pomerania, defended the town, but as he could not hope for prompt aid from his duke, turned for help to the Teutonic Knights in return for which he promised to defray all the expenses of war. The Teutonic Knights repulsed the invaders but then treacherously got inside the town of Gdańsk, drove out the Polish garrison and slaughtered the population of the suburbs, which they destroyed. They slaughtered also the settlement of German merchants who competed with their own town of Elbląg. They occupied eventually the rest of the country by force of arms and in this manner captured the mouth of the Vistula.

The newly uniting Polish State was at that time composed only of Little Poland, Kujawy, Łęczyca and Sieradz. Its ruler looked on helplessly as alien rule entrenched itself in one of his principal provinces. Only with great effort was the dangerous conspiracy of the burghers and German monasteries organized in favour of John of Luxemburg put down in 1311 by Albert, magistrate (*advocatus*) of Cracow and Bishop Jan Muskata, a Bohemian. It was Great Poland which took the step towards reunification when the collective rule of the five sons of Henry of Głogów proved to be inconsistent with the interests of the Polish knights and lords. The Archbishop of Gniezno laid a curse on the dukes and the knights of Great Poland defeated them arms in hands. In 1314 the conquest of Great Poland by Władysław the Short was completed.

Being very knowledgeable about international politics, Władysław the Short was able to establish his position in spite of the constant threats from the Luxemburg dynasty in Bohemia, as well as from the March of Brandenburg and the Teutonic Order. Władysław continued the alliance with Hungary and concluded new alliances with Denmark, Sweden and Norway, and with the dukes of Western Pomerania, Mecklenburg and Lithuania. In 1320 he was crowned King of Poland in Cracow, if not with the assent, at least with the assurance of Papal neutrality at the price of regulating Peter's Pence.

As Poland united, the political horizons of Władysław the Short and of his advisors, chosen from among the lesser nobility, grew wider. Władysław, once an insignificant Duke of Kujawy, became by his own ability and efforts a monarch who was fully enlightened on the subject of European political coalitions. His modest royal court became the school of political thought for people who had spent their youth in the atmosphere of regional particularism and the limited possibilities of rival duchies. Now they faced a challenge to which the capacity of the restored Kingdom was equal. The tasks clearly defined by the international and internal situation were: the defense of unity against foreign intervention and the reorganization of the State, its modernization to meet the conditions of the times—in short the consolidation of the Polish Crown.

TRANSITION OF POLISH CULTURE FROM THE ROMANESQUE TO THE GOTHIC

The territories most seriously menaced by the foreign influx, became in the thirteenth century the scene of the first national antagonisms. In Silesia, for example, some bishops of Wrocław conducted the defense of Polish holdings in Church benefices. Papal interests were threatened by the failure of the Germans to pay Peter's Pence. At the synod of Łęczyca held in 1285, the Polish Church adopted a resolution which provided that in order to nurture and develop the Polish language, "only those might be appointed masters of the cathedral, monastery and other schools who spoke Polish well, for they must be able to explain authors' works to the boys in Polish".

The written word was widely used, especially in legal practice, where a written document had the power of tangible evidence of transactions. Beginning with the thirteenth century the ducal chanceries protected the monopoly of notaries by registering all land transactions. The school system was expanded and parochial Church schools made their appearance in the towns. Quite early, in the thirteenth century, the German language was used in administrative court acts in towns where the Germans constituted a large proportion of the population.

The thirteenth century witnessed the first preserved examples of Polish prose and poetry, for the most part Church sermons and hymns. The Benedictine chorale was supplemented by the Cistercian chorale in the twelfth century. Far more popular became the Roman version of the Franciscan chorale and at the same time appeared a distinct diocesan chorale. These styles are fully illustrated by well preserved musical scores. Some of the compositions which have survived may well have been composed in Poland.

The historical chronicles are deeply national in their tone. Master Wincenty, Bishop of Cracow, who died in the Cistercian monastery of Jędrzejów in 1223, wrote a chronicle noted for its elegant rhetoric. He conceived the ambitious plan of linking the history of Poland with ancient history. This explains the literary versions of dynastic legends written in Latin, which in Poland performed the role of the *chanson de geste*. Although Master Vincent's chronicle praises the government of the lords and records the existence of regional duchies, yet Poland emerges in the chronicle as an ethnic whole. The *Chronicle of Great Poland*, written in the late thirteenth century, is a notable document, among other historical works outlining the ideology of state union and proving the fact that the West Slavs constituted a single community. The programme of state integration as noted in hagiographic literature was represented by the cult of St. Stanisław Bishop of Cracow, who was canonized in 1253 as patron of Poland. According to the *Vita maior Sancti Stanislai*, written by Wincenty of Kielce who lived at the time of the canonization, the quartered body of the martyr bishop miraculously grew together again—and this was also to be the fate of partitioned Poland.

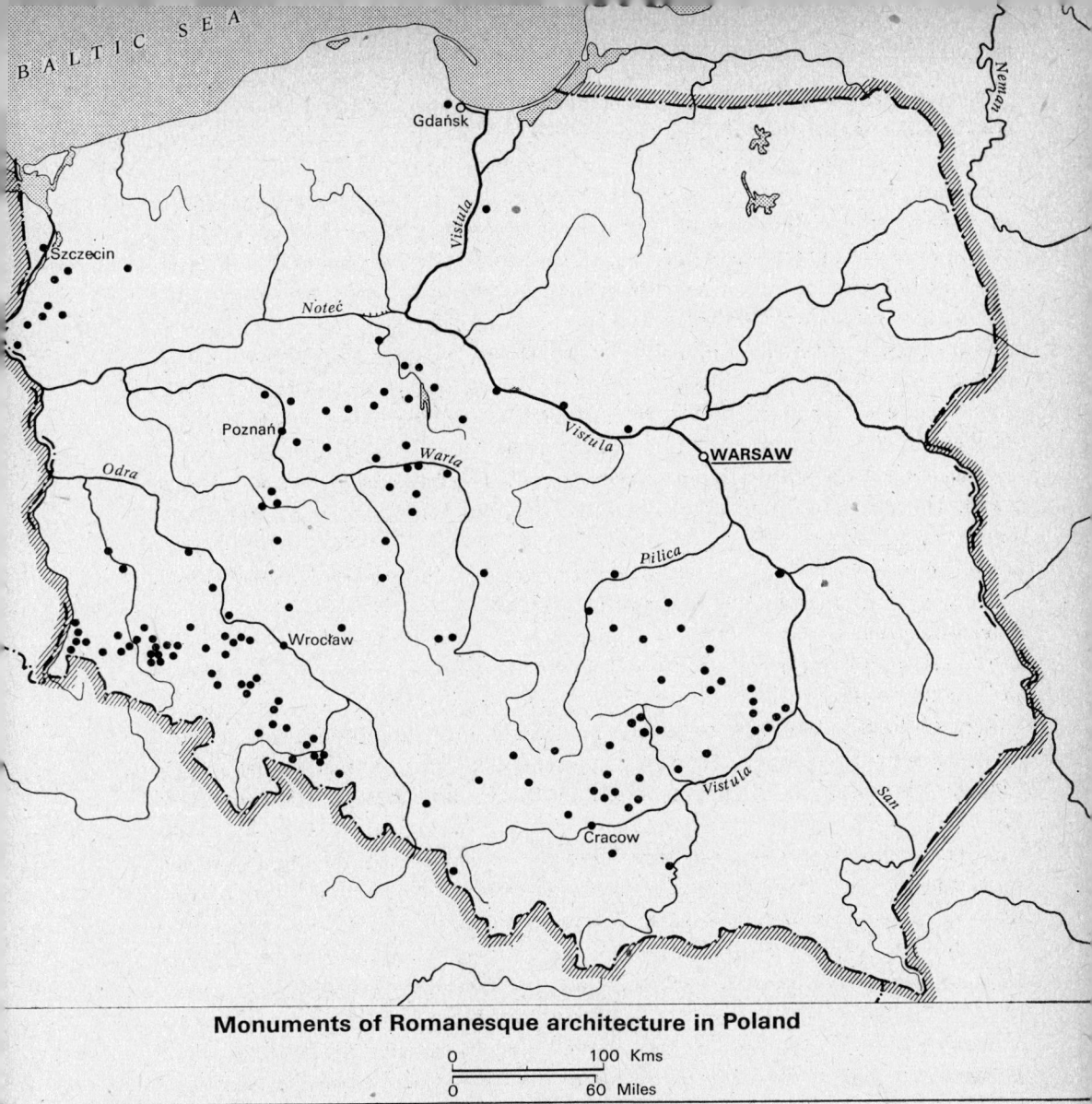

Monuments of Romanesque architecture in Poland

The growing network of schools multiplied the number of educated clergy, and in the thirteenth and fourteenth centuries the dukes and lords showed progress in learning Latin. Henry IV Probus, Duke of Silesia and advocate of Polish unity, composed love lyrics in German in the mode of the minstrels. The urban population rivalled the feudal courts in the field of intellectual and artistic proficiency. In the thirteenth century, Silesia produced the author of the historic treatise on optics, Vitelo, of a Polish mother and a Thuringian father, who worked in Italy and France. Silesia also produced Franco de Polonia, an astronomer, who improved one of the measuring instruments of the period. At the close of the thirteenth century and the beginning of the fourteenth century there lived and worked in Montpellier Nicolaus of Poland, professor of medicine, physician to Leszek the Black and author of medical works. In the field of jurisprudence and history the Dominican friar, Martin the Pole, born in Opava, nominated Archbishop of Gniezno and author of a popular chronicle of popes and emperors, was to become famous in the second half of the thirteenth century. Poles studied at the universities of Italy, mainly Bologna, and of France, principally Paris.

A few surviving fragments provide evidence of court and folk literature in the Polish vernacular, of ballads sung by the people about Duchess Ludgarda strangled on the order of her husband Przemysł II, of the battles fought by Poles, like the battle of Zawichost where Roman, Duke of Halicz, was killed in 1205 and vanquished by two brothers, Leszek the White and Conrad of Mazovia. Itinerant *ioculatores* appeared in the towns and markets bringing with them parables and satirical songs many of which criticized the social order of the times.

The social order was in greater danger from the heretical movement which also spread among the urban population of Poland. In the thirteenth century, the Valdensians preached liberty and equality. They were especially numerous in Silesia and despite the efforts of the inquisition were not suppressed. Some of them survived until the times of the great Hussite movement. Long processions of flagellants, who rejected the Church and its organization, passed through the Polish towns. The Beguines and Beghards, who remained longer within the Church, were persecuted in Silesia and completely suppressed in 1319.

The network of Cistercian monasteries grew in the course of the twelfth and the thirteenth centuries. The monasteries maintained close ties with the French, German and Danish abbeys from which they were derived, and had the obligation to take part in the general chapters at Cîteaux in Burgundy. The thirteenth century saw the rise of new monasteries which had no connexion with large estates as did the Cistercians, but were closely bound with vital urban centres. Mendicant orders spread quickly throughout Poland. The Dominicans and Franciscans appeared in the third and fourth decades of the thirteenth century and enjoyed the protection of some dukes of Silesia and Little Poland. They came with a different programme and introduced new religious ways and principles among the urban population and the rural population which flocked to them. They also introduced new forms of devotion and were influential in increasing the meagre number of Polish saints by new canonizations, most notable of St. Stanisław, the Bishop, and St. Hedwig, the Silesian Duchess. In addition to the missionary work in Poland they also sent expeditions to Ruthenia and Lithuania, and in 1245/1246 Friar Benedictus Polonus from Wrocław reached the capital of the Khan of the Mongols in the northern part of the Gobi desert.

Church influence grew with the expansion of the network of parish churches, based on the early castle-town chapels and private churches of the lords. In the course of the twelfth and the thirteenth centuries, this organization grew wider as new rural and town churches were founded. From the twelfth century the diocesan structure was reinforced by the creation of archdeaconries. In extent the diocese of Cracow was perhaps the largest in Catholic Europe. The episcopate was almost entirely Polish at the close of the twelfth century. Foreign clergy, however, were eager to come to Poland because they had better prospects of a career in Poland than in their own countries, as Guibert de Gembloux noted about 1150–1170. The number of foreigners in the Cistercian monasteries and Premonstratensian convents was noticeably larger. On the other hand the old Benedictine abbeys and the new mendicant monasteries were largely Polish.

The social and intellectual ferment of the age was not without effect on the arts. The two periods, the first covering the tenth and the eleventh centuries and the second starting with the middle of the twelfth, reveal a marked Latin influence. The journeys, pilgrimages and the dynastic and other contacts between the Polish ruling class and the western countries were important factors in sustaining this influence. The ruling group had both the opportunity and the means to satisfy its curiosity about the western countries. The climate was favourable for the acceptance of the intellectual and artistic questions which absorbed the minds of Europeans. Romanesque art, with its philosophic ideas and its moralistic and eschatological outlook, reached Poland through the agency of manuscripts, imported art objects and visitors to the country. Church art presented a vision of a society and a world designed to appeal to all the faithful. This society was nevertheless hierarchical, and the established hierarchy corresponded with the upper ranks of the ruling class. The cultural elite carried out the concept which held that certain branches of art were the domain of aristocracy. A striking example of this is the convent of the Premonstratensian nuns at Strzelno, a town on the border of Kujawy and Great Poland. Established here by a lordly family in the last quarter of the twelfth century, the nuns created in the course of a few decades a world that was distinctly their own. The pivotal centre of this world was the basilica with its finely-wrought sculptures imbued with the moral and philosophical erudition prevalent in this period. The desperate conflict of soul and body depicted in the columns, the discovery of some aspects of nature and the polymorphic symbolism, all were executed with the sure hand of stone carvers who skilfully adapted the sculptural styles of the Rhineland, Burgundy and Lombardy.

Although somewhat late in its reception, a flourishing Romanesque art found expression in quite a large number of major cathedrals and collegiate churches, like that of the Virgin Mary and St. Alexius in Łęczyca, and in the abbeys, like that of the Canons regular at Czerwińsk. Frequently ornamented with murals, it was the sculpture in the buildings which always represented a high standard of art. The most valuable works of Romanesque art are the great portal, found today in the Magdalene church in Wrocław, and a group of tympana found also in Wrocław. The Cistercians introduced an architectural style best illustrated by the monasteries in Sulejów, Wąchock and Koprzywnica. There the austere Romanesque ornamentation is wedded with the early Gothic forms of vault construction. The twilight of Romanesque art is represented by the works of the elegant stone-cutter workshop of Trzebnica. There we find work clearly inspired by the reminiscences of Provençal art. The concert of David and Bathsheba on the portal of the abbey church, is an interplay of form and poetic allusion in the mode of a refined courtly culture. The most notable examples of metal work are the portals of Gniezno which were produced in the last quarter of the twelfth century. The influence of the Meuse valley art is clearly in evidence here. The scenes, based on a native scenario, contain a wealth of ideological plots woven around the story of St. Adalbert, patron saint of Poland and Gniezno, and depicted in a style reminiscent of the love of nature that radiated from the school of Chartres.

With the second quarter of the thirteenth century a new building material made its appearance which revolutionized architecture and enabled countries which, like Poland, were poor in construction stone, to embark more ambitious church and secular buildings. Brick was used at first in Romanesque architecture, notably in the St. James' church at Sandomierz and the Cistercian churches at Kołbacz, in Western Pomerania. The introduction of brick affected architectural forms (noted at the earliest in Silesia) and was one of the creative components in the nothern version of Gothic art. The Franciscan churches in Wrocław, Cracow and Zawichost are the earliest examples of the new style. Particularly rich in early Gothic structures is Western Pomerania, notably Kamień, and Gdańsk-Pomerania, Gdańsk itself, Pelplin and Oliwa.

The second half of the thirteenth century marked the beginning of a large construction programme in towns, including churches, town halls and urban walls. The peak was reached in the next period. The churches were ornamented with Gothic sculpture including architectural detail, tympana and portals. The most impressive works were the early fourteenth-century tombs of dukes and bishops (Wrocław, Krzeszów, Lubiąż in Silesia and Wawel in Cracow). Only small though significant fragments of Early Gothic mural paintings have been preserved. An example is that found in the church of St. John at Toruń.

The scriptoria of the cathedrals and monasteries, where gifted illuminators were at work, handed down a rich heritage. Manuscripts were also imported from foreign countries. One of the richest storehouses of manuscripts was the library of the Gniezno chapter.

Chapter VI
THE *CORONA REGNI POLONIAE* AT THE HEIGHT OF ITS POWER IN THE FOURTEENTH AND THE FIFTEENTH CENTURIES

THE STATE APPARATUS CENTRALIZED

The growth of both town and country enabled Poland to regain a position in the international market at the close of the thirteenth century as an exporter of grain, cattle and hides, forest products and lumber, and soon afterwards of articles manufactured by craftsmen. Low priced Polish cloth competed successfully with cloth manufactured in the West. There is evidence that in the last years of the fourteenth century Polish cloth was known in southern Germany, in the region of modern Switzerland and among the southern and eastern neighbours of Poland. An economic and cultural community of central and eastern Europe emerged in the fourteenth century. It engaged in a lively trade which showed vigour up until the Turkish conquests. The community embraced an area from the Black Sea through Halicz Ruthenia and Novgorod Ruthenia, Lithuania and Poland to the Baltic Sea, Bohemia, Hungary, the German countries and northern Italy.

The political organization of central and eastern Europe showed a trend toward the creation of multinational monarchies with a major language group as backbone of the structure. In the course of the fourteenth century the Luxemburgs, Habsburgs, Angevins of Hungary, the Giedymins of Lithuania, the Piasts of Poland and soon afterwards the Jagiellons of Lithuania and Poland vied with each other to extend their sway over the widest possible economic and cultural areas.

The Polish Kingdom was called the *Corona Regni Poloniae* by the contemporaries to describe the moral if not political affiliations and the feudal, if not direct relations of all the Polish lands to the Crown. From the beginning, the Polish Kingdom pursued a national programme of reconstruction and rejected any attempt at linking these lands with other political organisms under a foreign sceptre. The Kingdom consolidated its machinery of power within the course of a few decades and then embarked upon a course of territorial expansion beyond its ethnic frontiers.

The unification of the State, or rather the creation of a Kingdom of Poland by uniting the major duchies demanded a continued political effort within the country, as well as for the purpose of establishing its frontiers. The greatest effort toward these ends was made during the reign of Casimir III the Great (1333–1370), the son of Władysław the Short. The programme of the unity of the State carried with it the concept of the King's authority over all the lands, both those ruled directly by the monarch and those still held by regional dukes. The introduction of the system of vassalage roused at first considerable resentment fed and fanned by foreign powers. Władysław the Short became the suzerain of the dukes of Kujawy and in the middle of the fourteenth century the dukes of Mazovia, who had vacillated between Poland, the Teutonic Order and Bohemia, became the vassals of the Polish Crown. As the Piast dynasties of Kujawy and Mazovia became extinct, their regions reverted to the Crown.

In the territories where the kings writ ran the earlier system of voivodships (palatinates) and castellanships as well as other offices to which the king appointed for life members of the lordly families continued to exist. These officials retained a wide authority and received grants, but the property immunities of the Church and the knights limited the scope of their efficiency. They still attended political assemblies representing the lords. However, in order to establish a more efficient administration directly subordinated to the king, it was necessary to appoint royal governors, the *brachia regalia* who on behalf of the king could rule the whole nation, over and above any immunities. In Poland this was the role of the capitaneus or *starosta*, an office first introduced by Wacław II of Bohemia and continued by Władysław the Short. The capitaneus was appointed or removed at the royal will. He kept a court register (*acta castrensia*) and the registers of Great Poland also included from the very beginning uncontested "perpetual" jurisdictional acts while other districts followed suit only much later.

The treasury and the chancery were centralized institutions. Because the old system of contributions levied by the dukes had broken down as a result of granting immunities, the chief tribute imposed by the kingdom was the relatively high and ruthlessly exacted plough tax (*poradlne, collecta generalis*). Further sources of income were the customs duties as well as the royal estates which were formed in the fourteenth century after an energetically conducted revindication of the lands lost by the Crown. The monetary system was a new feature of fourteenth century fiscalism. It developed apace with the growth of the money economy. The administration of the treasury was centralized in the hands of the Royal Treasurer who replaced the former treasurers of regional dukes.

During the reign of Casimir the Great, the regional chanceries of the earlier duchies ceased to exist. Through the agency of learned jurists at court, they were replaced by one efficient royal chancery headed by a chancellor and a vice-chancellor. The chancellor's office became the administrative centre of the internal and external affairs of state and widened its original role of secretariat by taking over the legal and judicial work of the Crown.

Cracow. St. Florian's Gate, 14th cent.

Cracow. St. Catherine's Church, 14th cent.

Whereas the towns were governed by the *ius municipale* and the tenures of peasants by a variety of German law, the nobles and peasants who remained under Polish law were subject to the *ius terrestre*. The oldest record of Polish common law, generally called the *Księga Elbląska* (Elbląg Book) after the place where its manuscript was kept, was compiled in the second half of the thirteenth century. Casimir the Great caused the Polish common law for Little Poland and Great Poland to be recorded in the middle of the fourteenth century. Local courts (*iudicia terrestria*) that operated in the individual territories had their powers strengthened, a kind of judicial self-government of the gentry also kept records of legal transactions, which was an extremely important function in a country where the public notary operated exclusively within the framework of Canon law.

Royal jurists subscribed to the principle of *unus princeps, unum ius, una moneta in toto regno haberi debet*. Separate ordinances regulated economic matters in such fields as mining, roads and customs duties. On the other hand a unified monetary system achieved with the introduction in 1338 of the big Cracow grosz (*grossi Cracovienses*) did not bring stability to the currency because of subsequent debasement by the royal treasury. The Hungarian gold ducat was most often used in foreign exchanges.

General assemblies of the lords were rarely convoked in the fourteenth century. The king's council appointed by the monarch assumed their prerogatives. As the royal residence was established in Cracow and the lords of Great Poland simmered with discontent throughout the reign of Casimir the Great, the lords of Little Poland (or Cracow lords) exercised an overwhelming influence in the royal council. From the beginning of the fifteenth century all the most outstanding dignitaries (bishops, palatines and castellans) sat in the council, with the king presiding over it, the council took all decisions with regard to foreign affairs and public appointments.

POLITICAL PROBLEMS IN THE REIGNS OF WŁADYSŁAW THE SHORT AND CASIMIR THE GREAT

The boundaries of the Kingdom were established by war and negotiation. Władysław the Short consolidated and left to his son alliances with Hungary, Lithuania, Halicz Ruthenia and Denmark. The claims of John of Luxemburg to the Polish throne brought an action against the Teutonic Knights for the return of Gdańsk-Pomerania and other annexed territories before a Papal tribunal in 1319/1320. The case ended with a verdict in favour of Poland against which the Teutonic Knights appealed to the Pope. An armed struggle followed in which Polish forces won the battle of Płowce in 1331, but both the lawsuit and the war failed to produce the desired result. The attempt to reunite Lubusz with the Kingdom by an alliance with Western Pomerania against Brandenburg also ended in failure.

From 1327 the Bohemian Crown began to reduce the Silesian dukes to vassalage, which the Polish Kingdom was powerless to resist. Thus political failure loomed along the whole of the western and northern frontiers. Both the military and diplomatic actions of the diminutive but valiant Władysław I, revealed the painful fact to the founders of the revived Kingdom that international forces were not balanced in favour of Poland whose military and financial resources were severely limited.

A realistic evaluation of the situation gained ascendency at the royal court when Casimir, the son of Władysław I, succeeded to the throne in 1333. The young King paid John of Luxemburg a large indemnity to buy off his claim to the throne and strengthened his own alliance with Hungary. In 1339 Casimir brought afresh legal action against the Teutonic Order, but the result was the same as before. The 1343 treaty of Kalisz, however, provided a compromise solution by which Casimir gave up his efforts to recover Gdańsk-Pomerania in return for the restoration of Kujawy and the Dobrzyń Land by the Teutonic Order. The Order for its part recognized the King of Poland as its founder. Casimir also gave his approval, specifically by the peace of Namysłów in 1348, to Bohemia's overlordship over the majority of the Silesian duchies. Only towards the end of his life did the King begin military and diplomatic preparations to take up the Silesian question again. By adopting Casimir, Duke of Słupsk in Western Pomerania, he created a possibility that as least part of that country might be incorporated with Poland. However, Casimir the Great left no legal heir and the heavy commitments of the Cracow lords in the east ruled out this political trend forever. The Polish-Lithuanian understanding, initiated by his father and furthered by Casimir at the close of his life, prepared the ground for a decisive stand against the Teutonic Order, whose growing power was a threat to both the states.

Poland's expansion to the East began in the middle of the fourteenth century as a result of the efforts of the Cracow lords. These were partly descendants of new clans advanced in power by Władysław the Short and Casimir, such as the Leliwas of Melsztyn and Tarnów, the Porajs of Kurozwęki, and also scions of old noble clans, like the Topors of Tęczyn and others. The policy of expansion in the East was welcomed by the patricians of Little Poland and by the Church. Like the King they were interested in the occupation of Halicz Ruthenia which at this time was coveted by Lithuania and Hungary. The western section of Halicz Ruthenia was thickly populated; it was also a gateway to the fertile fields of Podolia and farther eastward. The trade routes to the Genoese colonies of Kaffa, Kilia and Akkerman on the Black Sea passed through Halicz Ruthenia by way of Włodzimierz in Volhynia and Lwów.

In 1323 the Halicz branch of the Ruric dynasty died out and the boyars called Prince Bolesław George of Mazovia to the throne. He was subsequently poisoned by the boyars in 1340, but he had named King Casimir his succes-

sor, which gave Poland a claim to intervene in Ruthenia. While Lithuania promptly extended her grasp upon Volhynia, King Casimir conducted a grim struggle with the boyars for the remainder of the duchy which by its size and riches was to compensate for the failures in the West. There was one other element which the Polish statesmen kept in view. Besides Lithuania and Hungary, the Tartars still remained potential rivals of Poland for supremacy over Halicz and Włodzimierz, and their political activity made itself felt throughout the fourteenth century. Ultimately a fairly sizeable area of Ruthenia was united with Poland between 1349 and 1366. At first there was some hesitation whether to preserve a distinct *Regnum Russiae,* as the territory was called in the usage of the Royal Chancery. In the end, however, the territories were incorporated in the Polish Kingdom. In 1434 they were placed under the Polish land law as the voivodships of Ruthenia, Volhynia and Podolia. A Catholic archbishopric was established first at Halicz and later transferred to Lwów as the metropolis for several bishoprics of the Latin rite. It was instrumental also in assimilating the ruling classes of this province with the Polish community. At the same time, however, Casimir the Great reestablished a metropolis of the Greek rite in Halicz which was directly dependent on the Patriarch of Constantinople. In this manner the Polish State expanded beyond its ethnic frontiers and entered in the middle of the fourteenth century upon a multinational stage in its development.

The reign of Casimir the Great has become the subject of a national legend. Casimir has been extolled as a great builder and a monarch who was just to all the estates. He was even called the "Peasant King". Indeed the King was a wise statesman and diplomat with wide interests, ranging from economics, the promotion of peasant settlements, culture, science and learning. Surrounding himself with a group of devoted ministers, notably Chancellor Janusz Suchywilk, Vice-Chancellor Janko of Czarnków and Spytko of Melsztyn, the Castellan of Cracow, he managed to carry through the programme of internal consolidation despite separatist tendencies and to stabilize Poland's position and give it prestige. The Polish King's envoy could state to Emperor Charles IV that his lord owed allegiance to no one, whether to the Emperor or the Pope. The Congress of Cracow in 1364 was a demonstration of the Polish King's authority and of the international respect accorded him. It assembled the Emperor, the kings of Hungary and Denmark and many other princes in order to help Peter of Lusignan, King of Cyprus, to promote a crusade.

As King Casimir had no male progeny, the Polish crown had long ago been designated to his nephew, Louis d'Anjou, King of Hungary. Casimir tried, in his last will, to secure for his grandson Casimir, Duke of Słupsk, a privileged position in Poland and the eventual succession to the throne after Louis. This will was, however, annulled by the Polish lords. At the end of the fourteenth century Poland was turning away from the political scene in the West and looking to the North and East.

8 History of Poland

THE PERIOD OF ANGEVIN RULE

After the death of Casimir the Great in 1370 there were noticeable signs of feudal anarchy in Great Poland, when Casimir of Słupsk and another pretender, Władysław the White of the Piasts of Kujawy, tried to overthrow the foreign dynasty. However, the Angevin episode (1370–1386) succeeded in maintaining the supremacy of a centralized government. The attempt was all the more significant as King Louis did not rule Poland in person. The regency was held by an old woman, Queen Elisabeth, mother of Louis and daughter of Władysław the Short. Louis d'Anjou strengthened Hungarian influence in Halicz Ruthenia by handing over the administration of the country to a reliable viceroy, Duke Władysław of Opole, who enhanced the prestige of the Roman Catholic Church in that area. From 1381 Poland herself was governed by a regency of five persons representing the lords of Little Poland and headed by Zawisza of Kurozwęki, Bishop of Cracow.

The major problem of the Angevin House in Poland was to secure the throne for the daughters of Louis against the opposition of the episcopate and a section of the nobles. The candidacy was, however, looked upon with favour by the towns which saw a promise of wide foreign trade in personal unions of the royal dynasties of that part of Europe.

In 1372 Louis granted the privilege of Košice by which he secured the support of the nobles for the succession of his daughters to the Polish throne at the price of reducing taxes, while soon afterwards he gained the consent of the clergy by granting them similar concessions. Upon the death of Louis in 1382, however, the lords ruling the country would not accept his plans in full. The regents were determined not to allow a German prince to occupy the Polish throne. They were decidedly opposed to Sigismund of Luxemburg, husband of Marie, the daughter of Louis d'Anjou who had been named as successor to the Polish throne. They rejected as well Wilhelm of Austria, engaged to Jadwiga (Hedwig), Louis' second daughter. Siemowit of Mazovia, another pretender to the Polish throne, was also repulsed by an armed intervention of Hungary. Jadwiga was placed on the Polish throne and the personal union with Hungary was broken. In 1384 the 10-year old young Jadwiga entered Cracow, the royal capital, and assumed the title of King (*rex*). In fact Poland since 1370 was actually governed by a group of oligarchs who were fully aware of their aims and possibilities.

THE UNION OF POLAND AND LITHUANIA. THE STRUGGLE WITH THE TEUTONIC ORDER

The Cracow lords were fully aware of the benefits to be derived from an expansion in the East when Casimir the Great was still alive. At the close of the fourteenth century a new and significant factor made its appearance, the desire to draw closer to the Grand Duchy of Lithuania and to establish a partnership with her against the Teutonic Order, as well as to settle the affairs of Halicz Ruthenia in accordance with Polish plans.

The Lithuanian State was founded as a monarchy in the middle of the thirteenth century. In the second half of the fourteenth century it had reached the peak of its political power. Under the rule and alliance of two brothers, Kiejstut (Kestutis), Duke of Troki, and Olgierd (Algirdas), the Grand Duke of Lithuania, the State stubbornly defended its western frontiers from the encroachments of the Teutonic Order. At the same time Lithuania extended her original territories (Aukštote, the highlands, and Samogitia (Żmudź), the lowlands) to embrace vast areas of the future Ukraine and Byelorussia up to Smoleńsk, Bryansk and the Black Sea steppes. The military nature of the challenge that faced the State helped to concentrate all authority in the hands of the Grand Duke. While Lithuania proper clung to pagan beliefs despite the repeated attempts made from the middle of the thirteenth century to convert the Lithuanians, the Ruthenian population in the major part of the Grand Duchy professed Orthodox Christianity. Ruthenian customs and Ruthenian literary culture characterized the whole ruling class, including also the reigning house, but the native Lithuanian lords still played the leading role in the State government and were loth to share their power with the Ruthenian boyars. The population was not distributed evenly throughout the large state but its economy was by no means backward.

Jagiełło (Iogailas), son of Olgierd, removed from power his uncle Kiejstut, became the head of the Grand Duchy in 1382 and took the guidance of the political issues into his own skilful hands. The first concept of his entourage was a closer understanding with the Grand Duchy of Muscovy. Jagiełło was to accept the Orthodox faith together with the hand of the daughter of Demetrius Donskoi. Muscovy, however, as the centre of an effort to unite the Ruthenian lands, appeared already as a dangerous rival of Lithuania which was attempting the same task. Consequently the cause of an alliance with Poland prevailed among the Lithuanian lords. The direct threat to the western frontiers, especially in Samogitia and hence a community of interests with Poland against the Teutonic Order, was an argument in favour of the Polish alliance. Poland was fully aware of the value of such an alliance, which would enable her to regain lost territories with the help of the Lithuanians and would moreover strengthen her hold on her conquest in Halicz Ruthenia. These prospects seemed so attractive to the ruling groups in Cracow that they were willing to arrange a marriage between Jadwiga and Jagiełło. The conversion of the pagan part of Lithuania to the Roman Catholic Church played a major role in conciliating the Polish clergy to the union. This conversion also struck out the major argument used internationally by the Teutonic Order to justify its actions against Lithuania, and cast doubt upon the missionary programme of Teutonic expansion.

By an act drawn up at Krewa in 1385, a union was effected between the Polish and Lithuanian States. Jagiełło took the name of Władysław when he was baptized and upon marrying Jadwiga became King of Poland in 1386. Poland and Lithuania had actually established only a personal union. By this union, however, both States could prepare to carry out their external objectives, such as the removal of Hungarian garrisons from Halicz Ruthenia and the exaction of homage from the voivodes of Moldavia and Valachia, to be paid to Jagiełło and Jadwiga. Poland helped Lithuania to strengthen her eastern frontiers. Catholics obtained a privileged position within the Lithuanian State. The more important cultural and social consequences of the union were to emerge only with time.

There was however an unfavourably disposed group in Lithuania which was particularly hostile to the interpretation given to the union by Polish lords that the Grand Duchy had been incorporated into Poland. This faction was led by Witold (Vytautas), the able son of Kiejstut, who was at first allied with the Teutonic Knights and who after 1392 was accepted by Jagiełło as co-regent of the whole of Lithuania. Witold's ultimate aim was the royal crown which he planned to acquire after establishing Lithuanian supremacy over the whole of Ruthenia and subduing the Tartars with the aid of Khan Tochtamish, who had been driven out by Tamerlane. Witold's plans regarding the Tartars suffered a setback in the defeat of 1399 inflicted upon him by the Tartars on the Vorskla river, where a number of Polish knights, who had been sent to Witold's assistance, were killed in the battle. In 1401 Witold was recognized as the Grand Duke of Lithuania under the suzerainty of Władysław Jagiełło, as "Supreme Duke". The Teutonic danger was now the factor that drove them both into closer cooperation. At the same time Lithuania's relation to Poland was satisfactorily explained as a personal union in the person of Jagiełło. Although Jadwiga, heiress to the Polish throne, died without issue in 1399, Jagiełło was nevertheless recognized by the Polish lords as King of Poland.

The Teutonic Order found itself in a dangerous position. The Knights tried to take advantage of the difference within Lithuania and Poland arising from the interest of parties in both the States in an eastward expansion. Yet the Order could not avoid the "great war" in 1409–1410. A decisive encounter and one of the largest battles of the Middle Ages was fought on the flelds of Grunwald in 1410. The Polish and Lithuanian army, commanded by King Władysław, routed the Teutonic Knights at the end of a day's heavy fighting. The Grand Master and many dignitaries of the Order fell in battle. The Order was no longer a dangerous military neighbour. The peace condition satisfied only the war aims of Lithuania by returning Samogitia to the Lithuanian State. The military and financial power of the Teutonic Order, however, was considerably weakened by the war. Nascent political movements led several decades later to the solution which Poland desired in Pomerania.

The victory at Grunwald enhanced the prestige of the Polish-Lithuanian monarchy and added vigour to its political activity, while the circles that favoured Church reform were deeply impressed by the defeat of the Teutonic lords. The mood was reflected in a letter of congratulations addressed to Władysław Jagiełło by John Huss. The military and diplomatic struggle with the Teutonic Order drew the lords of Lithuania and Poland closer together. In 1413 a new treaty of union was signed at Horodło on the Bug and 43 Polish clans adopted a corresponding number of Lithuanian lords who were allowed to use the Polish family crests. Władysław and Grand Duke Witold granted the Lithuanian lords the same fiscal and judicial privileges as were enjoyed by the Poles.

The Polish delegation to the Council of Constance began to play an active role in 1415. The delegates to the Council were Mikołaj Trąba, archbishop of Gniezno; Paulus Vladimiri of Brudzeń, rector of the Cracow University and a brilliant jurist; Andrzej Łaskarz of Gosławice, Bishop designate of Poznań, a fervent conciliarist; and the famous knight Zawisza Czarny of Garbowo. The Council was also attended by a delegation of recently converted Samogitians, and by Gregory Tsamblak, Metropolitan of Kiev, and political adviser to Jagiełło and Witold. The Poles rose to the defense of John Huss. They presented also a treatise written by Paulus Vladimiri which dealt with the exercise of Papal and Imperial power over the unfaithful; the author opposed conversion by the sword and defended the rights of pagans to their land. These principles as stated by the Poles provoked a controversy and excited a sharp rebuttal from the defenders of the Teutonic Order. The Poles were supported, among others, by the University of Paris.

War with the Teutonic Order broke out again, but the Knights were forced by the peace of the Mielno lake of 1422 to give up all claim to Samogitia. In this manner the German expansion on the Baltic was halted for many centuries and with it the ambitious plans for creating a consolidated Prusso-Livonian State governed by German lords.

POLAND AND LITHUANIA IN THE HUSSITE PERIOD. THE UNION WITH HUNGARY

The Polish-Lithuanian federation now assumed the role of a great power in central and eastern Europe. Once the bastions of German expansion to the North had begun to crack, there emerged fresh possibilities of creating a front against its effective operation. The Bohemian national movement gained in vigour while Hungary's policy in the southern area of German expansion grew noticeably independent. Jagiełło and his descendants attempted to take advantage of this situation, but soon restricted their ambitions to the interests of their dynasty alone, without regard to Poland's vital interests on her western frontiers. Although several excellent opportunities arose for regain-

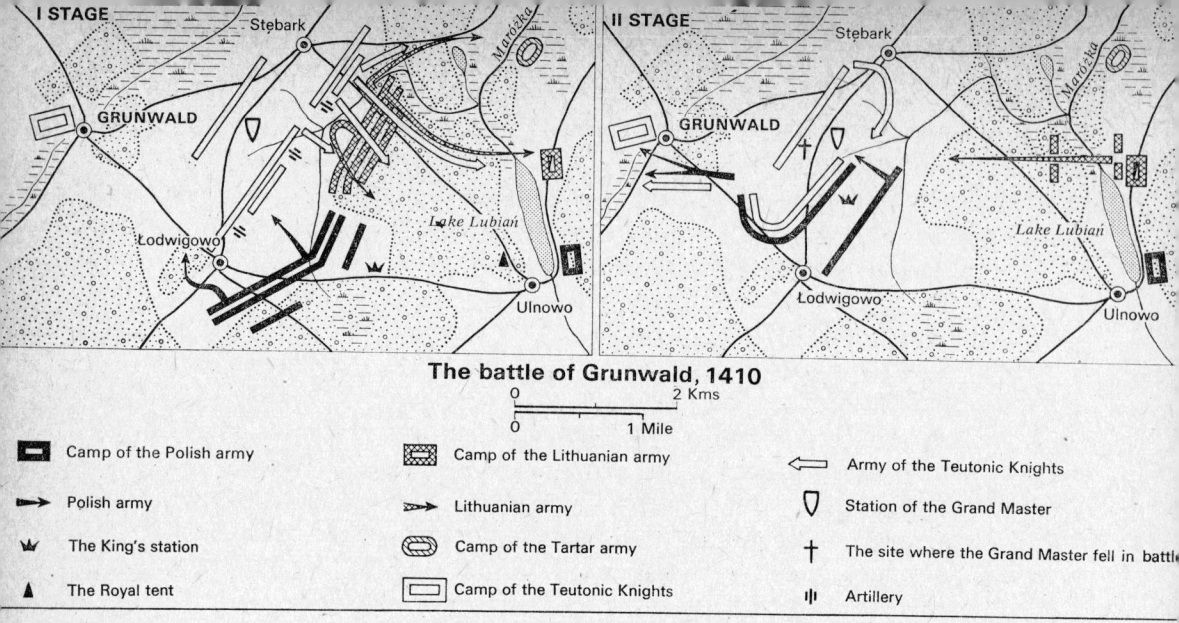

The battle of Grunwald, 1410

ing the lands of the Piasts, the political plans of the court were not concerned with the issue.

With the outbreak of the Hussite war in Bohemia in 1420, the circles which supported a national monarchy with a moderate social programme put forward the candidature of Władysław Jagiełło as a successor to the throne of Bohemia. The King declined the offer at the insistence of the Polish magnates who feared international complications and pro-Hussite sympathies among the gentry. The Grand Duke Witold, however, accepted a similar offer with the knowledge of the King and appointed as Victory of Bohemia the King's nephew Prince Sigismund, the son of Korybut.

All attempts at an alliance with the Hussite insurrection were frustrated by the Polish episcopate and the lords, headed by Zbigniew of Oleśnica, an outstanding figure in the politics of that period, who was Bishop of Cracow and at the end of his life also a Cardinal. At his bidding King Władysław recalled Prince Sigismund and in 1424 issued at Wieluń a severe edict against the Hussites and their allies. But the following year Sigismund played for a brief time the role of a "King elect" and even joined the uprising of the radical Taborites in Silesia.

At the birth of Crown-Prince Władysław, born to Jagiełło by his fourth wife Sophia, a Lithuano-Ruthenian Princess of Holszany, the King, became entangled in negotiations with the Polish lords to secure his right of succession. Jagiełło's son was sure of his succession to the title of Grand Duke of Lithuania because Witold had no heirs and the questions regarding the government of the Grand Duchy had already been settled. In Poland, however, the old King had to buy the right of succession for his son by granting a number of liberties restricting the royal power. Principal among these were: the 1425 privilege of Brześć, called *Neminem captivabimus nisi iure victum*, and the privilege of Jedlnia in 1430. Upon Witold's death in 1430, whose coronation had been prevented at the very last moment by the opposition of all the Polish lords, the King appointed Świdrygiełło (Svitrigailas), his last surviving brother, as Grand Duke of Lithuania. Świdrygiełło's programme for Lithuania aimed at complete independence from Poland and at equal rights for Russian and Lithuanian lords inside their State, while abroad his foreign policy stood in direct contradiction to the interests of Poland. The Grand Duke allied himself with Sigismund of Luxemburg and the Teutonic Order. Not until the death of the eighty-year old King Władysław Jagiełło in 1434 did Witold's brother, Prince Sigismund, son of Kiejstut, leading the Lithuanian opposition and its Polish supporters, finally quell Świdrygiełło's rebellion. Equal privileges for the Orthodox boyars and the Catholics, however, remained a permanent achievement of Świdrygiełło's reign.

The regency of Bishop Zbigniew of Oleśnica, which started in 1434, marked the ascendency of new magnates, principally from Little Poland, whose source of economic and political strength was derived from Halicz Ruthenia which they used to extand their power over the entire Kingdom. These actions evoked the dissatisfaction of the gentry and indeed of the peasants, who for many years have been coming under the influence of the radical movement whose fountain-head was Hussite Bohemia. The death of Sigismund of Luxemburg again gave the Hussite nobles and burghers of Bohemia the opportunity to propose a Polish candidate for the Bohemian throne. This time their choice fell on Władysław Jagiełło's second son, Prince Casimir. In the event of the candidate being supported by Poland, the suzerainty of the Polish monarch would then have been recognized by the dukes of Silesia. The royal court, under the leadership of the widowed Queen Mother Sophia, was favourably disposed to the idea and, despite the opposition of Bishop Zbigniew of Oleśnica, made military commitments against the Hapsburgs who clamoured for the throne of Bohemia. At the same time a section of the gentry, led by the fervent Hussite Spytek of Melsztyn, grandson of the Spytek who had collaborated with Casimir the Great, formed in 1439 at Nowe Miasto Korczyn a "confederation" against the bishop. The movement began to spread to the peasants, a fact which discouraged some of the nobles who, though opposed to the magnates, were nevertheless alarmed by the revolt of the peasants. The Polish Hussite revolt was broken in the battle of Grotniki on the Nida and the magnates compelled the Court to relinquish all dynastic plans in Bohemia.

The union with Lithuania ended in 1440. The Lithuanian lords murdered the stern Grand Duke Sigismund, son of Kiejstut, and the youthful Prince Casimir was sent to Wilno to rule as viceroy on behalf of his brother Władysław III. The lords of Lithuania, however, acclaimed him Grand Duke and thus dissolved the personal union with Poland. Without foregoing attempts to revive the union, the Polish lords quickly observed that they could compensate for this loss by reestablishing a personal union with Hungary.

After the death of Albert of Hapsburg, the Hungarian lords approached the court of the Jagiellons and offered the throne of Hungary to the Polish King. The main underlying reason was the threat of Turkey to the Byzantine Empire and Hungary. In spite of the opposition of the pro-Hapsburg faction, Władysław III was crowned King of Hungary at Buda in 1440 and thus allied himself with the anti-Turkish diplomatic and military coalition organized by Pope Eugene IV. In 1443 the King won a briliant victory in Bulgaria and signed a highly favourable truce, but he broke the agreement in the following year at the instance of Papal diplomacy, which induced him to conduct a war along the Black Sea coast, for which he was poorly prepared. Władysław III was slain in 1444 in the battle of Varna. Among the casualties were also the Papal legate and a great many Hungarian and Polish knights. The defeat sealed the fate of the Byzantine Empire and the Balkan Slavs, and the Turkish danger moved closer to central Europe.

THE GROWING POLITICAL ROLE OF THE GENTRY
THE RESTITUTION OF CROWN LANDS

The Polish lords called to the throne Casimir IV, the Grand Duke of Lithuania and brother of the slain Władysław III, hoping not only to reestablish the union with Lithuania, but also to incorporate its territories with Poland. Upon his arrival in Poland in 1446, the King recognized only the "fraternal union" of the two countries now under his rule, guaranteed Lithuania's frontiers as established in Witold's time and refused to recognize the privileges that restricted royal power in Poland. A talented and astute statesman, Casimir ascended the Polish throne with a programme which provided for the restoration of a strong central authority, for an extension of royal influence over central and eastern Europe with the purpose of forwarding the interests of the dynasty, and the restitution of the Crown lands. He carried out most of his plans in the course of a fifty years' reign.

In his struggle with the opposition represented by the magnates and Zbigniew of Oleśnica, the King was supported by the gentry and the "young barons of the Kingdom" who had been raised from the ranks of the gentry as well as by Great Poland. In the early years of his reign, Casimir also depended for support to some extent upon the towns. The royal party succesfully opposed the financial system of the Papal Curia, broke the opposition of the clergy regarding the appointment of bishops, and transferred this prerogative to the King. Casimir also acquired two small Silesian territories which were of vital importance because of their proximity to Cracow. In 1457 he obtained the Duchy of Oświęcim and suzerainty over Zator which together with the 1443 purchase of Siewierz for the see of Cracow moved the State frontiers to the west. In 1493 Zator became the property of the Crown. Casimir IV also mustered the support of the gentry for his plans for the restitution of Pomerania and the defeat of the Teutonic Knights. To further his ends the King granted the privileges of Nieszawa in 1454 which opened the way to the parliamentary system by widening the liberties of the gentry while restricting those of the oligarchy. The King swore on behalf of the Crown not to raise troops or impose new taxes without the approval of a convention of nobles known as land diets (*sejmiki*).

The State of the Teutonic Order was undergoing a political crisis. The wealthy towns, such as Gdańsk, Toruń and Elbląg, together with their German patricians, rose in revolt against exploitation by the Knights of the Order. The vassal knights of the Order, Poles as well as Germans, founded the secret "Salamander Society". After 1440, the Prussian estates, that is the knights and towns, established an official "Prussian Alliance" which conducted negotiations with the Teutonic Order, regarding tax matters chiefly. The repression of the Alliance by the Order was the direct cause of the outbreak of an insurrection by the Prussian estates. In 1454 Casimir IV received a delegation of the insurgents among whom were German speaking representatives of the towns and knights. Appealing to the claims of the Polish Crown, Casimir promulgated a writ of incorporation for Prussia. A Thirteen Years' War with the Teutonic Order followed, and its hardships were borne without the aid of Lithuania. International opinion was not favourably disposed to the elimination of the Teutonic State. The Pope intervened with an anathema against Poland, but this was ignored by the whole population, including the clergy. The war ended in 1466 with the peace of Toruń, by which Gdańsk-Pomerania as well as parts of West Prussia reverted to Poland. The new province was known henceforth as Royal Prussia. The sovereignty of the Teutonic Order was reduced to the remaining Prussian territory but without Warmia, Elbląg and Malbork. The Grand Master moved the capital from Malbork to Königsberg and bound himself to pay homage to the King of Poland whom he recognized as a suzerain of the Teutonic Prussia.

CASIMIR IV'S FOREIGN POLICY IN THE SECOND HALF OF HIS REIGN

The sole aim of Casimir's foreign policy in Bohemia and Hungary was to guarantee the thrones of these countries to his sons born of Elisabeth of Hapsburg. The Polish Crown's vital interests in Silesia were disregarded. Casimir would not be drawn into the Catholic coalition against George of Podiebrad, King of Bohemia, but tried to act as intermediary between him and the Emperor and Matthias Corvinus, King of Hungary. George agreed to name Władysław, Casimir's eldest son, as his successor to the throne of

Bohemia. Upon the death of George in 1471, the Czech diet actually elected Władysław King of Bohemia, but Matthias Corvinus established himself in Silesia, Lusatia and Moravia.

Matthias's death in 1490 offered Władysław of Bohemia a chance to ascend the Hungarian throne as well. With the support of the Hungarian magnates Władysław supplanted his younger brother, John Albert, the candidate of the gentry. John Albert was rewarded by being appointed a governor of Silesia. In this manner the Jagiellonian dynasty came to rule over vast, but not homogeneous territories, extending from the Baltic to the Black and Adriatic Seas. The diplomatic success of the dynasty failed to rouse enthusiasm in Poland, because it brought no political advantages to the Polish State. The fruit of the Jagiellonians' efforts, this harvest of royal crowns and lands, was to be seized by the Hapsburgs in the next generation. Meanwhile Casimir IV's policies averted the attention and the energy of Poland from growing complications in the East.

The Turkish capture of the Genoese Black Sea colonies of Kaffa (1475), Kilia and Akkerman (1484) was a severe blow to the trade with the East conducted by Lwów and Cracow. The Crimean Tartars ruled by the khans of the Girey dynasty became vassals of Turkey. They now became a hostile force raiding the borderlands of Poland and Lithuania. Casimir IV came to the assistance of Stephen, the Prince of Moldavia, who became Casimir's vassal in 1485. In the subsequent years Polish forces were successful in the military encounters with the Tartars. There was, however, no consistent policy in Poland. The King became embroiled in Hungarian affairs and signed a truce with Turkey thus recognizing her conquests and alienating the rulers of Moldavia.

Poland's entanglement in the dynastic struggle for territory had unfortunate consequences in the country itself, where the royal authority established by Casimir in the first half of his reign was now undermined. Issues of primary importance such as reform of the fiscal system and organization of the army were left unsolved. Royal policy had recourse to half measures.

FROM LAND DIETS TO A NATIONAL PARLIAMENT

The freedom granted by the King at the beginning of the Thirteen Years' War increased the prerogative of the land diets, assemblies of the gentry which congregated in each separate region. In the first half of the fifteenth century the King summoned the gentry only three times to obtain their approval for extraordinary taxes. By 1454 it became a fiscal and political necessity to convene the gentry every few years in order to win their support for war and other measures. This practice laid the foundations of the Polish parliamentary system and opened the way to the political supremacy of the gentry.

Cracow. Church of the Virgin Mary, 14th cent.

Cracow. Barbican, 1498–1499

The genesis of the Polish parliament may be traced to the colloquia or assemblies of the lords and the gentry, which in the thirteenth and fourteenth centuries were convoked in various regions and, less frequently, on a nation wide basis. Such conventions, attended by lay and Church lords and a small number of representatives of the gentry and the chapters, were summoned four times by Władysław the Short, but less often by Casimir the Great. They became a basis of government, however, at the close of the fourteenth century and were convoked once a year, generally at Piotrków, a town chosen for its central position. Apart from the general assemblies (*conventio magna*) provincial assemblies (*conventiones generales*) were held more frequently in the fifteenth century, separately for Great Poland—at Środa, Koło or Sieradz, and for Little Poland with Ruthenia at Nowe Miasto, Korczyn or Wiślica. The provincial assemblies were attended by the dignitaries of the province and by all the gentry who appointed representatives to the closed conference, and approved by acclamation the results announced to them. The assemblies debated issues of domestic policy, legislation and finance placed before them by the King. They manifested a great deal of initiative, especially at times when they acted as court of law.

The 1454 privilege of Nieszawa strengthened the third link in the parliamentary system, the land diets (*conventiones particulares*) of which there were eighteen at the close of the fifteenth century. The land diets were attended by local dignitaries and all the gentry. They established provisions of common law, gave their approval to the levy of extraordinary taxes, and chose two plenipotentiaries or regional deputies (*nuntii terrestres*) to attend the deliberations of the provincial and general assemblies. The provincial assemblies were more important in the second half of the fifteenth century, because they were more convenient to the king as well as to the gentry.

With the ascension to the Polish throne of John Albert (1492–1501), successor and son of Casimir IV, the general assembly (Seym) became an established parliamentary form, and the provincial assemblies were summoned less and less frequently.

The course along which the Polish parliamentary system developed in the fifteenth century did not lead to a full representation of the privileged estates, but to the transfer of legislative power into the hands of two feudal groups, the lay and ecclesiastical magnates, and the gentry. The parliamentary life flourishing during the reign of the last of the Jagiellons was filled with the conflict and the struggle for supremacy waged between these two groups.

WESTERN POMERANIA, LUBUSZ LAND AND SILESIA IN THE FOURTEENTH AND THE FIFTEENTH CENTURIES

The break-up of Western Pomerania into small duchies precluded any modernization in the political sense. The dukes of Western Pomerania maintained their comparative independence in the fourteenth century as a result of the friendly assistance of Poland, and also of Denmark in the fifteenth century. They were backed later by the three united Scandinavian kingdoms, headed by Eric I, a Duke of Słupsk. These factors saved Pomerania from becoming a vassal of Brandenburg. The spread of German influence continued however. Germans predominated among the knights. Towns like Stralsund, Szczecin and Kołobrzeg were completely Germanized, and Slavs were not allowed to become merchants or craftsmen. In the Church, too, the more important posts were filled by Germans. The University of Greifswald, a centre of intellectual activity, was founded in 1456. The majority of the rural population remained Slav. The peasants were subjected to harsh economic exploitation by the lords and by towns which conducted a vigorous trade as members of the Hansa. In the struggle with feudal anarchy and in the face of the danger from Brandenburg, Western Pomerania formed a political union in the second half of the fifteenth century. Bogusław X (1474–1523), the husband of Anna, daughter of Casimir IV, whose support he sought, introduced successful administrative and financial reforms. He established his capital in Szczecin where he ruled in collaboration with the estates represented in the diet.

From the fourteenth century Lubusz Land became known as the New March of Brandenburg. Frequent changes of the dynasties of the margraves offered Poland in the fifteenth century a number of missed opportunities for recovering this vital area. The Templars, and especially the Hospitallers, established here by the margraves, colonized the towns and villages with Germans. A major role was played by Frankfurt on the Odra, a town which controlled the trade in grain and timber. Frankfurt interfered with the transport of these products by its staple law that applied on the Odra and indirectly on the Warta. Both Great Poland and Western Pomerania voiced their grievance against these laws.

Silesia continued to lead the Polish lands in the economic field. Both the villages and towns, headed by Wrocław, prospered in the fourteenth and fifteenth centuries. The province was linked with the Polish Kingdom by major international trade routes leading to Gdańsk on the Baltic and through Cracow and Lwów to the Black Sea. The Polish territories supplied the raw materials for the crafts of Silesia, notably weaving, tanning and iron works. The towns of Silesia imported food from Poland and exported manufactured goods to her. The second half of the fifteenth century was marked by social discontent in the towns, unrest in the countryside, and an attack by the Church against the influence of radical ideas coming from Bohemia. Far reaching changes were noted in the political system. In the fifteenth century the kings of Bohemia gained direct control over several Silesian duchies, such as Wrocław, Świdnica, Ziembice and Oleśnica. Others were still governed by the Silesian Piasts as vassals of the Bohemian Crown. The last of these Piasts, the Duke of Legnica and Brzeg, died at the close of the seventeenth century. In 1471 Matthias Corvinus placed the whole of Silesia under a general magistrate (*starosta*). Władysław of Bohemia upheld these conditions by the franchise of 1498. Two of his brothers, John Albert and Sigismund held temporarily the office of viceroy of either the whole or part of Silesia. This Jagiellonian episode, however, left no lasting political imprint. As a province of the Church, Silesia remained under the authority of the Polish Archbishop of Gniezno.

By the fourteenth century German influence made deep inroads among the feudal lords and the clergy. The Piast dynasty was bilingual in Polish and German, and even spoke three languages on account of the strong influence of Bohemia, but was for the most part hostile to the Polish Kingdom. Among the exceptions was Bolko II, Duke of Świdnica and ally of Casimir the Great, and towards the end of the fourteenth century Louis I of Brzeg, an admirer of Silesia's national past. Both languages, Polish and German, were spoken in the towns because of the large influx of Slavs from the rural areas. The influence of Bohemian and Polish culture spread across the frontiers into the whole of Silesia. Many Silesians studied and lectured at the Jagiellonian University; the culture and art of Silesia influenced above all Little Poland and to a lesser degree Great Poland.

ECONOMIC LIFE IN THE FOURTEENTH AND FIFTEENTH CENTURIES

The Polish Kingdom owed its political success to the many-sided development of its energies, including its economy. The number of newly planted rural and urban settlements rose under Casimir the Great and throughout the fifteenth century. The scourge of the Black Death swept across Little Poland and Pomerania in 1348 and 1349, but it did not wreak such havoc as it did in western Europe. In the middle of the fifteenth century the population of the Polish State, within the frontiers of the Crown and without Royal Prussia, is estimated to have been over two and a half millions, with about 10 inhabitants to a square kilometre.

A vigorous colonization movement embraced, in the fourteenth century, the foothills of Little Poland. In the next century one may observe an ethnic expansion to western Ruthenia. Similarly Poles from Mazovia colonized Podlasie and the lake region of Teutonic Prussia (later called Mazuria).

The growth of settlements and increased population enabled the spread of more intensive forms of farming in which the three field system became general. Peasants began to rear cattle for sale. Various kinds of rent prevailed and were the most widespread form of feudal exploitation of the peasants. The German law embraced about half the villages; but the villages governed by Polish law were enjoying virtually the same legal and economic position. In the fifteenth century, the monastic estates were the first to expand their manorial farms, in order to increase grain production for the new and expanding markets. These farms were to base production on serf and not hired labour. These ambitions were carried out at the expense of the lands owned by the village mayors (*sculteti*), who according to a law of 1423 were "useless and recalcitrant". The holdings of the peasants were also reduced. The peasants were compelled to work for the lord one day a week per mansus (about 16 hectares) of land. The peasants resisted increasing exploitation by flight from their holdings and by fomenting local unrest. In 1496 legal restrictions were placed on the drift of peasants from the villages. These were the first symptoms of a social and economic regression of the Polish rural area. Until that time, during the fourteenth and a considerable part of the fifteenth centuries, Poland saw an expansion of settlement and production, while western Europe suffered an agrarian crisis.

Mining made progress in Silesia and Little Poland. Deposits of iron ore, copper, lead, zinc, sulphur and rock salt were discovered in the fourteenth century. In the course of the next century the mining centres of Olkusz and Wieliczka attained a high level of organization and technology.

The ascendancy of the commodity-money economy in exchanges between town and country, the formation of economic regions covering large districts and later the provinces of a united Polish Kingdom or parts of neighbouring countries, as in the instances of Silesia, Pomerania, Prussia and Mazovia were all factors contributing to the growth of towns. The progress of urbanization can be measured by the granting of municipal charters. In Great Poland 93 towns received charters in the fourteenth century and 153 in the fifteenth century; 40 and 83 towns in Mazovia received charters in the same centuries.

Local trade expanded and external commerce linked the Polish towns with western Europe and the Black Sea area. New roads to Lithuania were linked with the old network of trade routes. The total volume of trade grew to impressive proportions. For example, 30,000 ells (*postawy*) of cloth were brought each year to Cracow. The turnover in trade and money-lending grew from one decade to another, money being in general use in the sale of manufactured goods and agricultural products.

Technological organization of the crafts was improved. Appearing only occasionally in twelfth century Poland, but becoming more popular in the thirteenth, the watermills multiplied in the processing of iron, wool, timber, hides and grain. Better knowledge was gained of the raw materials and in various specialized crafts the production methods were refined. Craftsmen became highly skilled in their work and could produce in sufficient quantities to satisfy the demands of the whole population, which caused a decline of the crafts practiced in the countryside, though to compensate for this, less emphasis was placed on a higher output of farm products. In the fourteenth and fifteenth centuries, as a result of the division of labour and the use of money, trade activity reached a peak never again achieved in Poland under feudal conditions. The role of merchants as brokers between the peasant and the craftsman, became more important in the local market. The craftsmen were forbidden by law to engage in retail trade and in the course of the fourteenth century the merchants concentrated in their hands the trade in manufactured articles, raw materials and food. The burghers were not entirely freed from the necessity of growing their own food. Even larger towns cultivated the land granted to them under their charters. In small market towns, the burgher farmer devoted part of his time and effort to tilling the soil and to raising domestic animals.

At the end of the thirteenth and the beginning of the fourteenth centuries the guild was established as an association protecting the interests of craftsmen and enabling its members to perform their trades. The members of guild were masters, each working in his own workshop with his apprentices and journeymen. In the second half of the fourteenth and throughout the fifteenth centuries some of the masters owned several workshops and employed other masters as well as women, but the guilds opposed and prohibited this practice. An apprentice spent several years in learning his trade. He was then freed as a journeyman. At the end of a long period, which also included a journey that lasted at least a year and six weeks to other workshops within the country and abroad, the journeyman could render proof of his mastery in the trade by submitting evidence of his skill in the form of a specimen

piece of work upon the basis of which he could be made a master. The exploited journeymen staged revolts against their masters. Notable was the rebellion of the bakers of Cracow in 1375. The guilds were ruled by statutes, with which the town councils interfered. Owing to the advance in techniques employed in production there was an upward swing in the quality of the articles and greater specialization in the crafts. At the beginning of the fourteenth century there were 29 different craft guilds in Wrocław. In the leather trade alone distinctions were made between the tanners, white-, red- and black-leather craftsmen, suède and morocco leather craftsmen, purse-makers, belt, glove and robe makers, bookbinders, vellum makers, and furriers. In the metal trades there were blacksmiths, pewterers, coppersmiths, needle-makers, bell founders, goldsmiths, gold platers, gunsmiths, tinsmiths, spur-makers, cuttlerers and swordsmiths, armourers and locksmiths. It is obvious that all these specialists were not necessarily represented in every town, even in larger ones, nor did they always have their own guilds, being organized according to the raw material they used in production or according to some other criterion. In small towns all craftsmen who could not set up their individual guilds were members of a general guild. Finally, the guilds did not all possess the same economic status nor were they always able to maintain a balance of forces inside their organizations.

The guilds were interested in the collective purchase of raw materials, the processes of production, the quality and sale of articles, and regulated prices. They fought with the town councils, composed of merchants, for a share in the government of the town, in decisions on taxes, for revocation of the decree that compelled artisans to use merchants as middle-men in trade. The rising of weavers in Wrocław in 1333 which embraced all the poor of the town was directed against the town council. The guilds guarded the monopoly of production with varying success. The monopoly was gravely undermined by journeymen who, though not yet emancipated, worked in houses exempt from municipal jurisdiction or lying outside the town walls. Jewish craftsmen, not admitted into the guilds, were also competitive, as well as village craftsmen, like the weavers of the foothill villages of Silesia and Ruthenia.

The stratification of the town population varied and was related to the size of the town. At the beginning of the fifteenth century, large towns, such as Wrocław and Gdańsk with a population of 20,000, Cracow with about 14,000 and the smaller towns, like Poznań with about 4000 and Sandomierz with about 2000, were inhabited by three distinct groups of burghers, exclusive of the gentry and clergy who often constituted a sizeable proportion of the population. At the head stood a small group of merchant patricians who in the course of the fourteenth century assumed complete control over the political and economic life of the towns. They removed from power the hereditary advocatus and kept others away from the councils or at best admitted a small number of other representatives. In the years 1320–1350 among the 88 town councillors of Cracow only 14 were craftsmen. The

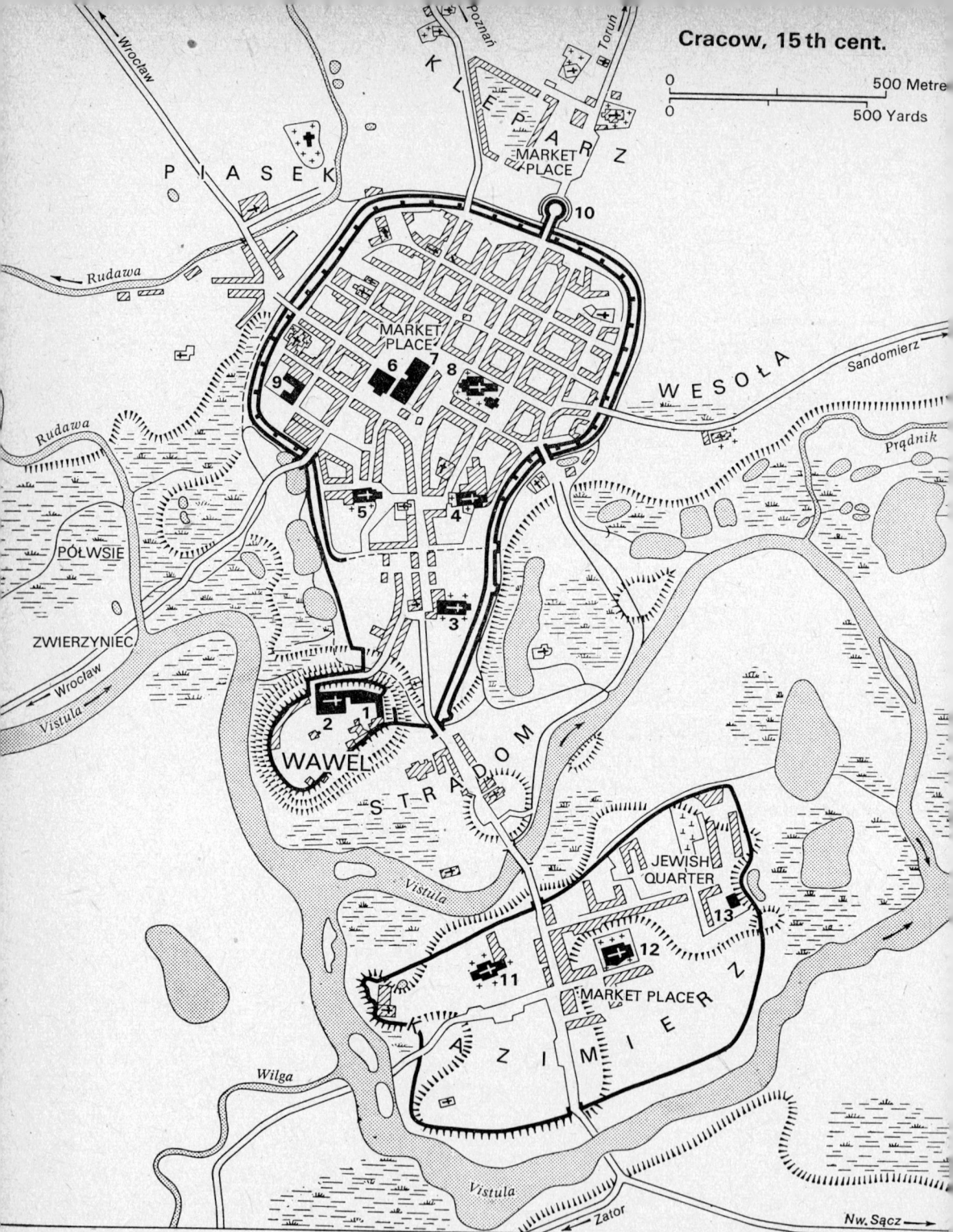

1. Royal Castle, 2. Cathedral, 3. St. Andrew's Church, 4. Dominican Church, 5. Franciscan Church, 6. Town Hall, 7. Drapers' Hall, 8. St. Mary's Church, 9. Collegium Maius, 10. St. Florian's Gate and Barbican, 11. St. Catherine's Church, 12. Corpus Christi Church, 13. Synagogue.

majority of these patricians were of foreign extraction and their native tongue for the most part was German, but there were also Italians (in Cracow) or Armenians (in Lwów). Nevertheless, when the conflicts during the period the Polish Kingdom's unification subsided, the patricians joined forces with the secular and church lords and with the Polish Crown, which gave them political support in exchange for financial aid. The patricians of Silesia adopted a similar attitude toward the Kings of Bohemia. On the other hand, the patricians of the Prussian towns, exploited by the Teutonic Order, pronounced in 1454 in favour of incorporation into the Polish State.

A second, far more diverse group as regards wealth, was the large mass of common craftsmen, who remained in both open or concealed conflict with the patricians. The third group were the poor, the servants and unskilled labourers, who remained outside the pale of town law. Thanks to the commoners and the poor the Polish language retained a strong influence even in towns like Wrocław which had been exposed to the constant influx of foreign elements. Elsewhere, Polish was either the predominant or the only language spoken. In Prussia, by contrast, in both large and small towns almost exclusively German was spoken. National antagonisms still yielded to class and political differences. The first powerful wave of unrest inundated Silesia and Little Poland in the 1360's. Opposition to the fiscal policies of the councils and strikes of local guilds continued until the close of the century. A second wave of revolts followed directly, inspired by Hussitism, culminating in the Wrocław insurrection of 1418, during which the town hall was captured and the councillors killed. The Polish Hussite movement was suppressed in the middle of the fifteenth century. Urban disorders, particularly in Great Poland, were suppressed in consequence. The counter-action of the Church by the Franciscan order took the form of the foundation of Bernardine monasteries in various towns.

The Jewish population of the towns constituted a separate national, religious, cultural and legal group. The liberties, granted initially by the Duke of Kalisz, Bolesław the Pious, in 1264, and some Silesian dukes were extended by Casimir the Great to the whole Kingdom, and confirmed once more by Casimir IV in 1453. It is true that these privileges were soon revoked by the Nieszawa Statutes; nevertheless they remained the fundamental guarantee of personal safety, inviolability of places of worship and freedom of trade of the Polish Jews. They were directly subject to the royal treasury and the jurisdiction of the voivode. The State, on the other hand, recognized the jurisdiction of the courts of the Jewish communities. These communities were established in the larger towns and were not very numerous. At the close of the fourteenth century the mass exodus of Jews fleeing from persecution in Germany swelled the numbers of the Jewish population in Poland and diversified the social structure of their Jewish communities. The Jews devoted themselves traditionally to money lending, an activity which promoted growth of the commodity-money economy, particularly when the Church remained adamant in its interdictions of usury as a trade for Christians. In the fifteenth century the Jews turned to the crafts, a fact which evoked a conflict with the town guilds. An agreement signed in Cracow in 1485 tried to regulate the standing of Jewish craftsmen in the guilds. There were clashes and even local riots as well as religious violence which were generally subdued by the State authorities despite the intolerant pronouncements of the lay and secular clergy. In the course of the fifteenth century many towns restricted Jewish residences to several streets and even set up separate districts (e.g. Kazimierz near Cracow). In isolated instances, as in Warsaw in 1483, the Jews were compelled to move outside the town walls.

The Armenian religious communities in the incorporated territories of Ruthenia retained their legal identity. Armenian merchant communities lived in the towns where they had settled in the middle of the fourteenth century. They were governed by Armenian law which they had brought with them. This law was codified in a statute granted to the Armenians by Sigismund I. Unlike the Jewish population, the Armenians were allowed to mix with the town population which professed other faiths and spoke other languages and were permitted to assume posts in the municipal government. Though they retained the Armenian language in the church services the communities began in the sixteenth century to adopt Polish culture and to speak Polish.

The Polish towns of that period were as varied in appearance as they were in size, ranging from Cracow, the capital of the Kingdom, Gdańsk and Wrocław which could be compared to any European town of that age, to the sleepy wooden hamlets with a population of several hundred which sprang to life only on market days. In the large towns the fifteenth century witnessed the construction of more brick buildings, including dwelling residential houses. The town accounts provide ample evidence of the concern for cleanliness, paved streets, order and precautions against fire. There was a marked expansion of municipal facilities, with construction of town halls, drapers' halls, yardarms, cloth cutters shops, baths, stalls, benches and booths in the markets, hospitals which were also asylums, parish churches, monasteries and mills. By the orders of Casimir the Great over 20 towns of his Kingdom were surrounded by walls. The towns continued to put up walls after his death. The Turkish danger that reared its head at the close of the fifteenth century was influential in changing the appearance of Polish towns into that of fortified strongholds, the kind that was to spring up in the early years of the introduction of firearms. The Barbican of Cracow was built in these years. The town churches were generally built of brick and stone as were the castles, residences of kings and of the *starosta* (capitaneus).

CULTURE IN THE FOURTEENTH
AND FIFTEENTH CENTURIES

The style of life at court and in the towns approached, especially in the fifteenth century, international standards in what has been called the autumn of the Middle Ages. Court festivals and tournaments, sumptuous feasts and rich dress contrasted sharply with the dire poverty of the towns with wooden and perpetually filthy streets. A life of pomp and splendour was led by the bishops and the new class of secular magnates, who had come into sudden wealth with the expansion to the East and who immediately adopted a princely mode of living.

There were no such sharp distinctions among the rural population. The wealthy tenant farmers lived on the same standard as the majority of the gentry. The wealthier knights lived in close harmony with the town patricians and eagerly adopted foreign habits either imported to the country or learned abroad in the course of travels. Regional differences began to emerge in the rural areas. Silesia and Little Poland led in the development of material culture followed by a part of Royal Prussia with Gdańsk, Elbląg and Toruń, then Great Poland with Mazovia at the very bottom of the scale. The new acquisitions of Poland in the East developed at an uneven rate.

From the middle of the fourteenth century, important events took place in education and in the organization of cathedral, parochial and town schools. A growing number of pupils were not so much candidates for the church clergy, as sons of burghers and the wealthier nobles who desired to acquire a minimum of knowledge and the ability to write, a skill they needed in commerce and in the municipal offices, such as the keeping of accounts and minutes in the city, land and provincial courts. The parish schools maintained by the town councils and the churches frequently evolved, as was the case in Legnica, into fairly large educational centres which prepared the pupils for university studies as did the cathedral schools. The sons of Polish burghers and nobles were enrolled in European universities. Maciej Kolbe of Świebodzin in the diocese of Poznań was the rector of the Paris University in 1480.

The University of Cracow, the second to be established in this part of Europe, was founded in 1364, shortly after the University of Prague, founded in 1348, but before the University of Vienna, founded in 1365. Casimir the Great introduced the Italian model where law was the principal subject of study, enabling the students to be state officials. Later reforms in 1400 followed the models set by the universities of Paris and Prague and included the study of theology. Maintaining contact with the intellectual circles of virtually all of Europe, the University of Cracow exerted an influence on neighbouring countries, among them Lithuania. The ferment caused by religious disputes aroused by the Hussites inspired many debates at the university. A passionate polemicist was Master Andrzej Gałka of Dobczyn, an adherent of the Hussites. In philosophy the university tended toward the doctrines of nominalism and subscribed to the principles of practical philosophy, while in politics it espoused, as did virtually the whole Polish episcopate and clergy, the conciliar doctrine within the framework of religious orthodoxy.

There were also social accents in the activity of the university. In 1447 Rector Jan of Ludzisko greeted Casimir IV with a speech in which he protested against the injustices inflicted upon the peasants of Poland. Members of the staff voiced their convictions outside the confines of the university. These were the theologians of European fame: Mateusz of Cracow and Jakub of Paradyż, the notable jurists Stanisław of Skalbmierz who developed the doctrine *"de bellis iustis"* in 1411 and Paulus Vladimiri of Brudzeń who has already been mentioned, author of the thesis stating that pagans had the right to their land and that neither the Pope nor the Emperor could dispose of it in any way. The school of astronomy and mathematics was founded in the middle of the fifteenth century through the agency of Marcin Król of Żurawica, Jan of Głogów, Wojciech of Brudzewo and others. Nicolaus Copernicus, one of the most illustrious scholars of the university, studied in Cracow from 1492 to 1496. Polish names appeared on the registers of the universities of Germany, France and Italy.

In the second half of the fifteenth century, Italian humanism was introduced in Poland by travellers and circulating manuscripts. Grzegorz of Sanok, Archbishop of Lwów, who died in 1471, had attracted a group of people seeking new literary forms and new secular themes. About 1490 another circle organized in Cracow was led by Filippo Buonaccorsi (Kallimachus) who opened the way for rationalism and criticism. The "Sodalitas Litteraria Vistulana" of the poet Conrad Celtis was active in the same period.

Latin still prevailed as the written language, as did Church writings. Many manuscripts were produced by the universities and schools. There was a proliferation of poetry, echoes of the *vagari* (strolling minstrels), songs, verses, political satire and didactic verse, a mountain of evidence of consistent and intensive literary pursuits. The keen awareness of history emerges in chronicles and accounts. Notable is the lively political memoir, hostile to the Angevin rulers, written by Janko of Czarnków, the Vice-Chancellor of the Kingdom, directly after the death of his beloved Casimir the Great. Another work, the *Chronicon principum Poloniae*, expressed the patriotism of its author, Piotr of Byczyna a Silesian burgher. There were collectors of ancient historical texts like Master Jan Dąbrówka, and writers of annals, like the *mansionarii* of Cracow chapter, who in this manner amassed a reference library for Jan Długosz. This fine historian, equally at home in diplomatic circles and as a teacher of princes, has left in addition to other works a history of Poland—*Annales seu cronicae incliti Regni Poloniae* composed in the style of an annual and brought up to the year 1480. Fashioned after Livy in style and technique and based on extensive research in primary sources, the work is a monument to patriotism and historical knowledge. Mention must be made of Jan Ostroróg, a secular political writer, whose memorandum on the system of the Polish State written in Latin in 1467 contains a broad programme of administrative and even social reforms.

National culture manifested itself more and more frequently in the Polish vernacular. There were translations of long works, like the Psalter for Queen Jadwiga and the Bible for Queen Sophia, the last wife of Władysław Jagiełło and a long list of translations of Hussite works for the populace. The Latin originals of the statutes enacted by Casimir the Great and by the dukes of Mazovia were translated into Polish in the fifteenth century. The first treatises on Polish orthography were written about 1440. Abundant evidence is provided by poetry written in Poland, which though still rough in form, covered a broad range of subjects from the religious to the profane. Secular music was written for one voice and set to Latin texts or to the vernacular like *Panno miła nie będziesz li ty będzie inna* (Sweet Maid, if it be not you, will be another), of the fourteenth century thrived side by side with large numbers of Church songs, some of them very fine in quality. There is evidence that from the late thirteenth century attempts were made to induce the faithful to take a more active part in the church services by participating in musical recitations of the symbols of faith, the decalogue and prayers. Soon afterwards, in the fourteenth century Easter songs were composed in Polish. *Bogurodzica* (Mother of God) was the song of the knights; it was sung in the fields of Grunwald in 1410. This fine piece of music calls for great skill on the part of the performers. In the fourteenth century or a little earlier, Franciscan cantors learned to sing in polyphony. The organ of Toruń was installed in 1343 and Polish organ tabulators appeared in the fourteenth century. Mikołaj of Radom, a famous composer of polyphonic music, emerged about 1430. There was likewise wide interest in the theory of music at this time.

Poland belongs to the countries which adopted and evolved printing at a fairly early date. The first printing shop was established in Cracow in 1473/1474. The first book to be printed in Polish appeared in Wrocław in 1475. The Cyrillic alphabet in printed books for the eastern and southern Slavs was used for the first time anywhere in Cracow in 1491. The libraries were filled with manuscripts and incunabula. There is reliable evidence of a relatively wide distribution of books in Latin and in *vulgari* in the last quarter of the fifteenth century.

In fine arts the activities of the artists underwent their own form of democratization. Most works were produced within the framework of the guild. The works of painters, sculptors, architects and goldsmiths were commissioned by clients, ranging from the royal court, the episcopate and the magnates to the urban communities and rural parishes.

Gothic style prevailed in architecture. The three leading provinces in art, Silesia, Little Poland and Prussia, interacted upon each other and were linked by numerous threads with the art of central and northern Europe. The most impressive buildings of the fourteenth and the beginning of the fifteenth century built within the area of the Polish State, were: the churches of St.

Mary, St. Catherine and the Corpus Christi in Cracow and the Cathedral of Archbishop Jarosław Bogoria in Gniezno. The most notable buildings outside the Polish Kingdom were: the town hall, cathedral and several large ecclesiastical buildings in Wrocław, the church of St. Mary in Gdańsk, one of the largest fortified complexes of Europe, the castle of Malbork, and the town hall and the churches of Toruń. The fact that the majority of the leading architectural centres were integrated into the Kingdom of Poland in the middle of the fifteenth century promoted an even more vigorous exchange of art experiences. A new form in architecture began to emerge at the close of the fifteenth century with such notable examples as the small fortified castle of Dębno and the Collegium Maius of the University of Cracow.

The churches and chapels were richly embellished with stained glass windows, murals and plaques, wood and stone sculptured figures, gold articles and textiles. Silesia and Little Poland led in sculpture and painting. Some of the works of that age, like the tomb of Władysław Jagiełło, represent a high level of European sculpture. Other works of art, paintings and sculptures, the product of guild workshops, reflect contemporary trends of European art and are faithful to the current ideas of the townsmen, gentry and wealthy peasants, who founded numerous small parish churches. The realism of daily life evident in their works helped immensely in conveying the reigning ideology to the enthralled spectators. Among outstanding works there is the exquisite figure of the Madonna of Krużlowa and the paintings produced by the Cracow and Sącz schools of artists, preserved in their best examples at Cracow and Tarnów. Wit Stosz (Stwosz), the celebrated sculptor of Nuremberg and Cracow, is preeminent among his contemporaries. His most important work is the altar of St. Mary parish church in Cracow, produced in 1477–1485, a gift of the town community. The precision of his observation of life and the sophisticated and stylized manners of the Late Gothic period is remarkable. In the vast expanse of the Polish and Lithuanian federation the influence of the Late Gothic period penetrated as far east as Wilno and Lwów. On the other hand, the influence of Ruthenian mural painting, developed in the days of Władysław Jagiełło in the Volhynian school and bearing the strong imprint of Balkan styles, and the art from the environs of Pskov in the days of Casimir IV reached the Wawel of Cracow, Lublin, Sandomierz and Wiślica. Many a notable work bears witness to this influence. The illumination of manuscripts spread, indicating that this select form of art frequently enjoyed the patronage of the Polish episcopate and some of the monasteries. Late Gothic gold articles attained a perfection of form and design which was to continue far into the sixteenth century.

The nationalities of the Jagiellonian State, the Poles, Ruthenians, Lithuanians, Germans, Jews and Armenians, played an important role in the lively exchange of cultural experience. Poland guaranteed privileges to the estates that emerged in the course of the fourteenth century, to the lords spiritual and temporal, the gentry, and the patricians. They were all united by sentiment and a common desire for a strong political foundation. The broad masses of the urban and rural population, of Polish and non-Polish language, were united by a loyalty to the State and its territory, a trait typical of the late Middle Ages. They saw an advantage in this political union. The mobilization of national forces in the period of the battle of Grunwald produced expressions of Polish nationalism in many ways, while the growth of a literature written in the vernacular strengthened the bases of Polish social consciousness. Writers of the second half of the fifteenth century were aware of the fact that the Polish *gens et natio* embraced all the people who speak Polish, from the royal court to the lowly peasant. The Tartar and Turkish danger gave rise to the belief in the mission of the Poles as defenders of Europe.

It may be recalled that on the eve of the outbreak of the Thirteen Years' War many of the citizens of Prussia who spoke German, declared their support for the Polish State in its form and substance. The *Regnum Poloniae* stood for a broad social and political union of many nationalities. This is the legacy that was bequeathed to the age that followed.

Genealogy of the Piasts (1)

(The tables include only the most important members of the dynasties until the end of the 12th century)

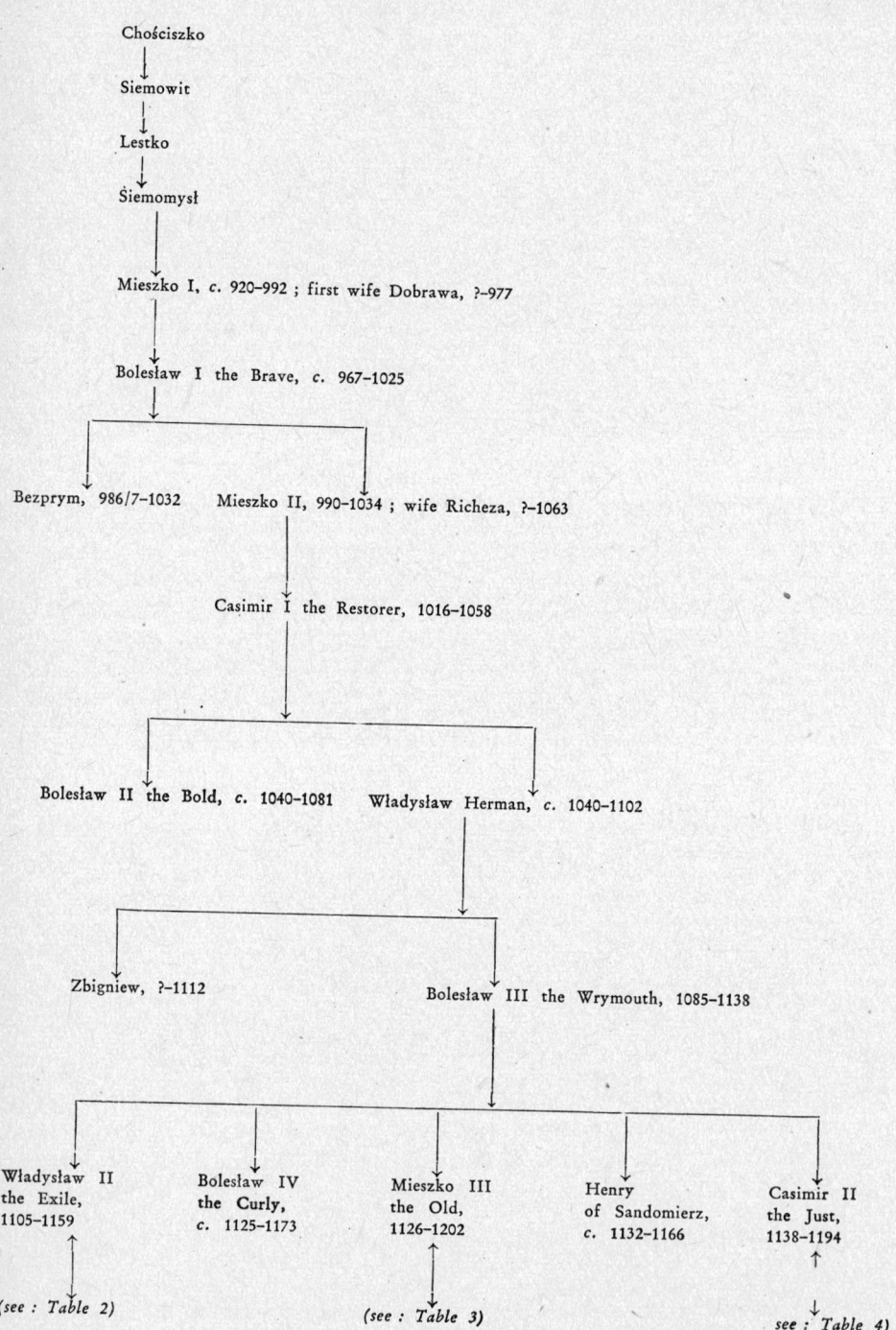

Genealogy of the Piasts (2)

(Silesian branch)

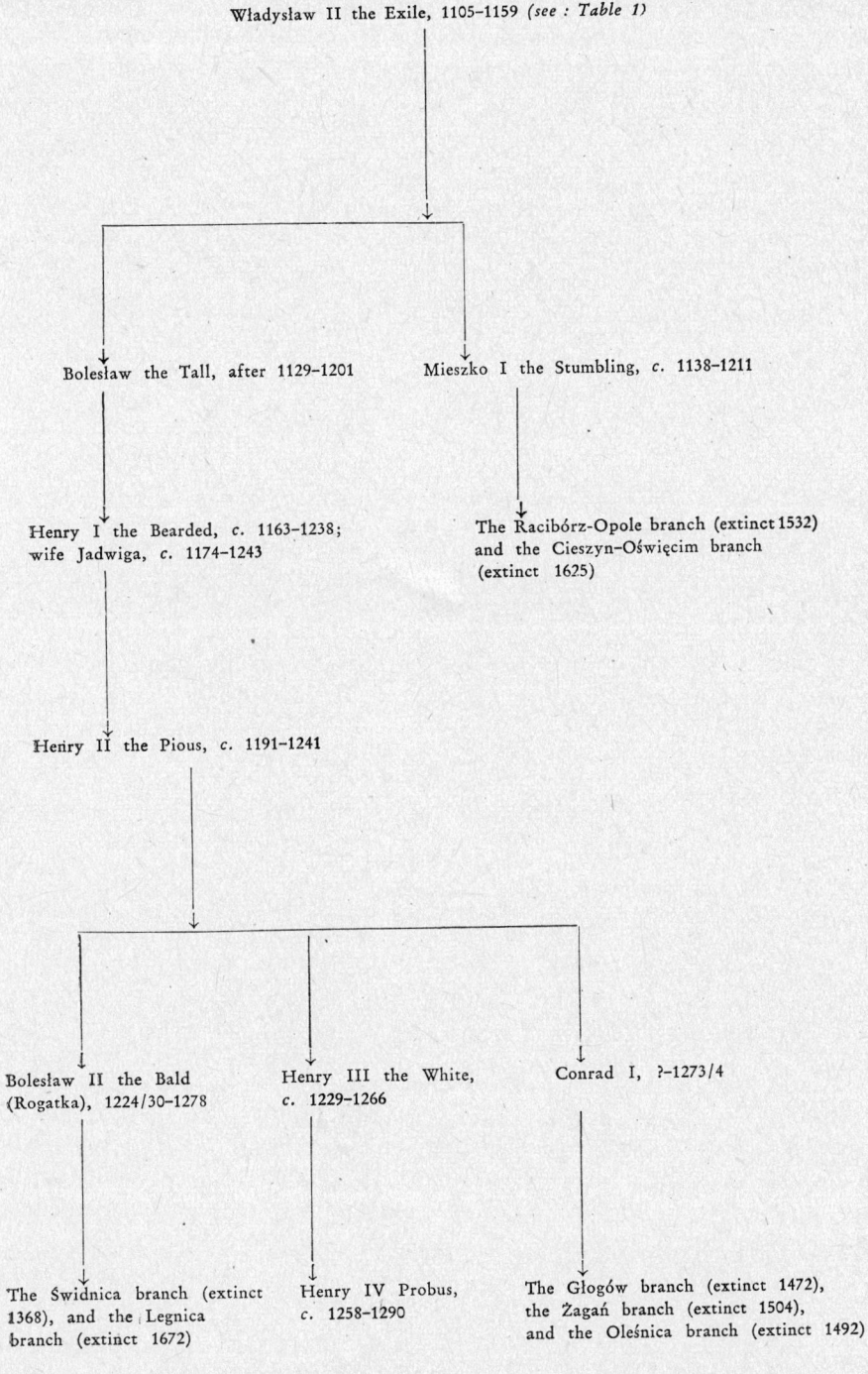

Genealogy of the Piasts (3)
(Great Poland branch)

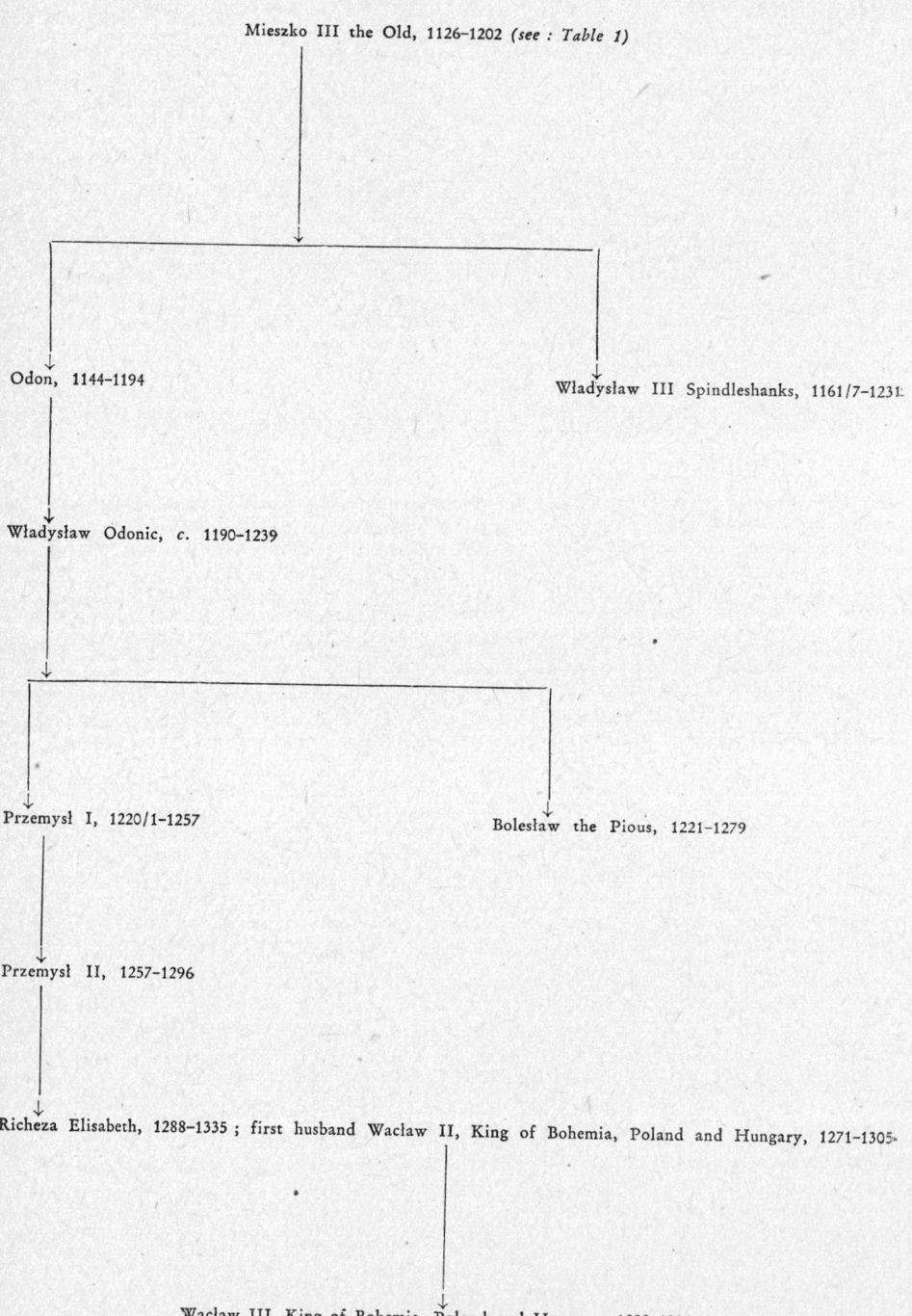

Genealogy of the Piasts (4)

(Little Poland, Kujawy and Mazovia branches)

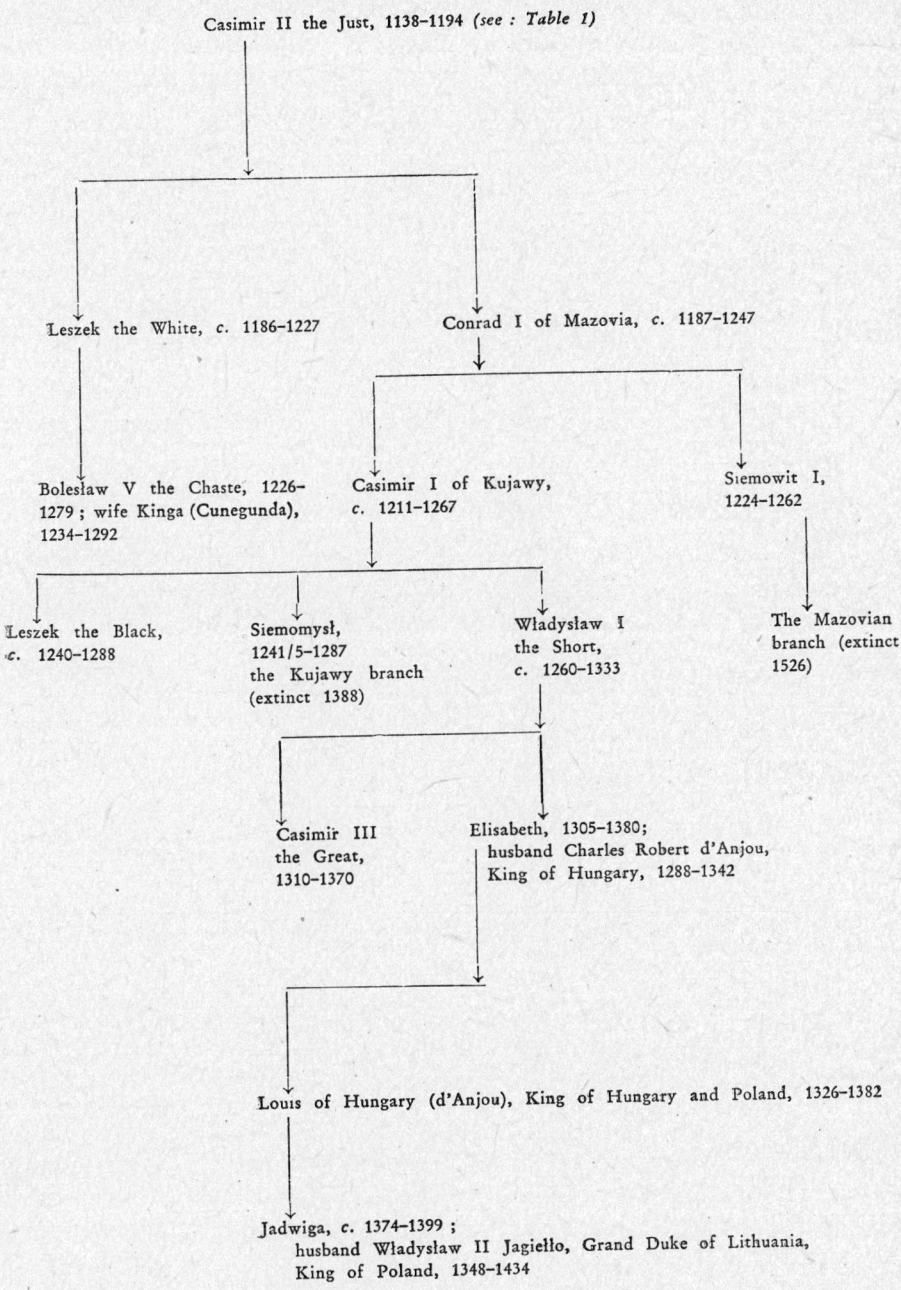

(see: Table of the Jagiellon dynasty)

THE COMMONWEALTH OF THE GENTRY

Chapters VII–IX
by Janusz Tazbir

Chapters X–XIII
by Emanuel Rostworowski

Chapter VII
POLAND'S "GOLDEN AGE" (1492–1586)

GENERAL CHARACTERISTICS OF THE PERIOD

The sixteenth century marked, in many respects, a turning point in Poland's history. It was a period of fundamental social, economic, political, cultural and religious change, the consequences of which were to be felt (or counteracted more or less successfully) by the subsequent generations. In the Polish Commonwealth of those days, though based on a voluntary and finally established union of two nations, everything was fluid, and therefore both a drive towards a strong central state authority and a further extension of the ruling class's privileges were still a possibility.

Whereas the seventeenth century could well be referred to as the "Golden Age" of the high nobility, the period of the rule of the last Jagiellons (especially the reign of Sigismund Augustus) witnessed the high point of influence of the middle gentry. They shifted their allegiance from the monarch to the magnates, at times supporting the king, on other occasions opposing him strongly. The limits of the gentry's political thought were set by narrowly conceived class interests; the gentry undoubtedly desired to improve the machinery of the State but, at the same time, they greatly feared anything that smacked of absolutism whose growth in the neighbouring states they watched with horror.

The gentry obtained considerable privileges for themselves which, simultaneously, resulted in restricting the freedom of activity, and even the freedom of movement, as in the case of the peasants, of other sections of the population. This class egoism, in a way a recurring and normal social phenomenon, would not have been so harmful in itself, had it been accompanied by the introduction of proper reforms in the political structure of the country reforms which were both feasible and within the limits of reality. Such reforms would have to lead to the creation of a standing army, a full treasury, and a smoothly working administration, and—above all—the establishment of an efficient parliamentary procedure. Too much, however, was left to the good will, patriotic feelings and political wisdom of the citizen. When these began to fail, it yielded immediately adverse effects on the entire system. The full implications of this state of affairs became apparent only later, but already in the sixteenth century certain signs of self-satisfaction with Polish achievements and an unwillingness to be involved in any armed effort which did not augur well for the future, became clearly visible among the gentry. Humanism made them conscious of the pleasures of life, and its practical side and for that reason they accepted most quickly and eagerly, a casual utilitarianism.

The splendour of the "Golden Age" was most striking in the cultural achievements of the period. They were often perhaps superficial and limited in scope, but they are unquestionable and generally acknowledged. In the sixteenth century therefore there were still no features which would point to a backwardness of Polish civilization with regard to the West. Poland at that period was, in every respect, superior to northern and eastern Europe and kept pace with the West not only from the point of view of economic development and political power, but also in the field of scholarly achievement, arts and literature. The greatest poet of the Polish Renaissance Jan Kochanowski, was of the same stature as Ronsard, and its most eminent political writer, Andrzej Frycz-Modrzewski was on the level of Jean Bodin. Scholars from all over Europe drew upon the magnificent discoveries of Copernicus. Throughout the Middle Ages everything that Europe knew of Poland could have been written in a few lines of print, usually confusing and inexact. Only in the sixteenth century was Poland "discovered" by Europe. The latter's horizons were, at once, extended by the knowledge of the New World and of Poland, a powerful and cultured country, perhaps somewhat exotic in the manner of its people's attire, but impressive in its wealth and size. To the West, which was then plunged in the chaos of religious strife, Poland appeared also as a sanctuary where a different manner of worship did not lead dissenters to death at the stake.

BETWEEN THE HAPSBURGS AND MUSCOVY

The reigns of the two sons and direct successors of Casimir IV, John Albert (1492–1501) and Alexander (1501–1506), were marked by bitter conflicts between the gentry and the magnates and the final shaping of the modern Polish parliamentary system. This period was of lesser importance for Poland's external affairs. These were marked by the simultaneous engagement of her forces in the East, against Muscovy and in the North, against the Order of the Teutonic Knights, and by the pursuit of dynastic claims to the Bohemian and Hungarian thrones. The dispersal of aims and forces was obviously bound to yield only transitory and impermanent successes.

Every victory over the Teutonic Order proved to be only a partial success

The dominions of the Jagiellonian dynasty, 15th/16th cent.

because it did not finally eliminate a state hostile to Poland on the Baltic. At the time of John Albert the Grand Masters of the Order ceased to pay homage to the Polish kings. Diplomatic measures to restore the former relationship were of no avail. Albrecht of Hohenzollern, who became the Grand Master in 1511, sought Hapsburg assistance, the military aid of German princes and even the support of Muscovy with which he concluded a formal alliance in 1517.

The new King, Sigismund I (1506–1548), the youngest of Casimir's sons, faced with intensive military preparations by the Teutonic Knights himself launched a war against them in 1519 in order to forestall an armed attack. After two years of hostilities a temporary truce was signed. In 1525 a compromise peace was negotiated and confirmed by the act of homage in Cracow, whereby Albrecht publicly recognized the suzerainty of the Polish

King. Poland abandoned the idea of completely dissolving the State of the Teutonic Order, which was now transformed into a secular state owing fealty to the Polish Crown. In secularizing the Order, Albrecht, at Luther's inspiration, adopted, together with his subjects, the Lutheran faith and acquired for himself the title of duke. The Duchy of Prussia, as it was since called, was to be ruled by his male descendants and, in the event of the expiry of their line, by the descendants of his brothers. A few people were then aware of all the negative implications for the future of this solution of the Prussian question, among them the Primate Jan Łaski, but even those who protested, for example, the Papacy, were indignant above all with Poland's consent to the secularization of the Order whose possessions were the fief of the Papacy. It was also the first case in Europe of a pact between a Catholic ruler and a Protestant duke foreshadowing the future separation of political and religious affairs.

In the East, the external policy of the last Jagiellons was aimed at recovering the territories lost as a result of the Turkish invasions, but the expedition undertaken in 1497 by John Albert not only failed to reach the Black Sea ports of Kilia and Akkerman, held by the Turks, but suffered a defeat whilst still on Moldavian soil. The defeat was inflicted by Hospodar Stephen the Great of Moldavia, whom John Albert planned to dethrone in favour of his own younger brother Sigismund. This failure, although its significance was to be overrated by future historians, showed nevertheless how ineffective was Poland's military effort in those days. It acted as an encouragement to Muscovy in its campaign to unify the Ruthenian lands begun in the second half of the fifteenth century.

This campaign led inevitably to a direct armed conflict with Lithuania which ruled over a considerable part of Ruthenian lands. The war, waged at the turn of the fifteenth century, brought several territorial gains to Muscovy which then seized a large part of the lands beyond the Dnieper and, in 1514, occupied Smoleńsk. The Lithuanian victory over the Muscovite army at Orsza, in the same year, did not change the situation. Taking part in the battles were also the Tartars who invaded, in turn, the Muscovite and Lithuanian lands. Their army was routed at Kleck (1506) during the reign of King Alexander by Prince Michał Gliński. The Tartar troops, however, did not form a regular army but only loosely linked detachments of cavalry, and their power could not be smashed decisively in one victorious battle.

Poland's growing engagement in the East, resulting from the activity of Muscovy, prevented the pursuit of a consistent policy in relation to the Danubian states. By the sixteenth century the ruler of Bohemia (including Moravia, Lusatia and Silesia) and Hungary was Władysław, son of Casimir IV. In 1515, at the Congress of Vienna, in which King Sigismund I also took part, Władysław concluded an agreement with Emperor Maximilian which through dynastic marriages gave the Hapsburgs a right of succession to the Bohemian and Hungarian thrones. These concessions were to induce the Emperor to withdraw from cooperation with Muscovy.

Throughout the sixteenth century the attitude to the Hapsburgs was to determine the two basic trends of Poland's external policy as well as the activity of two parties within Poland. The first of these parties, composed of part of the magnates and some representatives of the bishops sought, in alliance with Vienna, to provoke a war with Turkey and, later, in the period of elective kings, to seat a Hapsburg on the Polish throne. The second party represented the gentry and those of the magnates who opposed the absolutism of the Hapsburgs. This anti-Hapsburg party wanted to prevent Poland from becoming involved in a dangerous war with Turkey in the interests of Vienna and strove, above all, to preserve peace on the southern borders of the country. That peace was broken only once during the reign of the last Jagiellons by the Turko-Tartar invasion of 1524. A later attack on Pokucie (i.e. the Sniatyń and Kołomyja districts) by the Hospodar of Moldavia was repulsed by the brilliant victory of Hetman Jan Tarnowski at Obertyn in 1531. In 1533 an "eternal peace" was concluded with Turkey.

THE SOCIAL AND POLITICAL FOUNDATIONS OF THE "DEMOCRACY OF THE GENTRY"

The anti-Hapsburg party commanded strong support among the gentry which hated the Hapsburgs, seeing in them, and to some extent correctly, the advocates of absolutism and Germanization. It was the gentry (including 8–10 per cent of the population of the Crown), and especially the middle gentry which took the lead in the political life of the country during the Renaissance period. As already mentioned, in the second half of the fifteenth century the land diets of the gentry began to play an increasingly important role and their representatives were invited to attend sessions of the Seym in order to discuss common problems. In this way there emerged a separate chamber composed of representatives of the land diets from all over the country.

The earlier General Assembly to which only a few representatives of the gentry were admitted, was divided into a Chamber of Deputies (composed, for the time being, of some forty representatives of that class, two each from every land of voivodship) and a Senate created from the former Privy Council. Members of the Senate included all the bishops and those representatives of the magnates who occupied high government offices (chancellor, vice-chancellor, marshal, treasurer) or leading offices in the territorial administration (voivodes and castellans), in all over 80 senators. The principle of a two-chamber parliament had been consolidated during the first year of the reign of John Albert (1493) who had supported that success of the middle gentry over the magnates. The burghers were excluded from the Seym, whose privileges included the voting of taxes and amending existing laws. The representatives of Cracow and Wilno sat in the Seym but had no right to vote.

The senators, who until 1537 elected half the number of deputies at the land diets, did not surrender easily. Their conflict with the gentry was intensified when, after the death of John Albert, his brother Alexander, the Grand Duke of Lithuania, was installed on the Polish throne. The new act of union with Lithuania issued in Mielnik (1501) again brought a victory to the magnates because it placed all the matters of State in the hands of the Senate presided by the king. The act also stipulated the senators' right to refuse allegiance to the king in the event of his infringing their privileges, and made them responsible for all legal matters only to the Council of the Senate. The act of Mielnik was not accepted by Lithuania and the magnates soon lost their predominant position, following the adoption by the Seym of a law proscribing the holding of several of the highest State offices by one person (the so-called *incompatibilitas*). From then on, also, lands belonging to the Crown, which formed one of the foundations of the economic preponderance of the magnates, were to be distributed exclusively by the Seym and not, as hitherto, by the king according to his own will. Another important success of the deputies and senators was the famous constitutional law of *Nihil Novi* adopted by the Seym in Radom (1505) which stipulated that the king had no right to legislate without the joint consent of the two chambers. The same law established the scope of activity and the duties of royal officials and formally recognized the existence of a two-chamber parliament.

The next king, Sigismund I, made frequent attempts to disregard the principle of *incompatibilitas*. This inevitably led to a growing tension between the Crown which had the support of the magnates, and the middle gentry. The conflict, whose development was already evident in the 1520's, was brought to the surface as a result of the policy of Bona Sforza, King Sigismund's second wife. She sought to strengthen the King's position partly through winning the support of the aristocracy and partly also by increasing the estates and revenues of the Crown, which could thus become financially independent of the Seym. The court party composed of people won over by the distribution of high offices of State exerted a considerable influence in the land diets and the Seym, but the Queen's accomplices, just as she herself, were despised both by the gentry and by the old magnates who looked with apprehension at any extension of the royal power. This gave rise in 1537 to the "Hen's War", when the open display of opposition by the gentry gathered near Lwów in preparation for an armed expedition forced the King, Queen Bona and the magnates around them to accept a compromise.

At the root of the gentry's success lay also the consolidation of their

Nicolaus Copernicus

economic position. This was a result of the development of estates worked by serf labour, the size of which grew at the expense of the peasants who were removed from their holdings and given either smaller or less productive plots of lands. The productivity of the soil also increased at this time and, in the sixteenth century, the average grain yields amounted to 9 quintals per hectare.

The growing internal demand for, and the increasing export of grain to the West through Gdańsk caused an increase in the amount of compulsory labour and other duties rendered by the peasants to the manor.

Grain for export came chiefly from the large estates and, to a lesser extent, from the medium estates, but the peasants, too, had their share in this export

trade, selling the grain to the merchants who shipped it to Gdańsk. High prices for grain ensured a relative prosperity to those peasants who had a surplus for sale. The favourable prices, steadily maintained almost throughout the sixteenth century, guaranteed high profits from land and stimulated the expansion of the estates and the intensification of the labour services.

Numerous laws enacted by the Seym at the turn of the fifteenth century tended to restrict the personal freedom of the peasants and to reestablish serfdom, which had not been strictly enforced in the preceding period. The settlement of matters concerning peasants was gradually shifted from state to village courts thus strengthening the jurisdiction of the lord of the manor over the peasantry. The law of 1520 introduced one day a week as the minimum labour duty. The varied, though only sporadic, outbreaks of peasant resistance could not halt the process. Social unrest and discontent were partly relieved by the flight from the land. The labour duties, however, were not all introduced simultaneously and, at first, the peasants participated in the benefits derived from the continuous demand for grain. As a result, no large-scale anti-feudal risings occurred in Poland in the sixteenth century.

In the course of the sixteenth century the Seym enacted a number of laws directed not only against the peasants but also against the townspeople. The impact of these laws on the prosperity of the Polish towns must, however, not be overestimated. Throughout the Renaissance the towns continued to play an important role both in trade and in the crafts. Cracow, Poznań, Lublin, Warsaw, Gdańsk, Lwów and Toruń had a population each exceeding 10,000. The transit ports on the Vistula—Sandomierz, Kazimierz Dolny, Bydgoszcz—expanded and developed. Many towns conducted a brisk trade with foreign countries and the number of craftsmen's workshops grew continually. The developing exchanges in trade led gradually to the establishment of a national market.

The economic prosperity of the towns could not be thwarted by the laws of the Seym which exempted all goods purchased by the gentry and those manufactured in their estates from taxation. Identical laws in other countries did not have any adverse effects on the situation of the townspeople. There existed also in Poland, at the time, numerous mixed burgher-gentry trading companies which were faring quite well. The law of 1565, which barred the burghers from trading in grain and forbade Polish merchants to sell Polish goods abroad and import foreign goods to Poland, placed the big towns in a rather advantageous position as they thus became the only intermediaries in this trade. Foreign merchants were only allowed to display their goods there. Moreover, the law of 1565 never went into effect. Nor could the ban on the purchase of land by the burghers, which was enacted several times by the Seym, hinder the development of towns. On the contrary, it favoured investments of capital derived from trade in manufacturing enterprises.

Cracow. Wawel. Envoys Hall, 1529–1535

THE MOVEMENT FOR THE "EXECUTION-OF-THE-LAW"

The success attained by the gentry during the "Hen's War" gave rise to a movement which soon was to become known as the "movement for the execution-of-the-law". The name itself was in a way characteristic of a mode of thinking. The gentry believed that all evil resulted from the failure to observe old established laws and regulations. It was thus considered that the enactment of new laws was completely unnecessary, or even dangerous, and that all efforts should be rather concentrated on the proper execution of the existing, but inoperative constitutional laws. Contrary to what was generally being said, however, the programme for the execution of the law was a new one and consistent with the political and social aspirations of the sixteenth century gentry. It called for improvements in the four main spheres of the state's activity, treasury, armed forces, judiciary and administration.

The purpose of the fiscal reform was on the one hand to raise the value of the coinage (a number of not very successful steps were taken in this respect) and, on the other, to increase the royal revenues, among other means by abolishing the tax immunities of the magnates and the clergy. Attempts were also made to force the latter to cover a part of the expenditures for the defense of the country. The military value of the general levy, by which a levy of all members of the gentry capable of carrying arms is meant, was declining rapidly. Already the Thirteen Years' War had to be waged with mercenary troops, then a normal development in other countries, especially in western Europe. The maintenance of regular defense forces, however, along the open frontiers in the south and east was actually impossible in view of the State's meagre financial resources.

The "execution-of-the-law" movement sought, furthermore, to strengthen the executive and to put the ministers of State and the *starostas* under control of a superior body. This control was to be exercised either by the king himself, according to an earlier view or, as it was formulated in 1565, by the "instigators" elected by the gentry. The gentry also demanded that judicial organs be handed over to them through the establishment of elected tribunals.

The conception of a centralized administration was linked with the demand for safeguarding the State's sovereign rights in foreign relations, particularly with the Papacy. The oath of obedience to each new Pope taken by the King was considered, in part as a result of the influence of the Reformation, to be demeaning to national dignity. Individual leaders of the "execution" movement advocated also the return of lands which were lost to Poland in the fourteenth century. Poland's claims to Silesia or to the Lubusz Land were justified not by the fact that they were inhabited by Poles, predominantly townsmen and peasants with whom the gentry felt only very loosely connected, but by the feudal obligations of their rulers to the reigning Polish dynasty.

It would be an unwarranted oversimplification to look upon the "execution-of-the-law" movement as a uniform party pursuing a consistent policy. Various groupings existed each differing in their degree of radicalism and involvement in questions concerning the proposed reconstruction of the State. Thus identical demands, for example, the codification of laws, assumed different social content according to the particular person who had advocated it. For the distinguished jurist, Jakub Przyłuski it meant the introduction of a uniform legal system for the whole country to replace the old Magdeburg, Chełmno, Imperial or Papal laws. Andrzej Frycz-Modrzewski, on the other hand, fought for a completely new code of laws seeing in this the opportunity to put on an equal footing all sections of the population at least with respect to the criminal law.

The endeavours of such leaders of the movement as Mikołaj Sienicki, Hieronim Ossoliński, Mikołaj Rej or Rafał Leszczyński, all of whom were dissenters, often went considerably farther than the aspirations and the readiness for an active struggle of the mass of the gentry who supported them. As long as they shared certain demands, the Catholic deputies did not hesitate to support their Calvinist or Arian leaders in the struggle against the temporal and spiritual lords of the realm, but later that support was to be more and more often refused.

In the struggle against the rights and privileges of the magnates, the "execution-of-the-law" movement met also with the opposition of the King who was allied with the upper classes. Only after 1562 did King Sigismund Augustus, son of Sigismund I, favour an alliance with the middle gentry which, however, viewed with mistrust the attempts to place far-reaching powers in the hands of a monarch whose actions they wished to have under control. The progressive character of that movement was limited, on the one hand, by its fear of absolutism and, on the other, by apprehensions of competition from the burghers and an unwillingness to improve the lot of the peasants because that would reduce the incomes of the gentry. The internal dissension in the movement was thus responsible for its only partial success. This, in turn, resulted in the weakening of the energy and scope of the movement's further action.

The struggle was carried on, above all, at the Seyms which were held during the reign of Sigismund Augustus (1548–1572). The Seym of 1562–1563 passed a law which stipulated that the magnates must return to the treasury all the royal estates which they had illegally acquired since 1504. The execution of this law was, however, a very protracted affair and a complete restoration of these lands was never achieved. In 1567 the Seym agreed that the law was applicable only to estates pawned or distributed, in which case the royal rights of ownership were restored, but not to those leased or given for life where the royal rights were unchallenged. Since then, a part of the royal estates (so-called "table estates") remained allocated to the needs of the Court. The remainder were granted for life, partly as an endowment of the *starostas*, partly in consideration of special merits (*panis bene merentium*).

Both categories of estate were called *starostwa*. Their possessors were to pay one quarter of their nominal revenues for the army. The regular mercenary forces established under this provision were from then on called the "army of the quarter".

The demand for a reform of the high courts was pursued during the reign of Stephen Batory (1576–1586). Before that reform the King was the supreme judge for all estates. Now he renounced this right with respect to the gentry in favour of a Court for cases involving the gentry, called the Crown Tribunal. This supreme court, established in 1578, convened alternately in Piotrków for Great Poland and in Lublin for Little Poland. Shortly afterwards its activity was extended to the Ruthenian voivodships (1581), Lithuania as well as Royal Prussia (1585). This led to the further legal unification of Royal Prussia with the rest of Poland and was after the final incorporation of Mazovia (1526), another successful step towards the full integration of the country.

After the establishment of the Crown Tribunal the gentry took over, in part the rights of the judicial sessions of the Seym, passing verdicts in such cases as high treason and *lèse-majesté*. This carried in its wake a further considerable limitation of the royal powers. The King's judicial power was actually limited only to his subjects on the royal estates, whose cases were tried by referendary courts. Thus the curtailment of the monarch's judicial prerogatives proved to be the most lasting achievement of the gentry democracy.

SIGISMUND AUGUSTUS' FOREIGN POLICY

Towards the end of the reign of Sigismund Augustus, the last of the Jagiellons, a new conflict with Muscovy broke out. The struggle for the Dnieper basin (in particular for Smoleńsk) shifted Livonia to the basin of the Dvina river. From the thirteenth century onwards Livonia was dominated by the Order of the Knights of the Sword (Livonian Knights) which, until 1525, was closely linked with the Teutonic Knights in Prussia. After the secularization of the Teutonic Order, Livonia found itself isolated in face of Muscovy. Ivan IV the Terrible strove not only to open the route to the Baltic for Muscovy at the expense of Livonia, but also to subjugate the entire territory. His attempts were forestalled by Sigismund Augustus who, in 1557, by use of force compelled Livonia to conclude a military alliance with Lithuania directed against Muscovy. In the following year, Ivan the Terrible retaliated and invaded the territory of Livonia. In 1561 the Grand Master of the Livonian Order, Gotthard von Kettler, offered Livonia as a fief to both the Grand Duke of Lithuania and to Poland. In return King Sigismund Augustus granted Livonia self-government and guaranteed freedom for the Protestant faith. The same year Sweden seized Estonia with Reval. The Order of Knights of the Sword was disbanded and Kettler became a vassal duke ruling over a small portion of southern Livonia (Courland and Semigalia). The remaining parts of the territory became the joint dominion of Poland and Lithuania (1569). This led to a prolonged conflict over Livonia which involved, apart from Poland and Muscovy, also Denmark, allied with Poland, and Sweden which gave its support to Muscovy. The war was waged, with varying success for seven years (1563–1570) and ended with the peace treaty of Szczecin which, however, did not recognize Poland's right to Livonia. Independently of the treaty provisions the territory was temporarily given, by the decision of Ivan the Terrible, to Prince Magnus of Denmark as a fief, together with the Tsar's niece for wife, while Poland concluded a three-year armistice with Muscovy. The price Poland had to pay for the war consisted not only in the lives lost on the battle-fields and the huge expenditures from the royal treasury but also in the fateful concessions in favour of the Prussian ruler Albrecht of Hohenzollern, which were to bring disastrous consequences in the future. In exchange for promises of cooperation and assistance in the war against Muscovy, Sigismund Augustus granted the electoral branch of Hohenzollern the right of succession in Prussia (1563). Thus the possibility of uniting Prussia with the Commonwealth after the death of Albrecht was irrevocably lost.

This was, in part, caused by the ever deeper involvement of Polish policy in the East. The wars with Russia, and in particular the Livonian campaign showed that Lithuania could not by herself resist the pressure of Muscovy which was from time to time supported by the Tartars. Simultaneously the extent of political rights which the Polish gentry won for themselves became a growing attraction for the Lithuanian boyars. A closer union of the two States was also facilitated by the introduction in Lithuania, in the course of the sixteenth century, of central and administrative institutions identical with those already existing in the Crown. This situation called for a closer union of the two countries than envisaged by the Mielnik act of union of 1501, which was based on the person of a joint monarch. The establishment of such a union was opposed by the Lithuanian magnates who feared an increased Polish expansion in the territories of the Grand Duchy and the growth of importance of the Lithuanian gentry, at their expense. Eventually, however, the military threat from Muscovy compelled them to concede the consolidation of the Polish-Lithuanian union.

On July 1, 1569, following protracted negotiations a union was sworn in Lublin binding the two countries, Poland and Lithuania, into one State—the Commonwealth. In accordance with its provisions the Polish King, henceforth jointly elected, was to become at the same time the Grand Duke of Lithuania. Both countries were to have a common Seym and monetary system as well as joint decisions on alliances and declarations of war. On the other hand, the treasury, offices of State and the entire judiciary and administration were to remain separate. Sessions of the Seym were to be held in Warsaw situated nearer to Lithuania than Cracow, which lay in the distant south-western corner of the country. Thus in the second half of the sixteenth century Warsaw which, together with Mazovia, had only recently been incorporated into the Polish Crown began to acquire the character of the capital of the united states of Poland and Lithuania. It finally became the country's capital in 1596 when King Sigismund III transferred his royal residence there. In accordance with the provisions of the Union of Lublin the territories of the Polish Crown which thus far consisted of Mazovia, Great Poland together with Kujawy, Little Poland and Ruthenia, were enlarged by Podlasie, Volhynia and the Kiev region all of which were incorporated into Poland immediately prior to the Lublin agreement. In this way most of the Ukrainian lands, which formerly belonged to the Grand Duchy of Lithuania were placed within the frontiers of the Polish Crown. In this way the total area of the country which before the union was about 260,000 sq.km (including Royal Prussia and Warmia), after 1569 and after the incorporation of Livonia, increased to some 815,000 sq.km and its population numbered about 7.5 million.

This multinational state was given the name of the Polish Commonwealth (*Rzeczpospolita—respublica*) which in the terminology used in the sixteenth century did not necessarily mean a republican form of government. The Union, of course, did not eradicate all the social and cultural differences between Poland and Lithuania. These were to be partly eliminated in the future, as a result of the eastward expansion of the Polish element and through the adoption by the Lithuanian gentry of the ways and habits of their Polish counterparts. Yet simultaneously with this denationalization of the Lithuanian, Ukrainian and Byelorussian gentry, went the assimilation of numerous Polish peasants who, when settling in the eastern borderland of the Commonwealth, usually assimilated the customs, the language and often the religion of the local population. Another factor which played an important role in hastening the Westernization of Lithuania, distrustful as she was of the Catholic and Polish culture, was the Reformation reaching Lithuania from the West by way of Poland.

THE REFORMATION

The call for the reformation of the Church, initiated by Luther, did not, at first, find many adherents in Poland. It reached, in the first place, the townspeople in both Prussia as well as Silesia and the fringes of Great Poland—those regions which because of their national and commercial connexions were especially receptive to ideas and influences coming from Germany. These ideas contributed to the excitement of the already present social conflicts, which became glaringly evident in the revolts of Gdańsk plebeians and of peasants from the Duchy of Prussia. Both revolts, ruthlessly and speedily suppressed, had inscribed on their banners the demands for social and religious reforms.

The Polish gentry remained, for the time being, rather indifferent to the Reformation. Despite their dogged disputes with the ecclesiastical authorities in the Seyms of 1520–1537, over the Church's participation in the defense of the country, the abolition of tithes and ecclesiastical jurisdiction over laymen, the gentry did not connect these matters with the demand for the introduction of a new faith. Though adherents of the Reformation could occasionally be encountered among various social classes in the 1520's a mass movement for religious reform did not emerge until 20 years later.

Even then only a small proportion of the gentry adhered to it, although among those who did so were undoubtedly the best educated and politically most active representatives of that class. In the demands set forth by the Reformation they saw a very convenient weapon, though not the only one, with which to conduct their struggle for the execution of the laws, a movement directed against both the spiritual and temporal lords, but more against its anachronistic privileges completely out of tune with the current political and social trends. It was directed moreover against the huge landed estates of the Church and the vast incomes of the clergy, especially the bishops and abbots. The attack was all the more bitter because only a negligible proportion of the clergy came from the middle gentry. Indeed, it was the bishops from the aristocratic families, who disposed of the fattest benefices and the most profitable prebendaryships.

A separate organization of the Protestant Church arose comparatively early under the protection of the supporters of the Reformation among the gentry. In 1554 the first synod of the newly introduced Calvinist Church was held in Słomniki in Little Poland. This denomination was soon adopted by the majority of dissident gentry who objected to Lutheranism because of its nationally alien character and its submission to the ruler. In the Kingdom of Poland Lutheranism remained predominantly the religion of the burghers and gained a strong following in the towns of Royal Prussia which, during the years 1557–1558, were granted full freedom of religion by King Sigismund Augustus. The creed preached by the Bohemian Brethren, who arrived in Great Poland in 1548, likewise had no particular appeal to the gentry, despite its initial successes. The failure was partly due to the elements of social radicalism which it contained and its preference for clerical superiority over lay seniors.

In Calvinism, on the other hand, the gentry found the confirmation of its superiority over the crown and its administration. Calvinism granted the leading position in Church matters to lay elders and not to the reigning monarch. From the outset of its existence the new creed became in fact subservient to the interests of the gentry with the Calvinist ministers as mere tools and never as equal partners in Church affairs. The gentry were unwilling to cover the financial needs of the new religion, very seldom turning over to it the tithes which they now stopped paying to the Catholic Church. Thus money needed for the construction of Calvinist schools and printing shops, for the maintenance of churches and ministers was obtained with difficulty and in meagre quantities. The ministers, mostly of plebeian origin, appealed in vain to the gentry to relieve the lot of the peasants. The fact that the Reformation brought practicaly no tangible improvements in the situation of the peasants was probably one of the reasons for their indifference to the new creed. Only a minute percentage of the peasants adhered to the Reformation.

The establishment of the Calvinist Church by no means signified the abandonment of the idea of establishing a Polish National Church. At the Seyms of the middle of sixteenth century the King was pressed to take control of matters of faith in his own hands and demands were voiced for convening a national synod, for the abolition of clergy celibacy, for giving the gentry, or even all the faithful, the right to choose their own priests, for conducting church services in the Polish language and for communion in both kinds. Pope Paul IV, who was approached in 1556 on these matters, refused of course to give his sanction to these demands. Nevertheless the Reformation movement did score a number of important successes. At the Seym of 1562–1563 the *starostas* were finally instructed not to execute verdicts passed by ecclesiastical courts against laymen in cases of religion and disputes concerning tithes. The 1563 Seym compelled the clergy to contribute to the costs of the national defenses and the land tax was henceforth to be paid by the Church and by the peasantry.

These gentry successes, though only partial, were accompanied by strenuous efforts by the leaders of the Reformation to consolidate their camp through the unity of the Reformed Churches. The first step in that direction was the union which was concluded in 1555, in Koźminek, between the Calvinists and the Bohemian Brethren. The unification of the Protestant Churches was also the goal of the distinguished reformer Jan Łaski, a nephew of the Polish Primate, well known in western Europe as John a Lasco, who returned to Poland in 1556. His death in 1560 was a severe blow to these aspirations and the events of the next years hit them still more.

At the synods of 1562–1565 a split took place in the Calvinist Church and there emerged a separate religious sect of Antitrinitarians (Arians) which called themselves the Polish Brethren. They were joined by such eminent Calvinist leaders as Marcin Czechowicz, Grzegorz Paweł, Marcin Krowicki and Szymon Budny. At the root of the split there were differences in the doctrine; the Arians followed the teachings of Italian Antitrinitarians which were expressed, among other things, in their negation of the concept of the Holy Trinity. There were differences in social matters. Their radical wing condemned, especially in the early period of the sect's development, the enserfment of the peasants, the participation in war and the holding of office. The social and religious radicalism of the Arians compromised, in a sense, the entire Reformation and thus provided the champions of the Catholic faith

The Polish Commonwealth after the Union of Lublin, 1569

Legend:
- Kingdom of Poland
- Grand Duchy of Lithuania
- Prussia (fief of the Kingdom of Poland)
- Livonia
- Courland
- Lębork and Bytów (fief of the Kingdom of Poland)
- Spisz (pawned to Poland)

- Boundaries of the Commonwealth
- Boundaries between the Kingdom of Poland, Lithuania, Courland and Ducal Prussia
- Boundaries of voivodships, duchies and major lands

CRACOW — Capital of the Commonwealth
POZNAŃ — Capital of a voivodship or duchy

PWN Warsaw 1979

Imprint PPWK. Zam. 9074/79 — X – 30 218 – 10 285 egz.

with convenient arguments against it. This was one of the reasons which led to the exclusion of the Polish Brethren from the "Union of Sandomierz" concluded in 1570 between the Calvinists, the Lutherans and the Bohemian Brethren.

The Arians could still enjoy protection under the terms of the Confederation of Warsaw of 1573, during the interregnum after the death of King Sigismund Augustus. This act, issued at the time of fierce religious strife in the West, guaranteed the gentry full freedom to practise any religion of their own choice and forbade the secular authorities from persecuting people of other faiths. The dissenting gentry often accorded protection to their plebeian coreligionists. This assured an unhampered development of the Reformation movement though at the same time it perpetuated its division into many competing sects and groups.

The importance of the Reformation movement was not restricted to the religious and political life of the country. The struggle for the wider usage of the Polish language, the expansion of cultural activities, the development of printing houses, schools and writing, the striving for free discussion of matters of religion—all this was linked with the Reformation and had a proportional effect on Polish intellectual life during the Renaissance. It was therefore not accidental that all the leading intellectuals of that period were, in one way or another, connected with the Reformation. Even if they did not formally accede to any of its groups, they certainly sympathized with many of the demands advanced by the dissenters as did Andrzej Frycz-Modrzewski and Jan Kochanowski.

THE FIRST INTERREGNUM AND THE PERIOD OF ELECTIVE KINGS

The long interregnum (1572–1574) which followed the death of Sigismund Augustus and, with it, the end of the Jagiellon dynasty had serious repercussions on the constitution of the Commonwealth. The manner of electing the new king as well as the fundamental privileges he had to grant in favour of the gentry influenced the formation of Poland's political system for the next 200 years. Despite various proposals submitted by the deputies at several Seyms, all these matters were not regulated during the lifetime of Sigismund Augustus. His death without issue left the country facing not only the burning problem of electing a new king but also the still unsettled question how this election was to be conducted. It became a subject of controversy between various factions representing different political and social interests. Such leaders of the gentry as Mikołaj Sienicki, Stanisław Szafraniec and Świętosław Orzelski wanted the new king to be elected by an enlarged Seym, whereas a part of the magnates sought to give the decisive voice to the Senate. An

important success, above all for the Catholic magnates, was the appointment of the Archbishop—Primate of Poland as interrex in face of the opposition of the "execution-of-the-law", movement which put forward the candidature of the Calvinist Jan Firlej, the Grand Marshal of the Crown. The bishops were inclined to place the matter of election in the hands of the rank and file gentry, being fully aware that if the Seym were to be convoked in Warsaw the dominant position would be held by the Catholic Mazovians who had, thus far, resisted the encroachments of the Reformation. This view was shared by some of the magnates who believed that it would be much easier to control the thousands of poorly educated and politically immature gentry than to exert influence on experienced parliamentarians.

The legal basis for that mode of holding elections was provided by the young and still little known Jan Zamoyski. He advanced the principle of an election *viritim*, contending that in accordance with the established rules of the gentry's democracy all nobles of whatever rank had the right and the obligation to participate directly in choosing their king. The principle was accepted by the Convocation Seym held in Warsaw in January 1573. (This was, since the First Interregnum, the name given to the Seym held before the election.)

The Seym had to make its choice between three contending candidates—Hapsburg, French and Russian. All the candidates were members of dynasties with autocratic aspirations. For that reason the gentry sought appropriate guarantees against the introduction of such a form of government into Poland. In their struggle for the Polish throne the candidates bid against each other with all kinds of promises and concessions which would have been unthinkable on the part of any of the former Polish monarchs. It should be remembered that the powers and authority of the last Jagiellons were, in practice, very considerable; as Grand Dukes they could count on strong support in Lithuania which in turn, enhanced their position in Poland. Elective kings were deprived of that trump card and, being linked by dynastic ties with their own countries they did not hesitate to regard the new crown as a subject for bargaining.

Most important, however, was the fact that they had to accept two sets of conditions. The first, called *pacta conventa*, concerned the personal obligations of the elected king towards Poland, for example, of equipping a given number of troops at his own expense and replenishing the country's treasury. The second, which were of much greater importance to the shaping of the political system of the Commonwealth, were submitted for acceptance to the first of Poland's elective kings, Henry of Valois, henceforth called the Henrician Articles. These were presented to him by a Polish delegation which went to Paris in the autumn of 1573. The delegation, consisted of Catholics, led by Bishop Adam Konarski, and of Calvinists headed by Jan Zborowski and Jan Tomicki who used the opportunity to prevail upon Henry of Valois to make concessions in favour of their co-religionists in France. These concessions, called *Postulata polonica*, considerably eased the situation of the Huguenots.

Under the terms of the Henrician Articles the king recognized free elections, undertook to convene the Seym at regular intervals (once every two years for the period of six weeks) and not to call a general levy without the consent of the deputies. He could not proclaim new taxes and customs tariffs without the approval of the Seym. During the intervals between the sessions of the Seym the king was to be advised by a permanent council composed of 16 senators, sitting four at a time and changing every six months. The king was also required to reaffirm all the privileges gained thus far by the gentry, including the provisions of the Confederation of Warsaw which Henry of Valois accepted only very reluctantly. Yet he realized that his election by the gentry depended upon his agreement to all these conditions. In case of his failure to carry them out, the Henrician Articles released the gentry from their oath of allegiance and authorized them to declare against the king. That legal provision was, indeed, resorted to in the seventeenth century in the form of two mutinies, against a ruling monarch. In this way the privileges of the gentry reached their peak in the sixteenth century. Apart from personal immunity (no imprisonment without a court sentence), freedom of religion and exclusive jurisdiction over members of their own class, the gentry gained not only a share in the country's government, but also control over the king's activity.

The Henrician Articles (which, in course of time, were amalgamated with the *pacta conventa* into one law) were a classic example of the Seym's aspiration to attain supremacy over the king. The Seym controlled henceforth the actions of the government and of the king, influenced the course of foreign policy, decided on matters of taxation and the calling of the general levy. After the Union of Lublin the Seym was composed of some 140 senators and 170 deputies representing the gentry (of which 48 were from Lithuania). The Senate and the Chamber of Deputies debated jointly or separately though simultaneously, sending delegates to each other. In the sixteenth century a rule was established in the Seym, according to which any new law could be passed only with the unanimous consent of all deputies. At first, the disastrous effects of such a procedure did not make themselves felt. For a long time, when there was a difference of opinion among the deputies, attempts were made to reconcile the oponents of the particular bill and to convince them that if they did not intend to vote in the affirmative, they should, at least, refrain from protesting. The opposition's silence sufficed to recognize the unanimity of the Chamber. Such a compromise could be reached only thanks to the political experience and the high level of responsibility of the deputies and the relatively insignificant influence of the magnates. Already towards the end of the sixteenth century, however, lack of unanimity prevented a number of Seyms from operating.

The central offices of State, like those of the Marshal (who presided over the Senate and supervised affairs of the royal household); the Chancellor (who was in charge of external affairs and represented the king in the Seym);

S. Samostrzelnik, *Coat-of-Arms of the Szydłowiecki Family*, 1552

the Treasurer; and the Hetman or supreme commander of the army, were usually appointed by the king during the Seym. Local administration and judicial powers were exercised chiefly by *starostas* and, to a lesser extent, by the ancient regional officials, voivodes and castellans, whose offices were gradually assuming a purely formal character. Many other regional offices, held for life, usually unpaid and in most cases only honorary, served as a rule to satisfy the personal ambitions of the gentry rather than to contribute towards the efficiency of administration.

The revenues of the treasury were based on taxes granted in each case, by the Seym. The taxes were collected from the peasants and country squires (*pobór*—land tax), from the burghers (*szos*—property tax) and occasionally from the clergy (*subsidium charitativum*). The treasury also drew from the *czopowe* (a tax on beverages), customs, revenues from mining (salt, copper, silver and lead), port dues at Gdańsk, Elbląg and Riga, poll tax and profits of the mint. During the sixteenth century there took place a division between the public treasury, which provided chiefly for the maintenance of the army, and the court treasury, which furnished funds for the maintenance of the royal household.

The "army of the quarter" was small in number, not exceeding 3000 and then mostly cavalry, and was deployed along the southeastern borders defending the country against the invasions of the Tartars. The size of the army was increased only during the reign of King Stephen Batory who created a "selective" infantry which was formed by recruiting one soldier from every 20 *łan* (about 320 ha) of the royal estates. Thanks to the endeavours of the King and his chancellor (Zamoyski), the cavalry was also expanded, the infantry was equipped according to the Hungarian model and the first sapper units were formed.

THE POLICY AND WARS OF STEPHEN BATORY

The first election proved to be a discreditable affair. Henry, Duke of Valois, ceremoniously brought to Poland to be proclaimed King, after barely four months in Cracow learnt about the death of his brother Charles IX and escaped to Paris under the cover of night in 1574, to become the King of France. After his flight a double election took place. The senators chose Emperor Maximilian II, whilst the gentry elected Princess Anne, the sister of Sigismund Augustus, who was to marry Stephen Batory, Duke of Transylvania. The firm and resolute stand of the gentry prevented the outbreak of an armed conflict for the Polish throne. The followers of the Emperor who also had the support of the Papal Curia, finally recognized the legality of Batory's election to the Polish throne (1576). His election was resisted the longest by the city of Gdańsk. In order to crush its opposition Batory besieged the city in 1577. After several battles a compromise treaty was eventually signed;

Poznań. Town Hall, 1550–1560

the King consented to loosen the links of dependency binding Gdańsk to the Commonwealth and the city paid him a considerable indemnity.

That solution harmful as it was to the interests of the State, was the result of both the attitude of the gentry, unwilling to sacrifice blood or money for a war against Gdańsk, and of an unfavourable international situation. The King was preparing for a decisive showdown with Muscovy and sought alliances and money for the war. The full involvement in the East brought yet another and not less fatal decision, because the King and the Senate agreed to place the mentally incompetent Duke Albrecht Frederick of Prussia under the guardianship of the Margrave of Brandenburg, George Frederick of Hohenzollern (1578). Thus one more opportunity to subordinate Ducal Prussia to Poland was lost.

In Silesia, also, the situation turned to Poland's disadvantage. In the sixteenth century a number of Silesian rulers, descendants of the Piasts died without issue, which inevitably led to the decline in the number of sovereign Piast duchies. After the death of dukes without heirs, their lands fell into the hands of the Hapsburgs. In 1526 Bohemia came under the rule of Hapsburgs and in due course the centralist and absolutist aspirations of that dynasty were increasingly felt in Silesia.

Some of the Silesian rulers like the Piast dukes of Brzeg–Legnica did, however, resist these aspirations. The strong economic and cultural links between Silesia and the other Polish lands were still maintained. Although the urban patricians and the majority of higher clergy and gentry yielded to the growing pressure of germanization, the peasants as well as the plebeian elements in the Silesian towns, especially in Wrocław, remained Polish. Much weaker were the Commonwealth's ties with Western Pomerania which had recognized the suzerainty of the Emperor as early as 1521. Since the middle of the sixteenth century in particular, the economic links of Western Pomerania with Poland weakened and the victory of the Reformation brought that country closer to the German Empire in religion and culture.

The increasing Germanization and the consequent decline of the economic and cultural ties of Silesia and Western Pomerania with Poland were the outcome of the Commonwealth's growing political involvement in the East. The Union of Lublin drew the Commonwealth to an increasing extent, into the conflicts between Muscovy and Lithuania. In addition, the class interests of the gentry and the magnates compelled them to turn their expansion in the direction where they could obtain, with relatively little effort, the speediest and greatest advantages. In fact, at this period of history expansion eastwards was the policy pursued by practically all European States—from France to Muscovy, which precisely then, under the leadership of Yermak, was engaged in the conquest of Siberia.

This commitment did not mean that Russia abandoned her territorial ambitions in the West. In 1577 Ivan the Terrible invaded and occupied Livonia up to the Dvina river, with the exception of Reval and Riga. In this way Muscovy not only hindered the transit of goods along the Dvina but presented a direct threat to the Byelorussian lands within the borders of the Polish Commonwealth, and even to Lithuania proper. The reigning "King of Livonia", Magnus, turned for assistance to Batory who started military operations both in Livonia and Muscovy herself. In the first months of hostilities the Polish armies recovered the central part of Livonia and seized the town of Dyneburg. After the victories won by Poland in 1579–1580, when Polock capitulated and Velikye Luki was captured, Russia appeared to be ready for concessions. In the course of the 1581 campaign the Polish armies besieged the impregnable fortress of Pskov. The difficulties encountered during the siege however induced Batory to make certain concessions and to abandon the idea of further conquests. The King accepted the plea of the Tsar's envoys for a truce which was supported by the Holy See's diplomacy. A ten years' truce was finally concluded in Yam Zapolsky in January 1582. Under its terms Muscovy surrendered the area of Polock and withdrew her troops from the Livonian fortresses. Poland, for her part, returned the territories seized during the war. Notwithstanding these successes Batory did not abandon his plans first to subjugate Russia, and, afterwards, to strike, in alliance with other countries, at Turkey and thus to free the Hungarian lands from the domination of the Ottoman Empire. The death of the King (1586) interrupted the preparations for a new war against Muscovy.

BATORY AND THE GENTRY

Batory's death was met with relief among a large part of the gentry. They looked with apprehension at the King's attempts to consolidate his power and imputed to him absolutist tendencies of which the sign was to be the execution of a magnate, Samuel Zborowski, accused of high treason. The gentry, very expertly incited by some magnates, viewed this step as the first attempt to restrict their own liberties, forgetful that the same monarch granted them the separate jurisdiction for which they have long fought. The disintegration of the "execution-of-the-law" party went together with the rise of a new opposition to whom political trouble and the sowing of discord was the supreme purpose of activity. This opposition included members of the Catholic gentry, such as Stanisław Czarnkowski, as well as dissenters, like Jakub Niemojewski, a Calvinist, and Mikołaj Kazimirski, an Arian. The latter were prompted to opposition by the King's policy towards religion which was unequivocally pro-Catholic and favoured the Jesuits who were then generally disliked.

The attacks on the King were at the same time directed against his closest collaborator, his *alterrex*, the Grand Chancellor of the Crown, Jan Zamoyski. Thanks to his own abilities and the support of King Stephen this highly educated humanist and shrewd politician climbed quickly to the top of the ladder of State, not forgetting, in the meantime, his own personal advantage. Possessing only a few villages at the outset of his remarkable career, he became the owner of huge estates extending over an area of 6400 sq.km and the tenant of vast royal estates. Jan Zamoyski was the typical example of the new nobility which, taking the place of the old impoverished and moribund aristocracy, was gradually assuming power in the country.

The presence of Hungarian courtiers at the court of King Batory was the source of irritation to a growing national consciousness. They were accused of accumulating riches and aspiring to posts of eminence at the expense of the old Polish families. The King's cooperation with the Seym also did not run smoothly, although he somehow managed to induce the Seym to provide him, however reluctantly, with funds necessary for the conduct of the wars. On other questions, however, there was a mounting discord between the gentry and the royal court. Even Batory's military policy did not escape criticism, not so much on account of objection to the wars of conquest, because in those days few people were concerned with such subtleties, but rather because it was correctly assumed that, prior to any engagement in the East, the Prussian problem should be finally solved. Already at this stage the gentry's unwillingness to become involved in a military effort was apparent. That attitude stemmed not so much from a pacifist frame of mind as from a quietist reluctance to any armed conflict unless it guaranteed immediate material gains. The transformation of former knights into opulent gentlemen-farmers thriving on the grain trade was becoming a fact of life.

The reign of Batory did not bring any radical reforms which could, in the future, prevent the emergence of an omnipotent oligarchy, whose opposition to the King was to exert an ever stronger influence on the country's affairs. Assuming the posture of defending the nobles whose privileges were threatened by absolutism, the magnates skilfully exploited the gains of the gentry with the view to consolidating their own position. The principle of unanimity in the Seym, the election of the kings by the rank and file of the gentry (*viritim*) and the limitation of royal power by the Henrician Articles were all to become important weapons in the hands of the magnates in their bid for power.

HUMANISM IN POLAND

The period from the close of the fifteenth century to the end of the reign of Stephen Batory (1586) was the era of the Renaissance. The death of Casimir IV (1492) coincided in time with the discovery of America, which is generally accepted as the beginning of modern times.

Humanism did not emerge in Poland suddenly like a *deus ex machina* but was, in a way, a continuation of trends prevailing in Polish intellectual life and existing independently of foreign influences. It only multiplied and gave a powerful boost to the pre-humanistic undercurrents which had already existed in philosophy and historiography. Although at first humanism left a foreign, cosmopolitan imprint on many spheres of intellectual activity like poetry and architecture, it successfully merged with the local material and spiritual culture to give a highly original and specific mould to the Polish Renaissance. The refined character of the Italian Renaissance, which was brought to Poland either indirectly, through Hungary, or directly, was fully compatible with the aspirations of the royal court, the magnates, the gentry and even those of the wealthier burghers.

To the court of the Sigismunds, and especially to Queen Bona, the Italian example acted as a stimulus to centralize the authority of the State and to consolidate the power of the Crown at the expense of the privileges of the magnates and the gentry. The latter found in humanism a confirmation and an approval of their pre-eminent position. The study of the golden period of the Roman Empire inclined them to make certain comparisons and associations, so much the pleasanter that they enabled them to trace the origin of their class to ancient times. The flourishing of the Renaissance moreover coincided with the political and social advancement of the gentry.

The wealthy burghers, too, although lacking serious political aspirations, made full use of the achievements of humanistic culture. The more enterprising members of that estate used their wealth and influence to buy their way into the ranks of the gentry. Other representatives of the urban patricians saw in humanism, like many nobles and members of the clergy, a perfect means of making life more pleasant by acquiring new customs and habits attractive in form and content, and for displaying a growing interest in literature and works of art. Only a few of the burghers, such as Biernat of Lublin or Andrzej Frycz-Modrzewski, linked humanism with social protest and the striving to improve existing social relations. This reforming trend, however, was not limited exclusively to secular life; voices were raised for introducing changes also in the Church. The advocates of a radical transformation of the Church often shifted their loyalty to new religious organizations, hostile to the Holy See. In this way certain links were formed between humanism and the Reformation despite their opposing views on numerous issues.

Though the fixing of the exact period of Polish humanism could be a matter of discussion its beginnings, for example, had often been placed too early. The indisputable fact was that in its wake it brought fresh cultural values.

THE DEVELOPMENT OF A NATIONAL CULTURE

Humanism stimulated a deep interest in ancient history, cultures and languages, especially Latin, but, at the same time, it greatly enhanced the development of a Polish national culture. The knowledge of the contemporary man was extended not only by the discoveries of new lands and continents but was also affected by a mounting interest in the history and geography of his own country. The growing appreciation of the beauty of classical Latin was accompanied by the simultaneous process of ousting it from usage in many fields of life and supplanting it increasingly with the Polish language which was rapidly gaining ground. Polish came to be widely used in connexion with objects of everyday use such as names of tools, implements, and clothing. This period saw also the first drafts of legal documents, including constitutional laws adopted by the Seym in Polish. The decisions of the Cracow Seym of 1543 were the first legal publication in Polish. In that same year, 1543, the King decreed that documents of the courts of law, summons and verdicts, could be issued in Polish. Difficulties in introducing the Polish language were, however, encountered in those fields in which there was no adequate Polish terminology, which applied particularly to learning, especially philosophy, as well as to natural sciences and to political and social concepts.

The advent of the Reformation helped to introduce the Polish language to theological subjects. Despite the opposition of the Catholics, the Polish language was gradually replacing the formerly predominant Latin, its usage extending from Psalters to the conduct of highly involved dogmatic disputes. A new type of religious literature came into being which in a comprehensive and easily accessible form of writing expounded the position and views of the author and attacked the set of dogmas presented by the opponent. From the adherents of the Protestant faith the first Polish translation of the Bible of 1552 and 1563 came, as well as the first Polish grammar by Piotr Statorius, the first edition of a Latin-Polish dictionary by Jan Mączyński and, finally, the prototype of a national anthem written by Andrzej Trzecieski in the form of an anthem for the King and the Commonwealth. For the first time also, thanks to Łukasz Górnicki, the notion of "my country" as understood today came into usage.

This was one of the features of the developing Polish national consciousness. Though still uncertain and varyingly understood on account of the differences in comprehending the meaning of *gens* and *natio*, the concept of a Polish nation came to personify not so much a territorial community, as the common origin and birth, and, in many instances, also the common language of the people. The Renaissance idea of a nation, as reflected, for example, in the works of Frycz-Modrzewski, included as an integral part also the peasants whose sons were at that time admitted even to Cracow University.

The deepening and increasingly extending feeling of national consciousness, disseminated by literature (historiography and belles-lettres) had an influence in the Crown itself on that strata of the German patricians who had hitherto preserved a different language and different customs. Thus the sixteenth century brought about the final Polonization of the urban population in the Commonwealth. The second half of that century witnessed the victorious march of Polish culture to the vast expanses of Lithuania and Ruthenia. The granting to the local gentry of rights and privileges identical with those enjoyed by their counterparts in the Crown and the resulting adoption of Polish customs and way of life, brought in its wake the growing acceptance of the Polish language as more cultured and better suited to the requirements of the current political and intellectual life. The process of Polonization embraced also, at that time, the gentry of Royal Prussia. The identity of class interests as well as of social position was bound to lead, sooner or later, to the creation of a national unity of culture and customs.

The ethnically diverse State, split into supporters of Catholicism, the Orthodox Church and the Reformation, was to become united on the basis of the common origin of its people, allegedly descended from the ancient Sarmatians (inhabitants of the proto-Slavonic lands), according to the new chroniclers, Maciej Miechowita, Marcin Bielski and Marcin Kromer. The conception of the Commonwealth for this reason was often identified with that of Sarmatia whose eastern borders were supposed to have coincided exactly with those of the united Polish-Lithuanian State. This Sarmatian myth played, at the time of Sigismund Augustus, a completely different role from that in later periods when it served to set the gentry in opposition to the rest of the nation. The flourishing historiography of the Polish Renaissance became a great school of patriotism disseminating the feeling of love for the country and respect for the nation's past history. According to the historians (Bielski, Kromer and Bernard Wapowski), the past and the present, were linked by the memory of the life and history of the bygone generations.

A similar process could be observed in literature. The forms of its artistic expression were becoming ever richer, its horizons broadened and there grew the feeling of the responsibility of the writer and his involvement in the country's affairs. The language, still somewhat clumsy and primitive in the writings of Biernat of Lublin, was improved and enriched by Mikołaj Rej to reach perfection in the works of Jan Kochanowski. The popularization in Poland, during the 1520's, of the Roman type, which was taking the place of the Gothic type used before, was of considerable significance for the development of literature. This much clearer, easier and readable way of writing owed its popularity to Italian printers who had spread knowledge of it north of the Alps.

The period of the Renaissance in Poland witnessed a rapid growth of printing shops where belles-lettres and learned books were printed in hundreds of copies. The main printing centre was Cracow where such well known printing houses existed as those of Florian Ungler, Hieronim Wietor and Maciej and Marek Szarffenbergs. Printing offices were founded also in smaller localities, like Lusławice, Pińczów, Brześć Litewski, Nieśwież and elsewhere, playing an important part in the current political and religious conflicts. The printers boldly advanced the cause of the Polish language often drawing attention in the prefaces to the books they published, as did, for example,

F. Ungler, to the importance of the national language and the need to work on it.

Slowly and timidly the Polish language found its way to the schools also, though only at secondary level. As in other universities it was not accepted by Cracow University which, by the second half of the sixteenth century, was on the decline. On the other hand Polish was introduced into the curricula of the Protestant schools, above all into the Academy founded by Calvinists in Pińczów and the Lutheran schools in Gdańsk, Toruń and Elbląg. Some Catholic secondary schools soon followed suit like St. Mary's school in Cracow.

Education during the Renaissance period was strongly influenced by the ideas of humanism particularly in the Protestant schools. The followers of that faith waged a bitter struggle against scholasticism which prevailed, among others, in Cracow University. The interests of the entire Renaissance culture centred not only on the country conceived as a community of men, but also around man himself, his joys and sorrows, his thoughts and aspirations, his days of leisure and days of work. Jan Kochanowski did not hesitate to devote his *Treny* (Threnodies) to the sorrow of a father mourning the death of his child : Mikołaj Rej praised in his works the pleasures of the life of an average nobleman : Klemens Janicki wrote about the light and shade in the life of a poet who sought the favours of a mighty patron. Architecture which hitherto had been preoccupied with the erection of monumental edifices to the greater glory of God limited its interest to the building of chapels and reconstructing existing churches. Instead it showed a growing concern for decorating and beautifying mansions, castles, town halls and other public buildings. The reconstruction of the royal Wawel castle, begun by the Florentine della Lora was continued by Bartolomeo Berrecci. The result was a mixture of the Italian style with that arising from local requirements and conditions. In 1516-1517 the Sigismund chapel was completed on the Wawel hill. Formally a religious shrine, it was in fact a mausoleum extolling the king's greatness and power. There, too, the frivolous spirit of the Renaissance marked its presence in the rather suggestive grotesque decorations placed on the upper coffers, invisible to the faithful.

The example of the court was followed by the wealthy burghers. In many towns like Sandomierz, Chełmno, Tarnów, Biecz, and Poznań the old Gothic town halls were rebuilt in the Renaissance style or new ones erected. The same style prevailed in the newly built houses of the urban patricians and the manors of the wealthier gentry and magnates, like the palaces of the Boners in Ogrodzieniec, the Szydłowieckis in Szydłowiec and Chmielów, the Tęczyńskis in Tęczyn, the Tarnowskis in Tarnów and the Kmitas in Wiśnicz. The style of Polish Renaissance castle, modelled on the Wawel, was represented by the stately homes in Pieskowa Skała, Niepołomice and Baranów. The Sigismund chapel influenced the construction of similar mausoleums enhancing the prestige of the founder ; e.g. the Bishop Noskowski chapel in the Pułtusk collegiate church, or the chapel of the Myszkowski family in the Dominican church in Cracow.

Apart from the Wawel, numerous palaces of the aristocracy became centres of Renaissance culture. Some of the prelates, too, like the Bishops Lubrański, Padniewski and Krzycki took their part in patronizing and fostering the arts. Sculptures and paintings thriving under Italian influence, were used extensively to decorate the residences. They represented the realistic trend in which man and the flora and fauna about him were the centre of interest. The sitter's attire was carefully reproduced and in much detail; the gloves of Jan Kochanowski carved in stone on his tomb in Zwoleń were an example of the case in point. The painters more and often took as the subject of their works the representation of well known personages of the time rather than the images of the Saints. The sculptures, even if they were intended to be placed in a church, were concerned rather with presenting, in marble or in alabaster, the greatness of the deceased than with praising the glory of the Creator.

All this expressed the protest which in Poland, too, was beginning to emerge in the minds of the people of the Renaissance against the stringent control of their views, opinions and way of life by the Church in the name of religion. The bitter religious conflicts, during which Catholics and dissenters insulted and denounced each other, evoked among some representatives of the Polish intellectual elite, like Jan Zambocki, a courtier of King Sigismund I, and others, a feeling of despondency and scepticism towards all authority. They sought support for their views in the various branches of learning. The first to speak out against theology was astronomy. Copernicus' discovery not only destroyed the established belief that the sun revolved around the earth but also undermined the authority of the commentators on the Holy Scripture, who from its texts deduced their theory on the immovability of our planet. The Copernican heliocentric system was of tremendous significance for the development of the modern natural sciences. Based on a scientific attitude to the world it maintained that the fundamental criterion of truth was the compatibility of theory with practice and not with statements of ancient scholars. The banning, in 1616, of Copernicus' work *De revolutionibus orbium coelestium*, first published in 1543, by the ecclestiastical authorities, could not stop the triumphant march forward of his great discovery whose ardent supporters like Jan Brożek held chairs in Cracow University in the seventeenth century.

Historical writers of the Renaissance, too, endeavoured to establish laws governing history instead of attributing its course as had been hitherto maintained, to the direct interference of Providence. Lawyers were questioning the supremacy of the Church over the State. Polish jurists of the Renaissance period, like Andrzej Frycz-Modrzewski or Jakub Przyłuski, advocated the full sovereignty of the Commonwealth in its relations with the Holy See. In geographical writings names appeared of lands and peoples, which Holy

Scripture did not mention at all. Even in literature, in the works of Jan Kochanowski, Mikołaj Sęp-Szarzyński and Szymon Szymonowic, the names of ancient gods and goddesses were used instead of those of the Saints which, in the prevailing climate of opinion, signified something more than mere classical reminiscences. Equally noteworthy was the lay character of the foreign policy pursued by the last Jagiellons who maintained friendly relations with Lutheran Prussia and Mohammedan Turkey and firmly opposed the Papacy as long as it supported the Teutonic Order. Signs of religious indifference apparent during the Renaissance should not, of course, be overestimated. How weak and superficial they actually were, was proved by the rapid progress of the Counter-Reformation. The beginnings of the process of secularization of cultural life was to last for many centuries.

RENAISSANCE CULTURE AND LIFE

An essential feature of Renaissance culture was its close concern with everyday life and its involvement in the contemporary struggle for shaping a new political, cultural and religious face of the community and the state. Polemical literature was naturally engaged in that struggle. Any literary work of that period, beginning with Mikołaj Rej's *Krótka rozprawa między trzema osobami : panem, wójtem i plebanem* (Short Discourse Between Three Persons : the Nobleman, the Bailiff and the Parson), filled with allusions and innuendos, and ending with Jan Kochanowski's *Odprawa posłów greckich* (The Dismissal of Greek Envoys), the first Polish political drama, show how strongly contemporary literature was linked with the developments of the day. The same applied to the fine arts and to learning. Copernicus was an astronomer and mathematician but—when the necessity arose—he applied his knowledge of engineering in the defense of Olsztyn castle against the Teutonic Knights.

Geography served the needs of the country as well as the developing of trade. An important publication was the first modern geographical outline of the east European countries, written by Maciej Miechowita (*Tractatus de duabus Sarmatiae*, 1517). This was for many long years the chief source of information for the West about eastern Europe. An important achievement of Polish cartography was a great map of Poland made in 1526, by Bernard Wapowski on a scale of 1:1,000,000. Andrzej Frycz-Modrzewski postulated in his work *De Republica Emendanda* the rebuilding of the State in a spirit of greater social justice. He advocated not only religious reforms and the establishment of a national Church, but took a stand in the defense of the peasants against the growing burdens of serfdom, spoke for the rights of the townspeople and for equality before the law of all classes in criminal cases. He demanded as well the strengthening of the royal powers, the streamlining of State administration and the improvement of the country's defenses. His work was based on a modern conception of the State as a sec-

Jan Kochanowski. Tombstone at Zwoleń, 1584

ular organization, independent of, and superior to social classes and maintaining the balance between them. The novelty of the ideas propounded by Frycz-Modrzewski lay in the demand for extending the scope of the State's functions among which he also included ecclesiastical and educational affairs. The fact that Modrzewski's works were translated into German, Spanish, Italian and Russian clearly indicated that the ideas which he set forth were of topical and general importance far beyond the borders of a single country. Every nation embarking upon the path of modern development could find there advice and instruction. On the other hand many of his utopian ideas have not been put to the practical test either in Poland or in any other country.

T. Treterus, *Disputation of Cardinal Hozjusz with Protestants*, 16th cent.

It would be highly unjust to the Polish Renaissance to limit its achievements, as is often attempted, to the activities of those three intellectual giants: Copernicus, Frycz-Modrzewski and Kochanowski. Side by side with them there existed a galaxy of lesser creative intellects and they themselves often drew upon the achievements of their direct predecessors. The essential feature of the Renaissance was the scope and range of this cultural transformation. The number of copies of learned books which were then published on average in editions of 500–600 was symbolic for those times. Young people travelled in great numbers to foreign universities, predominantly Italian (Padua, Bologna), German (Wittenberg, Leipzig, Königsberg) and Swiss (Basel). The ranks of educated people grew steadily and in the course of the fifteenth century the number of parish schools more than doubled, from 253 to 650.

Cultural life was concentrated in the big towns with which the educated gentry had regular contacts. Small mansions were built by the gentry in the suburbs of Cracow and Lublin, (among others by Mikołaj Rej), where they used to spend their leisure time in pleasant company. This cultural life had not yet succumbed to rustic torpor and even smaller towns flourished under the rule of dissenting nobles. Printing houses were opened in such remote, parochial localities as Pińczów, Raków, Baranów and Węgrów. Writers and scholars converged on them to hold disputes and polemics on religious questions and the echo of these debates resounded all over Europe.

Thanks to the general use of Latin as the language of scholars, Polish thought and ideas spread and penetrated to the West, where the works of Modrzewski were widely read and commented upon with admiration. The treatises by Kromer and Hosius, directed against the dissenters were translated into many languages. The great discovery of Copernicus evoked lively discussions as well as strong opposition. The books by Miechowita and the popular sketches by Kromer (*Polonia*) extended knowledge of Poland among foreign readers. The arrival of Italians with Bona Sforza, of Frenchmen with Henry of Valois and of Hungarians with Batory enabled the average squire, who had never travelled abroad, to acquaint himself with the ways of these foreign visitors and to compare it with his own *mos polonicum*.

On the whole, the foreigners did not meet with an enthusiastic reception from the gentry. Their intellectual acumen and the manner in which they managed to acquire wealth and rank were a source of irritation to the average gentry. At the same time, however, there was only little evidence of a feeling among the gentry that because of their own superiority they had nothing to learn from other nations. National megalomania and xenophobia, which in later times were to poison the mind of the average nobleman, were not prevalent in his thinking though certain manifestations of these feelings were already apparent. The gentry were still tolerant towards other religious denominations, their way of life and political opinions. That tolerance stemmed partly from an attitude of indifference towards everything that had no direct bearing on the interests of their class, but in the final account nevertheless it was certainly propitious for the further promotion of cultural development. The scope of Poland's cultural life in the sixteenth century compared very favourably with similar developments in France or England and was undoubtedly much more extensive than in the immediately contiguous territories of eastern Germany and Western Pomerania which, at that time, were clearly passing through a period of cultural decline.

Chapter VIII

THE COMMONWEALTH AT THE TURNING POINT (1586–1648)

THE STRUGGLE FOR POWER

The Commonwealth of this time still drew upon the splendid traditions of the Renaissance and even seemed to continue them, conducting an expansionist foreign policy and extending the country's dominions. Thanks to the conquests in the East, confirmed by the peace treaty of Polanowo in 1643, it grew from 815,000 sq.km in 1569 to almost a million (990,000 sq.km). Of this, the area of compact Polish settlement comprised 180,000 sq.km and the Poles constitued about 40 per cent of the more than 10 million people who inhabited the Commonwealth in the first half of the seventeenth century.

The dilemma which then faced the kings of the Vasa dynasty at the time of the Thirty Years' War could be summarized as follows : either friendship with the Hapsburgs and the concentration of Polish interests in the East with a view to consolidating and extending the conquests there, or an alliance with the French-Protestant grouping and an active policy in the West with the hope of regaining Silesia and Pomerania. The former line of policy was supported by Sigismund III; attempts to pursue the latter were made, though not very consistently, by his son Władysław IV. They both came from Sweden and thus both cherished the hope of regaining, through Poland, the Swedish crown which was due to them in succession to Sigismund's father, John III.

The dynastic plans of the Vasas, however, miscalculated. The magnates, whose influence in Poland's political life was increasing regarded with apprehension any move in the country's foreign policy which seemed to involve excessive risk (and expenditure). In this attitude they had the backing of the gentry whose distrust of the monarch was coupled with a quietist contentment with the prevailing state of affairs. Hence already in the first half of the seventeenth century the central problem of the country's internal policy became the question of constitutional reform to strengthen the executive. Steps in that direction were taken by Sigismund III and continued by Władysław IV with the support of the leading circles of the Counter-Reformation. But all these attempts met with the unsurmountable opposition of the gentry who regarded any improvement in the machinery of State as the beginning of absolute rule.

The King, on the other hand, had hardly anybody to rely upon in his struggle for a consolidation of his authority. The towns, whose position in the Commonwealth was still rather weak, could not be counted on, while the Church in the seventeenth century refused to give support to the throne. The King sought to rally around him a part of the magnates upon whom he bestowed favours, but even they eventually found a common language with the anti-royalist nobles on the basis of common interests. This became clearly evident during the final stages of Mikołaj Zebrzydowski's rebellion and also found expression in the outcome of plans for a war against Turkey.

The reforming aspirations of the Court induced the magnates to seek a further weakening of the administration. The gradual restriction of the royal prerogative was coupled with the growth of the privileges of the great nobles, especially the magnates of the eastern marches, who had at their disposal their own armed forces, great wealth and numerous clients among the dependent local gentry. Thus, the individual magnates had everything that the reigning monarch was refused—abundant financial resources, a strong army and the support of a political party. They began also to exert a growing influence on the courts of justice which, at least nominally, were still in the hands of the gentry. Yet the verdicts of the courts could not be executed without the requisite force and the State was in no position to supply that force. The necessity therefore arose for the assistance of the magnates' own troops. Already at the beginning of the seventeenth century, individual magnates' families were engaged in private wars against one another, devastating the country and devouring its resources.

THE POLITICAL CRISIS OF THE COMMONWEALTH

After the death of Stephen Batory, the Hapsburgs, for the third time, made a bid for the Polish crown. Through the efforts of Jan Zamoyski, the throne was, however, given to Sigismund Vasa, the nephew of Sigismund Augustus, but the anti-Batory opposition, led by the Zborowski family and hostile to Zamoyski, proclaimed the Archduke Maximilian King of Poland. The Archduke crossed the Polish frontier at the head of an army. Defeated by Zamoyski at Byczyna in 1587, Maximilian was taken prisoner. Yet, the new King did not display the gratitude which Zamoyski had hoped for. The Swedish prince felt himself dominated by the personality of the Chancellor who sought to hold power, as during the reign of Batory, at the side of the young monarch. Their political plans also diverged. Sigismund III was despite everything, favourably inclined towards the Hapsburg whom Zamoyski, in

Genealogy of the Jagiellons and the Vasas

(The table includes only the most important members of the dynasties)

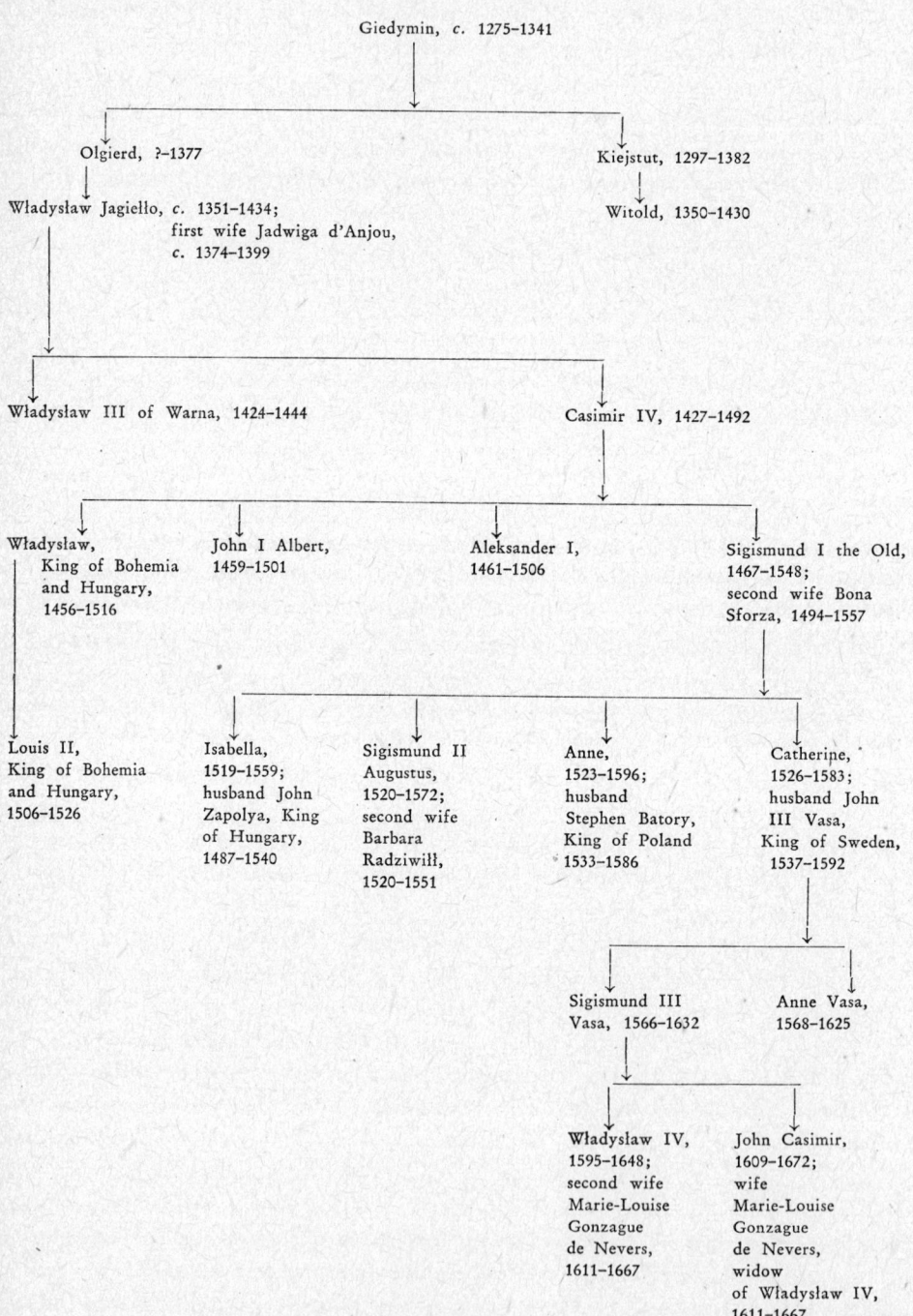

turn, hated so much that he was even said to be prepared to enlist the support of the Turks against them. When the old feud between the Zamoyskis and the Zborowskis flared up, the Commonwealth, soon after the election of the new King, became entangled in a serious political crisis.

The crisis was further deepened by the news of the behind-the-scenes dynastic bargaining between the new King and the Hapsburgs. In return for renouncing the Polish throne, Archduke Ernest promised Sigismund III substantial material benefits. The political differences were also accompanied by growing religious conflicts. The new ruler soon came under the influence of the Jesuits and opposed the strengthening of the provisions of the Confederation of Warsaw, by a constitutional law, under which those who violated religious peace in the towns would be liable to severe punishment. The dissenters, offended and shocked by this attitude began to draw closer to the opposition represented by Zamoyski's party which advocated religious toleration.

The ranks of the opposition were soon swelled by another religious group, the Orthodox. So far they had not been discriminated against because of their creed, nor were they coerced into accepting the Catholic rite. That situation changed, however, by the end of the sixteenth century when the Papal Curia in its desire to recover the losses sustained as a result of the Reformation, renewed its centuries old plans to bring about a union of the Greek Orthodox and Catholic Churches.

These plans also suited the Polish government which saw in religious unity the means of ensuring political unity in a vast state where so many different languages were spoken. This prompted the acceptance by the synods in Brześć held in 1595 and 1596, of a union which subordinated the Orthodox Church in the Commonwealth to the jurisdiction of Rome. It soon became evident, however, that the supporters of a union were in the minority. It was rejected by the peasants and the burghers for whom the old faith was an important element of their distinct national identity. Many of the Russian gentry as well as some of the magnates led by Prince Konstanty Ostrogski, also rejected the imposed union and joined the ranks of opposition to the King.

Meanwhile the King's relations with the gentry were steadily deteriorating as a result of his increasing involvement in the affairs of Sweden, the throne of which he formally acceded to after the death of his father John III (in 1592). His ill-timed military expedition against Sweden in 1598 ended in defeat. In keeping with the terms of the *pacta conventa* the King ceded Estonia, which belonged to Sweden, to the Commonwealth thus involving Poland in a new war over Livonia. The ensuing hostilities, in the course of which the Polish army, commanded by Hetman Jan Chodkiewicz, gained a resounding victory over the Swedes at Kircholm in 1605, had to be temporarily suspended because of the developments in the East.

The internal weakness of Russia, where Boris Godunov succeeded to the throne of the Tsars despite the resistance of the boyars, invited direct intervention by her neighbours, Poland and Sweden. A pretext for intervention was conveniently found in the appearance of an adventurer, said to be Gregory Otrepiev, a Russian monk who escaped to Poland claiming that he was the son of Ivan the Terrible, miraculously saved from the hands of Boris Godunov's henchmen. He enlisted the support of the magnates, in particular of the Wiśniowieckis and Jerzy Mniszech whose daughter he promised to marry upon his "return" to the throne.

The False Demetrius also found support among the court party including the King himself. Sigismund III, who was looking everywhere and at any price for allies in his struggle for the Swedish throne, hoped that he would find one in Russia under a new ruler. The clergy, particularly the Jesuits, saw in the person of the new Tsar the expectation of bringing Orthodox Russia within the fold of the Roman Church. All these hopes and aspirations were based on the promises which the power hungry Otrepiev lavishly gave to all and sundry. He adopted the Catholic faith, though, for the time being, he preferred to conceal this fact. An expedition against Russia met with the opposition of the local diets, who were critical of a foreign policy pursued by the unpopular monarch.

In autumn 1604, the False Demetrius with a several thousand strong army supplied and equipped by the Polish magnates crossed into Russia. Defeated on the line of march he would probably have perished, had it not been for the sudden death of Godunov which opened for him the road to the throne of the Tsars. Supported by the peasantry, the Cossacks and the boyars who despised the deceased ruler, Demetrius was crowned Tsar of All the Russias in 1605 and shortly afterwards married Maryna Mniszech, but his pro-Catholic leanings, his preference for Poles as well as his dissipation was bound to evoke mistrust towards him.

That mistrust was soon transformed into open hatred which led to the outbreak of a popular uprising in Muscovy in May 1606. Demetrius was murdered, the Polish garrison stationed in the Kremlin massacred and those who survived were thrown into dungeons. The boyars then proclaimed one of their own members, Vasili Shuiski, Tsar.

THE ZEBRZYDOWSKI REBELLION

In Poland all these events resulted not so much in a wave of Russophobia as in a growing resentment towards the already despised King who had involved the country in an unnecessary and bloody adventure in the East. The gentry's dislike of Sigismund was caused by all manner of grievances both great and small. They were irritated by his secret dealings with the Hapsburgs as well as by the presence of foreigners at the court, by his fondness of ball games and by the "incestuous", as they alleged, second marriage with the sister of his deceased wife. Yet undoubtedly the King's attempts to increase his powers were most feared. He was accused of absolutist tendencies in which he was supported by the court *camarilla* consisting of a group of loyal magnates led by Zygmunt Myszkowski and Andrzej Bobola, and some of the bishops. The programme of that party, unambiguously expounded in the books of Krzysztof Warszewicki and in Father Piotr Skarga's sermons, could well arouse anxiety among the gentry. What if the King's own preacher openly called for the abolition of most of the gentry's privileges, above all of *neminem captivabimus*, and for the reduction of the Chamber of Deputies to the status of mere advisory body?

The reasons which led the gentry into opposition were manifold. Though their avowed leader was Mikołaj Zebrzydowski, a zealous Catholic and a devoted friend of Jesuits, he succeeded in rallying around him adherents of the Orthodox Church as well as prominent dissenters. The Zebrzydowski or Sandomierz rebellion, so called after the town of Sandomierz which was the main centre of the movement, lasted for almost three years (1606–1609) and had a considerable influence upon the future course of the Commonwealth's history. Many words were then written by both sides, even more were angrily exchanged at meetings at Lublin, Sandomierz, Jędrzejów and Wiślica. Everybody spoke only of the welfare of the Commonwealth, but that welfare was conceived quite differently by the two contending parties.

The royalists defended the domestic and foreign policy of the Court. The opposition demanded further limitation of the royal prerogative. It wanted to deprive the King of the right to appoint state officials, strove to introduce a system of elective local officials, to pledge the deputies to obey instructions strictly given them by the local diet and finally to expel foreign Jesuits, the spokesmen of religious intolerance and ardent advocates of absolutism.

Eventually an armed clash took place after many attempts to find a negotiated solution had ended in failure. In July 1607 the royal armies routed the main forces of the rebellion at Guzów. The following year, the rebels, including Zebrzydowski, their leader, submitted to the King at a General Seym. It would, of course, be wrong to regard this act as a triumph for Sigismund III, because the rebellion destroyed, for years to come, all chances of enhancing the royal powers. The middle gentry, too, who were lured into the rebellion by slogans hostile to the magnates gained nothing by it. For them it was but a sad epilogue to the long years of struggle for the execution of the laws.

The sole victors to emerge from the rebellion were the magnates. That applied equally to those who had rallied to the King as well as to those who conspired with Zebrzydowski against him. The rebellion ended in a compromise by which the leaders of the opposition were assured a lenient treatment. The magnates made full use of the fact that changes in the State's structure were henceforth rendered impossible. Playing upon the slogan of Golden Freedom they were gradually taking over the control of the government. The efforts of the magnates were clearly understood by the Jesuits, who not only carefully expurgated from the next editions of Piotr Skarga's *Sermons* all praise of a strong royal authority, but even established censorship of all sermons to avoid anything that might offend the feelings of the increasingly powerful and watchful lords.

ATTEMPTS TO CHECK RUSSIA

The gentry, with their hopes for success frustrated, were left with an opportunity to look for partial compensation at least in the form of booty and military honour, in the vast expanses of Russia. On this occasion the expedition against that country was no longer a private affair of the magnates but was undertaken directly by the Polish Commonwealth. After the death of the first False Demetrius, another appeared claiming, as before, that he was the Tsar and that once again he had miraculously escaped death. The fraud was even more obvious than before although earlier Zamoyski already hinted that the affair was a "Plautus' comedy". But few cared now for any appearances of truth. Thousands of gentry rushed to the aid of the second False Demetrius to look elsewhere for the income satisfying the ambition and position which were denied to them in Poland. They sought to gain by the sword great fortunes in that rich and, to all appearances, defenceless country. The State on its part welcomed this opportunity of ridding the Commonwealth of the many fortune-seeking adventurers, a large number of whom had been former participants in the Zebrzydowski rebellion. When Tsar Shuiski concluded a defensive alliance with Sweden, Sigismund III decided that all courses of action were open to him and advanced into Russia (1610). In this he was prompted by his own dynastic considerations as well as by the Pope and the Jesuits who nourished the dreams of converting Russia and even Persia to Catholicism.

At the beginning the hostilities were concentrated around the fortress of Smoleńsk. The Russian army, together with Swedish contingents, which marched to relieve the siege, suffered a crushing defeat at Kłuszyn (1610), at the hands of Hetman Stanisław Żółkiewski, who boldly attacked the forces of the enemy four times larger than his own. This victory proved to be the turning point of the campaign. The road to Muscovy lay open, Shuiski was deposed and the boyars were ready to negotiate the election of Prince Władysław Vasa to the Russian throne. Sigismund III, however, himself wanted to be Tsar and, moreover, the question of the Prince accepting the Orthodox faith (which was the *conditio sine qua non* for ascending the Russian throne) was absolutely unacceptable to Polish Court. Negotiations thus dragged on without any hope for a successful outcome, the more so because in Poland's political plans the idea of annexation was gradually taking precedence over that of a personal union. This time, too, the Polish garrison in the Kremlin did not last long.

In 1612 an insurrection broke out in Muscovy, led by the burgher Kuzma Minin and Prince Dimitrii Pozharski. After gaining control over Muscovy a new Tsar was elected (1613). He was the boyar, Michael Romanov, the founder of the dynasty which was to rule Russia until the end of monarchy in 1917. Poland's hopes of any easy conquest had vanished. In order to maintain hold over its possessions, which included Smoleńsk, the Commonwealth was now compelled to resort to a protracted war.

This, however, did not restrain Sigismund III from pursuing his dynastic plans which by that time had become the *idée fixe* of his foreign policy. With his eyes set on conquest in the East, the King, just as Batory before him, made a disastrous move with regard to the future of Prussia. Following the death of Joachim Frederick of Hohenzollern, he agreed to the taking over of the Prussian fief by the electors of Brandenburg. Thus the Polish government once again entered the road of fatal compromise which was to lay the foundations for a powerful Prussian State.

In his attempts to win allies, Sigismund III turned again towards the Hapsburgs with whom he concluded a treaty (1613) which provided for political cooperation, covering also a campaign against the Emperor's rebellious subjects in Bohemia, Silesia and Hungary. In this way Poland took upon herself a kind of obligation to safeguard the interests of the Hapsburgs in countries once ruled by the Jagiellons.

All this was done with a view to regaining the Russian throne, this time for Prince Władysław. In 1617 he set out on a conquest of Moscov proclaiming himself the rightful Tsar. To his future subjects he solemnly promised that he would respect their faith, their rights and privileges, but at the same time he secretly pledged to his father that he would cede considerable parts of Russian territory to the Commonwealth. The campaign, in which comparatively small Polish forces were engaged, did not bring the expected success. Attempts to take Muscovy by storm ended in failure and the prospective subjects of Władysław did not show excessive eagerness for a change of ruler. On the contrary, they regarded Michael Romanov and rightly so, as a more trustworthy guarantor of the State's territorial integrity and defender of the Orthodox faith.

In that situation the only favourable outcome of the campaign were considerable territorial gains by the Polish Commonwealth which included the regions of Siewierz and Czernihów. These were ceded to Poland under the terms of a truce with Russia for 14 years concluded in 1618 at Deulino. Both sides adhered strictly to its provisions and only in 1632 did Russia make an attempt to recover the lost territories. A Russian army commanded by boyar Shein laid siege to Smoleńsk which the Poles, however, had transformed in the meantime into a strong fortress. The newly elected King, Władysław IV, hastened to check the Russian advance and to relieve the besieged stronghold. His military successes induced Russia to sign in 1634 a peace treaty in Polanowo. Poland retained for ever everything that she had gained under the Deulino Truce and, in exchange Władysław IV renounced all his claims to the throne of the Tsars. To make sure that his word would be kept, the Russian envoys even demanded the return of the document of 1610 declaring his election to the Russian throne, and were greatly dismayed when they learnt that the document in question was lost because of the disorder prevailing in the royal archives.

THE CONFLICT WITH TURKEY

The situation on the southern borders of the Commonwealth was much less favourable. A basic tenet of Poland's policy throughout the entire sixteenth century was to avoid a direct military engagement with the preponderant military power of the Ottoman Empire. Cossack forays into the Ottoman dominions and the Tartar incursions into Poland had repeatedly strained the relations between the two countries. Nevertheless, by "balancing on the brink of war" an open military conflict had in some way been avoided. This, of course, did not mean that Poland was not interested in the countries of the Danube basin, whether in Hungary, or in Moldavia and Valachia. At the turn of the sixteenth century Zamoyski had made several attempts to put on the thrones of these countries candidates who were amicably disposed towards Poland.

The further history of Polish-Turkish relations was shaped by two factors, the growing expansion of Turkey which reached practically to the threshold of the Commonwealth, and the continual incursions of Cossack forays into Turkish dominions. The Cossacks consisted of former serfs who had fled to freedom, and of the urban poor who settled in south-eastern Ukraine, colonizing the so-called Wild Plains, which extended along the Dnieper, between Polish and Tartar possessions. The Cossacks were organized in a military brotherhood, with their own authorities and their defensive stronghold of Sicz on the Dnieper island of Chortyca below the famous *porohy* or rapids of the river (hence the name of the region: Zaporozhe). Already Sigismund Augustus and Stephen Batory had attempted to use the Cossacks for the defense of the Commonwealth. Some of them had been enlisted into military service, constituting the "registered Cossacks" (enrolled in a special register). They were born warriors and adventurers who in search of loot and booty robbed Turkish galleys and invaded the dominions of the Ottoman Empire on the Black Sea coast.

Relations between Poland and Turkey had also deteriorated as a result of the decision taken by the Court and the King to side with the Hapsburg bloc. The reasons for that decision were manifold including the Commonwealth expansion eastward, the dynastic interests of Sigismund III (not to be identified with the interests of the Polish State) as well as the growing influence of the Counter-Reformation which more and more often abandoned political realism in favour of the aspirations of the Pope and the Hapsburgs. The Hapsburgs gained many important benefits from the alliance whilst it brought none to Poland. The only result for the Commonwealth was that it hastened the outbreak of a military clash with Turkey.

The Thirty Years' War was fought between the Catholic camp represented by the Hapsburgs, the Holy See and the Catholic League of the princes in the German Empire and the anti-Hapsburg grouping which consisted of France, the Netherlands and the Protestant union of the German princes. When an uprising against the Hapsburgs broke out in Bohemia, Sigismund III, who had been prevented by the opposition of the gentry from dispatching regular troops to relieve the situation, sent in units, which had been enrolled by Aleksander Lisowski (hence their name: Lisowski's men) during the days of the war against Russia.

These units composed of mercenaries typical of those times, inflicted severe losses on the army of Bethlen Gabor, Duke of Transylvania, who being at war with the Hapsburgs, laid siege to Vienna. Because Bethlen Gabor was a vassal of the Turks, the assistance given to his enemies was bound to affect Poland's relations with the Ottoman Empire. To add insult to injury the Cossacks had invaded and plundered the town of Varna. Faced with this situation Turkey, where the government had just been taken by the bellicose Sultan Osman II, renounced the "eternal peace" which had been concluded in 1533 and embarked upon war.

The small Polish force, under the command of the 70 year old Hetman Stanisław Żółkiewski, was routed in the battle of Cecora (1620) and the aged Hetman, who refused to seek his safety in flight, fell on the battlefield. The Commonwealth had to prepare for defense against an enemy which stood at its door. In the search for allies attention turned to the Cossacks. Their Hetman, Piotr Konaszewicz-Sahajdaczny brought an army of forty thousand men to the Polish camp at Chocim. In return the King had to close his eyes to the illegal reconstruction of the Orthodox Church's hierarchy in Poland. Since the unfortunate Union of Brześć its opponents now found in the Cossacks staunch defenders of the Orthodox faith. The Cossacks themselves, apart from their social demands for which they fought against the Polish Commonwealth under Semen Nalevaiko and Krishtof Kosinski (1595–1596) now found in the defense against the encroachments of Catholicism an ideological justification of their uprisings.

The Polish camp at Chocim (1621) resisted every assault of the Turkish army and, eventually, the Ottoman Empire was ready to start negotiations. The armistice, which was quickly concluded, came just in time for the Polish army which had only one barrel of gun-powder left in the camp. The peace treaty restored the position which had existed during the times of the Jagiellons. The frontier was to run along the Dniestr river; Chocim was to remain with Turkey and both sides undertooook to restrain their respective allies from invading one another's territories. In practice, however, the treaty prevented neither Tartar depredations in Poland nor the Cossack piratical raids to the Black Sea.

The preoccupation of the Commonwealth in the South, and above all, its inopportune interference in the affairs of Bohemia and Transylvania, weakened its position in the North. The opportunity thus created was seized by Sweden which launched an attack on Poland from that direction. In the years 1617 and 1621–1622 Poland lost in the hostilities a considerable portion of Livonia. Encouraged by these successes Sweden next attacked Royal Prussia and blocked the mouth of the Vistula which was vital for Poland's economic interests. The occupation of Royal Prussia was designed to check Polish attempts to recover Livonia and also to provide Sweden with a convenient base for an attack on the Catholic princes of the Empire and their Hapsburg allies thus joining the Thirty Years' War.

The three year long struggle in Pomerania (1626–1629) was waged with varying fortune. The Poles scored a victory in the naval battle near Oliwa (1627) while the Swedes emerged the victors at Górzno (1629). The terms of a six years' truce signed in Altmark (1629) placed Poland in a highly disadvantageous position. Sweden retained all the Prussian ports, with the exclusion of Puck, Gdańsk and Königsberg, as well as the Livonian territories up to the Dvina river. Poland was compelled to sign this humiliating treaty for the additional reason that the gentry refused to support the King's military effort though by this time the issue was not his dynastic claims, but the danger of Poland being cut off from the access to the Baltic Sea.

THE AGRARIAN CRISIS

During the closing years of the sixteenth and the first half of the seventeenth centuries, rural economy based on manorial farms employing serf labour continued to expand in Poland. The amount of land owned by the gentry grew not only by putting under cultivation temporarily abandoned areas, but also at the expense of peasants who were relegated to inferior or even fallow lands.

These methods inevitably led to the curtailment of the size of peasant holdings, as well as to a further social differentiation of the countryside resulting in a growth in the numbers of the village poor. This influenced the general standard of living of the rural population and was reflected in the steady decline of livestock and draft animals. The needs of estate management induced the gentry to increase the amount of labour dues. Where this, for varying reasons, was not possible, other peasant obligations towards the landlord were raised, such as extra labour days during harvesting or haymaking as well as payments in kind. The lord of the manor had moreover the use of numerous and burdensome monopolies which obliged the peasants to purchase certain commodities like vodka or beer exclusively in the inns run by the manor.

The possibilities of judicial action against mounting oppression were gradually being closed to the peasants on the estates of the landed gentry. Those who lived on the royal or ecclesiastical estates had the opportunity of appealing to the referendary courts and to higher Church authorities, though, as a rule, these took the side of the tenants or estate agents against the peasants. Yet even when the verdict went in favour of the complaining villager, there was still a long and arduous road before him before he could see that justice was done. In this situation the peasants, driven to desperation, resorted to flight to other estates where they were granted, at least in the initial period, certain reductions in the amount of labour and rent. The safest sanctuary was for a time the Ukraine, but it was too far away, especially for fugitives burdened with a family and possessions however meagre.

Thus, what was left to the overwhelming majority of the peasants, was the reluctant performance of labour dues (many complaint about their decreasing efficiency were then recorded), and the resort to an armed struggle for their rights. Though peasant uprisings led by the Cossacks, used to break out quite frequently in the Ukraine during the first half of the seventeenth century, in Poland proper such events occurred only sporadically. They occurred chiefly on the royal estates, above all in the Podhale region, where the living memory of former freedom and the mountaineers' skill in arms created favourable conditions for such uprisings in the defense of rights abused by the willfulness and tyranny of the *starostas*. In the district of Nowy Targ, for example, peasant disturbances lasted uninterruptedly for almost ten years (1624–1633). But apart from that region there were no major peasant riots and the charges levelled at, for instance, the Polish Arians by the followers of Counter-Reformation that they strove to incite a repetition in the Commonwealth of the bloody German events of 1525, were pure demagogy.

The possibility of a flight to the Ukraine helped to relieve the pressure of peasant resistance in other areas of the Commonwealth. There was likewise no unity among the serfs in the different regions of the country. The varying degrees of oppression and the lack of experience in the use of arms deterred the peasants from taking the course of direct armed action. Furthermore, on the ethnically Polish lands, the increase in labour and other dues towards the manor was a lengthy process extending over a couple of generations. In the Ukraine, on the other hand, the situation developed in quite a different manner. There in a comparatively short time the peasants were forced to perform serf labour to which formerly they had not been liable. In the

Ukraine, too, the insurgents found a common ideology which the Polish peasants lacked. That common ideology was expressed in slogans of the defense of freedom, of the Orthodox faith and of the emerging Ruthenian national consciousness. The insurgents rose in arms not so much against the medium sized manor farms of the gentry as against the huge estates which in the eastern regions of the Commonwealth covered most of the land. Thus, for example, Vasilii Ostrogski owned some 100 towns and castles while, in Volhynia, 60 per cent of the land belonged to the magnates. This rapid expansion of the great estates occurred after the Union of Lublin. In the Ukrainian areas there emerged new magnates' latifundia like those of the Wiśniowieckis, Ostrogskis or Koniecpolskis. On the other hand, many ancient magnate families had died out. Many Lithuanian and Ruthenian noblemen had moved to the Kingdom of Poland where they purchased or inherited new fortunes. As in a melting pot a reshuffle had taken place and new people had come to the fore within the magnate class. This was coupled with the further, rapid growth of its social importance.

THE GROWING IMPORTANCE OF THE MAGNATES

The aspirations of the magnates to dominate the entire gentry were not always successful. Symptoms of an antagonism between the gentry and the magnates had been evident throughout the whole history of the Commonwealth prior to the partitions. Its outward signs were visible in the struggles and disputes at the Seyms and in polemical pamphlets. But increasingly often the gentry were the losers in the conflict. The lesser gentry were employed in the administration of the magnates' estates and households: the middle gentry reduced to obedience by economic means (loans) as well as by the frequently occurring need to avail themselves of the magnates' protection. While the middle gentry could still resist the pressure of the magnates, who were not seldom unpleasant and troublesome neighbours, the lesser representatives of that class were, to a growing degree, becoming mere tools in the hands of the magnates. It was through them that the latter gained an increasing influence in the local diets and from among them that they recruited their private armies which were ready at any time to cut the throats of their adversaries.

Very characteristic of the progressing decentralization of the State was the fact that the armed forces in the service of the individual magnates were often equal in size to the peace time army of the Crown. Thus, for example, when in the middle of the seventeenth century this army numbered some four thousand soldiers, border magnates like Jarema Wiśniowiecki or Dominik Zasławski maintained regiments of two or even three thousand of their own men. In that situation both the defense of the country and the protection of

Portrait of a nobleman, 16th cent.

the interests of its ruling class ceased to be the concern of the central authorities but, to a growing extent, became the function of the magnates. Nor were the gentry any more interested in a strong, centralized administration; the latifundia of the magnates, their armies and courts provided ample opportunities for a career and good earnings, and the private forces of the "kinglets" as they were called, guaranteed adequate protection against revolts of their serfs and attacks by hostile magnates. Thus, the functions which, for example, in France or Austria were performed by the increasingly powerful central authority, in Poland were being gradually taken over by what, in fact, amounted to small sovereign States ruled by individual magnates. Their

influence, which grew in the eastern borderlands, penetrated deep into the Commonwealth, for their huge estates existed all over the country. The majority of the *starostwa* were also held by the most powerful families and, after a magnate's death, were granted not uncommonly to his son.

Observing the bitter struggles which the magnates waged among themselves, for example Stanisław Stadnicki with Łukasz Opaliński during the first half of the seventeenth century, and which at times developed into small civil wars, it was difficult to believe that somewhere there existed a superior royal authority. The economic power and the resulting political influence of the magnates permitted them to act in complete disregard of the State.

During the period of the first elective kings the prerogatives of the crown had been greatly reduced, among other reasons because of the necessity to reckon with the decisions of the Senate. On the other hand, the influence of the dignitaries of the Crown (ministers of State), most of whom came from the magnates' families and were appointed for life, increased considerably. The Senate was gradually becoming the chief centre in which the State's affairs were decided. The role of the Seym, which during the first half of the seventeenth century broke up six times without passing any laws, was visibly declining. The importance of the local diets on the other hand, was increasing (not without prompting by the magnates) and bound the hands of the deputies to the Seym thus hindering the possibility of reaching agreement at the Seym.

From 1613 decisions concerning taxation were, as a rule, transferred to the local diets. This decentralization of the fiscal system led to a situation in which some districts had to pay bigger taxes than others. The chaos was further deepened when the local diets were entrusted with the voting of taxes even for the defense of the State (1640). All this was bound to result in a decline of the revenues of the treasury which, in turn, rendered regular payments to the army virtually impossible.

The soldiers, who wed arrears of pay, organized military leagues or confederations which ravaged the country constituting dangerous centres of political ferment. The numerous wars (in which Poland was almost permanently engaged), however, made it imperative to continue the military reforms initiated by Batory. In addition to the old cavalry, "foreign regiments" composed of mercenaries had been organized. A number of Poles also served in these regiments. Specially created headquarters took command of the artillery which could boast of a high technical level raising its efficiency and fire power considerably. During the first half of the seventeenth century many new fortified outposts had been erected, especially in the Ukraine, where they were intended to keep in check the peasants and the Cossacks. Military operations carried out by Polish commanders were noted for their tactical brilliance; with comparatively small forces at their command they successfully conducted an active defense.

Krasiczyn. Renaissance castle, 1598–1614

Factors hampering the expansion of Poland's military power were, however, not only difficulties of a fiscal nature. Neither the gentry nor the magnates, in fact, desired it. The former, never themselves eager to enlist unless faced by enemy troops within the borders of the country, were against giving arms to peasants who could, if the need arose, turn those arms not only against a foreign invader. Both the gentry and the magnates regarded an efficient and well disciplined army as a potential source of support for the King's absolutist aspirations.

THE SITUATION OF TOWNS AND BURGHERS

At the turn of the sixteenth century, the Polish towns began to feel the effects of the steady development of the manorial farm economy based on serf labour. This applied, above all, to medium and small urban localities. The impoverished peasant was compelled to give up purchasing many goods produced by the urban craftsmen and to content himself with the products of the increasingly self-sufficient peasant holdings. Expansion of smaller towns was hampered also by the military confederations and civil wars. The situation of larger towns like Gdańsk, Lwów, Warsaw, Poznań and Cracow where the period of prosperity and expansion continued uninterrupted, was somewhat different. These towns were important commercial centres which, directly or indirectly, reaped the benefits of external trade.

Towns like Sandomierz, Kazimierz Dolny, Płock, Toruń and Bydgoszcz, situated along the route of the grain trade to Gdańsk also grew in importance. The export trade was on the increase on account of the expansion of the estates' productivity as well as the growth of the external demand for grain (from 52,000 last in the years 1562–1565, to 116,000 last in 1618. A last = c. 5000 kg). For the Gdańsk and Toruń merchants the export of grain became the source from which they accumulated considerable commercial capital. This process was practically impeded, especially during the reign of Sigismund III, by a monetary crisis which was reflected in rising prices and a decline in the value of money. As a result the State gave up its function of controlling the coinage, thus providing speculators of all kinds with an opportunity of making easy money out of the influx of foreign currency.

A different kind of towns were those founded at the turn of the sixteenth century on the lands of the magnates' latifundia. Among such centres were Zamość, which belonged to the Zamoyski family, Brody and Żółkiew, the property of the Żółkiewskis, Zborów, of the Sobieskis and Biłgoraj, of the Gorajskis. Their population worked mainly on the land while the local craftsmen worked for the needs of the surrounding estates. These townships being the property of the local lords were naturally subjected by them to increased exploitation. The supremacy of the nobility had also made itself felt in other urban centres. The royal towns were (since 1565) subordinated to the *starostas* who often, jointly with local authorities, composed of the town patricians, drew handsome profits from the exploitation of the population. In towns there were also districts, called jurisdictions which were the property of the gentry or the Church and as such were independent of the towns' administration and judiciary. The handicraft workshops in these districts, working on the commissions of the feudal lords, were often manufacturing goods which required high skills, for instance textiles, and found there conditions favourable for development, unrestricted by the prevailing laws and regulations of the guilds. Outside the guilds there were also the iron foundries which worked mainly for the needs of the army, and mines (chiefly salt mines in Wieliczka). The forges in ecclesiastical and royal estates were at that time leased to the gentry who, as a rule, brought them to a state of ruin.

The adverse effects of the political supremacy of the gentry and of the expansion of farm economy based on serf labour on Polish towns and handcrafts were to become evident only in later years, but the first signs of an economic crisis had been apparent already in the first half of the seventeenth century. The economic crisis was accompanied by a critical situation in the country's social, political and religious life. The later was closely linked with the progress of the Counter-Reformation in Poland.

THE DOCTRINE OF THE COUNTER-REFORMATION

The progress of the Reformation in Poland had markedly slowed down during the 1560's. The gentry and the magnates, after they had attained their main aims (exemption from the jurisdiction of ecclesiastical courts and ecclesiastical contribution towards the costs of the country's defense) began to return to the fold of the Catholic Church. They were impressed by the coherence of a Church which, despite the pressure of the Reformation movement, managed to preserve its basic privileges and the position of the dominating religion. The Church consolidated the unity of the gentry in the Commonwealth (acceptance of the Catholic faith constituted the last stage of the final Polonization of the Byelorussian and Ruthenian gentry). Catholicism marked Poland off from Protestant Sweden, Orthodox Russia and Mohammedan Turkey. The great value of the Catholic social doctrine was continually emphasized and, in a demagogic manner, counterposed to the "rebellious" teaching of the Reformation, especially of the Arians.

All this prepared for the triumph of the Counter-Reformation. Its influence was enhanced both by the arrival of Jesuits in Poland (1565) as well as by the improved intellectual level, though not the moral standards, of the local clergy thanks to the acceptance by them and partial realization of the decrees of the Council of Trent (1577). At a time when the activity of the Church embraced all spheres of life, it was only natural that the Counter-Reformation came out with its own concept of the State, especially of the social and political relations which, according to its spokesmen, ought to prevail in it.

Following largely the pattern of Hapsburg absolutism this concept included demands for granting greater privileges to the burghers and easing the lot of the peasants. Thinkers of the Counter-Reformation like Marcin Śmiglecki or Szymon Starowolski were specific in demanding the reduction of serf labour, maintaining rents and taxes in kind at an unchanged level and giving the serfs the right to leave the land. These demands resulting, in part, from the plebeian origin of their advocates aimed, as it was emphatically pointed out, at safeguarding the interests of the gentry. The excessive exploitation of the peasants resulted in the flight of peasants from the villages, an increase of the waste land and even, ultimately, peasants' revolts. In the political sphere the leaders of the Counter-Reformation spoke for the introduction of certain basic reforms. They demanded that the monarch's authority be strengthened, elective kings be replaced by hereditary rulers and that the State's administrative machinery be fully subordinated to the monarch.

It is obvious that these ideas could hardly evoke enthusiasm among the gentry for whom they heralded the transformation of Poland into another Spain or Austria, ruled by the same Hapsburgs, who during the successive interregna were so fervently supported by the Holy See and the Jesuits, as the prospective candidates to the Polish throne. On the other hand a strong monarchy, a Catholic one of course, was regared by Rome as a tool to be used for a speedy and ruthless extermination of heresy. As soon as it was realized, however, especially after the Zebrzydowski rebellion, that such theories gave rise only to distrust of the Church's intention and pushed even Catholic zealots into an alliance with Protestants, the Jesuits ceased to advocate them. More and more often, instead, they praised in writing and from the pulpit the system of Golden Freedom though, in fact, it amounted to approval of the growing omnipotence of the magnates.

The gradually developing decentralization of the State was bound to find reflection in the attitude of the Church, which began to attach a greater importance to cooperation with the gentry and the magnates than to an alliance with the king. Even during the reign of Sigismund III, who enjoyed the strong support of the bishops, the Papacy sought to realize, through Poland, not only its own political aims but often those of the Hapsburgs. That was because Poland, by rejecting absolutism, was not in a position to subordinate the Church to the interests of the State as had been the case in France in the seventeenth century and, even earlier, in Spain. Thus, religious considerations began to play an increasingly weighty role in Poland's foreign policy which was unheard of in the sixteenth century, an example of which was the alliance with the Hapsburgs and the military expeditions undertaken against Muscovy, among other reasons, on missionary grounds. In internal affairs, also, these considerations were gradually emerging.

THE METHODS OF THE COUNTER-REFORMATION

The Counter-Reformation had to take into consideration the specific features of the country in which it was to conduct its campaigns. Religious tolerance which had prevailed in sixteenth and seventeenth century Poland and attracted religious exiles from many European countries, did not secure equal treatment for the different social classes. The peasants, of whom only an insignificant number adhered to the Reformation, were reconverted to Catholicism by the crudest of means. Like the Calvinists before them, the Catholic lords did not now hesitate to apply pressure and to compel their subjects to attend religious services by fines, flogging or arrest. Similar procedures were adopted in the royal boroughs and in townships which belonged to the more zealous Catholic lords.

In larger urban centres the urban poor were won over to the Church by small scale philanthropy. This was pursued by the so-called Banks of Piety, interest-free pawnshops and by various benevolent brotherhoods. The sermons appealed to the religious ardour of the burghers and incited them to a ruthless destruction of the homes and the chapels of the "heretics". The appeals which invoked in equal measure the religious feelings and animosity of the Catholic plebeians towards the Protestant patricians, inevitably had their effect. At the turn of the sixteenth century the religious upheavals which took place in many towns (Cracow—1591, Poznań—1616, Lublin—1627) brought a total destruction of Protestant churches. Shops and even the homes of the dissidents were wrecked by the incited mob. The discriminatory practices applied against them by the guilds and by town courts also led to the rapid decline of their memberships. Some agreed to be reconverted, while others emigrated to Royal Prussia. In the towns of that province the Protestant majority revenged themselves on the Catholics by similar persecutions. On the other hand, during the Thirty Years' War, Lutherans expelled from Catholic occupied Silesia, and Bohemian Brethren, proscribed by the Hapsburgs in Bohemia, had been arriving in Poland and finding acceptance in many private estates. The Bohemian Brethren settled chiefly in Leszno, the property of their co-religionist Leszczyński. Thanks to the new arrivals the population of Leszno grew from three hundred families before 1628 to two thousand in 1656. The Counter-Reformation, victorious in Poznań, Cracow and elsewhere, was in no position to counteract these developments. Both the magnates and the gentry were joined together by class solidarity; actually their privileges lay at the root of the religious tolerance in Poland. The boundaries of private possessions constituted at least for a time an impregnable barrier which assured the safety of Protestant churches, printing offices and schools within them. In these circumstances the only way of dealing with dissenting magnates was by suggestion and persuasion backed by financial inducements. For a long time Papal nuncios had advised the kings to reserve State offices and grants of royal land exclusively for Catholics. Only under Sigismund III was that advice taken and even then not immediately.

The outlook and opinions of the young gentry were moulded in Jesuit colleges to which the gentry sent their children in great numbers, wanting to give their offspring a humanist education. The pupils were also prepared for public responsibilities. The graduates remained under close surveillance and those who displayed talents and obedience were promoted to positions of influence. In this way the Jesuits placed their own supporters in the Seym where the Catholic party systematically blocked all attempts to supplement the provisions of the Confederation of Warsaw with additional regulations which would guarantee its practical implementation. Graduates of Jesuit colleges were also present in the courts, which disregarding the prevailing laws of the land began, already in the 1620's to punish the adherents of Protestantism with heavy fines and imprisonment.

The sentence upon a Calvinist nobleman, Samuel Bolestraszycki, for translating a book written by his French co-religionist, Pierre de Moulin (1627) raised a commotion in the Commonwealth, but though the sentence was rescinded by the Seym, it nevertheless was an ominous sign for the future. The toleration of earlier years was gradually giving way to the fanaticism of the "new Catholics", as the dissenters called those who identified the gentry's interest with absolute obedience to the Church. Their first victims were the Arians. Although they were relatively small in number and although the social radicalism of the elder Polish Brethren had long since turned into a simple humanitarianism, their religious doctrines were too rational and tolerant even for the Calvinists. They thus continued to be considered a dangerous bogey.

During the reign of the tolerant King Władysław IV, who sought to come to terms even with the Orthodox Church by officially aknowledging the reconstruction of their Church hierarchy (1632), the main centre of the Polish Brethren, Raków, the renowned seat of their Academy and their printing office of European fame, was closed. Not satisfied with these successes, the Counter-Reformation initiated a campaign against anti-Trinitarianism which had spread to the estates of the Arian gentry in the Ukraine. An edict of 1647 finally forbade the Polish Brethren to maintain schools and printing houses.

It would, of course, be wrong to draw comparisons between all these developments in Poland with the militant intolerance which reaped its harvest in western Europe, whether in Protestant England or in Catholic Spain. It should also be borne in mind that the weakness of the executive authority of the State made a strict observance and execution of these bans and sentences difficult if not impossible. The general atmosphere in the country nevertheless visibly deteriorated. The Protestants for this reason began to look for assistance to Sweden. Transylvania and even Ducal Prussia. This in turn allowed Catholic propaganda to charge the Protestants with plotting high treason. Such propaganda was disseminated in many different forms,

Jesuits' and Dissenters' schools, 16th-18th cent.

- ○ Jesuits' schools
- ● Dissenters' schools
- ////// Boundaries of the Commonwealth, 1569
- —·—·— Boundaries of the Commonwealth, 1699–1772
- ------ Boundaries of the Kingdom of Poland, Lithuania and Courland

verbally from the pulpit, by such distinguished preachers as Father Piotr Skarga, and visually (Jesuits' school theatres and ecclesiastical art was very skilfully adapted to the needs of the struggle against heresy), as well as by the printed word. The latter included serious theological treatises (by Hosius, Białobrzeski, Powodowski) and small pamphlets (by Łaszcz, Wargocki) which sharply attacked not only the dogmas, but above all, their habits, way of life and political views. The propaganda of the Counter-Reformation presented the dissenters almost as atheists, enemies of Church and State, as basically antisocial elments always ready to conspire with the enemy. There was no hesitation in charging them with immoral and indecent behaviour.

The ostentatiously austere interiors of the dissenter chapels were pointed to by the Counter-Reformation and compared with the dazzling Baroque interiors of the Catholic church with its sculptures, gildings and the scent of incense. The rationalist Protestant religion was contrasted with a faith based on external and emotive manifestations of worship. The Jesuits, in particular, placed great emphasis on pilgrimages to miraculous shrines and images and on processions and relics, arguing that the surest way to the souls of the faithful was through their eyes. The imagination of the people was stirred by theatrical plays performed at Jesuit colleges and by public spectacles in the towns during which Protestant books and images of their leaders were burnt. Called to assist the lay and secular preachers in this campaign were the religious brotherhoods originating from the Middle Ages and now reactivated.

Though the Counter-Reformation was formally in many respects a return to the medieval conception of religion, it was in fact a new version of Catholicism adapted to the requirements of the new times, blended to a growing extent with local habits and traditions. Images of Saints, church interiors, cribs at Christmas and holy sepulchres at Easter were endowed with local decorative elements. Saint Isidore, the Spanish peasant, was depicted in the garb of a Polish villager. The after-life was represented as another version of life on earth in seventeenth century Poland. The heavenly court with Christ as King was described in words taken from the political life of the contemporary gentry and the Virgin Mary was presented as a good maiden from the manor pleading with the King of Heaven for her subjects. The earthly and heavenly hierarchies bore a close resemblance, with the sole difference that the magnate who had lived in wealth and luxury would have to beg the despised but virtuous serf to intercede for him.

For the gentry, Catholicism became an important element in their ideology. Although they respected and revered the clergy as the servants of God, they nevertheless sought to curtail the economic expansion of the Church by passing in 1635 a special law restricting bequests of land to monasteries. The traditional anti-clericalism of the gentry had out-lived the era of Counter-Reformation and the sharpest attacks on the Jesuits' insatiable lust for power and wealth came from the pens of Catholics. Polish antimonastic pamphlets, like *Monita Secreta* by Hieronim Zahorowski (1614) gained a European fame which endured well into the nineteenth century.

These attacks were not affected by the fact that during the first half of the seventeenth century, the ecclesiastical hierarchy had been infiltrated by the gentry. If at first the boldest advocates of both Protestantism and the Counter-Reformation in Poland were of plebeian or foreign origin, during the course of the next generation there was a marked predominance of priests of gentry origin who brought into the clerical order the vices and habits of their own class.

THE ELECTION AND REIGN OF WŁADYSŁAW IV

The lesson of the Swedish war (1626–1629) once more put on the agenda efforts to strengthen the royal authority. An opportunity was provided by the prospective election of a new king. The reign of Sigismund III, one of the longest in the country's history (1587–1632) was drawing to its close and the time was coming to think of how to elect his successor. Much attention was devoted to that question during the last years of the ageing monarch. Proposals were advanced for taking decisions by a majority vote (which, in a way, would be a solution for the recurring situation in which more and more often the Seym broke up without passing any laws). It was proposed also to exclude foreign candidates and designate a successor before the death of the reigning monarch. All the heated discussion on this subject yielded, however, no practical results because both the gentry, increasingly attached to the watchword of Golden Freedom, and the magnates, not excluding persons close to the Court, did not really desire to see the king's prerogatives strengthened and consolidated.

If the procedure of electing a king was controversial, the person of the candidate for the throne excited few reservations. Władysław Vasa knew well how to gain sympathy of the gentry. His attitude to his future subjects was one of frankness, chivalry and cordiality. In the controversy which raged between the supporters of a Swedish, short pointed beard and those who preferred moustaches *a la Polonaise*, Władysław was not referred to, as his father was, as representing the foreign, Swedish or German fashion, so much disliked by the gentry. Even the dissenters, whose protests and complaints during the 1632 interregnum were treated reluctantly and perfunctorily, regarded the new ruler as the harbinger of better times. It was not without good reason that the Papal nuncios in their reports to Rome, denounced a religious indifference bordering almost on heresy in the young monarch.

The entire election was nothing more than an enthusiastic acclamation of the only candidate for the Polish throne; which, nevertheless, did not prevent the gentry from seeking, at the very beginning of his reign, measures to impose fresh restrictions on the royal powers. The new king soon put a stop to these attempts and, within a few years, himself started to campaign for the extension of his prerogatives. He sought to achieve this aim by an alliance with the Church and the group of magnates who were close to the royal court. The task of recruiting new supporters was entrusted to an exclusive organization called "The Cavalry of the Order of the Immaculate Conception of the Virgin Mary" (1637). Yet all these endeavours were in vain. The plans of the King were rejected with indignation by the gentry who saw in them an attempt to copy the Spanish model hated by all as absolutist, and by the Protestants, moreover, as ultra-Catholic and likely to subject the conscience of the gentry to the authority of the Inquisition.

It may be added that the King's aspirations did not really horrify the rank and file of the gentry. It was generally considered quite understandable that every monarch should strive for an autocratic form of government, just as every nobleman should resist the implementation of these sinister plans. But such an attitude rendered any lasting political cooperation between the Crown and the gentry virtually impossible.

The gentry complacently enjoying their freedoms, privileges and wealth, rejoiced at the peace that reigned in the Commonwealth when the Thirty Years' War was just raging beyond its borders. The neutrality which Poland maintained during the reign of Władysław IV, despite attempts of the belligerents to draw her into the conflict, prevented the possibility of gaining any advantages from it, like the recovery of Silesia or, at least, reminding the world of her rights to that territory. The people of Silesia, especially when it was the direct theatre of the hostilities, more and more frequently looked towards Poland. The leader of the Protestant camp in Silesia, the banished Duke of Brzeg and Legnica John Christian, approached Władysław IV with the request to assume suzerainty over Silesia. This idea was, however, never realized, though in 1636 France undertook to support the Polish King's claims to Silesia in return for his entry into the war on the Franco-Swedish side.

Władysław IV would not agree to that because he had never abandoned his hopes for the Swedish throne. Following the previously mentioned successes against Russia, crowned by the treaty of Polanowo (1634), the King compelled the Swedes by force of arms to withdraw their garrisons from the Prussian ports which they had occupied since 1626, and to stop imposing customs duties on Polish trade. These conditions accepted by the Swedes in the truce signed in Sztumska Wieś (Stumsdorf, 1636), were considered by Władysław IV as a temporary armistice, only, but the Seym refused to support his plans for a new war. The magnates obstructed it and likewise the city of Gdańsk, where the customs duties imposed by the King proved very unpopular. Thus, however reluctantly, Władysław IV had to give up his Baltic plans for which preparations had already started with the expansion of the Polish navy at its base in Władysławowo. After 1641 all further work was abandoned and what ships remained were sold.

In 1637 Władysław IV established closer relations with the Hapsburgs, sealing them by his marriage to the Archduchess Cecilia Renata. This new alliance brought only meagre results. It is true, that the Duke of Prussia and Elector of Brandenburg Frederick William submitted and, failing to obtain the support of the Emperor, swore fealty as a vassal of the King of Poland

Kazimierz Dolny. Przybyła House, 1615

(1641) at the castle in Warsaw (this was to be the last Prussian homage in Poland's history). Władysław IV also received in pawn the Silesian duchies of Racibórz and Opole (1644) but this was the end of all advantages derived from the King's pro-Hapsburg orientation. The gains in the North-West were also insignificant. After the disappearance in 1637 (together with the death of Bogusław XIV, the last Duke of Western Pomerania) of a separate Pomeranian State, its territory was seized by Sweden. Poland succeeded in regaining in 1637 two Pomeranian fiefs, the Bytów and Lębork districts, which were incorporated into Royal Prussia. Atempts to regain the Duchy of Słupsk, rather inconsistently handled by the King, ended in failure.

THE COSSACK QUESTION

The gentry increasingly quietist in their attitude preferred to keep their military effort beyond the borders of the country to a minimum, particularly in view of growing internal difficulties which were not only of an economic nature. The source of the trouble was the Cossacks, who from being previously a loosely knit community of individual settlers seeking a better life in the borderlands of the south-eastern Ukraine, had grown into a military force presenting a threat not only to the Turks and Tartars. Their ranks were constantly swelled by the influx of people from other parts of the Ukraine who in the freshly colonized areas hoped to find freedom from the burdens of taxation and compulsory labour.

Indeed the lords of the vast Ukrainian estates had granted the newcomers considerable facilities releasing them for a period of several years from rent and labour dues. After the lapse of that period and sometimes even earlier the serfs were required to perform all the feudal obligations. This gave rise to an understandable opposition on the part of the population not only in the villages but also in the towns. Feudal oppression did not spare the townspeople, most of whom derived their livelihood from agricultural occupations.

Discontent grew also among the Cossacks themselves as attempts were made to put them, too, under strict control by establishing only a small number of registered Cossacks (in 1625, for instance, the number was fixed at six thousand whereas in actual fact there were already some 30–40 thousand of them). The remainder were to be relegated to the level of serfs and placed under the control of the gentry and the magnates. This gave rise to numerous rebellions which, here and there, were joined by the local population, who not only held in high esteem the military valour of the Cossacks, but also regarded them as defenders of the serfs' freedom and of the Orthodox faith.

Of the lesser Cosack rebellions three had assumed a greater significance, in 1630, 1637 and 1638. All of them were crushed. In order to keep the

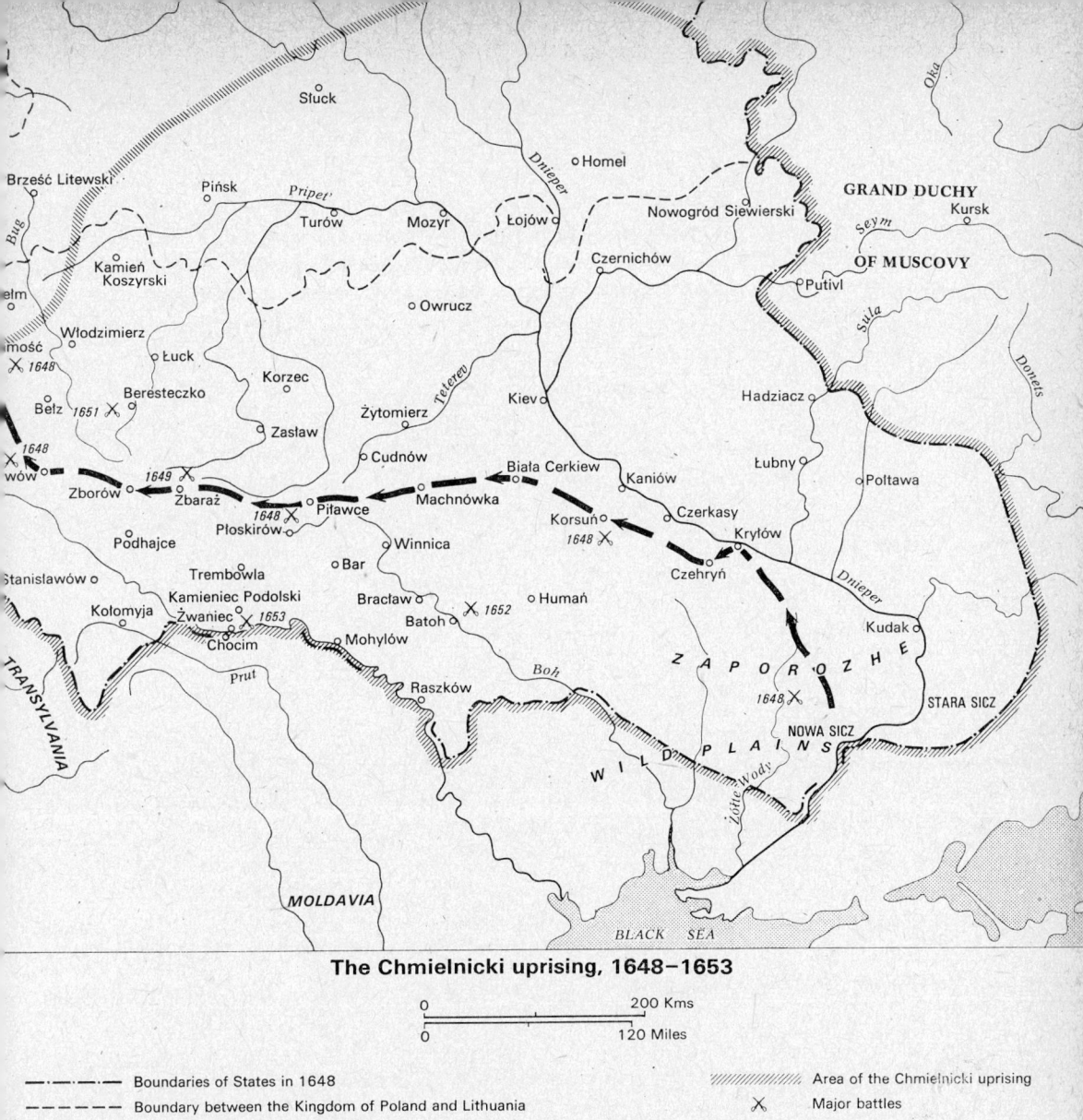

The Chmielnicki uprising, 1648–1653

- Boundaries of States in 1648
- Boundary between the Kingdom of Poland and Lithuania
- Chmielnicki's expedition in 1648
- Area of the Chmielnicki uprising
- Major battles

Cossacks in submission the fortress of Kudak had been erected on the lower Dnieper, above Zaporozhe. The number of registered Cossacks was further reduced and the Cossack military self-government was abolished. Ten years of "golden peace" (1638–1648) followed for the Ukrainian landlords who rejoiced at "the peasantry having been driven to the burrows", but the pacification proved to be transitory. Not only the Cossacks but also the majority of the remaining population nourished dreams of revenge for the wrongs they had suffered and of liberation from the growing oppression.

The peace was disturbed, involuntarily, by an action initiated by the King himself. His political and military ambitions were in glaring contrast to the general trends of the nobility. Being fully aware of this antagonism Władysław IV started preparations for a great anti-Turkish campaign, keeping them secret from the Seym. The King's plans were indeed grandiose. It was no longer a simple question, as suggested by the military (Stanisław Koniecpolski), of evicting the Tartars from the Crimea from which they constantly made incursions into Poland, but a less realistic concept of liberating the Balkans from the Turkish yoke and even hoisting the Polish flag over the Bosphorus.

These ambitious plans required the assistance of the Cossacks. The King gave them a secret order to start building a flotilla of small river crafts and rumours were circulating in the Ukraine about important privileges granted to the Zaporozhe Cossacks, the essence of which was, in the meantime, being kept secret. No wonder, therefore, that when nothing came from these plans the Cossacks felt deeply embittered. They were certain and not without good grounds that the failure was due to the intrigues of the magnates who were adamantly opposed to granting privileges to the Cossacks.

In fact, the affair had a wider aspect; at the Seyms of 1646 and 1647 the gentry and the magnates torpedoed the King's plans. Neither could see any advantages deriving to themselves in the planned expedition and both suspected that the King would emerge as the only winner, because in one way or another it would result in enhancing the royal power and in new taxes. As ever, on this occasion too, the foreigners were accused of being the instigators of these designs, so unpopular in the country. The King was let down also by his external allies. Muscovy concluded a treaty with the Tartars; Rome and Venice did not provide effective assistance, to say nothing of France to which Władysław IV came closer after his second marriage with Marie-Louise de Gonzague.

The frustrated Cossacks took up arms to win by force the privileges they were refused in negotiations. As their leader they chose Bohdan Chmielnicki, one of the Cossacks chiefs. Chmielnicki also hoped to avenge the personal wrongs which he suffered at the hands of Daniel Czapliński (an official of the magnate Koniecpolski) who confiscated his possessions and carried off his beloved wife.

Having reached an alliance with the Crimea Tartars, Chmielnicki set out, in the spring of 1648, from the Sicz advancing in a north-western direction deep into the Ukraine. He routed the Polish army at Żółte Wody and at Korsuń, thus convincing the people of the Ukraine, who had only waited for such a moment, that this time they were to witness events of an incomparably greater scope and power than ever before. The news of the victory rallied around him most of the local population. The peasants, the townsmen and the Cossack elders joined his forces, and they were soon followed by lower Orthodox clergy and even by the lesser and middle Ruthenian gentry.

In 1648 the King, who still had a certain moral authority with the Cossacks, died. The ambitious ruler who dreamt of gaining for Poland a lead-

Powroźnik. St. James' Orthodox Church, c. 1643

ing place among the European powers, left the country in an extremely precarious situation. This situation had been developing for quite some time and the successes scored by Chmielnicki merely brought forcibly to light all the basic weakness inherent in the constitutional and social structure of the multinational Commonwealth. Chmielnicki's armed uprising at first taken to be just another Cossack rebellion which would be easy to suppress, turned out to be the beginning of the military and political disintegration of the Polish State. This disintegration, however, had been prepared by the anomalies which had long been inherent in the entire system.

The lack of a strong, central government permitted the magnates to quell local anti-feudal movements and even sporadic Cossack rebellions. They were in no position to crush a massive uprising like that led by Chmielnicki. The reasons for the defeats of 1648 were to be found not only in the magnates' ruthlessness towards the Cossacks and the Ukrainian peasants, but also in their long struggle against any attempts to strenghthen the country. The founding of the Polish Commonwealth's internal and external security upon a federation of strong, but small dominions of magnates could not endure the test of experience.

Chapter IX

THE COMMONWEALTH IN THE YEARS OF CRISIS (1648–1696)

THE MAIN FEATURES OF THE PERIOD

The defeats sustained during the years 1648–1655 proved that the establishment based on Golden Freedom did not provide adequate safeguards for the political interests either of the State or of the ruling class. To some of its representatives led by the Court the successes scored by the Cossacks and the Swedes sounded an alarm which forced them to give serious thought to the need for far-reaching reforms; to others it was an indication that they should turn for help to foreign protectors.

That was the origin, on the one hand, of the attempts made during the reign of John Casimir to improve the constitution and, on the other, of the plans either to hand over the Polish crown to a foreign monarch, more powerful than a Polish ruler (the accession to Charles Gustavus of Sweden), or to carve out from the territory of the weakened Commonwealth a separate sovereign princely state (for example, the Radziwiłłs in Lithuania). In fact, those very same magnates who in their own country revealed themselves as the worst kind of trouble makers, like Bogusław Radziwiłł, were at the same time the most zealous followers and executors of the absolutist aspirations of foreign rulers. Radziwiłł behaved in this way as the governor of the Brandenburg elector in East Prussia.

The feverish endeavours to introduce reforms failed utterly, buried finally by the Lubomirski rebellion. The independence of the country, however, was for the time being preserved thanks to the patriotic drive of the people, including the gentry, during the Swedish invasion, known in Poland as the "Deluge". The peasants also rallied to the defense of the Commonwealth against aggressors of alien tongue, religion and customs. The gentry, too, fought with valour and bravery, especially when they were faced with the immediate danger of the invader on their thesheld. The self-sacrificing military effort of all sections of the population contributed to the preservation of the country's independence.

Another factor was that Poland's neighbours could not yet carry out the partitions planned by Sweden, Brandenburg and Transylvania in 1655–1657.

They were then still too weak and too much at odds, and, what was most important, these plans were not compatible with the interests of the future partitioning Powers, Austria nad Russia. On the other hand, the states bordering on Poland found a common interest in thwarting all attempts undertaken in the Commonwealth to reform the constitution. Moscow, Berlin, Vienna and Stockholm joined hands to prevent, by intrigues or bribery, any change for the better. They did not fail to conclude suitable agreements for joint action to counter any strengthening of the authority of the Crown.

This heroic feat of arms and a favourable international situation preserved the country's integrity, but it could not restore it to its former position. From 1648 Poland suffered continual territorial losses both in the East and in the South. In the 1670's the Commonwealth's foreign policy for a while was revitalized namely in the Baltic question, but already towards the end of the century Poland was only an object in international politics. The long wars combined with effects of the economic crisis, resulted not only in a marked fall in agricultural production and the beginnings of the decline of the towns, but also in the decay of the culture which in the first half of the seventeenth century, during the initial period of the Baroque had produced so many valuable and original works of art.

The growing class and national megalomania made the gentry turn a deaf ear to all calls for reforms and made them blind to the contemporary scientific and technical achievements in the West. In the course of the armed conflicts with enemies professing alien religions, the feelings of intolerance grew and religious fanaticism became for the gentry the sole criterion of *raison d'état*. The gentry considered that only they constituted the political nation and they therefore excluded all other social classes.

THE WAR WITH THE COSSACKS

The successes of the Cossacks during the first months of the Chmielnicki insurrection exicited a twin reaction in the ruling circles. The border magnates, like Jarema Wiśniowiecki, advocated the crushing of the rebellion by force without entering into any negotiations with the enemy. On the other hand, the more conciliatory party, represented by Chancellor Jerzy Ossoliński and the Voivode Adam Kisiel, sought to draw the Cossacks away from an alliance with the Tartars and, by granting them minor concessions, to induce them to come to terms with the Commonwealth.

The disastrous defeat suffered in the battle of Piławce where the regular army and the private regiments of the magnates together with their commanding officers ignominiously retreated from the battlefield, seemed to give substance to the opinion of the group which did not believe in the possibility of a military solution to the Cossack problem. This group scored another success by the election to the Polish throne of John Casimir Vasa, whose candidature was supported by Ossoliński. John Casimir married Marie-Louise, the widow of his deceased brother, Władysław IV. Chmielnicki reacted favourably to this election, but was not prepared to make concessions. He sought to liberate the entire Ukraine and not only, as was suggested, on the Polish side, to obtain agreement to increase the number of registered Cossacks and win the title of Hetman for himself.

Under the terms of the Zborów agreement in August 1649, however, Chmielnicki was forced to accept these proposals. The attacks of a combined Cossack-Tartar force failed to break the heroic resistance of the Polish units besieged in Zbaraż, while John Casimir for his part succeeded in winning over to his side the Tartar Khan, who himself did not really desire to see the emergence of a sovereign Ukrainian State.

The Zborów agreement raised the number of registered Cossacks to 40,000 but, at the same time, restored the domination of the gentry over the remaining Cossacks and the peasantry of the Ukraine. The agreement obviously could not last and was eventually rejected both by the Cossacks and by the Polish side where, following the death of Ossoliński (1651), the militant Wiśniowiecki party gained the upper hand. In this situation hostilities were resumed in 1651. The two sides prepared themselves very thoroughly for the new clash. Chmielnicki even thought of inciting subversion in the rear of the Polish army.

With that aim in mind he sent emissaries to Poland who aroused the peasants against the landowning gentry. These emissaries found a particularly fertile soil for their agitation, as the old social ferment in the Polish countryside got considerably stronger at the news of the success of the Ukrainian insurrection. The peasants of Great Poland, under the leadership of Piotr Grzybowski and Wojciech Kołakowski, and the Podhale mountaineers took to arms in 1651. The latter were led by Aleksander Kostka Napierski who used a forged royal "letter of credence" which allegedly entitled him to recruit for the army. Both those rebellions were ruthlessly suppressed. Kostka Napierski was besieged in the castle of Czorsztyn and impaled after the castle had been seized. Nothing certain is known about the contacts between Kostka Napierski and Chmielnicki; more probably he had links with George II Rakoczy of Transylvania. It is possible that Kostka Napierski only waited in Czorsztyn for the invasion of the Transylvanian army in order to attack the Commonwealth, when it was threatened from the east, between two fires. It seemed that this condottiere who had earlier offered his services to Queen Christina of Sweden, sought to use the anti-feudal struggle of the Podhale mountaineers to further his own ambitions.

The Podhale rebellions were suppressed chiefly by the militia of the Bishop of Cracow because the national army and troops of the general levy had departed for the Ukraine. Some of them returned hastily after the news reached them about the peasant rebellions, but in spite of this the forces of the Commonwealth gained a splendid victory over the Cossack-Tartar coalition in a three days' battle at Beresteczko (28–30 June, 1651). Chmielnicki's defeat was brought about by the military superiority of the Polish army and the withdrawal of the Tartars from the battlefield.

A new agreement was signed at Biała Cerkiew (Byelaya Tserkov), but after a short interval the war flared up again. The Tartar allies of Chmielnicki continued to play an ambiguous role and in these circumstances the Cossacks were unable to win a decisive victory. This compelled them to look for allies elsewhere. Chmielnicki, who had been aware of this situation for a long time, sought to establish closer relations with Muscovite Russia. The gradual rapprochement was eventually crowned by the Perejasław compact of 1654.

Tsar Alexis Mikhailovich who sought to make good the losses sustained in previous Polish-Russian wars, prevailed upon the *Zemsky Sobor*, the representative body of the nobility, in Muscovy to decide in favour of incorporating the Ukraine into Russia. This was approved also by the Cossacks, with the exception of some of the chiefs, and a section of the gentry and the higher clergy who saw in Russia a state akin in language and religion. The compact of Perejasław, though it did not make the Ukraine a sovereign state, nevertheless guaranteed her territory against attacks by Poland and aggresion on the part of Turkey which strove to convert the Ukraine into a protectorate of its own. It also brought about a complete reversal of alliances and became the cause of a prolonged war between Poland and Russia. The Tartars hitherto allied with the Cossacks went over to the side of the Commonwealth and helped to repel the combined Russo-Ukrainian attacks. The allied Muscovite and Ukrainian forces occupied parts of Byelorussia, Lithuania and the Ukraine, and penetrated as far as Lwów. In 1655 the Cossack army, after taking Lublin, reached the Vistula river, near Kazimierz Dolny and Puławy.

The situation was saved thanks to the Tartars, and Chmielnicki was even forced to recognize, though only formally, the suzereinty of John Casimir. A more decisive factor, however, which compelled Russia to withdraw from Poland and to make concessions was the military success of the Swedes who, in the summer of 1655, invaded the Commonwealth. Russia, fearing the rise of Swedish power, signed an armistice with Poland, the terms of which provided, among other things, for a joint campaign against Sweden.

THE SWEDISH INVASION OF 1655

From the very outset the new war took a disastrous turn for Poland. King Charles X Gustavus, under a formal pretext (John Casimir's persistent claims to the Swedish crown) broke the truce of Sztumska Wieś, hoping to conquer the Baltic provinces of the Commonwealth. In making his plans he was encouraged by the military weakness of the Polish State, exposed during the Cossack wars. He also believed, under the influence of the Polish magnate Hieronim Radziejowski, a traitor who fled to Stockholm after a private quarrel with King John Casimir, that Poland would be an easy prey.

Radziejowski's information turned out to be correct. The treacherous attitude of the magnates of Great Poland led by Krzysztof Opaliński enabled the Swedes in July 1655 to occupy that part of the country practically without fight. In the course of the following month the Lithuanian magnates, under the leadership of Bogusław and Janusz Radziwiłł, followed the example of their counterparts in Great Poland and surrendered Lithuania to the invader. Warsaw fell without a single shot being fired and shortly afterwards Cracow, defended by Stefan Czarniecki, was forced to surrender. The majority of the magnates and most of the gentry dependent upon them submitted to the invader. The gentry agreed to collaborate with the occupying power and the most eager collaborators were the dissenters embittered by the activities of the Counter-Reformation, but Catholic clergy also were to be found in the Swedish camp, led by some members of the episcopate. Barely three months after the beginning of the invasion King John Casimir had to take refuge in Silesia, while throughout the country the idea to dethrone him and elect Charles Gustavus the King of Poland was increasingly gaining ground.

Some gentry, remembering the persistent attempts by the Vasas to win the Swedish crown, consoled themselves that the proposed change would, in practice, amount to replacing one elected king by another. In reality much more important issues seemed to be involved. The gentry imagined that Sweden would help them in recovering the lost territories in the East because Poland was by herself in no position to achieve that goal. This defeatist policy was actually caused by the general state of the Commonwealth, which was not prepared to resist the forces of an invading army, trained and hardened in the Thirty Years' War.

The burghers, the peasants and the lesser gentry had but little to gain from the protection offered by the Swedes. On the contrary, they could feel the whole burden of that "protection". Looting and acts of violence by the Swedish troops, who had no respect even for the churches, to say nothing of their contempt for the safe conducts which the gentry so eagerly acquired, evoked general indignation and a strong desire for revenge. Already in the autumn of 1655 armed clashes with the invader occurred. They were waged by those units of the Polish army which did not go over to the enemy and by partisan groups organized by individual officers from among the burghers, the peasants and the patriotic gentry. The enemy, though still too strong to be defeated in an open battle was, at each opportunity, harassed and attacked by the partisans.

From his exile in Silesia John Casimir issued a summons for resistance. A general confederation was formed by the gentry in Tyszowce in December 1655, which declared itself for the legitimate King. The prevailing feeling of hatred towards the enemy was roused still further when in November and December the Swedes besieged the monastery of the Pauline Monks in Częstochowa, revered for its miraculous effigy of the Virgin. From the military point of view the siege was a complete failure and the widespread indignation which it aroused was eventually to bring disastrous consequences for the invader, the fact which was later skilfully exploited by the Counter-Reformation.

At the beginning of January 1656 John Casimir returned to the country. He was welcomed enthusiastically by the gentry who were disillusioned with Swedish rule and did not wish to be outdistanced by the partisan units of the people. With the King's return there began the period of liberation initiated already in December 1655 with the capture of Nowy Sącz by a several thousand strong detachment of peasants. In order to induce the common people to continue the struggle John Casimir solemnly swore in the Cathedral at Lwów, though in very general terms, to improve the situation of the serfs (1 April, 1656).

Hostilities, however, were to continue for a long time. They were waged by methods of partisan warfare, especially skilfully employed by Stefan Czarniecki, one of the most talented military leaders of the period. In June 1656 Warsaw was recovered for a short time but barely a month later it was retaken by the combined forces of Sweden and Brandenburg after a three days' battle on the outskirts of the city.

Realizing that he would not by himself be able to keep his Polish conquests, Charles Gustavus proposed to share the spoils with the Elector of Brandenburg who had joined forces with the Swedish King on the promise of obtaining Warmia and Great Poland, and of the recognition of his sovereignty over Ducal Prussia. The third partner in these plans of partition was to be Duke Rakoczy of Transylvania who indeed at the beginning of 1657 crossed the frontiers into the Commonwealth.

Poland, on her part, also thought of securing allies in the struggle against Sweden. Treaties were concluded with Denmark and Russia. The Elector of Brandenburg, who was induced to abandon his alliance with Sweden in return for releasing Ducal Prussia from fealty to Poland, was also granted the Lębork and Bytów districts (treaty of Welawa of September 1657). Reinforcements also came from Austria while Jerzy Lubomirski conducted a campaign of reprisal in northern Transylvania which forced Rakoczy to leave Poland hastily. His expedition thus ended in a complete failure and he found himself deserted even by Charles Gustavus who in June 1657 withdrew from Poland leaving Swedish garrisons in only a few towns. Hostilities then continued in Denmark and Western Pomerania whither Stefan Czarniecki set out with a Polish army corps. The eastern part of that province had recently been ceded under the terms of the treaty of Westphalia to Brandenburg, and the remaining territory, the coastal areas with Szczecin, had been left in Swedish hands.

THE PEACE OF OLIWA AND THE EASTERN QUESTION

After years of ceaseless struggle consideration was given to negotiations hastened by the defeats sustained by Sweden and the sudden death of her king. In the peace of Oliwa (May 1660), in which France acted as mediator, John Casimir renounced all claims to the Swedish throne. Sweden for her part, gave up all her territorial acquisitions in Poland, retaining only part of Livonia up to the Dvina river. Thus the *status quo* was restored, but at the cost of economic ruin for Poland and a political weakening of the State. The blame for the "Deluge" was laid on the invader, on Fate and, finally on the Arians. The latter who, as blasphemers, brought the wrath of the Almighty upon the country, were to be driven out from Poland by a decision of the Seym in 1658. The gentry failed to find fault with themselves, and were eager to cast into oblivion their own collective treason which not so long before had thrown the country wide open to the enemy.

As in the North and the West, in the East, too, attempts were made to restore, at the price of some concessions, the *status quo* of 1648. Following the death of Chmielnicki a compact was signed at Hadziacz in 1658 with the new Cossack Hetman, Jan Wyhowski. It provided for the creation of a separate Duchy of Ruthenia, covering the territory of the three voivodships of Kiev, Bracław and Czernihów, under the rule of the Hetman. The Duchy was to have its own officers of State and the Cossack leaders were to receive the same privileges as the Polish gentry. Their representatives were to sit in the Seym and the Greek Orthodox bishops in the Senate. The compact of Hadziacz which aimed at transforming the Commonwealth into a free union of three nations, Polish, Lithuanian and Ruthenian, came at least twenty years too late. Part of the Cossack leaders only decided to support it, but the rest no longer had trust in the good will of the Poles. The Ukrainian peasantry regarded the compact, and not without good reason, as yet another attempt to restore the rule of the feudal lords in the Ukraine.

A popular uprising against Wyhowski put an end to the Hadziacz compact. The would-be chancellor of the Grand Duchy of Ruthenia, the magnate Jurij Niemirich, was killed by the insurgents. Soon afterwards the Ukraine became one of the targets in the Russo-Polish hostilities which were resumed in 1659. The war lasted, with varying success, until 1664 when negotiations began leading only three years later to the truce of Andruszów (Andrusovo). Under the terms of the truce all Ukrainian territories on the left bank of the Dnieper as well as the provinces of Czernihów, Nowogród Siewierski and Smoleńsk were ceded to Russia, which also received Kiev for the period of two years, though in practice for ever. The treaty of Andruszów was a reflection of Poland's declining international position, which could have been resored only by a far-reaching reform of the country's political system.

ATTEMPTS TO INTRODUCE REFORM AND THE LUBOMIRSKI REBELLION

The defeats in the initial stages of the Swedish invasion impressed upon the royal court the urgent need for reforming the constitution. The conquest of the Commonwealth, territorially a much larger country with a bigger population than Sweden, by a relatively small Swedish army demonstrated the superiority of a centralized monarchy over a Poland, drifting towards anarchy. That same system of strong central authority was also behind the rising power of Brandenburg and Russia, both of which greedily looked towards the lands of their neighbour, the Polish Commonwealth.

On the other hand, the treason of the magnates who surrendered the country to the enemy, revealed that their class, embolded and encouraged by the growing chaos in Poland was even prepared to beg assistance from more powerful states in order to preserve its wealth and privileges. The omnipotence of the magnates was the outcome not only of the lack of a strong army and of a well-filled treasury, but also of defects in the parliamentary system. More and more often a minority opposition broke up the debates and in 1652 this was done by a single deputy. For the first time the deputy Władysław Siciński broke up the session of the Seym by his *liberum veto*.

In this situation the Court presented a plan for readjusting the manner of conducting the Seym debates (decisions were to be reached by a two thirds majority) linking this proposal with a bill which would enable the levying of regular taxes on the gentry. At the Seym of 1659 this scheme was, on the whole, favourably received. There was still a long way to its implementation and reliable supporters had to be found to carry it through. Those supporters could not come from the burghers, who were economically weak and not really interested in the affairs of the State. Nor could they come from the gentry, who, despite their enduring antagonism towards the magnates, were so distrustful of change in the existing system of government, that they could hardly be expected to help in the introduction of important reforms.

As at the time of Sigismund III, there remained only the help of a group of magnates (Mikołaj Prażmowski, Stefan Czarniecki, Jan Sobieski, Jan Wielopolski and others) who, in return for high offices and salaries, were inclined to support the plans of the Court. But that group alone was not sufficient, all the more that another (led by Jerzy Lubomirski) stood firmly against the introduction of any change in the political structure of the State.

The advocates of the reforms sought to find allies abroad. Assistance came from France, which was to be won over by the election to the Polish throne of Louis Duke of Condé or his son, during the lifetime of King John Casimir. The election *vivente rege* which would inevitably lead to the strengthening of the royal authority, was regarded by the gentry as an atempt to abolish free elections, one of the cornerstones of the gentry's democracy.

Their indignation and fears were readily exploited by the conservative opposition among the magnates; their wrath against the plot intending to infringe the Golden Freedom was generously subsidized by Vienna and Berlin, two capitals equally concerned to preserve the existing establishment in Poland. In those circumstances the opposition (Jerzy Lubomirski, Jan Leszczyński, Krzysztof Grzymułtowski) easily defeated the reform bills submitted to the Seyms of 1661–1662. The fire-brand magnates secured a powerful ally in the "Holy Union", a confederation of the armed forces. The soldiers confederated in the Union not only demanded their arrears of pay but also openly threatened, that they would cut to pieces all those who would dare to raise their voice in support of the election *vivente rege*.

In spite of everything the Court did not abandon its plans. The first step towards their implementation was to have been the removal of Jerzy Lubomirski, the leader of the opposition, from the political scene. Sentenced by the tribunal of the Seym to banishment and disgrace for high treason he refused to submit to the judgement and raised an open rebellion, the second in seventeenth century Poland.

Fratricidal war has been devastating the country for two years (1665–1666). Lubomirski defeated the royal troops at Mątwy (one of the most bloody battles in the history of seventeenth century Poland), but finally yielded to the King and left for Silesia. His death which occurred shortly afterwards (1667) put an end to further plots, which were simply high treason for Lubomirski planned to cede certain Polish territories to the Elector and to the Emperor both of whom had subsidized his activity. He also conducted negotiations with Muscovy. Lubomirski's own programme did not contain any constructive elements but, on the contrary, aimed at maintaining all the anomalies of the constitution and in this way prevented for a long period to come the possibility of introducing political reforms.

The Lubomirski rebellion was also a severe defeat for the King who therefore abdicated in 1668 and left for France. He died in Paris where King Louis XIV placed at his disposal the revenues derived from eight abbeys (among them Saint-Germain-des-Prés). The election which followed his abdication was a very turbulent one, because both France and Austria spared no effort to force through their candidates. Finally, however, a "Piast", which means a native Pole, was elected in the person of Michał Korybut Wiśniowiecki (son of Jarema). The new King, married to the Austrian Archduchess Eleanor ruled for only four years (1668–1673) which in view of all his deficiencies, was certainly too long. He was completely unable to cope with the internal difficulties of Poland and with the dangers which then threatened the country.

WAR WITH TURKEY

The most serious blow was the invasion of the Turks who strove to reduce the whole of Poland to vassalage. The peace of Poland's southern frontiers which had lasted since 1621, was broken after a lapse of more than forty years. Hetman Pietr Doroshenko, the Cossack leader in the Ukrainian territories on the right bank of the Dnieper, which remained under Polish rule submitted to the Sultan and called upon the Tartars for help. A combined Cossack-Tartar army was crushed by Hetman John Sobieski near Podhajce (1667), but the situation was not favourable for delivering a decisive blow to the invaders. The breaking up of consecutive Seyms, an empty treasury, the soldiers' confederations which time and again had shaken the country, all prevented the organization of a proper defense in the following years. It was not surprising therefore that in 1672 the army of the Sultan Mohammed IV, under the command of the Vizier Köprülü, began a triumphal march penetrating deep into the Commonwealth. Kamieniec Podolski fell to the Turks who then advanced to Lwów.

The victorious Ottoman Porte dictated ignominious conditions of peace which were accepted in Buczacz (1672). The Commonwealth lost the voivodships of Podolia, of Bracław and part of Kiev and had to pay, henceforth, a yearly tribute. This unprecedented humiliation was a healthy shock to the nation; all disputes and quarrels were abandoned for the time being, the Sultan was refused the tribute and taxes were voted for raising an army. John Sobieski was put in command. In 1673 at the battle of Chocim, a place already well known in the history of Polish-Turkish wars, Sobieski achieved a splendid victory over the Ottoman forces. Victory paved him the way to the Polish throne, vacant on the death of Michał Korybut Wiśniowiecki.

After his election (1674) Sobieski resumed the war with Turkey. The truce signed following his victory at Żurawno left, however, Podolia with Kamieniec in the hands of the Turks (1676).

The defensive battles fought in the East did not prevent the King from making attempts to recover Ducal Prussia which had been ceded to Brandenburg by the treaty of Welawa.

The idea was suggested by France. Even before his election Sobieski belonged to the French party, owing in part to the influence of his wife Marie-Casimira, daughter of the Marquis d'Arquien, a woman rather unpopular in Poland where she was generally known under the pet name of "Marysieńka". Sobieski's election was thus a success for Louis XIV. A secret alliance signed in Jaworów (1675) provided that Sobieski was to undertake a campaign against Ducal Prussia, while France, on her part, would prevail upon Turkey to restore to the Commonwealth the territories she had conquered from it. According to the plans of Versailles, the termination of the conflict with Turkey would enable Poland to invade Brandenburg or Austria, with whom France was then at war. These plans were, however, frustrated by the opposition of a group of magnates, who were bribed by Berlin and Vienna, with the aim of deposing Sobieski and giving the Polish crown to a Hapsburg.

Opposition came also from the Holy See and from the Polish clergy at the instigation of Papal diplomacy. The Papacy and Austria wished to prolong the Polish-Turkish war which prevented the Sublime Porte from attacking the Hapsburgs in Hungary, thus making it possible for the Emperor to wage the war against France. The rank and file of the gentry, too, among whom the conception of Poland as the "bulwark of Christianity" was by then firmly established, had no understanding for Poland's vital interests on the Baltic. Most important of all, however, was the fact that Turkey was not disposed to make any territorial concessions. In such circumstances Sobieski was compelled to abandon his plan to conquer Ducal Prussia. He set about instead the construction of an anti-Turkish league, though with scant success. Only at the beginning of 1683 did Austria, when faced with an imminent danger, conclude an alliance with Poland against Turkey. The Ottoman army was then standing at the gates of Vienna threatening the very existence of the Empire.

King John III at the head of an army consisting of 25,000 men hastened to relieve the city. Taking command over the combined Polish, Austrian and German forces, in all some 70,000 men, he defeated the Turkish army of about the same strength, in the battle of Vienna (September 1683). Aside from the *husaria*, Polish heavy cavalry, an important part in the victory was played by the effective cooperation of the other armed services, especially the infantry and artillery. The entire Turkish encampment fell to the victors. The reserve and hostility exhibited by the Emperor towards Sobieski and the Poles were more than compensated by the fame won by Polish arms all over Europe.

Less impressive results were attained in the pursuit of the retreating enemy. In Hungary the Polish army suffered a painful reverse in the battle of Parkany in which the King himself almost met his death. Political realities showed the expediency of the speediest possible conclusion of a peace with the now much weakened Turkey.

THE ANTI-TURKISH LEAGUE

In spite of the need for peace largely as a result of the activities of Papal diplomacy, Poland joined in 1684 the so-called "Holy League", an alliance between Poland, Austria, Venice and the Holy See. This step brought as its consequence new and exhausting conflicts with Turkey and the Tartars, from which only Austria benefited. The latter, striving to prevent the consolidation of Polish influence in the South, abstained from giving Sobieski effective assistance in his campaigns. Sobieski undertook several armed expeditions, in the years 1684–1687, 1689 and in 1691, in Podolia, to recover Kamieniec, and in Moldavia which he wished to conquer for his son Jakub. In order to obtain armed assistance Sobieski signed a military alliance with Muscovy in return for which he finally renounced (1686) all territories ceded to Russia under the truce of Andruszów.

All endeavours to conclude a separate treaty with Turkey were wrecked by the intransigent opposition of the magnates who were instigated, even openly bribed, by Brandenburg and Austria and strongly supported in their attitude by Rome. On the other hand, the Sublime Porte on its part was willing to return to Poland only Podolia with Kamieniec and that solely on the condition that the fortress would be demolished. Peace was eventually signed in Karłowice in 1699, three years after the death of Sobieski (1696). Under its terms Poland regained all the lands lost in 1672, not only Podolia (with Kamieniec), but also the voivodships of Kiev and Bracław.

It is not easy to make a general assessment of Poland's position at the period of her conflicts with Turkey. The wars were certainly an inescapable necessity because they were waged in defense of her national existence. On the other hand, the Commonwealth played only a secondary role in them, pulling Austria's chestnuts out of the fire. The decline of the country's political power, internal chaos and obstruction of the King's initiatives by the magnates at foreign instigation, resulted in the Commonwealth's diverting to herself the impact of a part of the Tartar-Turkish forces without gaining corresponding advantages, but opening the way for Austria to proceed to the conquest of almost all Hungary.

For the campaigns waged in the rear of the enemy, serving only to enhance the forces of Austria, a future partitioning Power, Poland payed with her military and economic exhaustion. Poland's situation contrasted sharply with the growing might of her neighbours. Fully aware of the fact that their strength lay partly in the weakness of the Commonwealth, the neighbouring states never relaxed their efforts at obstructing all attempts to consolidate the royal authority in Poland. Several secret treaties were signed between Austria and Russia (1675), Sweden and Brandenburg (1686 and 1696) and Austria and Brandenburg (1686), in which the contracting parties pledged themselves to work jointly to prevent the introduction of reforms in Poland and, specifically, the strengthening of the royal authority.

Who would sit on the Polish throne became increasingly a matter for the decision of foreign powers. The events which accompanied the election of 1697 were not only evidence of the decline of Poland's international position, but also a warning that her very existence as an independent State was in jeopardy.

ECONOMIC AND POLITICAL CRISIS

Protracted wars waged on the territory of the Commonwealth brought in their wake great devastation, not always caused by foreign armies. Moreover, as a result of these unsuccessful wars, the size of the State was reduced from 990,000 sq.km in 1634 to 730,000 sq.km in 1667 (following the truce of Andruszów), not to mention the temporary loss of Podolia and part of the Ukraine occupied by Turkey from 1672 to 1699. The population also decreased considerably; in the middle of the seventeenth century it was about 10 million, but the Cossack wars, the Swedish invasion and the important territorial losses reduced that figure by almost a half. Only towards the end of the seventeenth century did the population begin to increase again as a result of the period of stabilization attained during the reign of John Sobieski.

The decline of population and the devastations of wars and natural disasters brought about a marked fall in agricultural production: arable land reverted to waste, the number of livestock was greatly reduced and yields per acre fell considerably. The basic reason for this decline of agriculture, however, was the prevailing system of the manor farm economy based on serf labour and the serfs' consequent lack of interest in increasing production. Wars only hastened and intensified the process of decline in agriculture, but they were not themselves the essential cause of it.

The owners of the manor farms sought to improve the situation by imposing new dues upon the serfs. The number of days of labour service was raised and other burdens increased, like the manorial monopolies, rents and taxes. The peasants replied by mass flight, refusal to work and, in some parts of the country, even armed resistance. In addition to the peasants' rebellions 1651 mention should be made of the rising on the royal estates in the southwestern part of the Cracow voivodship (1669–1672), in the Podhale, in the Kurpie region (on the frontiers of Ducal Prussia) and on the Suraż estate in the Podlasie. Thus, as before, the main centres of peasant opposition were primarily on the royal estates.

Simultaneously with the ruthless suppression of the peasant rebellions, steps were taken by the owners of the manorial farms ruined by war to reduce the amount of labour dues and also to replace them to some extent, by rents. These changes were, however, of a transitory character and were introduced with a view to facilitating post-war reconstruction and to shifting its cost to the peasants who were also to bear the risk involved in the production of grain, the demand for which was steadily falling. Another reason for the greater use of rents instead of labour dues was the growing resistance of the peasants. Rents were introduced, above all, in the estates of the magnates, including Lithuania and Byelorussia, and in the royal estates. But those measures did not yield the expected results. A consequence of the prevailing shortage of labour and of the low level of cultivation was the recourse to extensive agriculture.

In this situation only the large estates of the magnates could be kept intact and only they could expand, mainly at the expense of the middle gentry, who lacking money for the economic reconstruction were compelled to sell them or to transform them into leaseholds. The extension of the magnates' latifundia strengthened their influence in the political life of the country. The clients of the magnates, the lesser and middle gentry, not only served loyally in the administration of their estates, at their courts and in their private armies, but also defended the interests of their protectors in the Seym and local diets.

It is no wonder, therefore, that out of 44 Seyms convened during the second half of the seventeenth century, 15 were broken up and two ended without passing any laws. The most important decisions were taken at local diets at which the magnates had control of the votes; their creatures broke up the sessions of the local diets and of the royal tribunals, questioning the legal status of the deputies. In the courts of law bribery became the chief instrument influencing the verdicts and the magnates brought pressure to bear on the judges to pass sentences favourable to their clients. The efforts of the middle gentry, who suffered most from these abuses, to restore order in the tribunals by way of legislative action were in vain. The competence of the courts of first instance, the castle courts (which examined the cases of the gentry but had their seats in towns) were extended. But in spite of the obviously biassed and corrupt administration of justice and the difficulties systematically encountered in carrying out a sentence the gentry willingly went to law and spared no effort and expense in protracted litigation.

The decentralization of the Commonwealth was reflected also in the fiscal system. There was no central supervising fiscal organ. The revenues of the treasury fell largely as a result of the monetary crisis brought about by the issue, after the Swedish wars, of almost valueless coins to the amount of twenty million zlotys, leading to a devaluation. From 1688 on the royal mints virtually ceased to function.

The treasury sought to find a source of revenue in new taxation. Instead of maintaining the army in winter quarters on the royal estates, a levy was imposed, the so-called *hiberna*, which was to cover the costs involved. Payment of the armed forces caused increasing difficulties a solution of which was sought by the introduction of a poll tax. The tax proved very unpopular with the gentry who in the end managed to get it rescinded.

Lack of money very adversely affected the numbers and the proficiency of the army. Cavalry continued to play the leading role as in the past, and only towards the end of the seventeenth century did the scales turn in favour of infantry and dragoon units. Apart from the *husaria*, cavalry distinguished by an armour to which were attached metal wings, which had always been dreaded by the Swedes and the Turks, light cavalry units, more mobile and less expensive to maintain were introduced. Sobieski reformed the structure of the infantry and raised its number considerably. He was the first Polish ruler who gave up altogether the service of the general levy, being fully aware of its doubtful military value.

Sobieski knew also how to coordinate the action of infantry and artillery whose effectiveness and fire power was greatly increased during the Swedish wars. His efforts to build a strong professional army met, however, with the resistance of the gentry who feared lest such an army would be used to increase the power of the Crown. Their fears were further intensified by the social composition of the army in which many people of plebeian origin not only served in the ranks but even held commissions. The peasants provided most of the infantry, while in the dragoon regiments there were many burghers even among the officers. The fact that the townspeople were eager to enlist in the armed forces was due not only to their patriotism, which they proved beyond any doubt during the Swedish invasion, but also to the economic decline of the towns and the shrinking possibility of finding employment there. The destruction of war reduced the population of Warsaw, Poznań and Cracow by half and losses were not made good even after the end of hostilities.

It was only then that the towns began to feel the impact of a manorial farm economy based on serf labour. The impoverished peasant bought less and less and the noblemen engaged in the export of grain made their purchases abroad or in Gdańsk. This inevitably led to the decline of both the urban trade and crafts. Manorial and rural crafts were serious competition to the craftsmen. Another reason for the decline of Poland's foreign trade was that the centre of international commerce had shifted to the Atlantic which was, the main route for overseas trade with the colonies, whereas Poland's main commercial interest lay in the Baltic. The mining of lead, silver, copper and salt declined considerably, the latter chiefly because of smuggling from abroad.

RELIGIOUS PROBLEMS

The deepening economic and political crisis caused a mounting wave of intolerance among the gentry. Those responsible for the prevailing ills were sought not only abroad but also at home, chiefly among the "heretics" who were continually accused of conspiring with the enemy. After the banishment of Arians (1658) a law was passed which made the abandonment of the Catholic faith a capital offence (1668). "Disloyalty" among the Catholics was enthusiastically hunted down. A Lithuanian nobleman, Kazimierz Łyszczyński, was even beheaded for his alleged, or real, atheism (1689). The influence of the Greek Orthodox Church was consistently pushed back. At the turn of the seventeenth century, after the loss of the Ukrainian territories east of the Dnieper, inhabited by adherents of the Greek Orthodox Church, the Catholic Church secured the abolition of the three Ortodox dioceses of Lwów, Łuck and Przemyśl and forced their bishops to join the Greek-Catholic Church, in communion with Rome.

The role of the clergy in the public and private life of the gentry had greatly increased. Indeed, a priest was the noblemen's companion from the cradle to the grave. The episcopate exerted a strong influence on home and foreign policy guarding, above all, their own interests as well as those of the Hapsburgs and the Holy See. An example is the confessor of King John III, the Italian Jesuit Maurizio Carlo Vota. The victory of the Counter-Reformation also adversely influenced the quality and learning of the clergy.

It is characteristic that Catholic thought in Poland expressed in polemical works, theological treatises and in preaching, flourished at the time of the struggles and disputes with the Protestants and as long as these struggles were not conducted by administrative coercion. As the Catholic Church gradually gained power and influence, and consequently greater freedom of action, it ever more frequently resorted to open pressure. Polemics were replaced by burning the heretical books, arguments gave way to insults and oral discussions—to massacres of the heretics. The victory of the Counter-Reformation submerged Catholic thought in inertia and quietism.

The numerous theological treatises, which then appeared, were only compilations and the contemporary disputes on the subject of divine grace and free will, which preoccupied Europe, generally did not reach Poland. Instead vast numbers of prayer books, moral dissertations and lives of the Saints were printed containing few original thoughts and often drawing upon medieval writings. The art of preaching could boast of only one prominent representative, the Jesuit Tomasz Młodzianowski, a writer of many works on theology, philosophy and ascetism.

The remaining preachers were a long way behind the standards of Skarga. They strove in the pulpit most of all to attain surprising effects by the use of a very elaborate manner of speech and strange comparisons. Polish words were intermingled with Latin, examples from Greek mythology were quoted as often as those from the Holy Scriptures. All this indicated a trend to achieve the exaggerated and purely theatrical effects, so typical of Baroque culture.

SARMATIAN BAROQUE

The Baroque which appeared in the West during the second half of the sixteenth century, came into its own in the Polish Commonwealth only at the outset of the following century. Its features were on the one hand a marked similarity with the European Baroque, for example, in its identical striving for an effective accumulation of contrasts, colours and decorative detail, and on the other, a distinctly regional manner of artistic expression and of customs differentiating it from the Italian or French Baroque. This separateness, which has led some historians to speak of a Slavonic Baroque, was expressed among other things in the orientalization of artistic tastes that became apparent in the decorative arts, in dress and interior decoration. These oriental influences in Poland were the outcome not only of the many contacts with Turkey, the Tartars and Muscovy, but also of the partial shifting of the centre of gravity in the cultural sphere from Little Poland and Great Poland, the ethnically Polish lands, eastwards to the Ruthenian and Lithuanian territories, now rapidly becoming Polonized, though this was restricted to the ruling classes only. From those eastern provinces came many prominent figures of the Polish Baroque—writers, scholars and artists. There, arose also the palatial residences of the Radziwiłłs, Czartoryskis, Potockis, Sapiehas, Wiśniowieckis and Lubomirskis, which constituted the centres for their patronage of the arts, made possible by the political and economic power of this class. Whereas in the West the royal courts, the ducal palaces and the towns were the main centres of Baroque culture, in Poland the order was reversed—the primary role in this respect was played by the manors of the gentry and the residences of the magnates and only afterwards by the royal court and towns. Political decentralization was accompanied by the decentralization of cultural life. This did not mean that the townspeople were not affected by the Baroque culture, and did not contribute to its development. From this point of view the influence of the Baroque on the community was probably broader than the earlier impact of the Renaissance.

The Baroque in Poland coincided with the period of gradual disintegration of social and economic life and, from the middle of the seventeenth century, with the political disasters which befell the Commonwealth. These events did not have an immediate effect on the Baroque culture and, until about the time of the Swedish invasion, it would be unjust to speak of a cultural regression in Poland. It was undoubtedly a qualitatively different period, which, however, did not mean that it was any worse than the preceding one. It would also be incorrect to identify completely the Baroque with the Counter-Reformation. Catholicism which triumphed in Poland certainly did leave its imprint upon it, but Baroque culture also embraced Protestant circles, influencing their literature and even the way of life of the dissenters. The cultural contacts with the West endured the longest and thus they became an important intermediary in bringing Baroque culture to Poland. As a result of their common social level and interests the Catholic magnates, like Krzysztof Opaliński or Aleksander Koniecpolski, could easily find a common language with the representatives of the Arian élite.

The Baroque period was, however, marked by certain contradictory trends. The growing religious irrationalism was intermingled with the rationalist attitudes expressed in the doctrine of the Polish Brethren, and the mounting fanaticism, with demands for tolerance advanced not only by the dissenters, but also by some Catholics who opposed religious persecution. The general trend of development was, however, clearly indicative of a growing cultural isolation displacing an open-minded attitude towards other ideologies, nations and civilizations.

The regressive tendencies in cultural life were enhanced by a reshaping of the Sarmatian myth. It attained its fullest and most mature form in the course of the seventeenth century, but had simultaneously a different ideological content than previously. It was above all the gentry which at this time looked for historic links with the ancient Sarmatians who, allegedly by conquering the local tribes, became the founders of the ruling class. Upon the gentry lay the historic duty to defend Christianity. The gentry, and only they were identified with the Polish nation, excluding other social classes, allegedly of different origin, from the national community. This concept of a nation of gentry, based on the community of a privileged estate, merged into a single entity the Polish nobility with the Polonized Ruthenian and Lithuanian gentry. This usurpation which contradicted the old Renaissance concept of a nation, proved to be an obstacle also to the process of the Polonizing the burghers of Royal Prussia.

If in the eastern borderlands even the burghers accepted, in part, the Polish language and culture, the population of Prussian towns remained, on the whole, faithful to the German way of life. At the same time, however, the inhabitants of Gdańsk, Toruń and Elbląg preserved deep loyalty to the Commonwealth, which was proved during the Swedish invasion. The existing political and economic ties made them feel closer to the people of Poland than to their compatriots in Brandenburg or Bavaria. One could speak, in this connexion, of the beginnings of the formation of a separate new-Prussian nationality, analogous with Belgian or Dutch. The continuation of the process was hindered by the Sarmatian myth which admitted to the Polish nation only the Prussian nobility and rejected those who could not boast of armorial bearings.

"Sarmatism" was not only a way of life, an original blending of Western and Eastern cultures. It also became an ideology. Its predominant feature was intolerance of other cultural, political and religious beliefs, an intolerance which clearly reflected the megalomania of the gentry who were convinced of their superiority not only over other social classes in Poland but even over other nations. The conviction grew among them that nothing could be learned from foreigners, because the system prevailing in Poland was perfection itself. This opinion implied that the foreigners for this reason sought to plot not only against the existence of the Commonwealth, but also against the freedom, the rights and the incomes of its inhabitants. Hence in the seventeenth century, a straight path led towards a growing xenophobia. Among the lower strata of the Polish community, especially among the peasants and in small townships, belief had spread about a devil dressed in a foreign, mostly German costume. As the popular tale had it, the devil ruled over witches who brought pestilence upon animals and death and illness upon people. Prosecutions for witchcraft which came to Poland from Protestant Germany, increased in frequency towards the end of the seventeenth century. Their victims were, as a rule, women of peasant and urban origin, but never noblewomen, who were protected by their class privileges. Royal privileges also guarded the Jews who enjoyed in Poland personal freedom and commercial rights. The Jews had their self-government exercised by the Jewish communities (*kahals*), and, for certain cases, their own courts of law. During the Renaissance period Polish Jews attained considerable prosperity, their cultural élite attained high standards of scholarship and could boast of such writers as Isaac of Troki, polemicist on questions of religion. During the seventeenth century Jewish communities in Lithuania sent rabbis to their co-religionists in the Netherlands, where they were highly esteemed for their piety and expert knowledge of the Talmud. The Cossack wars decimated the Jewish communities in the eastern areas of the Commonwealth, and the subsequent economic decline of the country undermined the prosperity of Jewish merchants and craftsmen.

LITERATURE AND ARTS

The effects of the growing intolerance and susceptibility among the ruling class found their reflection in the literature of these times. Its most valuable and boldest works were left unpublished; for this reason the seventeenth century is remembered as the century of literature circulated in manuscript. But the literary output of this period should not be judged by the standard of the devotional and panegyrical works published in large editions. Though the latter constituted almost one third of all publications which had been printed during the seventeenth century, nevertheless side by side with it there appeared poetical works of great value. Their authors came from among the Arians and circles close to the Arians (Wacław Potocki, Zbigniew Morsztyn and Jan Andrzej Morsztyn) as well as from among orthodox Catholics (Maciej Sarbiewski and Samuel Twardowski) who placed their pens at the service of the Counter-Reformation. The literature of the middle classes, especially at the beginning of the seventeenth century, contained many elements of social criticism (Sebastian Klonowic, Sebastian Petrycy of Pilzno, Szymon Szymonowic). Though not very well known, there was an anonymous literature of plebeian origin which in a sharply realistic manner described the exploitation of the peasants, the cruelties of the soldiery and the growing poverty, in a word, the progressive disintegration of the Commonwealth. The constitutional system was praised by Andrzej Maksymilian

Fredro in his *Maksymy* which were, for that reason, very popular with the gentry. Another author, Stanisław Herakliusz Lubomirski, criticized the system viewing with scepticism any possibility of its improvement. Numerous journeys, military adventures and experiences of the vicissitudes of life gave rise to a profusion of memoirs which appeared in the course of the seventeenth century. This literary form reached its climax in the memories of Jan Chryzostom Pasek who eloquently described the turbulent life and the narrowmindedness of an average nobleman of those days.

A realistic picture of contemporary customs and moods was painted by the theatre. This is evident not so much in the court theatre which mostly staged adaptations of foreign plays and dramas (in 1662 the Polish première of Corneille's *Cid* was held in Warsaw), as the urban theatres patronized by schools or towns. The truth about the situation in Poland, often a bitter truth, especially for the gentry, was brought to light on the stage of Jesuit school theatres which had at their disposal many able dramatists, the most outstanding of whom was Grzegorz Knapius.

The increasingly important position, of the lords spiritual and temporal found expression in the erection of new castles and palaces on their latifundia, as for example in Rytwiany by the Opaliński family, in Leszno by the Leszczyńskis, in Krzyżtopór by the Ossolińskis, in Łańcut by the Lubomirskis or in Kielce by the Bishop of Cracow. Their construction was accompanied by a flourishing development of sculpture and painting. Sepulchral sculpture, which continued to be under the influence of Dutch art (its exponents were Wilhelm and Abram van den Blocke and Sebastian Sala), as well as portrait painting served to depict the wealth and social importance of the founder. There appeared, too, a type of Sarmatian portrait painting of the school of M. Kober, Stefanowicz and others in which the graphic value gave way to a broad, and smooth coloured plane to portray accurately the magnate's attire in all its finery.

Yet side by side with the attempt to enhance the splendour of the family, portrait painting tried to achieve a true likeness of the subject. The burghers likewise were interested in having their portraits painted and the middle gentry honoured their ancestors by having their portraits painted on the coffins.

The triumph of the Counter-Reformation brought about the construction of many new churches and monasteries whose interiors were richly decorated with sculptures and Baroque painting. The flowering of ecclesiastic, Baroque architecture, the foremost examples of which were the St. Peter's and St. Pauls' Church in Cracow and St. Casimir Church in Wilno, owed its origin mostly to the Jesuits. Often old Gothic churches were reconstructed and given new external decorative elements. Sometimes they were enlarged by the building of new aisles (examples of such a reconstruction can be seen in the churches in Przeworsk, Szczebrzeszyn, Leżajsk and Kazimierz Dolny).

A notable builder of those times was Tylman of Gameren, who constructed the Krasińskis' Palace in Warsaw. The theory of architecture was represented by Stanisław Solski and Adam Freytag. The royal court was an important centre of the arts, primarily because of its patronage of the theatre and painting. The Italian Master Tomaso Dolabella worked in Poland during this period and under the patronage of the Vasas.

EDUCATION AND LEARNING

The high standard of non-conformist education, above all of the Arians (Raków) and the Bohemian Brethren with their Academy in Leszno (where one of the teachers was the famous Jan Ámos Komenský) reached only a minor part of the dissenting gentry. The majority of the Catholic gentry sent their children to Jesuit colleges, whose large network covered the country. The level of these colleges, was tolerably high in the beginning but declined gradually in the second half of the seventeenth century. The situation in the Jesuit Academy in Wilno (founded in 1578), and in the Academy of Zamość, established in 1595 by the great Jan Zamoyski, was no better.

In their efforts to gain control over university education the Jesuits encountered serious opposition from the Cracow Academy. In that school, too, despite its undoubted achievements during the first years of the seventeenth century, scholasticism was gradually gaining the upper hand and theology began to take precedence over the sciences. In this situation young noblemen, both Protestant and Catholic, preferred to pursue their studies at foreign universities, in Italy, France, the Netherlands and, to a lesser extent, in Germany. Higher education in Poland was provided mainly for commoners. Visits to foreign countries assumed a different character from the tours undertaken during the preceding century. The gentry were now more concerned, as can be seen in numerous diaries of these journeys, with acquiring a general Polish and a superficial knowledge of the world, its people and its customs rather than with a systematic education. Yet these voyages, too, came to an abrupt end with the Swedish Wars.

The "Deluge" was a dividing line in the development of Polish learning. Up to middle of the seventeenth century Polish learning continued to make creative contributions to knowledge. To some extent it developed parallel with the achievements of west European learning which, after the period of negation and destruction, so characteristic of the Renaissance, turned in the following century to constructive thoughts and ideas. The numerous polymaths of the West found a worthy counterpart in Poland in the person of Szymon Starowolski, author of works on history, politics, geography and war. Historiography likewise developed. Though its general conclusions and findings were largely erroneous and its main aim was to embroider the

Sarmatian myth, it nevertheless reveals evidence of a high standard. Apart from research into Poland's history (Wespazjan Kochowski and Jan Rudowski), the philosophy of history induced a wider interest in religious questions (Stanisław Lubieniecki) and in the study of the development of learning (Jan Brożek).

Learning, in fact, became the domain of the urban middle class whose representatives distinguished themselves in philology (Grzegorz Knapius), mathematical sciences (Jan Brożek, Stanisław Pudłowski), philosophy and logic (Sebastian Petrycy of Plzen, Adam Burski). Middle class scholars like Jan Jurkowski and Sebastian Petrycy approved of the Court's attempts to strengthen the powers of the monarch and to reform the administration with the view to limiting decentralization and putting an end to the lawlessness of the magnates.

The progress of learning and culture was hampered by the economic and political setbacks experienced by Poland. Attempts to rebuild the country after the havoc of the "Deluge" yielded only meagre results. In the second half of the seventeenth century, one can already discern the beginnings of decay of Polish culture. Yet it would be risky to make any hasty generalization. Even such people as Wojciech Tylkowski who wrote nonsensical tracts of a pseudo-philosophical character had merit in the field of mechanics and theory of agriculture.

The Counter-Reformation played its part also in the decline of Polish learning. It regarded every bolder achievement of scientific research almost as a heresy. The Counter-Reformation hampered the free flow of scholarly thought, broke all contacts with the Protestant world and forbade even university professors to read books placed on the *Index Librorum Prohibitorum*.

The universal lack of interest in scholarly research had a decidedly adverse effect. Neither the magnates nor the Court showed any concern for promoting scientific learning and by providing scholars with means to pursue their studies at leisure. Men of learning no longer enjoyed the respect of the community, a phenomenon which had first become apparent towards the end of the sixteenth century, higher education was held in contempt and considered unneccessary by the mass of the gentry. They had a purely utilitarian approach to learning from which they demanded enough to help them manage their financial affairs, or show their eloquence during debates in the Seym or the local diets. Legal education was acquired not at the universities but solely by working under experienced jurists.

The growing difficulties did not, however, stop the spread of Polish cultural influences eastward and westward. This influence was particularly marked in Russia and the Ukraine where Polish literature found eager translators, and Polish painting and music were widely followed and admired. Polish Culture also reached Rumanian lands (Valachia and Moldavia). Less impressive was the impact of Polish culture in the West. The rapid development of education and technology there created a gap between Poland and the West which was to be only partially closed in the period of Enlightenment.

Nevertheless it should be noted that the works of Arian philosophers, especially the monumental *Bibliotheca Fratrum Polonorum* published by the exiled scholars in Amsterdam (from 1665), met with a considerable response in England, Germany and France. Ideas propounded by such Arian writers as Jonasz Schlichting, Samuel Przypkowski, Jan Crell and Andrzej Wiszowaty who advocated a rational approach to matters of religion and religious toleration based on the separation of Church and State had some influence on the thinkers of the early Enlightenment. John Locke, Isaac Newton and Pierre Bayle held similar views, though on a number of points they disagreed with the Arians.

In the seventeenth century, the Silesians constituted a comparatively large group in the Arian movement. From their ranks came such vigorous leaders and talented writers as Szymon Pistorius, Joachim Pastorius and Tomasz Pisecki. Students from Silesia attended dissenter schools in Toruń, Raków and Leszno. Works by Polish poets and writers were widely read in the schools of Byczyna, Kluczbork and Wołczyn, thus maintaining the tradition of good Polish in these areas. The works of the great poet of the Polish Renaissance, Jan Kochanowski, translated by Marian Opitz, were especially popular. The mainstay of Polonism in Silesia were the burghers and not the gentry, most of whom were by that time already Germanized. Polish literary works created in Silesia expressed the thoughts and ideas of the burghers glorifying productive effort, like Walenty Rożdzieński extolling the toil of the foundry workers in *Officina ferraria,* or Adam Gdacius criticizing the vices of the nobles, their laziness and drunkenness, and preaching attachment to the land of the fathers from which they were separated by the present frontiers. Szymon Pistorius thus wrote of his native Opole: "When thou joineth with Poland, that bounteous and flourishing land, we shall all rejoice together with thee at the restoration of thy former condition".

Strong cultural ties existed also between the Commonwealth and the Polish element in Ducal Prussia. These ties were maintained above all by dissenters who went to study in Königsberg. On both sides of the border, identical hymn books were in use and successive generations were educated on Polish editions of the Holy Scripture. Polish dictionaries, grammars and readers were published in Königsberg. In the second half of the seventeenth century these contacts had slackened, to grow stronger again with the arrival of Arian exiles (Zbigniew Morsztyn, Samuel Przypkowski and others) and also as a result of the ceaseless efforts of the Prussian gentry to throw off the detested yoke of the "Great Elector"—Frederick William.

Chapter X
THE CRISIS OF SOVEREIGNTY (1697–1763)

GENERAL VIEW OF THE EIGHTEENTH CENTURY

Eighteenth century Polish history is usually divided into two contrasting periods: the "Saxon era" (1697–1763) marked by the decline of the Commonwealth, and the reign of Stanisław Augustus (1764–1795), regarded as a period of reforms and the age of Enlightenment, but which was also the period of partitions. There has been a tendency to link the reign of Stanisław Augustus with the nineteenth century rather than with the history of the Polish Commonwealth and to consider the year 1764 as marking the end of one era and the beginning of another.

The second half of the eighteenth century undoubtedly brought a change in the rhythm of Polish history; crucial and dramatic events occurred which resulted in "the revival of the Nation and the downfall of the State". The problem of "the Old and the New", of the end and the beginning in a continuous historical process, is usually an intricate affair but in this case the end stands out with exceptional, glaring clarity; it is the end of the Polish-Lithuanian State. The era of Stanisław Augustus was the last act in a political drama, in which the relations between Poland and her neighbours, with Russia in particular, provide the central theme. From the same point of view the problem of the beginning appears in a clear relief. The inter-dependence of Russian and Polish history points to the early eighteenth century as the crucial period. In the sixteenth and seventeenth centuries, the two Powers competed for ascendancy in eastern Europe and for domination over Byelorussia and the Ukraine, with the scales turning now in favour of one and now in favour of the other neighbour. They were two sovereign Powers in which the ruling classes had developed two diametrically opposing types of state: the centralized monarchy of the Tsars and the oligarchic Commonwealth of Poland. From the middle of the seventeenth century Russia had gained the upper hand, but Polish-Russian relations had not yet become the decisive factor in the history of the Polish-Lithuanian State and did not affect its internal affairs. With the reign of Peter I the situation changed fundamentally. Russia entered into the period of great-power development, while Poland sank into anarchy and passed through a period of crisis with the result, that the Poles could no longer control their own internal affairs. The Commonwealth opened the door wide to foreign political influence. During the reign of Peter I, Russian influence proved most important and, although weaker under succeeding rulers, it was to become decisive under Catherine II.

The uneven development of Poland and of her neighbours with regard to financial and military potential and the degree of political independence, left a distinct mark on Poland's history throughout the whole century, from the Northern War until the third, and last, partition of 1795. This was the background to the dramatic struggle for the reform and reconstruction of the Commonwealth in the era of the Enlightenment. The leaders in the second half of the eighteenth century had to bear the burden of the Saxon era.

THE PERSONAL UNION OF SAXONY AND POLAND

Sobieski's persistent efforts to secure the throne for his son ended in failure. Prince Jakub and the Queen-Dowager Marie-Casimira ("Marysieńka") did not enjoy popularity. Apart from the dislike of the Sobieskis the concept of a Polish candidate was undermined by the jealousies among the magnates of whom more than one were themselves aspiring to the crown. The interregnum of 1696–1697, disturbed by the mutinies in the army demanding arrears in pay and by an attempt at breaking-up the Convocation Seym, was dominated by the call to exclude a "Piast" from the throne. Quite a number of foreign candidates came forward. The odds were in favour of the French Duke of Conti whom Louis XIV supported with large sums of money. The seriousness of the French candidature induced the opponents of Versailles (Austria, Russia, Brandenburg, England and Holland) to a coordination action on behalf of the strongest opposing candidate, the Elector of Saxony. Peter I's position was of particular importance. For the first time Russia tipped the scale in a Polish election. In spite of the fact that the Frenchman was elected by a majority vote, the partisans of the Saxon conducted a second election. Conti had arrived by sea from far-away France to Gdańsk, but the candidate elected by the minority had himself crowned in Cracow (15 September, 1697). Faced with a *fait accompli,* the nation eventually accepted the Saxon King. (The final formalities were settled by the "Pacification Seym" of 1699). The Roman Curia played its part also because the head of the arch-Lutheran Wettin dynasty recognized that "Warsaw was worth a Mass" and became Roman-Catholic.

The Elector Frederick Augustus I who, as King of Poland, assumed the name of Augustus II, hoped to create a great power under his sceptre. Sovereign ruler of Saxony, he expected that the Electorate would provide the means which the elective kings had been hitherto lacking to curb the Golden Freedom. Industrialized Saxony and agricultural Poland were to complement each other economically to the advantage of the royal treasury. The territory separating the two countries (Silesia or a part of it) could be acquired by political and dynastic bargains. To safeguard the succession of Poland for the Wettins, dynastic sovereignty first had to be secured in the Danube duchies, Livonia or Courland. Did these ambitious designs present the Commonwealth with a historic opportunity for restoring the Jagiellonian splendour?

The union of Saxony and Poland often incurs unfavourable criticism with the Wettins' dynastic policies incorrectly interpreted in terms of the Teutonic "Drang nach Osten". Undoubtedly, however, Augustus the Strong, a nickname he owed to his unusual physical strength, attempted a task which surpassed his possibilities. If he was to succeed in creating a monarchy with great power status out of the union of a small duchy with an efficient government and a huge oligarchic Commonwealth, he had to break not only the resistance of the Polish gentry and magnates, but also that of the Powers interested in maintaining the *status quo* in central Europe. The Golden Freedom had too many powerful patrons. Augustus II remained up to the end a man of grand designs which he tried to carry out in an adventurous manner. Enmeshed in complex Polish and international issues, the higher he aimed the deeper he sank. As a last resort he was ready to propose a partition of Poland to his neighbours, provided he could at that price keep a part of the country under an sovereign and hereditary monarchy. During the reign of Augustus II, the idea of the Polish-Saxon union fell into discredit for this reason.

His successor abandoned these ambitious plans. To Augustus III (1733–1763) and his Saxon Court, the Polish crown meant a royal title for the Wettins, exalting them above the princes of the Empire. It enabled them to exploit the royal estates and the country's economic resources and to dispense sinecures. The Commonwealth was otherwise abandoned to its fate. Augustus III was the incarnation of the ideal shadow king, so dear to many Sarmatians. Augustus II attempted to rule from Warsaw; his son ruled only from Dresden. Up to that time, the monarch, in spite of all the limitations upon his power, had remained the keystone of the Commonwealth's political structure and the royal court had been an important institution in the cultural life of the country. After the collapse of Augustus II's ambitions plans, the Polish-Saxon union deprived Poland of that element. Batory could have kept in mind his native Transylvania, as the Vasa could think of Sweden, but these were kings residing in Poland, who identified their destinies strictly with those of the country. The situation which prevailed for 60 years, in which the Saxon kings remained strangers to Poland and absent from the country, was an important factor in the crisis of sovereignty.

THE NORTHERN WAR AND THE STRUGGLE FOR THE CROWN

The peace of Karłowice (1699) marked a turning point in Polish-Turkish relations. The century-long period of wars against the Porte came definitely to a close.

After the conclusion of the peace with Turkey, a party among the magnates believed that the time had come to abrogate the treaty with Russia and to recover the territory beyond the Dnieper. Augustus II tended in the opposite direction. As Elector of Saxony he entered into an alliance with Denmark and Russia aiming at partitioning Sweden's overseas possessions. Livonia was to be the share of the Wettins and not Poland's. It seemed an easy prey, but the surprising victories of Charles XII over the Danish and Russian armies in 1700 brought an unexpected turn to the war. The Swedes forced Denmark to conclude a peace and, taking the offensive, attacked Poland. She was to become the base for the decisive showdown with Russia.

Having routed the Saxon army in Livonia (July 1701), Charles XII entered Courland and demanded that the Commonwealth dethrone Augustus II. Without waiting for an answer, the Swedes occupied Warsaw (May 1702), defeated Augustus in the battle of Kliszów (9 July) and occupied Cracow. The Commonwealth was dragged into the war with Sweden, but it was politically divided and militarily passive. The programme put forward by Charles XII and endorsed by French diplomacy, providing for the deposition of the Saxon, a Polish-Swedish alliance and a joint war against Russia, found support with some of the magnates, but the looting by Swedish troops met with resentment and protest. The majority in consequence stood by Augustus. The Confederation of Sandomierz was formed by the King's side (1702) and a Polish-Russian treaty was signed in 1704, giving Russian forces the right to operate in Commonwealth territory. At the same time, in the territory occupied by Sweden, the Confederation of Środa was formed (1703) and later the General Confederation of Warsaw (1704) which proclaimed an interregnum. On 12 July, 1704 eight hundred of the gentry elected Stanisław Leszczyński King in a camp surrounded by Swedish soldiers. A year later a Polish-Swedish treaty was concluded in Warsaw, giving to the Swedish army rights similar to those which the Treaty of Narva had granted to the Russians. Thus there were two Kings in Poland, two Commonwealths (Leszczyński appointed new ministers and new officers of State) and, what is most important, two foreign protectors and two "auxiliary" armies fighting against each other. The Polish adherents of Augustus and Leszczyński played a secondary role, waging a guerrilla civil war on the fringe of the war between the Powers.

Before engaging in a final showdown with Russia, Sweden tried to consolidate her position in Poland. For this reason Charles XII entered the Electorate in 1706 and extorted from Augustus his abdication in Poland and the withdrawal of Saxony from the war. Leszczyński was recognized as King by most of the Powers, but did not gain general recognition within Poland. The adherents of Augustus deprived of their legal head, remained united under Russian protectorship. Charles XII and Leszczyński established contact with Mazepa, Hetman of Cossacks on the left-bank of the Dnieper. Till now subordinate to Russia, Mazepa aimed at unifying the Ukraine under the suzerainty of the Commonwealth. Relying upon Polish and Cossack help, the Swedes attacked Russia in the summer of 1708. The majority of the Cossacks, however, did not follow Mazepa and remained faithful to the Orthodox Tsar. The help of the Polish army also proved illusory. After an initial success, the Swedish army suffered a crushing defeat at Połtawa on 8 July, 1709. Charles XII and Mazepa fled into Turkish territory, Leszczyński withdrew into Swedish Pomerania and Augustus returned to Poland. The restoration of his rule took place at the General Assembly in Warsaw in 1710.

Meanwhile, Turkey, incited by Swedish and French diplomacy, but influenced in fact by her own designs for the annexation of Ukraine, attacked Russia. Mazepa's successor, Filip Orlik, recognized the suzerainity of the Porte. The combined Turkish, Tartar and Cossack expedition against the Ukraine was repelled by the Russian army, and Tsar Peter I entered Moldavia. There, however, he found himself encircled by the Turks and, threatened with captivity, signed a treaty with the Porte at his camp on the river Prut (23 July, 1711). Russia obtained the peace with Turkey at the price of her pledge to return Asov and not to interfere in Polish and Cossack affairs. This treaty was later to acquire the significance of a Turkish guarantee for Polish "freedom". Its origin in fact lay in Turkey's annexationist aspirations directed against the Ukraine; it was not until 1714 that the Porte officially renounced those aspirations when it recognized Augustus and renewed the peace of Karłowice with the Commonwealth. Annexationist plans were entertained also by the King of Prussia; (the title was assumed by the Elector of Brandenburg in 1701) but they met with Peter I's opposition. From 1710, Poland remained outside major war operations.

The Northern War, with famine and pestilence following in its wake, caused fresh devastation of the country. Though the frontiers of Poland were not affected, the political result of the war was disastrous to the Commonwealth. In Sobieski's time the country though weakened internally managed to accomplish feats of war and enjoyed prestige abroad. At the beginning of the Northern War Poland was still being treated as an equal partner by the Powers. Internal divisions, only superficially healed by the "Pacification Seym", were nevertheless in evidence since the double election. Trouble spots existed in both Lithuania and the Ukraine. The powerful Lithuanian family of the Sapiehas tyrannized the middle gentry to such an extent that a real civil war broke out in 1700. The Sapiehas, defeated in the struggle, turned to Charles XII seeking his intervention and taking the field at the side of the Swedes, while the opposite "republican" party placed itself under the protection of Tsar Peter. After the peace of Karłowice, the oligarchs of

Little Poland had wanted to eliminate the Cossacks within the borders of the Commonwealth. This resulted in a Cossack uprising led by Palij and Samuś (1702) with which the Crown forces could not cope. Tartar or Swedish support was considered but eventually an appeal was made to the Russians, whose help was rated to be the most effective. In this way the Poles themselves were encouraging foreign Powers to interfere in their internal affairs. At the same time, they proved incapable of independent military and political action on the side of either Augustus or Leszczyński.

The constitutional system of the Commonwealth was particularly conducive to acts of violence or foreign pressure under the cover of the legal paraphernalia of a confederation. In territories under the control of the Swedish, Russian or Saxon armies, pseudo-Polish authorities were established. Pressure by threat and corruption were sufficient to produce rival shadow governments with the help of one magnate group or another, and thus to force upon Poland an apparently legal decision. This was the easy lesson learnt by the neighbouring Powers from the experiences of the Northern War.

The balance of power among those Powers had changed. Turkey no longer threatened Poland and went on to the defensive as a result of Austrian and Russian pressure. Sweden, too, after the dazzling successes of Charles XII lost her great power status once and for all. Two new Powers expanded their influence in the Baltic at Sweden's expense : Russia and Prussia. The War of the Spanish Succession, waged at the same time as the Northern War, resulted in pushing away the Hapsburg from the south-west. Thus the aspirations of the dynasty to establish an universal monarchy came to an end. Instead the dynasty concentrated upon the consolidation of its dominions in Europe. As well as the modern Austria, France of Louis XV no longer played the same part in Europe as she had under the reign of the "Roi-Soleil".

From the time of the Northern War onwards, Poland's international situation was determined by three countries : Russia, Austria and Prussia.

THE CONFEDERATION OF TARNOGRÓD AND THE ARBITRATION OF PETER I

From the beginning of his reign Augustus II had been entertaining the idea of an royalist *coup d'état*, but the Northern War frustrated the implementation of these plans for many years. The Seym was not convened from 1703 to 1710 ; the decentralization of the administration therefore proceeded apace and the importance of the local diets, which raised taxes and recruited soldiers, increased. This lamentable state of affairs shocked the gentry out of their quietism. Amidst the misfortunes of war, political confusion and a growing antipathy for the oligarchic ministers, especially for the Hetman whose licence then had reached its climax, the thought of reforming the Commonwealth gripped the mind of the gentry. The spectacle of two rival

Kings claiming the crown discredited still more the authority of the ruler. Let Poland therefore become a true Commonwealth, a republic of the gentry, orderly, capable of defending her frontiers, but peaceful and living in harmony with her neighbours, because Kings, and not the Commonwealth had dragged the country into wars. In the political writings of the time these aspirations were most eloquently expressed by Stanisław Dunin-Karwicki. His programme advocated a strengthening of the Commonwealth's institutions and a curtailing of the royal powers.

Reform was being planned also by Augustus and his Saxon entourage, especially by Field Marshall Jacob Heinrich Flemming, but in the opposite direction to that of the gentry. The royal party aimed at introducing a hereditary monarchy and strengthening the government; the Saxon army was to be the main instrument for implementing this programme. At the General Assembly of Warsaw (1710), the two opposing trends did not, as yet, clash. In the short run, the chief opponents of both the Crown and the republican reformers, were the oligarchy of magnates and the power of the Hetmen, who were the dominating factor in the State.

The oligarchy was interested in maintaining the constitutional *status quo*. Its key-position lay in its power of mediating and holding the balance between royal authority and gentry republicanism. The scale turning one way or the other would curb their power to mediate and subordinate the magnates to the authority of the monarch or to that of an orderly Commonwealth. Let the King therefore keep his prerogatives, in particular his power to dispense patronage, so profitable to the magnates and let him use these prerogatives to keep the Golden Freedom in check. Let the liberty of the gentry, with the help of the magnates as mediators, at the same time prevent the King from strengthening his authority. If, however, the balance of power were endangered, and arbitration by the magnates proved insufficient to maintain that balance, then the help of foreign arbiters should be invited.

The Hetmen's opposition at the Seym of 1712 frustrated the attempts of the King to cooperate with the reformist group of the gentry. Augustus II resorted to drastic measures. The Turkish danger furnished the pretext for bringing Saxon troops into Poland in 1713. The behaviour of these troops was provocative. The Saxons sought to provoke a crisis, the pacification of which would allow them to establish a new order. The first riot of the gentry broke out in Little Poland in 1714. Within a year fighting had flared up on a larger scale. In addition to the gentry, peasants also joined the drive against the Saxons. These movements swept the whole country and a General Confederation was formed in Tarnogród (25 November, 1715) under the presidency of Stanisław Ledóchowski. The standing army ranged itself with the Confederation. The gentry movement was directed not only against the Court and the Saxon troops but against the Hetmen as well. Augustus II was again threatened with dethronement. Once again, however, the decisive role was to be played by a foreign power.

Augustus II, having secured his position on the throne with Peter I's aid, now aimed at shaking off the Russian tutelage. Negotiations for an alliance with France and an attempt to destroy the Russian party, headed by the Hetmen, were means to this end. Russia, therefore, excited the opposition against the King and had her share in inspiring the Confederation of Tarnogród. While both the provocations of Saxon troops and the Russian inspiration had played a part in initiating this movement, its momentum exceeded the intentions of those who had provoked or inspired it. It was the last spurt of gentry democracy, which engaged in fighting on two fronts: against the anti-Russian King, and against the Hetmen connected with Russia. The time had come for arbitration. The Hetmen were the first to turn to the Tsar for mediation. The Confederates followed suit and eventually King Augustus also accepted Peter I's mediation.

The Tsar's envoy, Grigory Dolgoruki, acted as mediator in the negotiations between the Court and the Confederates. The negotiations proceeded with difficulty until 18,000 Russian troops entered Poland. From then on, Dolgoruki was the master of the situation and it was through his influence that the treaty of Warsaw was signed and subsequently approved by an one-day Assembly called the Dumb Seym, because no one was permitted to speak, on 1 February, 1717.

Augustus II's Saxon-Polish policy had suffered a decisive defeat. The King was henceforth allowed to keep in Poland only 1200 of his Saxon guards and 6 officers of the Saxon Chancery. The attempt to achieve a closer union of Saxony and Poland was thereby frustrated. The gentry's programme of reforms was partly implemented in fiscal and military matters. Regular taxes were voted to cover 24,000 soldiers' "rations", out of which the officers were to have a fund for themselves. As a result a standing army of only 12,000 men was established. Hetmen authority and the autonomy of the local diets were somewhat reduced. A general amnesty was granted to both Confederates and Saxon soldiers. The restoration of order in military and fiscal affairs would have been a positive step, had not the budget and the credits for military establishment been fixed as if for a secondary state of the German Empire or of Italy, but not for one of Europe's largest countries, surrounded by the greatest military powers of the age. The fiscal and military reform was connected with a curtailment of provincial self-government which was not followed, however, either by a reform of the Seym or by the establishment of a local administration.

The Dumb Seym determined the Commonwealth's system of government for nearly 50 years; as a precedent it was of even greater importance. After Augustus II's grandiose plans and the effort of Tarnogród, a balance between "majesty and freedom" was established for many years, reflected in an atrophy of the legislature. There was, however, a specific reason resulting from the signature of Dolgoruki, the mediator. On the basis of that mediation Russia claimed the right to guarantee the resolutions of the Seym of 1717. The seventeenth century had already seen many agreements by the Powers with regard to Poland's internal affairs. The Russian interpretation of the Warsaw treaty, backed by force, introduced the concept of a foreign guarantee approved by the Commonwealth.

The growth of Russia's power alarmed many European states. Augustus II wished to take advantage of these fears to throw off Peter I's tutelage and regain Livonia. An anti-Russian alliance of England, Austria and Saxony was concluded in Vienna in January 1719. It was intended to draw the Commonwealth into the coalition by playing upon the dissatisfaction of the gentry with the protracted presence of Russian troops in Poland. The attempts of Augustus II to conduct an "emancipation policy" collapsed at the Seyms of 1719-1720 and 1720. The evacuation of Russian forces reassured public opinion and Poland refused to join the anti-Russian league. Not only the opposition of the Hetmen, who were connected for a long time with Russia, but the overwhelming majority of the gentry as well would not hear of another war. Augustus, in his disappointment, began to devise plans for a partition of Poland hoping to strengthen his power in a mutilated country. Peter I not only rejected these plans, but revealed them to the public in Poland. Thus the Tsar, as mediator and guarantor, was now defending the territorial integrity of the Commonwealth and its freedom, that is the existing system of government, and in particular free election. A vast but passive country, demilitarized and neutralized, would ensure peace at Russia's western frontier. To that end Russia concluded a number of treaties guaranteeing Polish liberties and a free election of the king: with Prussia and with Turkey in 1720, with Sweden in 1724 and with Austria in 1726. All these treaties were aimed against Augustus II's plans for the succession.

THE STRUGGLE FOR THE POLISH THRONE

Until the end of his life Augustus II persisted in vast political plans. He aspired to obtain the throne of Courland for the Wettins, which encountered Russia's opposition; as father-in-law of the Archduchess Marie-Josephine, he was counting on a share for Saxony in the division of the Habsburg territories (Silesia) after the death of her uncle, Emperor Charles VI, and he conducted negotiations with France to that end. His principal concern was to secure the succession to the Polish throne for his son. He was playing all the time with the idea of introducing a law making the monarchy hereditary by a *coup d'état*. In view of the resistance of the Commonwealth and of the neighbouring Powers these designs were only day dreams. Augustus also continued to entertain schemes of partition—his last remarks on that subject were uttered as late as three weeks before his death. King Frederick William I of Prussia listened to them with delight, but the collusion of the king-electors were not sufficient to change the existing system of the Powers. Augustus' multifarious negotiations did not inspire the trust of his partners.

The Saxon candidature had no chance of success in a free election in view of the attitude of both the Poles and the Powers. As in 1697, however, the odds suddenly turned in the Saxon's favour because he emerged as the only real contestant worth supporting against the French competitor.

One relic of the Northern War was Stanisław Leszczyński's royal title. Although Leszczyński conducted secret and protracted negotiations with Augustus II on renouncing his claims in return for an adequate compensation, the two parties never reached agreement. Leszczyński was hoping for a change in the international situation and counted on surviving his rival. After the conclusion of a peace between Russia and Sweden, and in the period of growing antagonism between Augustus and Peter I, Stanisław placed his main hopes on Russia. It was elsewhere, however, that he found firm support. France had not given up the idea of revenge for her defeat in the election of 1697. The Orleans faction contemplated obtaining the Polish throne with Russian support. The French Regent, wishing to use Leszczyński's claims for the purpose of his own Polish policy, granted him asylum in Alsace (1719). After the Regent's death, French diplomacy at once put up, in 1724, the candidature of Stanisław whose only daughter Maria was to marry a French royal prince and thereby bring a lateral branch of the Bourbon family closer to the Polish succession. The candidate to Maria's hand was first the Premier Louis Henri de Bourbon, but later it was decided to marry her to King Louis XV himself (1725). From that moment until the death of Augustus II, French diplomacy worked for eight years for Leszczyński's return to the throne.

Never before had a candidature *vivente rege* been prepared so long and so carefully. Ambassador Monti achieved much success in Poland. He effectively counteracted the consolidation of the Saxon's position, chiefly through a systematic disruption of the Seyms, in which French diplomacy cooperated with Russia. France won over to Leszczyński's cause the most influential— and competing—coteries of magnates, the Potockis and Czartoryskis. Stanisław as an anti-King who had been imposed by Sweden, was not popular during the Northern War. As the father-in-law of the King of France and a "Piast" he now gained general sympathy which France was encouraging with large sums of money. The task of French diplomacy in the international field was more difficult. In view of the basic antagonism between France and Austria, a counter-move by the Emperor was to be envisaged. The support of Sweden and Turkey was sought, but these countries were weakened and Turkey was involved in war against Persia. Russia's position was of crucial importance. It was believed in France that with the death of Peter I (1725) the position of Russia as a power would collapse and therefore not too much importance was attached to the negotiations with her. The attempts at a rapprochement did not yield results. The main difficulty consisted in the divergence of interests with regard to Turkey. France had traditionally been a friend of the Porte, while Russia was her principal antagonist, especially after the Baltic problems had been settled. It was also feared in Russia that Leszczyński's return to the throne might contribute to incite an undercurrent of revenge in Sweden. The result was that Russia remained faithful to her anti-Turkish alliance with Austria (1726) which proved to be one of the most durable alliances in the eighteenth century and of particular importance in Poland's international situation.

In 1732, a secret treaty between Russia, Austria and Prussia was signed, the so-called "Treaty of the Three Black Eagles", which excluded the candidature of both the Saxon and Leszczyński. The Powers declared themselves in favour of some neutral candidate, either a "Piast" or the Infant of Portugal. After the death of Augustus II on 1 February, 1733, however, Leszczyński's chances in the royal election proved so overwhelming, that the new Elector of Saxony with a handful of court creatures at his disposal was the only one who could cause a "conflict". He was, of course, unable to achieve anything without the intervention of the Powers. He purchased Russian intervention by promising the Duchy of Courland to the Tsarina Anna's favourite, Biron; with regard to the Emperor, the Elector renounced his rights to the Hapsburg succession and, abandoning his father's policy, guaranteed the Pragmatic Sanction.

The Saxon and Russian armies entered Poland forcing Leszczyński to withdraw to Gdańsk. A handful of nobles under the protection of Russian troops elected Augustus III King and a confederation was formed at his side. On Leszczyński's side the Confederation of Dzików was formed, but Polish military activity was so weak and the superiority of the 30,000 Russians and 10,000 Saxons was so great that hostilities did not assume major proportions. Before the capitulation of Gdańsk, Leszczyński sought shelter in Prussia; Frederick William I broke with the Alliance of the Three Eagles and, though lending no active support to Leszczyński, he nevertheless expected territorial rewards from him. The decision was to be brought about by the European war called the War of the Polish Succession of 1733–1735 and the final peace treaty of 1738.

Under the slogan of defending the freedom of the Polish election, France, Spain and Sardinia attacked Austria. To Spain and Sardinia Leszczyński's cause was, of course, only a pretext; for France it was the object of a political bargain. The victories of French armies on the Rhine and in Italy could not produce a decision on the Vistula. The scant help sent by sea to relieve Gdańsk was of no practical consequence, while more extensive operations in the Baltic zone would have provoked England into joining the war. Under such circumstances the military successes in the West were used to dictate to Austria conditions profitable to France and honourable for Leszczyński. He retained the title of King of Poland for life and received the Duchy of Lorraine which became Queen Maria's dowry. Augustus III was recognized and the "Pacification Seym" of 1736 brought about a normalization of conditions in Poland. The Saxon and Russian troops left the country.

The new King, an indolent ruler of mediocre abilities, was the opposite of his dynamic and adventurous father. The Saxon Minister Brühl governed on his behalf. During Augustus III's reign, the idle King did not infringe the noble liberties and the aspirations of the Court were limited to keeping the Polish throne for the Saxon dynasty. Yet, during the thirty years of Augustus III's reign, the Poles would now and again plan confederations against the King and the Saxon schemes of succession and would contemplate his dethronement. Abroad Stanisław Leszczyński was slow to abandon hopes for his return to the throne, and Louis XV's secret diplomacy would be contriving the *secret du Roi*, aimed at paving the way to Warsaw for the Duke of Conti, the grandson of the French candidate of 1697. First Prussia, later Russia were to dazzle the Polish magnates with expectations of the crown. During the reign of Augustus III the struggle for the throne did not assume such drastic forms as in his father's time, but none the less the precedents of double elections, two rival Kings and dethronements caused the position of the Polish King to be regarded lightly in the opinion of the Commonwealth and of Europe. The succession crisis entered a chronic phase.

DEMILITARIZATION AND NEUTRALIZATION OF THE COMMONWEALTH

The reign of Augustus II saw a series of wars in which the neighbours of the Commonwealth took part. The war of the Polish Succession had not yet ended when the war of Russia and Austria against Turkey (1735–1739) broke out. In 1740–1742 came the First Silesian War which overlapped with the Russian-Swedish War (1741–1743). In 1744–1745 the Second Silesian War was fought, as a campaign subsidiary to the general war of the Austrian Succession (1740–1748). Finally, eight years of peace, were followed by the Seven Years' War (1756–1763). Augustus III, as the Elector of Saxony, took part in the Silesian Wars and in the Seven Years' War. Saxony was twice invaded by Prussia; the Commonwealth remained neutral, but its neutrality was not respected by the belligerents. For the Tsar's army, the way to Balkan and German battlefields led across Poland. It was during the Seven Years' War that Russian troops established themselves in the Commonwealth, especially in Pomerania, for good. Prussian armies repeatedly forced their way into Poland, while Austrian forces did so sporadically. Upon those infringements of their frontiers, the Poles lodged ineffective protests and remained neutral.

The gentry society of the eighteenth century professed anti-militarism and pacifism. It had no thought of territorial expansion. The magnates of the borderlands still nourished feelings of nostalgia for the provinces lost in the East, but since the times of Peter I all talk of "torn away lands" was sheer rhetoric. It was not in Poland but in Saxony that plans were being made for a Silesian "bridge" to connect the Electorate with the Commonwealth (Brühl revived these Silesian designs during the wars with Frederick II). It was outside Poland, too, that plans were born for incorporating East Prussia into Poland in return for a compensation in Byelorussia or the Ukraine for Russia (Bestuzhev's plans of 1745 and 1756). The Poles did not think of expanding or shifting their frontiers, but feared foreign annexation. These fears were, however, not particularly strong. From the experience of the Northern War and the collapse of Augustus II's "grand designs", the conclusion had been drawn that the neighbouring Powers were watching each other with suspicion and would not let plans of partition be carried out. The threat to the fief of Courland alarmed Poland as an expression more of the Wettin's dynastic policy than of Russian expansion. The Poles wished to maintain the territorial *status quo*, protected, as they believed, by Providence, by the Powers and, in the last resort only by the mass-levy.

According to the republican ideology of the gentry the armed forces ought to be strictly for defense. Such had always been the concept of the mass-levy. Contrary to experience, much confidence was still placed in the effectiveness of this anachronistic instrument (the myth of 200,000 armed gentry). A numerous regular army, on the other hand, was considered dangerous as a potential weapon of royal absolutism or despotism of the Hetmen. The hardships suffered during the Northern War at the hands of unpaid marauding soldiers were indelibly inscribed on the memory of the gentry. A large regular army required taxes and recruitment—the gentry were not eager to bear the costs or to release peasant serfs for the army. The problem of taxation was moreover rendered more complex by the abatements granted to the Ukrainian voivodships. These tax reductions, justified by the havoc which those provinces had suffered at the time of the wars with Turkey and of the Cossack risings, were anachronistic by the mid-eighteenth century, but the gentry of the borderlands insisted on their privileges. The people of Great Poland, on the other hand, would not hear of increase in taxes until an equalization of burdens took place. This was the rock on which all plans for an expansion of the army were to founder. An increase in the army was also dependent on the changing international situation. It was to strengthen not only the Court or the Hetmen, but also the Powers with which the Court or the Hetmen wished to enter into alliance. Every plan to increase the army met with the opposition not only of the internal political forces, but also of foreign political factors.

Before the outbreak of the Northern War, the Commonwealth had an army which in principle consisted of 25,000 men, but was only 18,000 strong in reality, a trifle compared to other armies of the time. Even more important was the fact that in the course of the eighteenth century, the strength of armies elsewhere was constantly growing, whereas in Poland the opposite occurred. The Seym of 1717 carried out a reduction of the army to just over ten thousand, with the outdated old-style Polish cavalry amounting to almost a half of it. An attempt to increase the army, made at the Seym of 1718, was blocked by the opposition of the Hetmen and was not resumed again until the end of the reign of Augustus II. Under his son the Seyms witnessed passionate pleas in favour of a stronger army (especially in the years 1736–1748), connected with efforts to make Poland's foreign policy more active. The policy of the Court and of the cliques of magnates was fluid and equivocal, but it can be said that generally the Court aimed in principle at an alliance with Russia and Austria while the opposition (the Potockis) sought connexions with Prussia, Sweden, Turkey and France. The most serious confrontation took place at the Seym of 1744. Saxony, Russia and Austria strove to draw Poland into the anti-Prussian alliance and, for this reason supported not only an increase of the army but other reforms as well. The Potockis broke up the Seym with the cooperation of French and Prussian diplomacy. The Seyms of 1746, 1748 and 1750 were broken up under similar circumstances. In the course of these clashes the Potockis' plans for a confederation failed to be implemented, but the attempts of the Court to achieve reforms also collapsed. The reversal of alliances, preceding the outbreak of the Seven Years' War, completely upset the political balance of forces outside Poland. Plans for confederations, alliances and enlarging the army dissolved completely in the chaos of factional struggle and foreign intrigue.

Throughout all the fluctuations prompted by expediency, the Commonwealth of Augustus III came to play a stabilizing role in the "European system". The demilitarization and neutralization of Poland in fact suited the interests of all her neighbours. The political game of the Powers was limited to preventing an inert Commonwealth from being subordinated to the influence of one side or another. Whereas, under Peter I it appeared that a Russian protectorate would be established in Poland, in the plans of the Court of Versailles Poland was to take an active part, with Sweden and Turkey, in the France's system of eastern alliances. After the experience of several decades a system of balance and compromise was firmly established. This suited the Polish gentry quite well. The mechanism of inertia worked almost automatically and, if need be, disturbance of the balance could easily be adjusted by diplomatic pressure and corruption. The breaking-up of a Seym sufficed to secure this solution.

THE SYSTEM OF "ANARCHY"

During the reign of Augustus II, eight Seyms completed their work, but ten were broken up. Under Augustus III the second "Pacification Seym" (1736) was the only one to be held while the remainder, thirteen in all, were broken up. In breaking up Seyms Russian, Prussian and French diplomacy played the major part. France spent most money on that because in view of the distance involved, money was the chief argument in support of her policy in Poland, whereas Poland's neighbours had other means of pressure and persuasion at their disposal. A study of diplomatic correspondence may give the impression that Polish magnates were puppets pulled by strings from distant capitals, and that political struggles in Poland were waged by a Muscovite, a Prussian or a French party, with the outcome of sessions of the Seym decided by roubles, thalers and louis d'or. This would be, however, an over-simplified picture. The French, when drawing up the dismal balance sheet of their expenditure, came to the conclusion that those Seyms would still have been broken up, even if they had spent more money on making Seyms workable than in breaking them up.

The Polish nobles became accustomed to accepting foreign money and to discussing political action with representatives of the Powers, but they were governed in fact by their own family ambitions and interests. The unchallenged system of unrestrained licence of the magnates caused anarchy. Violence at elections and subsequent arbitration between "majesty" and "freedom", paved the way for the omnipotence of the oligarchs. The long process of its growth reaches its peak under Augustus III. The Saxon Kings were incapable of creating a Polish centre of government. Henceforth foreign influence from being a decisive factor changed into being an instrument used by the Polish nobles in their internal intrigues. The Potockis or Czartoryskis involved half of Europe in their affairs. The dividing line between doing suit and service to foreign reason of State and harnessing foreign forces in service of one's own family interests became blurred. The reconstruction of a centre of Poland's *raison d'état* could not come from Dresden but, under the existing conditions, only from one group of magnates gaining ascendancy. In such a situation the task of the Powers, interested in maintaining the *status quo*, was not difficult when the family groups themselves watched each other with suspicion.

The recovery of the south-eastern borderlands under the treaty of Karłowice and the cessation of Cossack and Tartar wars brought about a period of flourishing development for the Ukrainian latifundia. The "Wild Plains" were brought under cultivation. Skirmishes with the marauding *hajdamaks*, remnants of the Cossacks engaging in brigandage, were but a far cry from the wars and havoc that had filled the seventeenth century. At the time of the contest for the eastern borderlands the magnates had certain common aims demanding a coordinated action with the State. Now, this unifying factor ceased to operate. All that remained was family policy and the struggle for riches and honours.

In the middle of the eighteenth century Polish magnates were considered to be the richest private individuals in Europe, next to the English aristocra-

Main residences of magnates, 17th and 18th cent.

- ● Main residences
- ○ Localities (for reference)
- ▨ Boundaries of the Commonwealth, 1618
- —·— Boundaries of the Commonwealth from 1699–1772
- ——— Boundaries of Lithuania, Courland, Livonia

The names of the residences (first) and of the families to whom they belonged (second) are given below: Baranów—Leszczyński; Biała—Radziwiłł; Biała Cerkiew—Branicki (Korczak); Białaczów—Małachowski; Białystok—Branicki (Gryf); Bieżuń—Zamoyski; Birże—Radziwiłł; Brody—Koniecpolski; Buczacz—Potocki; Dukla—Mniszech; Gołuchów—Ossoliński; Jabłonna—Poniatowski; Kiejdany—Radziwiłł; Kleck—Radziwiłł; Kodeń—Sapieha; Końskie—Małachowski; Korsuń—Poniatowski; Korzec—Czartoryski; Krasiczyn—Krasicki; Krystynopol—Potocki; Krzyżtopór—Ossoliński; Leszno—Leszczyński, later Sułkowski; Łańcut—Lubomirski; Łubny—Wiśniowiecki; Nieborów—Radziwiłł; Nieśwież—Radziwiłł; Ołyka—Radziwiłł; Opole—Lubomirski; Otwock—Bieliński; Podhorce—Koniecpolski, later Sobieski, still later Rzewuski; Przeworsk—Lubomirski; Puławy—Czartoryski; Rydzyna—Leszczyński, later Sułkowski; Rytwiany—Opaliński; Rzeszów—Lubomirski; Siedlce—Czartoryski, later Ogiński; Sieniawa—Sieniawski, later Czartoryski; Sieraków—Opaliński; Słonim—Ogiński; Słuck—Radziwiłł; Stanisławów—Potocki; Tulczyn—Potocki; Wiśnicz—Lubomirski; Wiśniowiec—Wiśniowiecki, later Mniszech; Wołczyn—Czartoryski, later Poniatowski; Zamość—Zamoyski; Złoczów—Sobieski; Żółkiew—Sobieski.

cy. The source of their wealth, apart from hereditary fortune, lay in the acquisition of lucrative sinecures. In the Saxon period competition for vacant offices and ecclesiastical benefices was the main driving force in political activity. Distribution of vacant offices was the only real prerogative of the Crown, but manoeuvering with this power was insufficient to create a stable Court party. Appointments were made for life so that a magnate, once provided for, was not obliged to obey the Court any longer. On the other hand, too much favour to one clique could intensify the opposition on the part of other pretenders to the danger of internal peace. The Saxons came finally to accept the Polish system and were concerned chiefly with the future of their dynasty. To that end it was necessary not to estrange the influential nobles in the various parties. The controller of patronage Brühl, who received fees from the applicants, was governed by personal interests. As a result, the patronage policy of the Court, like the influence of foreign Powers, contributed to the maintaining of a balance among the cliques of the magnates.

Towards the end of Augustus II's reign, three men connected by family ties occupied an outstanding place because of their particular ability and a statesmanlike approach to politics. They were the brothers Michał and August Czartoryski and their brother-in-law Stanisław Poniatowski. The Czartoryskis traced their descent to an ancient princely family but, as far as fortune and honours were concerned, they were newcomers to the oligarchy. They owed the start in life to the patronage of the Saxon minister Flemming. Poniatowski rose from the medium gentry by revealing his military and diplomatic talents during the Northern War. The marriage in 1731 of August Czartoryski to Poland's richest heiress, Zofia Sieniawska, brought an enormous fortune to the family. As supporters of the Court they strove to obtain high office, but met with fierce resistance form the old oligarchy, especially from the Potockis. To prevent Poniatowski from receiving the vacant Hetman's baton the Potockis caused the breaking-up of the last few Seyms under Augustus II. The Czartoryskis lent support to the King, but not to the Saxon plans of succession because they themselves aspired to the crown. During the interregnum they sided with Leszczyński who was no longer young and had no male heir. After the Saxon's victory, they regained influence at the Court and until 1748 tried in vain to push through reforms. The so-called "republicans" or "patriots", which in Poland denoted groups opposed to the Court, with the Potockis at their head, successfully checked these efforts, but "The Family", the name commonly used for the Czartoryskis and Poniatowskis, because for so many years they had had a share in the State patronage, could promote their friends and consolidate their position in the country.

The Czartoryski party was notable for its coherence and high intellectual standards, but in the factional struggle they resorted to the same means as their adversaries. They entered into collusion with foreign Powers, planned confederations and broke up Seyms. From 1748 the Seym ceased to provide a platform to be used in the struggle for reform. The idea of achieving anything by parliamentary action was abandoned and the faction struggle was concentrated in the Tribunals. Efforts to dominate the administration of justice in order to settle accounts for the clique resulted in the complete decay of political life. From 1750 the Court and the Czartoryskis drifted apart. Brühl grew weary of their unsuccessful attempts at reform, to which the Saxon court attached no great importance, while "The Family's" arbitrary policy with regard to State appointments was burdensome to him. The Saxon minister found a more subtle dispenser of patronage in the person of his own son-in-law, Jerzy Mniszech. Owing to Mniszech's efforts an understanding was reached between the Court and the Potockis; the Czartoryskis passed into opposition. Under the rule of the so-called Mniszech camarilla political life in Poland became a hollow shell. Indeed, it is difficult to speak about programmes and orientation in foreign affairs even in terms of parties. The Commonwealth, having in fact neither a King nor a Seym, became a conglomeration of secular and ecclesiastical latifundia and gentry estates. The events which aroused public interest, were the scandals of the Tribunals, big court cases, appointments, grain prices, religious ceremonies, marriages among the magnates and their even more frequent divorces.

Such was to the satisfaction of Europe the condition of the Commonwealth. Not only Poland's neighbours (Russia, Prussia, Austria and Turkey) but France also arrived at the conclusion that any change in the Commonwealth would be dangerous. French diplomacy was the first to introduce the term "Polish anarchy"; it entered the political vocabulary as the description of a state of things which was looked upon with favour because it guaranteed a convenient demilitarization of the Commonwealth. The Poles themselves coined a brief, and not altogether disapproving definition of their situation: "Poland stands by anarchy" (*Polska nierządem stoi*). This maxim was not as absurd as is commonly believed. While the "anarchic" Poland presented the sad picture of a political market place, she nevertheless "stood" in the sense that her defenseless frontiers, though open to the entry of foreign troops, were not threatened with annexations. The Powers not only watched over Poland's neutrality; they were also on the alert lest any one of them should expand at her expense.

WESTERN POMERANIA AND SILESIA UNDER PRUSSIAN RULE

Though the Commonwealth suffered no territorial loss in the Saxon times, momentous and dangerous changes occurred none the less in the western teritories which had been lost by Poland in the Middle Ages. The development of the Brandenburg-Prussian State reached its climax when Prussia became an European power.

The division of Western Pomerania between Sweden and Brandenburg in 1648 did not satisfy the aspirations of the Hohenzollerns, who made several attempts in the second half of the seventeenth century to obtain possession of the mouth of the Odra. This goal was reached during the Northern War. The Prussian army occupied Szczecin in 1713; under the peace treaty of 1720, Sweden was forced to cede part of Western Pomerania including Szczecin to Prussia. The government proceeded with the elimination of Pomeranian particularism re-organizing the province, with strongly fortified Szczecin as its capital (1724). This thinly populated agricultural country of 300-400 thousand inhabitants became a domain of junker estates, with its sandy soil bearing not only rye and potatoes, but supplying the Prussian army with cadres of professional officers and with regiments of tough Pomeranian grenadiers. Gaining the command of the mouth of the Odra, gave Prussia the control of the Baltic gateway of the Warta basin. Twenty years later the whole of the Odra was to become a Prussian river.

In the early part of the eighteenth century, Silesia recovered from the devastation of the Thirty Years' War. Habsburg rule was consolidated at the expense of feudal particularism by the action of the Counter-Reformation. The German element was strengthened by an influx of Austrian nobles, bureaucrats and the Jesuits. Churches were being taken away from the Protestants, and this was connected with the ousting of the Polish language from churches. In the long run the consolidation of Roman-Catholicism in Silesia, a part of which belonged to the diocese of Cracow, with the diocese of Wrocław also subordinated to the Warsaw nuncio, was to prove advantageous to the survival of the Polish and Roman-Catholic consciousness of the Silesian people at the time when the province came under the rule of Protestant Prussia. Class conflicts of great intensity in the eighteenth century Silesia set the Polish peasants against the German gentry. For economic reasons the need to know Polish was felt even among the German burghers. Polish schools and printing presses continued to exist, and the enrolment of students at Cracow University in 1720-1780 remained on a level equal to that of the first half of the seventeenth century. With regard to language Silesia was largely still predominantly Polish in the middle of the eighteenth century. From the time of Sobieski, however, the Commonwealth did not care for the forgotten provinces in the West. Now, with the Austrian succession in question (after the death of Emperor Charles VI), Frederick II, with an ingenuity for legal chicanery typical of his family voiced the claim of Brandenburg to the inheritance of Silesia after the Silesian Piasts. His decisive argument consisted of an army of 100,000 men.

The annexation of Silesia accomplished in 1740, sanctioned in 1742 and finally confirmed in 1763 brought to the Hohenzollern monarchy a country which was vast (36,000 sq.km), populous (1,500,000 inhabitants) and rich. Frederick II now had not only new areas from which to recruit his soldiers and levy taxes but an industrious army of Silesian weavers and a multitude of miners and metal-workers whose number was growing rapidly. The Silesian metallurgical industry became the armoury of Prussia. This land, wedged-in between Saxony, Bohemia, Moravia and Poland, was for a quarter of a century the centre of strife in Europe, a stake in Prussia's power policy. The loss of Silesia would have ended the dreams of Hohenzollern power; the keeping of that province was the starting point for the further "rounding off" of their dominion.

For 300 years, the tradition of encroachments inherited from the Teutonic Order had been looming along the intricate course of the frontier between the Commonwealth and the Brandenburg-Prussian State. Now, a pincer arm was closing tight all the way from Wschowa to Pszczyna. The Electors of Brandenburg had already had under their sceptre the East-Prussian Mazurians, Lithuanians and the Pomeranian Kashubians, not to mention the Germanized Slavs. With the annexation of Silesia, Frederick II took another resolute step towards building a multi-national Hohenzollern power on Slavonic land. Prussia's further progress depended on a change in the European system with regard to Poland; in short, the replacement of the doctrine of static balance (anarchy) by the doctrine of dynamic balance (partition). A change of system in turn depended on what was going to happen within the Commonwealth.

SARMATIAN AND CATHOLIC CONFORMISM

In spite of the paralysis, or even atrophy, of its central government, regional particularism was not developed in the Commonwealth. A far-reaching differentiation among the peasant masses and burghers still prevailed in the multinational State, but the "gentry nation" was growing more and more homogeneous in its outlook. The process of Polonizing the Ruthenian nobility was completed (in 1697, Ruthenian was abandoned in judicial records). The Polish, Lithuanian and Ruthenian gentry, interrelated by thousands of family ties, were assimilated into one big family of brother nobles. The cultural patterns of Sarmatism, that is of the exclusively Polish Baroque, shaped in the seventeenth century, did not change in the first half of the eighteenth century, but were spreading and consolidating. Various factors worked for this intellectual conformism.

A Polish gentleman was called upon to speak on public matters and was brought up with this public duty in view. Elector of kings, potentially a member of Parliament and actual member of local diets, he should hold or, at least, voice some opinions. Although Seyms were broken up and under Augustus III there even came to the breaking-up of a Tribunal (1749), the local diets were held and lenghty instructions were drawn up at their sessions. Deputies and delegates from all over the country convened, made speeches and mingled with each other. A knightly estate in nàme, but in fact a community of landowners and jurists, settling their disputes under the land law, which was becoming more and more uniform in the Crown and in Lithuania, the gentry constituted a quarrelsome, but basically harmonious group used to obeying "elder brothers". The gentlemen-citizens voiced opinions which could not change anything under the existing conditions of anarchy but which one was supposed to utter. Patriotic ranting produced clichés which sounded similar, although spoken with a different accent, in one provincial town or another. In this way, generally accepted and obligatory axioms were inculcated in their minds, maxims on the honour of noble blood, on Golden Freedom, on despotism, the depravity of foreigners and the horror of heresy.

Besides an uniform judiciary and the declarative nature of political activity, another powerful factor in intellectual conformism was Jesuit education. Whether his manor was in one corner of the country or another, the average nobleman wrote and thought in the way he had been taught by the Jesuit fathers. The fathers proclaimed that all the calamities afflicting Poland were divine chastisement for indulging in heresy. Meanwhile, new grievances and new fears accumulated against the dissenters.

During the Northern War, as in the time of "the Deluge", dissenters sought Swedish protection. Saxon troops, against which the Confederation of Tarnogród was formed, were Lutheran. Saxons, backed by the Court, sought naturalization as Polish nobles and competed for Polish offices. Peter I was the protector of the Orthodox Church and an enemy of the Uniates. The Commonwealth, so submissive to the Powers, still behaved uncompromisingly in matters of religion. The Dumb Seym of 1717 passed a number of restrictions for dissenters. In 1724, a violent clash occurred between students of the Jesuit school and the Protestant burghers in Toruń. Sentenced by the royal (assessorial) court, the Mayor of Toruń and 9 burghers were beheaded. The Toruń affair aroused great resentment in Europe and had a powerful effect in shaping the unfavourable opinion on Poland which took root in Protestant countries and among the "philosophers". This opinion was certainly exaggerated, but it is a fact that Poland ceased to be the mainstay of religious tolerance, which she had been in the sixteenth century; in comparison with the rest of Europe, however, Poland remained a relatively tolerant country in the eighteenth century. In the West there has often been some confusion concerning the two concepts of religious toleration and of equality of rights of the dissenters. The execution of Toruń was a unique event and was exploited against Poland by an ill disposed propaganda. Poland was at this moment threatened with an intervention by Russia, Prussia and England in defense of the dissenters. Exceptionally, with regard to this issue an understanding was arrived at between the King and the Commonwealth. At the Convocation Seym of 1733, it was resolved to bar dissenters from all offices, from membership of the Seym and from the function of deputies in the Tribunals. The Protestant gentry against which these resolutions were aimed, was then already very small in number.

The struggle against the Orthodox Church, the faith of Ukrainian and Byelorussian peasants, was of a different character. The treaty of 1686 placed the members of the Orthodox Church in Poland under the protection of Russia, but at the turn of the seventeenth century all the Orthodox hierarchy in Poland turned Uniate. It was not until 1720 that an Orthodox episcopate was established in Mohylów by Peter I. The religious situation in the Ukraine and Byelorussia was fluid. The offensive of the Union did not cease in spite of Russian opposition, and the border gentry almost all adopted the Latin rite. The terms "Pole" and "Roman Catholic" were becoming more and more synonymous.

In the first half of the eighteenth century, the religious feeling of the people manifested itself in their taste for Church ceremonial and in religious practices which became a part of customs and tradition. Processions, saints' days, rigorous fasts and sumptuously celebrated sacred festivals were an annual feature. Home prayers marked weekdays. The need to belong to a community was met by fraternities and Third Orders. The cult of the Virgin was widespread and its most spectacular displays were the crownings of the effigies of the Virgin Mary, with the first coronation taking place in Częstochowa in 1717. The Polish religious rite had its own distinct pattern, with much in common with the Italian or Spanish Catholicism but was less marked by clericalism than in those Latin countries. The clergy were numerous and affluent, but for the most part not particularly scholarly; differing in the colour of their robes but not in their theological views, they played of course an important part as ministers of a cult that permeated the life of the nation. Yet, the friar with a collecting bag bowed low when entering the manor and the squire treated the parish priest as his personal chaplain. The clergy, greatly differentiated from the bishops of the senatorial order down to the poor plebeians in the rural parishes, occupied an intermediate social status half-way between the knightly estate and the people.

In spite of the undoubtedly well-grounded Roman-Catholic orthodoxy and the growth of intolerance and excessive piety in Poland of the Saxon period, the divergence between gentry and clergy and between the Commonwealth and the Vatican still smouldered. In the Catholic monarchies of the eighteenth century, relations between Church and State were often strained, but these matters took place on a high level between the Most Christian King or His Catholic Majesty on the one hand and the Hierarchy or Rome on the other, or else they took the form of doctrinal un-orthodoxy, like Jansenism in France. In republican Poland the collective opinion of orthodox and pious gentry prevailed instead. Although the gentry rejected heresy, the tradition of the sixteenth century disputes over tithes was still alive. The wealth of the Church, which had grown enormously at the time of Counter-Reformation, and its independence irritated the rank-and-file of the gentry, especially when taxes were considered. A programme of the gentry's demands was drawn up at the Seym of 1719 providing for taxes on the clergy for military purposes, a restriction of bequests to the Church, a lowering of fees for religious services and of the interest rate on the debts on landed estates owed to the Church, curtailment of the clergy's right to produce and sell spirits, a regulation of tithes and limitation of the competence of ecclesiastical courts. The conflict grew more acute in 1726 when the Seym went as far as to demand that the Nuncio be recalled. The immediate origin of the conflict was a dispute over appointments to certain abbacies; a compromise concordat was concluded in 1736 and put an end to a 10 years' crisis. In reality, a number of issues were involved. Apart from the demands of the gentry, there were also the aspirations of the Polish hierarchy to abolish the Nuncio's court in Warsaw; an inveterate antagonism existed between the Primates and the Nuncios. It was also desired to limit Church payments remitted to Rome. Owing to the paralysis of the Seym under Augustus III it was impossible to settle the relations between the Church and the laity, but the programme had the strong support of public opinion. The devout gentry exhibited a peculiar strait of anti-clericalism by condemning the legacies to the Church, the tithes, the inns belonging to priests, and the fiscal and judicial immunities of the clergy.

The gentry in the Saxon period still repeated the traditional maxim of the poorest country squire being equal to the voivode. This notion of equality did not, however, prevent the gentry cringing and bowing cap-in-hand to the magnates. While cultivating the "Sarmatian" way of life of their ancestors, they no longer possessed their martial valour and spirit of adventure. Vexatious litigation in court suited them better than prowess on the field of battle. The typical diarist of the time was the faction agent and constant litigant Matuszkiewicz rather than men like Pasek, the soldier. Over the length and breadth of Poland men engaged in lawsuits, but "the law is like a cobweb; the breeze will break through, but the fly will get caught and be blamed". Yet, in spite of the anarchy and the opresive domination of the great nobles, a peculiar legalism became deeply ingrained in the mentality of the gentry. The gentry had a highly developed sense of their Sarmatian and Catholic identity and reacted sharply against anything which endangered those values. Religious issues and slogans rather than political ones could rouse them to violent and even desperate action. Accumulated ideological residues remained idle in the Saxon times, but became an active force in conservative republicanism in the near future. But the sense of liberty was so deeply felt and linked to republicanism that it was later to characterize the Poles in their struggle against oppression.

LATE-BAROQUE CULTURE

The configuration of the Sarmatian and Catholic way of life was accomplished amid cultural stagnation and an atrophy of creative intellectual activity. The absence of change and new cultural contents was conducive to a consolidation of existing and permanent cultural values. Attempts have been made to explain that state of cultural ossification and regression in various ways, by war-weariness, by xenophobia checking outside influences, by a watering down in the "diluted culture" of the vast eastern territories and by the peculiar features of Turkish influence. It seems, however, that the main cause may be found in the preponderance of agrarian economy and in the fact that the urban element remained culturally unassimilated. The long decay of the towns reached its lowest point after the calamities of the Northern War. Gdańsk and other Pomeranian towns were still relatively prosperous, but they were Lutheran and German. The numerous Jewish communities constituting about 10 per cent of the population lived in even stricter cultural isolation. In modern Europe new cultural values were being created by the nobility who had settled in towns, the nobility in civil service, by the bourgeoisie and skilled craftsmen, whereas the Poles were a nation of landed gentry and serfs. The decay of the capital was particularly harmful to cultural life. The Warsaw of the Saxon times hardly deserved to be called a capital city. The Court residing in Dresden not only did not fulfil the role of a patron of arts and culture, but could not even be a centre of social life. Warsaw was neither a royal residence nor a political and administrative centre. Poland became one large province and cultural life drifted idly along a parochial course.

Amid the monotony of the countryside there glittered the magnates' residences and churches. The wealth of the magnates and clergy was displayed with grandiose ostentation. Palace and church architecture with appropriate painting and decorative sculpture produced the impressive works of the late Baroque period. In palace architecture, the Rococo style of France and Dresden prevailed and was accompanied by landscape gardening. The magnates built or rebuilt their many palaces in Warsaw, which, however, were not their homes. Their actual residences, furnished with every splendour, were constructed in the country. The first half of the eighteenth century saw the flourishing of church architecture. In addition to the prevailing Roman Baroque, Austrian and Czech styles affected more by the Rococo than the Italian exerted an increasing influence on this architecture. In the lively centre of Wilno, a north-Italian influence may be traced. In Warsaw and Lwów the classic Palladian elements also appeared. Amidst the multitude of models and influences entirely original concepts took shape and many beautiful churches were erected. In palace and ecclesiastical architecture architects of foreign origin held the lead (Italians, Germans, and Frenchmen), yet the number of Polish architects was growing. Stone buildings gradually supplanted wood architecture. In the most indigenous wood architecture traditional and Gothic-like forms yielded to imitations of Baroque stone architecture.

To a greater extent than in architecture, Polish tastes and the work of

Polish artists found expression in interior decoration. While the façades of churches and palaces were often kept simple, condensed luxury prevailed inside. In church sculpture stone and stucco were supplanted by wood. Polish carvers (Antoni Frączkiewicz, Piotr Kornecki and Antoni Osiński) were outstanding in their mastery of expressive and dynamic figurative sculpture. In altar painting the traditions of Roman Baroque prevailed (Szymon Czechowicz, Tadeusz Konicz). In the field of court art the nobles wished to have their palaces turned into little Versailles, with historical paintings patterned on ancient mythology and idealized official portraits. At the same time, however, the realistic "Sarmatian" portrait was widely cultivated (A. Misiowski, F. Rojecki, Ł. Orłowski), and to that we owe a rich gallery of expressive and lively pictures of moustached gentlemen in semi-oriental attire. The taste for the oriental found an expression in the decorative arts, with rugs and carpets manufactured at home appearing side by side with imported goods. The style of Polish country houses and manors was established at this time; their walls hung with rugs, ornate arms and Sarmatian portraits. Often their walls were covered with Baroque polychromes.

The splendour of religious ceremonies and court functions called for musical accompaniment along with plastic arts setting. Many magnates kept Italian orchestras. Church music continued in accord with the Old-Polish tradition (among the composers of the first half of the eighteenth century, mention should be made of Grzegorz Gorczycki, music master at Wawel Cathedral). Foreign visitors liked Polish music and dances. In the residences of the magnates, court theatre was also cultivated. The activities of Wacław Rzewuski at Podhorce and of Urszula Radziwiłł at Nieśwież were outstanding in this field. Among magnate courts, the most magnificent, it seems, was Białystok, the residence of Hetman Jan Klemens Branicki, who maintained a princely establishment, which has been called the Versailles of Podlasie. The courts of the magnates were wide open to clientele among the gentry. It was there that the youth received their "polishing-off", likewise the churches played their part in fashioning taste. Church and court art of the late Baroque period influenced the national taste inclined to sumptuousness and decorativeness, and this not only within the gentry; it penetrated into folk art as well. The cross-influences from East and West were instrumental in shaping a peculiarly and typical Polish style.

In the field of the fine arts, the Saxon times did not constitute a period of regression, but produced a picturesque expression of the civilization of the Roman-Catholic landed gentry. On the other hand, the stagnation of cultural life was marked in literature. The nobles and the clergy might live in ornate surroundings provided by architects, carvers, painters and masters of carpet-making, but in the realm of literature, they seemed to be self-sufficient. Much was being written and published but this rich production was for the most part dilettante scribbling or catering for primitive tastes. With

Białystok. Palace, 1728—1758

regard to form, the Baroque rhetoric degenerated into extreme mannerisms in pursuit of a far-fetched complexity of expression. Authors and readers amused themselves with bizarre versifications and childish diversions like rebuses, cryptograms with double meanings and symbolism obtained by means of typographical tricks. The Baroque manner achieved artistic results when the complex form was combined with intensity of thought. In the Saxon times this depth of thought was markedly weakened. With regard to content, literature was dominated by devotional and panegyrical writings in which the exaggerated cult of "armorial honours" and the glorification of alleged merit bordered on the grotesque. In epic poetry medieval and fantastic romances of adventure prevailed together with biblical motifs, lives of Saints and a legendary or naively heroicized history of Poland. The fiction of these years was represented by long-winded and clumsy books, which nevertheless showed the new demand for novels. The output of plays also grew, in connexion with the development of the school theatre of Jesuit and Piarist orders and of the court theatres maintained by the magnates. First attempts at adapting the works of Molière are to be noted. Satirical accents can be found in the plays by Franciszek Bohomolec, but on the whole the profuse moralism of the literature of this period directed its main attack against adultery, with drastic pictures of debauchery. Literary activity was cultivated by many magnates, a multitude of priests and, a feature which was new, by quite a number of women. Fresh and sincere notes

...on de Sa Majesté Stanislas Auguste, qui fut élu...
...anie ... le 7 Septbre 1764 peint par Bernardo Belotto
...rer relations et documents avec beaucoup de portraits de personnes...

appeared sometimes in lyrics. Almanacs issued by academicians in Cracow and Zamość spread astrological practices and gave advice on housekeeping and medical matters, with snippets of practical knowledge alternating here and there with superstition. This kind of literature for simple minds was cultivated all over Europe, but in the Poland of the first half of the eighteenth century it was the mainstream, not a margin, of literature. In the West even educated minds were then sensitive to the charm of astrological and alchemic speculation, but among the Polish gentry, vulgar superstition was spreading. This literature reflected the mentality of a stabilized and conformist society. Its trivial mannerism seemed shocking to the refined taste of a later period. Yet this literature may still interest and entertain the reader of today : it is not devoid of fantasy, imagery and expression, of a peculiar, though mostly coarse kind of humour. Some works of this epoch, like church hymns and proverbs, proved their vitality and became a component of the national culture. There were other fields of literature such as political writing and studies in history and law, on which the first half of the eighteenth century produced works of merit.

In the history of Polish culture the six decades of the Saxon rule can be roughly divided into two periods. Until about 1740 Poland lives on the increasingly sterile intellectual legacy of the seventeenth century. In the forties and fifties, in spite of the deep political degradation, a new trend appeared to overcome the cultural stagnation.

THE FORCES OF PROGRESS

After the Northern War, the Saxon period was one of a peace of uncommonly long duration in Polish history. Sporadic fighting with the Saxons in 1714–1715, peripheral hostilities at the time of the two Kings 1733–1735, and violation of the frontiers by troops of the neighbouring Powers during the Silesian Wars and the Seven Years' War, were the only minor disturbances of a peace of more than 50 years. Not only demilitarized Poland was not the scene of destructive hostilities, marches and billeting of armies, but it did not have to bear the burdens of maintaining a large standing army, either. Under these conditions a slow economic reconstruction took place. The course of this recovery was determined by the still prevailing system of a manor-farm and serf labour economy.

The convulsions of the Northern War were followed by a long-lasting stabilization of the value of money and fixed prices. This phenomenon, however, revealed not a dynamism of the economy, but its normalization, free of crisis. The incomes of landowners showed an upward trend. In an agricultural country, placing greatest emphasis on exports, the export of grain through Gdańsk serves as a reliable index. In 1700–1719 exports averaged 20,000 lasts a year, in the period of postwar normalization they

Canaletto, *Election of Stanisław Augustus*, 1778

rose to 30,000, and reached 50,000 a year in the 1760's. At the same time exports by land increased, owing to demand for supplies for the armies engaged in the Seven Years' War. Both townspeople and peasants were excluded from this growing prosperity whose major beneficiaries were the gentry and clergy, and above all the great estates of the magnates and the Church. The one-sided development of agricultural production, while the decay of towns continued and peasants were confined to a subsistence economy, dislodged the marketing of crops and hindered the effectiveness of the economic potential of the manor. In these circumstances, the *propinacja* (the Polish term for the manor's monopoly in producing and selling spirits) assumed increased importance. However, a wider process of industrialization also began.

It is not surprising that Poland was a country which attracted the particular interest of the French physiocrats in the second half of the eighteenth century, because this almost exclusively agricultural country had applied a peculiar liberalism for a long time. It was not an economic doctrine, but a practice resulting in a quite exceptional concept in the period of mercantilism, a complete absence of a national tariffs and industrial policy. The matter assumes a different aspect, however, if we consider the Commonwealth of the Saxon times as an amalgam of the magnates' latifundia.

Throughout the period when the predominance of the magnates was at its peak, the process of land concentration in the hands of great estate owners continued. The Polish magnate was more a wealthy man than an aristocrat. Wealth in land, however, was not always accompanied by ready cash. Money was scarce in Poland, credit was expensive and not easily available. Therefore magnates in their search for cash became bankers themselves after a fashion with whom their clientele among the gentry deposited money at an interest. This concentration of money made it possible for the magnates to spend huge sums for consumption purposes, for big transactions (purchase of new estates) and investment. Princely states, as the latifundia could be described, applied peculiar mercantilist policies, they were virtually closed economic organisms. A magnate, with his own means of transport and his own brokers, concentrated the exports and imports of a large agricultural area in his own hands. Within this area there was no liberalism, but rather a system of compulsion and monopoly. Owing to the use of serf labour and the natural resources of the latifundia, it was possible to undertake large capital investment not involving cash; it was possible at the same time to divert the currency into the lord's coffers by means of dues in money or in kind, and of the monopoly in consumer goods.

Those were the conditions which led to the establishment of manufactories in the latifundia. They produced not only for the manor's own needs (luxury goods), thereby reducing the import figures in the balance-sheet of "foreign trade", but for the internal market of the great estate as well (simple textile products, glass and metalware). This increased even more the flow of currency to the lord's treasury. Industrialized latifundia were not a common feature in the first half of the eighteenth century, except distilling and timber industries, but their growth revealed a significant trend. There also appeared factories producing goods for the national market, like the big manufactories of ornate waistbands worn by the gentry. Along the slopes of the Świętokrzyskie Mountains, the iron industry was encouraged largely by the initiative of the Bishop of Cracow, Stanisław Andrzej Załuski, and of the Małachowski family. In Great Poland a large region of textile industry was developed, connected with Lower Silesia and the Lubusz-District. In Warsaw, clearing houses transacting international business on a large scale appeared to meet the needs of their customers among the magnates.

The economic and social agrarianization of Poland had brought about an acute shortage of trained workmen and specialists in many fields. In this situation foreigners had to be called in; they were introduced to the manufactories and to nobles' courts as secretaries, librarians or private tutors. The newcomers came mostly from Saxony; among the most distinguished were Mitzler de Kolof, an economist, journalist and publisher and Jan Daniel Jänisch-Janocki, the librarian of the Załuski family, a noted bibliographer. Poland also attracted Frenchmen, Italians and Swiss. Foreigners not only entered the service of the nobility, but settled also in Poland as businessmen. Warsaw became an active centre of a middle class of foreign origin, but gravitating towards Polish culture.

The immigrant element joined in the efforts of the Polish intellectual élite to overcome Sarmatian stagnation. This élite consisted of men who had the means and opportunity to reach beyond the limited horizon of gentry provincialism. They sprang consequently from among the magnates and clergy. These two groups had always maintained a lively contact with abroad. The Franco-Polish court of Leszczyński in Lunéville and Nancy had in the thirty years from 1737 to 1766 been a centre spreading French culture. The magnates visited Dresden, Paris and Italy and began to take a livelier interest in Holland, England and Switzerland. These latter countries, which the Poles rated among republics, furnished examples of "orderly freedom". In the 1740's free-masonry began to spread among the magnates, enlivening international contact and breaking down conformist attitudes. The clergy remained in constant and close contact with Rome which under Benedict XIV saw attempts at the assimilation by the Church of certain scientific achievements of the age of Enlightenment. New intellectual trends in these years had a chance of penetrating into Poland only in so far as they were approved by Church circles (the Holy See and the central authorities of religious orders).

Persons in a position to make comparisons knew that there was nothing to be proud of in the political and intellectual state of the Commonwealth. Conscious aspirations for raising the country out of its sloth were born among these people. We are already acquainted with the political mechanism which frustrated reform in the field of government. However, their efforts found an expression in political writing, the only branch of literature to produce in the time of Augustus III such outstanding works as *Głos Wolny* (Free Voice), published by Leszczyński (probably not written by the King himself, but by the circle of his adherents), *List ziemianina* (A Landowner's Letter) by Stanisław Poniatowski, *Anatomia Rzeczypospolitej* (Anatomy of the Commonwealth) by Stefan Garczyński and, above all, Stanisław Konarski's *O skutecznym rad sposobie* (A Way to Effective Counsels). A certain animation in scientific research work found distinguished patrons in the brothers Załuski: Andrzej Stanisław, Bishop of Cracow, and Józef Andrzej, Bishop of Kiev, founders of the magnificent Załuski Library in Warsaw. In the field of historical and legal sciences prominent figures were Gotfryd Lengnich from Gdańsk, the Jesuit Kasper Niesiecki, and the Piarists Maciej Dogiel and Konarski. Reforms in the educational system were, however, of greatest importance.

These reforms are associated with the name of the Piarist Stanisław Konarski. The Collegium Nobilium, established by him in Warsaw in 1740, was not a large school but was a model, an example for others to follow. The general reform in the Piarist schools carried out by Konarski in 1754 was of wider importance. The Jesuits followed the Piarists. They established select colleges for young gentlemen modelled on the Collegium Nobilium, in Lwów, Wilno, Ostróg, Warsaw, Lublin and Poznań. At about the same time as the reform of Piarist schools, in the 1750's a modernization of instruction in all Jesuit schools was carried out. Cracow University also began to emerge from a long period of stagnation. Under the episcopate of Andrzej Stanisław Załuski, who as Bishop of Cracow was Chancellor of the University, its standards rose, especially in the Faculty of Law. The connexion of the University with its network of secondary schools grew stronger.

These reforms were preceded by a considerable expansion of secondary education in the number of both schools and pupils. At the end of the seventeenth century there were 9 Piarist schools but by about 1760 their number has risen to 29. As for the Jesuit schools, their growth may be shown in the following table:

Year	Size of school							
	large		medium		small		total	
	No. of schools	No. of pupils	No. of schools	No. of pupils	No. of schools	No. of pupils	No. of schools	No. of pupils
1700	8	4000	16	4000	22	2200	46	10,200
1770	17	8500	20	5000	29	2900	66	16,400

The number of teachers (equivalent to the number of classes) in the Jesuit schools grew even faster, from 244 in 1700, to 417 in 1773, which proves that the standard of schools was rising.

Whatever might be said of the curricula and the standards of instruction (especially prior to the reforms of the 1750's), the growth in numbers of the secondary schools was one of the determinant factors in the coming cultural revival.

The personalities of Stanisław Konarski, the great political writer and educator, or Andrzej Załuski, Chancellor of the Crown, the political collaborator of the Czartoryskis and the reformer of Cracow University, show how politics and education joined hands to carry out a reform of institutions and to spread general education.

THE POLITICAL DEADLOCK

The French Resident in Warsaw, Hennin, wrote in 1763 : "One would need volumes to present all that is being said and planned here. Confusion prevails in peoples' minds. No nation has ever been more deserving of sympathy. One is either a Russian or a Saxon—no one is a Pole. Inherent in the situation of this Commonwealth is a dilemma equal to the squaring of the circle. I fear that it will prove equally impossible to assure the happiness of this people, and then it would only remain to wish them eternal torpidity in their weakness and laxity".

Forces of revival were gathering in Poland, but their process of crystallization was extremely difficult. Among the magnates "The Family" of the Czartoryskis and Poniatowskis had no monopoly of reform ideas. Bold ideas and initiative were to come from the Potockis also, especially from Antoni, voivode of Bełz. The wise counsels of Stanisław Konarski were listened to in the "republican" circles around Hetman Branicki. The modern administrative practices of the Saxons gained adherents in court circles. But the rivalries of the oligarchical cliques held the balance and remained in deadlock. While individual magnates constituted the most enlightened and modern element in the Sarmatian Commonwealth, the magnate group as a whole made any change impossible. The *liberum veto* in the service of factional intrigue was an obstacle which could not be surmounted. In the four volumes of his well-known work O *skutecznym rad sposobie* Stanisław Konarski demonstrated the absurdity of the system of the unanimous vote. The bishops were discussing the use of religious sanctions against those who committed the "hideous sin" of breaking up the Seyms. Feelings of bitterness, shame and moral indignation were rising, but there was no practical solution unless one chose a *coup d'état* by forming a confederation, which would mean civil war. In view of the age-old connexion of the magnates with foreign courts and the interest of those courts in Poland's internal situation, a *coup d'état* was unthinkable without foreign interference and a civil war was bound to bring about a multilateral foreign intervention. After sixty years of the union of Poland and Saxony and anarchy nursed from outside, the Poles lost the ability as well as the power to solve their internal problems by themselves.

The formula that perpetuated the *status quo*, was the personal union of Poland and Saxony. At the time of the Seven Years' War, all the Powers that had an influence in the affairs of the Commonwealth, as well as the Holy See, which always pinned its hopes on the union for the progress of Roman-Catholicism in Saxony, favoured this personal union. Even Louis XV, having connected himself with the Wettins by the marriage of the Dauphin with the daughter of Augustus III and given up an active policy in Poland, finally abandoned the policy of the *secret du Roi* and declared for the Saxon succession, though with the retention of a free election. Augustus III was old and infirm and the time has come to consider the succession. The initial step towards the consolidation of the Saxon position in Poland was made when Prince Charles, Augustus III's son, took over the Duchy of Courland in 1758 with Tsarina Elisabeth's consent.

The Courland investiture became the cause of the final and radical breach of "The Family" with the Court and dynasty. The Czartoryskis and Poniatowskis decided to oppose by all means the perpetuation of the union and of the *status quo*. They had the support of a considerable section of the gentry, amongst whom anti-Saxon feelings ran high. During the Seven Years' War Poland was plunged into an acute financial crisis. In conquered Saxony Frederick II got hold of the mint which coined Polish money and began to issue debased coins on a large scale. The inundation of the country with depreciated money and a sudden and sharp rise of prices caused chaos. Among those who had their fingers in the pie were the Saxon jobbers as well as treasurers connected with Brühl. The gentry, accustomed to stable economic relations, condemned the Saxons for causing all the trouble by their war with Prussia and by their actual or supposed intrigues. "The Family" had a strong party at their disposal and the monetary crisis brought about acute tension in the country; it was a shock to Sarmatian quietism. This was not enough, however, to break the political deadlock.

The crisis in Polish affairs was to find its solution, as had happened so many times before in the eighteenth century, from outside Poland.

Chapter XI
TENTATIVE REFORMS UNDER RUSSIA'S TUTELAGE (1763–1788)

THE RUSSO-PRUSSIAN ALLIANCE

The abrupt turn in Russian policy after the death of Tsarina Elisabeth on 5 January, 1762 brought about a fundamental change not only on the field of battle but also in Poland's situation. The new ruler, Peter III, abandoned hostilities against Prussia and even began negotiations for an alliance with Frederick II, in which Polish problems played an important part. Russia and Prussia were to take the dissenters and the Polish "liberties" under their protection and to coordinate their action when the next interregnum occurred. The Russo-Prussian rapprochement resulted at first in the decisive ascendancy of Frederick II, because the new Tsar, a man of unstable intellect, caring more for his dynastic interests in Holstein than for the destinies of the Empire, was a fanatical admirer of Frederick.

Since the annexation of Silesia the King of Prussia entertained plans of conquest at the expense of Poland. In his Political Testament of 1752, he recommended that Royal (that is Polish) Prussia be "eaten like an artichoke, leaf by leaf", that one should pluck "now a town, now a district, until the whole has been eaten up". It was not only because of the configuration of her provinces that Prussia was particularly interested in territorial gain at the expense of Poland. The days of the Commonwealth's greatness and of Ducal Prussia's feudal dependence were not forgotten in Berlin. The thought that Poland might recover her power was a nightmare for Frederick II because he fully realized the degree to which the big power status of his small and disjointed monarchy was strained. The King of Prussia, the most vigilant guardian of Polish anarchy, dreamt therefore of a partition of Poland being, however, unable to accomplish it by himself.

The negotiations for a Russo-Prussian alliance were interrupted by Catherine II's *coup d'état* (9 July, 1762). The Tsarina was not as accommodating towards Prussia as Peter III and had her own ambitious plans with regard to Poland; yet she intended to carry them out in concert with Frederick II. Russia's attitude allowed Prussia to emerge safe and sound from the strain of the Seven Years' War and to conclude the peace of Hubertsburg (15 February, 1763), a result of the exhaustion, rather than the reconciliation of the Powers. Negotiations for an alliance henceforth proceeded between Petersburg and Berlin, to be crowned by a treaty of alliance. Its final signature (11 April, 1764) was already connected with the struggle for the succession to Augustus III. The rapprochement between Russia and Prussia was the genesis of the so-called "Northern system". The northern allies were united by common antagonism towards the participants of the former anti-Prussian coalition, the "Southern system" of Austria, France and Spain. Cooperation was needed to get the situation in Poland, a country on the border of the two "systems", under control. The position of Prussia and Russia, however, with regard to the problems of Poland did not coincide.

In Frederick II's intentions, which came near fruition during his negotiations with Peter III, the alliance with Russia was to contribute to a deepening of anarchy in Poland and to keep open the prospects of realizing his dreams of conquest which, until then, had met with opposition in Petersburg. To the Russia of Catherine II the "Northern system" was designed to maintain a dominant and lasting influence in Poland and to permit freedom of action against Turkey.

These two goals of Russian policy were closely connected because hegemony in Poland was a challenge to the Porte and, in any future Eastern War, a Polish auxiliary army and the territory of operations between the Dniester and the Dnieper could, to some extent, replace Russia's lost ally Austria. In the first half of the eighteenth century, Russia had several times given the Wettins support which had been decisive in maintaining their rule in Poland, but she failed to gain lasting ascendancy in the Commonwealth. The reign of the Saxons, which had its mainstay in the Electorate, beyond Russia's reach, and in the Wettins' family ties with western royal houses, was good enough to guarantee Poland's neutrality and anarchy, but something more was now at stake for Russia: she wanted hegemony not alliance. The immediate goal of Catherine II was, therefore, to prevent a prolongation of the union of Saxony and Poland. Russian troops expelled Prince Charles from Courland and reinstated Biron. As for the Polish throne, Catherine II had long before chosen her candidate to succeed Augustus III.

THE PLANS OF "THE FAMILY"

Everything started in the years 1755–1758, still during the reign of Tsarina Elisabeth, with a love affair between the Grand-Duchess Catherine and the 23 year old *Stolnik* (Steward) of Lithuania, Stanisław Poniatowski, who was then visiting Petersburg. The heads of "The Family", the old Princes Czartoryskis, Michał and August, saw in their nephew's amorous conquest political capital for their party. The assumption of power by Catherine II aroused great expectations. With this support "The Family" hoped to obtain the crown for one of their members (the old Princes would have preferred to see August's son, Adam Czartoryski on the throne, rather than Stanisław Poniatowski).

At the turn of 1762 and 1763, a council of "The Family" drew up a draft programme of reform, while Poniatowski laid down for Catherine II his own constitutional programme in the form of a philosophical allegory. The plan of the Czartoryskis' provided for decisions in the Seym by a simple majority vote. The Seym was to be in constant readiness to convene in extraordinary session, while collegiate organs of central administration were to be appointed by it. Like the work O *skutecznym rad sposobie* published at this time by Konarski (who collaborated with "The Family"), the programme was an interesting attempt to combine parliamentarism with the collegiate system of administration then widespread in Europe. Both the Czartoryskis and Konarski wished to eliminate the antagonism resulting from the duality of royal authority and the institutions of the Commonwealth, an antagonism on which the oligarchs thrived. The King was to be deprived of his only real prerogatives, namely the appointment of ministers, senators and officers of State, and the distribution of the *Starostwa*. The programme, conceived in the spirit of gentry republicanism, embodied two cardinal principles : 1) supremacy of parliament over government ; 2) election of ministers and officials by the Seym and the local diets. Moreover, the creation of ministerial committees (taking decisions by majority vote), was to take away the importance of the irremovable and uncontrolled ministers, appointed for life, who in practice had been the mainstay of oligarchical anarchy. The office of Hetman, the most exuberant and arbitrary institution, was to be abolished altogether.

Stanisław Poniatowski's constitutional programme was somewhat different. As a candidate for the throne he envisaged a reform of parliament along the same lines as the Czartoryskis', but he reserved for the king full power of appointment and distribution of patronage which made him the actual head of a strongly centralized government. Moreover, according to Poniatowski, the throne was to be hereditary. The differences between Poniatowski's constitutional monarchism and the Czartoryskis' republicanism were a sign of divergencies that existed within "The Family" which were to become more acute in the future.

The programme of the Czartoryskis' could not be carried out by parliamentary methods. "The Family" was opposed by two powerful parties of magnates, now reconciled in the face of the common danger : the Republicans, rallied around Hetman Jan Klemens Branicki, Franciszek Salezy Potocki and Karol Radziwiłł, and the Saxon party or "Mniszech camarilla". These parties could count not only upon most of the magnates and their rank and file gentry followers, but also on the army under the Hetman's command and on the private armies, the largest being the Radziwiłł's militia of 4000 men. The Czartoryskis therefore decided on a *coup d'état* by an armed confederation. For financial aid and arms, though not military intervention for the time being, they turned to Catherine II.

The idea of a *coup d'état* was conceived in connexion with Augustus III's illness. "The Family" intended to seize power while the King was still alive in order to have the situation under control during the anticipated interregnum. Russia approved the political plans of "The Family", but not their plans for government reform and at the Council of State held in St. Petersburg in February 1763 it was decided to give military and financial support to the candidature of Stanisław Poniatowski or Adam Czartoryski in event of an interregnum. The King's health, however, improved and the acute party struggle came near to civil war with the danger of "The Family" being crushed by the combined forces of the Republicans and the adherents of Saxony. In the spring, the Czartoryskis already asked for a Russian armed intervention under protection of which they would form a general confederation and conclude an alliance with Russia. Catherine II withdrew at the last moment, recommending delay until the death of Augustus III.

The background to the reversal of the decision in St. Petersburg, was the activity of Prussian diplomacy. Frederick II consented to support a candidate of the Tsarina's choice during the interregnum, but he rejected the idea of any change in the Commonwealth's institutions which were so convenient for Prussia. "The Family" found itself in a critical situation and was saved only by the death of the King (5 October, 1763). The Czartoryskis deluded themselves into believing they could make use of the Russian intervention for their own ends. When the interregnum occurred, they were not the leaders of a confederation deciding the country's problems, but a party striving for power, both threatened by, and dependent on foreign help.

THE INTERREGNUM (1763–1764)

After the death of Augustus III the Wettins' chances of keeping the Polish throne were apparently quite strong. They were backed by the majority of the magnates and enjoyed the support of the southern Powers. The Elector Frederick Christian, however, survived his father by a few months only, and his younger brothers, Xavier and Charles, each sought to obtain the Polish crown. There also existed in Dresden the concept of a compromise with the Republicans by placing upon the throne the elderly and childless Hetman Branicki during whose presumably short reign the 13-year old Elector Frederick Augustus would come of age. The discard in the Saxon House and the desire for a Piast, that is a Polish candidature, tacitly harboured by the

Republicans, hampered unity of action. Still more important was the fact that the southern Powers, exhausted by the Seven Years' War, while not sparing in declarations and promises, had no intention of becoming involved in the struggle for the Polish throne. Austria, being nearest to the scene of events, was effectively held at bay by Frederick II. Turkey, traditionally ill-disposed towards the Saxons, was not eager to intervene either. Thus Russia obtained a free hand in Poland.

Only then Catherine II informed "The Family" of her support for Stanisław. His candidature was thus a foregone conclusion. "The Family" mobilized its private armies and brought into the electoral campaign its efficient party which, with its enlightened and disciplined following, contrasted with the quarrelsome and incompetent Republicans. Most of the local diets ended in success for the Czartoryskis; the news of an advancing Russian army was also decisive. Under the protection of these troops a general confederation was formed in Wilno. The armed Republicans flocked to Warsaw to attend the Convocation Seym (May 1764) which they tried to break up. When the followers of "The Family" ignored this attempt, the opponents marched out of the capital. After an ineffective demonstration of armed resistance, Branicki withdrew to Hungary and Karol Radziwiłł to Moldavia.

At the Convocation Seym, the Czartoryskis only partially carried out their constitutional plans. This was connected with the attitude of the Powers. The Czartoryskis' programme was contrary to the traditional policy of Russia and especially to that of Prussia. If Catherine II wished to act as protector of Poland through her candidate, then the dualism of King and Commonwealth had to be maintained. A Seym taking decision by a majortiy vote, and enjoying a decided supremacy over the king, was a body more difficult to control than a king raised to the throne by Russia. For these reasons the efforts of Stanisław to strengthen the prerogatives of the Crown found a more favourable acceptance in St. Petersburg than the plans for a parliamentary reform. A number of Poniatowski's demands met with a favourable response ("What use do we have for a king who would be deprived of everything?"). On the other hand, the candidate to the throne was requested to support Russia's old claims with regard to a settlement of the frontier question, the protection of the Orthodox Church and the problem of fugitive serfs; he was also asked to persuade the Commonwealth "to request our guarantee for the preservation of its constitution and laws". That was tantamount to establishing a limit to attempts at reforming the constitution.

The Convocation Seym only slightly curtailed the use of the *liberum veto*. More was achieved in the way of constraining the oligarchic ministers and creating a nucleus of corporate administrative bodies by the establishment of a Military Commission and two Fiscal Commissions. Among many economic reforms, the most important were the abolition of private internal customs and the establishment of general customs at the frontiers of the country. A number of detailed resolutions contributed to an improvement in the situation of the towns and to the limitation of the clergy's economic expansion. The Seym made the important decision to continue the Confederation indefinitely (under August Czartoryski's presidency) which strengthened the executive power and opened prospects of further reforms being pushed through without the hindrance of the *liberum veto*, because confederated Seyms took decisions by majority vote.

With hopes of any help from abroad disappointed, most opponents recognized with varying degrees of sincerity the legality of the confederate authority. During the election the Russian troops withdrew for a distance of three miles from the capital and, under the protection of a few thousand private troops of "The Family", 5584 electors unanimously acclaimed Stanisław Poniatowski King on 6 September, 1764.

THE FIRST YEARS OF STANISŁAW AUGUSTUS

The new King was thirty-two years of age, of outstanding intelligence and careful education. In his travels abroad he developed a particular appreciation for England and her constitution. He was also impressed by the splendour of the absolute monarchy which he saw in Versailles and St. Petersburg. He was careful to preserve the prerogatives and revenues of the Crown and he used the income of the royal domain to become a patron of arts and literature. He established manufactories, built up the royal guard and chanceries. Flexible in his political tactics, he was consistent, almost doctrinaire indeed, in his pursuit of reform. An enemy of "sarmatism" and anarchy, he believed that Poland was in need of what he termed a "revolution". He had a lofty vision of his own cultural and legislative mission. Stanisław Augustus has often been charged with weakness of character, but it should be borne in mind that the position of a king in Poland was normally weak and Poniatowski's in particular. The old oligarchy, scornful of the "upstart" Poniatowski family, could not swallow the bitter pill of a mere Steward of Lithuania being so exalted. In his own party, "The Family", discord was growing deeper as the Czartoryski uncles lost hope of exercising tutelage over their nephew on the throne.

Stanisław Augustus, who owed his crown to Russia and was dependent on Russia's help, took little account of Catherine II's wishes in pursuing his own aspirations for independence in domestic and foreign policy. He was encouraged to bold action by his brothers and by the young men who flocked to his court. However until the King organized a reliable party of his own and won over to his side the social forces interested in restricting the oligarchy, his ambitious plans lacked a firm base.

Warsaw. Łazienki Park. The Water Palace, 1784–1795

The first years of his reign were a period of initiatives for sweeping reform in the field of finance (especially in the reform of the monetary system upset by Frederick II's debasements) and in the military field. In 1765 the King established the "Knights' School", the first really secular school in Poland, which aimed not only at training officers but also at preparing young gentlemen educated in the spirit of reform for public life. A great educational campaign was launched with the help of periodicals, belles-lettres and the theatre. From 1765, the periodical "Monitor", modelled on the English "Spectator", was published on the King's initiative. The "Monitor" criticized ignorance and conservatism, propounded religious tolerance and advocated the development of industry and improvement of agriculture. It wished to mould public opinion in favour of further reforms: the extension of the civil rights of the urban middle class and an improvement in the situation of the peasants. A close collaborator of the

Ignacy Krasicki

King, Andrzej Zamoyski (Chancellor from 1764), was vigorously active in municipal matters and organized commissions "for good city rule". Zamoyski, who presented the most extensive programme of reform at the Convocation Seym, was designated as the chief proposer of legislative reform at the Seym of 1766 at which there was to be a trial of strength.

The opponents of the King and "The Family", seeing the expectations for support from the southern Powers frustrated, turned now to Berlin and St. Petersburg, denouncing the prospective reform as being inconsistent with "Polish liberties". In 1765 Frederick II decided to compel Poland to abolish the general customs system: he established a customs-house imposing dues on goods shipped down the Vistula, through Polish territory to Gdańsk. Through Russia's mediation, the conflict was settled (the Kwidzyń customs-house was abolished but with it the Polish general customs). The Polish-Prussian conflict was a warning of the lack of cohesion in the "Northern system", as friendship with Prussia, moreover, was at this time the guiding-line of Russia's foreign policy. Stanisław Augustus' desire for an improvement of relations with Austria and France, was likewise alarming to St. Petersburg. Moreover, Warsaw delayed its answer to Russia's urgent demands with regard to frontier questions and dissenters.

This became for Catherine a question of personal prestige. Her first great and costly essay in foreign affairs ran the risk of being judged in Russia as a woman's whim, undertaken because of Poniatowski's charm, but with no profit to the Empire. Nikita Panin, who directed imperial foreign policy, was indeed in favour of bringing Poland into the alliance, strengthening her executive power and her armed forces, and carrying-out some of the Seym reforms; but he wished first to obtain satisfaction of Russian demands and to act in concert with Prussia. With that end in view he sent his close aide Saldern to Warsaw and Berlin in the spring of 1766. Frederick II rejected all idea of reform, declaring that "Poland ought to be kept in lethargy". Russia accepted the Prussian point of view.

When Zamoyski, at the Seym of 1766, put forward his programme of curtailing further the *liberum veto*, Russia and Prussia threatened Poland with war, demanded that the Confederation be dissolved and, assisted by England, Denmark and Sweden, made categoric demands that the dissenters be granted equal political rights. The King offered resistance by asking for concessions in the constitutional field in return. The conservative elements, to which the Czartoryskis fishing for popularity now looked, took the contrary position: they were readily willing to abandon reforms, but they were unyielding in religious matters. August Czartoryski dissolved the Confederation. The Seym did not settle these controversial issues. Europe was amazed at seeing a "rupture" between Catherine II and her "creature" Poniatowski only two years after his election. New Russian troops entered Poland and two dissenter Confederations were formed under their protection: one for Lithuania, at Słuck, and one for the Crown, at Toruń (20 March, 1767).

THE CONFEDERATION OF RADOM AND THE SEYM OF 1767–1768

To break the resistance of the King on the issue of reform and that of the Czartoryskis with regard to the dissenters, Russia decided to take advantage of the conservative opposition. It was clumsy alliance because the conservative elements with the Episcopate playing an important role, were the most unyielding on the question of dissenters. They were allowed, however, to delude themselves with the hope of the dethronement of Stanisław Augustus and for a return of the "Saxon times" (the young Elector of Saxony was growing up). The malcontent magnates under the direction of the Russian envoy, Repnin, formed local Confederations and approached Catherine II with the request that the "old government" be reinstated under a Russian guarantee. The Confederation was popular among the befuddled gentry, roused by propaganda against the "new-fangled ideas" of Warsaw and by religious slogans. Having humiliated the King and holding him at bay, Russia attained her goal. Stanisław Augustus bowed to pressure. The confederates, who had formed a General Union at Radom on 23 June, 1767 (under the presidency of Karol Radziwiłł), also witnessed the shipwreck of their hopes. Feelings of resistance against Russia began to run high.

In October 1767 the Confederate Seym assembled in Warsaw surrounded by Russian troops. To prevent discussion in the Seym, Repnin demanded that a delegation be appointed which would prepare draft resolutions which afterwards would be presented for approval to a plenary session. A section of the Confederates, led by Kajetan Sołtyk, the Bishop of Cracow, strongly opposed equal rights for the dissenters and the appointment of the delegation. Repnin responded with brutal reprisals (the arrest and deportation to Kaluga of the Bishops Sołtyk and J. A. Załuski, the Hetman Wacław Rzewuski and his son Seweryn). Russian troops blockaded Warsaw. The terrorized Seym, appointed a delegation and adjourned till February 1768.

During the four months of the delegation's work, the relations between the King and Repnin gradually improved. The conditions dictated by Russia with regard to dissenters were modified. The King obtained Repnin's consent for the establishment of a Permanent Council as a supreme executive authority, but the plan fell through because of Frederick II's unbending opposition. Far-reaching draft reforms with regard to peasants were not carried either, with the exception of the law depriving landowners of the power of life and death over serfs. In a number of secondary matters the Delegation continued and completed the work of reform. The principle of unanimity in the Seym was limited to "matters of State". Though this covered the most important spheres of legislation, it was no longer possible to break up a Seym for trivial reasons as happened under the Saxons. A definite limit was set, however, to reform aspirations. Five "eternal and invariable" cardinal principles were formulated upon which the stability of the political and social system reposed : 1) free election of kings, 2) *liberum veto,* 3) the right of renouncing allegiance to the King, 4) the gentry's exclusive right to hold office and to own land, and 5) the landowners' dominion over the peasants.

The resolutions of the Seym were placed under the guarantee of Catherine II and thus the Commonwealth was reduced even formally to the level of a vassal state. The Russian troops were, however, to leave the country, because Turkey insisted upon this point and Russia did not wish to break with her for the time being. Poland's place in the "Northern system" was to be defined by a Russo-Prussian agreement.

THE CONFEDERATION OF BAR (1768–1772)

The international situation had changed since 1764. Anxiety and the desire to take revenge against the "Northern system" were growing among the "southern Powers". The energetic foreign minister of France, Choiseul, was an exponent of this trend. He tried to set Turkey against Russia by pointing to the danger involved in the consolidation of Catherine II's influence in Poland. The Commonwealth, shaken by political crises, might become a seat of anti-Russian diversion. The troubles of Stanisław Augustus aroused hopes in Dresden where Elector Frederick Augustus had come of age. Some Radom Confederates, disappointed in Russia, decided therefore to take up the fight with the support of the southern Powers.

On 29 February 1768 an armed Confederation was formed in the Podolian town of Bar, 60 km from the Turkish border, proclaiming the defense of the faith and freedom to be its aim. The Confederation was headed by Józef Pułaski and Michał Krasiński, brother of the Party's chief diplomatic agent, Adam Krasiński, Bishop of Kamieniec. The movement had a markedly religious character, especially in the first period. A great influence was exerted over the Confederates by the Carmelite Father Marek Jandołowicz, who enjoyed the reputation of a prophet and worker of miracles. The nucleus of the Confederation's armed force was "The Order of the Knights of the Holy Cross". The Confederation spread quickly in the Ukraine. It was supported by most of the magnates, had the support of the rank and file gentry and part of the regular troops which passed over to the Confederates.

Repnin postponed the departure of Russian troops from Poland and sent them against the Confederates with royal regiments under the command of Ksawery Branicki marching with the Russians. A civil war flared up as a result of this foreign intervention. In addition an uprising by the peasants broke out.

The peasant discontent had been simmering in the Ukrainian borderlands for a long time. The pacification of those territories after the suppression of the Cossacks was followed by colonization. The privileges of the new settlers were now expiring and they became ordinary serfs. The growth of serfdom was accompanied by an intense Roman-Catholic missionary activity. The Ukrainian peasants had pinned some vague hopes on the Orthodox Empress and on her demands with regard to dissenters. The disappointment of these hopes by the armed intervention of the Catholic gentry was the immediate reason for the outbreak of an uprising under Ivan Gonta and Maxim Zhelezniak which spread over wide areas of the Ukraine in the spring and summer of 1768. The fighting cost many lives on both sides. Thousands of gentry and Jewish innkeepers perished at the hands of peasants, especially in the town of Humań. The pacification carried out jointly by Russian and royal troops, under Generals Kretchetnikov and Stempkowski, brought about an even greater loss of life. The peasant rising was a terrible shock to the gentry. The Confederation, in their blind hatred of the King, went as far as to put on him the blame for unleashing this Ukrainian whirlwind. For a long time, the terrible vision of the year 1768 was to be present in all debates on the peasant question and the religious and national problems of the Ukraine.

The capture of Bar by the Russians on 20 June, 1768 and the peasant war destroyed the Confederation in the south-eastern territories; the riots broke out again, however, in the region of Cracow (June–August), in Lithuania and Byelorussia (August–October). The Confederates were not an army, but a kind of a mass-levy of the gentry who long ago had become unaccustomed to warfare. The small Russian army (20,000 men) routed the Confederate groups easily, but was unable to pacify the country. The military inefficiency of the Confederates was compensated for by their anti-royalist political enthusiasm and by their religious and patriotic fervour. Russia now sought an understanding with the Czartoryskis, but negotiations came to standstill upon the news that the Porte had declared war on Russia (8 October, 1768); the "Polish War" as the Turks called it. The King ceased fighting the Confederates and adopted a wait-and-see attitude. In spite of the fact that Russia moved a part of her forces from Poland to the Turkish front the year 1769 failed to bring military success to the Confederation which had no unified command and supreme political authority. It was not until the autumn of 1769 that, under the pressure of France and Saxony, a "Generality" was formed at Prešov (in Slovakia).

Owing to the military reverses of the Turks, France wished to invigorate the Polish diversion by sending money and instructors with Colonel Charles Dumouriez to the Confederates. It was Dumouriez who, yielding to Saxon adherents, encouraged the Generality to proclaim the dethronement of Stanisław Augustus on 22 October, 1770. This step precluded all chances for an understanding between the Confederates and Warsaw. At the end of 1770 the military activity of the Confederation grew stronger. It had a strong foothold in Great Poland, where it was not impeded by the Prussians, because Russia's troubles in Poland were grist to the mill of Frederick II. In south-western Poland, an attempt was made with the help of the French to develop regular operations on the basis of newly formed infantry units and fortresses (in particular that of Częstochowa). Dumouriez thought of mopping up a fairly large area near the Austrian border in the spring in order to be able to carry out the election of a new king there. He was, however, defeated by Suvorov near Lanckorona in May. The last major military effort was Hetman Ogiński's rising in Lithuania, routed by the Russians in the battle of Stołowicze (September 1771). Soon afterwards (3 November) an atempt was made by the Confederates to kidnap Stanisław Augustus, which was condemned as attempted regicide and did much discredit the Confederates in the opinion of monarchist Europe. The Confederation was dying out when the news of the partition spread in the spring of 1772. The Confederates held out longest in Częstochowa, until 18 August, 1772.

The war of the Confederation demonstrated the military ineffectiveness of the gentry mass-levy when confronted with the military skill and organization of the second half of the eighteenth century. Genuine military talent was revealed only by Kazimierz Pułaski who scored several minor successes. These marginal successes as well the traditionalism taking little account of reality, explain the illusions about the value of improvised warfare by the gentry (*la petite guerre*) prevailing in Poland and among foreigners interested in Poland.

In its constitutional programme, the Confederation of Bar followed in the path of the Confederation of Radom, as a conservative movement with eyes fixed entirely on the gentry's Golden Freedom. On the other hand, original ideas were expressed by foreigners who devoted their writings to the cause of the Confederation : Rousseau (*Considérations sur le gouvernement de la Pologne*) and Mably (*Du gouvernement et des lois de la Pologne*). The Confederation thus played an indirect role in the West, stimulating the formulation of new opinions on civil liberty and national independence. The official historian of the French Ministry of Foreign Affairs, Rulhière (*Histoire de l'anarchie en Pologne*) helped greatly to popularize the legend of Bar. Kazimierz Pułaski who fought for the independence of the United States and fell in the battle of Savannah in 1779, carried the memories of Bar over the Ocean.

The Confederation of Bar was an important experience in the life of the last generations of independent Poland. The anonymous mass of Confederate veterans later to some extent helped to shape the opinion of the country gentry. During the Confederation war, while the magnate leaders quarrelled and in many cases preserved their fortunes by sitting on the fence, the younger members of the gentry took refuge in the forests and were deported to Siberia by the thousands. Resentment against the magnates grew among the Confederate soldiers. In spite of the leading part played by the factions of the magnates, the Confederation of Bar contributed to a growth of the gentry's political independence by making them sensitive to the issue of national freedom.

THE FIRST PARTITION

The Russo-Turkish war might have carried the seeds of the European war, if Austria had opposed Russia's advance in the Balkans. This would have set both systems of alliances in motion. It was against this background that the Prussian plan for a pacification of the Commonwealth was formed. As early as February 1769 Frederick II sent to St. Petersburg his so-called "Count Lynar's Plan", providing for a reconciliation of Austria with Russia and Prussia by means of a joint partition of Poland. The Tsarina's Court oscillated between Chernishev's tendency towards partition and Panin's policy of a Polish protectorate. Inability to deal with the Confederation swung opinion in favour of partition. The result of Russian policy in Poland had so far been somewhat unsuccessful. The Austro-Prussian rapprochement (the meeting of Frederick II and Joseph II on the battlefields of the Silesian Wars : at Nysa in the summer of 1769, and at Neustadt [Nowe Miasto] in the autumn of 1770) caused alarm in St. Petersburg. The petty greed of Austria (seizure of Spisz in 1769, and of three districts in the Tatra foothills in 1770) furnished a precedent.

In the spring of 1771, Panin made last attempt at pacifying Poland by dispatching Saldern to Warsaw. After the failure of this mission, negotiations with Prussia for a partition were started in June. All the circumstances assisted the Frederick's game : the unsuccessful rising of Ogiński in Lithuania and especially the warlike gestures of Austria. In July 1771 an Austro-Turkish alliance was signed in Constantinople ; the armies of the Emperor were concentrated in Hungary. Yet, in Vienna there was no firm resolve upon war. Since the downfall of Choiseul (December 1770) Austria could not entirely count on her French ally. France wanted to preserve peace and Choiseul's successor, d'Aiguillon, informed Frederick in August 1771 that he would have nothing against the annexation of Gdańsk and a small number of Polish districts by Prussia. This was not the price to detach Frederick from his alliance with Russia, the only guarantee of sure and permanent acquisitions in Poland. The loyal ally put his hand ostentatiously on the hilt of the sword, fully aware that this gesture would be enough and that he would not have to draw the sword from its sheath because the Franco-Austrian alliance was disintegrating. As long as the Austrians maintained their threatening attitude and restrained Catherine in the Balkans, they could induce her to seek compensation for herself (and for those who, though not engaged in war, were anxious to preserve the balance of power in Europe) in another direction, cherished by Prussia for so long. Russia eventually decided to give up Moldavia and Valachia and to make her peace with Austria by drawing her into the partnership in the partition. Maria Theresa entered into the negotiations for partition very reluctantly, but once her scruples were overcome and the decision taken in Vienna in 1772, Austria revealed herself to be the most acquisitive of the powers.

Thus Panin's "Northern system" disintegrated; it failed to play its role as a safeguard of Russian expansion in the Balkans and on the Black Sea coast. The "Southern system" also collapsed; its nucleus, the Franco-Austrian alliance, did not stand the test of the Eastern and Polish complications. Upon the ruins of those two "systems", an alliance of the three greatest military powers of the time was established. This event, dangerous for the balance of power in Europe, caused panic in Paris and dissatisfaction in London. Great Britain, however, did not go beyond defending Gdańsk against Prussia's annexationist plans, and the efforts of France were chaotic, belated and ineffective.

The year-long negotiations for partition proceeded in an atmosphere of hard bargaining and were accompanied by accomplished facts. St. Petersburg intended to continue her tutelage over a mutilated Commonwealth and, since the principle of the equality of the treaties had been adopted, Russia presented her territorial claims in a relatively modest manner thereby seeking to reduce the acquisitions of Austria and Prussia. They, on the other hand, vied with one another in their greed. Frederick II strove for Gdańsk with particular eagerness. Meeting with a determined resistance in that matter from Russia and the maritime powers (England and the United Provinces), the King of Prussia tried in vain to coerce the people of Gdańsk by all manner of vexations and pressures into a voluntary surrender to Prussian rule.

Under the treaties of 5 August, 1772, and subsequent delimitations, Prussia received 36,000 sq.km of territory and 580,000 inhabitants, Austria 83,000 sq.km and 2,650,000 inhabitants, Russia 92,000 sq.km and 1,300,000 inhabitants. Not satisfied with their spoils from the treaty, Prussia and Austria usurped further acquisitions in the course of frontier delimitations; these encroachments were, however, partly checked after a Russian intervention in 1776.

The importance of these annexations cannot be measured by area alone. In spite of the fact that Prussia's share in land and population was the smallest, she received the most valuable spoils on account of the vital economic importance of the mouth of the Vistula. According to Frederick II the Prussians became after the first partition "the masters of all Poland's products and entire transit". The Austrian annexation tore away from the Commonwealth rich and densely populated lands with valuable salt mines. Russia took possession of a comparatively poor and thinly populated area.

The ambassadors of the three Powers demanded that the partition treaties be ratified by the Seym. The Seym was to remain in session under the form of Confederation (the *liberum veto* was, in that case, inconvenient for its foreign protectors) and to appoint a Delegation, following the example of 1767. The Confederation was formed from teh corrupt circle of former Saxon and Russian creatures, under the presidency of Adam Poniński. Although the chamber of deputies had been carefully selected (the local diets had been held in the presence of the forces of the partitioning Powers), a few deputies headed by Tadeusz Reytan raised a strong protest against the Confederation. In the Seym, which however remained confederated, the followers of the King and of the Czartoryskis led a quiet opposition as a delaying action. Stanisław Augustus solicited foreign intervention and inspired in the West, especially in England, a campaign by pamphlets to show the illegality of the partition. The Powers responded to all resistance with the threat of extending their annexations further. The treaties were ratified on 30 September, 1773.

The enforced partition was supplemented by trade treaties, ratified in March 1775. The treaty with Prussia was disastrous for the Commonwealth being imposed upon the desperately resisting Delegation in a particularly brutal manner. With Silesia and, later, Pomerania and the lower reaches of the Vistula under Prussian rule, the overwhelming part of the Polish foreign trade had to pass through Prussian dominions. The treaty imposed heavy custom duties on goods leaving Poland, low duties on Prussian goods, and downright prohibitive charges on Polish transit trade passing through Prussian territory; the trade between the Commonwealth and Gdańsk was included in the latter category. In this way Frederick II, unable to get hold of Gdańsk, decided to ruin the basis of its prosperity by directing the Vistula trade to Elbląg which was already Prussian and enjoyed special custom privileges.

Apart from the immediate aims of exerting pressure on Gdańsk and seeking fiscal advantages, Frederick II was carrying out a long-term economic policy towards Poland which he had begun as early as 1765, when he thwarted the Polish customs reform. The Commonwealth, remaining under the political protectorate of Russia was faced with the danger of becoming economically a kind of Prussian colony.

With almost 30 per cent of its territory and 35 per cent of its population lost, the Commonwealth still remained one of the largest states in Europe; in area (520,000 sq.km) it surpassed Spain and was still equal to France. Within the boundaries of this multinational state, however, the ethnically Polish area with its main artery, the Vistula, was particularly mutilated in the north and south, cut off from the sea and from the natural boundary of the mountains and enclosed in the pincers of the Prussian frontiers. The first partition, moreover, worsened dramatically the international position of Poland which, virtually became a potentially "revisionist" country. The traditional policy of Poland's neighbours thus acquired a new reason for restricting her independence; the first partition constituted a precedent for future action.

CONSTITUTIONAL TRANSFORMATIONS (1773-1780)

The Delegation, appointed by the partition Seym (1773-1775), worked out new forms of government. The cardinal laws being in principle only a repetition of those of 1768 were again passed and the new form of government was subject to the guarantee not only of Russia, but also of the other two partitioning Powers. On the other hand, a rapprochement took place during the session between Stanisław Augustus and Russia, represented by the ambassador Stackelberg, who was responsible for the new course of the Tsarist policy. This rapprochement made it possible to proceed with the reforms. The establishment of the Commission of National Education in 1773, was the most momentous achievement. The breve of Clement XIV, abolishing the Jesuit Order, was used and, in spite of the Nuncio's resistance, the Jesuit estates were turned over to the State educational fund. Thus Europe's first Ministry of Education was created.

Most disputes centred around the projected Permanent Council. According to the original idea, this collegiate body was to take over all the royal powers, but according to the final draft (voted in 1775), it was the arbitrary magnate-ministers who were placed under restraint rather than the King. The Council was composed of 18 senators and 18 deputies elected by the Seym for a term of 2 years. The Council was presided over by the King. It was divided into five departments: foreign affairs, police, military, finance and justice (the Educational Commission was not subordinated to the Council, but remained directly under the King's authority). The Council submitted to the King three candidates for each senatorial seat. Every two years the retiring government gave the Seym an account of its activities. The establishment of the Permanent Council put into practice a plan which had long been proposed in Polish political literature.

The system of government created by the partition Seym was not free of ambiguities, particularly the definition of the terms of reference for the departments of the Permanent Council and those of the Commissions created in the years 1764-1766 (the Military, Fiscal, Marshal's and Assessorial Commissions); these Commissions were at one time directed against the ministers appointed for life. The ministers now saw them as a lesser evil than the new departments; the Military Commission in particular had, since 1775, become a tool in the Hetmens' hands. The Hetmen again came to the fore as the opposition aspiring to overthrow the Permanent Council and to have Stackelberg recalled from Poland.

A regrouping took place within the oligarchy. The old leaders died out or withdrew from political life. The long feud between the Potockis and the Czartoryskis gave way to solidarity in the fight against the royal authority and against the Permanent Council. Men of the former "Family" (Stanisław Lubomirski, Adam Czartoryski) now stood side by side with Ignacy Potocki, Ksawery Branicki (until recently a confident of the King and a conqueror of the Confederates, now Hetman and champion of the Golden Freedom), and Seweryn Rzewuski (deported in 1767, now Hetman, always an arch-conservative). Branicki was stirring the army to disobedience against the Council. The Seym of 1776, the first Seym not meeting in the rules of a Confederation since the beginning of Stanisław Augustus' reign, was to become a trial of strength. The opposition sought support in St. Petersburg (counting upon Potemkin against Panin), but they were disappointed: Stanisław Augustus obtained the protection of Russian troops for the Seym and the consent to form a Confederation in the Permanent Council.

The Seym of 1776 debated in an atmosphere of *coup d'état*. The opposition deputies were not admitted to the Confederation and excluded form the Chamber. The authority of the Permanent Council was extended, the Military Commission abolished, and the Hetmen deprived of their command. Besides, the Seym opened up the way to further reform by entrusting Andrzej Zamoyski, upon the King's proposal, with preparing a codification of the law.

Stanisław Augustus, encouraged by the success of the Seym, tried to engage in more active foreign policy by a normalization of Polish-Turkish relations and a rapprochement with France. These too independent steps were not liked in St. Petersburg. At the Seym of 1778 Stackelberg gave a free hand to the anti-royalist opposition, bringing Stanisław Lubomirski, Ksawery Branicki, Ignacy Potocki and Kazimierz Nestor Sapieha into the Permanent Council. During the term of office of this Council (1778–1780) the fate of Zamoyski's Code was decided. The draft Code, preceded by wide publicity and prepared with the help of a group of collaborators invited by Zamoyski (including Józef Wybicki and Joachim Chreptowicz) was already completed for the Seym of 1778. The work went beyond the limits of a mere codification of the law; it proposed a number of reforms in the social system and in the relations between Church and State. The draft Code recommended a considerable limitation of serfdom and an extension of the townspeople's rights (among them the right to send representatives to the Seym), while the landless gentry who constituted the magnates' clientele were to be deprived of political rights. In the relations of Church and State, the draft proposed to introduce the exequatur, making the consent of the State necessary for the publication of Papal bulls. The religious orders were to be subject to the jurisdiction of the national episcopate and age limits for entry into monasteries were fixed.

The Seym of 1778 deferred consideration of the draft for two years. It was opposed during this period by Nuncio Archetti who canvassed large numbers of the provincial gentry through the monastic clergy. The gentry were particulary alarmed by the concessions to the peasants, which the propaganda greatly exaggerated. Stackelberg likewise opposed the Code. The Seym of 1780 rejected the draft. The King proposed in vain to defer once more consideration of it, but a resolution was passed which prohibited the draft from ever to be conssidered by the Seym again.

The Seym of 1780 revealed the limits of reform under Russian tutelage when conservative opinions prevailed among the gentry. Henceforth, the King's party lost the initiative in introducing reforms; it looked only to Russia and found no encouragement there. After dramatic upheavals, the joint government by the King and the Russian ambassador became stable. In 1780, the Russian army left the Commonwealth after sixteen years.

GOVERNMENT BY THE PERMANENT COUNCIL

Russia's policy in the years 1776-1778 consisted in maintaining an uneasy balance between the King and the oligarchical opposition. One spoke at that time of two "Muscovite parties" in Poland : the Stackelberg (or Royal) party and the Potemkin party (or the opposition of the magnates). Such a state of affairs was not a result of differences in St. Petersburg, but of the tactics already adopted by Russia at the time of the Confederation of Radom.

The position of Stanisław Augustus was growing stronger. His renunciation of further reforms reassured the gentry in the countryside. The King attracted to himself a group of experienced political leaders like his brother Michał Poniatowski (Primate of Poland since 1784) and Joachim Chreptowicz, Vice-Chancellor of Lithuania, who skilfully managed the elections in the local diets. The core of the King's party was the newly-created senators, appointed from the middle gentry. The Senate lost its former character of a chamber of magnates and actually won supremacy over the Chamber of Deputies. The King commanded a majority in that Chamber, too. Debates in the Seyms tended to be sterile, because the more important issues which would have required unanimity as so-called matters of State were not put to the vote. For this reason the *liberum veto* had little significance. The Seyms elected to the Permanent Council candidates agreed upon by the King and Stackelberg. Stanisław Augustus organized a number of private royal chanceries, according to the structure of the departments. These chanceries being better qualified bodies, took over, actual leadership.

The Department of Foreign Affairs only formally had control of the foreign service created by the King (under Saxon rule, Poland had no permanent representatives abroad). The Department of Justice intervened in the judiciary and in disputes over competences. One of the primary reasons for the breakdown of the rule of law in the Commonwealth was the inability to execute sentences of the court. Now the courts resorted to military assistance which, it is true, brought about conflicts between the army and the civilian population, and kept the meagre armed force occupied. The King's endeavours to create a court militia were defeated by a strong opposition. Neither was the codification of law resumed after 1780, a matter which Stanisław Augustus had considered a burning need. Yet, not a little was done to uphold the laws. The Department of Police supervised order in the towns, the hospital system and the public health services. It was an institution with a limited personnel and only vaguely defined terms of reference. The King's plans for expanding the activities of the Department were opposed by Marshal Stanisław Lubomirski (marshals had traditionally exercised authority over the police in the capital). In the field of finance, a dualism between the Commissions of 1764 and the Department persisted. The supremacy of the Department was purely formal. The Fiscal Commissions had at their disposal the best trained administrative organization in the Commonwealth (the country was divided into ten fiscal provinces under superintendents). The fiscal revenues amounted to about 20,000,000 zlotys annually and increased slightly as the administration became more efficient. In addition to financial affairs, the Commissions' responsibility included industrial development and transportation.

The Military Department was virtually controlled by the King's military chancellery (General J. Komarzewski). The establishment of 1776 was now limited to 17,000 men. The tax system, which remained unchanged till 1788, did not permit raising more men. By taking advantage of budget surpluses, the army was slightly increased and reached a strength of 18,500 men in 1786. The structure of the Polish army did not correspond to the practice of the time. The cavalry (8000 strong) was still too large in relation to the infantry and was moreover unruly and archaic. The army had no system of conscription and voluntary enlistment was failing. The practice of sale and purchase of military commissions had an adverse effect on the quality of the officers. The Military Department and the King's military chancellery repeatedly took the initiative in army reform, but their attempts collapsed against the opposition led by Hetman Branicki. Much was done, however, to put the small army cadres in order; the artillery in particular was of a high standard. While the King aimed at bringing the Polish military system into conformity with the contemporary professional armies of Europe, the gentry considered that the Commonwealth should go its own way in those matters. Plans were advanced for basing the armed forces on civilian reserves, voivodship militias and the mass-levy. In that way, one expected to increase the armed forces without new taxes and conscription (which would have weakened the landowners' control over the peasants). The moral value of the citizen-soldier was used as argument. The magnate opposition counted on appropriating the supervision of a decentralized, provincial armed force.

Government by the Permanent Council was a step forward in comparison with the former anarchy and provided a school of administrative experience of great importance for the future; it was, however, a provisional arrangement, paralysed by the foreign guarantee. The Council and its Departments lacked authority and resources; nor was it backed by the sovereign will of the monarch, or by a parliament able to decide on "matters of state". It was the target of attack from the magnates' opposition which gathered momentum in the years 1784-1787.

The oligarchical opposition so often in the past disunited, now displayed considerable solidarity, which illustrated the extent to which the position of the oligarchy was in jeopardy. Yet, the opposition was not homogeneous. Branicki or Rzewuski represented the worst traditions of hetman anarchy, which gained in the conflict *inter maiestatem ac libertatem*. Of a different character was the group connected with Puławy, the Czartoryskis' residence (Adam Czartoryski, the brothers Ignacy and Stanisław Potocki); Puławy competed with royal Warsaw as a political and cultural centre. Coupled with a family pride, the idea of reforming the Commonwealth was current in Puławy, as well as the will to serve the country and faith in the ideals of Enlightenment. Apart from the political struggle another fight went on for cultural values.

Chapter XII

THE SOCIETY AND CIVILIZATION OF THE AGE OF ENLIGHTENMENT

THE ECONOMIC REVIVAL

For neutral Poland, the Seven Years' War provided considerable opportunities for economic development. This appeared in the increase of grain exports in Gdańsk (in 1762–1769, they reached 56,000 lasts a year which meant an annual income of about 20 million zlotys). It is true that Frederick II's debasement of the coinage had flooded the country with counterfeit money, but that kind of inflation, while resulting in a rise in prices, creating difficulty for the treasury and causing more than one devaluation, to a certain extent provided an abundance of money. Moreover money, liable to a decline in its value was correspondingly mobile, and was not worth hoarding at home, or accepted abroad. This period of a certain boom, an unquestionable growth of agricultural production and monetary chaos coincided with the accession of Stanisław Augustus.

The leaders of "The Family" were interested in economic problems and tried seriously to undo the effect of the State's traditional negligence. In 1764 it was resolved to establish a mint in Warsaw and to carry out a currency reform. Weights and measures were officially standardized, the General Post Office was established, control commissions were introduced in towns and a general custom tariff was introduced (as we already know). The individual magnates in the party of "The Family", in their concern to create conditions indispensable to economic development, showed their own private initiative. In 1765 Michał Ogiński launched the construction of a canal connecting the Neman with the Pripet', for which reason it was resolved to honour him with a monument. Fiscal commissions supervised the preservation and extension of the network of roads and waterways. The Lithuanian Commission undertook the construction of the "Royal Canal", connecting the Pripet' with the Bug. According to the original plans, those two large canals were to connect the country's eastern regions with the Baltic. Opened for traffic in 1784, under the changed conditions of the partition, they connected the basins of the Vistula and Neman with the Black Sea.

In these first years of hope and aspiration, a number of industrial enterprises were begun. These were not the manufactories seen earlier on the latifundia, but projects on a national scale. The first joint-stock company, "The Wool Manufacture Company" (under the direction of Andrzej Zamoyski) was formed with the government support in 1767. To meet the requirements of the army the King established an ordnance factory in Warsaw and a cloth factory; for the needs both of the Court and the general market as well, he established a faience porcelain factory at the Belvedere Palace. The King's most ambitious investment was the establishment in the royal demesne of Grodno, under the direction of Antoni Tyzenhaus, Treasurer of Lithuania, of a network of over a dozen manufactories with greatly diversified production. Most of them proved to be short-lived and failed not only because of the calamities brought by the Confederation of Bar and the first partition of Poland. The endeavours discussed here suffered from the dilettantism of the magnates and from lack of experts. In spite of the fact that they were based on the theory of the unpaid labour of serfs, these manufactories proved unprofitable. Serf labour was inefficient and difficult to exact, luxury goods did not withstand foreign competition, while ordinary products were not easily sold because of the low buying capacity of the market. The industrialization of an underdeveloped country, bureaucratically conceived from above, planned at a desk, might have overcome its first difficulties in the hot-house conditions of an absolute monarchy. Such conditions did not exist in Poland. Among projects on a national scale, the most durable achievement of those years was the stabilization of currency (1776) but even here a mistake was committed in striking silver coins which were too valuable and leaked out of the country in great quantity. This led to the reduction of the bank rate in 1786. The law of 1774 on negotiable instruments facilitated and safeguarded credit transactions.

The first partition introduced a basic change in the economic situation of the country. The loss of Pomerania and the trade treaty with Prussia resulted in a more than twofold decrease of grain exports via Gdańsk (down to 23,000 last a year). This loss was not compensated for by an increase in the export of agricultural products through Elbląg and Königsberg. The Prussian frontiers, hampering seriously Polish exports (with the exception of raw-materials sought by Prussian industry, like wool), provided an open gate for imports from Prussia. According to official Polish data the adverse balance of trade for the years 1776–1777 amounted to 44 million zlotys. This situation alarmed public opinion. The call for balancing trade by savings and the development of home industries was one of the most popular programmes. Nevertheless, Poland remained an agricultural country, with her farm production continuing to expand.

With the national territory in the Vistula basin mutilated, and the Baltic trade hampered, the Ukrainian territories and the prospects for Black Sea trade (opened up as a result of Russia's victory over Turkey) began to acquire economic importance. The network of waterways was re-orientated in that direction. With support from the Seym, the Company for Black Sea

Trade was established in 1782, with the magnate-banker Prot Potocki at its head. Poland concluded a trade treaty with Rusia for this purpose and opened a consular office in Kherson. The Company's ships appeared in the Mediterranean. Trade with Moldavia was also developing and in this connexion work was undertaken to make the Dniester navigable. The Black Sea trade was halted after the outbreak of the Russo-Turkish war (1787), but army contracts provided a compensation for grain producers.

The increase in grain production and in stock breeding was to some extent related to the progress in farming techniques. The second half of the eighteenth century witnessed a great development of agricultural literature. There even appeared the first books on agriculture designed for the peasants. We know of estates where new techniques and new crops (clover, alfalfa and potatoes) were introduced, but these were just modest beginnings in the great agricultural changes which were to take place in the nineteenth century. In the reformers' writings, the demand that labour dues be replaced by money rents, enjoyed much currency. The social and economic advantages of such a reform were emphasized because the peasant's initiative would be encouraged by making him interested in the results of production. The commutation of services into rents, carried out in the estates of Andrzej Zamoyski, Joachim Chreptowicz, Paweł Brzostowski and Stanisław Poniatowski (the King's nephew) achieved considerable fame and were held up as an example to others. Some of the great estate owners were attracted to the rent economy by the prospect of the estate administration being greatly simplified (compulsory labour in the latifundia required a large personnel for supervision and coercion). The success of these reforms depended on the development of the local market (that meant sales facilities for the peasants). The rent economy and the replacing of serf labour in manor farms by hired labour took place on a large scale in the economically developed territories of Great Poland. In the overpopulated territories of Little Poland where manor farms were not lacking in manpower, the commutation of labour dues into money rents was applied according to the temporary needs of the owners. In the Ukraine, in connexion with chances for exports, the changes went in the opposite direction: from rents towards serf labour. Nationally, the manor farm and serf economy not only held its dominating position, but was expanding wherever possibilities of large scale grain transactions existed, specially on the estates of the middle gentry. On the other hand, the demand that peasants should pay their dues in money instead of labour was often caused by difficulties in the sale of manorial produce and was tantamount to burdening the peasant with these difficulties. The question of the sale of farm products, connected with the balance of trade, presented another important question. Here we have the two aspects of the main problem, namely the stimulation of the home market.

In economic literature a simple remedy was repeated over and over again: the development of the towns and of industrial production would

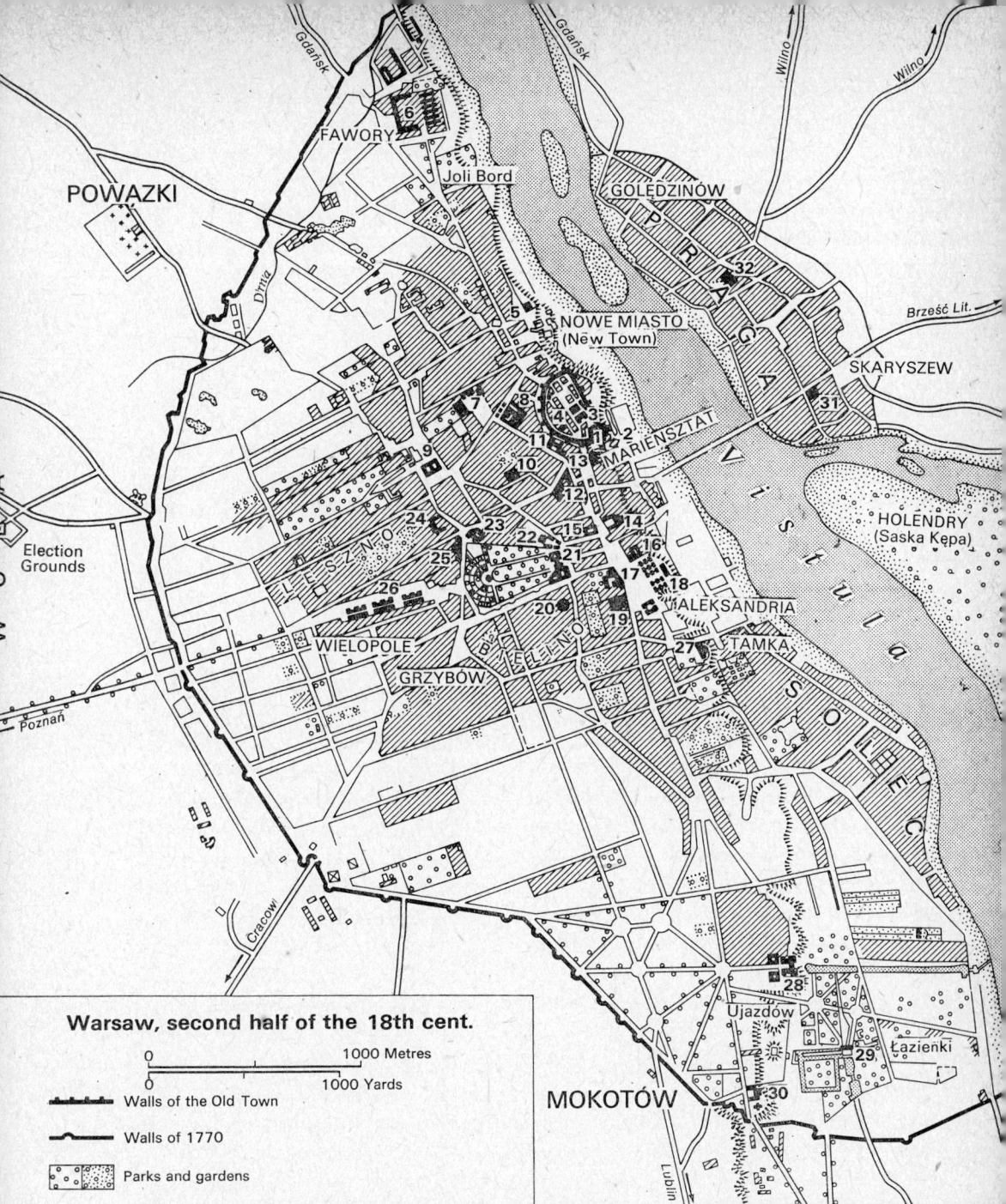

Warsaw, second half of the 18th cent.

- Walls of the Old Town
- Walls of 1770
- Parks and gardens

1. The Royal Castle, 2. The Palace "Pod Blachą", 3. St. John's Church, 4. St. Martin's Church, 5. St. Mary's Church, 6. Royal Guards barracks, 7. The Palace of the Republic, 8. Piarists' College, 9. The Arsenal, 10. The Załuski Library, 11. The Branicki Palace, 12. The Primate's Palace, 13. Black Friar's Church, 14. The Radziwiłł Palace, 15. The Czartoryski Palace, 16. Sisters of Visitation Church, 17. The Czapski Palace, 18. The John Casimir Palace, 19. St. Cross Church, 20. The Protestant Church, 21. The Royal Saxon Palace, 22. The Brühl Palace, 23. The Blue Palace, 24. The Ogiński Palace, 25. The Bieliński Palace, 26. Horse Guards barracks, 27. The Ostrogski Palace, 28. The Ujazdowski Palace, 29. The Royal Palace Łazienki, 30. The Belvedere, 31. The Parish Church of Praga, 32. Black Friars Church in Praga.

increase the volume of exchange between town and country. Industrial activity was presented as the duty of a patriot. This motive as well as the current fashionable ideas should not be underestimated in the activities of some of the magnate-industrialists, but economics remained economics. The latifundia manufactories of the Saxon times continued to exist, new ones were established, more or less profitable, more or less durable. This was undoubtedly an element of progress, but it was not adequate to the country's needs. Nevertheless, deeper changes in the economic development were also taking place little by little.

Warsaw, a town of less than 30,000 inhabitants in the first years of Stanisław Augustus' reign, reached a population of 120,000 by 1792. This large capital became, as a matter of fact, an important centre of domestic trade, of urban industry, crafts and trade as well as of something new in Poland, of numerous banking houses. Under the difficult conditions of being on the Prussian borderland, the important centre of Great Poland's cloth and linen industry maintained its position as a producer, while handicraft production in this region was dominated and organized by commercial capital to an ever greater extent. In the region of Kielce, on the basis of the old ironworks, modern blast furnaces replaced the former primitive ones. The Mines Commission, established by the King in 1782, resumed the exploitation of abandoned mines and conducted geological surveys (after the loss of the Wieliczka and Bochnia salt-mines, the search for salt deposits became an urgent problem). The mining of hard coal was started. A characteristic phenomenon of the 1780's was the establishment of numerous joint-stock companies with mixed gentry and urban middle class capital. The most important among them was the "National Linen Factory Company", formed by the Primate Poniatowski in 1787. The enlargement of the army to 60,000 during the Four Years' Seym was an incentive for the development of a national industry which met to a large extent the needs of the army. A great deal of building construction took place in the country, especially in the expanding city of Warsaw.

When dealing with economic revival, one ought not to overlook the element of conscious effort. The fascination of the people of the eighteenth century with economic problems and their faith that the economy could be consciously shaped, were a striking feature. An abundant economic literature, a multitude of theoretical projects proposed both by private individuals and by government departments, specially by the fiscal commissions, and the continuous search for new ways and solutions were also dynamic elements of development appearing in this short and difficult period. The difficulties were indeed great and not only of an external nature. Specific projects were conditioned by the weakness of investment capital and by dear credit; the whole of economic life was determined by the division of society into estates. It was against such a background that this unique plan for an "Economic Constitution" came to life in 1791.

THE SOCIAL TRANSFORMATION

Out of about 12 million inhabitants, (without Courland) Poland lost about 4·5 millions in 1772. Within the next twenty years the population of the dismembered country grew by natural increase form 7·5 million to about 9 million (in 1791). The approximate social structure of that population (we have so far at our disposal rather inexact data only) was as follows:

Gentry	700,000	8·0 per cent
Clergy	50,000	0·5 per cent
Burghers	600,000	7·0 per cent
Jews	900,000	10·0 per cent
Peasants	6,500,000	72·0 per cent
Miscellaneous (Armenians, Tartars, Orthodox "Old-Believers")	250,000	2·5 per cent

In the multinational Commonwealth, the Ukrainians, Byelorussians and Lituanians accounted for about one half of all peasants and burghers excluding the Jews. On the other hand, the process of complete Polonization of the gentry in the Commonwealth's eastern territories was already concluded.

This social structure does not reflect the occupational structure. The peasants were overwhelmingly farmers, though there were among them persons engaged in rural crafts (especially the timber and textile industries). The Jews were mostly tradesmen, middlemen and artisans. Two-thirds of them lived in towns and thus were actually burghers, though they did not belong to the burghers' estate. Besides the 600,000 burghers in the formal sense, as the citizens of the towns, there lived in the towns as many Jews, a certain number of clergy and gentry with their servants and the craftsmen employed by them who did not belong to the municipal community. The urban population can thus be estimated at about 1,300,000, with the reservation, however, that most small towns were in practice agricultural settlements. Finally, with regard to the gentry, less than a half owned landed estates (about 300,000). For the most part, they were leaseholders, farmers inhabiting separate villages (the so-called *zaścianki*) and small holders, tilling their land themselves. The manorial staff, the court and the militia of the magnate, were also composed of empoverished gentlemen. In the course of the eighteenth century, a process of social differentiation occurred within all the estates.

The factor levelling out the peasants' financial position was the manor farm economy which was demanding that those who supplied a determined quantity of labour (with their own draft animals) should have an adequate economic potential. The gentry manor farm and the serf village were an integrated whole. When conversion from labour dues to money rent took place, or hired labour was introduced in the manor farm on a larger scale, the levelling role of the manor decreased, and the social division of labour and financial differentiation progressed. In the second half of the eighteenth century, new methods of farming, agricultural literature and general education sporadically began to reach the peasants. Towards the end of the century, the peasants reacted quite strongly to such political events as the Constitution of 3 May, 1791 and the Kościuszko Insurrection. The impact of the peasants on the moulding of the "peasant question" took place above all through acts of resistance against serfdom. The peasants used their limited possibilities for presenting their claims and bringing complaints (we have a large number of peasant petitions from this period). They refused to perform duties and escaped from the "bad master's" village. The Ukrainian rising of 1768 left an unforgettable impression upon the gentry, and new peasant disorders in the Ukraine caused serious fears in 1789.

The implementation of peasant reform was much more difficult in the Commonwealth than in an absolute monarchy; it had to pass through a Seym composed exclusively of members of the gentry. The Seyms of 1767–1768, 1773–1775 and 1780 rejected the proposals for reform although they were not at all radical. They proposed only to mitigate personal serfdom and to give the peasants the possibility of seeking justice in courts. The struggle for peasant reform went on outside the Seym in political writings.

The Jewish population, almost one-million strong, underwent an ever greater differentiation. The *Kahals*, responsible for Jewish debts, had from the seventeenth century onwards controlled the granting of credits and for practical purposes performed the function of banks. These flourishing associations dominated by a wealthy *élite*, disposed of considerable capital, deposited with them at interest by the gentry and clergy. They in turn lent money, not only to Jews. Owing to the *Kahal* banks a considerable concentration of usurious and commercial capital occurred of a scope reaching beyond Poland's borders. On the other hand, the majority of Polish Jews lived in extreme poverty.

The south-eastern borderlands of the Commonwealth produced in the eighteenth century two religious sects which had an important influence on the transformation within the Jewish community. The popular mystical Chassidic movement begun by Israel ben Eliezer, generally called Beszt, contributed to a firm isolation of the Jews from outside influence. The equally mystical anti-Talmudist sect formed by Jakub Frank developed in an opposite direction. The Frankists eventually adopted Christianity; a section of them was knighted and Polonized. The mass Chassidic movement and the much narrower Frankist movement made it difficult for the ideas of the Jewish Enlightenment according to the Berlin Haskala to spread in Poland; the disciples of Moses Mendelssohn were active in the Commonwealth, though under difficult conditions. Among the Maskils (advocates of the Enlightenment) the most distinguished was Mendel Levin from Satanów (a protégé of Adam Czartoryski).

The Jewish self-government known as "Seym of the Four Provinces" was abolished in 1764. The right of Jews to settle in towns and to engage in trade and crafts was restricted. Demands were made for the Jews to be settled on the land and for the *Kahals* to be abolished. The Christian burghers strove, through fear of competition, for an increasingly greater legal and economic curtailment of the Jewish population's rights. The reformers among the gentry desired assimilation by administrative pressure. The Jews felt that religious and national identity was threatened. The question of a Jewish reform was becomming an urgent problem. The estate barrier between the burghers and the Jews was an obstacle to the transformation of Polish towns into truly modern urban centres.

Within the estate of the burghers a slow disintegration of the guild organization took place. The purpose of the continued existence of guilds was questioned in many quarters. The differentiation of the burghers was most noticeable in Warsaw. On the one hand, the germs of a modern big bourgeoisie came into being. Bankers, rich merchants and industrialists had political and cultural aspirations. They built palaces for themselves and became partners of the gentry in more than an economic sense. The desire to emulate the magnates often had adverse effects because capital was turned over to consumption. However the desire of the rich burghers to purchase landed estates was a reflection of a normal tendency to secure a sound investment. On the other hand, Warsaw experienced a great concentration of town people which, at critical moments, exerted an important influence on the country's political climate. Warsaw, a great and dynamic city, abounding in contrasts, was an entirely novel phenomenon in the Commonwealth.

The prominence achieved by the burghers in intellectual life was likewise a new feature. The middle class provided not only university professors, jurists and learned priests as before, but also the leading political thinkers like Stanisław Staszic and Józef Pawlikowski, who demanded and planned the reform of the Commonwealth. The municipal reforms, undertaken in the 1760's and 1770's, had broadened the control of the State over the towns. The work of the control commissions and of the Permanent Council's Police Department contributed to putting the municipal finances in order and to the launching of public utility projects. This was, however, interference by the gentry authorities and was accepted reluctantly by the municipal authorities. The burghers aimed at emancipating themselves, supervising their own affairs and gaining a share in the central government of the Commonwealth. The people of Warsaw became a potentially revolutionary element.

The formal equality of "brother-gentlemen" had always been a fiction which became particularly glaring under the magnates' oligarchy. The great differentiation of the electoral body did not lead, however, to the formation of separate parties of the magnates, the middle-gentry and of the lesser gentry. In the first half of the eighteenth century, a score or so important families commanded all the votes, the poorest gentry being most dependent on them. Under the conditiions of anarchy, a system of patronage and clientship had developed; while it did not have a legal form, it was in essence similar to the process of feudalization in the medieval meaning of the term. The social trend of the government reforms in the second half of the eighteenth century was mainly the struggle against oligarchy. The strengthening of the central authority and the enforcement of law automatically loosened the bonds of patronage and clientship. Apart from this, domestic upheavals, specially the Confederation of Bar, shook many a magnate's fortune. Private armies were abolished. The now smaller courts of the magnates did not attract as many courtiers and hangers-on as before. The independence of the middle gentry was growing encouraged by deliberate policy of the royal party. The lesser gentry, on the other hand, remained dependent on the magnates, especially in the eastern borderlands. This was an ignorant element, in principle obedient to the magnates but turbulent, quick to grasp for the bottle and the sword. Poverty sometimes made them prone to radical tendencies. The social stratification and tension within the gentry were reflected in the problem of reforming electoral law.

The process of stratification or even partial disintegration of the traditional estates of the Commonwealth resulted in the emergence of new social classes. There was a category of people which did not fit into the accepted division: the migratory element, composed of peasants drawn away from the land, or artisans drawn away from their workshops, who made their living by hiring themselves as casual labour in various trades or in beggary. The apperance of itinerants was not novel but it was a particularly noticeable feature of this period and so was the tendency to employ them as manufacturing workshops workers. The problem of the proletariat had begun to present itself in Poland.

A process more evolved and characteristic for the Enlightenment was the formation of professional classes. In a society divided into estates, the role of the intelligentsia was played primarily by the secular and monastic clergy. An ecclesiastical career opened up the road to promotion, however limited, for people from lower estates. That is why so many able and ambitious people took holy orders in the eighteenth century. The novel aspect was that their membership of the ecclesiastical estate became in many instances purely formal. The dissolution of the numerous Jesuit order contributed to this development, but more fundamental causes were at work: the intellectual laicization of many priests and the fact that new types of secular careers became open to them. Educational reform secularized the teaching profession. The growth of periodicals and of all kinds of literary works made it possible for editors and writers to make a living from their professional work. A literary and artistic milieu appeared in Warsaw. The expansion of the civil service and the army drew some landowners away from the rustic way of life and attracted the lesser gentry. In the law, the bourgeois barristers began to make their mark. Laicized priests and ex-priests, teachers and tutors, scholars and artists, young civil servants, officers and lawyers, made up an element receptive to the ideas of Enlightenment and free of social prejudice. In this respect Warsaw, as a great city, was moving ahead of the rest of the country. A growing disparity arose between the progressive capital and the conservative provinces, a phenomenon which had not existed in the epoch of oligarchic decentralization.

CONFLICT OF FASHIONS AND IDEALS

Wąsy i peruka (The Moustache and the Wig) was the title of a comedy, in which a nineteenth century playwright expressed the contrasts in the cultural life, customs and manner in the times of Stanisław Augustus. On the one hand there was "sarmatism"; the old fashioned moustached nobleman, his head half-shaven, wearing the *kontusz,* an overcoat with split sleeves, following a semi-Turkish fashion and perorating in schoolboy Latin. On the other hand, there was "foreignism": the dandy in a powdered wig, a snob, forgetting not only Latin, but even Polish for the sake of French.

"Sarmatism", colourful, original with a cultural coherence of its own, experienced ossification in the eighteenth century. Social and political thought became sterile as a result of the gentry's self-congratulation; literature degenerated into Baroque and macaronic writing. To the contemporaries, "sarmatism" was synonymous with conservatism. The Confederation of Bar with its abundant political and religious poetry and with its anti-reform lampoons, was a powerful manifestation of "sarmatism", not only in the political but also in the cultural field. "Sarmatism", appealing to the Polish identity, drew its inspiration from the dislike of the foreigner.

The sixty years of Saxon reign in Poland favoured the spread of foreign fashions and that way of life in the residences of the great nobles. The negative aspect, however, had a greater significance: the absence of a natural centre for the nation's cultural life which a capital should be. The source of foreign influence was not so much the court of Dresden as travel in the West, especially in France, which became an almost obligatory part of the upbringing of the scions of noble families. In drawing-room conversation, correspondence, reading and the education of children, French supplanted the native tongue. The traditional Polish and Catholic customs ceased to be attractive. Divorce increased in aristocratic circles, as well as "fashionable marriages", in which both sides agreed to full sexual freedom. Drinking was less fashionable, but gambling for large sums of money became common. The partition Seym of 1773–1775 was engraved on contemporaries' memories as a continuous carnival. All that had, in fact, little in common with the "foreign plague". The magnate enjoyed himself better wearing a wig than the *kontusz*, but it was not the wigs that determined his attitude to a life of self-indulgence without sense of responsibility.

Much thought has been given to the question of the extent to which the Enlightenment in Poland was an import from abroad. This dilemma is unreal. The Enlightenment was an European feature and Poland, for all its Sarmatist ossification, was a part of Europe. Intellectual currents traversed the old continent in various directions and reached the Commonwealth by different ways. If Poland in the second half of the eighteenth century was more than ever before open to the international exchanges of ideas, it was not because the country had been conquered by outside influences, but because the political and cultural stagnation of the Saxon times had been surmounted within the country.

An important part in removing the barriers of social privilege was played by the freemasonry. The first lodges had already appeared in Poland under the Saxons, but freemasonry did not spread widely until the reign of Stanisław Augustus, especially after 1767. In 1782 the Polish Grand Orient lodge was established. The highest masonic offices were held by prominent persons like Andrzej Mokronowski, Ignacy Potocki, Szczęsny Potocki and K. N. Sapieha. Besides the magnates, foreigners settled in Poland were particularly active members of the lodges (the statutes of the Grand Orient were drawn up by the King's secretary, Maurice Glayre, a Swiss). Stanisław Augustus himself was a freemason. By the late 1780's the majority of progressive politicians among the gentry had found their way into the lodges. The ties of masonic brotherhood, linking magnates with people not belonging to the gentry, for there were even valets among them, contributed to spread the ideas of humanism and the natural equality of men. In the eyes of Sarmatians, those were "foreign fads".

New ideas from the West reached Poland by various channels. Stanisław Augustus employed many foreigners in his chanceries and as confidential agents abroad. Some of those men played a prominent political role, in particular Father Scipione Piattoli. The Italian Enlightenment found followers among some of the priests travelling to Rome (Stanisław Konarski, Hugo Kołłątaj). Some representatives of the Confederation of Bar, which in principle was conservative (Michał Wielhorski, Ignacy Massalski), established close contacts with Rousseau, Mably and with French physiocrats. The well-known physiocrat, Dupont de Nemours, was engaged by Bishop Massalski as secretary of the Commission of National Education. A number of Frenchmen became engaged in Polish political literature by writing treatises and memoranda intended for the Poles. The works by French, English and Italian philosophers, economists and legal theorists (not to mention novels), were translated into Polish in great numbers. Erudite German works furnished material for Polish periodicals. The spate of theatrical production consisted mainly of adaptation of French and Italian works.

Yet, while the Polish economists took much from the physiocrats or from Condillac and the Polish playwrights based their plots on foreign models, it was not merely passive imitation. In the social sciences, foreign inspiration was adapted to Polish conditions, in literature to Polish customs and local colour. As years went by, original creative work grew up in all fields of writing. The same, though to a lesser extent, was true of the fine arts. In architecture, painting and sculpture, the leading artists were Frenchmen and Italians, permanently settled in Poland and, for the most part, enjoying royal patronage: like Merlini, Fontana, Bacciarelli, Canaletto, Le Brun, and Norblin. To foreigners goes the credit for the reconstruction and redecoration of the Royal Castle in Warsaw; its decoration was dominated by national themes, both historical and allegorical. The King's summer residence, the Łazienki, was the highest achievement of the "Stanislavian style". In later years, Polish artists made their mark: Stanisław Zawadzki, Piotr Aigner, and Jakub Kubicki in architecture, Aleksander Kucharski, Franciszek Smuglewicz and Kazimierz Wojniakowski in painting. In music Polish opera appeared beside the Italian. The rhythm of the national dance, the Polonaise, had earlier already made an European career. Now, alongside of the Polonaise (cultivated by Michał Ogiński, Hetman, constructor of the canal, and himself a composer), folk tunes (mazurkas) appeared in the works of Polish composers. Various ingredients were thrown into the melting-pot of Polish culture to produce the alloy of new conventions and attitudes, a new style replacing the sterile "sarmatism" and the superficial imitation of foreign way of life.

The age of Enlightenment waged a struggle against the errors, vices, weaknesses and eccentricities which had multiplied during the period of the oligarchic anarchy. Sarmatian complacency was replaced by the spirit of criticism, though with an optimistic background. The people of the eighteenth century believed in the better future for which men should fight. They liked, at the same time, to look back to the nation's glorious past and drew upon the cultural legacy of the Polish Renaissance. National consciousness increased considerably during this time. This can be seen in the conscious care for, and in the modernization of the language, which was cleansed of degenerate accretions and a macaronic style and thus entered a period of splendid development. The old national institutions were permeated with a new ideological and social content. The traditional Polish freedom of the gentry was translated into the language of European Enlightenment and modernized, without breaking with the parliamentary and republican heritage.

The development of satirical literature was a characteristic mirror of the awakening criticism. The satire on customs and manners had two targets. The gallery of types ridiculed in poetry and comedy included on the one hand the ignorant, superstitious and brutal Sarmatians, on the other hand the ladies and dandies, indulging in "fashionable" dissipation, posing as foreigners and scorning national customs. In the dispute between "the moustache and the wig", the men of the Enlightenment declared for the head, whatever adornment it possessed. From about 1788, however, a change occurred in fashions, indicative of the rising national consciousness, of the attachment, and to a certain extent, return to national customs. Among the progressives, the Polish costume (the *kontusz*) came into fashion again. The first man to create a sensation in the Warsaw society in 1788, by changing ostentiously from French frock into a *kontusz*, was Jan Potocki, a young aristocrat educated abroad and the author of distinguished journalistic, scholarly and literary works, written exclusively in French. Such gestures should not be underestimated. The problem epitomized in the conflict of "moustache or wig", the problem of a civilization full of contrasts, arising from temporary backwardness, had been surmounted.

THE INTELLECTUAL UPHEAVAL

For services in the field of education during the Saxon times, Stanisław Augustus honoured Konarski with a medal bearing the following inscription: "To him who dared to be wise". The greatest poet of the next generation, Ignacy Krasicki, wrote: "Learn we must, for the golden age is over", by which he meant the age of the Saxon kings. Indeed, thought which had once been an act of courage, now became a duty. Striking indeed was the country's general situation first in the restriction, then in the release of talents. A stimulating role was now played by royal patronage and by some of the magnate's courts (Puławy of the Czartoryskis, Łańcut of the Lubomirskis, Słonim of the Ogińskis). Warsaw was a magnet attracting the intellectuals. Men of great ability appeared simultaneously in different fields of creative activity.

A great upheaval took place in literature. Franciszek Bohomolec's comedies still moralized more than they amused. Adam Naruszewicz still wrote turgid panegyrics and conventional bucolics, but in satire he achieved a pungent sarcasm and racy humour. A great master of satire, fable and heroicomic poem was to appear in the person of Ignacy Krasicki. The distinguished stylist, Stanisław Trembecki, raised topical poetry and descriptive poems to a high level of artistry. Akin to Trembecki in libertinism was the young Voltairian, Kajetan Węgierski, author of numerous satires and lampoons. Franciszek Zabłocki displayed considerable skill in the writing of comedy. Julian Ursyn Niemcewicz brought to political journalism the effective form of fable and comedy. A master of the stage was Wojciech Bogusławski, an actor, theatrical director and producer of many plays. In sentimental lyrics, Franciszek Karpiński and Franciszek Kniaźnin set new tones which foreshadowed the coming of Romanticism.

The writers of the Stanislavian era achieved artistic perfection in minor forms and in traditional literary fashions. Novels or historical dramas were still experiments. Krasicki's didactic novels of manners were not equal artistically to his fables or satires, but they were an important literary and social phenomenon which found imitators. This rich literary output was strongly engaged in the great educational campaign. Much of it was declamatory and declaratory, abounding in stereotyped characters meant to represent positive values, but satire and comedy pulsated with life and realism in the presentation of negative or ridiculous types. Laughter indeed became a formidable weapon.

Learning saw important achievements such as the critical history of

Poland in the Middle Ages written by Naruszewicz, a Polish grammar by Onufry Kopczyński, the mathematical and astronomical works by Jan Śniadecki, and Krzysztof Kluk's writings on botany and agriculture. The pace of intellectual development was set, however, by talented popularizers and compilers and by men who put their knowledge to the direct service of daily life. These were, on the one hand, economists and jurists like Antoni Popławski, Hieronim Strojnowski, Ferdynand Nax, Wincenty Skrzetuski and Teodor Ostrowski, on the other chemists and geologists, connected with industry and mining like Józef Osiński or Jan Jaśkiewicz. On the frontier of the social sciences and current politics there developed a rich political literature which was to produce its greatest work during the time of the Four Years' Seym. During the period of the Permanent Council, this practical and didactic approach left a mark common to belles-lettres, journalism and learned writings.

It has been mentioned above, that the alliance of politics and education was a characteristic feature of the Polish Enlightenment. Statesmen like the King, the Primate Poniatowski, the Vice-Chancellor Joachim Chreptowicz, Andrzej Zamoyski, Andrzej Mokronowski, Adam Czartoryski or Ignacy Potocki were educational leaders. Educationalists like Hugo Kołłątaj, Franciszek Jezierski and Franciszek Dmochowski, came upon the political stage from their work at school. The presence of the highest dignitaries in the Educational Commission added to its prestige. The "Society for Elementary Books" was a more specialized body, presided over by Ignacy Potocki but with Grzegorz Piramowicz as its moving spirit, the most outstanding Polish educationalist after Stanisław Konarski. The Commission had recourse to the country's finest traditions, established in Konarski's Collegium Nobilium (Ignacy and Stanisław Potocki were its pupils) and of the "Knights' School" (under the command of Adam Czartoryski). Foreign models were found in the Austrian Studien-Hofkommission and in the French plans for a reorganization of the educational system, likewise connected with the abolition of the Jesuit Order.

All schools throughout the country (with the exception of the "Knights' School") were subordinated to the Educational Commission. The country was divided into two school provinces (the Crown and Lithuania) at the head of which stood the Principal Schools, the reformed universities of Cracow and Wilno. Directly subordinated to the Principal schools were the divisional schools (higher secondary schools), beneath which were the subdivisional schools (lower secondary schools). The latter had parish and private schools for girls under their supervision and care. The Principal schools were the chief element in this organization. The reform of the Cracow Academy, accomplished by Hugo Kołłątaj, was a major achievement; this moribund school, sunk in medievalism, was transformed into a modern university. A rather superficial reform of the Wilno Academy was carried out by the ex-Jesuit astronomer, Marcin Poczobut. The Principal

Schools performed the combined functions of universities, learned societies, teachers colleges and education offices. The great amount of administrative and supervisory work they were burdened with adversely affected their purely academic activity. Yet, the main goal of the "educational revolution" was the reform of secondary school system and in that domain the school system fulfilled its task quite well.

Polish became the medium of instruction in secondary schools (Latin was taught from a modern Polish textbook). Mathematics and natural sciences were introduced on a wide scale, with particular emphasis on their practical application, including instruction in farming and surveying. Young people were to be prepared for public life by instruction in Polish history, the laws of the land and "moral science" by which ethics was understood. Paramilitary training was also introduced. In 1781–1790 about 17,000 pupils annually attended 74 secondary schools. In many schools young people from other classes than the gentry made up more than one half of the pupils. Compared with the Jesuit and Piarist schools, however, the total number of pupils fell as a result of difficulties of organization and finance caused by the re-organization. Among the sons of the well-to-do gentry many studied at home and not a few abroad.

In the first years of the Commission's work much attention was devoted to the problem of the parish schools. This concern was an aspect of the popularity of physiocratic doctrines. Elementary education was designed to increase the peasants' productive capacity. The Commission drew up curricula and a model primer, but the plans for the creation of a wide network of parish schools fell through for lack of funds. The maintenance of elementary schools continued to depend on the initiative of the parish clergy, but the Commission exercised supervision over those already in existence. The number of these schools was nevertheless growing. During the Four Years' Seym the government began to make greater efforts to make the parsons manage the schools in the parishes.

The Educational Commission met many difficulties, such as the partial dissipation of post-Jesuit property, the lack of textbooks and competent teachers and opposition on the part of former monastic teachers and the conservative gentry. The "Society for Elementary Books" supplied textbooks of a high standard, for instance the handbook of logic was written for the Commission by Condillac and the excellent mathematical textbooks by the Swiss Simon L'Huillier. The number of young secular teachers, already trained in the Commission's colleges, increased gradually. With the new curricula, the introduction of new textbooks and new teachers taking up their work, internal conflicts within the teaching profession and the outside opposition against the Commission however gathered momentum. Among the provincial gentry ideological differences between the old and the young generation became more and more clearcut. The opposition to the Permanent Council had many currents. The opposition to the Educational Commission was uniformly and unmistakably conservative. In practical matters of education, on the other hand, the cooperation between the Commission's "patron", the King, its President, the Primate Poniatowski, and such people as Ignacy Potocki, Adam Czartoryski and Hugo Kołłątaj, developed harmoniously. It was a promise of the consolidation of the party of reform which came to fruition with the Constitution of the Third of May.

Chapter XIII

THE STRUGGLE FOR THE INDEPENDENCE AND FOR THE REFORM OF THE COMMONWEALTH (1788–1794)

THE END OF THE GUARANTEE

In the quiet years of the Permanent Council's rule, the alliance of Russia, Austria and Prussia was gradually disintegrating. With regard to the problem of the Bavarian succession a rupture between Austria and Prussia took place in 1778–1779. The relations between Russia and Prussia also cooled which soon found expression in Russia's attitude towards a correction of the Polish-Prussian frontier (1776) and in the constant pressure exerted by Prussia upon Gdańsk. During the life-time of Frederick II (until 1786), appearances were maintained. From 1780, however, Austro-Russian cooperation was imminent against Turkey and, partly, against Prussia as well. In St. Petersburg the Austrophile trend represented by Potemkin prevailed over the old policy of the Prussophile Panin who fell into disfavour in 1781.

Stanisław Augustus had always considered that Prussia and the Prussian influence upon Russia was the greatest danger to Poland. He now expected that the anticipated Russo-Turkish conflict would allow the Commonwealth to play an active part at the side of Russia and Austria. The King hoped that Poland's participation in a military alliance would carry Russian consent to further constitutional reforms and to an increase in the army, that it would assure a containment of the magnate opposition and open broader prospects for economic expansion in the direction of the Black Sea. The possibility of territorial expansion at the expense of Turkey was also taken into account in Warsaw. Counting on Potemkin's support, the leaders of the magnate opposition made offers of alliance to Russia, competing with those of the King. According to their plan, Poland's participation in the war against Turkey was to be achieved through an anti-royal Confederation which would overthrow the rule of the Permanent Council. With Russia's help the Confederation would set up its own armed force, intended partly for the creation of an auxiliary corps to be used at the side of the Tsarist army.

On the occasion of the meeting of Catherine II and Joseph II, in the spring of 1787, the magnates hastened to Kiev and Stanisław Augustus to Kaniów. Both sides were disappointed. Russia had no intention of allowing further changes in the Commonwealth's guaranteed system of government. The only proposal contemplated was the possibility of using a Polish auxiliary corps, but without consent to reforms. The offers of the magnate opposition were also declined for fear lest the Commonwealth should again become the scene of disturbances and foreign intervention. The maintenance of the *status quo* in Poland suited Russia. In the event of a war with Turkey it assured peace on the western frontier and a supply base on the right flank of the Ukraine. Under these circumstances an alliance with the imperial courts did not open the road towards the Commonwealth's further reform. On the other hand, Russia and Austria, unlike Prussia, recognized the inviolability of the frontiers of 1772. On 16 August, 1787 the Russo-Turkish war began. It was soon joined by Austria. This was a turning point in Poland's history.

The disappointment of Kiev resulted in a split on foreign policy in the ranks of the formerly united magnate opposition. Szczęsny Potocki, Branicki and Rzewuski stuck to their plans of a Confederation by Russia's side. Ignacy and Stanisław Potocki and Adam Czartoryski gave up solliciting Russian support and turned to Prussia, as did the Lithuanian magnates, Karol Radziwiłł and Michał Ogiński. Prussia's interest in Poland was motivated by highly ambiguous designs. Since the war of the Bavarian Succession Hertzberg's exchange plan had been played with in Berlin. With Prussian assistance Poland was to recover Galicia and, in return, she would cede Gdańsk, Toruń and a part of Great Poland to Prussia. The thought was also nurtured in Berlin of provoking an anti-royalist Confederation which would throw the country into civil war, clear the way for an armed intervention and, eventually, lead to a partition as the Confederation of Bar had done. For the time being the most important thing was to prevent a Polish-Russian alliance. The broader background of these schemes was the great power policy of Frederick William II of Prussia who, having entered into alliance with England and Holland, and having encouraged Sweden to declare war on Russia, threatened Austria and Russia. The prospect was presented to Poland of becoming a part of a powerful alliance of Prussia, Britain, the United Provinces, Sweden and Turkey. The broad prospect of alliance and wars obscured to the Poles the annexationist schemes of Prussia. Those opposed to the King and the Permanent Council found external support and the patriotic elements perceived the chance of emancipating Poland from Russia's tutelage and throwing off her guarantee. Very quickly a wide movement sprang up, deceptively called the Patriotic Party or the Prussian Party.

The political upheaval of 1788 arose because of mounting discontent with the humiliating "proconsulate" of Stackelberg. Vigour and self-confidence were growing among the gentry. The men of the Enlightenment were calling more and more impatiently for social and constitutional reforms, while the conservatives were counting on the return of "good old times". In the King's words a "ferment of ideas" affected the whole country. A great variety of elements allied against the system of guarantee and the Council. This loose coalition, inappropriately called a "party" was to gain a decisive majority in the Seym.

Russia did not consent to Stanisław Augustus' plan for forming a Confederation within the Permanent Council, which would have assured ascendancy to the royal party from the very beginning. A Confederation Seym was formed on 7 October under the presidency of S. Małachowski and K. N. Sapieha; its task, according to Stackelberg's original idea, was to push through a resolution for the increase of taxes and the army, and to conclude an alliance with Russia. From then on the events followed with lightning speed. On 13 October the Prusian envoy read a note in which he protested against an alliance with Russia and proposed a Polish-Prussian alliance. It created a sensation in Warsaw and in St. Petersburg. Russia withdrew the plan of alliance. On 20 October the Seym voted amidst general enthusiasm for an army increased to 100,000. Who was to exercise command over it? On 3 November, after a hard struggle, the War Department was abolished and a War Commission was constituted, elected from among the Seym. Stackelberg protested against such a breach of the guarantee. Prussia responded with a declaration that she considered herself bound only to guarantee the Commonwealth's independence, but had no intention of restricting Poland's freedom to legislate. On 9 December the Department of Foreign Affairs was abolished and replaced by the Seym Deputation for Foreign Affairs. On 19 January, 1789 the Permanent Council itself was abolished. The Seym prolonged its powers for an indefinite period and decided to govern by itself.

THE SEYM CONTROL

The Poles made up for the long paralysis of the parliament by making it all-powerful for a few years. It was a provisional arrangement, to be sure, but in keeping with the republican trends, so important in Polish constitutional thought. By the overthrow of the Permanent Council not only the central organ of government was abolished, but also the Police and Justice Departments, which were not replaced. The Educational Commission survived because of its autonomous position, but found itself under very heavy fire. The conservatism of the gentry found fuel in the financial problem. Increasingly numerous demands were made for educational funds to be allotted to the army and for the schools to be turned over to the religious orders again. The Confederated Seym, taking decisions on all questions by a simple majority vote, took into its own hands, through the Commissions and Deputations, military affairs, the Treasury and foreign policy.

The implementation of the resolution calling for an army of 100,000 proved impossible, because it was not followed by adequate resolutions on taxes and conscription. The strength of the army was reduced to 65,000. As a result of the efforts of the Hetmen's party the dragoon regiments were turned into gentry cavalry of the Polish type, and its number was so unproportionally increased that it amounted to a half of the whole army. By filling the ranks with petty gentry Branicki counted on winning popularity, but he did not manage to regain the command over the army. This big increase in the national cavalry led the Polish army away from the line of development laid down by the King and the War Department.

The introduction, in March 1789, of the tax of incomes from land (10 per cent) and the corresponding taxation of clerical estates (20 per cent) was of greatest importance among the tax laws. This was the first tax imposed directly upon the gentry. It was estimated that it would yield 16 million zloty annually, but the sytem of assessment (based on the taxpayer's own declaration) and the method of collection failed to produce more than 9 million. Fiscal revenues from all sources reached a total of 40 million which was double the figure of 1788, but still not enough for the needs of the military increases. New sources of income, outside of taxes, were therefore anxiously sought. In 1789 the latifundia of the bishopric of Cracow were taken over by the Treasury. It was intended to do the same with other episcopal estates, with a system of salaries for the bishops, and to carry out the sale of privately held state domains (*starostwa*). Thus the problem of "national domains" promised to become acute in Poland.

In connexion with the increase of the army and treasury, the matters calling for government intervention grew more numerous. The Seym, while abolishing the administration from above, began to reconstruct it from below. Organs of local administration, previously non-existent in the Commonwealth, were called into being towards the end of 1789. Mixed civilian and military commissions for public order were elected by the gentry in local diets. It was a first step, and a very important one though not systematically carried out, towards the building of a new form of government.

The Seym's foreign policy was influenced by public opinion to an extent previously unknown. There occurred an explosion of anti-Russian feelings with men from Branicki's circle unexpectedly playing the leading part in abusing Russia and this from a group including former Confederates of Bar. Peasant disorders in Ukraine in the spring of 1789 were attributed to Russian intrigues. The Marshal of the Partition Seym, Adam Poniński, was banished by a court of the Seym as a traitor. Public opinion, however, also thwarted the aspirations of the Prussophiles by opposing any territorial concessions, in particular, the cession of Gdańsk and Toruń.

In 1790 the question of an Austro-Prussian war and the plans for regaining Galicia were hanging in the balance. In Warsaw, the skilful Prussia envoy, Lucchesini, gained considerable influence upon the leaders of the

Seym, but the negotiations for a Polish-Prussian alliance were being dragged out. Although Stanisław Augustus was no longer the controller of foreign policy because the Seym had created a new diplomatic service, subordinated to itself, he made difficulties demanding in particular that the trade treaty of 1775 be revised. It was eventually decided in Warsaw and Berlin to postpone the controversial matter of tariffs and cessions to a later date, and the Polish-Prussian defensive alliance was signed on 29 March, 1790. The treaty was in point of fact aimed at Austria's ally, Russia, whose access to the eventual theatre of war lay through Polish territory; the entrance of the Russia army into Poland would constitute the *casus foederis*.

The Prussian influence in Poland was of an entirely different character from the Russian tutelage in the years 1764–1788. It is true that the Prussians did not favour a strengthening of the Commonwealth and were covertly working against it, but Berlin's policy towards Poland had a variety of cross-currents. Events might take various turns and the Polish cavalry could prove useful. Finally, it was by exploiting the theme of independence that the Prussians had effectively supplanted Russian influence in Poland and they were netiher willing nor able to establish their own proconsulate in the Commonwealth. For the first time for many years the country's political life developed under the conditions of full sovereignty. This is why the history of the Four Years' Seym has particular significance. It shows what could be achieved by the Commonwealth of the gentry, imbued with the spirit of Enlightenment.

The fall of the joint rule of King and ambassador allowed various tendencies and social forces unhampered expression. In the local diets the provincial gentry expressed quite freely their opinions which were sometimes strange and old fashioned. Debates in the Seym were far from systematic and orderly, a display of traditional Polish oratory and quarrelsomeness. As we already know, for those opposed to the Permanent Council, the overthrow of the system of guarantee was a common point of departure from which, however the roads led in different directions. The extreme conservatives rallied around the Hetmen of whom one (Branicki) was performing strange political acrobatics in Warsaw, between anti-Russian bombast and toadying to Potemkin, while the other (Rzewuski), having left the country, was peddling a story of lament over the fall of ancient Polish liberties in the capitals of Europe. Many of the gentry who stayed at home, however, combined conservatism in constitutional and especially social questions with sincere patriotism and dislike for the leadership of the magnates. The young republicans, enthusiasts for the supremacy of the Seym, took up the ideas of Konarski and of the old "Family". The latter's traditions were revived by Adam Czartoryski and Ignacy Potocki, who gained a decisive influence over the Speaker of the Seym, Małachowski. The houses of Małachowski and Czartoryski became meeting places for members of the Seym; there draft resolutions were elaborated and strategy and tactics in the Seym outlined.

The analogy with the old "Family" cannot, of course, be drawn too closely. During 25 years much had changed in Europe and in Poland where ever-louder echoes of the French Revolution were heard. The patient and flexible Stanisław Augustus consistently held to the line of reform planned long before. Having suffered many humiliations at the beginning of the Seym, he was slowly regaining importance, while the former allies were drifting farther and farther apart, and the majority in the Seym of 1788 was splitting into the Hetmen's "zealots" and the "true patriots" (with Małachowski and Ignacy Potocki at their head). Their positions were clarified in connexion with the drafting of a new constitution, undertaken at the end of 1789. This process took place in Warsaw with its concentration of middle class and intelligentsia who however did not remain passive spectators of events on the stage of the Seym.

POLITICAL LITERATURE

Side by side with the debates in the Seym, a discussion led by the political writers took place, no less verbose than in the Seym, but covering a wider social range and a greater variety of problems. It is hard to describe briefly, without falling into schematism, the enormous quantity of pamphlets, brochures and extensive tracts. It may safely be stated that in political journalism, the adherents of reform prevailed over conservatives, not only in the quality, but also in the quantity of their writings.

The most distinguished and most widely read political writers were Stanisław Staszic, Hugo Kołłątaj and Józef Pawlikowski. Staszic, a burgher's son from the little town of Piła, who had chosen the priesthood to devote himself to study (which he pursued in Germany and in Paris) and later became a tutor to the children in the household of Andrzej Zamoyski. Another priest was Kołłątaj, descending from a gentry family of moderate wealth, the renowned reformer of the Cracow University and an outstanding political tactician. Józef Pawlikowski was educated in schools reformed by the Educational Commission; a poor townsman from Piotrków, he published his principal works anonymously at a remarkably young age and was later known as a leader of the radical Left, described as the Polish Jacobins. The works of these three writers gave the most comprehensive presentation of the problems with which the Polish political literature was preoccupied; its character was one not so much of abstract deliberation as of practical counsel.

Until the outbreak of the French Revolution the Commonwealth was the largest parliamentary state on the continent. Western estimates of the Polish parliamentarism and gentry republicanism led to misunderstandings. Rousseau was too susceptible to the charms of the idealized Golden Freedom, accepting even the *liberum veto.* The French Jacobins fell into the other extreme by seeing in the Commonwealth of the gentry with a king at its head only another form of aristocracy. Under Polish conditions, there existed no possibility either of monarchical absolutism or of plebeian revolution. Social reforms could be achieved only through a modification of the principle of representation. In pre-reform Poland, the gentry, which, incidentally, constituted a very numerous and greatly diverse community, was considered to be equivalent to the nation. The Seym represented that "nation" within which there existed formal equality and a general franchise. Now, however, the conviction grew that the nation comprised not only the gentry, but all the inhabitants of the Commonwealth.

Recognizing all the people as full citizens was a utopia under the then existing conditions, but this utopia created an ideological perspective. That is why the political writings, especially those of Staszic, reveal a dualism of maximalist egalitarian theories and of what was attainable at the moment. Pawlikowski spoke of "eternal truths" and of "truths for the time being". Kołłątaj appealed for the forbearance of future generations in order to justify the limited scope of reforms which were considered possible in the eighteenth century. It was Kołłątaj, too, who defined most clearly the new principles of representation. The nation should be divided into three estates : 1) owners of landed property, 2) owners of urban property, 3) persons owning no property. Full electoral rights should be granted only to landowners and the urban owners of property. The Seym should consist of a landowners' chamber and a chamber of the towns. The interest of the plebs should "for the time being" be defended by three tribunes of the people, elected from among the gentry by the landowners' chamber. Staszic demanded that an equal number of landowner and burgher deputies be sent to a common chamber. Pawlikowski called for parliamentary representation of the burghers and clergy, as taxpayers. Gentry who owned no landed property were to be eliminated from the local diets. Thus the general franchise within the gentry nation was to be replaced by the principle of representation based on property.

Alongside the principle of property qualifications, typical of bourgeois parliamentarism in its early phase, there appeared a specifically Polish concept of modifying the notion of the gentleman-citizen. Kołłątaj, a political leader with practical common sense, realizing the difficulties in introducing a wide burghers' representation into the Seym, proposed an automatic ennoblement of men of wealth and persons achieving distinction in the army, in civil service and education. Ignacy Potocki argued that all men (*hommes*) who become gentle (*gentils*) should be recognized as gentlemen (*les gentilshommes*). A minor political writer made the suggestion that the whole nation should be ennobled gradually. It may be admitted that Kołłątaj's concept of the gentry as an open civic estate, with a constant influx of new fortunes and new talents and with a departure of the gentry without property, was a variant of the principle of representing property, realistic enough under the then prevailing Polish conditions. The Commonwealth of the gentry was to become a commonwealth of men of property in which the landed gentry would retain a political predominance, but not a monopoly of political rights.

In social matters Staszic, Kołłątaj and Pawlikowski agreed in principle. To all three of them the magnate oligarchy and serfdom were Poland's main calamities. Peasants should be personally free, but they should make contracts with the landowners, convert from labour services to money rents as far as possible, and be placed under the protection of public law and of the State. There was no question yet of granting land to the peasants. Differences appeared in the approach to the Jewish problem. The burghers' dislike for Jews is noticeable in Staszic's writings. Kołłątaj called for the assimilation of Jews by radical administrative measures. The most liberal programme of making the Jews citizens and re-educating them, while respecting their religion and customs, was formulated by Pawlikowski. In the writings of this plebeian, one senses a deep solidarity with the common people of Polish villages and small towns. It is no mere accident that Pawlikowski's views on the government of the State differed markedly from those of other authors.

Kołłątaj and Staszic were republicans in the Polish sense of the term in as far as they recognized the king as the titular head of the Republic. In order to avoid the disorders of interregna they even proposed to make the throne hereditary, the king being, however, deprived of power. All officials and dignitaries as well as corporate administrative bodies were to be elected by the local diets and the Seym. The Seym, always ready to be convened in the view of Staszic, or permanently in session according to the proposal of Kołłątaj, would become the government. The deputies and senators should comply strictly with the wishes of the constituents as expressed in instructions of the local diets. Kołłątaj developed most consistently the theory that the dualism of king and Commonwealth caused a conflict of powers which ought to be eliminated by "making the Seym a monarchy". The king, according to Staszic, was always the "natural" enemy of freedom and would strive to found a despotism, if only the means at his disposal permitted it.

Pawlikowski took a different attitude. He maintained that Poland would not for a long time be mature enough to achieve a "really free government and legislation". He had no confidence in the Seym composed of gentry whose authority he sought to limit. Poland should "mature" under the paternalist rule of an enlightened monarch, the crown being hereditary in the Poniatowski family. The royal power of appointment was to be extended to include all offices in the administration and judiciary. The king was to have the advantage of legislative initiative in the Seym. Collegiate governmental organs were to carry out his will. It was not an absolutist programme, but one for a constitutional and parliamentary monarchy with a strong central executive. Pawlikowski often referred to Montesquieu, keeping to the spirit rather than the letter of Montesquieu's teaching. The king's share in legisla-

Hugo Kołłątaj

tive and judicial power was an infringement on the principle of the separation of powers but, under Polish conditions, it was to answer Montesquieu's idea of balance by compensating for the enormous social ascendancy of the gentry. Pawlikowski gave philosophical form to the popular tendency to appeal to the "good king" against the "bad masters". This young monarchist and later Jacobin professed advanced liberal views in social and economic matters.

The ideas proclaimed by Kołłątaj, Staszic and Pawlikowski are to be found, in a more or less diluted form, in the profuse journalistic production representing reforming and progressive trends. In the group of writers rallied around Kołłątaj and called "Kołłątaj's Forge" (Franciszek Dmochowski, Antoni Trębicki), an outstanding personality was Father Franciszek Jezierski, a passionate enemy of the magnates and a tribune of the people. The munici-

Jan Śniadecki

pality of Warsaw inspired and financed an extensive journalistic campaign in favour of a municipal reform (Świniarski, Mędrzecki, Barss, Baudouin de Courtenay). For the first time, Jewish journalists appeared writing in Polish (Herszel Józefowicz, Salomon Polonus and Szymel Wolfowicz). Zabłocki abandoned the writing of comedy to become a master of rhymed lampoons in which he in particular derided and disparaged the Hetman Branicki.

The conservatives in literature adopted a defensive role, repeating hackneyed clichés about Golden Freedom, seasoned with the phrases of J. J. Rousseau. They could, however, count on a response from the gentry by raising the sceptre of an absolute monarchy which allegedly was waiting to destroy the gentry's freedom with the aid of the lower orders. An especially fierce opponent of hereditary succession and defender of the hetmen's authority, the shield of traditional Polish freedom, was Seweryn Rzewuski. Demagogy found a chance to show what it could achieve in the defense of the political rights of the impoverished gentry which the magnates used to dominate the local diets. Some of the ideologists of the conservative party refreshed their vocabulary by appeal to the federalist ideas fashionable in the West (under the Polish conditions, the autonomy of provinces would have benefitted the magnates who controlled the voivodships), and to Montesquieu's separation of powers (arbitrary ministers as a "mediating" link between the king and the gentry). Szczęsny Potocki and Jan Suchorzewski were the first in Poland to advocate the abolition of monarchy. In their plans of a federal republic without a king they invoked the example of the United States. Those were, however, isolated voices. The conservative ideal was the Commonwealth with a king, as it had existed prior to 1764.

THE CONSTITUTION OF 3 MAY, 1791

On 7 September, 1789 the Seym appointed a Deputation to prepare a draft Constitution; the principal role within this body was played by Ignacy Potocki. Soon afterwards, in the middle of November, delegates from 141 towns assembled in the capital upon the initiative of Jan Dekert, Mayor of Warsaw, and formed a kind of a bourgeois confederation. They submitted a petition, composed for them by Kołłątaj, demanding admission to the Seym and to official posts and the right to purchase landed estates. The uproar made by the conservatives about a revolution on the French pattern being allegedly in the making in Poland was greatly exaggerated. Direct political action by the bourgeoisie was nevertheless an unusual event in the Commonwealth. The Seym appointed a special Deputation to work out a draft law for the towns and thereafter the two Deputations: The Constitutional Deputation and the Deputation for Towns were working at the same time.

Work progressed slowly for various reasons. In the period of a war scare in 1790, controversial constitutional disputes were deferred, but, the Austro-Prussian convention signed at Reichenbach and Sweden's withdrawal from the war with Russia (August 1790), foreshadowed the end of the favourable international situation to which Poland owed its temporary liberty. The tension between Russia and Prussia still existed but at the end of 1790 and in the beginning of 1791 the international situation spurred the Poles into achieving a constitutional *fait accompli* before the question of war or peace was finally settled. There existed, however, serious differences between Stanisław Augustus and the Constitutional Deputation.

The draft prepared by Ignacy Potocki followed the republican line subordinating the Seym to the local diets and the executive to the Seym. The king was to be hereditary but without power. These plans were opposed by Stanisław Augustus who was gradually recovering importance in the country and in the Seym. As for the leaders of the patriotic party (one can already speak of such a party at this time), they encountered ever greater difficulties on the part of the Hetmen's "zealots" and were unable to achieve their ends in the Seym without the support of the King. The shift in the balance of forces was strongly marked towards the end of 1790. The Seym resolved to extend its term for two more years while at the same time including a new body of deputies. The elections of 16 December strengthened the position of the King (the new deputies included many of his followers); on the other hand, the instructions voted in the local diets during these elections revealed the conservative attitude and often frank hostility to the reform of the provincial gentry. The programme of the Deputation was, however, based on confidence in the "sovereign legislative will" of the local diets. The result was a crisis of confidence. In consequence, Ignacy Potocki decided to enter into a closer cooperation with the King. Scipione Piattoli, an Italian, whom both the King and Potocki employed in preparing constitutional drafts, was very instrumental in reconciling their views.

Stanisław Augustus worked out his programme at the beginning of 1791. The throne in his view ought to be hereditary in the Poniatowski family. The King was to retain his former prerogatives, in particular the power to appoint senators, ministers and officials. He was to preside over the council of ministers, or the "Guardians of the Law", as they were called, who made their decisions by a majority vote and were responsible to the Seym, unlike the King, who was not responsible. Ministers were not appointed for life, but appointed by the King to the body of Guardians for two years. The ministers, sitting as Guardians, were at the same time the presidents of the collegiate governing bodies, elected by the Seym; the Commissions of War, Foreign Affairs, Justice, Finance and Education. The King presided over the Senate which had almost equal legislative power with the Chamber of Deputies. The deputies were not bound by the mandates of the local diets. Sixteen deputies of the towns sat in the Chamber, and 2 burghers sat in each of the government Commissions. The contracts between peasants and landowners were placed under the protection of the government. The peasants were permitted to leave the village, while a peasant who had served his term of years in the army gained his freedom.

The King's draft became the basis for secret discussions, at first within a very narrow circle (Ignacy Potocki, Piattoli, Kołłątaj and Małachowski), but afterwards in a wider group of deputies of the patriotic party brought into the secret. The passing of the Constitution was to be accomplished in the Seym by a procedural trick which amounted to *a coup d'état*. It was decided first to satisfy the aspirations of the burghers, and thus secure their support. On 18 April the Seym passed the law on municipal reform, based on a draft prepared by the King and Joachim Chreptowicz. The law met in principle the demands in the petition of 1789 except that it limited the number of town plenipotentiaries to 22 members who were entitled to vote only on matters relating to the towns and commerce. On the other hand, the law of 18 April gave the bourgeoisie the opportunity of achieving the status of nobles. The law on local diets, passed at the same time, excluded the landless gentry from them.

In the course of these secret consultations, the King's draft Constitution underwent considerable alteration aimed at weakening its monarchical tendencies. Potocki wished to secure the succession to the throne for the Hohenzollerns, while Małachowski, following in this respect the more general public opinion, preferred the Saxon dynasty. In view of the uncertain international situation, the Elector of Saxony did not wish to commit himself and it was eventually decided that the Seym on its own would proclaim his daughter, Augusta, heir apparent to the Polish throne, in the expectation that she would found a dynasty. The King anticipated that she would marry one of his nephews. The King's power of appointment was reserved to Stanisław Augustus only for life. After prolonged disputes, it was agreed, in accordance with the King's proposal that the Guardians of Law should be composed of the primate and four ministers only; the King's choice was limited, however, to 16 ministers (4 chancellors, 4 hetmen, 4 marshals and 4 treasurers), previously appointed for life (now they could be recalled by a vote of the Seym). The centralization of government was weakened by the stipulation that the same ministers could not sit on the board of the Guardians and preside over the Commissions. The government Commission of Justice was rejected as incompatible with the principle of the separation of powers. The Speaker of the Seym was appointed by the Guardians in order to give him an insight into the actions of the government and to enable him, in case of need, to convene the Seym in extraordinary session even in opposition to the King. The Guardians thus conceived did not take their decisions by majority vote; the King's position "prevailed". The King's resolution was binding as soon as it was countersigned by one of the ministers sitting on the board of the Guardians and responsible to the Seym in virtue of his signature.

In the field of legislation the range of matters to be decided by qualified majority was increased, and the role of the Senate was diminished by comparison with Stanisław Augustus' draft. Confederations and confederated Seyms were abolished. With regard to the peasant problem, all detailed provisions were passed over and the Constitution limited itself to a general declaration of the "protection of the law and the government" to all the peasants and to assuring freedom to immigrants from abroad.

The final text, worked out mainly by Kołłątaj, was thus a compromise between the monarchical and constitutional programme of Stanisław Augustus, and the republican scheme of Ignacy Potocki. In one matter Stanisław Augustus obtained more than he had proposed, when he was granted a decisive voice in the council of Guardians. With ministerial posts filled as they were at the time, the "patriots" were not sure of a majority; they placed more trust in the King than the ministers, because he was bound to them by having engaged in the plot.

The events of 3 May, 1791 were carefully staged. Advantage was taken of the fact that the number of deputies present in Warsaw was small (182) and, being assured in advance of the support of about one hundred of them, they acted by surprise. Troops were paraded in force, the burghers turned out in crowds, the galleries in the Chambers were filled by people in favour of the Constitution. The opposition was confused and intimidated. By circumventing normal procedure the draft law was read and voted at the same session.

A compact patriotic and royal party was formed around the Constitution under the slogan of: "The King with the People, the People with the King". Kołłątaj, who was appointed vice-chancellor, was playing an increasingly important part in the Constitutional party. He organized a political club, called "The Assembly of Friends of the Constitution", which enrolled both deputies and political leaders from outside the Seym. At the meetings of the Club, laws were drafted and parliamentary tactics worked out. Members of the Club serving as Seym deputies were bound to solidarity. The "Assembly" had a press organ of its own entitled "Gazeta Narodowa i Obca" (The National and Foreign Gazette). It was Poland's first political party to be organized on modern lines. The burghers all over the country were enthusiastic about the Constitution. The reservations of the provincial gentry were gradually overcome, as can be seen from the resolutions of the local diets. Agents from Warsaw were active in the provinces and propaganda in favour of the Constitution was also carried out by the army. The Constitution party purchased the broad support of the gentry by refraining from a bolder measure of peasant reform. In many places the peasants interpreted the Constitution as a release from serfdom and renounced obedience to their masters. The Guardians issued proclamations against such "misinterpretation of the government protection" and called upon local authorities (mixed military and civilian commissions) to use troops against recalcitrant peasants in the event of need. Peasant reform in the long run was not, however, given up.

The basic law of 3 May as well as laws on towns, local diets and on the mixed military and civilian commissions, were the first stages of a thorough constitutional reform which was to be completed by detailed laws. The Guardians, the main commissions and the local commissions were Poland's first extensive and hierarchically centralized government machinery. Kołłątaj announced that after the completion of the "political constitution", steps would be taken to introduce an "economic constitution" and a "moral constitution". The latter plan was connected with the work undertaken on the codification of law, under the name of the Code of Stanisław Augustus. Within a few months, the work of the Deputation of Codification was greatly advanced. It was there that the legal status of the peasants was to be more closely defined. The peasant problem also played an important part in the plan for an "economic constitution".

Kołłątaj worked on this project jointly with Michał Ossowski, manager of Prot Potocki's commercial and banking enterprises. The "economic constitution" was to cover: 1) property relationships, 2) the protection of labour, 3) investments. Polish economists always had a predilection for liberal theories. In the 1770's physiocratic doctrines were spreading and now Adam Smith gained wide popularity. It was realized, however, that Poland's feudal economy was not ripe for a free flow of wealth and labour and the "economic constitution" was to create proper conditions by means of administrative measures and government intervention. A reform of the ecclesiastical estates and the *starostwa* was designed to secure uniformity in property relations. Peasant reform was to stimulate the economic activity of primary producers and bring about a clear social division of labour and create a labour market (a strict separation of agriculture and rural industry, even by means of compulsory transfers of population). Investments were to be stimulated by reducing the rate of interest (5 per cent) and by the establishment of a National Bank granting long-term loans at a low rate of interest (under 4 per cent) for industrial investment. Only the two closely related matters of the Bank and the *starostwa* were submitted to the Seym in the form of a bill. According to Ossowski the Bank was to issue a paper currency covered by the income from selling the *starostwa* (they accounted for about 10 per cent of all landed estates). In view of international developments, the resolution of the Seym was tardy. The National Bank was not established. The *starostwa* were to serve as security for a loan contracted abroad.

The question of reforming the law relating to the Jews was closely connected with economic problems. The Seym Deputation had been considering it since 1790, but it was not until the beginning of 1792 that the matter took a more concrete form. The initiative was mainly in the hands of the King, Kołłątaj and Piattoli who had direct contact with the Jewish elders. The Seym voted the abolition of *Kahal* debts and some minor laws securing a measure of emancipation. The course of political events, however, interrupted work on broader reforms.

　*From the passing of the Constitution of 3 May to the outbreak of the Polish-Russian war, there elapsed barely one year. In order to estimate properly the importance of the "political constitution", it should be reviewed in conjunction with all the steps taken during that year to give effect to the reforms. It had been instituted on this occasion under conditions of full sovereignty and on a broad political and social basis. The conservative opposition sought to block reform by obstruction in the Seym, but was unable to undertake "counter-revolution" (as it was called at the time) on their own. Time worked for the government which was getting stronger and for the ruling party. Kołłątaj's unwearying activity made its mark in all fields. It is impossible to extrapolate the broken line of development and reflect upon what Poland might have achieved. The dynamism of this line was, however, indisputable.

THE RUSSIAN INTERVENTION AND THE SECOND PARTITION (1792–1793)

Having learned of the Constitution of 3 May, the Prussian Minister Hertzberg wrote: "The Poles have given the *coup de grâce* to the Prussian monarchy by voting a Constitution much better than the English. I think that Poland will regain sooner or later West Prussia, and perhaps East Prussia also. How can we defend our State, open from Memel to Cieszyn against a numerous and well governed nation". The old minister from the school of Frederick II, who had always seen in Poland not only a victim, but also a potential danger as well, was too pessimistic.

　The peace of Jassy (9 January, 1792) brought the Russo-Turkish war to an end. Prussia, having abandoned her anti-Russian policy, was returning to the traditional plans of partition and found a pretext in claiming that the alliance of 1790 was no longer valid in view of the change in the form of government in Poland. Russia for her part regained a free hand. Although Austria advised acceptance of the situation, Catherine II and her favourites were determined to stamp out the "French plague" in Warsaw and demanded the restoration of the system of guarantee. The victorious army of the Black Sea was ready to hand. A pretext for the intervention was furnished by Poles: the Hetman Seweryn Rzewuski, a fanatic of the idea of the "sacred baton", Szczęsny Potocki, the Ukrainian magnate consumed by personal ambition and Russia's henchman Ksawery Branicki. These magnates with a handful of their clients and followers signed in St. Petersburg on 27 April, 1792 the act of Confederation which was later promulgated under the false

The Polish Commonwealth during the partitions, 1772-1795

date of 14 May in the border town of Targowica. On behalf of the "Commonwealth" they condemned "the monarchical and democratic revolution of 3 May" and, under the terms of the guarantee, called for the help of Russian troops. Those crossed the frontier on 18 May, 1792, two weeks after celebration in Warsaw of the first anniversary of the Constitution.

At the last moment, on 22 May, 1792, the Seym agreed to increase the army to 100,000 men. The Poles had deluded themselves too long with the Prussian aliance (at present Prussia made it impossible even to purchase arms abroad). Poland had at her actual disposal an army of less than 60,000, with a disproportionate number of cavalry. Against 97,000 Russians, Poland put into the field 37,000 men (the rest of the army constituted a reserve). Prince Józef Poniatowski, the King's nephew, took command on the Ukrainian front. The defensive battles of Zieleńce (17 June) and Dubienka (18 July) could not halt the continued retreat. Stanisław Augustus, Kołłątaj and Ignacy Potocki tried to open negotiations with Russia, by offering, in return for the acceptance of the Constitution, the succession to the Polish throne to Grand Duke Constantine (the grandson of Catherine II). The Empress refused to enter into any negotiations and demanded the King's unconditional accession to the Confederation of Targowica. While the war was not yet lost, its continuation did not hold out hope of victory and seemed likely to bring with it the danger of partition. At the session of the Guardians on 24 July, the majority (including Kołłątaj) declared for the accession of the King to the rebel Confederation. Stanisław Augustus joined the Confederation and ordered that hostilities be stopped. Some scores of officers (among them Prince Józef Poniatowski and Tadeusz Kościuszko) submitted their resignations. The parliamentary leaders led by Kołłątaj, Małachowski and Ignacy Potocki left the country.

As the Russian forces advanced, the number of Confederates in the occupied territories grew. There were among them some sincere admirers of Golden Freedom, a greater number were corrupt opportunists and the majority was merely intimidated. It was not a spontaneous movement as the Confederation of Radom had been. Szczęsny Potocki was under no illusion on that account. In December 1792 he warned Rzewuski that the makers of the Constitution "have no need to win over opinion, because it is already on their side ; if only they waited for the occasion and proper time, they would have the nation behind them. What I am saying here, is the incontrovertible truth". The leaders of Targowica reluctantly yielded to Catherine II's demands concerning the King's accession to the Confederation. They feared, not without good grounds, that Stanisław Augustus might resume his earlier role in the "Russian system". The leaders of the Confederation, having wrecked the administration, added to the chaos and economic depression caused by the cost of a lost war and Russian occupation. When, in the early spring, the Prussians occupied Great Poland, Toruń and Gdańsk (with the people of Gdańsk offering armed resistance to the

Prussian army), the men of Targowica found themselves in a position of political bankruptcy. They had not anticipated a fresh partition of Poland (Catherine II had given them assurances in this respect). Their protests against the Prussian invasion were unavailing. The Confederation, discredited in Polish eyes as treason and in the eyes of the partitioning powers by its inefficiency and attempts at resistance, no longer justified its existence. Szczęsny Potocki, Branicki and Rzewuski laid down their offices and left the country.

The negotiations for partition which led to the Russo-Prussian convention, signed in St. Petersburg on 23 January, 1793, were conducted against the background of the war of Austria and Prussia with revolutionary France. Austria, dependent on the help of her Prussian ally and seeking consent for her plans to annex Bavaria, declared her *désinteressement* in Polish problems. Prussia demanded from Catherine II, the instigator of the anti-French action undertaken by monarchical Europe, a reward for her difficult efforts on the Rhine: the reward was to be accretions of territory on the Vistula and the Warta. The robbery of Polish territory was to cement the coalition and the partition, according to the intentions of the Powers, was to extinguish the potential fire of revolution in the East more effectively than the Confederation of Targowica. Prussia obtained 58,000 sq.km and Russia 250,000 sq.km. The ratification was to be made by the Seym, convened to Grodno for 17 June, 1793.

In spite of the fact that the deputies were carefully selected, the Seym put up a much more stubborn resistance than it did in 1773. Arrests, sequestration of estates, threats, the surrounding of the Chamber by troops and bribery played their part. The treaty with Russia was ratified on 17 August and that with Prussia on 23 September (the resistance of the Seym in this matter was particularly strong and the pressure particularly drastic). During the Grodno Seym, it was not the men of Targowica who came to the fore, but Stanisław Augustus and some earlier adherents of Russia. The new form of government reestablished the Permanent Council, the fundamental laws and the guarantee, though some of the reforms of the Four Years' Seym were retained. This was not a constitution compatible with the aspirations of the men of Targowica. According to Russia's intentions, Poland (with an area of 212,000 sq.km and a population of about 4 million) was to remain a buffer state, "a barrier between the Powers", with the executive power centralized to an extent sufficient to allow the Russian ambassador to be the actual ruler of the country.

THE EMIGRATION AND THE SITUATION AT HOME

The political emigration, concentrated in Saxony, adopted at first an attitude of wait-and-see. They wished to discover whether the King could succeed in reaching an understanding with Russia over the heads of the authors of the Confederation of Targowica and in achieving a tolerable *modus vivendi*. The Second Partition clearly upset calculations of a peaceful development in the country. The political leaders of the emigration not only refused to reconcile themselves with the loss of three-fifths of the territory, but feared lest the partition should foreshadow the final elimination of the Polish State. It was decided to resort to a last fling: to mobilize the maximum military effort which had not been called up in 1792 for fear of partition and in the hope of negotiations with Russia.

As early as the spring of 1792 Kołłątaj and Ignacy Potocki were considering for a time the idea of an alliance with France, in view of the fact that the outbreak of the war of France against the first Coalition coincided with the outbreak of the Russo-Polish war and with the treason of the Prussian ally. This idea now became the guiding line of the foreign policy of the emigration. It sought to take advantage of the great authority enjoyed by the famous "soldier of liberty" Tadeusz Kościuszko. Born in 1746, cadet of the Warsaw "Knights' School", he studied military engineering in Paris, later took part in the American War of Independence, distinguished himself in the construction of fortifications and was promoted to the rank of general. Appointed to serve with the Polish army by the Four Years' Seym, he won fame in the battle of Dubienka in 1792 and had been made honorary citizen of the French Republic. Kościuszko went to Paris in the beginning of 1793 with a memorandum announcing that Poland would establish a bourgeois republic with abolition of monarchy, equal civil rights for all citizens and a limited franchise based on property qualifications and that the republic would declare war on all three partitioning Powers (of whom Austria and Prussia were then at war with France). While words of encouragement came from the French government, interested in a diversion in Poland, Kościuszko obtained no specific promises from either the Girondists or Jacobins. The Poles could not count on help either from France or from Turkey, from whom, after France, most was expected. The hopes of Prussian, or at least Austrian, neutrality were illusory. In their struggle against the three partitioning Powers the Poles were left to their own resources.

An alliance with revolutionary France failed. What remained was France's example. The victories of the French greatly impressed the Poles both at home and abroad. Hugo Kołłątaj was fascinated by the effectiveness of revolutionary methods in mobilizing the nation for a tremendous effort; the vision of a general "war of the peoples against tyrants" had a magnetic spell. The pamphlet O *ustanowieniu i upadku Konstytucji 3 Maja* (On the Passing and the Overthrow of the Constitution of 3 May), written jointly by Kołłątaj, Franciszek Dmochowski and Stanisław and Ignacy Potocki, was a vehement indictment of Stanisław Augustus and reveals the growth of radical opinions. After Kościuszko's return from France it was decided that he should assume dictatorial powers as the leader of the insurrection. Kościuszko counted upon the cooperation with the regular army of the armed masses of the people throughout the country. This idea was suggested by the American experience, but it had also been very much alive in Polish political thought. The peasant armies of the absolutist monarchies were kept in the tight grip of military discipline. In the improvised armies of citizens fighting for freedom, morale was a factor of major importance. The fundamental social problem in an insurrection lay in the question: in the name of what freedom should the serf fight?

The political direction of the preparations for an insurrection was with the émigrés, but the situation at home was decisive in determining the outbreak. The country went through a grave economic crisis. The six largest banks of Warsaw declared their insolvency in 1793. The maintenance of an occupation army of 40,000 and the billeting of troops were a heavy burden. During the winter of 1793/1794 there came to Warsaw crowds of vagrants. Social conflicts were increasing in the guilds and manufactories. Death and poverty were growing. Against such a background, the luxury displayed by the notables of Targowica and the Seym of Grodno, despoiling national property, was particularly shocking. Revolutionary songs, pamphlets and posters were multiplying, and in them the hated "traitors" increasingly were called "aristocrats". As early as February 1793 the mass of the people of Warsaw appeared as a political force, making it impossible for the Russians to seize the Arsenal.

The situation in the army was most explosive. The new Hetmen appointed by Russia were the most despised. In accordance with the decision of the Grodno Seym, the army, about 50,000 strong (a part of the soldiers was in areas cut off by the new Russian frontier) was to be reduced to 15,000. The soldiers were threatened with unemployment or enlistment into foreign armies. The army, the importance of which had increased considerably during the time of the Four Years' Seym, and, which had been toughened in the campaign of 1792, represented an ardently patriotic and organized section of the community.

The situation in Warsaw and other urban centres (Cracow, Wilno), and in the army, was the basis upon which conspiratorial organizations developed after May 1793. In the ranks of the conspirators, beside army officers, there were many representatives of the radical intelligentsia from the old "Kołłątaj's Forge", sympathizers with the French Revolution. Equally active were men of moderate opinions, whose programme advocated a return to the consitutional system of 3 May. This trend could count on the support of the greater part of the gentry and of the wealthire bourgeoisie. Among the moderate conspirators, some maintained tacit contact with the King. The conspirators at home exerted pressure on the leadership of the emigration to launch an insurrection. Kościuszko hesitated, reviewed the development of the international situation, and urged a more careful preparation of the general mobilization, postponing the call to arms. Meanwhile, the Permanent Council resolved on 21 February, 1794 to proceed with the reduction of the army. A few days later arrests were made among the conspirators. Under these circumstances the decision was taken in the country. On 12 March, General Madaliński's brigade set out for Cracow, where Kościuszko was awaited.

THE INSURRECTION OF 1794

On 24 March Kościuszko proclaimed in Cracow the act of insurrection which, with its subsequent decrees (especially the Manifesto concerning peasants, issued at Połaniec on 6 May) served in its way as a provisional constitution. Dictatorial power was assumed by the Commander-in-chief of the armed forces who established an insurgent government, called the Supreme National Council. The Council was to appoint criminal courts with the power to inflict the death penalty upon the opponents of the insurrection. Regional authority was vested in the commissions for public order. The gentry and bourgeoisie were to sit in the courts and commissions in equal numbers. The lowest organs of administration were controlled by the superintendents (*dozorcy*) over an area comprising 1000 peasant farms each. They were to supervise the execution of government decrees in the countryside and to intervene in the relations of the peasants and the gentry. Conscription was designed to exact one infantry man from every five households and one cavalry man with full equipment from every fifty (the conscription was to furnish 100,000 infantry and 10,000 cavalry, in order to counteract the predominance of cavalry in the previous structure of the army). All men between 18 and 40 years of age were to be enlisted into the mass-levy to undergo military training and to cooperate with the army in local operations. Peasants were to obtain personal freedom (the right to leave the village) and to enjoy security of tenure. The labour dues were limited to 25–50 per cent of te previous assessment. All these decrees were binding until the end of the insurrection, upon which the government would surrender its power to the Seym and render an account of its activities. The Seym was left to decide upon the future form of government.

Thus the act of insurrection did not stabilize revolutionary authority, but gave it emergency powers. This decision reflected not only respect for legality, but also the basic political tactics of the insurrectionist authorities. They counted upon the support of the gentry, the bourgeoisie and the peasants. Advanced radicalism might deter the gentry from participation in the insurrection, excessive conservatism could hurt the mass of the people. The provisional decrees issued by the dictatorial authority made it possible to adopt a flexible social policy depending on the military needs. Political

Tadeusz Kościuszko

and social accomplished facts created in the course of war would, however, determine the character of the future constituent assembly.

Kościuszko at the head of 4100 regular soldiers and 2000 auxiliary peasant troops achieved a success in the battle of Racławice on 4 April. The road to the capital was, however, barred by the Russians and the Commander-in-chief would have found himself in a difficult situation, if an insurrection had not broken out in Warsaw on 17 April. A major part in the street fighting was played by the populace, led by conspirators among whom the shoemaker, Jan Kiliński, became a legendary figure. The Russian garrison was routed and the embassy captured. Soon afterwards, on 22 April, an insurrection broke out in Wilno. Towards the end of the month, the whole Polish army came into action with the units cut off by the frontier forcing their way through to the Polish side. Thus the insurrection swept over almost all Polish territory within the frontiers of 1793. Political differences at this point made their appearance. In Wilno power was assumed by the Jacobins (Colonel Jakub Jasiński) who adopted a strong attitude against the Confederates of Targowica (the hanging of Hetman Szymon Kossakowski). In Warsaw the radical conspirators did not try to seize the power which was assumed by moderate elements, connected with the King; they formed the Provisional Substitutional Council. The Council was reluctant to satisfy the demands of the populace, which called for revolutionary justice against the men of Targowica. On 24 April the so-called Jacobin Club was formed in Warsaw; it was opposed to the Council. Under the pressure of the Club and the townspeople, the criminal court sentenced, on 9 May, several leaders of the Confederation of Targowica (the Hetmen Ożarowski and Zabiełło, the Chairman of the Permanent Council Ankwicz, Bishop Kossakowski) to death by hanging. Kościuszko disowned both the Provisional Substitutional Council and the Supreme Council of Wilno. In the Supreme National Council created by the Commander-in-chief there were "Moderates" as well as men connected with the Jacobins.

The social and military objectives of the insurrection were not entirely realized. The municipal militia of Warsaw did not fail, it is true; it reached a strength of 18,000. The gallant part played by peasants armed with scythes in the first battle of the insurrection at Racławice was an important fact in Polish morale which has given rise to a lasting legend; its hero was the peasant Bartosz Głowacki, who was promoted to the rank of officer; its symbol was the peasant russet-coat assumed by Kościuszko. In fact, however, the peasant mass-levy did not play its expected role. There was no time to give the peasants military training, there were not enough arms for them and no successs was achieved in exciting a lasting enthusiasm for the cause of the insurrection. The decrees aimed at alleviating the lot of the peasants were frustrated by the gentry; besides, these concessions were of provisional nature and did not eliminate the forced labour system. On the other hand, a radical agrarian reform during the war was impossible, both for political considerations and for economic reasons. Under the system of compulsory labour, the village and the manor farm were a unit and its breaking up was bound to have an immediate effect upon the food supply, a problem the insurrection was confronted with in the last weeks before the new harvest. That is why the insurrectionist authorities were instructed not only to defend the peasant's rights, but to watch lest the peasants should refuse work on the manor farm. The command over the peasant levies was to be entrusted to landowners and their agents. Under such circumstances, the prospect of a massive transformation of serfs into "soldiers of liberty" had to remain an utopian illusion. On the other hand, the peasant recruits swelled the ranks of the regular army of the insurrection. They could feel themselves citizens in the insurgent army more than in the backwaters of a village.

The strength of the army changed. At the height of the insurrection it reached 70,000. During the insurrection (April–October), some 140,000 men passed through its ranks. The supply of munitions and arms for an army larger than that established by the Four Years' Seym, in the small and constantly shrinking area under insurgent control, was a major achievement. The production of gunpowder, guns and ammunition was satisfactorily organized. A rifle factory was lacking. For this reason an important part was played by arming soldiers with pikes and adapted scythes and in tactics by interesting attempts to combine artillery fire with a mass attack, to get to close quarters with the enemy.

In the insurgent government, the mobilization of resources for the needs of the army was energetically supervised by the Departments of Treasury, Food Supply and War Needs. The Department of the Treasury under Kołłątaj introduced a system of progressive taxation, carried out requisitioning on a large scale (especially with regard to Church silver for the minting of coin), printed Poland's first banknotes (60 million were issued, 8 million went into circulation). The government took over industrial plants, exacting compulsory deliveries and organizing food supplies not only for the army, but for the civilian population of Warsaw as well. These activities included certain elements close to what has been termed "war socialism" in the historiography of the French Revolution. The Department of Instruction (under Franciszek Dmochowski, a close collaborator of Hugo Kołłątaj) managed propaganda and the press. In the educational and agitational work among the peasants, the administrative machinery and the Church were employed. The attitude of the insurgent authorities towards the Episcopate was critical (two bishops discredited by their collaboration with the Confederation of Targowica had been hanged), but they could count on the support of the lower clergy, within whose ranks there were some ardent Jacobins. The scenes most reminiscent of revolutionary Paris were the public executions in the town squares. The gallows surrounded by armed crowds were the counterpart of the guillotine. The activities of the criminal courts and the problem of

Ożarów. Manor House, second half of the 18th cent.

terrorism were the two questions in which the differences between the "Moderates" and the Jacobins were most conspicuous.

The Jacobins were so called by their opponents, though they were not, of course, affiliated to the Parisian clubs. They were mostly groups of young enthusiasts aged between twenty and thirty who wished to combine the struggle for independence with permanent political and social change. They were working directly among the people, especially among the townsfolk, but were not themselves *sans-culottes*. They came for the most part from the impoverished lesser gentry who had settled in the towns. We find them among the army officers (Jasiński, Zajączek, Chomentowski), lawyers and jurists (Orchowski, Maruszewski, Taszycki), journalists and writers (Pawlikowski, Dmochowski, Szaniawski), and finally among the lower clergy (Mejer, Jelski, Loga). Their activity exerted a material influence upon the democratization of the insurrection and of its various bodies. They spread a revolutionary atmosphere by their agitation and writings (especially numerous poems and songs). Their goal was to establish accomplished facts, to build a republic with equal rights for townspeople and gentry and freedom for the peasants. With the slogan "The Country in Danger!", they called for a radical mobilization of all forces, and a revolutionary seizure of the resources of rich individuals and institutions. Terrorism was to drive

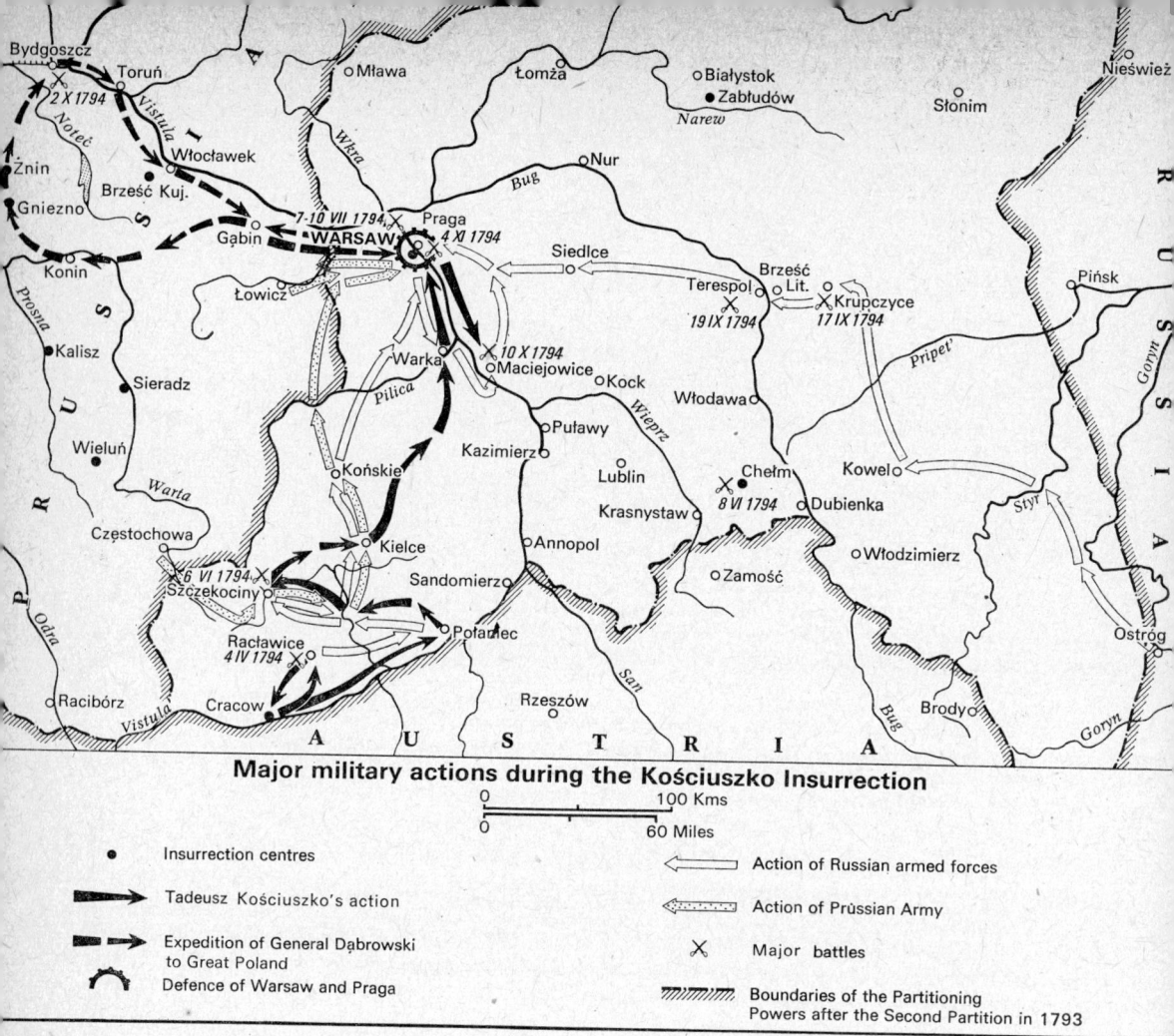

Major military actions during the Kościuszko Insurrection

- Insurrection centres
- Tadeusz Kościuszko's action
- Expedition of General Dąbrowski to Great Poland
- Defence of Warsaw and Praga
- Action of Russian armed forces
- Action of Prussian Army
- Major battles
- Boundaries of the Partitioning Powers after the Second Partition in 1793

the insurrection onto the path of ruthless determination and block the way of retreat. The Jacobins were also called "Hugonists" after Hugo Kołłątaj, who enjoyed a great authority among them. In radicalism, however, the disciples went beyond the master. To the "Moderates" (the majority of generals, the political leaders of the Four Years' Seym, like Ignacy Potocki, and the wealthy bourgeoisie), the republican dictatorship of the insurrection was only a means of regaining independence when the constitutional system of 3 May could be restored. The King declared his adherence to the insurrection. While not allowed to share in power, he had his men among the "Moderates". His nephew, Prince Józef Poniatowski, fought in the insurgent army. Kościuszko attempted to preserve the "unity of action in the general movement". The attitude of the Commander-in-chief towards the various political groups changed according to the development of the military situation.

In May the Prussian army entered Poland. On 6 June Kościuszko lost the battle of Szczekociny (12,000 Poles against 24,000 combined Prussian and Russian troops). On 15 June the Prussians seized Cracow. The Polish forces retreated towards Warsaw. Military reverses increased the revolutionary ferment among the people of Warsaw and excited the activity of the Jacobins. On 28 June the mob broke into the prison and a number of people accused of treason were hanged without trial. Kościuszko took severe measures against the terrorists (sentences of death, mass arrests, drafting suspects into the army) and brought the national cavalry, composed of gentry, into the capital. Jasiński was removed from command of the Lithuanian army. In July Russian and Prussian troops encircled Warsaw. The Commander-in-chief wished to maintain political unity. He declared that "the revolution would not turn against the King" but at the same time made a concession to the Jacobins by handing over to them the Army Criminal Court. Reprisals against the participants in the June riots ceased. The government appealed to the generosity of the people of Warsaw who responded by creating enormous earth works around the capital. The battles before Warsaw (20,000 Poles against 40,000 Russians and Prussians) and the fortification and defense of the city were the greatest military achievements in the history of the insurrection. Kościuszko exhibited outstanding talents as an engineer. For the second time (since April), an important part was played by the people on the ramparts and their work. The siege of Warsaw lasted for two months; in the meantime an insurrection broke out in Great Poland; between 20 and 23 August it spread over the whole territory annexed by Prussia in the Second Partition and even farther into Pomerania. This forced the Prussians to withdraw from Warsaw (on 6 September). The Russians likewise raised the siege. To aid the insurrection in Great Poland a division was dispatched under General Jan Dąbrowski who reached far to the north, captured Bydgoszcz (on 2 October) and entered Royal Prussia (on 6 October). The Prussians were driven out from the main theatre of the war. From the south, however, the country was occupied by the Austrians, and in Lithuania the territory controlled by the insurrection was shrinking with the fall of Wilno on 11 August.

Immediately after the siege of Warsaw was raised, political struggles flared up again. Kościuszko restricted the work of the Army Criminal Court, which resigned as a mark of protest. The Jacobins began to criticize the Commander-in-chief severely. Meanwhile, the war entered into its decisive phase. Russia, having obtained Turkey's pledge to keep the peace on 8 August), decided to throw new forces aginst Poland. A strong corps under the outstanding military commander, Suvorov, set out by forced marches from the Ukraine in the direction of Warsaw. Kościuszko gave up the idea of a peasant mass-levy, ordered a draft of recruits on 18 September (it was expected to raise about 20,000 men), and prepared an extensive operation to prevent Suvorov from establishing contact with the army of occupation. Upon leaving the capital, the Commander-in-chief gave temporary authority to the Jacobins. The rapidity of Russian movements defeated the plans of concentrating Polish forces. In the battle of Maciejowice on 10 October Kościuszko's corps of 7000 men was destroyed after a heroic struggle; the Commander-in-chief himself was wounded and taken prisoner. The defeat at Maciejowice was a moral shock out of all proportion to the loss of one army corps. The Jacobins could not make up their minds whether to seize power. On 12 October the National Council elected a new Commander Tomasz Wawrzecki as a compromise candidate "able to unite the minds". Kołłątaj formed a new club in which Jasiński called for a radical uprising which would make capitulation impossible (among other things by putting the King to death). On 4 November Suvorov took Praga, the suburb of Warsaw on the right bank of the Vistula, by storm. Out of the 14,000 defenders only 4000 escaped to Warsaw. General Jasiński, poet and revolutionist, fell on the ramparts, fighting till the last. Suvorov's troops carried out a massacre of the civilian population. Praga was to be a terrifying example. Kołłątaj and Zajączek left Warsaw. The surrender of the capital was signed by the Municipality. Wawrzecki withdrew to the south with the army. Under the pressure of the Russian pursuit, the remains of the army were dispersed. On 16 November Wawrzecki was taken prisoner.

THE EXTINCTION OF THE POLISH STATE

It is not clear whether prior to the outbreak of the insurrection, it was Russia's intention to preserve permanently a rump-Poland, or whether further partition was merely a matter of time. With regard to that problem, there were different tendencies at the Tsarist court. Stanisław Augustus received assurances that Russia would check the annexationist aims of Prussia and Austria, provided the Poles kept quiet. It is, however, hard to guess what turn events would have taken, because only six months elapsed between the ratification of the partition and the signing of the Polish-Russian treaty in Grodno and the outbreak of the insurrection. The final liquidation of the Polish State was now a foregone conclusion. In September 1794 Seweryn Rzewuski promised Catherine II to pacify Poland for good, if he was given dictatorial powers. He promised not to repeat the "mistakes" of Targowica which "gave rise to the present revolt by giving strength to the party of the King and the Constitutionalists". After the fall of Praga, Ignacy Potocki renewed the proposal of 1792 of giving the throne to Grand Duke Constantine. No attention was paid to those offers in St. Petersburg. The only essential problem needing solution was the determination of the new frontiers.

Negotiations between the partitioning Powers were going on during the hostilities. As in 1772, the occupation forces tried to create accomplished facts. Never was bargaining for the division of spoils so determined. Austria and Russia attempted to limit Prussian claims. The conferences on the partition of Poland ended in a deadlock. On 3 January, 1795 Austria and Russia concluded an aliance against Prussia. The embroiled Powers were making war preparations. France took advantage of this situation because Austria was compelled to reduce her forces in the West and Prussia had concluded peace in Basel (on 5 April, 1795). Prussia, as a result of her exhaustion, gave up her resistance in August. The final agreement was signed on 24 October, 1795. The Prussians occupied Warsaw, captured by Russia, and in return they ceded Cracow, taken in the course of the final campaign, to Austria. The new frontier line between the three partitioning Powers ran along the Pilica, middle Vistula and Bug. This frontier passed through the immediate vicinity of the tollgates of Warsaw. No ratification from Poland was needed on this occasion. Stanisław Augustus abdicated on 25 November, 1795. In an atmosphere of friction, the work of frontier delimitation was completed on 2 July, 1796. The final settlement of problems connected with the new territorial changes like the liquidation of the Commonwealth's debts and of those of the King, was determined by the Convention of 26 January, 1797. In a secret additional clause, the three Powers undertook that the very name of Poland would be erased forever from the vocabulary of international law. A year later, on 12 February, 1798, the last King of Poland died in St. Petersburg.

For 150 years research on the reasons for Poland's disappearance from the map of Europe centred upon two concepts: Poland's own guilt and the guilt of others. Poland's guilt consisted in making insufficient efforts to defend the country, the egocentricity of the gentry which resulted in the cause of the Commonwealth failing to become a cause of the whole nation, political mistakes and treason: guilt of the others consisted in the political crime of the partitioning Powers and the indifference of the West. The soul searching examination of Polish and foreign consciences played an important part in shaping the political, social and emotional attitudes of the post-partition generations. Closest to a scholarly approach to the problem, however, were these historians and thinkers who reached back into the remote past in tracking the internal causes of the fall of Poland. While rejecting the concept of guilt, we shall follow their arguments.

In the seventeenth century, a basic disparity appeared between the development of Poland and that of her neighbours in those fields which were decisive for a country's strength. There is no reason to believe that in the eighteenth century some fate necessarily doomed the weaker State to be devoured by the strong one. A weak country was often a convenient neighbour for the great Powers. Poland, however, found herself in an extremely difficult, one might say, dramatic situation, marked by two great mutually incompatible aims: the armed struggle for independence and the desire to improve the country under peaceful conditions. To govern herself in accordance with her own will, the Commonwealth, surrounded by great

Powers, would have to be a greater power herself. Poland's situation compelled her either to have a great power status, equal to her neighbours, or to an inertia convenient to them. Transition from weakness to strength is not achieved by good intentions alone. Stanisław Augustus was not lacking good intentions in the ambitious years of 1764–1766, nor were the leaders of the Four Years' Seym or the chiefs of the 1794 Insurrection. What they lacked were means. And means had to be powerful, if forces capable of resisting the neighbours were to be mobilized from a multinational country, with society divided into estates, with oligarchic decentralization, an administration in a state of atrophy and an almost entirely agricultural economy. As for Poland's neighbours, if they were not "natural" partitioners, with the exception of Prussia, they certainly were "naturally" opposed to a power growing at their frontiers.

It was no accident that the partitions took place not at the moment of Poland's greatest weakness, but when she began to grow stronger. There exists a dramatic rhythm between the reforms of 1764–1766 (and the Confederation of Bar which was their result) and the First Partition, the work of the Four Years' Seym and the Second Partition, the Insurrection of 1794 and the final disappearance of Poland as a State. Poland was slipping from Russia's grasp, Prussia lay in wait upon her frontiers, while the principle of the balance of power automatically drew Austria in. Closer analysis of events permits reflection upon merits, errors and guilt of individuals and social groups, upon the intellectual and moral character of the principal actors of the drama, like Catherine II, Frederick II, Stanisław Augustus or Kościuszko. When surveying the events in their broad perspective, however, the conclusion arises that in the seventeenth and at the beginning of the eighteenth centuries, there occurred in central and eastern Europe historical processes which brought the Commonwealth to the point of humiliating inertia. Great risks attended Stanisław Augustus trying to walk the political tight-rope without having enough power to lead the parliamentary Commonwealth consistently along with him. In fact, both the King and all the men of Enlightenment took a mutual risk in their efforts to achieve the political, cultural and economic advancement of their country. Their reforming zeal and patriotism cannot be denied; they cannot be accused of a particular class egoism (they were what they could be, in the social sense) or inclination to treason (under the conditions of half-sovereignty the dividing line was flexible). They lost an uneven struggle.

It was not the old system of oligarchical anarchy which destroyed Poland. Polish society in fact demonstrated its fundamental vitality at a time when the Polish State was struggling to maintain its existence against the old order of Europe. This experience infused into the Polish nation the desire to resurrect the Polish State by internal reform, in alliance with the European revolutionary movement, in defiance of the defenders of the old order, the very powers which had partitioned Poland.

POLAND UNDER FOREIGN RULE 1795–1918

CHAPTERS XIV–XVII
by Stefan Kieniewicz

CHAPTERS XVIII–XXI
by Henryk Wereszycki

Chapter XIV
THE NAPOLEONIC ERA (1795–1815)

THE ENFRANCHISEMENT OF THE PEASANTS AND THE NATIONAL UPRISINGS

The downfall of the Polish Commonwealth was by no means an unprecedented event in the political practices carried on by the big powers in the eighteenth century. The unique feature, however, was that Poland deprived forcibly of her statehood was a nation of 10 million people and fully capable of independent existence. The partitions interrupted brutally Poland's vigorous economic, social and cultural development. Even though the disaster was a consequence of Polish errors in the past, even though the Targowica group had played its part, the Polish people regarded the partitions to be an act of violence perpetrated by perfidious neighbours.

The patriotic majority of the Polish people could never reconcile themselves to this outrage. Attempts undertaken by the three partitioning Powers to denationalize or to assimilate Poles remained unsuccessful, especially when in the nineteenth century national consciousness and patriotic feeling ran high in Europe. Moreover, Poland's struggle for independence found a ready response in all European countries under foreign rule whether in the Hapsburg monarchy, Turkey or in Tsarist Russia. Poland's resistance to the three "Northern Courts" remained for a period of 120 years a steady ferment disturbing the balance of power in Europe and was favourable to revolutionary upheavals.

The nineteenth century, the era of the industrial revolution and of the victory of capitalism, was for Poland an age of oppression. While other European nations were accumulating wealth and power in their bid to conquer the world, Poland was subject to foreign exploitation. Economically as backward as the rest of eastern Europe, she had experienced in the first quarter of the nineteenth century the same process of the abolition of feudal conditions: serfdom, labour dues, and the guild system, the same process of building up her factory industry and capitalist landed estates. But in Poland this process of economic and social evolution took a course different from that of either Germany or Russia because it developed in the context of national subjection. Polish patriots from Kościuszko onwards saw in the class struggle the means of liberating the nation, and appealed to the people, proclaiming that a reborn Poland would offer freedom and equality. The agrarian question became, therefore, the key problem in all Polish uprisings; it determined the attitude of all social groups and political factions and hastened the introduction of reforms by the propertied classes and by the governments of the partitioning Powers.

The turning point in this dual process was to be the enfranchisement of the peasants which made it possible for a peasant to become owner of the land. This reform, started in the part of Poland under Prussian domination early in the nineteenth century, was completed in Prussian and Austrian Poland by 1848–1850; in the Russian dominions it was carried out only in 1861–1864. The reform was spurred on and accompanied by revolutionary upheavals and national uprisings. With her peasants enfranchised, Poland entered the era of modern capitalism. Simultaneously, the agrarian question ceased to provide the motive power of revolutionary movements. Very soon labour problems became the main source of social unrest.

Thus the years 1795–1864 were in Poland's history a period marked by the introduction of capitalism, by a gradual emancipation of the peasants, and by large-scales national risings. This period of seventy years may be divided into two almost equal phases:

(a) 1795–1831. During these years, the crisis of feudalism was only beginning to take shape. Remnants of a Polish State still existed in the Duchy of Warsaw and the Congress Kingdom. Independence movements and the struggle for social justice were still led by the gentry. The period reached its climax with the November Insurrection (1830–1831).

(b) 1832–1864. The agrarian crisis entered then an acute stage, with a simultaneous intensification of national oppression. This gave rise to more radical ideologies and political programmes: plebeian voices now made themselves heard among the leadership. The culminating point of the crisis coincided in the parts under Prussian and Austrian rule with the revolutionary movements of 1846–1848 and in the Russian part with the January Insurrection (1863–1864).

POLAND AFTER THE THIRD PARTITION

The three States, which had carved up the Polish Commonwealth, presented in the late eighteenth century different shades of enlightened absolutism. All three tried to assimilate the newly acquired Polish territories as quickly as possible and to exploit their resources to the full. The large landowners, who had been the masters in Poland, were now excluded from power. The traditional voivodships were replaced in the Prussian portions by the provinces of West Prussia, South Prussia, and New East Prussia; in the

Austrian dominions by the provinces of Old and New Galicia; and in the Russian dominated part by a number of gubernias or provincial governments. The new administrations were manned by freshly arrived foreigners, and Polish was banned as the official language from government offices and courts of justice. The Prussian government was more drastic than the Austrian government in its efforts to Germanize the population. Settlers were brought from the West, and German was imposed as the compulsory medium of instruction in all schools. With the same end in view the partitioning Powers took over the *starostwa* as well as a considerable part of lands of the Church. The Russian and Prussian governments sequestrated or confiscated the large estates of persons who had taken part in the last insurrection.

The political disaster had a far reaching effect on the economic development of the country. A large number of manufactories (particularly in Warsaw) went bankrupt, and rent reform was checked. In addition, Polish territories were subject to intensive fiscal exploitation and to conscription. Greatly increased taxes were collected far more efficiently than they had been under Polish rule. As for conscription, the toll of lives taken from Polish peasants was most heavy under the Austrians, who were then waging a bitter and unsuccessful war in the West.

After 1795 conditions in Russian Poland differed essentially from those in the two other areas: it covered in effect regions inhabited preponderantly by Ukrainians, Byelorussians and Lithuanians, where only the gentry and a part of the urban middle class were Poles. The Russian government did not take this into account in its political dealings at that time. Russia, like Prussia and Austria, was a State with a feudal, conservative system. All three imprisoned and persecuted Polish patriots in order to repress irredentism; yet, at the same time, they sought to combat Jacobinism born of the French Revolution, which equally threatened them. For this reason, they maintained class privileges in Poland and sought support among the country's aristocracy and wealthy gentry. Progressive social reforms introduced by the Four Years' Seym and during the Kościuszko Insurrection were abolished; the lord remained the master of the peasant; discrimination against the urban middle class continued and with it oppression of the Jews; the magnates were cultivated but the petty gentry were harassed. Ecclesiastical privileges were curtailed and attempts were made to bring the Church under State control; however, Orthodox Russia as well as Protestant Prussia looked upon the Catholic hierarchy as a desirable ally from the angle of social conservatism.

More pronounced was the difference in policy adopted by the three partitioning Powers with respect to the peasantry. Austria began by introducing progressive reforms. A series of letters patent granted by the Emperor Joseph II (1780–1790) assured the peasant security of tenure and laid down that his burden might not be increased; the maximum labour service he had to render to the lord was fixed at 3 days a week and the manorial administration was to be supervised by the district commissioner. These reforms were, however, carried out only in part: the intended general change over from labour dues to rent never took place: and the right granted the peasant to complain about his master at a district office proved ineffective in practice.

The Prussian government proceeded to introduce rents of the State lands; with regard to private estates it confined itself to appointing justices authorized to settle disputes between peasants under government control though acting in the name of the squire.

Under Russian rule, the peasant was worse off, because he was assimilated to conditions prevailing in Russia. Serfdom there had all the attributes of personal slavery and labour dues were calculated not according to the size of the plot of land, but to the number of male "souls" in the village.

These divergences in the agrarian policy of the three Powers were due, in part, to the different levels of their economic development. Prussia, who had withdrawn from the war in the West and was carrying on a vigorous trade with both belligerents, could afford to offer benefits to agriculture. High grain prices were an incentive to enterprising landowners to modernize their estates, expand their manors at the expense of the peasants and employ more hired labour. Equally profitable conditions existed after the partitions in the Ukraine owing to the opening of the waterway enabling grain to be carried on rafts down to the Black Sea port of Odessa. In the conditions which prevailed in Russia this could only encourage the large wheat producers to increase the exploitation of the Ukrainian peasant and to demand more serf labour. Galicia's economic situation was far worse: ruined by the continuing war and cut off by tariff boundaries from the natural outlets for her exports she had to stick to old methods much longer. The decrees of Joseph II, which were binding in theory but ineffective in practice, did not encourage social and economic progress.

ATTITUDE OF THE POPULATION AND THE INDEPENDENCE MOVEMENT

The downfall of the Commonwealth was beyond doubt a serious blow to the aristocrats and the wealthy gentry, because it took the reins of power out of their hands. For the moment, however, they accepted the new state of affairs, especially when the partitioning Powers averted potential revolution by maintaining the system of serfdom and labour services. The loyalty of the gentry was particularly evident in the Russian dominated territories where the new Tsar Paul I, who succeeded Catherine II in 1796, had released numerous Polish prisoners, including Kościuszko and had restored to the gentry the privilege of appointing minor administrative and judical officers.

The magnates, who had not lost hope of Poland's resurrection, counted mainly on conflicts that might arise among the partitioning Powers, and on one of the latter restoring Poland to full sovereignty. Actually, a conflict of the sort was looming ahead in 1795–1796 in connexion with the frontier delimitation. Tension between Prussia, on the one hand, and Austria and Russia on the other, continued even after a compromise had been reached. While hoping for a conflict between the partitioning Powers, a number of magnates, engaged in political activities took good care to maintain a loyal attitude towards "their own" partitioning government. A considerable part of the middle gentry retired into private life. In the Prussian zone, the post-partition period was referred to as the "golden years", because the price of grain rose and credit was cheap. Prussian State institutions invested large sums of money in mortgages on landed estates. The Polish gentry spent money lightheartedly with little thought of using it to raise their property's economic level; the government expected to recuperate the investment eventually by chasing the Polish debtors off their land.

Resistance to the partitioning Powers stemmed from those groups of the population which were most vitally affected by the loss of independence. This section of the community included the lesser gentry and the petty bourgeoisie, but mainly the professional intelligentsia and the officer corps. Immediately after the insurrection had failed, clandestine connexions were established between all three parts of partitioned Poland, quite often under the cover of masonic lodges with the aim of restoring a free Poland. The movement was joined by individuals among the gentry and even the aristocracy; the latter were more inclined to suggest diplomatic methods in preference to armed uprising. A group of Galician conspirators sent Stanisław Sołtyk to Paris, where he was to contact the Directory. In January 1796, a group of conspirators in Cracow drew up an act of Confederation which contained the pledge to take up arms at the call of the French government. A secret committee was founded with its seat in Lwów under the name of the "Centralizacja" with dependent branches in the Russian and Prussian provinces. About one thousand of the soldiers who had served under Kościuszko, led by Colonel Joachim Denisko, assembled in Moldavia, then under Turkish rule, with the intention of marching into Poland.

It was the time of Bonaparte's brilliant campaigns in Italy. The Polish people expected a total defeat of the Austrians, Russia's entry into the war and the arrival of the French in the Balkans. Bonaparte, however, signed an armistice at Leoben (1797), the attempt of Denisko's forces failed, the Lwów conspiracy was discovered and Austrian and Russian prisons were filled with Polish patriots.

The first conspiracy had no definite social programme, but it had been joined by radical elements from the former Jacobins. One of them was

Franciszek Gorzkowski, an impoverished noble and a land surveyor by profession, who acting in agreement with the Warsaw conspiracy, started a campaign among the peasants in Podlasie which was then under Austrian rule. According to him, all peasants in Poland ought to take to arms on the same day, remove the lords from the land, march on to meet the expected French forces and jointly with them liberate Poland. In his campaign among the illiterate population Gorzkowski used lithographed pictures which showed the difference in numbers of peasants and the gentry, or illustrated the peasant's misery of today and compared it with his prosperity of tomorrow in a free Poland. The first country squire who came across this propaganda, surrendered Gorzkowski to the Austrians (1797); thus ended an immature, but nevertheless important attempt at revolutionary propaganda among the peasantry.

After the arrests in Galicia and in Lithuania, the conspiracy continued in the Prussian-dominated areas. In 1798 a new secret centre was founded, namely, the Society of Polish Republicans. Its membership included former officers, writers, lawyers, small merchants and even some landed gentry. The Society's "Supervisory Body" drew up the directives for Poland's future government. It was modelled on the French Constitution of Year III, which meant that it advocated the abolition of privileges and rejected cooperation with any of the partitioning Powers. It promised the peasants personal freedom in general terms, without declaring that they would obtain their freeholds. The Republicans recognized Kościuszko as their leader: he was then in France, having been released from captivity. They also kept in touch with Kołłątaj who was detained in an Austrian prison. While awaiting new French victories, the members of the society restricted their activity to ideological propaganda, military intelligence for France, and to helping volunteers who were joining the Polish Legions in France, and Italy. The conspirators had no strong backing in Poland; they counted mainly on the arrival of the French. The group was never discovered, but it dissolved gradually and ceased all activity after 1800, when peace in Europe was restored. The Polish revolutionary forces were neither numerous nor strong enough to take up the fight alone.

THE LEGIONS

When the Kościuszko Insurrection collapsed a few thousand officers and politicians emigrated. The majority of them soon assembled in Paris, where a semi-official Agency of the Insurrection government was active under the leadership of a Warsaw lawyer, Franciszek Barss. The Agency was supported by the more moderate elements among the émigrés, while the Jacobin wing, headed by the writers Franciszek Dmochowski and Kalasanty Szaniawski, set up its own Deputation, and tried to enlist the help of the French government. The Deputation considered the idea of provoking an uprising in Poland, whereas the members of the Agency were opposed to this course and tried mainly to organize Polish military units to serve under the French. Neither of these attempts had, at the beginning, any chance of success. Most of Poland's territories were at that time in Prussian hands and therefore any action undertaken to secure Poland's independence was considered as anti-Prussian. France had meanwhile made peace with Prussia at Basel and was in no mood to annoy her by raising the Polish question seriously. The Directory was at war with Austria, but it was a war waged for France's "natural frontiers" and not for spreading revolution. The leaders in Paris used the Polish body without the slightest scruple to put pressure on Austria, but they did not intend to tie their hands by creating Polish units in French service.

Bonaparte's victories in Italy, however, offered opportunities for raising such units. There were many recruits from Galicia among the Austrian prisoners of war and many able officers could easily be found among the Polish émigrés. The suggestion was made to the Directory by General Henryk Dąbrowski, who had arrived from Warsaw. The Directory sent him to Milan, where Bonaparte gave the matter serious consideration. The hero of Arcole was presenting his government with accomplished facts. He was already attempting to establish his independence of Paris. One of his plans was to create an Italian army, but as yet he could not discover where the required number of volunteers might come from. The idea of a Polish Legion as an auxiliary unit in his army in Lombardy appealed to him. In this spirit Bonaparte drafted the agreement which was signed in Milan by General Dąbrowski and the Lombard government on 9 January, 1797, and formally approved by himself as Commander-in-chief. The legionaries were to obtain Polish uniforms, Italian epaulets and a French cockade. They were assured that they would return to Poland if the national cause should demand it.

Dąbrowski issued an appeal inviting his compatriots to join the ranks of the reborn army and himself engaged in recruiting men in the prisoner-of-war camps. By the time the armistice of Leoben was signed, he already had 3600 men under arms. Within a year, their number reached 10,000. In spite of the peace negotiations, the legionaries longed for an armed return "from Italy to Poland". This idea found its expression in a song composed by Józef Wybicki, Dąbrowski's friend, in 1797, *Jeszcze Polska nie zginęła, póki my żyjemy* (Poland is not yet lost, so long as we are alive). This song, which all the soldiers adopted, was in time to become Poland's national anthem.

Meanwhile France had signed the peace treaty of Campo Formio. The legions were transferred to serve the new Cisalpine Republic. One of the legions was garrisoned in Rome and distinguished itself in 1798 during the campaign in Naples. The Poles were also employed to put down popular revolts against the French. This revealed the dual character of their duties. On the one hand, these Polish legionaries were the soldiers of revolutionary France, adopting the example of her democratic army, pledged to fight for the rights of man; with Poland in their mind they accepted instruction in the art of war under the leadership of the greatest commander of the time. On the other hand, they were used in Italy as the tool of fresh oppression and there was nothing to guarantee that they would one day have a chance to serve their own people. The Deputation group opposed the Legions, both on principle and because they were the creation of a rival party. This, however, did not prevent many radicals from joining the ranks of the Legion. The most gifted among them, Józef Sułkowski, became Bonaparte's aide-de-camp and tried to win his sympathy for the Polish question (he died in street fighting during the Egyptian Expedition).

In the ill-starred campaign of 1799 the Polish legions suffered great losses. One of them was handed over to the Austrians after the capitulation of Mantua, while the other was bled white in the battle of Trebbia. A new Legion was then formed on the northern front, the "Danube Legion" under the command of General Karol Kniaziewicz which played a decisive role in bringing about the victory of Hohenlinden (1800).

There came another brief spell of peace in Europe, during the period of the Consulate. The treaty of Lunéville left Poland still subject and even specified that neither France nor Austria would give assistance to the internal enemies of the other. Many Polish officers and soldiers resigned while others revolted against the despotism of the First Consul and made contacts with the Republican conspirators in France and Italy. Bonaparte, in turn, considered the Polish units superfluous and undesirable. The greater part of the Legions (about 6000 men) were therefore despatched to San Domingo (the modern Haiti) to put down the Negro rebellion (1802–1803). Nearly all of them perished there killed either by the climate or in battle, fighting for the ignoble cause of a colonial war. This episode brought the idea of the Legions into disrepute.

Yet in spite of this sorry ending, Dąbrowski's Legions had been of some use to the Polish cause. During the five years of their existence some 20,000 men had received training and this nucleus made possible the resurrection of a national army in the Duchy of Warsaw. The Legionaires were imbued with the democratic and civic spirit of the French Army; they were the hard-core radiating hope and confidence in Poland's liberation even though they placed their hope on help from abroad.

When this hope failed to materialize and Bonaparte betrayed the cause of liberty after the 18th Brumaire, the Polish Jacobins began to seek new means of salvation. One of them, Józef Pawlikowski, who was then secretary to Kościuszko, published an anonymous pamphlet with the striking title *Czy Polacy mogą się wybić na niepodległość?* (Can the Poles achieve their own liberation ?) (1800). His answer was, of course, in the affirmative but on condition that the mass of the Polish people would rise and fight for national liberation and for improving their lot. The booklet was confiscated by Fouché's police and made no deep impression at the time; but in the succeeding generation it became the credo of Polish patriots.

ADAM CZARTORYSKI AND THE PUŁAWY PLAN

After 1800 conspiracies had lost their *raison d'être* in Poland. Many politicians and officers of the former legions were returning from their exile and seeking other kinds of public activity. This they could find in the field of science and culture. A nation threatened with disappearance was bound to salvage at least the relics of its past, to promote education and to preserve its cultural treasures. Many enlightened magnates like J. M. Ossoliński and S. Potocki established scientific libraries in those years. Many collections of books owned by monasteries which were closed, were thus preserved to serve future generations of research workers. Princess Isabella Czartoryska established in her residence in Puławy the first Polish museum of historical relics; she called it "The Temple of Sybil". In 1800, thanks mainly to the efforts of Staszic, the Warsaw Society of the Friends of Science was founded. Here a small number of aristocratic patrons assisted a group of distinguished scholars who set themselves the task of drafting a comprehensive programme for the study of the various branches of science and learning. The most important work published under the aegis of the Society was the *Dictionary of the Polish Language*, compiled by Samuel Linde; its first volume appeared in 1806.

The most favourable conditions for educational work at this time existed in the Russian-occupied part of Poland. The new Tsar Alexander I had made friends with the young Prince Adam Czartoryski, who became his confident and was appointed Deputy-Minister of Foreign Affairs; together, they drew up projects to liberalize Russia. Czartoryski also became the curator of the Wilno Educational District and in 1802 he opened a Polish University in Wilno which soon reached a very high academic standard. At the head of the University stood the Śniadecki brothers, one of them a mathematician, the other a natural scientist. Sponsored by this institution, a network of secondary and primary schools was established in the Educational District of Wilno which embraced Lithuania, Byelorussia and the Ukraine. The organization of this educational system followed closely the model drawn up by the pre-partition Commission of Education. An exceptionally high level was attained by the Lyceum (secondary school) of Krzemieniec in Volhynia which owed its foundation to the efforts of a magnate and distinguished historian of law, Tadeusz Czacki. Czacki's main aide was Hugo Kołłątaj, who had gone back to educational work after his release from prison.

Tsar Alexander's friendship with Czartoryski and his generosity towards Poland had a deeper political reason. Russia indirectly took advantage of the weakening of Austria as well as Prussia after the revolutionary wars to reassert her expansionist policy in central Europe. The liberalism of the new Tsar was intended to attract not only the Poles, but also the Slavs in Austria and the Balkans. Czartoryski worked wholeheartedly for the restoration of a united Poland in union with Russia under Tsar Alexander. He saw in the approaching decisive showdown with revolutionary France prospects for the success of his schemes. When Napoleon Bonaparte proclaimed himself Emperor and Great Britain was organizing the Third Coalition, Czartoryski conceived an intricate scheme for joint action by Austria and Russia to attack neutral Prussia and recover all the Polish lands in her possession; the war with France was to be the second stage. In 1805 Alexander I arrived in Puławy (then under Austrian domination), and was welcomed enthusiastically by the Polish aristocrats there as their future ruler. But the "Puławy Plan" proved to be a will-o'-the-wisp. Russia was simply blackmailing Prussia to force her to join the coalition. Straight from Puławy Alexander went to Potsdam to conclude an alliance with Frederick William III. Notwithstanding this unexpected disillusionment, the majority of Poland's aristocracy was still attracted by the pro-Russian orientation. In the coming great showdown, Tsarist Russia was to prove the mainstay of the old feudal order.

JENA AND TILSIT

The 1805 campaign ended in a brilliant French victory at Austerlitz. The *Grande Armée* then halted on Poland's threshold, keeping in mind the ambiguous attitude of armed, though neutral, Prussia. Only a year later war with Prussia was to compel Napoleon to deal with the Polish question. After Jena and Auerstädt and after the lightning occupation of the Prussian fortresses the road into Poland was open to the French.

Napoleon residing in Berlin, negotiated with the King of Prussia and, at the same time, encouraged the Poles to rise in arms. On 3 November, 1806 Dąbrowski and Wybicki issued a revolutionary appeal to the population dictated by Napoleon. In it they quoted the Emperor's words: "I want to see whether the Poles deserve to be a nation". Napoleon was not promising the Poles anything; he was even ready to strike a bargain with the King of Prussia at their expense. But the Russian army was drawing near on its way to reinforce the Prussian forces and hard fighting lay ahead of the French on the Vistula. Under these circumstances they were compelled

General Jan Henryk Dąbrowski entering Poznań on November 6, 1806

to enlist the support of the Polish people. They entered Warsaw and Poznań without a shot being fired. Dąbrowski organized a provisional Polish administration, calling upon the gentry to rise and join the army, and demanding that the landlords provide the recruits from among their peasants. The common people, the petty bourgeoisie and the petty gentry were full of enthusiasm. The magnates sent delegations to pay homage to Napoleon, but in general they were rather reserved. Many of them possessed properties in the neighbouring areas under Russian or Austrian rule and disapproved of the "usurper". On the other hand, there were Jacobin politicians, headed by General Józef Zajączek, who offered their services to Napoleon and appealed to him to bring about radical reforms in Poland. The Emperor, however, calculated that the left-wingers would be loyal to him anyway and that it was much more important to win over the Polish aristocrats who supported Russia. Prince Józef Poniatowski hesitated for a long time before accepting the post of director (or minister) of war offered to him by the French. He finally had to agree under the pressure of public opinion; the alternative might have been the appointment of either Dąbrowski or Zajączek as Commander-in-chief. In January 1807 Napoleon transferred the temporary administration of Poland's occupied territories to a Government Committee of seven. Most of its members were aristocrats, former leaders in the Four Years' Seym, heated by Małachowski and Stanisław Potocki. The Committee's principal task was to ensure that the *Grande Armée* received its supplies during the winter campaign ahead.

Nearly twenty thousand Polish soldiers under Dąbrowski were engaged in this campaign: they had pushed the Prussians down the left bank of the lower Vistula and later played a major role in the siege of Gdańsk. The Polish people in general were convinced that service under Napoleon was bound to result in their country being reinstated within its former frontiers, but the Polish question was left in abeyance. The fierce battle of Eylau had brought no decision, and Napoleon was careful not to create any accomplished facts so far as Poland was concerned. After the battle of Friedland the Polish question became a bargaining point in the Franco-Russian negotiations.

In the course of secret parleys that took place in Tilsit in 1807, Napoleon declared himself ready to hand the Poles over to the Tsar, whereas Alexander in turn suggested that Jerome Bonaparte should be put in charge in Warsaw. Both Emperors dreamt of a division of the world, but none of them was ready to sponsor the troublesome Polish question. A compromise was finally struck and the new King of Saxony, Frederick Augustus, was appointed to rule in Warsaw. Russia received, as a meagre compensation, the district of Białystok. The choice of a Saxon prince as "duke of Warsaw" was proof of the temporary character of the Franco-Russian agreement. For the time being, the Duchy of Warsaw was to remain a French outpost in eastern Europe. Later, depending on the march of events, the territory might serve another purpose. It might, for example, be either ceded to Russia in exchange for other advantages, or used in rebuilding all of Poland as a bulwark against Russia.

THE CONSTITUTION OF THE DUCHY OF WARSAW

The small new State was artificially carved out of the Prussian part of Poland; it covered an area of 104,000 sq.km with a population of 2.6 million; ran in a narrow strip from the Warta basin to the lower course of the Neman. It was so pitifully small a part of the former Commonwealth that the great general disappointment caused by the Tilsit decision need

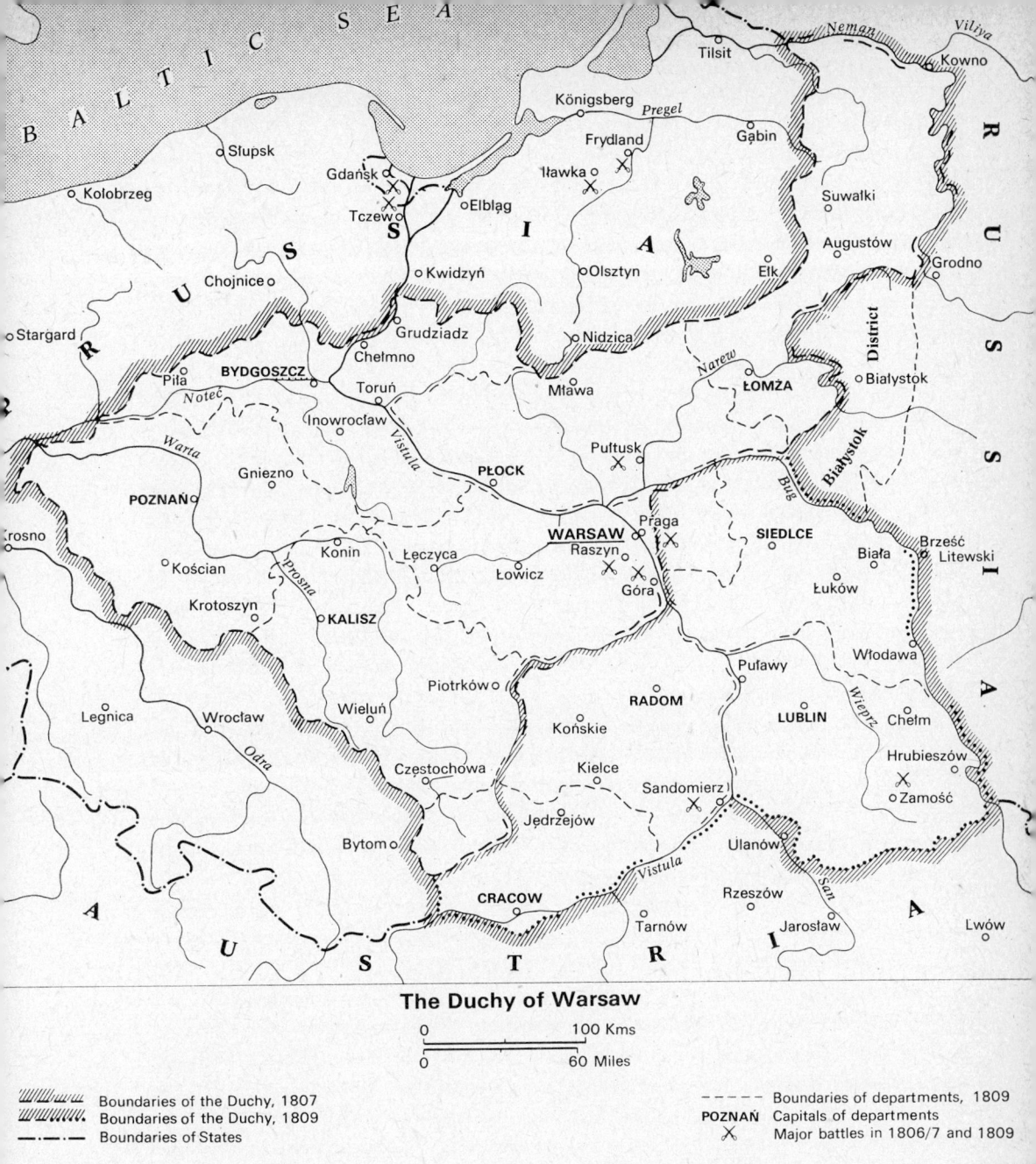

The Duchy of Warsaw

| 0 | 100 Kms |
| 0 | 60 Miles |

▨▨▨ Boundaries of the Duchy, 1807
▨▨▨ Boundaries of the Duchy, 1809
—·—·— Boundaries of States

- - - - Boundaries of departments, 1809
POZNAŃ Capitals of departments
✗ Major battles in 1806/7 and 1809

cause no surprise. Yet this small strip of land produced a Polish government and raised and trained Polish armies. To the people it meant the first promising step towards restoring the independence of the entire country.

In July 1807 Napoleon summoned the members of the Governing Committee to Dresden and there dictated to them the main principles of the new Constitution, taking little account of their opinion in the matter.

These principles were an adaptation of the Constitution of the French Empire (of the year VIII) and similar to those granted by the Emperor to other vassal states in Germany and Italy, but with allowance for conditions prevailing in Poland. The whole power was put into the hands of the king; the Seym had, however, the right to vote on bills relating to taxation and law. The administration followed the French pattern (6 prefects heading the departments of Poznań, Bydgoszcz, Płock, Łomża, Kalisz and Warsaw). Each department was divided into districts under a subprefect. The Constitution made no mention of civil rights but declared the abolition of "slavery" (which meant the serfdom of the peasants) and proclaimed the equality of all citizens before the law. Moreover, it introduced the Code Napoléon. The composition of the Seym followed more or less the same lines as in the past. The members of the Senate were by appointment, bishops, voivods and castellans. In the Chamber of Deputies the majority were to be representatives elected in the local diets from among the gentry; in addition, however, 40 per cent of the deputies were to be elected in communal assemblies in which landowners, merchants, master craftsmen, officers and a part of the intelligentsia had voting rights. All offices were reserved for the citizens of the country and the "national" language was introduced into the administration. These provisions gave a Polish character to this new minute State.

Those were the legal provisions. Matters turned out differently in practice: King Frederick Augustus resided permanently in Dresden and the country was ruled by a State Council closely supervised by the French Resident. The Polish army provided by the Constitution was under the orders of Marshal Davout, commander of the French occupation corps. The bourgeois legislation imposed upon the Duchy did not abolish the rule of the gentry in spite of appearances. The economic weakness of the Polish bourgeoisie made it possible for the great landowners to retain their political supremacy even under the new form of government.

This became most obvious in the manner in which the Constitution was applied with regard to the peasant question. The provision contained in article 4: "slavery shall be abolished", did not settle the basic question, namely, the recognition of the peasants' right to own land. Left-wing writers advocated a gradual enfranchisement of the peasants. Some ministers agreed that the payment of rent was to be accepted at least in the case of "national" that is State landed estates. But the selfish point of view of the landowners again prevailed. Their main spokesman was Feliks Łubieński, Minister of Justice. Under his influence the royal decree of 21 December, 1807 did indeed confirm the right of the peasant to leave his land freely, but reserved the right of the squire to keep the land with its buildings and inventory as his property. Moreover, the decree by implication empowered the squire to remove the peasant from the land at will. Thus the rural population, though it was freed theoretically, remained in reality dependent on the goodwill of the squire, and was forced to render labour service under threat of eviction.

ECONOMIC AND SOCIAL CHANGES WITHIN THE DUCHY OF WARSAW

Right from the beginning, the new little State was confronted with economic difficulties. It was unable to exist independently, it had no real sovereignty and in addition, it was systematically exploited by the French occupation forces. Napoleon levied contributions from the liberated Polish territories, he took over all Prussian State assets and claims and debited the Duchy's treasury for the armaments furnished to the Polish army. In its balance of payments the Duchy was always in debt to France, compelled to ask for extension of dates for payment, or to borrow the required amounts from French banks at usurous rates. About a dozen French generals were granted awards from Polish State properties.

A typical example of the methods used in this financial exploitation was the case of the mortgages held by Prussian government institutions on the majority of Polish estates. Napoleon transferred all claims to his own account as spoils of war, assesssed their value at 49 million francs and ceded them to the treasury of the Duchy by the treaty of Bayonne (1808) for a sum of 21 million francs payable within four years. In practice these claims were irrecoverable owing to the general decline in the income of the gentry. The continental blockade had brought in its wake a sharp reduction in the price of grain. The years of carefree living were now over and the ruling circles were faced with the threat of losing their estates. Because the government did not wish to put them under the hammer and thus could not raise the instalments (known in Poland as "Bayonne sums") it repaid the debt in "cannon fodder", by supplying recruits to the Army. The petty Duchy maintained at first 30,000 and later 60,000 men under arms. In addition to this compulsory contingent, Napoleon organized out of Polish recruits other units which he incorporated into the French forces. Over ten thousand Polish soldiers were employed for four years in the cruel and bloody war against the Spanish people.

The agricultural crisis made it impossible to take proper advantage of the new conditions arising from the abolition of serfdom. Hardly any landowner could afford to make investments and pay for hired labour. Most of the estates retained the old system of labour dues which cost nothing but the peasants expected that the arrival of the French would bring them complete liberation. There were areas where they refused to render services and regions devastated by the war, which they simply deserted making use of their new freedom. The government tried to check migration and, on the whole, defended the interests of the gentry. The contributions imposed upon the country, in the form of taxes, compulsory deliveries, levies of troops and construction of fortifications were borne, predominantly, by the poor rural population.

Three military campaigns within six years were not conducive to a rational economy. Memoirs recorded that the gentry remembered the Duchy of Warsaw as a period of hardship caused by falling incomes, wartime requisitioning and difficulties in obtaining credit. It can hardly be said, however, that there was general ruin in the country; it was rather the question of some fortunes tottering and others growing up. Big landowners experienced difficulties but the weaving industry of Great Poland and other trades prospered. Warsaw came to life again; army contractors amassed fortunes, and the peasants found life easier at least for a while. The temporary currency difficulties were overcome by devaluing the worthless coins left behind by the Prussians and issuing a national currency. The trade balance of the Duchy was favourable, at least while peace reigned. The very fact that the tiny country was able, in spite of the turmoil of war to cope with its considerable difficulties, find the means to raise an army and to set up a new administration, was proof enough of its capacity to survive.

The fact remains, however, that the treasury of the Duchy had to struggle hard to overcome its difficulties. In its search for new sources of income the government increased indirect taxes and issued banknotes, an operation which proved unsuccessful. Tax collection was slow and the military budget devoured 2/3 of the income. By 1811 treasury arrears exceeded 90 million Polish zlotys. Civil servants did not receive their salaries and even the payments in the army were delayed. In despair, the ministers appealed in vain to Paris for financial assistance.

The hard times brought with them a series of important fundamental changes. The new Constitution did not help the peasants much, but it did raise the social standing of the petty bourgeoisie. The aristocracy was still in control, and the Seym was preponderantly gentry in character, but in the officer corps and in the administration the number of commoners increased and many of them took advantage of the right to acquire land. From the Warsaw money lenders emerged, during those years, a close-knit group of financiers and bankers who were soon to become a very powerful factor.

The Jewish population was excluded by special royal decree from the privileges granted to the bourgeoisie. The "temporary" suspension of the civil rights of the Jews denied them the right to hold office, and was the starting point for further restrictions including the concentration of urban Jews in segregated districts. Jews were also excluded from military service and compelled to pay a special tax instead. This discriminatory legislation was motivated, as usual, by the view that the Jews belonged to an alien civilization. This in turn retarded their assimilation. Very few groups of progressive Jews were favourably disposed towards the new régime and gave their support to the Polish cause. Special fame was won by Berek Joselewicz, leader of a Jewish regiment during the Insurrection of 1794 and later squadron commander in the army of the Duchy, who fell in battle during the 1809 campaign.

Two new social groups came to the fore during the Napoleonic era, the bureaucracy and the army. The constitution established a new administrative machinery, until then unknown in Poland. Towards the end of the Duchy's existence the number of civil servants and local-government officials had reached the figure of 9000. A Law and Civil Service School was established in Warsaw to train them. The wealthy gentry were unanimous in grumbling about the expense and incompetence of this new machinery. The fact remained that the civil service opened a new career for both the bourgeoisie and the impoverished gentry, and that it helped to emancipate the emergent Polish intelligentsia.

In the general view, the Army was the chief *raison d'être* and support of the Duchy and thus enjoyed great popularity. Recruits were levied by drawing lots and they had the right to provide a substitute. Wealthier people took advantage of this privilege, so that in practice the rural poor joined the ranks. Conditions in the army were tough but training was good, morale usually high, and military efficiency of quite a high standard. To the soldier military service was a school where he learned his civic duties; military service was considered a form of social advancement. The most valuable cadre within the officer corps were the officers of the legions; many young volunteers came from the landed gentry and frequently they rose from the ranks. Service under the national banner, with its prestige and prospect of speedy promotion, had general approval. Also, the troops had faith in Napoleon and believed that he would revive their motherland.

The Church hierarchy looked upon the new régime with disfavour. The State ignored the privileges of the Church, which it tried to make serve its needs. The feud between Napoleon and the Pope had repercussions in Poland. Time and again disputes with the bishops flared up concerning divorces and civil marriage provided for in the Napoleonic Code. The compensation due to the Church for expropriated Church estates was not paid, while clergymen were recruited into the army. Some religious orders campaigned among the people against the French. The bishops branded some ministers as freemasons. The clergy declined to perform the duties of registrars as instructed. An open conflict between Church and State never arose, but secret animosity was widespread and a large number of patriotic, englightened citizens looked upon the Roman Catholic Church with disfavour.

THE YEAR 1809

Early in 1809 the first Seym was convened in Warsaw, an event which brought life to the political scene. The government headed by Stanisław Potocki and Feliks Łubieński was faced by a twin opposition. The conservative party among the landowners complained publicly of exorbitant taxes and of the costly bureaucracy; privately they worked to undermine the system in order to get back the former privileges of the gentry. On the other side stood the ex-Jacobin leftists almost completely excluded from power, who sharply criticized the new rulers of the Duchy and, in support of the progressive principles in the Constitution, advocated their expansion. The two most outstanding writers of the Enlightenment, Staszic and Kołłątaj, expounded their point of view in pamphlets which enjoyed a large circulation. They were in favour of the Napoleonic system and expressed their belief that it would bring about Poland's liberation, social progress and economic prosperity. Staszic sat in the State Council, where he played a useful part; the ambitious Kołłątaj, however, who had been described to Napoleon as a dangerous Jacobin, was not entrusted with office.

The first elections revealed a majority for the gentry; none of the radical politicians entered the Chamber of Deputies. In accordance with the rules of the constitution, the session of the Seym was limited to two weeks and only fifteen members elected by the Chamber to the three Seym Committees had the right to deliver speeches. Under these conditions, the Seym meekly adopted the government's proposals for new taxes; the opposition could air its views only at informal meetings of the deputies. The international situation was tense and nobody in Poland wished to risk an internal conflict.

In the spring of 1809 Austria made an attempt to retaliate against France by taking advantage of the fact that the greater part of Napoleon's forces were tied up in Spain. Napoleon treated Poland as a territory of no importance to the military operations which were to take place on the Danube. The Duchy was therefore stripped of troops. Quite unexpectedly Archduke Ferdinand d'Este's army corps, 30 thousand strong, crossed the Duchy's frontier. This move was political rather than strategic, because Austria wanted to hold Polish territory as a counter when bargaining for an alliance with Russia or Prussia. Meanwhile, Prince Józef Poniatowski barred the way to the invader at the approaches of Warsaw. The battle of Raszyn on 19 April, where 12,000 Poles fought against 25,000 Austrians, was a day of glory for the Polish infantry which stubbornly defended every inch of ground. The Poles were masters of the battlefield, but had to withdraw to Warsaw on the following night on account of the heavy losses.

After this honourable encounter Poniatowski negotiated with the Austrians, surrendering Warsaw to them and withdrawing his army to the right bank of the Vistula. This stratagem proved most effective: the Austrian army corps was compelled to station part of its forces in the turbulent Polish capital. This weakened them considerably, and the Polish army thus regained freedom of action. While the Archduke on the left bank of the Vistula sought in vain to subdue the western districts of Poland, Poniatowski, on the right bank, boldly launched an offensive into friendly and undefended Galicia. The Polish cavalry, enthusiastically welcomed by the population, occupied the districts of Lublin and Sandomierz almost without a shot. They at once set about raising new Polish regiments in these territories.

Poland's successes caused uneasiness in St. Petersburg. In 1809 Russia, though formally allied with Napoleon, wished Austria success. A Russian army corps entered Galicia, not with a view of fighting Austrians, but simply to prevent further Polish conquests. Prince Poniatowski's forces were now placed in a difficult position. Archduke Ferdinand's army corps left Warsaw to defend the Austrian dominions and the Polish commanders could hardly depend on the Russian "ally". The outcome of the campaign was decided on the Danube, by Napoleon's victory at Wagram. The Austrian army corps retreated towards the Moravian Gate, pursued by the Poles who took Cracow before the Russians could get there.

It took three long months of nervous diplomatic manoeuvres by France, Austria and Russia before the peace treaty of Schönbrunn was signed. As far as Poland was concerned, this meant another compromise; the Duchy of Warsaw was enlarged by 4 new departments (Cracow, Radom, Lublin and Siedlce) because they could not be denied to the Poles who had conquered them by force of arms. But they obtained only a part of Galicia, to avoid provoking Russia, to whom Napoleon assigned the Tarnopol district as compensation.

The fact that the territories of the Duchy were thus nearly doubled again kindled the hope that all Poland would sooner or later be liberated. But the merger of the "old" and the "new" departments did not proceed without political friction. The Lublin and Sandomierz regions were poorer and economically less developed than Great Poland and their gentry was even less ready to accept the new reforms. Here also were the residences and the spheres of influence of some of the great Polish aristocratic families: Puławy—the property of the Czartoryskis' and the Zamoyski estates. In 1809 Count Stanisław Zamoyski declared himself firmly for Napoleon and assumed the presidency of the provisional Lublin government. He hoped to be able to maintain a separate administration for the four departments at least until the time when the Constitution of 1807 would be revised and rendered more conservative. His hopes were disappointed. Under a royal decree the new departments were incorporated in the Duchy without reservations. The provisions included the Napoleonic Code, the abolition of serfdom and the December decree depriving the peasant of the right to own land. The incorporation of the new territories strengthened the hands of the right-wing elements in the Duchy. On the eve of the war against Russia Napoleon himself attached ever more importance to securing the support of the Polish aristocracy. Ideas of reforming the administration and the judicial system and the revival of the ancient rights and privileges of the gentry were frequently discussed in 1810-1811, but were usually shelved for financial reasons. This accelerated the rivalry between the two most influential ministers, Łubieński and Matuszewicz. The former, the Minister of Justice, represented the progressive minority of the gentry favouring a gradual evolution toward the capitalist system. The latter, the Minister of the Treasury and a client of Puławy, represented a conservative tendency.

During the same period changes were taking place within the ranks of the left-wing opposition. Out of touch with the masses and with no prospect of obtaining Napoleon's support, many ex-Jacobins, though capable, ambitious, and eager for action, became disillusioned. The most outstanding of them, Kołłątaj, died in 1812 in complete isolation. Many of his former supporters sought personal promotion. At all cost they wished to become influential and to take revenge on their right-wing opponents. Looking for allies to combat the party in power, they tried to join forces with the conservative opposition, and in 1809 even supported the Lublin provisional government against the centralist policies of Warsaw. Some of them, like General Zajączek and Szaniawski, went still further. They espoused the Russian point of view and renounced the ideals of their youth. Others, like Gorzkowski, withdrew altogether from political life. A few, particularly among the officers, conspired against Napoleon and renewed their former underground ties with the Republican opposition in France, and with the German Tugendbund. These were dangerous steps: in the prevailing balance of power in Europe, a struggle against Napoleon could benefit only the reactionary coalition. In Poland herself, all progressive and patriotic elements, fascinated by the Emperor's genius, followed him faithfully, believing that they would regain Poland. The epigones of Jacobinism could not make up their mind to swim against the prevailing current of opinion. Incapable of practical action, all they could do was to transmit the tradition of their revolutionary youth to the succeeding generation.

THE DOWNFALL OF THE DUCHY OF WARSAW

From 1807 international conditions were favourable for Poland, due not so much to the Tilsit compromise as to the antagonism latent between the two leading continental Powers. The compromise between France and Russia had relegated the Polish question to the rank of an object of local bargaining. A decisive victory of France or Russia for this matter would destroy the hope of any country in Europe becoming independent. But so long as the struggle for power between France and Russia continued, Poland held the balance and this compelled both Napoleon and Alexander to make far reaching promises to the Poles.

The beginning of 1810 saw the last attempt to save the Tilsit system, and to prevent war. The French ambassador, Caulaincourt, was discussing in St. Petersburg the possibility of a marriage between Napoleon and Grand Duchess Anna; in return France was to pledge that "the Kingdom of Poland would never be restored". The negotiations were broken off at the last moment and from that time an armaments race began on both sides of the frontier. The Tsar now tried to win over Poland, and especially the Polish army, to his side. He approached Prince Poniatowski through Czartoryski, promising to revive Poland under his own sceptre in her frontiers of before 1772. Poniatowski resisted the temptation and informed Paris accordingly. He had two good reasons for his refusal. First he knew that neither the army nor the people would agree to give up the French connexion and secondly, he felt rightly that Russia was insincere in her promises. Having failed in his efforts to win over the authorities in Warsaw, Alexander tried to get a foothold in Lithuania. He offered to restore the Great Duchy of Lithuania, and to revive the Constitution of 3 May. But even Czartoryski declined this ambiguous offer, because he did not wish—as he put it "to set one altar against another". Only a small group of Lithuanian aristocrats remained on Alexander's side.

In 1812 Napoleon hesitated to embark on the difficult campaign. To the very last moment he counted on being able to force the Tsar to yield, and this is why he avoided provoking him by raising the Polish problem openly. On his march to the East, he by-passed Warsaw; he issued orders that the Seym be convened in an extraordinary session, and that a Confederation and the renewal of the union with Lithuania be proclaimed, but this was a pure façade. The delegates of Confederation who were sent to meet Napoleon at Wilno, obtained only vague statements. The Emperor carefully restrained the enthusiasm of the Poles and avoided committing himself with regard to the future of their country.

For this "Second Polish War" the Poles raised the largest contingent of all allies of France, nearly 100,000, of whom 40,000 served in a separate army corps under the command of Poniatowski. It was believed in Poland that this tremendous effort would bring liberation. There was something ambiguous in this famous expedition against Moscow. The victory expected in Poland would restore the old frontiers on the Dnieper and the Dvina and the domination of the Polish gentry over the Lithuanian, Byelorussian and Ukrainian peasants. In Byelorussia, the peasants greeted the French as liberators; they began to refuse labour services and in some instances they even rose against their landlords. The Provisional Government of Wilno ordered them to continue performing their services and said nothing about improving their lot. Peasants, who rose against the manors, were severely punished by the gendarmerie under Polish command. On its march the *Grande Armée* lived off the land and devastated the country. Lithuania's enthusiasm quickly disappeared and yielded few recruits to the army.

The Poles paid a heavy price for their participation in the war. At Smoleńsk and Borodino the 5th army corps fought in the front line and suffered tremendous losses. In the disastrous retreat the Poles often covered the disintegrating columns of their allies. At the Berezina they helped to rescue Napoleon from imminent disaster. They rescued all their guns and banners in the general debacle, but their losses reached 70 per cent of their effective strength in dead, wounded, and prisoners.

The rout of the *Grande Armée* was not equivalent to a total defeat for Napoleon, but it was obvious that he could not hold the line on the Vistula. With the approach of the Russians, the Polish aristocracy immediately changed its attitude. Already in the autumn of 1812 the Warsaw ministers began negotiations with Alexander using Czartoryski as an intermediary. Now that the situation had changed, Czartoryski reminded his friend, the Tsar, of his promise to restore Poland.

Early in 1813 the Russian armies entered Warsaw. The Polish forces under Prince Poniatowski were then concentrated round Cracow. Once again his aristocratic relatives tried to persuade the Commander-in-chief to join the Russians with his army and thus to earn Alexander's favour. Poniatowski, however, stood firmly by his soldier's oath. There was a time when his army corps, pinned down at the Austrian border, seemed doomed. Napoleon's offensive in Saxony averted this. After the battle of Lützen the Austrians agreed to allow the Polish army corps pass through Austrian territory. The Polish troops went westwards and fought shoulder to shoulder with the French until the battle of Leipzig, where Poniatowski, now a Marshal of France, died a hero's death when retreating across the Elster river.

This heroic finale marked the end of Poland's Napoleonic epic. For a brief period the best part of the Polish nation had pinned its hopes on a man of genius, a foreign conqueror. These hopes were in vain, because Napoleon could never have reunited the Polish territories without dominating Europe. Even if he had succeeded in establishing a world monarchy, he would have subjected Poland equally with the rest of Europe. The tremendous effort, however, which went into Poland's struggle at Napoleon's side was not without value. It drew tens of thousands of people from all walks of life into the struggle for independence, and redeemed, at least in part, the shame of partition. It reminded Europe that the Polish nation did not accept its loss of independence. A short lived Polish State and its national army were to survive the general catastrophe.

Yet, this period in which Poland underwent momentous internal changes had a still deeper significance. The French régime marked the beginning of the end of feudalism in Poland and the rise of a new bourgeois society. During those years serfdom was abolished, the Code Napoléon was introduced together with a modern administration, the bourgeoisie achieved social advancement and the privileges of the Church were curtailed. All these reforms were received from the top and did not arrive from the country's own efforts, or own revolutionary endeavours. Success was only partial. Under the Code Napoléon, the landed gentry remained the ruling class, and forced labour was still the mainstay of the rural economy. Nevertheless, new initiatives gripped the countryside and paved the way for later development.

Succeeding generations for whom every decade brought new disappointments were fascinated by the Napoleonic era, with its glorious victories. Mickiewicz felt this strongly and expressed it in his masterpiece *Pan Tadeusz*. The memory of these few years, pregnant with hope, for a long time to come, inspired young people to embark upon new ventures with faith in ultimate success. Such was the positive side of the Napoleonic legend. It had its negative aspect also, which only later became apparent, in the form of confidence that help for Poland would come from the West like a miracle, the belief that liberty could be attained without a social upheaval. Such misconceptions weighed heavily upon the national risings in the succeeding epoch.

Chapter XV
THE KINGDOM OF POLAND AND THE NOVEMBER INSURRECTION (1815–1831)

PEASANT REFORM IN PRUSSIAN POLAND

The process of abolishing the feudal system of peasant exploitation had its origin in the development of the productive forces and in the necessity and possibility of improving rural economy. But it demanded the breaking down of the age-old privileges of the gentry. This was accelerated by the resistance of the oppressed peasant masses. In some cases the impetus came from outside.

By the end of the eighteenth century, Poland's western territories were ripe for the abolition of labour service which had become less and less efficient. Their incorporation into the Prussian monarchy had retarded the trend towards the introduction of a system of rents. The administration of the junker State in practice vigorously defended the property rights of both the German and the Polish landowners. While pretending to watch over the peasants' interests, the Prussian administration, recruited mainly from the landed gentry, ruled with an iron hand and exacted from the country people the bulk of the taxes and the provision of recruits for the army. The offences against the manor were severely punished.

The junker régime met with the strongest opposition in Silesia. This province conquered by Frederick II in 1740–1742, was never reconciled to its new master. For half a century—from the Seven Years' War to the Napoleonic era, ferment was brewing in Silesian villages, erupting time and again in local disturbances among both Polish and German peasants. The linguistic border in Silesia ran towards the end of the eigtheenth century more or less along the meridian of Wrocław. Tension was particularly acute in 1766–1768, 1784–1786, 1793-1795, and 1798–1799. Here and there the peasants would abandon their work and march on the manor or town with scythes and pitchforks. They resisted military coercion and in the 1790's opposition was particularly marked in the Sudeten foot-hills with the insurgents openly admitting that they took their example from the French Revolution. All these risings were local revolts extending, at most, to a few districts, and lacking skilled leadership; it was relatively easy for the troops to deal with them. But the very persistence with which revolts occurred made the Prussian bureaucracy realize that it was high time to introduce agrarian reform.

The necessity for such reform became urgent with Prussia's collapse in 1806. Silesia was temporarily occupied by the French, and there was even talk of annexing it to Poland. When serfdom was abolished in the Duchy of Warsaw in 1807, Prussia had to follow suit. Stein's programme of reform, which was evolved with an eye to modernizing the State and preparing it for a military revival, clearly had to include the emancipation of the peasants.

In 1807 personal serfdom was abolished in the Prussian State; a year later the peasants were enfranchized in the State lands. Labour dues continued for the time being on private estates, and the landowners prevented any further plans of reform. This caused a fresh wave of revolt in Silesia in 1811, which was more violent than ever before. Now disturbances broke out in the southern Polish part of Silesia. The peasants burned down manors, they demanded publication of a decree which was supposed to have abolished labour service. Again the movement was suppressed by the army, but reform could no longer be postponed. In the course of the year, the "Settlement Decree" was issued for the entire State.

The Settlement was to be a voluntary agreement between the landlord and the peasant. If no agreement were reached, State authorities were to impose the conditions. The peasant was to become the owner of the land but in return had to surrender one third of it, or even one half if his rights were less explicit, to the landlord as compensation. Thus the reform was onerous to the peasant, the more so because it was carried out in stages extending over a long period of time, during which the peasant remained dependent upon his master.

During the new wars of liberation waged in 1813–1815 little was done in Prussia to emancipate the people. And when the war came to an end the monarchy no longer needed to curry favour with the peasants with the consequence that the old Junker methods once more prevailed. A new royal Declaration of 1816 limited the scope of the Settlement with regard to a number of essential provisions. It was to apply only to larger holdings of peasants who performed labour service with animals and who had held the land for more than twenty years. Certain provinces enforced local decisions which restricted the peasant's rights even further. Upper Silesia, inhabited by a poor Polish population, was treated most severely.

An indispensable supplement to these provisions was the law of 1821 concerning the redemption of still outstanding peasant dues. It applied to "settled" holdings as well as to former tenants, but in practice only the more wealthy peasants could afford the expense.

This legislation was applied in two Polish areas under Prussian rule, in Silesia and Pomerania. After the Vienna Congress of 1815, the Grand Duchy of Poznań, forming the western part of the Duchy of Warsaw, also came under Prussian rule. The new agrarian legislation was extended to this area after a delay of some years. As a first step, in 1819, peasant evictions were prohibited and in 1823 the Settlement law was promulgated in the Poznań area. Some of the paragraphs appeared to be more favourable for the peasants; later, however, in 1836, the landlords of the Duchy of Poznań obtained a royal declaration which restricted the scope of the Settlement to bring the law in conformity with that in other provinces.

Thus the Prussian reform which did away with archaic rural conditions, was imposed by the State; the state, however, acted above all in the interests of the larger estates. In practice it was left to the landowner to decide if, when, and at what speed new settlement was to be carried out; he also fixed the period during which labour services were to continue. This meant that a landowner wishing to modernize his estate received encouragement from the State to convert to a system of hired labour, while less enterprising landowners could spread the evolution over decades. A key to the Prussian reform lay in the fact that it embraced only a minority of the peasantry. The poor peasants who were excluded from the settlement, were to remain as the labour force necessary to enable the manorial farm to carry on. In Upper Silesia the Junkers evicted nearly the entire rural population; the proletariat created by this means was to serve as the manpower in the Silesian mines and foundries. In the Poznań area evolution was slower; the gentry did not dispense with all the small tenant farmers quite as quickly; on the contrary, they used them to get a certain amount of free or cheap labour during the difficult period of adaptation to the new conditions.

From the point of view of the village, the Prussian reform split the uniform rural population into two strata. The "settled" peasant, if he was not required to pay exorbitant redemption instalments, could gradually achieve independence and even become a well-to-do small producer. The poor peasant left out of the settlement was doomed to lose his land sooner or later, leave his village, or be reduced to the status of a farmhand. It was precisely this split in the village community which made peasant resistance to the new laws so ineffective. We do know from the documents that many peasants raised claims against the new settlement and that there were acts of resistance to certain provisions in Pomerania, Silesia, and the Poznań area. But nowhere was there mass protest and even in troublesome Silesia the rural areas remained quiet for a period of more than thirty years.

When the reform was promulgated, it met with the protest of the conservative part of the landowners who deprecated state interference as an encroachment upon their property rights. But when they saw the manner in which it was enforced, even the conservatives realized that the settlement really served the interests of the landed gentry. As a result, the more enterprising landowners in other Polish provinces themselves tried to adopt the Prussian pattern. In fact, Prussia was the first country in central Europe to effect the abolition of feudalism and the transition to capitalism by a reform enforced by the government without experiencing revolutionary disorders. Lenin called this, at the end of the nineteenth century, "the Prussian road towards the advancement of capitalism in agriculture". This path was taken at different times and in different conditions, by all European countries east of the Elbe, including Poland.

ESTABLISHMENT OF THE CONGRESS KINGDOM OF POLAND

In 1813 almost the whole of Poland, including Warsaw, Gdańsk, Poznań and Cracow was under Russian occupation. It seemed that Alexander I would carry out the promise he had made earlier to the Poles. But Napoleon had not been finally defeated. The coalition needed the aid of Austria and Prussia to win the final victory and these Powers demanded that Russia return to them their share in the dismembered Poland. Alexander tried to evade the issue and played for time avoiding taking a clear stand in the Polish question for fear of offending his allies.

It was not until 1814, when the allies entered Paris and Napoleon was exiled to Elba, that Russia regained her freedom of action. Alexander, ostentatiously accepted remnants of the Polish forces who had been fighting to the bitter end on France's side, under his wing and allowed them to return to Poland with their arms. He also declared publicly that he was ready to "work for the happiness" of the Poles and looked to them for support in the expected diplomatic conflict. His guidance was enthusiastically followed not only by the Polish aristocracy under Czartoryskis' leadership, but also by a large number of Napoleon's generals. They imagined that it would be possible, with Russia's backing, to re-establish Poland within her pre-partition frontiers under a conservative régime.

The Powers were opposed to too great an expansion of Russia and resisted these plans at the Vienna Congress. The Tsar succeeded in getting Prussia's support in exchange for backing her claim against Saxony. As for England, Austria and France, they even threatened to resort to military action, in order to prevent Russia from establishing herself on the Vistula. The attitude of the Powers towards Poland reflected their relationship with Russia. In public, the ministers Metternich, Castlereagh and Talleyrand, affirmed their readiness to see the former Poland re-established; in private they intrigued actively to revert to the 1795 post-partition frontiers. Having agreed eventually to the proposal that the Kingdom of Poland was to be united with Russia, they tried to reduce its frontiers in the west; simultaneously they advocated that Poland be granted wider freedoms, with an eye to possible Russo-Polish conflicts in the future. Alexander resisted these intrigues backed by the unanimous support of Polish public opinion. Czartoryski himself played an important role at the Congress as a member of the Russian delegation.

A compromise was reached in February 1815. Russia ceded to Prussia the western part of the conquered Duchy of Warsaw, including the towns of Poznań and Toruń. A tiny neutral state was formed out of Cracow and its surrounding district. The rest of the former Duchy was left to Russia as the "Kingdom of Poland" commonly called "Congress Poland" or "Congress Kingdom". The definite creation of this last province was strongly influenced by Napoleon's sudden return from Elba. On the eve of another struggle with the "Corsican", the Congress dared not provoke the Poles. The peace treaties concluded by Russia with Austria and Prussia on 3 May, 1815, and later incorporated in the Final Act of the Congress, declared that the Kingdom of Poland was forever united with Russia "in virtue of its constitution" and that Tsar Alexander reserved to himself the right to undertake any "internal expansion" of its boundaries. Other provinces of former Poland would also obtain "national institutions", the scope of which was left to the discretion of the monarchs. In this manner another partition of Poland was carried out in Vienna, which provisionally guaranteed a more extensive autonomy to only one Polish area. The main decision was the entrusting of Poland's central areas to Russia which had, until then, annexed only some eastern and mostly non-Polish territories of the Commonwealth. Because Warsaw, notwithstanding the new frontiers, remained a centre of attraction for the whole country, Poland's fate was, after 1815, indirectly linked for a century with the destiny of Russia and with the outcome of the struggle which was to take place in Russia between the Tsarist régime and the revolutionary forces.

The Constitution of the Kingdom of Poland had been mentioned in the Final Act of the Vienna Congress and was thus guaranteed by the Powers, but the text of the Constitution was worded as determined by Alexander himself; the draft prepared by Czartoryski was changed by the Tsar in a more autocratic spirit and was solemnly proclaimed in Warsaw in November 1815. There were a number of provisions in it adopted from the Constitution of the Duchy of Warsaw, namely, the authority of the Crown, the composition of the State Council, the Senate and the Chamber of Deputies, together with the provisions abolishing serfdom and establishing equal rights for all before the law. "General guarantees" were extended to civil rights which included freedom of the press and personal freedom, but they largely remained a dead letter. The rights of the Seym were slightly extended. On the other hand, there was a clear return to collegiate government; commissions were established in preference to ministries and voivodship com-

Sielpia Wielka. Factory shop, first half of the 19th cent.

The Congress Kingdom of Poland and the Free State of Cracow, 1815

mittees instead of individual prefects. A number of the most important offices was reserved specifically for landowners.

The manner in which the law was to be applied depended in a great measure on the persons appointed to key positions. The highest office, formally, was that of Viceroy or Lord Lieutenant (*namiestnik*) who presided over the Administrative Council (or government) and in whom an important part of the King's rights was vested. It was generally thought that Czartoryski would be chosen for that post. Alexander, however, preferred to entrust the function to a more obedient person. General Zajączek was appointed, a former Jacobin, but now a martinet devoid of political ambition. The Grand Duke Constantine, brother of the Tsar, was placed in command of the Polish army; in practice, he was more important than the government. In addition, the Russian senator Nikolai Novosiltzow became a member of the Administrative Council in his capacity of "imperial commissioner" and acted as the unofficial supervisor of the Polish government. Thus, contrary to the letter of the law, the destiny of the Kingdom lay in the hands of two men each of whom were either unfavourably disposed or opposed to the freedoms which had been promised to the Polish people.

THE AGRARIAN QUESTION IN THE KINGDOM OF POLAND

The Napoleonic years had depopulated and devastated large tracts of land and had disturbed the balance of social relationships. More and more peasants deserted the land. In 1813–1815 entire hamlets would cease to perform labour service and approach the authorities with demands that they be allowed to pay rent instead of labour dues and even be allowed to rent demesne.

The "Reform Committee" which was set up during this period of transition under Czartoryski's chairmanship issued a questionnaire asking the local authorities and courts together with private persons for their opinion regarding rural conditions. The result of the enquiry was negative. The majority of landowners stated they were in favour of a continuation of labour dues and opposed to State intervention in agrarian matters. The Constitution therefore did not alter the *status quo*; the decree of December of 1807, which had made the peasant a free tenant without any right to the land, remained in force.

The continuation of labour service made the peasant's formal freedom an open question; attempts were made repeatedly to restrict this freedom even further. In 1818 a royal decree entrusted to the landowners the duties of mayor of the village (*wójt*), thus giving them administrative powers over the population in their estates. A further decree of 1821 concerning journeymen made it difficult for an agricultural worker to leave his employment of his own free will. The new provisions could not again bind the peasant to the soil but in general they consolidated the practice of the State refusing to examine the complaints of peasants working on private estates and taking the gentry's side in any case of insubordination by the village.

The general economic situation did not favour progressive agriculture. Grain prices fell because the Kingdom was cut off from its natural commercial outlet at the mouth of the Vistula and growth was courtailed by the prohibitive corn laws in Great Britain. A considerable number of estates were burdened with heavy debts and could only carry on because the moratorium was extended year after year. The owners of demesnes, especially those in the western part of the country, were turning from the unprofitable production of grain to growing potatoes and to sheep breeding. New methods of distilling allowed them to make easy money by inducing the local population to consume alcohol, and the growing textile industry was a customer for their wool. Cultivation of the potato imposed more work on the peasants; sometimes in the form of "additional" days of labour service but more often through imposing a system of compulsory cheap labour. A system of loans to the peasants, mostly in grain, pasture or firewood, to be paid for later in the form of labour, secured for the demesnes a sufficient amount of cheap manpower.

By the middle 1820's the big landowners were emerging from the crisis. Prices ceased to fall, and the State established the Land Credit Society (1825) which enabled landed gentry to pay their earlier debts. Nevertheless, rural conditions were still unfavourable to technical progress and consequently to the abandonment of the labour services. After 1815 the government, as a result of developments on the State land, began to "settle" these estates and to convert the peasants from labour services to money rents, payable directly to the State. This attempt at reform was soon abandoned because it only offended the opinion of the gentry. Ksawery Lubecki, Minister of the Treasury, who was trying to find the money to launch his big investment schemes, succeeded in forcing through a decree, in 1828, by virtue of which all State lands were to be sold to private individuals. The inhabitants of these domains were to be deprived both of the right to own land and of the right to State protection which they had enjoyed hitherto.

The State lands were at that time the chief centre of peasant resistance to oppression. This resistance took the form of petitions demanding conversion to rents or legal action against the more oppressive tenants. The moving spirits of those demonstrations and lawsuits were agitators who were mostly *déclassé* intelligentsia from outside the village, and sometimes educated peasants who led the legal opposition of the community. Among the better known agitators was one, Kazimierz Deczyński, a man of peasant stock and the village teacher in Brodnia, in the Kalisz region. As a punishment he was enrolled in the army. Deczyński left an interesting diary dealing with his activities and with the contemporary situation of the peasantry.

THE BEGINNINGS OF MODERN INDUSTRY IN THE KINGDOM OF POLAND

While agriculture made only slight progress owing to the unfavourable conditions, developments in industry were quite remarkable. These years gave birth to Łódź as a textile centre.

Earlier attempts to attract skilled workers from abroad had failed. Now that conditions in Europe became stable after the Congress of Vienna, they were crowned with success. Spinners and weavers from the Duchy of Poznań, Silesia and Saxony, whose livelihood was threatened by the competition of factories in western Europe, willingly moved to the east where they were protected by new custom barriers and where they could maintain contact with the markets of the East. Many of these textile workers were introduced by enterprising landowners into voivodships of Mazovia and Kalisz. It was in this way that small industrial centres were established at Aleksandrów, Konstantynów, Tomaszów and Zduńska Wola. Each immigrant was given a plot of land and building material and was granted several years' tax exemption, while the squire reserved for himself the profits yielded by the fulling of cloth and more especially by the sale of liquor. The State adopted a similar line about 1820 when it created industrial settlements like Zgierz, Łódź, Pabianice, on its own domains. At first there was only hand-woven cloths and linen in single workshops, but soon, capitalist entrepreneurs arrived after the workers, and began to organize manufactories. The government gave them assistance by offering loans on easy terms. Industrial enterprises were established not only in the new manufacturing centres, but also in the towns of Kalisz, Sieradz and Warsaw. They adopted various forms of organization, like the cottage industry, the putting-out system or centralized production. The fulling and finishing of cloth generally required water-driven machinery. At the close of the 1820's the first steam-driven mechanical spinning machines began to operate in Przedbórz, Łódź, Warsaw, and in other centres.

The first place among textiles was held, at that time, by cloth woven from wool, the quality of which was steadily improved by breeders in Poland's western districts. At first the chief customer of cloth was the Polish army, but very soon, markets opened up in the East, thanks to the advantageous customs agreement with Russia which had been arranged by Lubecki in 1822. Polish cloth was then going freely to Russia and to China, but by 1830, woollens encountered a competitor in the cotton industry. The cheaper foreign raw material enabled manufactures to reach the vast and less exacting market within the country. In 1829, Poland produced 6.9 million ells of wollen cloth and 3.7 million ells of cotton cloth.

The textile industry based mainly on a line running through Łódź and Warsaw, benefited greatly from the influx of immigrants including Germans, but also Poles from the Prussian zone. Basically, however, it was a native creation backed by local capital and using the rapidly expanding local labour force, home produced wool, and in the case of cotton was sold to the local customer. The textile industry contributed to the establishment of several new urban settlements, among them Łódź, which grew to be a large city.

Heavy industry, encouraged mainly by the State, developed along somewhat different lines. Staszic, head of the Department of Industry and the Arts in the Commission of Internal Affairs, elaborated the first plan for the expansion of State mines in the "Old Poland Basin", situated between Kielce and the Kamienna river. The basis for mining was State-owned property. "Mining estates" were allocated to the particular establishments and were required to furnish the necessary serf labour. A "miners' corps" organized on military lines, was established to provide skilled labour. The miners joining it were "sworn in" and enjoyed a number of privileges and social security benefits, like old-age pensions and sick-benefits, but they were not allowed to leave the service.

In 1824 the mining administration was transferred to the Commission of Incomes and Finances, under the control of Lubecki, who accelerated the pace of its development. A temporary boom on the European market indicated the need to boost zinc production. Iron production, however, was more important to the economy. Lubecki started the construction of a large combine on the Kamienna river, consisting of four blast furnaces and sixteen puddling process furnaces with casting and rolling mills. The technique employed was old-fashioned, being based on charcoal as fuel and waterpower. Water transportation was to solve the problem of carrying raw materials and semi-manufactured products. Meanwhile, zinc production, concentrated more to the west, in the Dąbrowa Basin, brought with it an expansion of the State's coal mines. Coal mining, which had begun before the partitions, now made progress and it was possible later, after 1830, to take a further step toward metallurgical techniques.

The development of the pig iron and steel production furnished the basis for the national metal and machinery industry. The most important plants of this type were situated in Warsaw, the works of Evans Brothers, English industrialists, founded in 1822, and the State "Machine Construction Works". They produced mostly agricultural implements and distillery appliances. In addition to these metallurgical plants, there were a number of smaller workshops in Warsaw which engaged silver-plating and the produc-

Stanisław Staszic

tion of precision instruments. There were also some textile mills in the city, but they never played an important part.

The speedy development of industrial enterprises created conditions for the growth of a working class, consisting of townspeople, craftsmen from the guilds and country people attracted to the urban centres. In the mining industry compulsory labour provided by the miners' corps and labour service contributed by mining estates still played an important role, whereas the textile industry had already adopted a system of wage labour. It is difficult to speak of a homogeneous working class at this time, if one considers the differences in background and religion which kept the Polish-German and Jewish workers apart in any factory. Also, the borderline between the cottage weaver still theoretically free and the real proletarian was fluid.

Warsaw. Polish Bank, 1825

Statistical data from various contemporary sources permit us to arrive at the hypothesis of a working class of 30–40 thousand persons.

There was no legislation governing hours and conditions of work, and no restriction as regards the work of women and children. Old-age pensions an sick-benefits which were financed out of the dues contributed by the workers, existed on a modest scale only for the miners' corps. There was no limit to the exploitation of workers; this was particularly true with regard to cottage workers, whose workshops were busy round the clock without interruption, the entire family labouring hard to eke out a miserable existence.

The working class showed no signs of organization. There were some disputes in the textile industry and sharp attacks were made on the factory owners by weavers who were threatened with ruin; but those were only sporadic clashes. To our knowledge only two strikes took place in Warsaw, in 1824 and 1830 but they were of a purely incidental character.

OPPOSITION AND CONSPIRACY

The decisions of the Congress of Vienna were received with satisfaction by the propertied classes of the Kingdom of Poland. The Constitution gave the landed gentry political power and enabled them to exploit the peasant at their will; Tsar Alexander kept up the hope that the annexed provinces of Lithuania, Byelorussia and the Ukraine would be reunited with Poland.

Yet the Constitution of the Kingdom proved rather unstable. The very concept of a personal union between a huge Russia, ruled autocratically, and a small constitutional Kingdom seemed indeed unnatural. At first, it was expected that Alexander would continue on the road to liberal reforms within Russia, but already in 1820, reactionary tendencies got the upper hand in the system of the Holy Alliance. Perceiving the danger of a possible revolution in Europe and the situation in Russia herself, Alexander began to curtail the liberties he had granted to the Poles. Being himself the author of the Polish Constitution, he did not feel bound to respect its provisions.

The first source of disagreement was the Polish army, which Grand Duke Constantine ruled with caprice and brutality. The ordeal of day-long parades, the steady browbeating of the men and the complete disregard for human dignity had led a dozen or so officers to commit suicide. Then followed the restriction of civil liberties: the secret police was increased considerably and special commissions of investigation were used to supplement the ordinary process of enquiry. In 1819 censorship was introduced and the opposition press was suppressed. Novosiltzov ruthlessly tracked down any secret organization, above all students' organization. He did his best to make the Tsar distrust the Poles and was intent on securing the abolition of all constitutional liberties.

In this reactionary mood, the Tsarist government made use largely of newly created aristocrats, the Sobolewskis, Gutakowskis, Grabowskis who were appointed to the highest posts. The Tsar also secured the support of the episcopacy in exchange for some concessions in the law of marriage. At the request of the bishops, Stanisław Potocki, Minister of Education, was dismissed in 1820. He was the last of the prominent men of the Enlightenment period, a follower of Voltaire and an advocate of subordinating the Church to the State. During his term of office, he was instrumental in expanding the network of elementary schools. Stanisław Grabowski, who succeeded him, deliberately discouraged the growth of these schools and thus deserved his nickname of "Minister of Public Obscurantism".

Ksawery Lubecki, the Minister of Finance, from 1821 acquired an independent position. When he assumed office he found the treasury in a desperate state on account of excessive military expenditure and speculation by corrupt officials. The very independence of the Kingdom seemed threatened. Lubecki won the confidence of the local bankers and obtained the necessary credits. He collected ruthlessly all arrears of taxes and succeeded in balancing the budget. By exploiting the State monopolies of the sale of salt and tobacco he collected ever higher taxes from the peasants. Lubecki assisted the big estate owners to pay back their debts and launched a policy of large-scale investment. Backed by the Tsar, he secured a favourable customs tariff for Polish textiles. As mentioned above he increased the number of State-owned foundries. In 1828 he founded the Bank Polski. In short, he succeeded within a very short time in turning a poor and backward country into an exporter of industrial goods and a producer of machinery. Thanks to this achievement, Lubecki's prestige was very high in Petersburg, which circumstance enable him to defend the Kingdoms' independence successfully against Novosiltzov's intrigues. On the other hand, Lubecki had no respect at all for constitutional freedoms and was unpopular in progressive and in liberal circles among the gentry. The only groups who backed Lubecki wholeheartedly were the big bourgeoisie, making fortunes on loans and government orders, and some aristocrats with capital invested in industrial enterprises.

There were two trends of opposition in the Kingdom of Poland, the one legal and the other clandestine. Both of them at first set themselves the aim of defending the Constitution against the encroachments of the Tsar. The wealthy gentry in western Poland interested in policies of capital investment, were hard hit by the agrarian crisis. At the same time, they failed to understand the government's policy of investing capital in the industry. With no influence on the government in Warsaw, they attacked the policy of the ministers, declaring at the same time their loyalty to the constitutional monarch.

A group of Kalisz deputies, led by the brothers Wincenty and Bonawentura Niemojowski, voiced their criticism of the government already at the first session of the Seym in 1818. In the following session in 1820, criticism grew much stronger and Wincenty Niemojowski demanded that two of the government ministers be indicted for having endorsed the decree on censorship. Under his influence the Seym rejected most of the government's bills. On closing the session, Alexander gave vent publicly to his annoyance. The next Seym was convened only after another 5 years had elapsed. Meetings of the chamber were no longer open to the public and the leaders of the opposition were excluded from it. The Kalisz deputies were reduced to silence; at the same time the economic situation of the landowners improved and the unrest among the gentry subsided.

During the 1820's the liberalism of the gentry was openly modelled on the ideas of the French parliamentary system. The Kalisz deputies refused to cooperate with subversive forces, the obvious ineffectiveness of legal opposition in the Seym inclined even some of the Kalisz group to make contact with the underground conspirators.

Secret associations flourished in Poland after 1815 as they did in other parts of Europe, among the intelligentsia which had no influence on the affairs of the State. University students and the officer corps wished to see the tiny Kingdom's frontiers widened to encompass a united Poland but they disliked the propertied classes and showed a marked sympathy with the common people. It must be borne in mind, however, that the conspirators were themselves of noble origin, impoverished and *déclassé* gentry, yet traditionally attached to their class. The movement which we today call "revolution of the gentry", gradually evolved its aims in the period 1815–1830. These aims were as follows: full national independence, the improvement of the standard of living of the common people and the need for an armed rising. To the very end, however, the movement remained confined to an élite, having no contacts whatever with the peasantry or even with the urban poor. And for a long time the leaders of the movement rejected the idea of direct preparations for a revolution. On the other hand, they quite early on were in touch with similar organizations in other countries— with the German Burschenschaften, French Carbonarism, and later with the Russian Decembrist movement.

The first secret society called *Panta Kojna* ("Everything in Common") was created at Warsaw University in 1817 by a small group of students at whose head stood Ludwik Mauersberger. The group confined their activity to theoretical discussion and was not discovered until several years later, when it had already discontinued its meetings in Warsaw. Of far greater importance was the succeeding students' organization, The Union of Free Poles, which was founded in 1820. Some of its members later became well-known revolutionaries, like Tadeusz Krępowiecki, Wiktor Heltman and Maurycy Mochnacki. The Union skilfully extended its influence among the students, preparing them for the struggle for liberation and, among other things, for rousing the masses of the population. The Union published a legal monthly magazine, "Dekada Polska". After several months of existence the Union was discovered by the police and its members placed under arrest.

Student's unions at Wilno University had a longer career. In 1817 a small group of friends, including among others Tomasz Zan, Józef Jeżowski and Adam Mickiewicz, established the Society of Philomaths with self-education as its prim aim but with the broader vision of eventually transforming the nation and society by means of education. These high-minded gifted young men matured beyond their years, in their idealism believed in the efficacy of a systematic long-term activity which would, some day, make them the leaders of the country and enable them to take up the fight for independence. This was, of course, a dream. As time went by and the Philomaths completed their studies and entered the world, their activity clearly began to evolve in the direction of a political conspiracy. In 1823 the authorities by accident found traces of their organization. Wilno became the scene of arrests and investigations conducted by Novosiltzov. Not all branches of the Philomath organization were discovered, but the most important of its members, among them Mickiewicz, were exiled to the interior of Russia, which brought about the collapse of the organization.

Quite independently of the student conspiracies, the officers had established an important underground movement. The moving spirit was Major Walerian Łukasiński of the 4th Infantry Regiment. Taking advantage of the government tolerance of semi-legal freemasonry, he founded in 1819 an independent organization called "National Freemasonry". The humanitarian phraseology and symbolism were replaced in his lodge by patriotic slogans. Łukasiński's aim was the reunification and liberation of Poland. There was no statement on how these ends were to be achieved. One of his associates the lawyer Jakub Szreder, stressed the importance of considering the peasant question. The secret organization was very soon joined by some representatives of the gentry, who sympathized with the Kalisz group and were opposed to any radical policies.

Threatened with discovery by the secret police, Łukasiński dissolved the National Freemasonry and founded in 1821 the "Patriotic Society". The members of this secret organization were divided into three grades. In theory, the Society embraced all the Polish areas, but the officers were grouped in a separate "military province". The aims of the organization were not revealed: members thought that they should meet a possible attack by the Tsar upon the Kingdom's independence. A number of the gentry joined the society in Lithuania and in the Ukraine, prompted mainly by their desire to see those provinces united with the Congress Kingdom, if possible, without any armed conflict. In 1822 Łukasiński was arrested and eventually sentenced to 9 years imprisonment: he never regained his freedom and died behind bars in the Schlüsselburg prison in Russia, after 38 years of captivity. The leadership was then assumed by Lieutenant Colonel Seweryn Krzyżanowski, who was far more compliant with the views of the landowners in the conspiracy. There followed a marked decline in the society's activity.

Meanwhile, Russian secret organizations, especially the "Southern Society", approached the Poles with a proposal of collaboration. In 1824 Krzyżanowski and, a year later, Prince Antoni Jabłonowski discussed the matter with the Russian conspirators in Kiev. The object was to reach an agreement on a joint revolutionary action, the form of the future political structure of Poland and the mutual relationship of the two liberated nations. Both parties realized the need for common action against a common foe, but they also sensed the differences inherent in their respective programme and aims. The Patriotic Society placed the national question before the social one, and their republican and democratic views appeared to be considerably weaker than was the case with the Decembrist Left. The Russians, moreover, did not wish to recognize the Polish claim to the 1772 frontiers. Thus the Kiev agreement was couched in rather general terms. The more radically inclined individuals among the Poles made closer contact with the Russian conspirators. The friendly relationship between Mickiewicz and the Petersburg and Odessa Decembrists is well known. Julian Lubliński, a young Polish revolutionary, was co-founder of the republican United Slavs Society in the Ukraine.

The events of December 1825 took the Polish conspirators by surprise. After the death of Alexander I, the Decembrists attempted a *coup d'état*, but it ended in complete failure, as they were neither sufficiently prepared, nor backed by the mass of the population. The Patriotic Society was only a passive witness, but investigations in Russia led to the discovery of the Polish conspiracy. Krzyżanowski and many of his comrades were arrested and the famous prison within the walls of Warsaw's Carmelite convent became once more the scene of the criminal investigation police's brutality. Novosiltzov endeavoured to apply the Russian criminal procedure to the Polish offenders, but Lubecki successfuly opposed this and the constitutional procedure was adopted. Offenders accused of high treason were to be tried by a Seym Tribunal composed of members of the Senate. The new Tsar, Nicholas I, agreed to this solution after long hesitation. He reckoned that after passing sentence on the conspirators the Polish senators would be forever committed to remaining on the Tsar's side. The Seym Tribunal, however, which met in Warsaw among a population seething with excitement, cleared all the accused of the charge of high treason, chiefly at the instance of Czartoryski; it passed lenient sentence on them, merely for their participation in clandestine organizations (1828). The representatives of the Polish aristocracy dared not condemn publicly revolutionaries of gentry origin.

Tsar Nicholas took this sentence as a personal defeat. For the following two years he had to take into account Russia's difficult international position and continued therefore to treat the Poles with consideration. In 1829 he even came to Warsaw for his coronation as King of Poland. He was determined, however, to curtail the Kingdom's liberties at the first opportunity which presented itself. The Poles were aware of this and although underground activity subsided to a certain extent after 1825, Polish patriotic opinion realized the danger looming ahead.

NEO-CLASSICISM AND ROMANTICISM

The fifteen years of calm after the Congress of Vienna created conditions favourable for the development of Polish cultural life, which had been halted during the time of the partitions and the Napoleonic wars. Polish science and education, together with Polish journalism, were in many respects a continuation of the traditions of the Enlightenment and were carried on to some extent by the same people. They took up once more the struggle against "Sarmatic" obscurantism and the class prejudices of the past, on behalf of reason, liberty and tolerance. At the same time, they were opposed to extremist tendencies in the realm of both ideology and artistic principles.

Side by side with the old universities of Cracow and Wilno, Warsaw University, founded in 1818, was growing in importance. It had set itself the aim of training for professions, lawyers, teachers and physicians. The country's industrial advancement demanded the immediate establishment of a mining college followed by the opening in Warsaw of the first Polish Technical University. The Society of the Friends of Sciences, continued to carry on valuable research work, specializing in humanities, history, economics, and philology. Slavonic studies were a subject of particular interest, because they investigated the cultural heritage common to all Slav nations. The most noteworthy results in this field were achieved by Zorian Dołęga-Chodakowski, a self-educated research worker in the field of the folk culture of the Ukraine and of Byelorussia. Next to Wilno, Warsaw became the main centre of intellectual life. The press developed considerably, and even though political publications with liberal tendencies declined because of press censorship, the number of general newspapers increased. The literary and social journal "Pamiętnik Warszawski" (Warsaw Record) stood on a very high level. Other periodicals specialized in jurisprudence, natural sciences and industrial techniques.

Attracted by Warsaw life, young intellectuals from all corners of Poland now flocked to the capital to work in the civil service and private offices and enterprises, or for newspapers. Coming mostly from impoverished manors and provincial backwaters, these young people disliked the way of life and the artistic tastes of the propertied classes. Thus, while the aristocrats in their drawing rooms still adhered to the literary traditions of the eighteenth century, the younger generation would gather to debate in coffee houses and in editorial offices seeking new content, new themes and forms in literature.

The Classical School in Warsaw was patronized by a cultivated aesthete, Stanisław Potocki. It really achieved something, when, for example, it printed in Wilno paper an article featuring a squire cynically offering for sale a new invention, a machine for beating peasants, or when a pamphlet written by Potocki himself, *Podróż do Ciemnogrodu* (The Journey to Darktown) made fun of the backwardness of the Polish clergy. When it came to literary criticism and the creative arts, the works produced by classicists were artificial and lifeless; examples are the descriptive poem *Ziemiaństwo* (The Landed Gentry) by Kajetan Koźmian or Alojzy Felińki's tragedy, *Barbara Radziwiłł*. The novels written by Julian Niemcewicz and Fryderyk Skarbek followed more or less the foreign models of W. Scott or Sterne. In the field of comedy in these years the great individual talent was the playwright Aleksander Fredro, closely connected in his sympathies with conservative circles, but rejecting conventional standards whether classical or romantic. The best of Fredro's works, moreover, appeared after 1830.

Though an older school in literature, the neoclassical, still dominated the fine arts. Among the artists, Antoni Brodowski, whose great compositions dealt with mythological and religious topics, was also the painter of expressive and subtle portraits. Architecture was allowed to develop neoclassical forms of building. Many manors and palaces in the countryside with their columns and porticos, the new government buildings in Warsaw like the Bank Polski, the Society of the Friends of Science, built by Corazzi, the buildings of the voivodship offices at Kalisz, Radom, Suwałki and elsewhere, bore witness to the impetus in town planning and to the highly developed aesthetic taste of this period. Bent upon straightening out crooked lanes and sweeping away unnecessary slums, the planners of the period felt so superior that they contemptuously destroyed numerous Gothic and to their mind barbarian monuments of the past. Many ancient city halls and churches were demolished in this period, including the fortifications round the cities of Cracow, Warsaw and elsewhere. The romanticists were too late in their defence of these treasures of medieval art.

The appearance of the first works of Romantic literature gave a death blow to the concepts of the Classical School. The first volume of Adam Mickiewicz's poems was printed in 1822 and Antoni Malczewski's poem *Maria* in 1825. Romanticism broke with the rigid forms, and opposed sentiment to the cold reasoning of the Classical School. The culture of the salons was challenged with popular motifs and interest in the fate of the common people. Contrary to what was happening in western Europe, Polish Romanticism did not cultivate the worship of the medieval knight errand, but adopted a tone of animosity against the magnates and struck a note of freedom. This is not surprising, because the leading Romantics were at the same time members of secret organizations. Mickiewicz's *Oda do młodości* (Ode to Youth) reflects the programme of the Philomaths, and his *Konrad Wallenrod* describes in the form of an allegory the life of a nation in captivity. *Zamek Kaniowski* (The Castle of Kaniów), a poem by Seweryn Goszczyński written in 1823 reminded the deeply shaken reader of the 1768 rising of the Ukrainian peasantry against the Polish gentry. The Romantic poets transformed the language, the tastes and the manner of expression of their whole generation. They imposed their own aesthetic outlook even on the political circles of their opponents. Their leading theorist, Maurycy Mochnacki, made it quite clear in his work O *literaturze polskiej XIX w.* (On Polish Literature of the 19th century) in 1830 that one of Romanticism's main tasks was the awakening of national consciousness.

Two men of great talent opened the way for Romanticism in their respective fields. One of them, Joachim Lelewel, a professor in the University of Wilno, modernized the methods of historical research in Poland. He also pointed out the importance of studying the history of the entire nation, not only that of monarchs and ruling upper classes. Although Lelewel steered clear of politics for many years, he was the idol of the younger generation and had a powerful influence in a patriotic and progressive sense. The other was Fryderyk Chopin, favourite of Warsaw's salons, a child prodigy and composer, who introduced the extraordinary wealth of Polish folk music into his works and elevated Polish music to the level of the world's masterpieces.

Romanticism was the artistic outlet for the ideolgical ferment which was stirring the whole nation. The feeling of insecurity and injustice caused by the decisions of the Congress of Vienna and the presentiment of the coming struggle for independence and social justice inspired both Mickiewicz and Chopin. Although only a very few groups among the young intelligentsia readily accepted the revolutionary ideology, romantic poetry made an immediate conquest of the hearts and minds of the educated population.

THE ORIGINS AND THE OUTBREAK OF THE NOVEMBER INSURRECTION, 1830

The news of the French July Revolution of 1830 electrified the Polish population, but neither the ruling aristocrates and landowners nor the wealthy bourgeoisie connected with them had the least intention of breaking with Russia. No disappointments they had suffered under the Tsars could alter the fact that a popular uprising would involve enormous risks.

Discontent was, however, growing among the population. The international tension had a direct impact on trade and industry. Wages were tumbling, unemployment was widespread, and the cost of living rose sharply. The poor people of Warsaw bitterly complained against the existing conditions.

For over a year a new secret society had been active in Warsaw; its members were mainly cadets of the Infantry Officers School. These young people, who saw no prospect of being commissioned and were tired of the senseless parades and drill round Warsaw's Saxon Square, were eager for revolt. Piotr Wysocki, their leader, kept in touch with Warsaw literary circles and university students. He had no political ambitions and was far from formulating radical programmes of any kind, but he was ready to give the signal for battle, if the necessity arose, and he was convinced that the nation would follow him.

The upheaval in France and Belgium made a European war seem quite probable. Nicholas I was trying to get Prussia and Austria to join in an intervention against the revolution in the West. However, the patriotic circles and secret societies in Germany, Italy and Poland, some affiliated to the Carbonari organization, sided with France and Belgium and were ready to go to their assistance. The Polish army was to take part in the proposed intervention of the Holy Alliance; if that army marched towards the west, the Kingdom would be placed under Russian occupation, and that meant that the Tsar Nicholas would have a free hand to carry out his plan and

Attack on the Belvedere Palace, November 29, 1830

abolish the Constitution. The Polish conspirators reasoned therefore that they must start their struggle before the army was sent abroad. Thus, when the first mobilization order appeared in the Warsaw press on November 19 and 20, it was decided to begin the struggle within the next few days.

The leaders of the conspiracy were not agreed on immediate political aims. Mochnacki was the only one among them who pointed out the necessity of setting up a revolutionary government of their own. His comrades looked towards prominent personalities, popular generals who were known to the patriots, and members of the opposition in the Seym. They approached Lelewel in person, who remainded aloof, but gave them some encouragement. Only during the very last few days before the outbreak did the conspirators begin canvassing support directly in the districts on the banks of the Vistula among the craftsmen and the poorer population and in the Old Town in Warsaw.

On the evening of 29 November, a group of civilian conspirators attacked the Belvedere Palace, intending to kill Grand Duke Constantine. Simultaneously, the Officer Cadets made their assault on the Russian cavalry barracks near the Łazienki Park, while the officers called upon the Polish regiments to rise. The synchronization of these movements failed. The Grand Duke hid and was saved. The Cadets were pushed back from Łazienki and had to fight their way through the centre of the city amid the general indifference of the bourgeois districts. Most Polish generals categorically refused to take part in the insurrection and several of them were killed by the conspirators as a reprisal. The tide turned that night when the populace spontaneously stormed the Arsenal, armed themselves and engaged the Russian detachments. By the dawn of 30 November the Old Town of Warsaw was in the hands of the revolutionaries. The Grand Duke Constantine held the southern part of the city with Russian cavalry and the Polish detachments, which had not deserted him. He dared not, however, fight in the narrow streets of the centre of the town, but rather expected the Polish conservatives to quash the revolution.

Even after this victory the insurgents did not manage to set up a revolutionary government. The power they could have had for the acting was taken in a swift move by the adversaries of the revolution.

THE POLITICAL STRUGGLE TO CONTROL THE INSURRECTION

Before the night of 29 November was over, Lubecki, the most prominent member of the government, and Czartoryski, the most influential of Poland's magnates, had joined hands to oppose the revolt. When they learned that Grand Duke Constantine did not want to act single handed, they called in the Administrative Council and on their own authority appointed several popular conservatives to join it. The Administrative Council issued an appeal which was posted on all the street corners, deploring the "regrettable incidents" of the night before and calling upon the population to restore peace and order.

Only then did the rebels take action in defence of their aims and turn to the armed population for support. Mochnacki organized a revolutionary club. At a stormy meeting he demanded vigorous action including the disarming of the Grand Duke's troops and the establishment of a new government. The people staged a demonstration and compelled the government to dismiss all members, who openly sided with Russia and coopt several members of the revolutionary club. The conservatives mastered the situation by making some concessions to patriotic feeling. A Provisional Government was set up and the newly coopted members of the revolutionary club were discarded. The Grand Duke was prevailed upon to send the Polish regiments which were still with him back to Warsaw. Finally the convocation of the Seym was announced and simultaneously the club was broken up by a gang of armed students.

The counter-revolutionaries found a convenient tool in the person of General Józef Chłopicki. The General, a Napoleonic officer known for his valour and popular because of his personal disagreement with the Grand

Duke Constantine, was generally considered the best man to head the uprising. In fact, he did not believe that war with Russia was possible and he was vehemently opposed to any revolutionary action. On 5 December, backed by the army, he proclaimed himself dictator, seized the arms which the population had captured from the Arsenal, and re-established law and order in the city. Some fine appeals to patriotism cloaked his real intention, which was to find a way to an agreement with Tsar Nicholas. He let Constantine leave Poland with his Russian troops unmolested and sent Lubecki with conciliatory proposals to Petersburg.

The conservatives did not succeed, however, in restraining the popular movement. The provincial towns followed Warsaw's example and enthusiastically declared their solidarity with the rising. Groups of volunteers arrived from Galicia and Poznań. The middle gentry, swayed by the wave of patriotism, declared their readiness to fight for independence, and the Kalisz faction linked up with Warsaw radicals to oppose the dictatorship. On 18 December the Seym unanimously adopted a Manifesto recognizing the national character of the insurrection. Chłopicki protested and offered to resign, but finally he came to terms with the Kalisz group. The dictatorship continued, though under the control of a delegation of the Seym. The Kalisz faction obtained some ministerial posts and Chłopicki pledged that he would hasten the country's rearmament.

The factor which secured an understanding between the patriotic majority of the gentry and the counter-revolutionary group, was the common fear of revolutionary tendencies in the country. News of the November Rising prompted the peasants to refuse labour service and troops were used to coerce them. Anxiety and fear of the masses induced the Kalisz faction to rally to the support of a strong government. The former left-wing conspirators and members of the disbanded revolutionary club countered by demanding that the broad mass of the population be made to join a national war. Their organ, "Nowa Polska", sharply criticized the activities of the dictatorship.

In about mid-January 1831 the results of the Petersburg negotiations were revealed. Nicholas I refused categorically to make any concessions to the "rebels" and demanded their unconditional surrender. The disheartened Chłopicki yielded his authority to the Seym without reservation. Warsaw was in a ferment. The Left wing founded the Patriotic Society and brought pressure to bear on the chamber by means of the press, street demonstrations and the aid of friendly deputies. Patriotism did not permit the Seym to capitulate disgracefully. This meant that preparations must be made for a war with Russia. In spite of the passive opposition of the conservative wing, the Seym resolved on 25 January to dethrone Nicholas I and thus close the door to further negotiations. The monarch's rights and privileges were vested in the Seym, which elected the members of the government and the commander-in-chief. A coalition government under Czartoryski was formed. It consisted of two conservatives, two members of the Kalisz group, and the representative of the Left, Lelewel. Thus they could count upon public support. There was, however, no agreement on the course of action to be adopted. The commander-in-chief appointed by the Seym was to become independent and more powerful than the government. Under the circumstances, the generals, who disliked the war and were opposed to all revolutionary activities, were to exert a decisive influence on the political course of the revolution. Because Chłopicki refused to accept the appointment, Prince Michał Radziwiłł was to be the nominal commander-in-chief, with Chłopicki as his private adviser.

THE POLISH-RUSSIAN WAR

Early in February 1831, a Russian army 115,000 strong under the command of Field Marshal Diebitsch marched into Poland. The Polish army had a peace time strength of 40,000 well-trained soldiers. Chłopicki had intentionally neglected to enlarge this force because he had intended to fight the Russians with a regular army, to suffer an "honourable" defeat, and thus have a pretext to capitulate. The Polish General Staff had a number of prominent military experts, among them the highly capable General Ignacy Prądzyński, but they were short of commanders able to command larger units and to take major decisions.

The Poles failed to take advantage of the winter to launch their offensive in the direction of Lithuania and thus steal a march on the enemy. After a few minor delaying actions, came the pitched battle of Grochów near Warsaw on 25 February. The Russian forces outnumbered the Poles and the fighting was fierce and bloody. Chłopicki was in command, substituting for the incompetent Radziwiłł. When he was severely wounded, the Poles withdrew behind the river. Diebitsch did not dare cross the Vistula near Warsaw, and waited for the ice to flow downstream with the intention of attacking the city from the south.

By the end of March, however, an offensive launched by the new Polish commander Jan Skrzynecki forstalled Diebitsch's plan. Swift attacks undertaken from Warsaw in an easterly direction, smashed the Russian right wing in a series of battles, at Wawer, Dębe Wielkie and Iganie, but Skrzynecki dared not take advantage of the victory to defeat Diebitsch in a decisive battle and withdrew to Warsaw.

In the spring the insurrection spread throughout Lithuania and Byelorussia and part of the Ukraine. The Russian armies had difficulty in keeping open their lines of communication in the rear; this allowed the Poles to manoeuvre successfully. Diebitsch was still in the area of Lublin. Prądzyński therefore outlined a plan for a bold attack of the total Polish forces against the élite corps of Russian guards marching down from Białystok.

There was a real chance to deal the opponent a decisive blow. Skrzynecki, however, a temporizer by nature, was opposed to any definite decisions as a matter of principle. He did not believe in victory and pinned his hopes exclusively on help that was to come from abroad. Another reason was that he did not wish to expose the army to any risk, because it might eventually prove a good weapon against the Left. He was reluctant to accept the plan of attacking the guards and carried it out half-heartedly. At the crucial moment he cut short the pursuit and thus let victory slip through his fingers. As a result he now found himself in a critical position. When Diebitsch caught up with him on 26 May on the retreat from Ostrołęka, he defended himself clumsily and suffered heavy losses. His troops were almost routed and he had to fall back on Warsaw.

He then redoubled his efforts to remain in power and to bar the road to the Left. For two months Skrzynecki concealed the extent of his defeat from the public and pretended to be extremely busy engaging in minor operations. In reality, he displayed an irresponsible and almost criminal inactivity. The Lithuanian rising was in the meantime crushed and the Polish troops despatched to its rescue had surrendered their arms at the Prussian frontier. Paskevich, the new Russian Commander-in-chief appointed after Diebitsch's death, boldly crossed the Vistula on his march from Pułtusk through Nieszawa and threatened the western districts which had, until then, remained untouched by war. The Polish High Command did not even try to stop the enemy's pincer movement. Not until August, when the main Russian forces were threatening Warsaw from the west, did the Seym finally decide to dismiss Skrzynecki. By then, however, the situation had become altogether hopeless.

THE REVOLUTIONARY LEFT AND THE PEASANT QUESTION

The only possibility of victory in the uneven struggle against the overwhelming Russian forces seemed to lie in the mobilization of the peasant masses, but the peasants, who were burdened with contributions in kind and conscription for guard duties, and who were still forced to render labour services, remained quite indifferent, sometimes even hostile to the war being carried on around them.

The question of enlisting the support of the peasants was under discussion in Warsaw. The Kalisz group tabled a bill in the Seym which provided for the introduction of rents for the peasants in the national estates. This step accorded with the general idea of evolution towards capitalism and it did not directly affect the interests of the landowners. Nevertheless, the bill was opposed by the die-hard conservatives in the Chamber, who obstructed

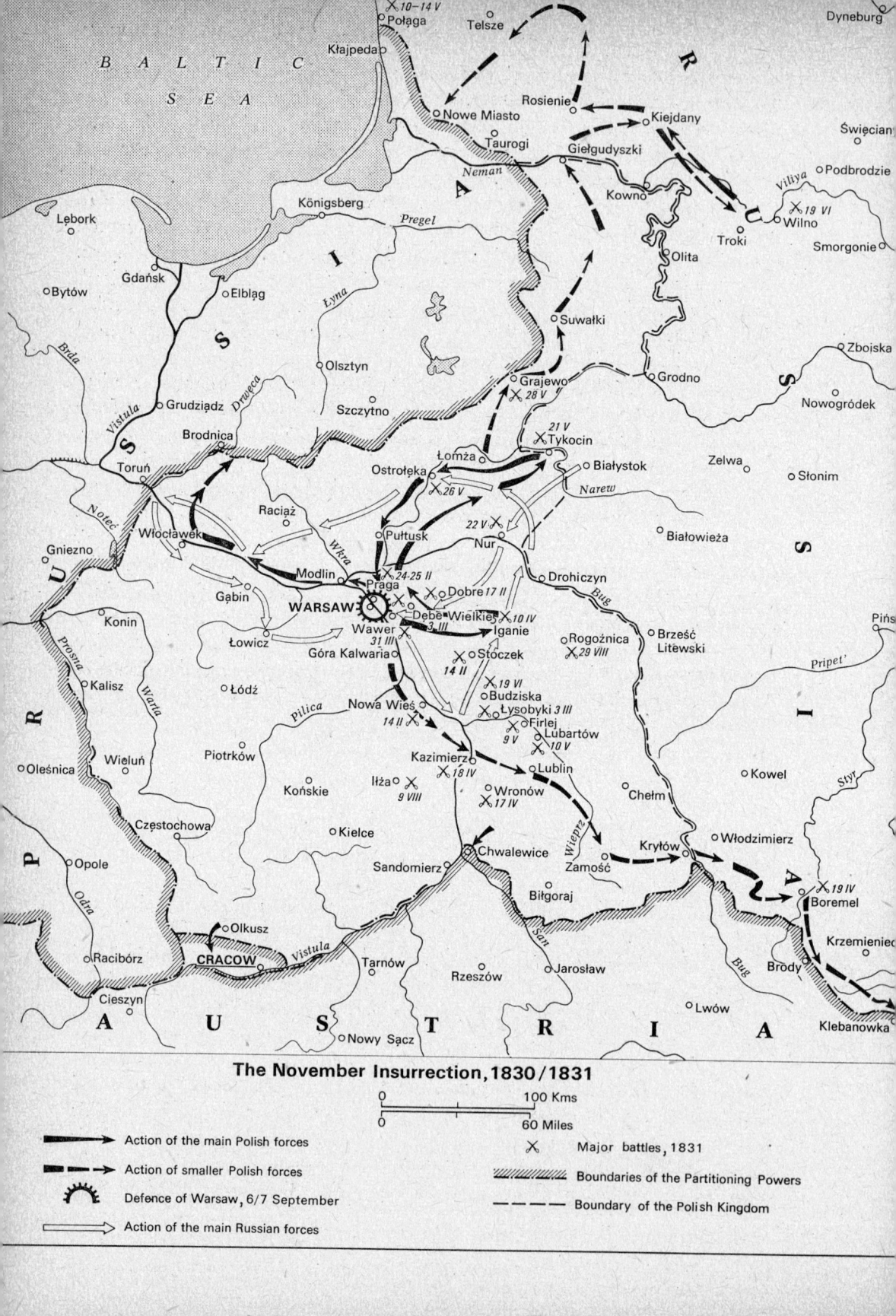

its passage by dragging out discussion and finally had it taken off the agenda. One of the few radical deputies, Jan Olrych Szaniecki, submitted a motion that went even further and provided that all peasants be granted their freeholds with compensation for the landlords; he received no backing from the majority of the deputies. Thus, the leaders of the insurrection did nothing to improve the lot of the peasants, and this fact was reflected in the attitude of the country people. As summer came, desertions from the army multiplied in the villages, and there were cases of peasants rising against the manors.

The agrarian question was also discussed in left-wing circles. Excluded from power, they created a campaign platform in the Patriotic Society and had for their use several newspapers including "Nowa Polska" and "Gazeta Polska". Membership of the Patriotic Society consisted mostly of the radical intelligentsia and, to a lesser extent, of the lower middle-class. Its nominal chairman was Lelewel, who thus combined in a strange way his functions as a member of the government with those of the patron of the opposition. In fact, he expected with the help of the Left Wing to bring pressure to bear upon the government in matters of policy and war strategy. The members of the Society agreed that vigorous military action was imperative. They demanded the dismissal of ineffective commanders and of any officers suspected of treason. They advocated a mass-levy and consequently they were in favour of alleviating the burdens of the peasants and abolishing feudal labour services. Members of the Society were not unanimous with regard to social questions. Mochnacki, one of their most prominent spokesmen at the begining, had become more moderate in his views, whereas the extreme Left produced a group of more radical speakers and journalists including men like Krępowiecki, Gurowski, Czyński and Father Pułaski. Their demands were clear and unambiguous: they pressed for the establishment of a republic, the emancipation of the peasants and capital punishment for traitors and spies. Yet even this radical minority in the Society had no direct contact with the populace of Warsaw, and wielded no real power.

The political struggle grew more tense after the defeat at Ostrołęka. The conservatives tabled a bill in the Seym demanding that the government be reformed. Their aim was to set up a dictatorship capable of resuming negotiations with the Tsar. Alarmed by this turn of affairs, the Kalisz faction, supported by the Left Wing, rejected the bill of reform. Military reverses increased tension among the population and, when Skrzynecki in his search for scapegoats arrested a few senior officers, the infuriated mob demanded their trial by court martial and punishment. Only with great effort was the populace pacified.

In August the Seym had at last to bow to public opinion and dismiss Skrzynecki. His successor, General Dembiński, had distinguished himself during the uprising in Lithuania and wished to continue the war, but, for the same reasons as Skrzynecki, he did not want to expose the army to any risks, and when the moment came to fight the long expected battle, he retreated with his troops to Warsaw. A storm of excitement broke loose in the city on 15 August. The Patriotic Society held a violent meeting and despatched a large delegation to the government demanding a drastic change of policy. The mob took the prison by assault, summarily tried and lynched the arrested generals for treason, and hanged several agents of Grand Duke Constantine's former secret police, who also were under arrest. The left-wing leaders were utterly perplexed in the face of this spontaneous outburst. They never thought of taking advantage of the situation to overthrow the government and take power into their own hands.

The events of 15 August caused surprise and alarm among the propertied classes. In thier anxiety to restore order, the conservatives, the liberal Kalisz group, and even the Right Wing of the Patriotic Society, joined hands once more. The Seym nominated General Krukowiecki to head the government and vested him with quasi-dictatorial power. Krukowiecki ordered the army to occupy the city; he had a few second-rate participants in the riots executed by firing squad as a warning to the population. He loudly proclaimed his readiness to continue the war; but secretly, he was preparing to capitulate.

THE INTERNATIONAL SITUATION AND THE COLLAPSE OF THE RISING

The November Insurrection was obviously instrumental in preserving Belgium and even France from the intervention of the Holy Alliance. Russia had her hands tied on the banks of the Vistula for almost a year. During that time, the French July monarchy was able to stabilize its position and Belgium to establish her independence. In view of these circumstances, the progressive elements throughout Europe developed a warm sentiment for the Polish "knights of liberty". French and German democrats were enthusiastic about Poland, Hungarian and Czech patriots were influenced by the Polish movement when formulating their own more progressive political programmes. Volunteers of many different nationalities joined the Polish ranks. The Polish insurgents turned to the Russians with the appeal: "for our freedom and for yours" and paid homage publicly to the memory of executed Decembrists. This attitude received a favourable response from many Russian revolutionaries.

The European courts in Paris, London and Vienna, took advantage of the Polish-Russian war to further their respective interests, but did not think of assisting Poland. On the contrary, the Powers tried to localize the conflict lest it spread to the rest of Europe. Polish diplomacy failed to understand this. Its head, Czartoryski tried in vain to enlist the help or mediation of the Powers; nor did he succeed in convincing their cabinets of the legal and non-revolutionary character of the Polish movement. He was particularly eager to obtain Austria's ear, and ready, to Lelewel's dismay, to offer the Polish crown to an Austrian archduke, even at the cost of giving up the Constitution. His efforts were in vain because although Austria was pleased with the difficulties confronting her Russian neighbour, she considered the insurrection a dangerous revolutionary movement and wanted it to fail. Prussia kept an army corps at the frontier of the Kingdom and rendered the Russian every assistance posible without violating her neutrality. The British Whig government declined to take a stand in Poland's affairs. The July Monarchy in France was mindful of public opinion, but confined itself to a rather general expression of sympathy with the Polish plight. The Holy See treated the insurrection as a rebellion against the legitimate power and condemned it solemnly, after it had collapsed.

With nothing to fall back upon except its own resources, the Polish insurrection took the brunt of the whole Tsarist might for eight months, but neither patriotism nor the valour of officers and soldiers could overcome the enormous difference in means and arms. The leaders of the rising could not decide upon arming the peasants, nor did they do anything to win the peasants' support for the cause of independence. When dissatisfaction with the ineffective leadership led to the savage riots of 15 August, the conservative camp, which feared the possibility of a revolution deliberately hastened the collapse of the insurrection.

Towards the end of August Paskevich's army reached the capital's outer defenses in the west. Krukowiecki had just despatched an army corps under General Ramorino towards the east, thus reducing the Warsaw defenses by 20,000 men. The most discredited leaders of the uprising, with Czartoryski at their head, had left Warsaw with that corps. The Russian army attacked the city on 6 September. Between 35,000 and 40,000 Poles had to man the vast ramparts and face 77,000 Russian troops whose artillery was more than double that of the Poles. The battle lasted two days. In spite of the heroic resistance offered in various sectors, the enemy broke through to the toll bars. General Józef Sowiński, veteran, who defended the suburb of Wola, fell in battle. The Polish commanders were above all concerned with preventing any arms reaching the civilian population and fighting on the barricades. Krukowiecki started negotiations for total surrender. It is true that the Seym rejected it at the Kalisz group's suggestion and deposed Krukowiecki. Only Warsaw was abandoned to the enemy, while the army retreated to Modlin.

The Left Wing in the Seym and many officers demanded that the war be carried on, but the generals pressed for surrender and forced through the election of General Maciej Rybiński as Commander-in-chief. Ramorino's corps marched south and crossed the frontier into Austria without trying to join Rybiński. Rybiński started negotiating with Paskevich, but pressure from his subordinates prevented him from surrendering to the enemy. On

5 October the remainders of the Polish armies still numbering some 20,000, crossed the frontier near Brodnica and were disarmed by the Prussians.

The November Insurrection had collapsed in an unequal fight without having been able to muster all the forces available to the nation. Fundamentally, this was due to the fact that the rising was dominated by the gentry. The signal for the outbreak had been given on 29 November by revolutionaries from the gentry, men ready to fight for freedom and independence, but incapable of imposing their will on their own social class. Their vacillation and their lack of any programme, which stood out so glaringly in the attitude of the most prominent members of their group, like Lelewel or Mochnacki, were the reason why leadership of the national movement was taken over by the propertied classes. The government and the army were thus led by men who did not desire the insurrection, who did not believe in victory and who were, above all, frightened by any revolutionary activities. For these very reasons they wasted the finest assets they possessed, an excellent army and the enthusiasm of the people.

Engels later referred pointedly to the November Insurrection as a "conservative revolution". This definition, which was interpreted in various ways, did bring out the dual character of the rising; its weakness as well as its positive meaning. The rising was led and brought to the point of collapse by the conservatives, but it was essentially a revolutionary act which, though it failed, left a lasting imprint on the future of the nation. The war fanned the patriotism of tens of thousands of soldiers, it shook to the roots not only the Kingdom but also the neighbouring sectors of the partitioned country which provided many volunteers. Last but not least, it accelerated the formation of new progressive and far-reaching programmes. At the same time the November Insurrection played a large part in European history by enhancing the chances of revolutionary movements in other countries. The close link between the fate of Poland's cause and the fate of the revolution in Europe was a characteristic feature of the decades that followed.

Chapter XVI
ON THE EVE OF AN AGRARIAN REVOLUTION (1832–1849)

REPRISALS AFTER THE INSURRECTION

The defeat of the November Insurrection brought the revenge of Tsar Nicholas upon Poland. The Tsar declared the Constitution null and void. He abolished the Seym, as well as the Polish army. For appearances' sake, in 1832 he promulgated an Organic Statute for the Kingdom guaranteeing the country its separate administration and civil rights. The Statute, however, was never enforced and the country was kept in a state of emergency. Paskevich, the conqueror of Warsaw, was named Viceroy (*namiestnik*) and became the autocratic ruler of the Kingdom. The Administrative Council was relegated to the position of a passive instrument executing his orders. Similarly, the civil authorities in the provinces were placed under Russian military commanders. The country had to pay the cost of Russian occupation forces and the cost of building fortresses. A Citadel was erected in Warsaw as a means of intimidating the rebellious capital.

The Tsar announced an amnesty for all participants in the insurrection except the principal leaders who had to face trial and exile to Siberia. All property belonging to persons who had been sentenced or who had escaped abroad, was confiscated. Many state domains were granted in right of primogeniture to Russian generals and dignitaries, who had shown their zeal in crushing the insurrection. Reprisals extended to the cultural field as well. The Society of the Friends of Science was closed down as were the universities of Warsaw and Wilno, while precious scientific collections were taken out of Poland. Tsar Nicholas' régime clamped down on learning and education throughout the State, but particularly ruthless methods were applied with regard to Polish culture.

The process of Russification was now greatly intensified in the western provinces of the Empire. In 1839 the separate Uniate Church was abolished and several million Byelorussians and Ukrainians were forcibly converted to the Russian Orthodox faith. The Kingdom kept its separate administration with Polish as the official language, but the highest posts in the government were held by Russians. The adaptation of local conditions to Russian standards was undertaken by stages. In the course of a decade or so, the voivodships were gradually converted into Russian-type provinces (*gubernia*). The Russian currency was introduced and so likewise was the Russian Criminal Code. The Government Commission for Religious Denominations and Education was abolished and all educational matters were placed directly under the Ministry of Education in St. Petersburg. The ultimate aim envisaged was the complete incorporation of the Kingdom into Russia.

Russian reprisals were reflected in the remaining parts of partitioned Poland. During the preceding fifteen years the Prussian and Austrian governments had been paying attention to the liberties granted to the Poles by Alexander I. Thus the King of Prussia promised to respect Polish nationality in the Grand Duchy of Poznań and appointed Prince Antoni Radziwiłł as *namiestnik*. In Lwów a Seym was established on the lines of the old system of estates, though without real authority. Permission was granted to open the Ossolineum, a Polish scientific institute founded by a generous magnate, J. M. Ossoliński. After 1831, however, the tendency towards Germanization was more pronounced and the three signatories of the Holy Alliance collaborated more closely to counteract European revolutionary movements and particularly the Polish cause. In 1833 a Russo-Austrian agreement was signed at Münchengrätz, to which Prussia adhered later. It provided, among other things for the cooperation between the police of the three partitioning Powers in combatting Polish conspiracies, and for the reciprocal extradition of political refugees.

The new anti-Polish trend had its impact on the Cracow Republic. This miniature State of 1164 sq. km, and 88,000 inhabitants had been granted a constitution in accordance with the decision of the Congress of Vienna, with the right to elect its Senate and a representative assembly, and received a guarantee that it might develop on national lines. The Senate was in the hands of the local aristocrats who refused to allow the wealthy liberal bourgeoisie a share of power. In general, however, Cracow and its district fared well enough and enjoyed the advantages of free trade. In the Cracow district the labour dues had been replaced almost completely by rents. After the November Insurrection, however, the liberties of the city were curtailed. Power was taken over by the Conference of Residents, composed of the representatives of the three "protecting" Powers, and the Senate was relegated to the role of their passive tool. A secret Austro-Russian understanding envisaged the abolition of this last vestige of Polish statehood at the first opportunity.

ECONOMIC DEVELOPMENT IN THE THREE PARTITION ZONES

Years which for Poland were particularly hard in the political and cultural sense were marked, however, by economic expansion. This progress was not uniform in all Polish territories and did not affect all branches of the economy equally.

Agriculture began to flourish, because the price of grain rose and west European urban centres were a good market. This induced landowners to intensify production and invest capital in farming; crop rotation gradually replaced the three-field system and steel ploughs and scythes were used; manorial farm buildings were improved, greater care was taken in animal husbandry and horse breeding, while forestry was rationalized. This progressive trend was particularly noticeable in the Prussian zone, where the agrarian reform created favourable conditions. In the Congress Kingdom economic progress was more evident in the northern and western parts, in the voivodships of Płock and Kalisz, than in the voivodships of Kielce, Lublin and Podlasie; it occurred as a rule on the larger and more advanced estates. In Galicia, which was rather backward, farming continued in general along traditional lines.

The demesne farm, which had every political and economic advantage over the villages, introduced progressive techniques mostly at the expense of the peasants. The landlord reorganized his estates either with the help of the government as in the Poznań region or from his own resources as in the Congress Kingdom, which meant that he transferred the peasants to poorer plots and reduced the size of their holdings. He now used his own teams of animals to work the land, needing mostly manual labour to cultivate potatoes and sugar beet. He therefore transferred richer farmers from labour duties to rent, he evicted most of the others, or let them stay on diminished holdings as cottagers. He limited the peasants' traditional right to collect fire wood and graze their animals in the manorial woods. Evictions assumed disastrous proportions in some parts of the Kingdom, where barely one fourth of the arable land was left to the peasants. Peasants who paid rent enjoyed more favourable conditions. They were more numerous on state-owned land as well as in some of the large latifundia (especially in the Zamoyski estates) and in many middle-sized private properties in the western part of the country. On the whole, however, the welfare of the tenants depended on the amount of rent they had to pay, and was sometimes exorbitant. Moreover, no contract of tenancy made the peasant a landowner, nor did it provide him with security for the future.

Industrial development was more and more uneven in the various provinces of Poland. There was stagnation in some parts of the country; Galicia, for example, still had its primitive handlooms, and a few iron or glass works, operating under the old labour service system. In the Grand Duchy of Poznań, the weaving industry collapsed completely on account of the far more efficient competition of western Europe. The peasant weavers in the Silesian Sudeten foothills were also experiencing a crisis. Yet the Wrocław textile mills were prospering and heavy industry—ironworks and collieries—in the Upper Silesian district made spectacular advances.

In Congress Poland, the Tsarist government retaliated after the November Insurrection by obstructing the export of Polish cloth to Russia. This caused a crisis in the textile industry and a number of producers moved east from Congress Poland across the new customs frontier; this marked the development of the textile industry in the Białystok region. The crisis did not affect the cotton industry which supplied only the local market. Its production increased from 3.8 to 22.6 million ells during the period 1830-1844. In the mid-1830's the first large-size mechanized spinning factory of Ludwik Geyer was commissioned in Łódź; several hundred weavers working on handlooms also found employment there.

In heavy industry Lubecki's investment policy was taken over by the Bank Polski which completed the building of the combine on Kamienna river and constructed a big modern metallurgical works in the Dąbrowa Basin, the Huta Bankowa. The Huta consisted of six large coke furnaces, an iron foundry, a puddling furnace, a rolling mill and mechanical workshops. This important plant was out of proportion to the actual needs of the home market and was therefore not exploited to capacity for many years. However, the construction itself which was financed by the Treasury, accelerated the accumulation of capital in the hands of entrepreneurs and financiers with close links with the government. The 1830's and 1840's were a golden age for many speculators who used the credit extended by the Bank Polski to found or operate a variety of enterprises and to amass fortunes amounting to millions of zlotys. The most famous of them, Piotr Steinkeller, whose career ended in a spectacular bankruptcy, had the reputation of being a distinguished pioneer of Poland's industry. Others, more adroit, survived the crisis and formed the nucleus of the Warsaw and Łódź big bourgeoisie. This bourgeoisie was completely loyal to Paskevich and established close relations with that section of the big gentry which was itself engaged, like the Łubieński brothers, in financial speculation.

It was during the 1840's that the first railroads were built in Poland. Tracks leading towards the foundries and collieries of Upper Silesia were mapped out almost simultaneously from Vienna, Berlin and Warsaw. The Warsaw-Vienna line was a project of Steinkeller; after his financial disaster the Russian government extended it up to the Austrian frontier (1848). About the same time the Berlin-Wrocław-Cracow line began operation. Poland thus established comparatively early rail connections with western Europe.

THE LIBERAL CAMP AND "ORGANIC WORK"

Capitalism developed in Poland under conditions of political subjugation. The Polish propertied classes were acutely conscious of their dependence on foreign rulers, who took no account of the interests of the conquered provinces and often retarded their development. Paskevich's régime left no room for an accommodation with the partitioning power or for open political action. The Polish landowners, however, did not hide their dislike of illegal political activity, conspiracies or preparation for uprisings. They considered them too risky steps which might unleash the revolutionary forces which were liable to woo the peasants with promises and create difficulties for the gentry. Many landowners sought a middle-of-the-road solution between an unpopular accommodation with foreign rule and a socially dangerous conspiracy. They thought to find it in legal, but non-political activity, namely, in the effort of raising the social, economic and cultural level of the country. It was customary at the time to call this complicated concept of activity "organic work" as opposed to plotting revolutions and insurrections. "Organic work" was to promote the development of the country and its evolution towards capitalism. It was to safeguard the interests of the landed gentry in these new conditions and at the same time show their readiness to serve the public interests. Finally, it was designed to neutralize the revolutionary movement and oppose it by suggesting more positive and effective means of reform.

The birthplace of "organic work" (the term came into use in the middle of the nineteenth century) was the Grand Duchy of Poznań. There the liberal gentry changed over faster to a capitalist economy and had relative freedom of action. The Prussian monarchy, harbouring the ambition of uniting Germany, was beginning to pay attention to German liberal opinions. This fact brought about a marked coolness in its relations with Russia after 1840 and a more lenient attitude towards the Poles. In Poznań the censorship was relaxed and the authorities interfered much less with the establishment of Polish associations.

The leadership of the "organic work" in Poznań was assumed by Dr. Karol Marcinkowski, a prominent physician and philanthropist who had gained the confidence of the leading landowners of the province. Thanks to Marcinkowski's efforts Poznań built its "Bazar", a hotel building which was also to serve as a centre for Polish commerce and to house Polish social organizations. In the same spirit, the Society for the Promotion of Education was founded, a vast organization which awarded scholarships and trained Polish intellectuals and artisans. Moreover, local agricultural associations began to be set up. The advocates of "organic work" claimed that their aim was to strengthen the Polish middle classes, bourgeoisie, intelligentsia, and later on the wealthier peasants, but in reality, they were trying to place the middle class under the thumb of the landed gentry.

The possibilities of carrying on "organic work" were more modest in the other parts of Poland. In the Congress Kingdom Andrzej Zamoyski, an aristocrat and civic leader who had introduced the system of rents for many peasants in his family estates, tried to rally round himself a group of active landowners. He arranged annual gatherings in his residence at Klemensów to discuss economic and social questions and inspect a farm where crop rotation was applied. The publication "Roczniki Gospodarstwa Krajowego" (Yearbook of National Husbandry) became the mouthpiece of the Klemensów group. The influence of this group was narrow, even among the gentry. In Galicia, another magnate, Prince Leon Sapieha, was trying to bring life into the old-fashioned and moribund institution of the Seym, based on the old estates. After many years of effort Vienna granted permission to open a saving bank in Galicia, the Land Credit Association and the Agricultural Society. There also were some timid attempts made in the Seym to introduce some agrarian reforms without, of course, trespassing on the interests of the big landowners. These attempts have to be viewed against the background of the growing menace of a peasant rising and the democratic propaganda spreading in the country. Almost at their inception all attempts were interrupted by the outbreak of the 1846 uprising.

A specific variety of "organic work" were the temperance brotherhoods which enjoyed tremendous publicity in the villages in the 1840's. Technical progress in distilling brought in its wake an enormous increase in vodka production, lower liquor prices, and a disastrous spread of drunkenness. The Roman Catholic clergy began to organize mass teetotal meetings patterned on the Irish temperance movement where people pledged themselves to stop drinking alcohol. The movement began in Upper Silesia and spread to other districts where it attracted millions of followers. In fighting the social evil of drunkenness, the priests were at the same time increasing their influence among the people and expected to divert attention from revolutionary ideas. Yet, the mass participation of peasants in the temperance brotherhoods was, on the contrary, their way of showing their animosity to the gentry who produced and sold the spirits. The closing down of inns run by the manors caused anxiety among the gentry. The Tsarist government looked upon the brotherhoods as a politically dangerous element and prohibited them in its zone, at the same time increasing taxes on the manufacture of alcohol in order to reduce consumption. The mass temperance movement subsided during the years of the 1846–1848 revolution.

The example of the temperance brotherhoods shows the two main difficulties which confronted "organic work". On one hand, the foreign government was obstructing their development, on the other hand, the institutions founded by the organic group were becoming tools of revolution. The golden mean between armed resistance and losing one's national identity was combatted among the gentry itself on the one hand by the ultraconservatives, on the other hand by ardent patriots. As the revolutionary situation grew more tense, even the most zealous advocates of "organic work" joined the revolutionary movement, some for tactical reasons, others under pressure of public opinion. Polish liberalism which was artificially limited to non-political and social activities, broke down whenever it was put to the test.

THE NATIONAL QUESTION IN SILESIA AND POMERANIA

The two areas of the Prussian zone, which had come under foreign domination earlier than the rest of Poland, developed along different lines. Some parts of these provinces, Lower Silesia and Western Pomerania were almost completely Germanized; wherever the Polish language had survived, it was used by the common people. In Upper Silesia, Warmia and along the lower course of the Vistula, the remaining Polish gentry were either Germanized or had sold their properties at the beginning of the nineteenth century.

Thus in the regions of Opole, Warmia and Mazuria, and partly in Gdańsk-Pomerania, national and class divisions began to coincide. The Polish peasant and worker had their opponent in the German junker, merchant and official. When the Upper Silesian industrial region suddenly expanded at the beginning of the nineteenth century, Polish miners and foundry workers became once more objects of exploitation by the German lord of the manor who had become an industrialist. The Polish intelligentsia was represented in Silesia and Pomerania solely by a small group of priests and village teachers of peasant stock. This peasant community had no links with the other Polish districts and their culture was shaped by the gentry and the landowners. Attached to their native tongue and local custom, these communities had no distinctly national consciousness. There were a few scholars and writers in Warsaw or Cracow who did take an interest in the Polish national character of Silesians and Mazurians. The generation of the gentry revolutionaries failed to see that this community, though it did not belong to the gentry class, was an integral part of the Polish nation.

This feeling of mutual strangeness began to change in the 1830's. The development of capitalism, progress in town planning, the expansion of education—all of these processes served as incentives to the hitherto passive rural population. The November Insurrection found a warm response in Silesia and Pomerania. Volunteers from both regions took part in the war. A fact like the internment of the Rybiński corps in Pomerania for a period of several months after they had laid down their arms contributed to establish close ties between Polish soldiers and the local population. The civic leaders in the Poznań district also began to draw closer to the neighbouring provinces under Prussian rule.

National consciousness in those territories crystallized still faster when measures were taken directed against the Polish language. Up to the nineteenth century, the Prussian government undertook no systematic action to Germanize the common people and did not care what language they spoke. In Silesia, the official theory claimed that the dialect which was scornfully dubbed as "wasserpolnisch" had nothing whatever in common with Polish. After 1815, however, the requirements of an expanding industry, of the capitalist manorial farm, and military service, compelled the administration to pay more attention to the language of the local population. Repeatedly orders were issued introducing the German language in Catholic and Protestant churches and in the primary schools. After 1830, German became the medium of instruction in all schools of the villages and small towns, irrespective of the nationality of the children.

This attack upon the Polish language was bitterly resented by the population of Pomerania and Silesia. Any peasant and worker realized that the banning of the Polish language in administrative offices, courts and places of work made it difficult for him to defend himself against the exploitation by the German ruling classes. The more stubbornly did he hold on to his native tongue and fight for its equal rights. From the 1820's onward, entire rural parishes in Silesia and Pomerania—both Catholic and Protestant—frequently came forward demanding that Polish remain the language in which church services and teaching be conducted.

Popular resistance was sometimes taken up in intellectual circles. Gustaw Gizewiusz, a pastor at Ostróda in the district of Mazuria, defended the native language of his people. In his well-known work *Die polnische Sprachfrage in Preussen* (The Polish Language Question in Prussia) of 1843 he underlined the Polish features of large areas of Pomerania and Silesia, and condemned the government's attempts at Germanization. He secured the minister's consent (nominally, at least) to the continuation of some partial use of the Polish language in the Mazurian schools.

In Upper Silesia, Józef Lompa, a modest primary school teacher of peasant stock, was the first propagator of national culture and consciousness. Lompa was a prolific writer and published popular pamphlets on many subjects, including economics, folk custom, religion, topography, and history. Presenting his material in a way accessible to peasants and workers, he taught them to read Polish and inculcated in their minds respect for their own national tradition. Like Gizewiusz, Lompa kept in close contact with the educational centres of Warsaw, Cracow and Poznań and was consciously working for a union between Silesia and the motherland, though he steered clear of political activity. It is hardly possible to assume that, prior to 1848, either Silesia or Pomerania had a broader understanding of the question of Poland's independence. But there was that awakening among the masses, the feeling of being nationally different, which later found its expression in the revolutionary movements of 1848.

THE GREAT EMIGRATION

After the debacle of 1831 came the exile of those participants in the insurrection to whom the Tsarist amnesty did not apply and also of those who refused to live under alien oppression. The French government, taking account of its own public opinion, received the exiles, granting them a modest allowance and placing them under police surveillance. The Polish "knights of liberty" wandered westwards, welcomed and cheered on their way by progressive circles in Germany and France. They numbered about eight thousand, and among them were prominent political and cultural leaders, statesmen, generals, journalists, poets and artists. Most exiles were junior officers, because the regular soldiers had been forced for the most part to accept the amnesty. Seventy five per cent of the refugees were of gentry stock, though very few of them possessed substantial means.

This emigration was given the adjective "great" in later years to distinguish it from other waves of political refugees. From the very beginning this group of exiles was to play an exceptional role in the life of the country. Suddenly, they found themselves in an atmosphere, where political freedom reigned and where they could keep in close contact with the progressive currents of the West; they experienced a rapid ideological evolution and, their eyes lifted toward the homeland, they shared their new experiences with their mother country.

During the first few months the exiles imagined that they would soon return home arms in hand, taking part either in the expected war or in a world revolution. In this mood Adam Czartoryski pleaded with the western governments to create armed Polish military units as a nucleus for new legions. The Left Wing made contacts with French progressive thought and above all, with the secret Carbonari organization, the "Supreme Vente of the World", and its leader Buonarroti.

By the end of 1831 the group of newcomers to Paris, composed mostly of intellectuals, elected a Polish National Committee with Lelewel as its leader. The most active among the former members of the Patriotic Society had joined it. The Committee prophesied a fresh uprising in the near future and emphasized the unity between Poland's cause and the cause of all oppressed peoples. Lelewel, however, who feared internal dissention, was opposed to outlining of the programmes relating to social and constitutional matters. This state of affairs led to violent discussion among the Poles in Paris. In March 1832 several left-wing members including T. Krępowiecki, K. Pułaski, J. Czyński and J. N. Janowski, refused to obey the Committee claiming for themselves the freedom to associate with people of the same opinions. The dissidents founded the Polish Democratic Society.

The followers of Lelewel as well as the conservative group among the émigrés made every effort to attract the most numerous group of the exiled officers who had been placed in provincial "dépots" by the French government. Proposals were advanced to elect a new committee or "council of generals" and to recognize the leadership either of Czartoryski, former president of the National Government, or of Rybiński, the last Commander-in-chief. Attempts were also made to revive in exile the former Seym of the Kingdom of Poland. One after another these attempts failed. The exiles as a whole were against submitting to the former authorities and formed political groups instead, according to their political beliefs.

Lelewel's Committee tried for a whole year to arouse world opinion to take an interest in Poland's cause. They issued many appeals, organized campaigns to raise funds and other demonstrations. At the end of 1832 the Committee was disbanded by the French police. Lelewel had already initiated an underground movement which was to prepare the ground for a revival in the following year of partisan activities in Poland under Józef Zaliwski. He reckoned that Carbonarist revolutions would break out almost simultaneously in France, Germany and Italy.

Lelewel, however, was outdistanced in the Carbonari underground movement by his main rival Krępowiecki, who was appointed head of the "Polish National Venta". The Carbonarists failed to provide assistance in 1833, the expected revolutions in Germany and Italy proved a flash in the pan and Zaliwski's partisan movement collapsed. Several hundred exiles started out too early from their base at Besançon to take part in the German revolution and eventually found refuge in Switzerland.

These adventures were accompanied by violent ideological quarrels in which the causes of the failure of the November Insurrection were discussed, its conservative leadership was condemned and new proposals were put forward for the future. The ideology of gentry revolutionism had outlived its usefulness; the left-wing exiles pronounced more or less resolutely for democracy and the liberation of the country by the people.

It was soon apparent that democracy could be interpreted in various ways. On the second anniversary of the November Insurrection Krępowiecki took the rostrum during a public celebration in Paris with a violent oration in French. He condemned the pernicious theory of "national unity" which during the last rising had become a tool of the counter-revolution. He criticized the gentry and declared his solidarity with the peasants in their class struggle, extolling the traditions of Chmielnicki and Gonta. His speech provoked a riot; not only the conservatives, but also a considerable number of democrats protested against so sharp a break with the noble traditions of the Poland of the gentry. Krępowiecki had to resign even from the Polish Democratic Society. There followed a schism in the democratic camp. The moderate majority among the democrats believed that it would be able to win over all classes of the nation, both the gentry and the people, to support the cause of independence; theirs was a type of "gentry democracy" characteristic of social conditions in Poland. The radical minority rejected all compromise with the gentry and adopted the point of view known today as "revolutionary democracy".

The group of Polish refugees interned in Switzerland linked up with Giuseppe Mazzini and took part in 1834 in his abortive expedition to Savoy. This military venture led to further collaboration in the form of the alliance of fraternal organizations, "Young Italy", "Young Germany", and "Young Poland". It was in this way that the Polish Left Wing shook off the dictatorial authority of the Carbonarist "Vente" and formed its own, autonomous organization within the framework of the general European revolutionary movement.

Lelewel, who had been expelled from France, settled in Brussels and took over the leadership of "Young Poland". It was intended that it should remain a small secret organization working to control other groups of exiles by infiltration. It did not succeed in this aim, but it was joined in 1835–1837 by many active men of ideas and initiative who returned to Poland as emissaries and played an important role there. Depleted by this main effort, "Young Poland" suspended its activity in the following years. Some of its members, like Karol Stolzman, continued to maintain contact with Mazzini in London.

During this period the Democratic Society's membership rose to several thousand persons and spread throughout France. Members living together in one locality formed a section of the Society and kept in contact by corresponding with the leading of Central Section in Paris. The Society was founded by the Left Wing which had seceded from Lelewel's Committee. The first statement issued by its founders in 1832 contained some revolutionary-democratic accents and spoke in a general way about "the land and its fruits being common to all". Gradually however, new people joined and the scales were tipped in favour of a more moderate point of view. The Central Section of the Society moved from Paris to Poitiers. After debates which lasted several months, the revolutionary-democratic opposition was purged from the Society in 1835. Work then began on a more detailed programme. A project outlined by Wiktor Heltman was after a public discussion accepted as binding by a vote of the Society.

This programme, called the Poitiers Manifesto of 1836, was the result of a carefully constructed compromise between the liberal gentry tradition and the revolutionary-democratic programme. Its cardinal principle was: "Everything for the people, everything by the people"; it declared that all classes were to be equal and that serfdom and labour services were to be abolished. It tried nevertheless to present these slogans in a manner acceptable to the gentry. It stated therefore that the revolutionary government would, on the day of the rising, grant full property to every peasant who tilled even the smallest strip of land. This appeal was to spur the people on to fight for their liberty, without discouraging the participation of the gentry. In fact, the manifesto did not suggest taking away manorial farmland from the gentry nor did it propose that landless peasants should be given land. The doctrine of the Democratic Society was deliberately vague on this point. It permitted the Society to appeal to the patriotic sentiment of all classes, but it created a state of permanent uncertainty in Poland. Many members of the Society believed that the Poitiers Manifesto was the first step toward a larger and more just settlement of the agrarian problem in a liberated Poland. Other less radical members would have been quite satisfied if the manorial farm had continued to exist in Poland alongside with peasant ownership. Yet the continued existence of manorial farms would have meant leaving a large number of peasants without land.

Far away from the country and with an uprising a long way off, it was easy to cloak these controversial questions and insist upon the Society's Manifesto as a dogma, while leaving the question of interpretation open for the time being. The Democratic Society adopted a rigid set of rules; it only accepted members whom they considered safe, demanded strict discipline, and purged anyone for the least deviation from the programme. Power lay in the hand of a five-men Central Board ("Centralizacja") elected every year by postal vote of all members. The Board had its seat first in Poitiers and then, after 1840, in Versailles. It kept in close touch with the sections by means of circular letters and various news sheets. In practice, the members of the board were always elected from among a dozen or so persons belonging to the same group. Wiktor Heltman and Wojciech Darasz represented the democratic tendencies while the right-wing Tomasz Malinowski inclined towards the liberals.

The Democratic Society's compromise doctrine was opposed by the extreme Left Wing led by Krępowiecki and Pułaski. This latter group was backed by several hundred soldiers, who had landed in Portsmouth in 1834, many of whom were of peasant stock. When the insurrection collapsed they were ruthlessly persecuted in Prussia. Because they refused to accept the Tsarist amnesty, they were jailed in the fortress of Grudziądz. They were ultimately expelled from the country and in Portsmouth found a haven in old barracks where they received a pitiful allowance. At first they joined up with the local Democratic Society section, but soon became critical of its programme. Under the influence of Krępowiecki and Stanisław Worcell, they broke with the Society and formed, in 1835, the "Grudziąż Commune of the Polish People". Following its example, another Commune was formed in St. Hélier on Jersey Island. This group was composed of a small number of intellectuals and called itself "Humań", a name which recalled the peasant uprising of 1768 in the Ukraine.

Both Communes rejected the programme of the Democratic Society, claiming that it did not satisfy the needs of the people. The proposed grant of freeholds, in fact, favoured the landed peasants and ignored the landless; it perpetuated the existence of the big landowners and, though it abolished caste privileges, it maintained the privilege of money. The members of the Communes adopted a utopian-socialist line, denying the right to private property, claiming that all land belonged to the people. They imagined that the government of the people would distribute land and individual workshops for life. The basic feature of their programme was the abolition of the gentry's property rights, and the assumption of power by the people.

With such views, the Communes remained isolated among the exiles, and

Joachim Lelewel

did not succeed in establishing continued contact with the homeland, in spite of the fact that their publications did influence revolutionary democrats there. Owing to their isolation from society, the Communes became less active as the years passed. Their most prominent members, Krępowiecki and Worcell, withdrew and this dwindling refugee group became a kind of political sect with a growing inclination to mysticism. The slogans it had uttered, however, were revived later in the underground movement at home.

After 1840, the extreme Left Wing and the moderate centrists around

Lelewel lost much of their importance. Numerical strength lay with the rival groups of the Democratic Society and the Czartoryski clan. The latter had the support of the majority of notables in exile and the less politically conscious emigrants who respected authority. In exile, Czartoryski had gradually changed his point of view, from conservatism to liberalism, a fact which reconciled the former Kalisz group to him. He believed in constitutional monarchy, his group adopted the name "Third of May" and considered the old prince as "the *de facto* king". Czartoryski tried to persuade his confidants among the Polish aristocracy of the necessity to abolish serfdom (it being understood that landlords would receive compensation). He also tried, though in vain, to induce them to make preparations for another uprising which he considered a means of counteracting a social revolution. In making his revolutionary plans Czartoryski counted upon a European war which might break out as result of the Anglo-Russian conflict in the Near East. He therefore maintained relations with British and French diplomatic circles who used the Polish question as a trump card in their dealings with the Holy Alliance. From his Paris residence, the Hôtel Lambert, Czartoryski despatched his agents to the Balkans and the Near East trying to win over the Turkish government to his side and to gain favour with the Rumanians and South Slaves. The activity of Polish agents contributed in a certain measure to awakening the national consciousness in the Balkans and in the formulation of their political programmes. It was of little immediate use, as far as the Polish cause was concerned. Czartoryski invariably appealed in his policy to two parties who were unwilling to lend him effective support, the big landowners in Poland, who opposed the uprising on principle, and to the governments of France and Britain, to whom the Poles were only a convenient tool.

Closely connected with the political struggle of the exiles was their cultural activity, especially in the field of poetry, music, painting and creative science. The influence of the exiles on the homeland in matters of politics and culture was exceptionally strong. They supplied the ideological content and the aesthetic criteria which inspired the nation in the succeeding generation. We must not forget, however, that the exiles, immersed as they were in the currents of western-European affairs, were concerned above all with their national problems, the most acute question being the crisis of the feudal system and the imminence of an agrarian revolution. This was the focal point of interest in every group of political exiles. They could do little, in a practical sense, except point the way and elaborate theories and programmes. The actual liberation had to be undertaken by the country itself.

CONSPIRACY WITHIN POLAND

Attempts to prepare the country for another uprising after the failure of the November Insurrection met with the general opposition of the propertied classes. At the same time the mass of the population could be reached only with great difficulty by patriotic propaganda. In these circumstances, the underground movements of the 1830's and 1840's found their recruits mainly among the poor or *déclassé* gentry, the employees on the estates, the city intelligentsia and students. The propaganda for these secret associations was at first carried on mainly by emissaries from the emigration and only gradually did the country emancipate itself from their tutelage.

In 1832 many insurgents found a temporary asylum in Galicia and Cracow. In collaboration with them Lelewel's Committee planned to begin a fresh struggle in the Russian zone. Colonel Józef Zaliwski, who had returned from Paris, assumed that small detachments of revolutionaries could operate in the woods and effectively hold the enemy army in check; he expected the partisans to win over the peasants with vague slogans about social liberation. In the spring of 1833 the first partisan groups crossed the frontier from Galicia and Pomerania. The attempt failed: the partisans were either caught or forced to withdraw. Some of them died on the scaffold, while others were exiled or confined in Austrian prisons for many years.

These failures caused the conspirators to put off their preparations for revolt and concentrate instead on ideological propaganda. This action was undertaken in Cracow and Lwów by various secret organizations in cooperation with the Carbonarists and later with "Young Poland". In 1835 an emissary of "Young Poland", Szymon Konarski, was instrumental in forming the Association of the Polish People, a secret society which soon extended from Cracow across Galicia and throughout Russian Poland. The Association evolved democratic principles which were not very clearly defined and tried to mobilize the people for the fight for independence. Clandestine groups were formed by students in schools and universities, and among junior officials, tenant farmers and the provincial gentry. Konarski himself was very active in the Ukraine and succeeded in rallying important groups of the Ukrainian landowners to the cause.

Soon, however, opinions began to differ within the Association in respect of tactics and policy. The moderate wing wished to postpone undertaking armed action to a distant future. For the time being, they wished to work exclusively among the educated section of the population. A typical spokesman for this point of view was Franciszek Smolka, a Lwów lawyer. The radical wing stressed the necessity of disseminating propaganda among the common people and appointing an early date for the uprising. Members of that wing, especially the Cracow University students, campaigned personally among artisans, while others went to enlist Polish and Ukrainian peasants for the revolution. Radical circles began to display their feelings against the gentry. Gustaw Ehrenberg's popular song gave vent to these feelings in its mocking refrain: O *cześć wam, panowie magnaci!* (Hail, Milords the magnates!). Konarski, however, was forced to seek the support of the wealthy gentry east of the Bug. He made concessions to them in his programme, and though issuing slogans for the liberation of the peasants, he made the solution of the peasant problem dependent upon the goodwill of the gentry.

In 1837 there was a crisis within the underground movement. The Left Wing in Galicia founded its own organization which began to carry on more open propaganda for an uprising among the peasants. This resulted in mass arrests involving the Warsaw movement as well. Smolka tried to find his own way out of this situation by suspending all the activities of the Association. The Galician underground survived a few years under different names, but almost all these groups were eventually discovered. Konarski, who worked in the Wilno area, was arrested and shot in 1839, after having heroically endured the ordeal of a brutal criminal examination. Thousands of Polish patriots were in prison, either at the Warsaw Citadel or in the former Carmelite building in Lwów. Hundreds were deported to penal servitude in Siberia, or rotted in the Austrian fortresses of Spielberg and Kufstein. The dragging out of underground activities over so many years had led in practice only to many new victims.

In 1839 a new stage of underground activities began in direct collaboration with the Central Board of the Polish Democratic Society at Versailles. Its emissaries organized a secret Committee in Poznań which was headed by Karol Libelt, a philosopher and educationalist. This Committee abstained from large-scale recruiting, but made good use of the possibilities offered by legal publications to popularize democratic principles. Prussian censorship having been relaxed, journalism began to blossom in Poznań. Progressive weeklies and monthlies like "Tygodnik Literacki" (Literary Weekly) and "Rok" (The Year), prepared the minds of the "enlightened" readers for the acceptance of the principles of the Poitiers Manifesto. The same kind of activity was envisaged for Warsaw, where the periodicals were to publish economic and literary articles under the cover of which political ideas might be propagated.

The long term propaganda inspired by Versailles paid little attention to feeling current in Poland. Unrest among peasants compelled to perform labour service in Galicia and Congress Poland and among the evicted peasants in the Poznań province was reaching boiling point. Artisans and factory workers were beginning to organize their own conspiracies against both the partitioning Powers and against oppression by the employers. In view of these explosive sentiments many of the local consiprators were inclined to break with the attitude adopted at Versailles and to bring forward the date of the rising. This view gained the upper hand, especially in the secret organization in the Kingdom which went at that time under the name of the Association of the Polish Nation.

The moving spirit of the radical wing was Edward Dembowski, a very able young landowner who contributed his talent, his wealth and in the end, his life to the cause of the revolution. He turned Warsaw's "Przegląd Naukowy" (Scientific Review) which he had founded, into the chief organ of progressive political thinking. With considerable courage, he began to unite the independent secret organizations which sprang up spontaneously among the Warsaw artisans, in provincial towns and even among peasants. Threatened with arrest, he fled to Poznań in 1843. There he spent about a year publishing many articles on philosophical and literary subjects which always contained strong political allusions, and extolling, though watchful of the Prussian censorship, the revolutionary spirit and the democratic ideology, proposing the return of the land to the people and the abolition of the gentry's rights over it. In Poznań Dembowski made contact with two secret organizations, Libelt's Committee, which was growing ever more dependent on liberal circles among the gentry, and an independent radical organization, called Union of the Plebeians. The latter was led by the owner of a printing shop, Walenty Stefański, who conducted a mass campaign among artisans, college students and sometimes peasants, reaching the small towns in the Poznań area, Pomerania and Silesia. His aim was to speed up the outbreak of insurrection. True to his habit, Dembowski established relation with the "Plebeians", as well as with some patriotically minded landowners. He encouraged both to oppose Libelt. Expelled from Poznań by the Prussian police, he soon appeared in Galicia, where he started an adventurous career as an emissary of the revolution.

In 1844 a new underground venture flared up and collapsed—the Peasant Association—founded by Father Piotr Ściegienny, son of a peasant from Kielce district, and a village parson in Lublin voivodship (province). He had been campaigning among the peasants in both regions for a number of years rousing in them a national and revolutionary spirit. A "Letter by Pope Gregory XVI" which was, of course, apocryphal, distributed by him, called upon the peasants and poor townspeople to rise against the masters and put an end to class exploitation. He also predicted, that common people of Poland and the Russian troops would join hands and fight together against the squires and the Tsar. Ściegienny was in contact with the national underground movement. He was arrested just at the moment when he was ready to launch his mass campaign. Deprived of his holy orders, he was pardoned under the gallows. His death sentence was commuted to hard labour for life and he was sent to the Nertchinsk mines in Siberia.

The case of Ściegienny, the priest and patriot engaged in conspiracy was not exceptional. While the higher ultramontane clergy, obedient to directives from Rome, condemned the attempted insurrections and at best supported "organic work", some provincial priests conducted patriotic and even revolutionary agitation among the people. Roman Catholicism, as opposed to Orthodox Russia and Protestant Prussia became a pillar of Polish nationality. It is true, however, that the religious, mystic and romantic patriotism, widespread in Poland in the nineteenth century, had not much in common with a sense for politics and also obstructed the development of a democratic philosophy, on which the success of the insurrection depended.

The spontaneous extension of secret mass organizations gave leaders of the Central Board food for thought. The chief exponent of the country's opposition to it was Henryk Kamieński, a wealthy landowner from Congress Poland and a well known author of works on economics. Kamieński was a level-headed, devoted patriot. Having once resolved that the mass participation of peasants was a precondition for a victorious insurrection, he accepted the Poitiers Manifesto and sought only the right opportunity to apply it. He had no faith in the effectiveness of conspiracies inspired by agents coming from abroad. He advised instead a mass propaganda campaign elaborating democratic principles, to be expounded by the educated classes to the people. A population properly indoctrinated would rise and take up arms as one man. The "People's War" launched by the masses could quickly overpower the enemy. Because social revolution was indispensable for such a war, anyone standing in the way of revolution should be threatened with the death penalty. Such were the views Kamieński published anonymously in his *Prawdy żywotne narodu polskiego* (Vital Truths of the Polish Nation) and, in an abbreviated form in the *Katechizm demokratyczny* (Democratic Catechism). Both pamphlets published in 1844–1845 were distributed clandestinely throughout the country, inciting the people to rise and adding a radical twist to the movement, most probably quite contrary to the author's intention. On the other hand, the upper classes to whose patriotism the "Vital Truths" were appealing, condemned the author as a bloodthirsty terrorist proposing the massacre of the gentry.

The Central Board at Versailles concluded that further postponement of armed action might lead to spontaneous local risings and to general disaster. They let it be known therefore in 1843 that they agreed to an early uprising which they fixed for 1846.

This decision, determined by the internal situation, influenced the development of the conspiracy. Membership increased and former opponents among liberal landowners adhered to the movement. Their action was prompted by the prevailing wave of patriotism as much as by the conviction that they would have to be present at the decisive moment in order to have a say in future decisions. All influential positions, like those of the "provincial district commanders" were taken on the eve of the outbreak by the landed gentry.

This development caused anxiety among the radical Left Wing. Would the new gentry conspirators be sincere in carrying out the necessary social revolution? Dembowski joined forces with Stefański's "Plebeians" and tried, at the end of 1845, to overthrow the Poznań Committee and to put genuine democrats in power. At the crucial moment, one of the Poznań landowners simply denounced Stefański to the Prussian police. The leader of the "Plebeians" was put behind bars, and the leadership of the conspiracy remained in the hands of the "Moderates".

Ostensibly, the conspirators accepted the Poitiers Manifesto and agreed with the principle of peasant emancipation. In practice, however, the Left Wing alone stood for a "People's War". The Right Wing was afraid of such a war and encouraged an uprising only in the hope that the struggle for independence would neutralize the threatening class struggle. Wherever it was possible, the progressives went to the villages to preach revolution. Disguised as peasants, they explained to the illiterate villagers that the overthrow of the foreign government would free them from labour services and make them owners of their land. Such approaches frightened the gentry members of the underground. They held the view that the uprising ought to originate from outside the common people, with the gentry and their servants. Only when the gentry had power firmly in their hands would they announce the liberation to the peasants and keep them well under control with the regular army. This was the idea of Ludwik Mierosławski, whom the Central Board of Versailles had appointed Commander-in-chief. The leaders of the underground therefore opposed attempts at campaigning beforehand among the peasants. In fact, such action had only too often contained overtones of propaganda directed against the gentry.

The conspirators were starting a war against the three states of the Holy Alliance without international force to back them, without arms and without being properly organized. They began it because they could wait no longer. The country was facing a social upheaval and the peasants were liable to march against the manors. There was a possibility of combining the class struggle with the liberation movement. This chance was not taken advantage of because the moderate leaders hoped instead that a national insurrection would stop the peasant upheaval. This lack of consistent tactics on the part of the revolutionaries plunged the country headlong into disaster.

THE DISASTER OF 1846

Galicia was, for many reasons, the worst trouble spot in Poland in the 1840's. Economically, it was the most backward area. Agriculture was on so low a level that it did not provide enough food for the peasant smallholders. Serfdom and labour service were still in force. The introduction of money rent was prohibited and the exploitation of peasants by the gentry was more and more oppressive. Though the patents issued by Joseph II permitted the peasants to file lawsuits against the manor and to complain to the district commissioner, such lawsuits were as a rule lost and this only increased the bitterness of the country people. The Austrian bureaucracy in principle kept watch over the feudal system in the villages but it made use of the growing class antagonism to keep the Polish gentry within bounds. Democratic propaganda collapsed in the 1830's when the local underground centres had been broken up and became active again on a very small scale only shortly before the rising. The left-wing conspirators could not muster sufficient support in the impoverished and backward small towns. Preparations for the rising were undertaken by the gentry and this sufficed to arouse the suspicion and anxiety of the country people.

The time for the nation-wide rising was set for Shrovetide, 22 February, 1846. Yet in some places, especially the Tarnów region, the peasants had been arming themselves several weeks beforehand, they placed guards along the roads and attacked travellers. In order to forestall the peasant movement, the conspirators pretended that there was an imminent danger of arrests, and advanced the date for the attack on Tarnów by four days. The Austrian chief of the district, Breinl, appealed to the peasants, promising them liberty and imperial favour if they marched against the insurgents. On that momentous night some peasant groups stopped the Polish armed units as they advanced on Tarnów, took them prisoner and delivered them to the Austrians. The attack on Tarnów was halted and the following days saw the whole peasantry of central Galicia rise against the manors.

Specially appointed members of the National Government gathered in Cracow to await the outbreak of the revolution. Cracow, this last free morcel of Polish territory was to sound the call for battle. Instead, the Austrian army marched into the town on 18 February. Simultaneously mass arrests by the Prussians were reported from Poznań (as a result of treachery among the landowning circles). Thus the best organized region, the Poznań area, was itself unable to fight. The leaders, who had remained in Cracow, began by cancelling the call to revolt, but later they decided nevertheless to start it. Owing to the avalanche of preventive arrests and to contradictory orders issued by the leaders, the plan of a simultaneous rising of all Polish districts was frustrated completely. In less than a score of places small groups rose in revolt, but they soon disbanded themselves realizing that the country as a whole remained immobile.

In Cracow, however, street fighting broke out on 20 February. It was followed up by peasants in the neighbourhood taking up arms. Three days later the Austrian General Collin retreated from the city with his tiny army corps and retired to the Silesian border. On 22 February the National Government came out into the open in Cracow. It comprised Jan Tyssowski, Ludwik Gorzkowski and Aleksander Grzegorzewski. A manifesto was published announcing equality for all citizens, abolishing labour services and rents without compensation for the squires, and offering state lands to volunteers who would participate in the rising. These provisions were somewhat wider in scope than those of the Poitiers Manifesto.

On 22 February, all attacks against the partitioning Powers except those in the Cracow area had already been squashed. A movement against the gentry was spreading in central Galicia. Peasants attacked the manors and plundered them killing the gentry and their agents. The fate of the country depended on whether or not the two elements could be merged, on whether the peasant class struggle could become a part of a nation-wide agrarian revolution. Dembowski tried to bring this about when he arrived in Cracow, but he found that the situation had changed, because Tyssowski had dismissed his colleagues within two days and had proclaimed himself dictator. Dembowski persuaded Tyssowski to appoint him as secretary and went to work with a feverish activity. He issued new, more radical appeals, sent propaganda agents into the villages, organized a club, set up a revolutionary press and warded off attacks on the government undertaken by the conservatives. All these desperate efforts proved in vain. An Austrian column was marching from the east on Cracow and its commander, Colonel Benedek, was openly inciting the peasants to fight against the gentry. A small detachment sent out against him was defeated and routed near Gdów, Dembowski was shot by the Austrians in the Cracow suburb, Podgórze, where he was trying to meet the peasants at the head of an unarmed procession. After Dembowski's death the collapse followed. Tyssowski took the remainder of the revolutionary units out of the city and handed their arms over to the Prussians. Cracow was occupied by the Russians and the Austrians. Several months later the area of the Free City was formally incorporated into the Austrian State.

Austrian bureaucracy knew how to make use of the peasants to counteract the Polish uprising at the decisive moment. This does not mean that the peasants rose to defend the Emperor, or that their movement was the work of the Austrians. The peasants had risen spontaneously against feudal oppression while in many regions they fought the partitioning Powers as well. The village of Chochołów in the Tatras participated openly in the national uprising, mobilized by the teacher Jan Andrusikiewicz. The Austrians, in turn, employed force to pacify the peasants when they were not confronted by the insurgents.

Within a few days peasant movement resulted in the ransacking of some 400 manors and about a thousand casualties. Labour services virtually ceased to be performed throughout central Galicia and soon the resistance movement spread to the rest of the province. The peasants, moreover, found a leader, a villager from Smarzowa, by the name of Jakub Szela, who presided over the lynching of his masters, the Bogusz family, then surrounded himself with armed bodyguards. He secured the obedience of the peasants within an area of several score square kilometres and negotiated with the Austrian authorities.

The Vienna government praised the Galician peasants before the world for their loyalty to the Emperor, but it was in no mood to grant them concessions at the expense of the gentry. Peasant resistance was put down by a large number of troops with the help of mass floggings. Szela was interned, and the Galician villages were once more compelled to perform labour service. Nonetheless, the suppressed *jacquerie* had established certain incontrovertible facts which had their repercussions even beyond the boundaries of the province.

The world-wide publicity given to the incidents in Galicia, utterly discredited Metternich's régime and convinced the conservatives throughout the Hapsburg monarchy and abroad of the necessity to make concessions to the people. This explains the eagerness with which agrarian reform was introduced in Austria, Germany, Hungary and elsewhere, as early as 1848. Another result of the Galician uprising was that it encouraged peasants to rise in other countries in Rumania, Lombardy and France. In the Congress Kingdom by 1846 whole districts had ceased to render labour service. The Tsar made haste to issue an ukase forbidding the eviction of peasants and any arbitrary raising of labour dues, but even then it was difficult to get the peasants to return to order. To sum up, even though it failed, the peasant movement had strengthened class consciousness in the villages throughout Poland.

The movement had failed because of the fundamental error the peasants had committed by letting themselves be used against the Cracow insurgents who were promising them freedom. The Cracow rising was crushed, and this fact left the peasants isolated against the Austrian troops. It was a serious defeat for the Polish democratic group. The peasant on whom the insurgents had counted turned against them, mainly because of the mistakes the democratic conspirators had committed.

The year 1846 shook the entire nation to its roots. Margrave Aleksander Wielopolski reproached Metternich for his perfidy in a widely publicized open letter. He advised the Polish gentry to give up the idea of independence and to merge with Russia on the basis of a voluntary association. This was a sign of the growing tendency among Poland's aristocracy to seek accomodation with foreign rule. The democrats did not wish to give up hope of winning over the people to support the national cause, but there was the fear of another massacre, and care had to be taken more than ever less slogans be issued against the gentry. It took the left-wing conspirators defeated in 1846 a long time to recover from the blow, and a long time before they again found a common language with the peasants.

In spite of the grave consequences which followed the Galician peasant movement, one can hardly overlook the fact that in its historical perspective it did have some positive effects. Though fraught with tragic mistakes, the national movement attacked the very foundations of the feudal system and speeded up the abolition of serfdom and the labour services. The liberation of the peasant from the yoke of feudalism was the indispensable prelude to his achieving political maturity and becoming nationally conscious. Inasmuch as the Tarnów *jacquerie* hastened the emancipation of the peasant, it also advanced the cause of Poland's independence.

THE POZNAŃ RISING OF 1848

The events that had taken place in Galicia were a prelude to the revolution which swept across Europe two years later. The demands of a bourgeoisie for power, the desire of oppressed nations to liberate themselves, the new demands of the peasants, and the first demands of a young working class were the issues that caused the outbreak of a long series of stormy events which began in Italy and France and later shook central Europe.

The 1848 Revolution often called "Springtime of the Nations" placed the Polish question once more on the order of the day. 1846 had reminded Europe of that nation of revolutionaries who were always ready to ally themselves with any subversive force. Both the revolutionary leaders and the defenders of the old order realized that the Poles would rise against the Holy Alliance, if there was a revolution, that they would liberate themselves if the revolution was victorious, or go down with the revolution if it failed. On the eve of the French February uprising, the national celebrations staged by Polish exiles in Paris, London and Brussels were occasions for the local revolutionaries to demonstrate. Marx and Engels fraternally embraced by Lelewel were also among the speakers. The leaders of the Communist Union declared that Polish independence was indispensable and that the prerequisite for her liberation was the agrarian revolution. By the end of February 1848 the people of Paris had overthrown the monarchy of Louis Philippe. Three weeks later street fighting broke out in Vienna and in Berlin. Two of the partitioning Powers were in a state of crisis and two parts of Poland therefore seemed to have regained their freedom of action, but they were not ready for the struggle after their recent defeat of 1846.

The Grand Duchy of Poznań had just witnessed the trial of the participants in the earlier rising. Sentenced to death or to terms of imprisonment they were awaiting their fate at the Moabit prison in Berlin. Some of their comrades, who had been released were again agitating in Poland, distributing leaflets in towns and villages about the imminent revolt. The news of the victory of the revolution in Berlin caught them by surprise on 20 March. If the Germans supported the cause of freedom, they would certainly fight Tsarism in alliance with the Poles. This hope caused the Poznań "Plebeians" to postpone storming the Citadel which threatened the city.

They were also checked by liberal landowners, like Maciej Mielżyński and Gustaw Potworowski. These two leaders of the "organic work" movement (after Marcinkowski's recent death) now joined the revolution in order

Poles in Berlin after their Release from the Moabit Prison, 1848

to "legalize" it. They calculated that the uprising might induce the government to grant the province home rule at least. In fact the Prussian authorities were too frightened to oppose the first Polish demands. A National Committee was speedily elected in Poznań and a delegation was despatched to Berlin. Its members, mostly moderates, presented no claims, but merely asked the King for a "national reorganization". At that time the Berlin population was cheering and welcoming the Polish prisoners released from Moabit prison. Mierosławski announced a Polish-German crusade against Tsar Nicholas. He advocated the speedy rearmament of Poland, but without provoking the Germans.

Throughout the Poznań area detachments of riflemen and scythemen were hastily formed. The poor people in town and country were eager to take up in the hope of finding better living conditions in liberated Poland. Upon an appeal issued by the National Committee, the gentry joined the movement assuming leadership of the subdistrict committees, in order to prevent "excesses", and to keep the mass of peasant volunteers in check. The Left Wing saw in these revolutionary cadres the beginnings of a national armed force, while the right wing treated the armaments as a demonstration and a means of bringing pressure upon the government in order to obtain the desired concessions. The new Prussian government composed of liberals, seemed to yield to the Poles, but the generals and the local bureaucracy who had recovered their nerve after the first scare, were already preparing to repress the Polish movement. Dominated by the moderates, the National Committee failed to take advantage of its initial opportunity to attack. It put off proclaiming radical principles and confined its activity to one single province.

By the end of March Mierosławski had arrived in Poznań and took over personal command of the Committee's War Department. He promised to revive the plans which had been frustrated two years before of having two revolutionary armies coming from Poznań and Galicia to attack Warsaw simultaneously. Yet Mierosławski had no confidence in the men with whom he was to collaborate. He suspected the landed gentry of harbouring counter-revolutionary designs, and accused the peasants of thinking solely of massacring their masters. According to him, Poland's future should be assured by the "Polish middle class", meaning the impoverished gentry and the urban poor. Out of these elements, and especially out of officers returned from abroad, he wanted to create cadres for the regular army of his dreams. While he thus dreamt, he neglected to advance the cause of the revolution.

Meanwhile, the Prussian government sent General Willisen, a liberal friendly to the Poles, to Poznań, with the instructions to pacify the province by persuasion because German opinion was still favourably disposed towards the Poles. Willisen promised the members of the National Committee that the local administration of the province might be taken over by the Poles; but he demanded in return that the Polish volunteer detachments be disbanded. The Right Wing agreed to this but dared not force a surrender in the face of 20,000 armed insurgents. This difficult task was given to the democrats, Libelt and Stefański. Mortally afraid of an armed struggle, which might cause the peasants to rise against the gentry, they, too, agreed to concessions. Negotiations took place on 11 April at Jarosławiec, at a moment when the Prussian columns were preparing to attack the insurgent camp at Środa. In the course of feverish debates Mierosławski succeeded in forcing Willisen to agree to let some 3000 soldiers keep their arms temporarily.

After concluding the Jarosławiec agreement, the landowners considered that the revolutionary movement had come to an end. It was exceedingly difficult to keep down the revolt of the scythemen. In pleading with them to disband, each volunteer was promised 3 morgs (3/4 ha) of land. Playing thus into Willisen's hands, the gentry presumed that they would be given authority over the province. The Prussian army, however, were ruthlessly pacifying the country, while the local bourgeoisie and the German settlers armed against the Poles. The Prussian government refused to reorganize one part of the province which they maintained was "German". The mass of the peasantry was eager to obtain arms in order to retaliate against the Prussian provocation. Fearing an armed conflict which might degenerate into a social revolution, the Right Wing forced the National Committee's hand at the end of April, and compelled it to adopt a resolution agreeing to total disarmament. The resolution was rejected by Mierosławski who commanded the four military "camps", which had been established after the Jarosławiec agreement. These camps might have become the nucleus of a nation-wide insurrection. Mierosławski, however, did nothing to establish the necessary links with the peasant movement spreading throughout the province. The Prussian army pacified the villages and then turned against the Polish camps. Mierosławski succeeded in concentrating his forces and repelled the assault of one of the Prussian columns at Miłosław on 30 April. Two days later he won another battle at Sokołowo but suffered heavy casualties.

There was still a chance of rousing the population to fight against the foreign enemy. The gentry officers exerted all their efforts to forestall a struggle which might bring disaster, if it was lost, or prove an even greater calamity, if it degenerated into a victorious revolution. Some officers deserted, others encouraged the soldiers to desert, while still others began negotiating with the enemy behind Mierosławski's back. Within ten days they succeeded in dispersing the unit several thousand strong of the victors of Miłosław. A lawyer by the name of Jakub Krotowski (Krauthofer), who was one of the most enterprising local democrats, organized a partisan movement in the Poznań area. These efforts, however, were soon frustrated.

After the province of Poznań had been pacified by force, the "reorganization" scheme was abandoned. Quite obviously, a revolutionary movement, which had not gone beyond the boundaries of one province, had to yield to the superior force of the enemy. The Congress Kingdom, intimidated by Paskevich's army of occupation, did not rise in 1848 and the conspirators working in Warsaw decided not to call a revolt. Galicia did not stir either. The Poznań area thus remained isolated, but the importance of the events which took place there in the course of seven stormy weeks went beyond the boundaries of the province.

The greatest surprise of the Poznań rising was the behaviour of the peasants. The poor people of the countryside, farm hands, day labourers and smallholders, were in the front line, but even the yeomen farmers joined them in opposing the Prussians when their gentry leaders no longer wanted to fight. This was proof of the awakening to a higher degree of national consciousness among the masses of this economically advanced province, a fact which warmed the hearts of all patriots after the recent Galician tragedy.

The propertied classes, in turn, were less prone than ever before to undertake revolutionary ventures. In the presence of Prussian oppression, however, they were compelled to keep up their opposition to the government, though obviously this was a legal opposition. Their principal aim was thenceforth to enlist the support of the middle classes, the bourgeoisie and the wealthier peasants, calling upon them to defend the faith, the Polish language and their native land. Anti-German propaganda adopted from this time onwards

Polish participation in the European revolutions, 1848

Legend:
- International boundaries
- Boundaries of the Congress Kingdom of Poland
- Boundaries of the German Union, 1815–1866
- Centres of revolutionary fighting with Polish participation
- Major battles of the Mickiewicz Legion and of the Polish Legion in Hungary
- Major centres of the revolutionary movement in the Grand Duchy of Poznań, in Silesia and Galicia

PWN Warsaw 1979

nationalistic overtones and the Catholic clergy played an important role in this respect.

While freedom of the press and freedom of association still existed in Prussia, some liberal leaders founded in 1848 the Polish League, a mass organization to ensure the legal protection of Polish national identity. The League was soon forbidden to function, but the guiding principles it had laid down were followed throughout the second half of the century. The impact of Germanization, which threatened all Polish social classes in Prussia, facilitated the task of the upper classes in their call for solidarity and weakened the position of the radicals.

The third surprise of the revolution in the Prussian-dominated zone was the national awakening in Pomerania and Silesia. Before that time, these provinces had taken little part in patriotic activity within the Poznań area. Now, the Gdańsk area of Pomerania joined first the Poznań movement, and then the Polish League. From this time they continued to work hand in hand with Great Poland. As for Silesia, the revolutionary movement of 1848 comprised both Poles and Germans. The tide of peasant risings extended to Polish and German districts, Polish and German revolutionaries jointly defended the barricades in Wrocław. Independently of this movement, the Silesian Poles developed a national movement of their own. Upper Silesia elected mostly Polish peasants to the Berlin National Assembly. On their behalf Father Józef Szafranek tabled a motion demanding equality of rights for the Polish language. Polish political clubs and other societies were founded, and the "Dziennik Górnośląski" (Upper Silesian Daily), a paper with a pronounced national inclination, began publication. Józef Lompa himself was among the more active members of the movement. All these Polish organizations in Silesia were disbanded when the revolution collapsed. They had issued no call for independence and were associated only indirectly with the Poznań national movement, but even this limited activity was considerable step forward in the national thinking of this area and of the first collective effort undertaken to defend Polish national rights.

When the German revolution was defeated in the first half of 1849, Polish nationals lost the civil rights which had been granted them, but the revolution did have a beneficial effect on the progress of the agrarian reform. Under the pressure of the peasant movement in which Silesia had played an important role, the Berlin Assembly was compelled to revise the settlement laws. Smallholders were now included in the arrangement and could own their land. All peasants were permitted to buy out their landlord's rights by instalments and some other dues were abolished without compensation to the landlords. Thus the revolution of 1848 destroyed feudal institutions that had existed in the areas of the Prussian part of Poland. By the middle of the century, this province entered an area of advanced capitalism.

GALICIA IN 1848

After the revolution in Vienna, the Austrian part of Poland, Galicia, was granted more freedom of action than was allowed in the Prussian sector, particularly as a result of the precarious conditions prevailing in the Hapsburg monarchy. Galicia, however, was in no position to take advantage of the opportunity offered and the revolutionary movement in that area remained rather weak, although it did last much longer.

As soon as the first news of the events in Vienna reached Cracow and Lwów, street demonstrations forced the local authorities to release all political prisoners. The liberal bourgeois leaders in Lwów under Smolka's leadership presented a petition to the Emperor to grant them civil rights, to institute Polish as the official language in the administration, the courts and the schools, and to abolish labour service. This petition was also signed by many landowners. The delegation sent to Vienna was carried away by revolutionary fervour and went beyond the contents of the petition, demanding national independence. Naturally, there was hardly a chance of winning this fight single-handed. The peasants were indeed suspicious of the Polish nationalist movement and, after the experiences of 1846, no one dared to proclaim their emancipation because it might give rise to a new social upheaval. A National Committee was set up in Cracow with the participation of members of the Versailles Central Board, who had returned home from Paris. Even that Committee did not go beyond calling upon the landed gentry to liberate the peasants from labour dues of their own free will. Only a very few of the landowners responded to the appeal, although everybody was aware that labour services could not be perpetuated. Other questions were also involved, especially the compensation of the landlords and the peasants' rights of access to woods and pastures. Count Franz Stadion, the Austrian governor, availed himself of the gentry's hesitation to announce that the Emperor had ordered the abolition of all labour services in Galicia and to promise that the landlords would receive compensation from the government. Thus he gained favour with the countryside and weakened the opposition of the landed gentry. Now the Austrian army could clamp down on the revolutionary movement which was brewing in Galicia. After brief street skirmishes, Cracow was shelled on April 26. The local Committee was disbanded and the returned exiles were expelled from the town.

In the meantime, the Austrian Constitution granted freedom of association and freedom of speech to Galicia as well. A National Council was set up in Lwów with a large membership, which sought to centralize all political activities in the province. Similar councils were established with the participation of the bourgeoisie and the urban intelligentsia in other cities and towns. Moreover, units of the National Guard, wearing uniforms reminiscent of the Polish pattern, were organized in some towns. Publication was started of a number of political dailies and general elections to the Vienna parliament took place. This vigorous movement, however, dared not to resist the occupying power. For one thing, it could not count on the support of the peasants, while on the other hand, the Ukrainians in Eastern Galicia experienced a political awakening in opposition to the Poles. Both gentry and intelligentsia in the Lwów area ignored the existence of another nationality in Galicia and refused the Ukrainians the very civil liberties they were trying to obtain from Vienna. This conflict between the two nationalities was exploited by the Austrian bureaucracy.

Under the pressure of revolutionary events the majority of the Polish landowners joined the movement and supported the National Council. Later, however, their own personal interests gained the upper hand and caused them to change their attitude. In the summer of 1848, conservative lobbies were created in an effort to get government support against the Polish revolutionary movement. The National Council was about to split when internal events precipitated the collapse of the revolutionary movement. The reactionary forces destroyed the working class revolution in Vienna and the same happened in Lwów. The Austrian commanders instigated street fighting and shelled the city, crushing the resistance of the barricades on 2 November, before it could spread. In consequence the Polish National Councils were dispersed and the national guards disbanded. The Polish journals closed down and military rule held sway once more in the province.

Though the revolution failed, its greatest gain survived, in the form of the emancipation of the peasants, which was assured throughout the Austrian Empire by a special act of parliament. The reform, which had been forced through at the time of upheaval by the solidarity of the peasants themselves, went far beyond what had been granted by earlier reforms in Prussia. It provided that everyone, even the least smallholder, should own his land. Freed from serfdom and labour dues, the peasants obtained their land theoretically free of charge; in reality, the fact that the gentry were promised an indemnity from the government resulted in the peasants having to pay compensation of a kind, though the amounts were reduced and well concealed because the indemnity fund was to debit the peasant taxpayer as well. Stadion's first announcement guaranteed the peasants their grazing and forest rights, but a few years later at the time reactionaries were in power, the validity of this right was generally denied. The villages with their small, scattered holdings and an acute lack of fire wood and grazing grounds, remained economically dependent upon the manors. Nonetheless, the act of abolishing feudalism had opened the road to capitalism in the Austrian part of Poland as well.

Seven months of political freedom revitalized that most backward province where, until that time, only a very few groups of the intelligentsia had taken part in underground activities. In 1848 thousands of people, from the aristocrats down to the peasants, consciously participated in public life. During this period, also, political programmes and attitudes were established that were to be characteristic of this province until the end of the century.

There was the conservative programme of the landowners looking to the Crown for support against the social movements; the programme of the "democrats", or rather of the bourgeois liberals defending civil and national rights, but powerless before the government because they had no mass backing; and the social programme of the peasants who demanded "forests and grazing grounds" and laboured under the illusion that they might win favour with the Emperor. Finally, the essential feature of the conditions prevailing in Galicia was the weakness of the revolutionary-democratic element, which might have lent staunch support to the peasants and won them over to the fight for national independence. This movement had a spokesman in the person of Julian Goslar, the son of a manor official. The young Goslar had worked closely with Dembowski and had been imprisoned several times for his political activities. He was hanged in 1852 after another revolutionary incident. There was no one in the succeeding generation to emulate him in this economically backward country, which was still haunted by the memories of 1846.

POLES IN EUROPEAN REVOLUTIONARY MOVEMENTS

The events that took place in March 1848 caused crowds of exiles to flock back to the country. Before long the defeat of the Poznań rising gave the signal for a new migration towards the West. The former émigrés were joined by new young exiles fleeing from oppression or looking for other battlefields to fight for the cause of freedom.

By the middle of 1848 the European revolution was entering its crucial stage, but it had not yet broken down. Bitter political struggles were in full swing in France and in Germany. In Italy and in Hungary the fate of the revolution was being decided on the battlefield. Exiled Poles were ready to engage in any of these struggles, confident that the cause of progress was their own cause. From private to general, they were welcomed everywhere with open arms, as faithful and reliable allies of every revolutionary movement.

In Italy, the national movement began even earlier than the Paris February Revolution. Through his agents, Adam Czartoryski appealed to "liberal" Pope Pius IX to create a Polish legion to fight on Italy's side against the Austrians. At the beginning of his pontificate Pius IX had shown favour to the Poles; but he did not want war with Austria and refused to agree to the scheme for a legion. Mickiewicz then appeared in Rome on his own. Received by the Pope, he called upon him to back Poland's cause and the cause of freedom in the world. Conservative compatriots regarded Mickiewicz as a dangerous revolutionary and made it impossible for him to extend his stay in Rome. The Polish poet summoned a handful of enthusiastic young men and proclaimed at the meeting on 29 March, 1848, the "Set of Principles" (*Skład zasad*) of the Polish Legion. It was a poet's revolutionary creed, couched in lofty language. Mickiewicz's idea was to create a Polish army unit at the side of the Italians which would attract and enrol all Slav soldiers serving in the Hapsburg army. In response to Mickiewicz's call several hundred Polish exiles hurried to Italy. One of their companies commanded by Colonel Mikołaj Kamieński took part in the war of 1848 in Lombardy. Another one fought a year later in defence of Republican Rome. In Milan, in Genoa, and in Florence the Polish legionaries fought on the side of the people against the reactionary forces. In 1849 Mickiewicz himself became the editor of the newspaper "La Tribune des Peuples" published in Paris. The editorial board comprised democrats of different nationalities, and the aim pursued by the paper was to act on French soil as a defender of all nations who were fighting for liberty. "La Tribune des Peuples" in which Mickiewicz published excellent articles, cooperated with the French leftists and was suspended when the reactionaries gained the upper hand.

At that time in 1849, Mierosławski, the former leader of the Poznań insurgents, still commanded Italian forces in Sicily and later on German forces in Baden. The conservative General Chrzanowski was at the head of the Piedmontese army which was beaten at Novara. Agents of the Polish Democratic Society took part in the German uprising in Dresden. Earlier, General Józef Bem, who had become famous as artillery commander during the November Insurrection, gallantly defended besieged Vienna. After the fall of that city, he left for Hungary looking for another battlefield.

The Hungarian uprising directed against Austria was the last great military undertaking of this revolutionary period and all Polish patriots looked to it with great hope. Several thousand young Poles secretly crossed the Carpathian Mountains and fought gallantly in dozens of battles under the leadership of General Józef Wysocki. The Commander-in-chief in Hungary at various times was General Dembiński. The most famous among the Poles was General Bem who was appointed commander of the Transylvanian army and recaptured that province which had been all but lost to the enemy; he pursued a strategy of constant attack, never lost his temper in defeat, and was beloved by his subordinates and respected by the local population.

During the Hungarian campaign the Poles were confronted with the thorny Slav problem. 1848 awakened political consciousness in many nations subjected to the Hapsburg monarchy, the Czechs, Slovaks, South Slavs and Rumanians. Polish scholars and politicians made, in the preceding years, a contribution to the national revival of the Czechs, Slovaks and South Slavs, but the Poles opposed Panslavism inspired by Russia which appeared to them as a tool of Tsarist policy. The year 1848 should have united all Slavs under the banner of freedom. All of them were soon in conflict with the Hungarians whose leaders refused to treat them on a basis of equality. The imperial government was not slow in taking advantage of these antagonisms and exploiting them against Hungary. Thus the Czechs, the Croats, and the

Transylvanian Rumanians, or rather the leading groups of their urban intelligentsia joined the reactionary camp. Most of these minorities were Slavs; and the idea of all Slavs being brothers met with a lively response in Poland. A large Polish delegation attended the Slav Congress in Prague in June, 1848. Polish patriots never tired in their endeavour to get all Slavs to join the revolutionary movements. Thus, for example, they made contact with the Left Wing in Bohemia and induced them to join the struggle against the Hapsburgs. In Hungary the agents of the Hôtel Lambert tried to convince the Hungarian authorities that the granting of equal rights would induce national minorities to stop their collaboration with the reactionaries.

When Nicholas I sent Paskevich's armies to help the Austrians, he declared in his manifesto that he would fight not only the Hungarian, but also the Polish rebels. Soon after, the Hungarian army laid down its arms before the Russians, while the Polish legionaries under Bem and Dembiński sought refuge in Turkish dominions. Poles were to be found in the revolutionary camp up to the very last. The logic of events demanded even that the Czartoryskis work hand in hand with the revolutionaries, if they wanted to do anything for Poland, whereas those Polish conservatives who aligned themselves openly with the party of "order" actually renounced their country's independence.

The same relationship to the Polish question prevailed in various other political camps in Europe. The united reactionaries were firm and systematic in combatting all Polish aspirations. The French and German liberals proclaimed their friendly feelings for Poland, as long as they were backing the revolution; but they turned against the Poles the more fiercely, the faster their conversion to the counter-revolution had taken place. Only genuine revolutionaries remained faithful to their friendship for Poland. This was true particularly of the leaders of the working class. The "Neue Rheinische Zeitung", published in Cologne, condemned in 1848 the old outrage of Poland's partitions, as much as the new outrages committed by the Prussians in the Poznań province. It commended the services rendered by the Poles to the revolutionary cause and declared repeatedly that "the establishment of a democratic Poland is the first condition for the establishment of a democratic Germany".

POLISH CULTURE IN THE ROMANTIC PERIOD

The period of the greatest national calamities experienced after the November Insurrection became, paradoxically, a time of unusual achievements in art, poetry, music, painting and the humanities. The talents which had been maturing in the preceding decade seemed to have acquired depth in the atmosphere of defeat and were broadened by their experience of exile. They assumed the mission of showing the nation the new paths ahead. At a time

Adam Mickiewicz

when Polish politicians were either losing their contacts with the country, or had to go underground, patriotic poetry reached ever wider circles and the authors achieved in the eyes of the people the rank of teachers of the nation, of national "bards". All institutes of higher learning, with the exception of Cracow, were closed in Poland. Systematic research, especially in the field of science, was rendered difficult. These were the reasons for the one-sided development of Polish learning and culture directed towards the study of humanities.

Juliusz Słowacki

Contemplating the disaster that had come upon Poland, the great Romantic poets devoted themselves almost entirely to the task of digging deep into the meaning of the nation's history. In *Dziady* (Forefathers' Eve) Mickiewicz contended with God himself over the martyrdom of Poland; in *Księgi pielgrzymstwa* (Books of Pilgrimage) he tried to outline for the exiles a model programme for the fighters for liberty. In *Pan Tadeusz* he evoked the unforgettable image of a vigorous, living country, with a treasure chest of emotions, for a nation of prisoners and exiles. During the same period Juliusz

Słowacki, Mickiewicz's undaunted rival, was writing *Kordian*, the drama of the gentry revolutionaries, while in *Grób Agamemnona* (Agamemnon's Tomb) he hurled his indictment against Poland's gentry-tainted past; in *Beniowski* he settled his accounts with the émigré groups and coteries, dazzling the reader at once with the masterly handling of the poetic form and an extraordinary blend of concealed feeling, irony, and subtle witticism. The third man of the great Romantic trinity, Zygmunt Krasiński, proceeded from a conservative position and took up the topic of the impending social revolution which was disturbing Europe. His *Nieboska komedia* (Undivine Comedy) was an apocalyptic vision of the ultimate clash between a corrupt aristocracy and the plebeian rabble. The works of these "bards" served to inspire several generations of Poles.

Their poetry did not propose a practical way out of the tragic reality of the present, but proclaimed only the mystic creed that Poland, exalted to the figure of a "Christ" or a "Winkelried" among the nations, would some day rise from the dead, as had Christ. Polish idealistic philosophy took the same line, with Cieszkowski, Trentowski and Libelt transposing Hegel's concepts to meet the requirements of Polish Messianism which promised the martyr nation an era when "the Holy Ghost" would descend to deliver its people. The most extreme type of Polish Messianism was the doctrine of Andrzej Towiański, whose teachings directed his disciples to redeem the nation and the world by exercising their willpower and raising their moral standards. For a number of years Towianism held sway over many brilliant minds, among them Mickiewicz and Słowacki, a fact which prejudiced their creative talents.

Polish historiography followed a different line, largely owing to Lelewel. Domiciled in Brussels, he was involved continuously in problems of his exiled countrymen which he could not influence directly. He gained the stature, in the eyes of his compatriots and those of strangers, of an ideological patriarch of Polish democracy. Foreigners considered him an excellent connoisseur of medieval numismatics and historical geography. For his compatriots, he created an optimistic concept of national history. Communal institutions peculiar to Poland since time immemorial, which had been distorted in the course of centuries by the influence of the magnates and by those who aped foreign customs, would be reestablished in a vivid and liberated Poland. This philosophy of history became the basis of all programmes of Polish democracy in this period. Lelewel himself and Mickiewicz, professor of Slavonic literatures at the Collège de France, were the main spokesmen for Polish learning and culture in the eyes of progressive Europe.

In Poland creative writing developed along different lines according to the means of expression and upon the political point of view. Aleksander Fredro, an original playwright, produced his best comedies soon after the November Insurrection, *Zemsta* (Vengeance), *Śluby panieńskie* (Maidens' Vows), and *Dożywocie* (Life Annuity). He did not bore his audiences with any political problems, but enchanted them with the charm of his dialogue and scintillating humour. Reaping success from the very start, his plays have remained in the repertory of Polish theatres. Apart from Fredro, the writings of the conservative authors were tainted with a clear ideology. They defended the time-honoured traditions and customs of the gentry and contrasted them with the progressive "alien" ideas, either in the form of a historical novel, as for instance in Henryk Rzewuski's *Listopad* (November), or in rhymed tales like those by Wincenty Pol. The liberal trend of advocating moderate reform and "organic work" found its medium in the contemporary novels popularized by prolific writers like J. I. Kraszewski and J. Korzeniowski. The realistic novel of the period usually dwelt on the topic of evolution and changes occurring in the society of the landed gentry. It is significant, however, that the fate of the peasant gets sympathetic consideration in these novels.

A third trend in literature was inspired by the democratic ideology. Here, the poetic form was preferred, and quite often anonymous verses made the rounds. The main exponents of this concept, which was concentrated on the impending insurrection, were the Warsaw Bohemians closely allied with Dembowski who consistently exposed the hypocrisy of salon society, the so-called Enthusiast Circle fighting for the emancipation of women, and in Poznań Ryszard Berwiński, author of a revolutionary *Marsz w przyszłość* (March into the Future).

In 1845 the impending agrarian revolution was reflected in a peculiar poetic controversy. Zygmunt Krasiński was deeply shocked by the *Katechizm demokratyczny* (Democratic Catechism), whose author, Kamieński, threatened the foes of the insurrection with the death penalty. The poet protested in his *Psalm miłości* (Psalm of Love) against the propaganda directed against the gentry. He countered it with a slogan, most popular afterwards, in right-wing circles, "Z szlachtą polską polski lud" (The Polish people with the Polish gentry). Słowacki answered Krasiński with a beautiful poem declaring himself unambiguously on the side of the people and the revolution. As had been seen, Mickiewicz too was roused from his mysticism by the revolution. He served the idea of the Polish Legion and became editor of "La Tribune des Peuples".

In two fields of the arts, music and painting, Poland produced two unique talents of European stature. Fryderyk Chopin became world famous in Paris as a composer and virtuoso. In spite of the strong ties that bound him with the traditions of classical music, he introduced novel elements into piano harmony and technique. To his countrymen he was the exponent of the romantic pathos of the struggle for liberation, to the world he remained the explorer of the treasury of melodies drawn from Poland's folk music. "By birth a Varsovian, by sentiment a Pole, by his talent a citizen of the world", as Norwid beautifully said. At the same time Piotr Michałowski became one of the great romantic painters in Paris. His works portrayed scenes of village life and were a combination of brilliant modern technique with a keen realistic gift of observation. Michałowski's way of painting was a generation ahead of

Cyprian Kamil Norwid

the tastes, which prevailed in Poland at the time. His works were hardly known in the homeland and did not influence his contemporaries.

Only a very thin stratum of Poland's society was familiar with these achievements in Polish art. Poland's cultural life was stultified by a backward educational system, discouraged by foreign rule, especially in the Congress Kingdom and Galicia, and in the villages by the landowners. The problems, feelings and aspirations of the mass of the people were mirrored in the

Fryderyk Chopin

national poetry, music and philosophy, but the masses themselves did not benefit from these achievements at the time.

The era of the "three bards" came to a close after 1848, though there remained a number of romantic successors: K. Ujejski, T. Lenartowicz, M. Romanowski and W. Syrokomla, and their poems later inspired the young revolutionaries of 1863.

A man almost unknown and never understood by his contemporaries was Cyprian Kamil Norwid, a great artist, thinker and pioneer of new forms

P. Michałowski, *Portrait of an Old Peasant*

and content in the reflective lyric. In his firm belief that the country would be revived by the common people and that a new Polish art would grow from popular roots, he was likewise a man of his epoch, but what he wrote about the essence of art and the role it plays in stimulating the minds of the people in everyday life could only be understood by the third generation.

In the 1850's Warsaw once more regained its position as the main centre of Poland's intellectual and cultural life. The city was growing fast and improving, new dwelling houses and public buildings were erected, like the Vienna Railway Station, Europejski Hotel, the Land Credit Association, all designed by H. Marconi in the Renaissance style. Like Paris, Warsaw planned big arteries of communications, gas and running water were piped to the houses and horse-drawn buses came into being. The newspapers changed rapidly and became a profit-making concern. In the Wielki Theatre Stanisław Moniuszko's operas, *Halka* and *Hrabina* (The Countess), saw their first performances and aroused the patriotic feelings of the audience. The Warsaw School of Fine Arts produced a group of young painters like W. Gerson, F. Kostrzewski, J. Szermentowski and others who went into the countryside to study the landscape of the Polish village and the characteristics of the village and the peasants. In Warsaw, too, J. I. Kraszewski and Korzeniowski were writing their novels.

Intellectual activity which had been disorganized after the 1831 débâcle, began to revive in a number of quarters, such as the Cracow Scientific Society, the Poznań Society of the Friends of the Sciences, and finally also in Warsaw's Main School (Szkoła Główna). Besides history and philosophy, the physical sciences, physiology under Professor Majer, geology under Professor Zejssner, medicine under Professors Dietl and Chałubiński, began to have a share in the achievements of these institutions. Even before the January Insurrection bourgeois circles began to take a lively interest in practical and technical problems, in the worship of labour, thrift, and cautions politics, all of which foreshadowed the coming of the era of positivism. In the meantime, however, more and more attention and space was devoted in novels, in poetry and on the stage, by the artist painter, and particularly by the journalists, to the most vital issue of the day, the peasant problem.

Chapter XVII
THE PERIOD OF THE JANUARY INSURRECTION (1850–1864)

THE REVOLUTIONARY SITUATION IN RUSSIA AND POLAND

In the 1850's the Russian part of Poland was the last sector where the peasant did not own his land, where he was subjected to the authority of the manor and compelled to render labour dues. The extent of compulsory labour in the Kingdom was dwindling, though, and conversion to rents was taking place. Arbitrary eviction of peasants from the land was officially prohibited by the ukase of 1846, but the peasants were less patient in their submission to remaining feudal conditions. Backed by the Tsarist government, the landowners aimed at introducing agrarian reforms which would leave in their hands the larger part of arable land and all forests. If this happened, a considerable part of the peasantry would become complete proletarians. The peasants on private estates complained more generally against such a reform. They were striving not only to get rid of labour dues, but also to recover the land which had been taken from them, to keep their right of entering the woodland and perhaps even to divide the landlords' estates among themselves. The expected conversion to freeholds could become the starting point of a social upheaval and therefore could also become a powerful factor in the national liberation movement.

In the early 1850's, reaction got the upper hand in Europe, while Russia was still subject to the autocracy of Tsar Nicholas. The crisis came during the Crimean War of 1854–1856. This war which was waged against Russia by the western Powers did not, however, fulfil the hopes of the Polish exiles. Napoleon III and Palmerston used Poland as a trump card in their game of diplomacy, but were by no means eager to unleash a revolutionary struggle, which might serve to liberate the oppressed peoples of Europe. Nonetheless, the defeat in the Crimean War revealed the weakness of Nicholas' Russia and marked the beginning of reforms which had repercussions on conditions in Poland as well. The new Tsar, Alexander II, received a friendly welcome in Warsaw. Yet he disappointed Polish hopes when he sternly told the representatives of the gentry: *"Points de rêveries, Messieurs, point de rêveries"*. Nevertheless, the general line of approach was more liberal and this, coupled

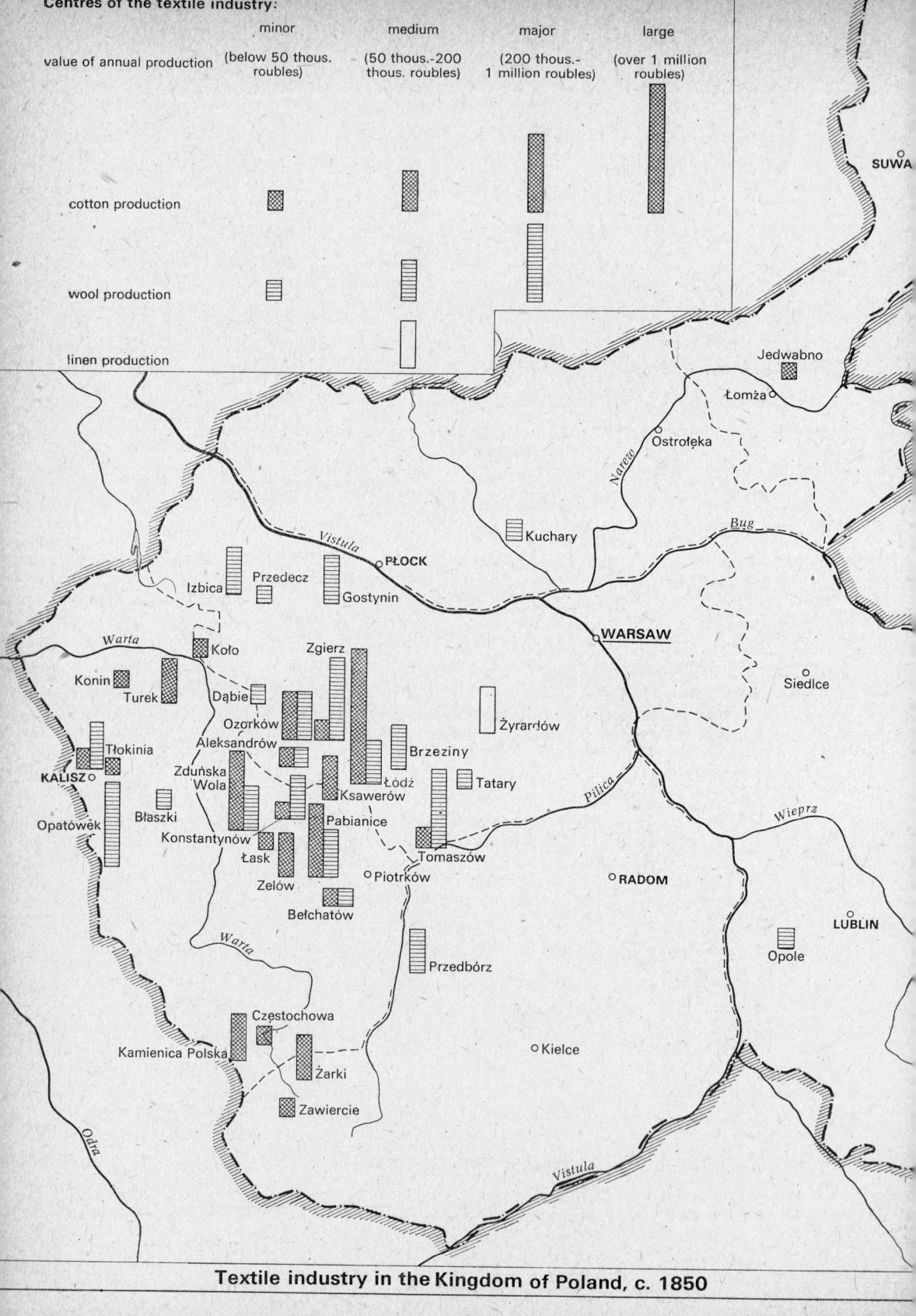

with Russia's temporary entente with France, began to ease the situation in Poland. An amnesty brought the release of many political prisoners. Censorship was relaxed. The government granted permission for the establishment of an Agricultural Society in Warsaw and for the opening of a Medical Academy. In the more liberal atmosphere of the post-Crimean period new political groups were formed within a very few years.

At the head of the Agricultural Society, which had immediately attracted several thousand landowners as members, stood the well known leader of "organic work", Count Andrzej Zamoyski. The Society pursued the economic aim of improving agricultural techniques and the social aim of achieving gradual abolition of labour services in a manner which would be as advantageous as possible to the gentry. This aim, which was of vital importance in view of peasant opposition, could not be achieved without government support. Zamoyski and his advisers had therefore no intention of antagonizing the government by presenting political demands. All they could do was to count on favourable circumstances in the future which might force St. Petersburg to seek an accomodation with the Poles.

The bourgeosie was ready to go somewhat further. Its potential power and economic influence were growing fast. In 1851 the Kingdom had been incorporated into the Rusian customs area, which assured Polish textiles a wider access to eastern markets than ever before. This quickened considerably the concentration of the textile industry in the Łódź district. In 1854 the first completely mechanized cotton mill of Scheibler started operating there. The Warsaw metallurgical plants also were equipped with machinery. In the early 1860's a few factories in Warsaw were already employing several hundred workmen each. A new branch of industry, sugar production, came into being, based mainly in the western part of the country. Warsaw was connected by rail with Vienna, Berlin and St. Petersburg, which made it a busy emporium. The local industrialists and financiers had close connexions with the banks in Berlin and Paris. They purchased real estate and used gentry capital in their enterprises. These circles had an interest in seeing the autonomy of the Kingdom increased. They were particularly eager to obtain municipal selfgovernment and equal rights for the Jews. Naturally, no thought was further from the big financiers than engaging in revolutionary activities, but among the well-to-do Warsaw intelligentsia patriotic circles existed which had the intention of influencing public opinion. An influential figure in this milieu was Edward Jurgens who was an opponent of conspiracy. The Left Wing called his circle the "Millenary Group" for its alleged desire to postpone the fight for Poland's freedom for a thousand years.

Once again, the real conspiracy was begun by university students. Several thousand Poles were studying in the universities of the Russian Empire, mostly sons of landowners and impoverished gentry families. They had their semi-public organizations for mutual aid and smaller closely-knit groups of political leaders engaded in conspiratorial activity. At the General Staff

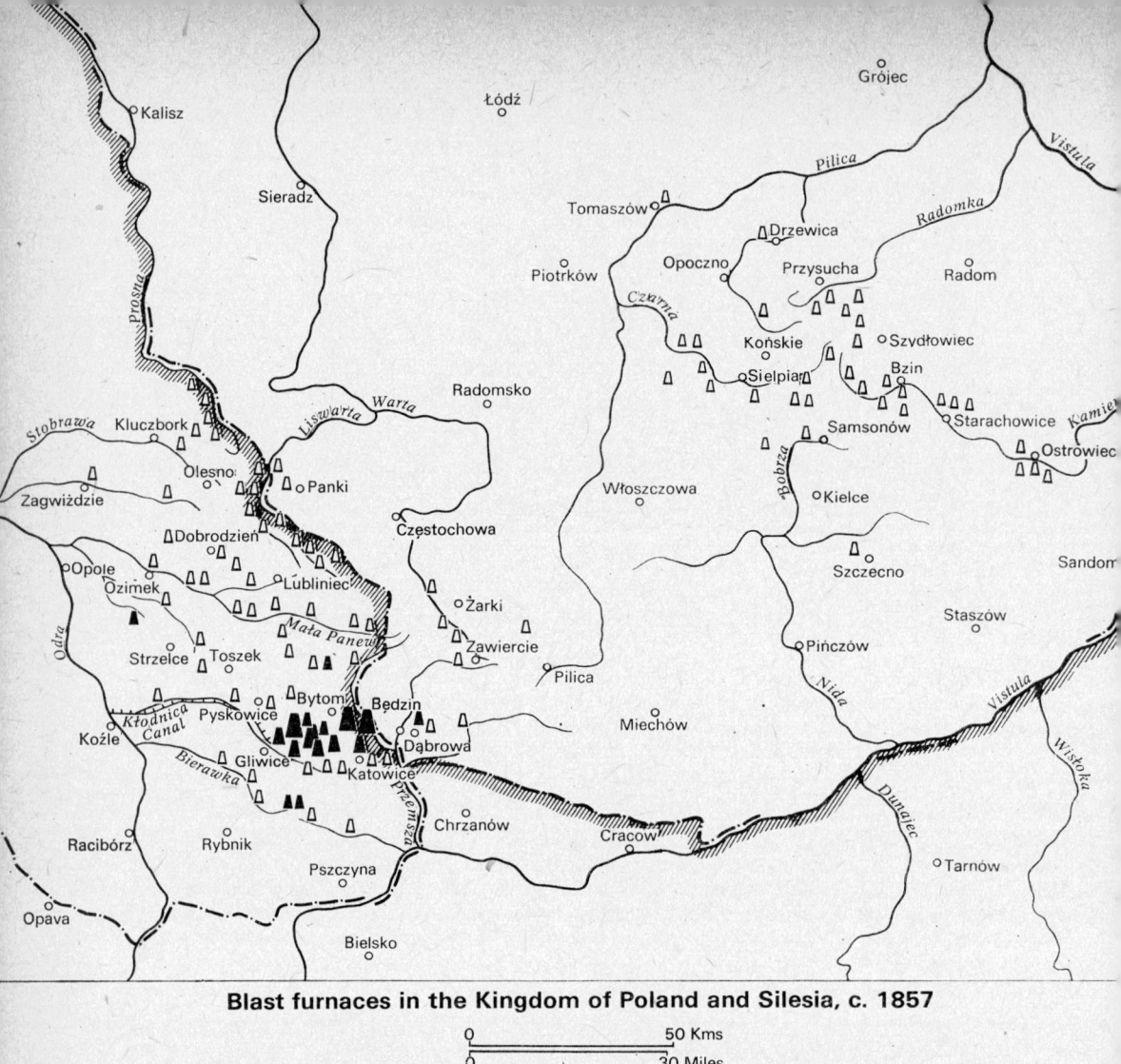

Blast furnaces in the Kingdom of Poland and Silesia, c. 1857

△ Charcoal blast furnace   ▲ Coke blast furnace   ▲ 2 coke blast furnaces   ▲ 3-7 coke blast furnaces

Academy in St. Petersburg was a group of capable Polish officers gathered round Zygmunt Sierakowski. They established contact with Russian revolutionaries, with Tchernyshevski and Dobrolyubov, and made plans for a joint action against the Tsarist system at some time in the future. Concurrently, Polish exiles in London, especially Stanisław Worcell, collaborated with Hertzen and with the editors of the famous "Kolokol" (The Bell).

The opening of the Medical Academy in Warsaw in 1857 permitted the expansion of student circles. They went on gradually from semi-public work for united aid to planning revolutionary activity and established relations with Russia and in the West. The man they accorded the greatest respect was General Mierosławski who lived in Paris. It was generally known that he belonged to the circle of Prince Napoleon Bonaparte, the radically-minded cousin of Napoleon III, and he was expected to obtain the support of the Second Empire for the coming Polish insurrection. In his public speeches in Paris Mierosławski violently attacked the doctrine of "organic work" and threatened the gentry with ruin, if they did not take part in the revolution. In Poland he had the reputation of being a Red extremist, but he could more appropriately be called a demagogue trying to establish his authority over the conspiracy, always with the illusion that "Poland's third estate" would subdue both gentry and peasants in the coming insurrection.

The Franco-Austrian war of 1859 and later the unification of Italy electrified Polish public opinion. It was possible to think that, thanks to French help, a Polish Cavour or a Polish Garibaldi would emerge and achieve a similar success. Mierosławski cooperated closely with Garibaldi, and because there was a fair possibility of a new Austro-Italian war breaking out at the end of 1860, Mierosławski sent directives to the young people of Warsaw asking them to be more audacious in their public demonstrations. The Hôtel Lambert group also encouraged the aristocracy at home to assume the leadership of the Polish cause. The crisis of the labour service system in the Russian part of Poland, the obvious weakness of the Russian Empire and the unstable international situation were all factors in awakening long repressed hopes in Poland. Once more the regaining of national independence seemed within reach. Few people in Poland counted on an early armed insurrection, but many circles yearned to demonstrate their national feeling in the open.

PATRIOTIC DEMONSTRATIONS

In June 1860 the funeral of the widow of General Sowiński, one of the soldiers of the November Insurrection, gave rise to the first public demonstration in Warsaw. In October of the same year the population of the capital openly ignored the meeting of the three monarchs (the Emperors of Russia and Austria, and the Regent of Prussia). Later in the same year, on the memorable anniversary of November 29, the people sang for the first time in the streets of Warsaw the patriotic religious hymn *Boże coś Polskę* (God who hast Poland), as well as the anthem (*Jeszcze Polska nie zginęła*). The disconcerted police did not deal effectively with these demonstrations.

The demonstrations were controlled by a number of allied students' groups. Some of them had links with Mierosławski and aimed at mobilizing the Warsaw streets, perhaps looking forward to a possible armed rising, if a European war should break out. Other groups of young men were in contact with the "Millenaries", who looked favourably upon popular restiveness because they believed that such demonstrations might bring the government to seek a compromise and introduce reforms. The patriotic spirit pervaded the petty bourgeoisie, tradesmen and factory workers and Warsaw vibrated with militant recollections of 1794 and 1830.

At the beginning of 1861 everyone expected the long promised Tsarist ukase, which was to abolish serfdom in Russia. Some agrarian unrest could be envisaged in this connexion. In February the peasant question was to be discussed at the annual Warsaw meeting of the Agricultural Society. The Polish landowners did not want the government to steal a march on them in settling this crucial problem. The "Millenaries" proposed that a political appeal be addressed to the Tsar, but Andrzej Zamoyski firmly rejected this suggestion. The Warsaw bourgeoisie decided therefore to stage demonstrations in order to put pressure on the landowners and force them to present an appeal. At the same time, the conspiratorial circles believed it possible that a real mass demonstration might lead to a clash with the army and perhaps even to revolution.

On the thirtieth anniversary of the battle of Grochów, on 25 February, 1861, the organizers led a procession carrying patriotic emblems to the market place of the Old Town. It was dispersed by the police. Two days later, on 27 February, a larger crowd demonstrated in the street, in the Krakowskie Przedmieście, one of Warsaw's main streets. A military detachment fired one volley into the crowd, killed five and wounded almost a score. Wary of the aroused people, Viceroy Gorchakov withdrew his troops to the barracks and refrained from any further repression.

The bloodshed forced the propertied classes into action. That very night a gathering in the Merchants' Club selected a Delegation from the leading representatives of Warsaw's bourgeoisie. Jointly with the leaders of the Agricultural Society, they drafted an adress to the Tsar which recalled in very general terms the historic rights of the Polish nation. In the negotiations which followed Gorchakov agreed to a solemn funeral of the five victims. The members of the Delegation tried to convince the Viceroy that they alone, if given a free hand, could prevent open revolt. At the same time they were explaining to the craftsmen and the angry students that only a dignified, calm approach and "moral" force could compel the government to grant concessions. By this manoeuvre, the Delegation kept the situation under control. The funeral of the victims was absolutely without incident although a very large crowd attended. The young revolutionary leaders could not bring themselves to issue a call to arms. The Tsarist authorities, taken aback by the extent of the movement, remained passive at the time, but had no intention of backing down on matters of principle.

The political crisis had its repercussions throughout the country. Cities and towns staged demonstrations on the Warsaw pattern, committees were formed, and occasionally some unpopular officials were forced to resign. In Łódź a crowd of weavers demolished in several factories the new machines, which had deprived them of work. Peasants, excited by the news of emancipation in the neighbouring provinces of the Empire, stopped performing labour dues. Resistance against compulsory labour extended to more than 160,000 farms in April and May 1861, and this example incited peasants to disobedience. Tenant farmers stopped paying rents, farm hands demanded land from the demesnes. To save themselves from the threatening peasant revolt, the government temporarily announced that from the autumn peasants could change from labour services to rents.

In the political field, St. Petersburg also retreated step by step, obliged to avoid an open clash with the Poles at a time of internal and external difficulties. An ukase issued by the Tsar announced the nomination of a State Council with advisory functions and the inauguration of elected urban and district councils. Margrave Aleksander Wielopolski was appointed a member of Administrative Council. Thus the government offered the Polish aristocrats a share in authority in exchange for their assistance in subduing the revolutionary movement. In order to carry out this policy Wielopolski disbanded both the Agricultural Society and the Municipal Delegation. A demonstration in protest against these measures, which took place on 8 April, was dispersed by the army; several hundred people perished in the bloody massacre on Warsaw's Plac Zamkowy.

In the general indignation which followed these reprisals, neither the Polish gentry nor the bourgeoisie saw their way clear to follow Wielopolski. On one hand, the concessions granted by the government seemed insufficient, even to the circles close to Andrzej Zamoyski. For one thing they embraced only the Congress Kingdom and ignored the interests of the Polish gentry in Lithuania, Byelorussia and the Ukraine. On the other hand, the pressure exercised by public opinion kept the landowners from entering into an agreement with the occupying Power. It they did, left-wing patriots might easily take radical step of backing the peasants against the gentry. Therefore the landowners and the bourgeoisie though accepting the Tsar's concessions, did not openly dissociate themselves from the opposition exhibited by the entire nation. Demonstrations continued in spite of vexatious behaviour by the police. The population wore mourning, patriotic hymns were sung in the churches and the people obeyed the directives of secret organizations. This propaganda spread among the poor of the urban centres. Its slogan that all creeds were equal excited the Jewish population. It tried to attract the peasants and reached out to Lithuania and to the other parts of partitioned Poland. In spite of class antagonism which divided the country, there seemed to be complete solidarity as far as the demand for independence was concerned. The government was unable to cope with the movement. In October 1861 the martial law was proclaimed in the Kingdom and troops forced their way into two of Warsaw's churches, arresting the majority of the faithful attending a patriotic Mass. After this act of violence, demonstrations ceased and the national movement went underground.

THE NATIONAL ORGANIZATION

The period of demonstrations and "moral revolution" was not favourable to the establishment of a distinctive revolutionary party, but it facilitated the recruitment of members for spontaneously created secret organizations. In the spring and summer of 1861, many groups were formed in Warsaw and in the provinces by young people of the intelligentsia and by artisans. They all called themselves "Reds", which amounted only to the belief, that no armed insurrection was possible in Poland, without some social reform. In the beginning, part of the Red groups were under the influence of the "Millenaries" but soon there emerged a Left Wing, to whom demonstrations were not merely a means of arousing patriotic feelings or putting pressure on the government, but a means to enrol the support of the masses in preparing for an insurrection. An outstanding radical figure in the movement was Ignacy Chmieleński who bitterly accused the "organic work" party of betraying the national cause for the sake of their own petty class interests. In October 1861 immediately after the proclamation of martial law, several of the Red circles united as a result of the efforts of the writer, Apollo Korzeniowski. A City Committee was formed, whose members decided upon the amalgamation of all secret societies in the capital. The Committee's delegates, mostly young people, including the brothers Frankowski, Szachowski, Wasilewski and others toured the provinces to organize additional cells there.

Following the principle that the leaders of the movement should reside within the country, the City Committee did not accept Mierosławski's leadership, but got in touch with the Sierakowski circle in St. Petersburg. This circle sent Jarosław Dąbrowski to Warsaw, who, while acting publicly as a staff officer of the Tsarist army, soon became "the Head of the City of Warsaw" and of its Red organization. Dąbrowski based the conspiracy mainly on the metal-workers. By spring 1862 the unification of all of Warsaw's secret organizations had been accomplished. The City Committee was already at that time calling upon the propertied classes to accept its authority.

These classes, the landowners and the bourgeoisie, anxiously watched the development of the conspiracy, afraid of the possible insurrection as well as of the radical programme of the Reds. Nonetheless, the camp of the "Moderates" (or White Party) could not make up their minds to come to terms openly with the Russian government, firstly because the state of martial law gave no evidence of Russian willingness to make concessions and, secondly, because even the die-hard conservatives had to take public opinion into account. The Whites therefore sought a middle road between striking a bargain with the foreign ruler and accepting a revolution. They thought they could find that middle road, as before, in the programme of "organic work" embellished with patriotic phrases and promises of an insurrection at some time in the distant future. The White Party was composed, in the countryside, of former members of the Agricultural Society. It was directed, since the end of 1861, by a secret Directory in which Leopold Kronenberg, a Warsaw banker, played a leading role. The Directory had considerable financial resources at its disposal but, torn with dissent, it remained rather inactive.

The state of martial law did not pacify the country with its undercurrent of conspiracy. The villages, too, were in ferment and refused to agree to conversion to rents on the onerous terms imposed by the government. In May 1862, St. Petersburg decided to make further concessions to the Polish upper classes with a view to pacifying the country. The Grand Duke Constantine (brother of the Tsar) was appointed Viceroy. Wielopolski was appointed chief of the civil administration. The Tsar approved the ukases as elaborated by the Margrave in respect of compulsory conversion to rents, the granting of equal rights to Jews, the expansion and Polonization of public education. The University of Warsaw, suppressed after 1831, was reopened under the name of Main School. All these reforms were designed to appeal to the gentry and the bourgeoisie and were intended to draw them away from the struggle for independence. The Right Wing of the big landowners among the Whites were impressed and inclined to come to terms with Wielopolski.

At this very moment in May and June, Dąbrowski, the chief of the Warsaw conspirators, was planning to launch an armed attack without delay. At the same time he was head of the secret "Officers' Committee of the First Army" composed of several hundred officers stationed in Poland, both Russian and Polish, united in the revolutionary movement. The organization cooperated with the revolutionary movement in Russia, the "Zemlya i Volya" (Land and Liberty) Committee, as well as with the St. Petersburg group led by Sierakowski. The alliance with the Russian revolutionary movement opened new vistas to the Red conspiracy. The officers of the Russian garrison in Warsaw engaged in the conspiracy were ready to open the gates of the Citadel to the insurgents. This audacious plan caused anxiety among the moderate wing of the Red camp. Various groups of the centre, until then divided among the Whites and the Reds, were now pressing hard for the two organizations to unite, to reject any compromise with the Russian government and, at the same time, to postpone the armed struggle. Dąbrowski foiled this attempt and preserved the Committee's existence by maintaining a separate Red organization. He had, however, to give up the idea of an immediate armed rising and to agree to admit some moderates as members in the Committee. Some time earlier, the Russian high command had got wind of the revolutionary organization within the army. Three officers of the Warsaw garrison (Arnholdt, Śliwicki and Rostkowski) were shot. During the summer, Ignacy Chmieleński, in agreement with Dąbrowski, organized in Warsaw several attempts on Constantine's and Wielopolski's life. The attempts failed and the men directly involved died on the gallows. But the revolutionary terror coupled with Tsarist reprisals made it difficult for the Whites to go over to the side of the government. The negotiations between the Grand Duke Constantine and Andrzej Zamoyski were torpedoed. The Whites advanced demands, which seemed unacceptable to the Russians, that the reforms should also apply to Lithuania and Ruthenia (Ukraine). After this fiasco the Tsarist government exiled Zamoyski from Poland.

Meanwhile, the secret Red organization was expanding. Its network embraced cities and towns in Russian Poland and extended as far as Poznań and Galicia. The organization took the title of National Central Committee and, operating underground, proclaimed itself the supreme national authority. In the meantime, in August, Dąbrowski was arrested and Agaton Giller, the representative of the right wing Reds enjoyed the greatest influence in the Committee. He established the principles of building a "secret Polish State" which was to harness the entire nation and compel the people to obedience. The organization possessed an efficient network of local authorities. It had an underground press and established a national tax, which it collected under pressure of public opinion even from those who opposed the movement. The Central Committee announced to the peasants the conversion to freeholds, while promising the gentry that they would be compensated by the government for its loss of income. Giller expected in this way to be able to rally all classes to the national cause. Giller and Zygmunt Padlewski (Dąbrowski's successor as Head of the City of Warsaw), went to London to negotiate with Hertzen and Ogariev, the editors of "Kolokol". In the agreement they concluded it was stated that the Polish movement was democratic in character, that it was intended to give the land to the peasants and that it recognized the right of Lithuania and Ruthenia to self-determination. In exchange, the leaders of the revolutionary movement in Russia promised the Poles assistance in their fight against the Tsarist Empire.

It took time to prepare the insurrection, in particular to buy and import the necessary weapons. In agreement with the Russians of the "Zemlya i Volya" Committee, the Central Committee planned the armed insurrection for the late spring of 1863, Wielopolski frustrated this plan by putting forward his scheme for the conscription of politically disloyal young men. The levy was announced in advance, but the exact date remained a secret and so did the list of the victims. In this manner, the Margrave expected either to smash the Red organization, or else force it to start fighting at a most inconvenient moment. In fact, the rank and file of the Red organization brought pressure to bear upon the Central Committee and demanded that it give the signal for the insurrection as soon as the conscription was started.

At the last minute the right wing of the Committee with Giller in the lead did their utmost to prevent the insurrection, but the scales were tipped by Padlewski supported by an enthusiastic group of "voivodship commissars" who had come to the meeting from the provinces. The day before the levy, on 14/15 January the younger conspirators left Warsaw secretly and went into hiding in the neighbouring woods. A week later, on 22 January, the Central Committee as the Temporary National Government issued the Manifesto for the Insurrection and called the nation to arms. The Manifesto announced that all peasant landholders should own the land they cultivated. All labour service and rents were consequently abolished and the landowners were promised government compensation. The landless population were promised 3 morgs of land from government estates, provided they took part in the fight for liberation.

THE ARMED STRUGGLE OF 1863

During the night of 22/23 January, 1863, small units of insurgents attacked the Russian garrisons in some 20 places. The odds were heavy, for only a small part of the 20,000 conspirators took part in the fight. There was a shortage of arms, because supplies from abroad had not been brought in on time and the Tsarist regular army occupying the Kingdom had 100,000 men under arms. Though attacking by surprise, the insurgents were successful in only very few of the first engagements, but the Tsarist commanders realized the danger they were facing and ordered the garrisons to concentrate.

The Whites were opposed to the insurrection, which they expected to fail quickly and did what they could to persuade the armed units to disband. The insurrection continued however, thanks to the spirit and devotion of a few revolutionary volunteers. In the regions of Podlasie, Sandomierz and Kielce several units, numbering a few thousand men each, went into action in February. They were composed mainly of artisans, workers from the mining areas and petty gentry. The outbreak of the insurrection caused fresh peasant revolts. In many districts peasants raided and pillaged the manors, bound the owners and their employees with ropes and carted them to town. The Russian troops tried to put down the *jacquerie* in defence of the gentry and fought the rioting peasants as they did the insurgents. Simultaneously the insurgents promised the peasants their freeholds and called upon them to join the fight. The gentry were anxious because they feared that further resistance to the movement might turn it against them and bring on social revolution.

At the same time Bismarck took advantage of the Polish insurrection as a welcome opportunity to offer the Tsar Prussia's military assistance. The Russo-Prussian Convention, signed by General Alvensleben in St. Petersburg on 8 February, made the Polish Insurrection into an international problem. Napoleon III intervened with the obvious design of exploiting

A. Grottger, *Battle*, 1864–1866

the situation against Prussia. He succeeded in drawing Austria and England into the diplomatic game which did not exclude the possibility of military action. Having once resolved to take advantage of the Polish Insurrection, Napoleon wished to make sure that it would not collapse too early. He put pressure on the Whites through the intermediary of the Hôtel Lambert, demanding that the insurrection be continued and gave some hope of military assistance. These suggestions from Paris fell on fertile ground, because the Whites realized, that they could no longer stand aside while the nation had risen in revolt.

In the second half of February, the Whites decided to join the insurrection. The Directory led by Kronenberg at once endeavoured to wrest the leadership from the Reds and to take the radical content out of the movement. Their plan was made easy by the difficult situation of the Reds. On the eve of the revolution the Central Committee had appointed as dictator Mierosławski, the only prominent commander linked with the camp of the Reds. Mierosławski arrived in Poland, but was defeated in two ill-fated skirmishes and returned to Paris. The members of the underground government travelled around the country looking for a convenient place to establish themselves in the open under the protection of the insurgent army. In practice, the head of the revolutionary movement was Warsaw's "Head of the City", Stefan Bobrowski, a dedicated and energetic young man. Faced with this situation, the leaders of the Whites assembled in early March in Cracow, where they usurped the power of the National Committee and appointed General Marian Langiewicz dictator. This popular commander was to serve as a screen for a new completely White government, but Langiewicz's unit was dissolved a week later and the unhappy dictator imprisoned by the Austrians. Bobrowski then announced that the secret Temporary Government was taking command once more. For a time the insurrection was safe, but within the next few weeks the Whites, in cooperation with the right wing of the Reds, achieved a change in the composition of the government and Giller was once more placed at the head. The separate organization of the Whites was disbanded. The gentry and the bourgeoisie joined the movement, making sure that their influence would prevail.

The insurrection had one peculiar aspect right from the beginning. It was directed by the National Government hiding in Warsaw, which issued its instructions under its famous anonymous seal. The civilian chiefs of voivodships, districts and towns were named by and subordinated to the government. The organization extended its efficient supervision throughout the country and was well obeyed by the population. It levied taxes, settled disputes, punished traitors and spies. Last but not least it waged war against the Russian Empire which gradually mobilized some 300,000 soldiers for the fight.

The Polish units consisted at first of a few thousand men and because such units could hardly cope with the enemy's overwhelming strength, they quickly disintegrated. Instead, smaller partisan units came into being, each of them consisting of about 500 men and capable, if well commanded, of holding its own for several months, harassing the enemy, avoiding capture and even attacking occasionally and scoring successes. In the latter part of the spring and during the summer several scores of such units were active in the field. The partisan movement embraced all regions of the Kingdom, Lithuania, and part of Byelorussia; Galicia and Prussian Poland sent volunteers and funds across the borders. The principal problem was the lack of weapons. Large sums were expended for their purchase from armament manufacturers abroad, but the supplies reached the camps only with considerable difficulty, so that most of the partisans were equipped only with scythes. With their supreme devotion to duty the insurgents might have been able to keep the strongest European army in check, but they could never defeat it, nor hope to hold a single district for any length of time.

Without outside help the Poles could be victorious only if the mass of the people rose and if the movement were changed into an agrarian revolution and spread to Russia as well. The leaders of the left wing of the Reds, Sierakowski, Dąbrowski and Padlewski, were thinking in these terms. The Whites, however, prevented moves in this direction, as soon as they came into power. The Polish peasants, who had hesitated at first, showed more and more sympathy for the movement, when they saw that the promises made to them were being kept faithfully. Labour dues and land rents had ceased to exist and the national government saw to it that they were not reimposed. Freeholds thus became a reality, but the government was directed by the Whites and did not countenance further peasant demands. It granted no land to the landless and postponed calling the whole population to arms to some time in the future. Pinning all their hopes on an intervention by the Powers, the Whites were reserving their forces for the expected European war. For the time being they wanted to survive and indulged only in armed demonstrations. In the early summer war seemed imminent, because the Russian government refused to accept the diplomatic notes addressed to it from Paris, London and Vienna, but Napoleon, yielding to the arguments of his partners, did not go to war and, in spite of the loss of prestige, left Poland to her fate.

The Red politicians were quite aware of the fact that the insurrection was in danger of collapse. Twice, in May and September 1863, they succeeded in wresting the famous official seal from the rival Whites and forming their own National Government. Both attempts were short-lived, and the Whites returned to the helm after a few weeks. In the late autumn dictatorial power was at last assumed by Romuald Traugutt, who was to carry out the Red's national programme of relying on the peasants. Preparations were made for a mass-levy as opposed to reliance on the help of the western countries. Relations were to be established instead with the revolutionary movements. This new policy had come several months too late. The people were exhausted and worn out by the unequal struggle. The best had either fallen in battle or been betrayed. Warsaw's city organization, which had been protecting the government, had crumbled away. Muraview, Governor General in Wilno, the cruel "Hangman" as he was called, had put down the rising in Lithuania by applying mass reprisals. Thanks to the energetic attitude of Traugutt and his closest friends, especially General Józef Hauke-Bosak, the units of the revolutionaries survived the bitter winter in the southern part of the Kingdom. In April 1864, however, Traugutt was arrested and hanged soon after. The secret organization was wiped out, and the armed insurrection had come to an end.

THE EMANCIPATION OF THE PEASANTS AND THE END OF THE PERIOD OF NATIONAL RISINGS

No sooner had the threat of a European war disappeared, that the Tsarist government openly changed its policy in Poland. Wielopolski was the first to leave Warsaw and Grand Duke Constantine soon followed him. General Berg was appointed Viceroy and decided to break down Polish resistance with the brutal use of force. Permanent pacification of the country was, however, unthinkable without a preliminary settlement of the agrarian question. The decree of the National Government, which had granted freeholds to the peasants, was an incontrovertible fact, and the Tsarist government could do nothing but confirm it. Abandoning the policy, he had been following up to this time of backing the interests of the landed gentry, the Tsar entrusted the execution of an agrarian reform in Poland to Russian liberal bureaucrats headed by Nicholas Milyutin. The relevant ukase issued by the Tsar on 2 March, 1864, gave the peasants the land they cultivated and granted the proprietors compensation from State funds. All further promises, such as the granting of land to the landless and the return of land illegally taken from the peasants, were to be fulfilled only in a very small measure. In fact the Tsarist reform simply sanctioned the state of affairs created by the insurrection. Consequently it granted the peasants more land on much easier conditions, than those provided by the Russian reform of 1861. A similar measure applied as well to the western provinces of Russia, where the Tsarist government has been obliged to revise the provisions of the 1861 reform to the advantage of the peasants, soon after the outbreak of the Polish Insurrection in the spring of 1863. The January Insurrection had, then, contributed to improving the standard of life not only of the Poles, but also of the Lithuanian, Byelorussian and Ukrainian peasants. The immediate effect of this move was all to the advantage of Russia. The peasantry discontinued its armed struggle and tried to ingratiate themselves with the Russian commissars, while they awaited the distribution of the land, but, contrary to the expectations of the bureaucrats, the peasants who had been granted land did not become in the long run loyal subjects of the Tsar.

The end of the insurrection marked the end of the process of abolishing feudal conditions in Poland. In all of the three parts of the country under foreign rule, however, this was carried out only partially. The reforms were introduced from the top, by governments whose hands had been forced either by the popular masses and by the revolution, or by the state of international relations. The reforms abolished labour dues, the power of the lord of the manor over the peasant, some other privileges and class differences. They were not genuinely democratic reforms. In the new bourgeois society, the landowner had to maintain his economic dominance over the landless peasants and the small-holders. The reform in Galicia proved more radical than the Poznań reform, while the reform in the Kingdom was more radical still. The more advantageous the conditions offered by virtue of the reform, the greater were the possibilities for a swift development of capitalist relations.

As has been mentioned before, from the end of the eighteenth century on the issue of peasant emancipation and the struggle for independence were closely intertwined. This was due not only to the fact, that Polish patriots were promising freedom to the peasants to encourage them to join the struggle for national liberation. There was another reason as well, namely, that the abolition of feudal servitude created a nation of new, free citizens, conscious fighters for freedom, whether in the present or succeeding generations.

The series of insurrections did not bring about Poland's independence. The defeats caused material losses, reprisals, and continued restriction of national liberty. We have seen what was the cause of these defeats. The greater strength of the enemy and the indifference of the European Powers were not the only reason. Causes may be also found in the inconsistency of the patriots themselves and the opposition of Polish counter-revolutionaries. And yet the balance-sheet of a century of effort did not show only losses. Even the lost revolution paved the way for a broader and clearer national consciousness. Each successive national movement embraced a greater number of people and was larger in scope. The army of the Duchy of Warsaw had been led by aristocrats. The November Insurrection was started by gentry revolutionaries. The first to join the ranks of the January Insurrection were young workers and craftsmen, and the last to leave the partisan struggle were the peasant volunteers. Finally, 1863 created in Poland the conditions necessary for the development of capitalism with its accompanying labour movement, which in later years caused the collapse of the partitioning Powers. Already in the early twentieth century the sons of the peasants who had been emancipated by the National Government began to struggle by word and deed for Poland's independence.

J. Malczewski, *The Last Stage*, 1883

Last but not least the international aspect of Poland's fight for independence must be remembered. For 70 years risings were ever imminent and at times were extremely effective as a factor counterbalancing the hegemony of the Holy Alliance. In this respect alone they were an encouragement to all progressive efforts in Europe and all peoples struggling for national independence. This found its expression not only in the participation of Polish volunteers in the Hungarian campaign, in Garibaldi's march, or on the barricades of the Paris Commune. The November Insurrection certainly contributed to the establishment of Belgian independence, and Poland's example awakened national consciousness in the backward peoples of the Balkans. Nor was it an accident that the Polish question had the lasting sympathy of all progressive circles in Europe. Volunteers from all corners of the world fought in the Polish ranks, including many Russians and Germans. Leading revolutionaries of the nineteenth century, with Marx and Engels at their head, were unanimous in their defence of Poland.

As is generally known, the "Polish Meeting" which was convened in London in July 1863 became the starting point for the discussions which led to the foundation of the First Working Men International. Its first General Council declared a year later: "The struggle for independence was carried on by the Poles in the common interest of the nations of Europe. That is why its defeat is at the same time a heavy blow to the cause of human civilization and progress. Poland had undoubtedly the right to demand universal support for her efforts to win independence from the leading nations of Europe."

At this time, in 1864, this resolution was only a token of friendship. The future was to show that the revolutionary labour movement could become one of the deciding factors which brought Poland her desired liberation half a century later.

Chapter XVIII
POSITIVISM AND TRI-LOYALISM. THE BEGINNINGS OF THE WORKING-CLASS MOVEMENT (1864–1885)

THE AFTERMATH OF DISASTER

For the politically conscious elements of society the defeat of the January Insurrection was the greatest blow that the nation had suffered since the partitions. Between 1861 and 1864 Poland had, in fact, believed in the immediate possibility of regaining full independence within extensive state frontiers. The autonomy of the Kingdom gained in 1862 was generally considered insufficient. In the spring of 1863 the armed intervention of the Powers was expected to result in independence. Simultaneously, the conviction was current that the peasant problem, the most outstanding social issue of the time, would be solved in such a way as to return the peasant into a conscious citizen and patriot. The gentry hoped, at the same time, to preserve its privileged position in society. The bourgeoisie was even more of the opinion that after agrarian reform the peasants would become the basis of national strength and the foundation on which the modern capitalist Polish State would rise.

The year 1864 dispersed all these hopes. Reality appeared so terrible by comparison with the recent illusion that it was regarded only as a disaster offering no prospects for a better future. The peasant had just receive his land from the hands of the Tsarist government and for another generation would not become a basis for the national struggle for freedom. There was no realization that a land reform, more advantageous for the peasants than that in Russia, would shortly hasten the development not only of the class consciousness, but also of the national feelings of the peasantry and that already by the end of the century the Polish village in the three areas of partition would become an essential factor in the growth of national strength.

The fact similarly was often overlooked that the land reform offered some parts of the country possibilities for rapid economic progress. In the Kingdom and in Silesia the second half of the century saw the development of large-scale industry, thus giving rise to a factory proletariat, which was not only to mark a new direction in social development, but also to contribute a powerful force in the struggle for national liberation. Thus, the social upheaval, which was regarded by the bulk of the conservative propertied classes as a national disaster, contained within it the seeds of a better future. This, however, was to appear only in the next generation, that happier generation which not only struggled for independence but gained it. One thing was regarded at this time, and for that matter two generations later, as an undoubted disaster, the weakening of the Polish element in the eastern borderlands. Looking at this matter from the perspective of the hundred years which separate us from Muraviev's persecutions, one comes to the conclusion that in one way or another the fate of the Polish elements in these lands was already sealed. The dominant force which eliminated the Polish element from the eastern borderlands was the awakening of the national feeling of the masses in central and eastern Europe. In the final analysis, it is this process which shifted the Polish political border from the areas between the Dnieper and the Bug to the area between the Vistula and the Odra. Thus, this historic period, which began with the disaster of the January Insurrection and ended with the downfall of the post-1919 Poland, created all the conditions for the emergence of the State which lies at this present time within the Polish frontiers.

THE POST-1863 EMIGRATION

It was a tradition of Polish history in the epoch which followed the partitions, that after disasters many individuals in danger of persecution by the conqueror would seek their salvation in emigration. In their new home they would attempt not only to continue their conspiratorial activity, but, above all, would devise new social concepts and political programmes. The same occurred after 1864. The influence of this new emigration on the country, however, cannot be compared with that of the Great Emigration, whether politically, ideologically or culturally. After 1831, as after 1794, the country lapsed into lethargy ; in the social sense things returned, at least superficially, to the state existing before the insurrection and the country entered a period of reaction. After the January Insurrection of 1863/1864, on the contrary, a basic transformation of economic and social conditions took place. The elimination of the last vestiges of feudal conditions in the Polish countryside occurred. This went on at a more speedy pace in the Russian area than had taken place first in the Prussian and then in the Austrian zones. In addition, in the Prussian area the ending of the "Settlement Reform" came at the end of the 1850's. In Austria it was the 1860's which saw the rapid destruction of the peasants' traditional rights and the consequent struggle for "woods and pastures" conducted with great intensity by the village and manor. As a result, all the three areas underwent, more or less simultaneously, profound social changes. Soon a rapid industrialization of the Kingdom occurred and brought with it demographic changes. In the face of these great transformations the role of the political emigration remained limited and its influence on the shaping of political life in the country—small. In the immediate future the Austrian area became the centre of relatively free political life and thus numerous individuals returned to the country to engage in some work, but in the main their activities were professional.

This does not mean that there were no outstanding thinkers among the post-1864 exiles, capable of creating new and even viable political and social conceptions. Their Left Wing sought a new approach to the problem of the historical territories of the former Polish State. There was an attempt to find a solution which would rescue the idea of the Jagiellonian State and uniting the "Three Nations", in face of the awakening national consciousness of the Ukrainians and Lithuanians. In these ideas a programme was put forward, in one form or another, of a federation of these peoples in a spirit of equality and fraternity based on a revolutionary social ideology, which in that generation could only, in effect, be socialist. This is the reason why the supporters of these concepts, like J. Dąbrowski and W. Wróblewski, found themselves on the barricades of the Paris Commune in 1871 and became the connecting link between the tradition of the January Insurrection and the modern revolutionary movement.

The participation of Poles in the First International was quite considerable and it is they who, after the fall of the Paris Commune, sought, as envoys of the International, to bring the socialist movement into Russia by way of the Polish territories. This had no immediate or essential impact on the development of the ideology of those active in the country. It was only years afterwards, when the issues resulting from the direct effects on the January Insurrection had been solved in the country and new social movements began to arise, that the ideas which had been preserved in exile began to influence the views of the younger generation.

THE RUSSIANIZATION POLICY IN THE KINGDOM

The most important social problem which faced the Kingdom after the collapse of the insurrection was the peasant problem. The 1864 ukase granted the peasants the ownership of the land in their possession as well as the lands which had been illegally taken away from them since 1846. The peasants were not required to make direct payment for the acquisition of the land, in contrast to the peasantry of the rest of Russia, while the previous owners received their compensation in bonds. On the other hand, the peasants were made to pay a relatively high land tax.

The new organization of the Kingdom and, in particular, the execution of agrarian reform was to be supervised by the Executive Committee, composed of Russian officials vested with extensive powers. The initial premise of the Executive Committee was to gain the favour of the peasantry for the Russian government and to weaken the gentry politically. In the course of putting into practice the ukase the anti-gentry policy was considerably relaxed, especially in relation to the wealthiest landowners. The uneconomic aspects of the reform appeared, after a certain period of time, in a manner most unfavourable to the peasants. No re-allotment of land was carried out and the peasants' rights to woods and pastures were not abolished, in expectation that this would become a cause of dispute between the village and the manor. A separate machinery of local and central authorities administering peasant affairs was set up with the purpose of keeping the peasants under government tutelage. In the long run this also turned out to be unfavourable to the peasantry's economic interests. The Executive Committee likewise did not intend to abolish the manor farms and had no concern for the fate of landless peasants. They received such small allotments that they could not support themselves from them. The peasants received only 27 per cent of the state and secularized Church lands. Most of these estates were used to reward, as after 1831, a new group of Russian dignitaries. In all, the area of land cultivated by the peasant increased as a result of the reform from 8 to 10 per cent and at the beginning of the 1870's amounted to 8,2 million morgs. This area increased afterwards, steadily but slowly, as a result of a voluntary division of manorial lands, and reached a total of almost 11 million before the First World War. It was primarily the wealthiest section of the peasantry which benefited from this process. The land hunger caused by the population increase resulted in a recurrent proletarianization of a considerable part of the rural areas, finding its expression in the division of holdings, an increase in the number of the landless and a growing wave of emigration.

While in the early years land reform improved the peasant's position, it simultaneously weakened very considerably the position of the gentry. It was in the first place the medium gentry which, economically weaker, could not find at the outset sufficient resources to make the transition to new methods of management not based on serfdom. Because it was precisely the medium gentry which had sacrificed a great deal for the cause of the insurrection and suffered from repression, it becomes clear that the reform resulted in the ruin of many estates. This caused numerous gentry families to seek employment in the cities, in trade, industry and the professions, a movement which was rendered difficult, because at the same time the administration was being russified, which deprived them of those possibilities which existed, for example, in the Hapsburg monarchy, where the road to government appointments was open to the *déclassé* gentry.

In this difficult situation for the ruined gentry of the Kingdom the role of women, who had to find employment in these new conditions, increased. This resulted in a movement towards emancipation earlier, than was noted in western or central Europe.

A result of the increased influx of the gentry to the cities was the cultural transformation of urban life. The towns, hitherto largely populated by German and Jewish inhabitants, as was true for all this part of Europe, now became more closely connected with a Polish culture of specifically gentry character. This affected, above all, the rapidly growing intelligentsia. This social group, the most active culturally, now transmitted gentry traditions to broader sections of the community, which were only, at this time, awakening to a full cultural life. Thus, both the urban proletariat and the entire Polish bourgeoisie, took on many of the Polish gentry traditions. Here we have a distinct feature of Polish culture, which gives it its uniqueness among European nations. The nineteenth century saw the triumph of bourgeois culture in all of Europe, but in Poland the picture was different and for casual observers it created the appearance of inferiority or backwardness in Polish cultural life. It made it more difficult for foreigners to understand many of the phenomena of Polish social, cultural and political life.

Political repression was the prime factor in aggravating the crisis of the landowners. Already during the insurrection Muraviev, the Governor General of Wilno, proceeded to attempt the eradication of the Polish element in Lithuania. He carried out land reform in such a way as to weaken the Polish gentry. The western provinces of the Empire were not granted institutions of local self-government (*zemstva*), which in Russia strengthened the position of the landlords. The government confiscated a large number of Polish estates, and exiled to Siberia entire villages inhabited by small landholders of gentry origin who considered themselves Poles, because in these lands belonging to the gentry was equivalent to feeling oneself to be a Pole. The Polish language was eliminated from government correspondence and the Roman Catholic clergy was prohibited from keeping civil registry books in Polish. In these provinces Catholicism was usually synonymous with Polish nationality and it was only in the native Lithuanian areas that the Catholic peasants spoke Lithuanian. The Polish language was prohibited in schools and eliminated from shop signs and commercial correspondence. Poles, not only gentry but peasants as well, were forbidden, once and for all, to buy land. In addition, all Polish landowners had to pay a permanent, special tax or contribution. The result of these regulations was a considerable decline in the percentage of the Polish population in Lithuania, Byelorussia and the Ukraine.

The action of the government in the Congress Kingdom was somewhat different and more long range. The land reform laws provided for new structure of village administration. Single village units were created, under the name of a *gromada* (sub-commune) from which the gentry estates were excluded. These units were not set up in the villages inhabited by the petty gentry. Several sub-communes were joined together with the adjoining manor estates into larger units called *gmina* (commune). Their village-elder (*wójt*) was formally elected by a meeting from which, however, both the rural poor and the estate owners and priests were excluded. A strict supervision was exercised over the *gromada* and *gmina* by government officials, called "commissars for peasant affairs". All this was to serve the purpose of rendering cooperation between the Polish educated classes and the rural population impossible.

On the basis of the emancipation laws the government could undertake a policy of unifying the Kingdom with the Empire and of suppressing an independent Polish existence. In 1866 the Council of State and the Administrative Council were abolished and the Kingdom's budget incorporated into that of the Empire. A year later the various government commissions were abolished, eliminating thereby the administrative separateness of the Kingdom from the Empire. The Commission of Justice maintained itself for a few more years; after its abolition new courts on the Russian pattern were introduced. The Napoleonic Civil Code, however, remained in force. The administration was reorganized in 1867 when ten smaller provinces (*gubernie*) were set up. When Berg died in 1874 the office of Viceroy was abolished. The supreme civil and military authority in the Kingdom was henceforth exercised by the Governor General. This new administration was staffed entirely by Russians. Simultaneously, the institutions of self-government (*zemstva*) which existed in the Empire were not introduced into the Kingdom, because they could have been taken advantage of and fallen into the hands of the Poles.

The government expended its greatest efforts on the Russianization of education. This policy was still more severe in the western provinces of the Empire, which had belonged to Poland before the partition, than in the Congress Kingdom, where the process took place gradually and could not be fully implemented. The Main School in Warsaw was replaced as early as in 1869 by a Russian University. In the course of the next few years the secondary schools were Russianized. In 1885 Russian was introduced as the language of instruction in primary schools and only the Polish language and religion were to be taught in Polish. Russian teachers were not introduced, however, into the primary schools on the correct premise that they would antagonize the peasant children and render their Russianization impossible. As a result in remote localities teachers' colleges were set up where peasants' sons, mostly those of illiterate parents, were educated according to Russian precepts. Teachers educated in this way were to carry out the Russianization of the Polish peasantry. During the first generation a considerable section of these teachers answered the hopes placed in them, but their sons, often also teachers, became in the future the first Polish educational and social leaders amongst the peasantry.

The second factor, apart from education, which had a strong influence on the peasantry's attitude was the Church. In order to make the clergy its obedient instrument the government decided to make the Catholic hierarchy dependent upon itself and to sever its connections with Rome. The majority of monasteries were closed down, Church property was confiscated and the entire clergy was to be paid by the State, thus becoming, to a considerable degree, materially dependent on the Russian authorities. The Tsarist government broke the Concordat with Rome, and the Polish bishops were placed under the authority of the Spiritual College in St. Petersburg. The Catholic hierarchy opposed these steps and numerous bishops were exiled as a result. Their dioceses were accordingly left vacant. In time, the resistance of the upper hierarchy began to weaken, but the ranks of the faithful remained staunch and the threats of the government to introduce Russian for sermons, singing and prayers proved ineffective. After 1871 the Russian government began to retreat from this hopeless struggle. On the other hand, the liquidation of the Uniate Church was carried out to its completion. The tool of the Tsarist government, Michał Popiel, the administrator of the Uniate diocese in Chełm, went over in 1875 with a majority of the communes to the Orthodox faith. This gave rise to a fanatical resistance of the faithful who did not wish to relinquish Catholicism. The government punished the resisting peasants with flogging and entire Uniate villages were exiled to Siberia. In spite of this, numerous Uniates baptized their children in secret and had secret weddings in Galicia or in the forests celebrated by disguised Catholic priests. The result of these persecutions was to bring about a closer identification of the Uniate population in the Russian areas with Polish nationality, a process which was the opposite of that taking place simultaneously in the Austrian area, where the Uniate Church became synonymous with the rising Ukrainian national consciousness. Ultimately, it was only after the election of Leo XIII as Pope that the relations between the Vatican and St. Petersburg were normalized. In 1882 the Concordat was renewed and the vacant sees were again filled.

Thus, in general, one can describe the policy of the Tsarist government towards the Poles after the January Insurrection as one of repression, Russianization and the destruction of all social forces which could offer resistance to Russian rule in Poland.

THE POLISH PROVINCES OF PRUSSIA. THE *KULTURKAMPF* AND THE NATIONAL REVIVAL IN SILESIA

In the Prussian area government policy up to the end of the 1860's was less determined. Bismarck's government fought, of course, against all Polish national aspirations but the Polish community after the failure of the 1848 uprising, and even more so after the disaster of 1863, did not consider illegal action and saw the proper field for the national cause in economics and education. A struggle for the land was waged between the Poles and the Germans and, for the moment, it was the Polish gentry which suffered, losing its supremacy in the amount of the land it held by comparison with that held by German landowners. This took place with extensive assistance from the authorities. In 1880 the Prussian junkers in the Poznań area held 50 per cent more land than the Polish gentry, whom the Prussian government considered to be the essential political strength of Polish nationality. In Pomerania this relation was still less favourable to the Polish gentry, not to speak of Silesia, where there was no large property in Polish hands at all. The reprisals for the assistance which the Poles in the Prussian area gave to the January Insurrection were relatively mild. The great trial, which took place in Berlin in December 1864, of the organizers of assistance for the insurrection resulted in eleven death sentences but these were all against persons who were absent. The rest of the accused were sentenced to a year of imprisonment or two. In 1866, after the victory over Austria, an amnesty was proclaimed from which the Polish prisoners also benefited. In any case, Bismarck could not conduct too bitter a struggle against the Poles in Prussia, because at this time he was in conflict with the liberal opposition, while in the international arena, in preparing for a diplomatic victory over Austria and France, he made effective use also of the Polish question. It was only after the final unification of Germany in 1871 that the situation changed. An almost complete Germanization of the school system took place and, simultaneously, the government undertook the persecution of the Polish element in the Church.

The *Kulturkampf*, in its wider German meaning, was an expression of the struggle of the bourgeoisie for the completion of the building of an unified German State. The aim, above all, was to secularize the German school system in order to utilize it for strengthening German national consciousness. In the political field this was a struggle against particularism which had been so strong in Germany since medieval times, but in the Polish provinces this struggle of the Prussian State assumed a different character. Bismarck's purpose was to gain for the struggle against the Catholic Party, which in Prussia had the sympathies also of non-Catholic conservatives, a part of the junkers, who always had very strong anti-Polish traditions. That is why Bismarck strongly emphasized the anti-Polish character of the *Kulturkampf*. As a result, he provoked the resistance of broad masses of the

Polish population which, up till then, had not been particularly hostile to the Prussian State. In particular, the *Kulturkampf* brought about an awakening of Polish consciousness in Upper Silesia, where, precisely at this time, the masses were beginning to take an active part in political life.

The *Kulturkampf* was carried out both in the German Reich and within the Kingdom of Prussia. But it was precisely the Prussian Diet and government that were most deeply involved in it, just as they were in any anti-Polish campaign. One of the reasons was that there existed in the German Parliament powerful parties, such as the "Zentrum" and the Social Democrats, which opposed anti-Polish legislation and were generally against any anti-Polish campaign.

As in Germany, so also in the Polish provinces of Prussia the hierarchy of the Church committed itself to the struggle against the government with the greatest distaste. Mieczysław Ledóchowski, the Archbishop of Gniezno and Poznań, a cosmopolitan prince of the Church, with little consciousness of Polish patriotism, represented an ultra-loyal position with regard to the government up to 1872. The law, which deprived the Church of its supervision over education, was the most important factor affecting conditions in the Prussian area. The Prussian government used it for the purpose of eliminating Polish from the schools in order to make the educational system a tool of Germanization. There followed the laws of May 1873, which subjected the clergy to the control of the State. It was these which finally forced Ledóchowski, who up to now had not even opposed the teaching of religion in German, to adopt a decidedly hostile position. In 1874 he was arrested, along with a large number of Church dignitaries in Prussia. From then on, the entire clergy entered into the struggle against the pressure of Germanization which, as a result, made Polish nationalism and Catholicism identical in this area. This had immediate effects beneficial to the national cause, especially in Upper Silesia, but in the next generation it also resulted in the fact that the western Polish lands became a stronghold of clericalism, which prevented new and more progressive social ideas from penetrating to the masses.

It was due to the *Kulturkampf* that the Prussian area first obtained civil registry offices, but, like the secular school, it served the purposes of Germanization in the Polish lands.

In Silesia the Polish national movement was connected to a considerable degree with the very rapid growth of industry. The peasant, divorced from the land, came into contact with a socially more mature environment and became a more politically conscious individual. If one compares an analogous situation in Mazuria and Warmia, where there was no industry and the peasant population also spoke Polish, it becomes clear that in Upper Silesia it was the Polish industrial working class which constituted the fundamental element in the national revival in this area. The pioneer of this movement was a Silesian school teacher, Karol Miarka. In his youth he considered himself a German. It was only when he was 33 years old that, after becoming acquainted with the Polish literary language and with the richness of Polish literature, he became aware that he was a Pole and from this moment on, he devoted all his energy to the cause of awakening the national consciousness of his compatriots. He began to write stories for working people, helped in this by Paweł Stalmach, a worker in the national movement in Austrian Silesia and the editor of the "Gwiazdka Cieszyńska" (The Cieszyn Star). From 1896 on, Miarka edited his own paper, "Katolik" (The Catholic), in which he declared his views clearly in defence of the Polish language, though maintaining, at least superficially, an attitude of loyalty to the Prussian State. This paper became extremely popular and though it faced financial difficulties, especially in the period of the *Kulturkampf*, when the editor was fined and imprisoned, it became a political power and decided the vote of the Polish miners and peasants at elections. Elections to the Reichstag were universal, direct and by secret suffrage. Miarka allied himself with the leaders of the Catholic "Zentrum" and ensured that the only deputies elected from Upper Silesia were those who had his support. Miarka was an opponent of a class-conscious labour movement, while the "Zentrum" which he served, represented neither the interests of the people nor the Polish cause. However, the fact that Miarka mobilized his readers to offer resistance to the government for the sake of the defence of Catholicism advanced the cause of national development of this province. The great majority of the population of Silesia realized that it was Polish, though this was then still understood primarily in ethnic and linguistic terms. The political consequences, inducing a different attitude towards Prussia as an alien state, which might arise from this feeling, could not yet become strongly marked. The struggle for the rights of the Polish language was waged in alliance with the clergy which, in its upper ranks, was not Polish at all.

About 1878 Bismarck realized that the struggle against the Catholic Church had become pointless. Under pressure from the upper bourgeoisie and large-scale industry he made the transition to a protectionist trade policy and, drifting away from the liberals, he sought the support of the conservatives and the "Zentrum". In this connexion he moderated his hostility to the Vatican, which had gone on for a number of years, but this did not, however, in any way lessen the severity of the policy of Germanization as applied to the Poles.

THE AUTONOMY OF GALICIA

At the same time as the Congress Kingdom lost the last remnants of its autonomy and the Germanization tendency in the Prussian area became sharper, Galicia obtained broader political freedoms. This was a result of the crisis of the Hapsburg monarchy which, in the face of social changes and separatist national aspirations, had to seek a compromise with the propertied classes in the various provinces. The beginning of this development came with the Austrian defeat in Italy in 1859 when the representative of the Galician conservatives, Count Agenor Gołuchowski, was called to join the government. A year later the October "Diploma" of the Emperor Franz Joseph promised the granting of autonomy to the "historic" units of the monarchy. In 1861 Galicia, like the other provinces, obtained its own Provincial Seym with, it is true, much restricted rights. The landowning majority in the Seym was fully prepared to reach an understanding with the government on the condition that they would take control of the country into their own hands. Nevertheless, when the January Insurrection followed, the leaders of both the Red and White factions in Galicia cooperated with it. This resulted in reprisals and in February 1864, when the movement was already declining, a state of emergency was declared in Galicia.

These repressions turned out to be more vexatious for the Poles than harmful. The head of the government, the centralist Schmerling, was faced with such strong opposition in the monarchy that he could not wage a struggle with the Poles on a large scale. In any case, the Polish politicians, who in Galicia were almost exclusively representatives of the wealthier gentry, had many interests in common with influential circles among the Austrian aristocracy. Thus, they were not faced with far-reaching reprisals. Immediately upon the fall of Schmerling's government the state of emergency was lifted and the new Prime Minister, Belcredi, made it possible to start again the quest for autonomy. In the autumn of 1865 the Seym met again. The electoral law of 1861 for Galicia provided for a division of electors into four curiae: the curia of large holdings where the owners of large estates elected 44 deputies, the two curiae of towns and commercial-industrial chambers represented by 26 deputies, and the curia of the small holdings, by which was meant the peasants, which in two-stage, indirect elections chose 74 deputies. The elections were open without balloting which, as a result of the low level of political consciousness of the peasants, made it possible for the administration to exert considerable influence on the results. The law was extremely unfair, because one deputy to the Seym was chosen by 10–20 electors in the curia of the large landowners, while a deputy from the peasant curia represented, at times, tens of thousands of voters. Up to 1873 the Galician Seym elected a delegation to the Vienna Parliament (Reichsrat). After 1873 there were direct elections in the country based on a law similar to that for the Seym.

Political activity in the Austrian area was particularly vigorous in 1866–1873, when a struggle was waged in the entire monarchy for the establishment of the constitutional system on a firm basis. After the war of 1866 the Polish politicians perceived new international prospects. Beust, the Austrian chancellor, was prepared to seek revenge for Sadova and sought to reach a political and military understanding with France. The Polish diplomats from the group of Prince Czartoryski assumed that the moment had arrived for renewing diplomatic manoeuvres aimed at coordinating French and Austrian policy directed against Russia and Prussia. As is known, all these schemes became unreal with the outbreak of the Franco-Prussian war in 1870, while the defeat of France and the unification of Germany dealt, it appeared, the final blow to the Polish hopes of regaining independence with the assistance of European powers.

Nevertheless, it was precisely this unstable international situation which helped the Polish politicians of Galicia to a considerable degree in gaining a broad autonomy which was preserved up to the fall of Austria and the rebuilding of an independent Polish State. The Polish politicians in Austria were basically supporters of the federal programme and opponents of centralism. They could not, however, oppose decisively any Vienna government, even a centralist one, because in the event of war such a government might favour a solution of the Polish question. It was not only this consideration which weakened the Polish opposition against centralist cabinets. A more significant role was played by the social and national problems in the province.

The main social problem of Galicia at this time was the question of woods and pastures left in abeyance by the legislation of 1848. The struggle for the rights of the peasants to woods and pastures was for them an extremely important issue. The moment these rights were lost the peasant was forced to buy building material and fuel from the manor and to rent pasture. This forced him to seek work in the manor and revealed a new form of dependence, not feudal but capitalist in essence, of the peasantry on the manor. The gentry, in struggling for autonomy, in effect for taking over the administration in Galicia, thus fought for a solution of the problem of woods and pastures on terms advantageous to themselves. In practice, disputes concerning woods and pastures were referred to the courts, but cases usually ended in favour of the manors. The state of acute class struggle between the peasant and the gentry had repercussions also on the attitude of the peasantry to the national question. In the eyes of the peasantry Polish nationality was represented by the gentry and for this reason the overwhelming majority of the peasantry did not wish for generations to admit to a solidarity with Polish national aspirations. It was where serfdom and questions of woods and pastures had been settled earlier, as in the former area of the Free City of Cracow, or where serfdom had been less arduous, as for example in the mountain areas, that the peasantry's consciousness of being Polish developed more rapidly. In the remaining areas the peasantry for many years, up to the end of the nineteenth century, did not consider themselves Poles.

The low level of political consciousness among the peasantry had its roots in the general economic backwardness. The country was agricultural and the villages were overpopulated, but the sale of agricultural produce was not profitable because of the long distances from markets. The extension of the railways caused a flooding of Galicia with industrial goods produced in the western parts of the Hapsburg monarchy. This ruined the meagre beginnings of local industrial manufactures. Galicia, which had been one of the most fertile Polish provinces, became the poorest of the three partition areas. From the mind-19th century, but especially towards its end, the oil industry began to develop in Eastern Galicia, but it did not play a considerable role in the economy of the province as a whole. It employed only a few thousand workers and the profits went mainly to foreign capitalists, who had invested in Galician oil and who sought to obtain a tariff policy which would give Galicia the smallest benefits.

The second factor which weakened the political position of the Galician gentry in Vienna was the awakening of national consciousness among the Ukrainian population of Eastern Galicia. Once the Ukrainian peasant had been aware only of his social and class interests. Because the Polish landowner, however, spoke a different language and adhered to another religious rite, these factors hastened, or at least facilitated, the awakening of national feeling among the Ukrainians.

At the outset the Ukrainian, or Ruthenian, as they were called at the time, intelligentsia in Eastern Galicia was composed primarily of the Greek Catholic clergy and a few government officials, lawyers and doctors. In these years, the national feeling of this intelligentsia in a modern sense was only just taking shape. To some extent they adhered to the traditional connexion with the gentry, though this was weakening, and thus with the old Polish tradition, but only a few considered themselves still to be politically and nationally Poles of Ruthenian origin (*Gente Rutheni natione Poloni*). A much stronger group felt a community of interest with Russia and considered the Ukrainian language to be one of the Russian dialects. This group, known as the Russophils and later as the Old Ruthenians, considered themselves in effect to be Russian. They were highly conservative and strongly supported by the Greek Catholic clergy of the metropolitan Curia in Lwów. Though loyal for the time being towards Austria, they had decided sympathies with St. Petersburg. The weakest group at the time were those who considered the Ukrainian, or "Little Russian", to be separate and distinct and who thus considered the inhabitants of Eastern Galicia and the Dnieper region a single separate nation. This idea had already emerged in the declarations made by the Galician Ruthenians at the Slav Congress in Prague in 1848. It was from these factors that the Ukrainian national movement was in the course of years to arise and the very name of Ukraine, which took root only in the last years of the nineteenth century, was to play a considerable role in the moulding of distinct national consciousness.

The Polish politicians of the 1860's and the 1870's who came in contact with the Ukrainian problem were mostly of the opinion that a separate Ukrainian nationality did not exist at all and that the Greek Catholic population of Eastern Galicia, even if it did not speak Polish, was only a separate Polish tribe like, for example, the Kashubians in Pomerania or the Highlanders in the Tatra mountains. This illusion could not, however, be maintained. When the Ruthenian deputies in the Seym undertook the defence of the peasants' interests and had recourse to Vienna with their national demands, account had to be taken of this factor. Therefore the Polish political leaders tried to achieve a settlement of the Ruthenian questions. The Ukrainian politicians aimed at an administrative division of Galicia into an eastern region, where the Ukrainian population was in a clear majority, and a western or Polish region. This point of view was energetically rejected by the Polish gentry politicians who feared that the division of Galicia would do away with the existing monopoly of power enjoyed by the wealthy East Galician gentry to the advantage of Ukrainian intelligentsia, among whom, moreover, radical ideas were already spreading in the 1890's. The Polish bourgeoisie of Eastern Galicia saw also a danger to its own position arising from the Ukrainian national movement. Only some West Galician politicians and a very few representatives of the East Galician magnates, therefore, could agree to the idea of granting the Ukrainians concessions in the field of culture, especially in regard to the school system, to which the peasant nation, awakening to a new life, attached special importance. The conservative-minded Ukrainian politicians, following the example of the Poles, at this time thought that the only road forward lay in complete loyalty to Vienna.

In 1866–1878 the government in Vienna was mostly in the hands of the Centralists, but it had to take into account the position of the Polish deputies in the Reichsrat. The Poles, on their side, did not support the federal programme proclaimed by the Czechs. This skilful game succeeded in obtaining for them far-reaching concessions leading towards the extension of Galician autonomy. An important part was played in this by Count Agenor Gołuchowski, the Minister of State in 1859–1860 and the Viceroy of Galicia in 1849–1859, 1866–1868 and 1871–1875. The general policy of the dynasty in internal politics was in any case established for the entire period of the last years of the Hapsburg State, once the agreement with Hungary had been reached at the end of 1867. In the countries of the Crown of St. Stephen power now passed into the hands of the Hungarians, while in the lands west of the Leitha river it was reserved for the Germans. The Germans were, however, weaker in the western half of the monarchy than the Hungarians were in the eastern. For this reason they needed a reliable ally. Towards the end of the 1860's Polish conservative politicians counted on an European war in which the Hapsburg monarchy would be their ally. This made possible the conclusion of a compromise between the Polish gentry in Galicia and the dynasty, which was to endure for half a century. It did not lead to Poland's independence and it preserved at the same time the supremacy of the conservatives opposed to economic and social progress. In spite of everything this alliance gave at least to one of the Polish areas the possibility of a free national life.

The Galician politicians did not reconcile themselves immediately with the new political situation in the Hapsburg monarchy. In December 1866 the Seym declared the loyalty of the Galician gentry to the dynasty in the famous address which ended with the words, "At your side, Sire, we stand and wish to stand". The Austrian Constitution, which was enacted a year later, however, narrowly restricted once more the extent of local autonomy. In September 1868 the Seym passed a resolution in which it demanded separation almost as far reaching as that obtained by the Hungarians. A struggle to implement this resolution was waged in the Reichsrat in Vienna. When in 1870 the moderate federalists led by Alfred Potocki came to power for a short time, the government was prepared to consider the Galician resolution, but it came on the agenda only during the succeeding government of Hohenwart, who did not have a parliamentary majority. The resolution was not passed, but Galicia obtained during this period a number of concessions enacted by imperial decrees. In addition, it became a custom from this time onwards that at least one Polish minister should sit in the government as minister for Galicia. The Galician school system, including the universities, was Polonized together with the entire civil service and the courts. In 1872 the Academy of Sciences and Letters was established in Cracow, the only scientific institution of this type in Poland. It should be added that after the abolition of the Warsaw Main School in 1869 the only Polish universities were in Cracow and Lwów. Up to 1915 the Viceroy of Galicia was always a Pole and, in fact, real power over the country lay in his hands.

THE DEVELOPMENT OF INDUSTRY IN THE CONGRESS KINGDOM

A feature which probably had the greatest significance for the life of the nation was the development of large-scale industry in the Kingdom of Poland after the January Insurrection. This industry was based on foundations built in earlier years, especially under Lubecki, but the solution of the agrarian problem and, later, the commercial policy of the Russian Empire established the basic direction of development. A significant part was played here by foreign capital which was invested in the factories in the Kingdom in order to get inside the Russian tariff barrier, which from 1877 was rising ever higher. The Congress Kingdom had its own source of cheap manpower, but at a higher stage of development than in the interior of Russia, which made possible its use in factories demanding skilled workers. Industry found its supply of workers in craftsmen who were being turned into proletarians as a result of the industrialization. The necessary credit institutions already existed and commerce was highly developed. Foreign capital was interested in penetrating the immense Russian market. For this reason Polish industry was not established to serve Poland's needs and did not draw much benefit from such investment. As a result the needs of the country were met either by the handicraft industry, the goods of which were more expensive than factory goods, or by imports. Industry did, however, introduce modern conditions into the life of the country. Industry and trade, with their attendant credit institutions provided employment not only for the landless or small-holding peasants, but also for the intelligentsia of gentry descent. All this gave rise to new social problems. Already in the 1870's the working class appeared as a factor which from the outset, through its mere existence and later through its own consciousness, transmitted new impulses to political life. In the twenty years after the insurrection it multiplied threefold from 50,000 to 150,000.

Between 1865 and 1880 the technical revolution in industry was completed. Mechanical looms were introduced in most factories, in both the cotton and woolen industries. In the metallurgical and engineering industries large-scale plants, where the basic processes of production were mechanized, likewise played a dominant role. Similar progress took place in the sugar industry as well. Only the foundries lagged behind in technique for a while. In 1865 180 plants employed steam power, with 375 engines developing 3746 h.p., but in 1878 there were already 674 plants with 807 engines developing 14,627 h.p. Simultaneously, the productivity of labour was doubled between 1864 and 1880. An ever greater degree of concentration may be seen in industry. In 1886 there were 11,000 factories in the Kingdom employing 70,000 workers, but in 1880 there were less than 10,000 employing 120,000 workmen. The value of production in these plants was estimated in 1866 to be 52 million roubles rising in 1880 to 170 million.

An essential condition for the development of industry was the expansion and intensive use of the railways. The transport of coal on the Warsaw–Vienna main line increased elevenfold in this period. A number of new railway lines were constructed. In 1866 Łódź was linked up with the railway network by means of a branch of the Vienna line. From 1870 Warsaw was linked with Moscov through Terespol and Smoleńsk, and from 1873 with Kiev. In 1877 the Vistula line linked Warsaw with Mława on the Prussian border in the north and with Volhynia through Lublin in the south. In 1885 the Dąbrowa Basin was connected with the Vistula line at Dęblin. In this way the network increased in the Kingdom from 635 km in 1862 to 2084 km in 1887, but the Congress Kingdom, nevertheless, had one of the poorest railway networks in Europe. At the end of the nineteenth century

Poland under foreign rule, c. 1870

there was one kilometre of railway to 4700 inhabitants in the Kingdom while in Russia the ratio was 1 : 3200 and in Germany 1 : 1400. Only Turkey, Bulgaria and Greece were in a worse position than central Poland. This was a very clear example of the discriminatory economic policy of the Tsarist régime.

Up to the end of this period, however, the impulse of spontaneous economic development was stronger than the deliberately harmful action of the Russian government, and it was decisive for the development of industry up to the second half of the 1880's. The value of industrial production reached 200 million roubles, trebling itself since 1863. The general growth of the Kingdom's industry in the years 1887–1889 was estimated at almost fivefold, whereas in the same period industrial production in the Empire increased only twofold. This was particularly so in the cotton industry which rose in the Kingdom almost forty times, but only twice in Russia.

Such a rate of industrialization changed not only the demographic position by causing a sharp growth of the population in general and a particularly marked one in the towns, but by bringing into existence new social conditions it had a decisive influence in shaping new ideologies. These were the social sources of the intellectual concept known as positivism.

POSITIVISM

Warsaw positivism was not a distinct philosophical school as in the West, but manifested itself in a specific approach to social and national problems. It was primarily a return to the slogans of "organic work" known already in an earlier period. Its main concern was for economic advancement and its utilization for the national cause, because the acquisition of the education which would make work possible in the new economic conditions would lead to the spread of education and Polish national consciousness among the masses and imbue them with the national tradition. In short, this was the ideology of a burgeoisie growing in strength and numbers, opposed to both political romanticism and gentry traditions, yet, at the same time, preaching to the peasants and workers the principle of class solidarity. If the ideals of the previous generation had proclaimed insurrectionary struggle as the national aim, it was now in humdrum, but steady work in the economic and social field that a solution was seen of a situation which after the collapse of the insurrection in 1864 and of France in 1870, whose aid had been counted upon, seemed to hold no hope for Poland.

The positivists proclaimed a break with the philosophy of insurrection and declared their reconciliation with the existing conditions which seemed to have stabilized after 1871. The foregoing of aspirations to independence was to be accompanied by a retreat from participation in political affairs, a retreat which was, of course, only an apparent abnegation, because it was linked with the highly political stipulation of loyalty towards foreign rule. This concept, adopted in Galicia for current political needs, after a certain time took on a different meaning. It gave rise to a general conception called "tri-loyalism" by which was meant the reconciliation of every Polish province with its own foreign government. The upper classes of the landowning aristocracy and great financiers saw in this principle a safeguard of their own social position.

The political programme of the Galician conservatives was formulated as early as in 1869 in a satirical pamphlet entitled *Teka Stańczyka* (Stańczyk's Portfolio) after Stańczyk who was the clown of King Sigismund I, in which the passion for conspiracy was ridiculed and plots were condemned as the greatest danger to the national cause. This pamphlet was written for current needs in opposition to bolder democratic views demanding autonomy from the Austrian government. It was only in the course of time that the ideas expressed in "Stańczyk's Portfolio" took on a more general meaning and the name "Stańczyk" became the nickname for conservative West Galician politicians. They were regarded with respect, however, by conservatives in other areas, because they were the only politicians who by their willingness to compromise had obtained concrete political advantages.

The political conclusions drawn from "organic work" were contrary to the national traditions and could not take permanent root in the consciousness of socially active elements in the Polish nation. Nevertheless, positivism left a permanent mark on the attitude to national issues of both contemporaries and succeeding generations. The programme of the positivists was put into effect up to the end of the period of subjection. Above all, they insisted upon the duty of spreading education amongst the masses. This was carried out by dedicated persons in the Kingdom under most difficult conditions and here their work was to be a substitute for the lack of Polish schools in opposition to the policy of Russianization evident in official education policy. Among the pioneers in this movement were Konrad Prószyński, writing under the pseudonym Promyk, who from 1881 began to publish the "Gazeta Świąteczna" (Holiday Gazette). He wrote an excellent primer which was widely used as an instrument for combatting illiteracy. Another prominent person was Mieczysław Brzeziński who popularized the natural sciences and edited the journal "Zorza" (The Dawn), which was similarly designed for a wide readership.

The centre of learning at the beginning of this period was the Main School in Warsaw which operated in the years 1862–1869 and maintained close contacts with contemporary European learning. It had important scientific achievements in the field of biology—the Warsaw School of Henryk Hoyer, Sr. and in chemistry through the works of Jakub Natanson. Many eminent scholars emerged from this school like the linguists, Jan Baudouin de Courtenay and Adam Kryński, as well as writers and journalists like

Bolesław Prus

Aleksander Świętochowski, Henryk Sienkiewicz, Bolesław Prus and Adolf Dygasiński. The closing of the Main School in 1869 was a particularly painful blow. Learning in Warsaw flourished afterwards as a result of the efforts of individuals or small groups of scholars, assisted by the intermittent support of private patrons. In these primitive conditions and in spite of the obstacles created by the Tsarist authorities it was, nevertheless, possible to initiate and go a long way towards completing such collective enterprises of major importance for learning as the *Polish Geographical Dictionary*,

Maria Konopnicka

the *Dictionary of the Polish Language* and the *Great Illustrated Encyclopedia*. Eminent scholars like the geographer W. Nałkowski, the ethnographer O. Kolberg, and the sociologist L. Krzywicki were active in Warsaw during this period.

Learning in Galicia enjoyed a greater freedom and could draw on the resources of the universities. The Cracow Learned Society, which was converted in 1873 into the Academy of Science and Letters became an institution embracing all Poland, enrolling outstanding scholars from all three

Henryk Sienkiewicz

J. Matejko, *Stańczyk*, 1862

regions of the country. The humanities were particularly distinguished by the development of historical studies. The "Cracow School", recognizing the need for a critical and severe appraisal of the past, sought to show that the cause of Poland's downfall should be sought in Polish society itself. The historians of this school, like W. Kalinka, J. Szujski and their younger contemporary, M. Bobrzyński, adopted the point of view of the ruling "Stańczyk" group, condemning the worship of conspiracy and revolutionary romanticism and exalting strong monarchical rule. This does not alter the fact that they raised the critical analysis of sources and historical method to a higher level. Lwów University also followed suit and here K. Liske's seminars produced a host of energetic and talented historians.

In the physical sciences the achievements of Z. Wróblewski and K. Olszewski, who first achieved the condensation of oxygen and nitrogen obtained international recognition. Many Polish scholars continued their work

Maria Skłodowska-Curie

in western Europe, where many of them occupied chairs or became heads of institutes. Thus Maria Skłodowska-Curie, twice winner of the Nobel Prize, became while in Paris one of the discoverers of radioactivity; E. Habich was the organizer of the oldest technical college in South America. Among the Poles exiled to Siberia there were also outstanding scientists who explored and investigated the country like B. Dybowski, A. Czekanowski, J. Czerski.

While the most important achievements in literature of the romantic period were poetic works of high quality, it was prose, serving the needs of the times, and, in particular, the novel which flourished in Poland and abroad.

A pioneer of these new ideas was Aleksander Świętochowski, an extremely versatile writer, whether as a journalist, novelist or playwright, who condemned class prejudices and clericalism bitterly and fought for the emancipation of Jews and equal rights for women. He was firmly convinced of the progressive role of the bourgeoisie, but at the same time opposed all political activities aimed at fighting for independence and resisted the working class movement from its very inception. He urged political solidarity and while he condemned the clericalism of the upper classes, he recognized the social function of the clergy which, according to him, "constantly and over a large time shall exercise tutelage over the ignorant masses". Eliza Orzeszkowa fought in her novels for the emancipation of women, for rescuing the village from poverty and backwardness, sharply criticizing religious fanaticism and obscurantism and passionately demanding rights for the Jews. The ideas of "organic work" were expressed in her novel dealing with the life of the petty gentry *Nad Niemnem* (On the Neman). Bolesław Prus (1845–1912), whose real name was Aleksander Głowacki, was a writer, journalist and thinker. In his novel *Placówka* (The Outpost) he presented the struggle of the Polish village against German oppression as a model for society illustrating the ignorance and backwardness of the Polish peasant. *Lalka* (The Doll) was the first great novel in Polish literature about the Polish urban middle class presenting a broad picture of life, social problems and conflicts in the period after the 1863 Insurrection.

Frequently in this period the expression of sociological concepts and ideas of freedom took the form of historical themes, even in remote times, like Bolesław Prus's *Faraon* (The Pharaoh). A similar didactic aim is evident in the works of Henryk Sienkiewicz, the writer of colourful historical novels such as *Krzyżacy* (The Teutonic Knights), the trilogy *Ogniem i Mieczem* (With Fire and Sword), *Potop* (The Deluge) and *Pan Wołodyjowski*, and *Quo Vadis,* a novel about Nero's Rome and the first Christians, for which the writer received the Nobel Prize. The influence of French naturalism showed itself in the novels and short stories of Dygasiński and the novels and plays of Gabriela Zapolska.

The poetry of this period was represented by the introspective poet Adam Asnyk and by Maria Konopnicka, a fighter for progress and enlightenment, who drew much of her inspiration from folk art.

Journalism, which developed considerably during this period and in which the best writers engaged, likewise served to proclaim the slogans of positivism.

Art in this period, while deprived of state support, received private encouragement, no longer from the aristocracy as had been earlier but from the wealthy bourgeoisie. It severed its links with romanticism, though that tradition was to some extent continued by the paintings of Jan Matejko. Closely connected with the Cracow school of history and working in Cracow, he created his great historical tableaux. He imposed on Polish society his own vision of the past to such effect that to the present time the average Pole visualizes the national heroes as represented by this great painter in his compositions like the *Battle of Grunwald, Stańczyk* and *Skarga's Sermon.*

A. Gierymski, *Sand-diggers*, 1887

It was realism, however, which became dominant in art thanks to painters of everyday life of such ability as Józef Chełmoński, Maksymilian Gierymski. The most eminent of the realist painters, Aleksander Gierymski, became a precursor of Polish expressionism. It should be noted that Polish art did not so much follow the fashion of St. Petersburg, Berlin, or Vienna, as that of Rome and especially Paris and was linked in this period even more closely with west-European art.

THE BEGINNINGS OF THE POLISH WORKING-CLASS MOVEMENT

The growth in numbers of the working class gave rise to a labour movement simultaneously in all the three regions of Poland. Although political and social conditions were different in each of these areas, the working-class movement constituted the first political and social movement in the period after 1863 embracing the entire Polish nation.

Its beginnings may be found in the most industrialized region of Poland, in Silesia. Working-class organizations began to arise in Germany in the

1860's, led first by F. Lassalle and later developed by the Marxists, A. Bebel and W. Liebknecht. At this time Lassalle's emissaries were already active in Wrocław and in the general election to the North German parliament of 1867 the socialists obtained 4000 votes in Upper Silesia. The greater part of the German and Polish workers voted together in solidarity. In 1875 the unification of the two socialist parties in Germany took place and in the 1878 elections 23,000 votes were obtained by the socialists in Silesia, of which Polish votes certainly constituted an important part. The same region was also a field of activity by trade unions directed by liberal bourgeois leaders, which pass by the name of the "Hirsch–Duncker Unions". When in 1878 the anti-socialist legislation in Germany went into effect, the socialist movement in the Polish provinces of Prussia ceased to exist. It revived shortly afterwards, but inspiration for this came, not as in earlier years, from the German socialists, but from the Polish movement in the area belonging to Russia.

In the Congress Kingdom the working-class movement was rooted in native conditions, drawing its strength from the old revolutionary traditions among the handicraft workers. This spirit was reawakened by the initiative of young intellectuals who had made contact with the socialist revolutionary movement at Russian universities. The most outstanding of these young men was Ludwik Waryński, who came from a gentry family in the Ukraine. During his studies in St. Petersburg he belonged to a circle of Polish revolutionaries, who in 1874 decided to start their action in Poland, where socialist groups were beginning to arise among the Warsaw workers. In 1878, under Waryński's influence, "Resistance Funds", little groups formed for the purpose of agitation, were formed. These Warsaw socialists, among whom a prominent theorist, Aleksander Więckowski and his successor, Stanisław Mendelson, drew up the first Polish socialist programme, which was printed in Geneva in 1878, known, however, as the "Brussels Programme" because for reasons of secrecy Brussels was given as the place of publication. It was, on the whole, expressed in general terms, but it stressed the class struggle and international solidarity. It shows that the young revolutionaries, opposed the rejection by the positivists of the struggle to change the existing situation. While they did not ignore national aspirations, they proclaimed, above all, the international slogan of a general revolution of the peoples.

In 1879 Waryński had to escape from Warsaw and leave for Galicia. In this economically retarded area there was virtually no industrial proletariat. The first socialist groups arose in petty-bourgeois and handicraft circles under the inspiration of former members of the left-wing democratic movement in Lwów which had supported the 1863 Insurrection. A leading part was played by printers who in this part of Europe were always the most politically conscious element among the working class. For several years Bolesław Limanowski, an exile from Lithuania, who had taken part in the demonstrations before 1863 and had been deported to Siberia, had been foremost in these activities. In years to come he was to become the first outstanding Polish socialist to lay more stress on national than on class aims. Shortly afterwards he was compelled to leave Poland for a long time and became primarily a prolific writer and historian of the democratic school combatting, almost alone, the ideas of the Cracow school of history.

It was Limanowski who introduced Waryński to the socialists in Lwów. Waryński, a born conspirator, wished immediately to set up a secret socialist organization in Lwów. The Lwów socialists determinedly opposed this step, considering that in constitutional Austria conspiracy was unnecessary and even harmful. The twenty-two years old Waryński departed for Cracow, where there was no socialist organization at all, and there formed a conspiracy which was immediately discovered by the police. An investigation was begun in which the Austrians collaborated with the Prussian and Russian police. The result of their discoveries were arrests in Warsaw and a trial in Cracow in 1880, followed for two months with the greatest interest by the public. During this episode ultra-conservative circles and their Cracow newspaper "Czas" (Time) strongly denounced socialism, seeing in it the principal danger to society. More democratic and liberal papers defended the accused. Ultimately the 35 accused were set free and several foreign subjects were deported. A most important part in this famous trial was played by Waryński and Mendelson. Afterwards they both imigrated to Geneva, from whence they conducted agitation in Poland. In Galicia the Cracow trial was a stimulus to the growth of the socialist movement. Already in 1879 a socialist programme for Galicia had been elaborated, but its extremely moderate demands showed the backwardness of this area. Perhaps the most significant fact for Poland as a whole was that one of the Lwów socialists, the young poet, Bolesław Czerwieński, in 1881 wrote the words to the anthem *Czerwony Sztandar* (The Red Flag), which in the history of socialist movements in Poland played a more important role than many well-written pamphlets. The song became well known throughout Europe.

After the Cracow trial Waryński, Mendelson and Limanowski came together in Geneva. Limanowski was already publishing there the paper "Równość" (Equality) in 1879. A dispute arose between them about the question of independence which was to be continued by three generations of socialists in Poland. Limanowski, as an advocate of independence, shortly afterwards left the paper, and the attitude of Waryński and Mendelson was represented at a celebration in Geneva of the fiftieth anniversary of the November Insurrection by Kazimierz Dłuski, who ended his speech with the words, "Down with patriotism and reaction, long live the international and the social revolution!" Patriotism in this sense was understood as the separation of the Polish question from general revolutionary aims and as a position in which the influence of a gentry mentality was dominant. For the moment this was a somewhat theoretical question, because the hopes of socialists for a speedy social revolution were in any case illusory and the struggle for independence did not have any chance of success, but it was precisely on this basis that a division of the Polish working-class movement into two mutually hostile sections arose.

Mendelson with a few companions departed shortly afterwards to the Prussian area to organize the socialist movement there among both Polish and German workers. He wished to give proof in practice of his internationalism. The activities of this small group in Poznań lasted for only a month because the police took them into custody.

Waryński went back to Warsaw at the end of 1881 and the fruits of his activity there were most serious and important. Fascinated by the "Narodnaya Volya" movement, the leading revolutionary organization in Russia, which aimed at the overthrow of the Tsarist régime by means of conspiracies and terrorist activity, he resolved to establish a similar organization in the Kingdom.

THE "PROLETARIAT"

The secret organization established by Waryński, which had already taken on the characteristics of a political party, called itself the "Proletariat". Its first political pronouncement in August 1883 had revolutionary and internationalist overtones. The party organized strikes and one of them in the textile factory in Żyrardów involved 8000 workers and ended in victory. The year 1883 saw the greatest flourishing of the party. Outside Warsaw it was active already in Łódź, Zgierz and Białystok. In September 1883 a secret paper also called "Proletariat" began to appear, the first of its kind to be published in the Kingdom after the collapse of the January Insurrection. It was, however, precisely at this time that Waryński was arrested. After this misfortune the party was led for a time by Stanisław Kunicki, who was connected with the "Narodnaya Volya" and was inclined to follow its example in the use of terror. At this moment the "Proletariat" concluded an agreement with the "Narodnaya Volya" as the two organizations which expected to undertake the struggle for power, the one in Russia, the other in Poland. It followed from the agreement that the "Proletariat" was to conduct its activities where the majority of the population spoke Polish. "Narodnaya Volya", moreover, guaranteed the "Proletariat's" complete independence and agreed to work in collaboration. Shortly afterwards the two organizations were discovered by the police, but this agreement and the activity of the "Proletariat" gave rise to a tradition of revolutionary class struggle. In the summer of 1884 the police arrested Kunicki and Ludwik Janowicz, the leaders of the "Proletariat", and shortly afterwards

Ludwik Waryński

two hundred of its members were imprisoned. Twenty-nine of them were tried by a court martial. The case lasted a month and Waryński emerged as a hero. He delivered a magnificent speech which was his last great political act. On 30 December, 1884 judgement was announced, condemning six of the defendants to death by hanging, i.e., those who had been tried for acts of terror. S. Kunicki, P. Bardowski, a Russian judge, M. Ossowski and J. Pietrusiński, were hanged on the slopes of the Warsaw Citadel. They became heroes in the tradition of the revolutionary working-class movement.

At the same time the trial showed that the country, which had languished in lethargy since the disaster of the Insurrection of 1863 was awakening to a new life and that the struggle, interrupted in 1864, was renewed upon the basis of combining the old insurgent traditions "for your freedom and ours" with the new ideals of the revolution. Though the mode of expression was different, the content was to be to a considerable degree the same, because it was a struggle for the freedom of the Polish people.

The rest of the accused were sentenced to deportation and penal servitude. Waryński was imprisoned in the notorious Schlüsselburg where he died of tuberculosis in 1889. He was the outstanding figure of this period of the struggle for liberation.

After the trial of the "Proletariat", arrests did not cease, but the Tsarist government, not wishing to give publicity to the revolutionary working-class movement, deported those arrested to Siberia by administrative means. Of these many perished in the extremely severe conditions there. This was the fate of Maria Bohuszewicz, who up to 1885 had led the activity of the moribund party.

In 1887 a few intellectuals revived the organization, but this activity was on a much smaller scale and lasted only one year. Very soon they, too, were imprisoned. This was the "Second" or "Little Proletariat" and for this reason the first organization was traditionally referred to as the "Great Proletariat". From this time on, however, there was a labour movement in existence which continued to develop and, even if particular organizations were broken up by the gendarmerie, the movement resurrected itself time and again, gaining ever more experience, developing new forms of organization and continually perfecting its ideology.

THE BEGINNINGS OF THE PEASANT MOVEMENT

During this same period, when the working-class movement emerged in the Polish territories, an independent peasant movement also began. It was in the Prussian area that Polish peasants first revealed activity of an economic nature. From 1862 onwards J. Kraziewicz established in Pomerania peasant organizations, or "agricultural circles". This movement spread quite rapidly so that in 1867 a "diet" of peasants was convened in Toruń. The first agricultural circle in the Poznań area was set up in 1866. It is only then that the landowners decided to assert their leadership over this spontaneous movement. In 1873 tutelage was established over the agricultural circles under the direction of Maksymilian Jackowski, an outstanding and dedicated man. Soon, the number of circles increased to 150 and they contributed in a considerable degree to raising the level of agricultural techniques among the peasants of the Prussian area. Later, when the Prussian government began its struggle against the Poles for the ownership of the soil this had a decisive importance on the successful repulsion of this dangerous attack.

The peasant movement in the Prussian area, under the patronage of the landowners, did not have a class character. It was the Austrian area which saw the beginnings of a peasant political movement. The Galician gentry did not take the initiative in spreading education in the villages. It was customary to regard the peasantry as a hostile element. When the gentry had obtained autonomy in Galicia and taken the administration into its own hands, it felt safe with regard to the peasantry and did not in the least consider it a duty to raise the level of education among the former serfs. The primary and secondary school system was controlled by the Provincial School Council, which included a number of devoted and energetic educationalists. The Council was, however, dependent on the Viceroy and the Seym, which approved the school budget. The landowning majority in the Seym hamstrung the activity of the School Council and the expansion of the school system, with the result that the opportunity which autonomy offered for promoting the national cause and winning over the peasantry was not taken. Just as in the question of woods and pastures, an obstinate class egotism had prevailed with regard to the school question, which was considered only in the light of keeping the peasants in a state of dependence in order that they might easily be exploited. The gentry found an ally in the clergy which was under the direction of an ecclesiastical hierarchy, closely linked with the gentry and its interests. Care was taken that the badly paid teachers did not gain authority in the countryside.

The initiative in organizing an independent peasant movement did, however, come from a priest in opposition to the hierarchy. This was Stanisław Stojałowski, endowed with unusual organizing abilities, but at the same time something of a demagogue. From 1875 he edited "Wieniec" (The Wreath) and "Pszczółka" (The Bee), papers which had up to that time been published for the purpose of keeping the peasants obedient towards the upper classes. Stojałowski began a tremendous political drive in which, though he formulated no far-reaching programme, appeal was made to free the villages from their dependence on the gentry. Stojałowski proclaimed the necessity of thrift, education and the establishment of circles of an economic character. In a short time he gained such popularity that thousands would come to his meetings. In 1883, on the 200th anniversary of the relief of Vienna, 12,000 peasants appeared in Cracow on his orders. The authorities realized that Stojałowski had become a political power and soon launched a struggle against him, which was to make him a tribune of the people.

THREE PROVINCES AND ONE NATION

The policy of the three Powers dominating Poland in the first years after the insurrection took on a different aspect in each of the three areas. Each area entered the era of capitalism under different conditions not only in the political, but also in the economic and social sense. Galicia had the broadest political possibilities, but also the least advantageous economic conditions. It had none of the conditions for industrial development, the modernization of its social relations and the raising of the general level of culture. The Congress Kingdom, subject to brutal political oppression, simultaneously entered an era of rapid industrialization which led to rapid modernization. Finally, the Prussian area, where the possibilities of political life were very restricted, nevertheless, benefited from the achievements of a modern state and drew benefit from belonging to a power whose economic development was extremely rapid. Though the Poznań and Pomeranian territories remained agrarian, agriculture in both these provinces was raised to a high level of efficiency, which strengthened the Polish community in its struggle against oppression. Upper Silesia, on the other hand, became a great mining and metallurgical area. While it is true that the Poles could work in these industries only as unskilled workers and that they took second place to the Rhineland, with the result that the workers were paid on a lower scale than in other provinces of the Reich, it was precisely the existence of this great industrial basin which established the basis for a national revival in the province.

The growing significance of the Congress Kingdom, by comparison with the other areas, was shown by the growth of its population. In the second half of the nineteenth century the population of the Kingdom increased from 4.8 mln to 10 mln, or by 108 per cent. The population of Galicia from 4.6 mln to 7.3 mln (59 per cent); the population of the Poznań province, most strongly affected by emigration, from 1.4 mln to 1.9 mln (36 per cent).

The differing conditions of life in the three areas also entailed the closer connexion of the Polish territories with the three foreign States, to which they had heretofore belonged only in an administrative sense. The expansion of the railway network played a very important role in this respect. It connected the individual Polish areas with Russia, Germany and Austria and absorbed them into foreign economic systems, with a consequent growth in the influence of foreign culture and ideas. This in turn threatened the nation with a dissolution of its cultural unity which up to this time had remained homogeneous, not withstanding the loss of independence.

It was precisely in this field, however, that the Polish nation displayed unusual vitality and powers of resistance. It developed and enriched its own culture, common to all the three areas, by drawing into it an ever widening mass of the people.

The progressive emancipation of the peasantry was of particular importance in this respect, which had its basis in the fact that from the end of the Middle Ages up to the time of the January Insurrection the amount of land in peasant possession had shrunk with each generation. From this time onwards a contrary process took place. In all three areas under foreign rule, the peasants began to buy land back from the landlords. In the Kingdom this took place in the years 1864–1890, largely as a result of the settling of the woods and pastures question. In the Poznań area, somewhat later, after 1880, the peasants took advantage of unfavourable world prices for agricultural produce, which severely affected the great landowners, and enlarged their holdings by purchase of land. The situation was most difficult in Galicia, but even there the peasants had also secured their position against the estate and soon began to attack the weakened medium landowners by means of land purchase, thus increasing their total holdings by comparison with the holdings of the gentry.

All these social and economic features increased markedly in the following two decades and gave rise to political changes within Polish society. The general economic development, though uneven in the different areas, strengthened democratic tendencies in all of Poland. The working class became stronger, especially with the increased concentration in industry. The position of the peasantry also was stronger, while the bourgoisie enriched itself and the landowning gentry was on the whole able to adapt itself to the new economic conditions. Further development of literature and journalism and in learning and the arts was apparent. All this gave the leading groups in Polish society a feeling of power and strengthened that faith in the future of the nation, which had been weakened by the disaster of the insurrection.

Chapter XIX
THE FORMATION OF MASS POLITICAL PARTIES. NATIONALISM AND SOCIALISM (1885–1904)

THE PRUSSIAN EXPULSIONS. THE COLONIZATION COMMISSION

In the middle of the 1880's changes of attitude took place among the socially conscious sections of the nation. The influence of positivism had come to an end. The appearance of a revolutionary working-class movement was in itself proof of the fact that the political passivity proclaimed by the positivists was out of date. The publication of Sienkiewicz's *Trilogy* in 1884–1888 may be regarded as the sign of this change. Because of the author's obvious talent it immediately gained a wide readership and became an important factor in shaping Polish thought. These novels were a glorification of Poland's gentry in the past, for which reason conservative circles gave the author, until recently a positivist, their support, but the younger generation found in this historical novel, with its seventeenth century theme, an extollation of Poland's former strength and moral comfort for the present. The younger generation, disarmed physically and spiritually by the disaster of the Insurrection of 1863–1864 and the slogans of "organic work", now once more yearned for military action and the tradition of knighthood. It rejected political passivity and felt that the sober slogans of the positivists served to mask the selfish class interests of a bourgeoisie growing in wealth.

At this juncture, when the attitude of political passivity was disappearing, a new blow was dealt to the Polish nation. In March 1885 the Prussian government expelled from the eastern provinces of the State all foreign citizens of Polish nationality. About 30,000 Poles were involved in these "Bismarckian expulsions" and in a very short time they were expelled from homes which had been theirs often for many years. This regulation, issued at a time of complete peace, gave rise to general indignation against Prussia, not only in Poland, but also throughout Europe and even among a large part of the German people.

There had been insufficient time to recover from this unexpected blow when the King's speech in the Prussian Parliament on January 1886 foreshadowed new and much more significant moves in the struggle against the Poles. In April 1886 the Prussian Parliament established a special fund of 100 million marks for the purpose of purchasing land from the Poles, on which German peasants were to be settled. From this time onwards the struggle with the Poles entered a dramatic phase, because it was already clear that the aim was to extirpate the Poles from their western territories.

In his speeches Bismarck proclaimed that he had begun a struggle with the Polish gentry and did not in the least aim at the Polish peasant, whose loyalty towards the State, he pretended, had remained unchanged. But the struggle on both sides spread to an ever greater part of the population and was transformed into a struggle between the two nations, giving rise to fierce national feeling on both sides, a development which Bismarck, who was always guided by reason of State, did not favour at all. Just as in the period of the *Kulturkampf* Bismarck's motives, when he began this struggle, were different from those of the social forces which supported him in the campaign. Once more these proved to be the stronger. The National Liberals, with whose support Bismarck established the Colonization Commission, regarded the settlement campaign more as an experiment on a much broader scale than a mere struggle against the Polish gentry. They desired a general change in the agrarian system. Their aim was the creation of a strong and prosperous peasantry, which would socially and, therefore, politically counterbalance the power of the Prussian junkers. The growth of chauvinism in Germany was to their advantage; the bourgeoisie abandoned its liberal ideas and regarded nationalism as a useful instrument in the struggle with the growing socialist movement. It was for this reason that to the very end of the Prussian monarchy it was precisely the National Liberals who remained the most determined advocates of expelling the Poles from Germany's eastern borderlands.

Bismarck, on the other hand, took his stand, as always, upon immediate political expediency. In the 1870's the *Kulturkampf* had, in his view, the internal aim of smashing the "Zentrum", the bastion of particularism, and the external purpose of opposing the threatening Franco-Austrian-Catholic coalition. Now such a coalition was not a threat, because from 1879 Austro-Hungary had been an ally of Germany. The aim now was, on the contrary, to strengthen and implement the alliance with Austro-Hungary. Bismarck was aware that the *Dreikaiserbund,* concluded in 1872 and renewed again in 1881, did not fully guarantee the preservation of good relations between Russia and Austria. Fearing a possible Austro-Russian conflict, he knew that Germany would be forced to side against Russia. He understood that in such a case the Polish question would again present a problem. He considered, therefore, that before such an eventuality should happen, it was necessary either to exterminate or at least to weaken the Polish element in Prussia to such a degree that a reconstituted Polish State would have no cause to claim Poznań or Pomerania. He desired, at the same time, to remind Russia, by the very fact of pursuing a struggle against the Poles, that the three partitioning Powers had in common an important problem, more vital than expansion in the Balkans, namely the Polish question.

These were the motives of the Prussian government when it began its struggle to wrest land from the Poles in Poznań and Pomerania. Once the struggle had begun, the initial causes gradually lost their significance. The results of the struggle, however, were permanent. The different classes of Polish society experienced a great shock and it was clearly understood that the nation stood in mortal danger. Though it is true that in the Poznań area resistance was not organized immediately, especially when the activity of the Colonization Commission in its first years was not too dangerous and met with serious technical difficulties, both sides realized that the further development of the conflict was inevitable and that alternative methods would be utilized in the struggle for ownership of the soil.

THE POLISH LEAGUE

Probably the first tangible political result of the German attack was the creation in Switzerland of the so-called Polish League. The initiative for this step came from Zygmunt Miłkowski, one of the more eminent members of the democratic emigration after 1863–1864, himself a well-known novelist. In 1887, a year of tension in international relations as a result of the Balkan crisis and an expected Austro-Russian war, he published a famous pamphlet entitled *Rzecz o obronie czynnej i o Skarbie Narodowym* (Regarding Active Resistance and a National Fund). He proclaimed that it was time to break with political passivity and that a positive attitude coordinated in all the occupied areas, would force the enemies to change their conduct towards the Poles. In the pamphlet, preparations for insurrection were not recommended, but a deliberate abandonment of the concept of insurrection was condemned. Miłkowski put forward the idea of establishing a national fund to be used for propaganda abroad. The pamphlet made a tremendous impression on the youth of Poland. It was a challenge to the prevailing positivist ideology and to the slogans of "tri-loyalism". It was followed immediately by the idea among the emigrants of establishing a secret organization, which would direct Polish politics in all the three areas. Thus, the Polish League was established, headed by a committee with the traditional name of "Centralizacja", under the chairmanship of Miłkowski. The social principles proclaimed in the League's statute may be considered to be generally democratic. They were not, however, elaborated in detail, though on the other hand considerable attention was paid to the possibility of a conspiracy for the purpose of preparing the Poles for the event of European conflict.

This organization would have remained an ephemeral émigré project, had it not been joined by a group of young men in Poland connected with the periodical "Głos" (The Voice), established in Warsaw in 1886. The most important among them was Jan Popławski who had been sentenced to deportation in 1878. While in exile he had met the Russian "Narodniks" and absorbed some of their ideas of agrarian socialism. After his return to Poland he collaborated at first with positivist journals, but, at that time, his anti-gentry views became more marked. To Popławski the common people embodied all the positive characteristics. "Without traditions and even without culture, the Polish people have preserved their nationality more fully and strongly than the educated classes". It was these ideas which this group introduced into the Polish League, of which they soon completely took control. Zygmunt Balicki, Popławski's close collaborator, was responsible for the establishment of a large organization of university students called the Union of Polish Youth (Związek Młodzieży Polskiej, abbreviated to "Zet"). Modelling itself on the Free Masons, it had at first three and later two degrees of initiation. This organization remained under the leadership of the Polish League and it was active in all university centres where Poles studied, at home and especially abroad. The organization was a political force for many years and those who had been its members adopted an attitude of mutual solidarity, which gave them an immense influence on the whole of Polish political and social life up to the reestablishment of independence and later. Soon "Zet" began to establish itself in the secondary schools also and in the self-education circles which were being organized and which, though they usually arose spontaneously, quickly came under the influence of the "Zet-Brotherhood". Thus, around 1890 a general political awakening took place in which the young intelligentsia played a leading role.

This movement was connected with the general abandonment of the attitude which had prevailed since the collapse of the insurrection in 1864. At first the general public, frightened and passive, regarded illegal social work as likely to lead to fresh persecution which was to be avoided at all costs, but in 1885 changes in the attitude of a large section of the intelligentsia could clearly be seen. This showed itself not only in illegal political action, but also in educational and cultural work which was almost as dangerous for the foreign rulers.

The illegal campaign of popular education in the Kingdom was one of the finest achievements of the period. Gradually an entire network of secret schools was established, whether primary for the mass of the population, or secondary of all types, reaching ultimately to university level. This organization was active not only in Warsaw, but also in other towns and small communities of the Kingdom. Everywhere the illegal teaching of the Polish language, history and geography was carried on. According to Russian official sources, in 1901 clandestine teaching embraced a third of the country's population and the majority of the peasants owed their literacy to the secret school system. This effort had, of course, not only an educational significance. It brought about an awakening of national and social consciousness and, because those who participated in this work, come from a variety of groups with different points of view, it stimulated both nationalism and socialism.

In practically all the state secondary schools of the Russian part of Poland secret self-education circles were established, effectively resisting attempts at Russianization by the authorities and teachers. Secret courses of Polish history and literature also were held. The major role in this effort was played by women. The historian Władysław Smoleński, who took part in this work, writes about them as follows, "Imbued with the mission of struggle for national existence, in their homes they taught with undaunted zeal children who were deprived in the secondary schools of their native language, history and literature; they lit up with the torch of Polish culture the basements and attics of the workers, the provincial towns and the manor houses".

A clandestine course of higher education was established for women in which the most eminent Polish scholars in Warsaw lectured. It was called the "Flying University" because the lectures were obliged continually to change from one place to another. It had twenty-or-so lecturers and several hundred students. Its courses lasted for twenty years and became legal only after the 1905 Revolution. In addition, all girls' private schools gave secret courses in Polish history and literature; clandestine secondary schools for girls were also established.

Whole areas of social and cultural activities were forced underground as a result of the pressure of the Tsarist government, which did not permit Polish initiative in the cultural field. The Poles were assisted by their old tradition of conspiracy, inherited from the 1863 Insurrection. In this respect, no other people in this part of Europe had as fine a record. A nation, deprived of sovereignty, was able to establish in the cultural and educational field a network of organizations which, in practice, were immune from the persecutions of foreign governments. All those who participated in this work were of course well aware of the personal risks involved. Though immediately after 1864 all illegal work was frowned upon by the great majority of the well-to-do, in the middle of the 1880's an increasing number of persons working with dedication in the field of secret education, were accorded recognition among the educated classes. A large part was played in this by literature which glorified the heroes of this activity and found a common language with the Polish readers, in spite of the severity of censorship, which, as is usual in such cases, was not able to break down the conspiracy of understanding between the author and the reader.

THE SOCIALIST MOVEMENT

In this period the socialist movement also took on a new scope. In Galicia it benefited from those gains which had been won by the proletariat in its struggle in the western and more industrialized provinces of the monarchy. Simultaneously with the establishment of an all-Austrian party, a Social-Democratic party was organized in Galicia in 1892, led by Ignacy Daszyński, an able speaker and agitator. Galicia was also, in spite of its general backwardness, slowly entering the era of capitalism. For military reasons the Austrian government enlarged the railway network and this entailed an improvement of conditions in industry. A more rapid development of the oil industry in the area, first at Jasło, and then at Drohobycz and Borysław, hastened the growth of the working class. Thus the basic conditions for the development of the socialist movement had arisen. The newly-formed party ultimately called itself the Polish Social-Democratic Party of Galicia and Cieszyn-Silesia and played in the life of this province a much more important part than was warranted by its essentially weak social basis. Its full significance dates from the time it began to send deputies to the Austrian Parliament. This became possible after a constitutional reform introduced in Austria an electoral class (*curia*) based on universal suffrage in 1897.

As in all of Poland, in Galicia the decision to celebrate the workers' holiday on May Day became a stimulus for the movement. In 1890 May Day was held in Lwów, Cracow, Warsaw and Łódź. The Polish proletariat thus gave evidence of its political existence.

In the Congress Kingdom the working-class movement grew with the expansion of industry. The value of industrial production in the next twenty years again doubled, from 200 to 400 million roubles. The number of workers in the Kingdom increased at the same time from 150,000 to 270,000. What was still more important, however, was that an increasing number of workers were employed, as a result of concentration of industry, in large industrial plants. This increased the working class feeling of strength and hastened the development of its experience.

Along with the growth of the working class, a rapid urbanization occurred. The population of Warsaw increased almost fivefold in the period from the Insurrection of 1863–1864 to the outbreak of the First World War rising from 200,000 to 900,000. Łódź, the textile centre and the most important industrial town in the Kingdom, grew tenfold from 50,000 to 500,000. This process was aided by a fundamental change in agriculture. At this time the Kingdom ceased to export grain, because the European markets were flooded by cheap American grain. Local grain was sold at lower prices to towns and factory areas with a consequent lowering of the cost of food for workers and townspeople in general.

Under such economic and social conditions the working-class movement gained strength in spite of repression. In 1892 a strike accompanied by disturbances occurred in Łódź on the occasion of May Day, with troops being sent out against the workers. It was clear that the proletariat in the Kingdom was mature enough for the formation of a mass socialist party. Once more the exiles were responsible for its organization. In the autumn of

1892 a famous meeting was held in Paris under the chairmanship of Limanowski and with Mendelson as its principal organizer. The meeting set out a programme of the Polish Socialist Party and the Union of Polish Socialists Abroad was formed, with the aim of assisting the movement in Poland. The programme, modelled partly on the recently formulated Erfurt programme of the German Social-Democratic Party, was reformist in nature. It aimed at the creation of a democratic Polish republic, but fully socialist aims were postponed to a later stage. Thus this working-class party linked the emancipation of the working class with simultaneous national liberation. It was this feature of the party which attracted to it, along with sincere socialists, also those for whom socialism was only a slogan to win the masses to a political programme of struggle for national independence.

In 1893 the Polish Socialist Party (PPS) was established in the Kingdom and controlled by a Central Workers' Committee. The party at once began a skillful campaign of agitation. Above all, it distributed secret literature at first smuggled in from abroad. The secret paper "Robotnik" (The Worker) was published regularly from 1894. It symbolized the strength of the party, inasmuch as the gendermerie could not for a long time discover its printing works or interfere with its distribution. Józef Piłsudski soon became its editor and the *de facto* leader of the party. He had returned in 1892 from exile in Siberia and had joined the Wilno branch of the Polish Socialist Party.

At the same time, in 1893, a second socialist party was established. It was internationalist in character and consistently put more emphasis on the class struggle. This was the Social Democracy of the Kingdom of Poland founded by Rosa Luxemburg and Julian Marchlewski. It considered itself to be continuing the work of the "Great Proletariat" and held the view that the slogan of a struggle for national independence was at that time injurious to solidarity with the working-class movement of Tsarist Russia, whose government was its common enemy. After temporary setbacks, the party became active again under the leadership of Feliks Dzierżyński under the name of the Social Democracy of the Kingdom of Poland and Lithuania, abbreviated as SDKPiL. This party stressed its close links with Rusian Social Democrats. Rosa Luxemburg continued to be its principal theorist. In opposition to the exploitation of patriotic slogans by the propertied classes, she maintained that the Kingdom, as well as the other two areas, had grown economically as a result of association with the larger states to which they belonged and were therefore "organically incorporated" in them. Thus, economic reasons were an obstacle to regaining political independence. The social revolution, by abolishing social and political oppression, would also thereby do away with national oppression in all its manifestations. Rosa Luxemburg and Marchlewski soon afterwards went to Germany, where they were active in the German Social Democratic movement without ceasing to maintain their contact with the SDKPiL. In the Kingdom the antagonism between the

SDKPiL and PPS became deeper. The dispute on the national question in Poland deepened the divisions existing on a world-wide scale between revolutionary and reformist views in the working-class movement.

At the same time as the Polish Socialist Party arose in the Kingdom, a Polish Socialist Party of the Prussian area was established. Its organ was the "Gazeta Robotnicza" (The Workers' Paper) which had begun publication earlier in Berlin. In 1901 the paper was transferred to Katowice in order to strengthen Polish socialist agitation in Upper Silesia. At the outset the Polish Socialist Party of the Prussian area was considered a branch of German Social Democracy, which assisted it financially, but soon disagreement between the two parties arose, because the German Socialists did not agree to nominating Polish socialist candidates in Upper Silesia, on the grounds that the country had never belonged to Poland. The German Social Democrats were not united in their attitude on the question of Poland's independence. Wilhelm Liebknecht was an outstanding friend of Poland, but he died in 1900 and the new leader of the party, August Bebel, in spite of his sympathy for Poland, inclined rather to the views of Rosa Luxemburg. As a result the Polish Socialist Party of the Prussian area ultimately in 1913 set up an organization separate from that of the German party.

The influence of the PPS in the Prusian area was relatively small. Since the *Kulturkampf* the masses in this area had come under the strong influence of the clergy, who were opposed to class agitation and had organized a labour movement under their own sponsorship, both in the Polish lands of the Prussian State and in Germany itself, especially in Westphalia, where there were numerous Polish workers. The clergy under the influence of Leo XIII's encyclical *Rerum novarum* of 1891 undertook this campaign precisely at the time when the mass socialist parties were being found. On the initiative of Archbishop Florian Stablewski, "Societies of Polish Workers" began to be organized in 1892. Since 1905 the paper "Robotnik" (The Worker) edited by Father Adamski was published, while the Gniezno theological seminary held courses on social questions. Polish workers' unions were established still earlier. The strongest was the Bochum Polish Workers' Union, founded in 1902, which later led to a unification of all the unions of this type.

ATTEMPTS AT COMPROMISE WITH THE GERMAN AND RUSSIAN GOVERNMENTS

These workers' unions, which pursued a policy of class conciliation, tended in the national question likewise to put forward passive slogans, defending the *status quo*, and were not in the least dangerous to the Prussian State. This resulted from their desire to gain the support of all those, both Poles and the Germans, who wished to oppose the danger of socialism. Immediately after Bismarck's fall in 1890 Polish conservatives launched a broad political campaign aimed at creating some type of a *modus vivendi* with the Prussian State. These attempts at conciliation were connected with the activity of the landowner, Józef Kościelski, who, through his connexions at the Court, came into contact with the new chancellor, Caprivi, at a time when he was in a difficult situation in the Reichstag and wished to win over the Polish deputies.

Caprivi's first significant move in the international field was the refusal to renew the 1887 secret treaty, which linked Berlin and St. Petersburg diplomatically, but which was undoubtedly at variance with the Austro-German alliance. This severance of established links between the two northern courts, which was in a way the foundation stone of Polish subjection, was of immense significance for the future fate of Poland. At the time it gave rise only to a temporary relaxation of the German anti-Polish policy. It lasted barely as long as this brief first Russo-German tension, which manifested itself most sharply in a customs war, resolved by the signing of a ten-year trade treaty in 1894. Both Powers found a new area for imperialist expansion in the Far East, where they worked together against Japan.

It was not only international circumstances which frustrated a Polish-German conciliation. The basic cause lay in the fact that the German bourgeoisie, abandoning liberal ideas in the new period of imperialism, adopted extreme nationalist slogans at home as the best antidote to socialism. The bourgeoisie was likewise aware that these slogans made it possible to mobilize the energies of the broad masses for imperialist aims. In order to put into effect the building of a navy in the interests of heavy industry, it was necessary to create a huge propaganda machine. For this purpose the "Allgemeiner Deutscher Verband" (General German Union) was established in 1891, renamed the "Alldeutscher Verband" (Pan-German Union) in 1894.

The Polish Parliamentary Club in the Reichstag gave the government their support not only for its projects of military and naval expansion, but also for its economic policy, which during Caprivi's time stressed more the interests of large industry than those of agriculture. In this way Polish conservatives agreed even to a policy which was contrary to the economic interests represented by them. They were willing to sacrifice a great deal in order to stop the ruthless oppression and extermination begun by Bismarck. In effect, some relief was obtained. Perhaps the most essential was the granting of the right to have its own inspectors, to the Union of Polish Cooperatives. This made it possible for the Polish cooperatives to extend their activity very considerably, which was of great importance in the struggle for land ownership. The concessions which the Poles obtained in the field of education proved, however, to be temporary. In general, the government had exhausted the possibilities of a compromise, which could be reconciled with the ideas of growing nationalism. All legislation of an anti-Polish nature, including that in respect of the Colonization Commission, remained in force and was to be still further enlarged.

The attempts at conciliation ultimately came to an end in 1894 shortly before Caprivi's fall. During four years the Polish deputies had shown considerable subservience to the government's requests in Parliament, without receiving any further concessions in return. In the end they had to give up this policy under the pressure of indignant Polish opinion. It was clear that the policy of conciliation was that of the Church hierarchy and the aristocracy and was of an anti-democratic character. The Polish bourgeoisie and petty bourgeoisie also regarded socialism as an enemy, but the socialist movement was still weak in the Prussian area. Thus it was considered that the dominance of the aristocracy and Church hierarchy constituted a much greater danger. The Prussian area was undergoing the same changes as the other parts of Poland, drawing the broad masses into political life. The emergence of mass political parties, first the socialist, then the bourgeois and petty-bourgeois, and finally the peasants, made impossible a policy of conciliation in Germany, just as similar attempts failed within the Tsarist system.

Simultaneous attempts at a compromise with Russia were of a somewhat different nature. It was stressed here that national salvation was to be found in conciliation with Russia, on the basis of Pan-Slav solidarity and the community of economic interests linking the two countries. These ideas were voiced in the Petersburg paper "Kraj" (The Land) founded and expertly edited by W. Spasowicz. A lawyer by profession, living in St. Petersburg, he was close to the Russian liberals, admired Russian culture and at the same time was aware of the merits of Polish intellectual culture. As a literary critic and journalist, he worked for a cultural rapprochement of the two peoples. He saw a possibility of a Russo-Polish union, setting forth as his ideal a multinational, liberal state like Switzerland. Spasowicz was connected with the Polish aristocracy and the great financiers, who supported the paper and regarded the ideas expressed in it as corresponding to their social and economic interests.

Repeated attempts to obtain a more liberal attitude from the Russian authorities in the Kingdom met with absolute unwillingness on the part of those directing Tsarist policy. Such attempts were made by Zygmunt Wielopolski, the son and heir of the Margrave Aleksander Wielopolski, who had connexions with the Court. The government of the rigid Alexander III with the administration of Hurko, the Warsaw Governor-General, and of Apukhtin, the curator of the Warsaw school district, was a period of ruthless persecution of all things Polish in every cultural field. Alexander III's death in 1894, when the conciliation attempts in Poznań had broken down, seemed to be a turning point. All those who wished for an understanding with the Tsarist régime placed their hopes in the young Nicholas II. After Hurko's retirement, the new Governor-General in Warsaw, Count Shuvalov and later Prince Imeretinsky, knew how to give support to these illusions by their polite behaviour and the maintenance of good relations with the Polish aristocracy.

The Tsar's visit to Warsaw in 1897 was the climax of these illusions. He was presented with a million roubles raised by public subscription, which he donated to be used for the building of a Polytechnic. He also allowed the erection of a monument to Mickiewicz. The donations for this monument revealed the immense change in the attitude of the Polish peasants, who contributed what they could by the thousand. Basically, however, the Kingdom did not obtain real concessions. Shortly afterwards the advocates of the policy of compromise were brought into discredit by Piłsudski's publication of a memorandum by Imeretinsky, which was spirited away from St. Petersburg. He spoke contemptuously of the party of conciliation with Tsarism and considered the parties opposing the Tsarist government as the real factor to be taken into account. The publication of this memorandum was a painful blow to the policy of compromise.

POLISH NATIONALISM AT THE TURN OF THE CENTURY

It was after 1900 that a new attempt at conciliation with the government was made by the National Democratic Party, which had emerged from the Polish League. Within a few of after its foundation, an essential change of outlook had taken place in the League. The heirs of the January Insurrection, believing in the old ideals of fraternity between nations, had lost influence and their place was taken by a young group, led by Roman Dmowski, then a university student. In 1893 Dmowski, together with Balicki and Popławski, transformed the Polish League into the National League. In the next few years this organization developed a pronounced nationalism, departing from democratic ideas. This ideology corresponded to the attitudes prevalent among the bourgeoisie of practically all Europe. It was a sign of the arrival of a new area, the era of imperialism.

It should be emphasized, however, that the origins of Polish nationalism differ somewhat from similar movements in western Europe. French nationalism, whose beginnings were in Déroulède's "League of Patriots", Pan-Germanism which started in Austria but was supported by west German big industry, as well as Imperialism in Great Britain, were connected to a large degree with the establishment of great monopolies which sought to mould public opinion for the purpose of opposing socialism and gaining support in the struggle for markets and colonies. Although in Poland the nationalist movement had similar local roots, especially in the Russian area, it was also a reaction to what was happening in other countries. On the one hand, it was an answer to the attack of German nationalism, on the other, it resulted from the ideological influence emanating from France and England with which the Polish intelligentsia always had intellectual, artistic and literary connexions. It is true that in Poland, too, financial institutions arose which took control of important branches of economic life, such as, for example, the Commercial Bank in Warsaw. These institutions could not be indifferent towards politics. It was a fact, however, that the Polish nationalist movement during its formation was not dependent on commercial bodies, and the parties or social organizations, established by the National League or secretly led by it, were not at that time connected with industrial monopolies. That took place later during the 1905 Revolution, when it was shown that these parties could serve the interests of the propertied classes.

Up to the outbreak of the 1905 Revolution the nationalist movement adopted, at least in theory, an anti-Russian attitude aimed at securing independence. In 1894 Dmowski sought to organize a demonstration on the occasion of the hundredth anniversary of Kiliński's uprising in Warsaw, which resulted in reprisals by the authorities against members of the League. The paper "Głos" (The Voice), which up to this point had represented the point of view of this group, ceased to appear, and Dmowski and Balicki had to take refuge in Galicia. The "Przegląd Wszechpolski" (The All-Polish Review) began to be published by Dmowski in Lwów as a theoretical paper. In Cracow Popławski edited "Polak" (The Pole), which was intended for agitation among the peasants and smuggled into the Kingdom.

The National Democratic Party was formally established in 1897 and soon became the strongest political representative of wide sections of the urban population with considerable support among well-to-do peasants. In the near future the party was to evolve still more clearly along nationalist lines.

THE PEASANT MOVEMENT IN GALICIA

During this period the first modern mass peasant party was born in Galicia. The initiative came from intellectual groups with a point of view close to that of the Warsaw "Głos", whose organ was the "Przegląd Społeczny" (The Social Review) founded in Lwów in 1886. It was founded by Bolesław Wysłouch, who had become acquainted with socialist ideas while studying in St. Petersburg. After imprisonment in Russia he took refuge in Galicia and played an important role as the promoter of the peasant movement.

It was precisely in this period that the situation in Galicia became more acute. The conservative politicians understood that the broad masses were awakening from political lethargy, as was shown by Stojałowski's activity and the first socialist circles. In 1888 Count Kazimierz Badeni, a man who believed in strong government, came to power in Galicia as Viceroy. The first political problem with which he dealt was Russophilism among the Ukrainians. The activity of Tsarist agents among the Uniate clergy, which began to develop favourable leanings towards the Orthodox Church, had been discovered. Badeni successfully combatted these tendencies among the Uniate hierarchy and, moreover, reached in 1890 a compromise with the Ukrainian politicians, giving the Ukrainians some concessions in the field of education. From this time onwards the Greek Catholic hierarchy became the mainstay of the Ukrainian national movement in Galicia.

In the same year Michał Bobrzyński, a historian of the Cracow school and one of the outstanding Galician conservative politicians, became the head of the Provincial School Council. His achievement was the development of primary education in the area under Austrian rule which until now had been sunk in illiteracy. Many criticism can be made of the social direction which Bobrzyński gave to the Galician school system, but it is true that it is from his time that a serious effort to develop general education in this province began.

Badeni, as Viceroy, fought against the peasant movement with police repression which had the principal result of hastening of its radicalization. The Peasant Party was founded in 1895 and its real leader was Jan Stapiński, a young agitator of peasant family. He edited, first with the help of Wysłouch and afterwards on his own account, the periodical "Przyjaciel Ludu" (The Friend of the People). This paper waged an unflinching struggle against the great landowners. In the meanwhile Stojałowski, persecuted and imprisoned by Badeni, attacked with mounting fervour the ruling classes of Galicia, though often in demagogic terms. The peasant leaders soon found a political platform. Badeni, having become prime minister of Austria, introduced a fifth curia, based on universal suffrage, to elect members of the Vienna Parliament. In the 1897 Parliament Polish deputies appeared who did not join the Polish Club. These were the Socialists led by Daszyński, an extremely able parliamentary orator, and the Peasant Party followers of Stapiński. This showed clearly that the political hegemony of the conservative "Stańczyk" group was coming to an end. At the same time the conservatives had compromised themselves politically in the Prussian area, when Kościelski's policy of compromise broke down in 1894. Socialist parties and the National Democrats came into existence in the Congress Kingdom, and a socialist and a peasant party were formed in Galicia. It could be clearly seen that, in spite of the borders and differing political and constitutional conditions, Polish society, as a whole, underwent simultaneous and identical political changes.

THE DEFENCE OF POLISH NATIONALITY IN THE PRUSSIAN AREA

During the last years of the nineteenth century which saw the formation of democratic political parties in the Austrian and Russian areas, the Prussian area likewise underwent social and economic changes. The provinces of Poznań and Pomerania had to fight, above all, against the intensification of Germanization and make ever greater efforts to retain ownership of the soil for the Poles. In this field, effective means of defence were soon discovered. On the basis of a law dating from Caprivi's time concerning vested property, the Land Bank began to divide up and settle peasants on landed estates. The Bank was created with some financial assistance from the gentry in Galicia and the Congress Kingdom. It was followed in its operations by the Land Purchase Bank, which succeeded in attracting even west German capital because of its high dividends. The Polish peasant succeeded in paying a high price because of his desire to own his own land. It soon became clear that the Poles were conducting their own settlement campaign more effectively than the Colonization Commission, which received ever greater financial support from the Prussian State.

Perceiving the ineffectiveness of the methods adopted against the Poles, the Prussian government abandoned the principle, sacrosanct until now, of equality of all citizens before the law and in 1904 issued a decree which permitted the authorities to prohibit the erection of houses in the new settlements if these new villages contradicted the aim of the law of 1886, designed to preserve the German element in the population. The Poles sought to overcome this obstacle by settling purchasers of the new holdings in former estate buildings. This decree gave rise to the famous case of the peasant, M. Drzymała, who when the authorities refused to grant him permission to put up a house, lived in a wagon on his property. The German government fought the Poles not only by depriving them of land. From 1898 onwards more new laws against the Poles were issued. The policy of Germanization became sharper and more extensive, especially in the field of education. The introduction of religious instruction in German in the primary schools led in 1901 to the notorious Września (near Poznań) affair, where a teacher used corporal punishment to force unwilling children to follow his subject in German. The parents supported their children and, in consequence, scores of people were given prison sentences of many months. Once again the affair received wide publicity all over Europe.

The Germanization of the Polish areas under Prussian rule was given a spurious authenticity by changing place names. Attempts were made to change the spelling and often the sound of Polish surnames when birth certificates were issue. This often resulted in friction with the population.

It was also sought to enlarge the Prussian administrative machinery in the Polish areas in order to increase the number of German officials, who were brought in from other provinces and given special bonuses to encourage them to remain in a foreign environment. Attempts were made to establish German cultural institutions and large funds were earmarked for this purpose. All this had the aim of strengthening the German element in the eastern borderlands annexed by Germany.

Initiative came not only from the State, but from private sources as well. In 1894 the "Deutscher Ostmarkenverein" (The German Union of the Eastern Marches) was set up in Poznań. It was called the H.K.T. ("Hakata") by the Poles from the initials of its founders Hansemann, Kennemann, and Tiedemann. This society was founded by the Prussian junkers who had become active politically during Caprivi's government and formed the Agrarian Union to defend the economic interests of the landowners against the influence of big industry. Soon the "Hakata" became closely linked with the government, but it always preserved an appearance of independence in pursuit of its tasks of conducting a constant anti-Polish agitation. It also initiated some government action, representing it as the realization of the desires of the German community itself.

The anti-Polish campaign was conducted in a planned and systematic way. New settlements, at first haphazardly established, were carefully located. Because rural population was greater than the urban some towns were surrounded by German agricultural settlements, in order to create strong German islands in an ethnically Polish area. Such a policy of settlement would indeed have proved effective in the long run, but there was insufficient time for its fulfilment.

The Germanization of many towns failed, in spite of the fact that the Germans had at their disposal, in the struggle with barely a few million Polish subjects, all the resources of the most powerful European state. Thus, for example, Poznań was 50.76 per cent Polish in 1890 and 57.07 per cent in 1910, according to official statistics which, as was proved later, were falsified to the advantage of the Germans.

In this same period the Polish national movement in Upper Silesia made further progress. After the termination of the *Kulturkampf* the clergy, being reconciled with the government, ceased to support the Polish cause in Silesia and even began to assist the government in its campaign of Germanization. In this province, where there were practically no native intellectuals, it was very difficult for the Polish population to free itself from the influence of the clergy, but the national movement, once awakened, could no longer be suppressed. A Polish press, independent of the "Zentrum" began to develop. It was run by journalists of Silesian origin and newcomers from Poznań and Pomerania. The most important papers of that time were the "Nowiny Raciborskie" (The Raciborz News) and the "Gazeta Opolska" (The Opole Gazette). Their editors were opposed to the "Zentrum" and the clergy's sponsorship of the Polish revival came to an end. In the first years of the twentieth century, at a time when the Polish Socialist Party was al-

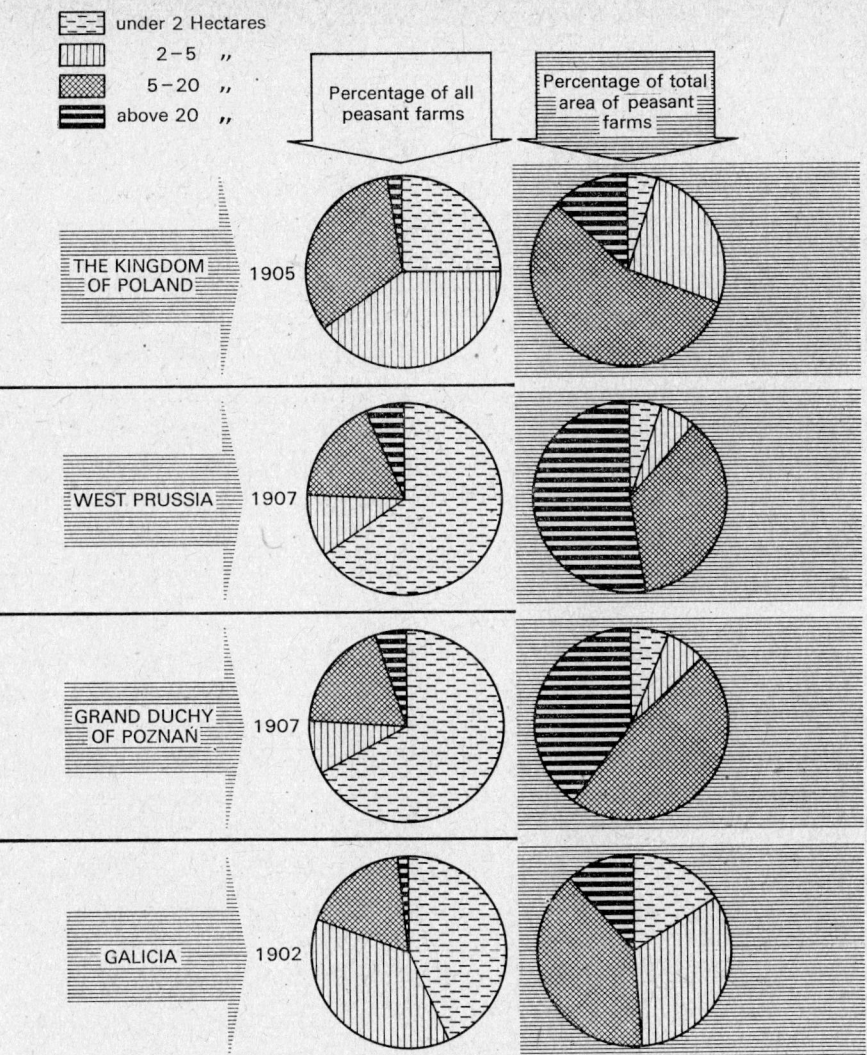

III. Structure of peasant farms in Poland c. 1900's

ready active in Upper Silesia, the influence of the National League also began to spread. From its ranks came the most vigorous of the younger generation of Silesian politicians, Wojciech Korfanty. In the 1903 elections to the German Parliament Polish candidates, independent of the "Zentrum", were put up in the seven Silesian constituencies. Against the wishes of the "Zentrum", a Polish candidate was elected, Korfanty, who in the final vote received the support of the Polish Socialist Party. This first Polish electoral victory is considered correctly as a turning point in the history of the province. It showed that the struggle against German clericalism had been won and from this time onwards the Polish movement had a completely independent character.

The development of national consciousness among the Mazurian and Warmian population of East Prussia and among the Kashubians in Gdańsk-Pomerania was much slower. There, too, 1848 had marked the beginning of a national revival, but in Mazuria and Warmia the movement remained weak in spite of the efforts of individuals from other provinces and even from Warsaw. The essential cause lay in the fact that this was an agricultural territory without industry. The Mazurian peasants were, moreover, mostly Protestant like their junker masters. Prussian propaganda was even able to use the Polish language in its encouragement of Mazurian particularism. The economic backwardness of these lands did have the result that the peasant, remaining in his village, preserved his Polish, but, on the other hand, social advancement in Mazuria and Warmia was possible only by the acceptance of German culture and language. The situation was better in Kashuby, where the proximity of the industrial area of Gdańsk and the Catholicism of the local peasants and fishermen always resulted in the election of a Polish deputy to the German Parliament from the maritime Gdańsk-Pomerania district of Kartuzy, Puck and Wejherowo.

ECONOMIC EMIGRATION

It can be stated that in general by the turn of the century Polish social and political life had become much more democratic. The mass of the people began to have an increasing influence over the attitude of the nation as a whole. This was the result of economic expansion. One of the important factors which strengthened the position of the ordinary people of Poland was emigration, which took on a tremendous scale in the last decade of the nineteenth century. The first wave of emigration came from the Prussian area in about 1870 and consisted mainly of craftsmen. In the 1880's it was the peasantry from the province of Poznań who emigrated primarily to the United States, but also to the west German industrial areas. In the 1890's peasants from the Congress Kingdom began to emigrate, first to Brasil and then to the United States. Galicia was the last to experience emigration, but it was here that the largest exodus of Polish peasants took place. The total for Galician emigration has been estimated at about half a million. Apart from permanent emigration, seasonal migration also had increasing importance. Landless peasants or small-holders, mainly from Galicia, went to undertake agricultural work in the eastern provinces of Germany, especially in Western Pomerania, where their labour, because of shortage of workers among the local population and the departure of Germans for west Germany in the *Ostflucht* (Flight from the East), was vitally necessary to agriculture.

Whether the emigrant returned home or remained abroad, he sent money back to his family, with which land was bought. Emigration, involving

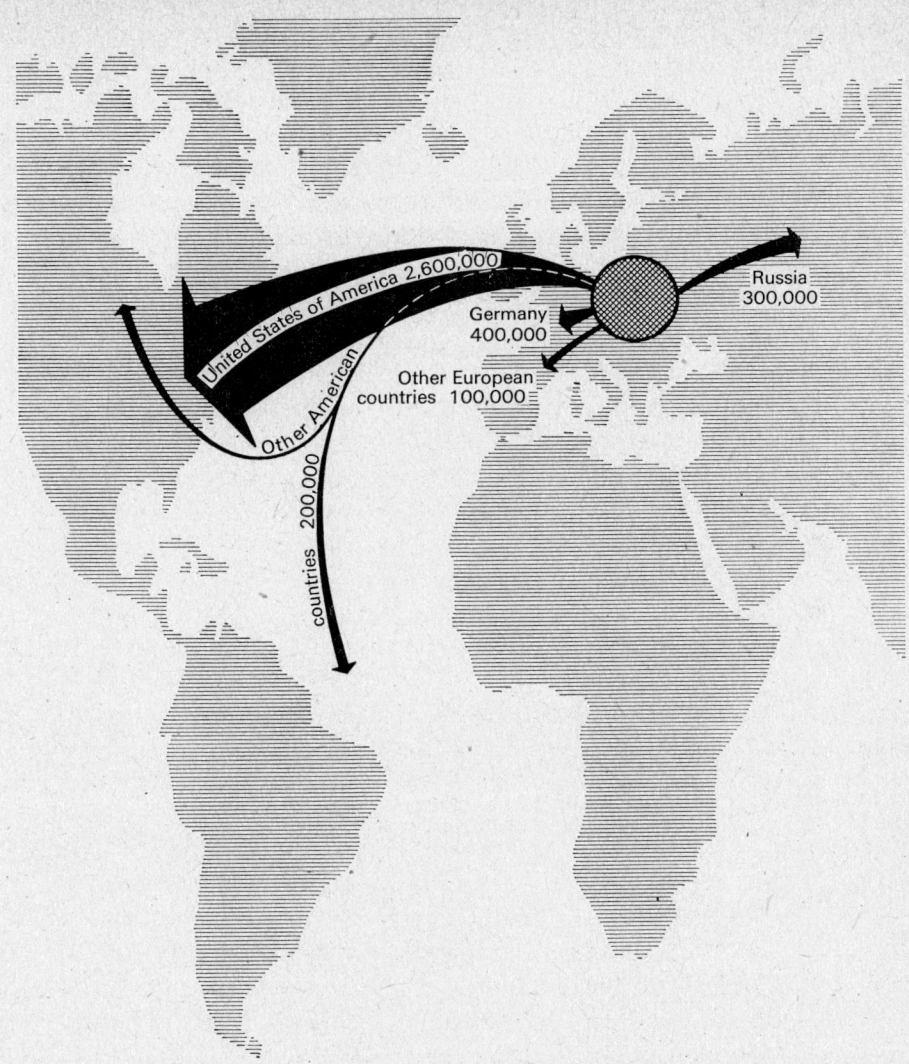

IV. Emigration from Polish lands, 1870–1914

millions of people, on the whole helped considerably in raising the economic and cultural level of the Polish countryside.

Thus large Polish centres were formed abroad, especially in the United States, where the Polish masses were at first organized by the clergy, but later by more progressive, lay intellectuals. The beginnings of Polish organizations in America date from the political emigration after the January Insurrection, which founded a Polish press. As a result, by the end of the century the general level of political consciousness of the Polish peasant was probably higher among the emigrants in America than at home. The future showed that the general balance-sheet of emigration, though a negative phenomenon, in the long run had some positive aspects. It enriched the

Polish village and it produced an important political factor for the national cause, the influence of the Polish community in the U.S.A.

One must not forget either the great contribution made by Polish workers, peasants, technicians and intellectuals to foreign civilizations in the nineteenth century. This is especially true in Russia. Increasingly large numbers of Polish professional people, technicians and traders, emigrated to the interior of the Tsarist State, attracted by the possibilities offered by expanding industry. They frequently became prosperous and, on the whole, were respected. In earlier periods emigration from Poland to Russia had been that of political prisoners, who were settled in the eastern provinces of the Empire, especially Siberia. The Polish prisoners contributed a good deal to the economic and cultural development of those remote lands, and indeed to the scientific study of them. Many of these people won the sympathy and gratitude of the local population. In 1883 a general amnesty made possible the return from Siberia of thousands of deportees. Many of them, however, remained there permanently. It is characteristic that they became the pioneers of a Russo-Polish rapprochement among the most progressive circles of both peoples. A similar role was played by the subsequent wave of deportees, who were sent to Siberia for participation in the working-class movement and the 1905 Revolution. The economic emigration, mostly of professionally qualified persons, strengthened sympathy for the Poles in all ranks of Russian society and its contribution to raising the cultural level of the eastern regions of the Empire was considerable.

"YOUNG POLAND" AND THE ARTS

The social and ideological transformation at the turn of the century was also reflected in the field of culture. In the twilight of positivism Polish literature, as ever reflecting trends current in Europe, passed into a new period corresponding to modernism, which in Poland was referred to as the era of "Young Poland". Its main centre now was Cracow.

Stanisław Przybyszewski, who had earlier made a name for himself in Berlin as a writer in German, arrived in Cracow in the last years of the nineteenth century. The periodical "Życie" (Life), under his editorship became, along with the Warsaw "Chimera" edited by Zenon Przesmycki-Miriam, the organ of a new literary and artistic trend voicing aesthetism and the cultivation of form and, simultaneously, the criticism of uninspired, Philistine attitudes. Poland witnessed once more a wave of lyrical, verbose poetry, enamoured of eroticism and complicated symbolism, and consciously harking back to romanticism. A cult of Słowacki was born in Poland, though he was interpreted and understood in a peculiar fashion. Thus the poet gained a posthumous victory as it were over Mickiewicz in Polish public opinion. The outstanding poets of this generation were Kazimierz

Stanisław Wyspiański

Tetmajer, an admirer of decadence; Jan Kasprowicz, a peasant's son, who dealt with social and religious problems in his lyrics and drama; and Leopold Staff, whose work enjoyed a vogue for a long time after this period. The greatest creative artist of this generation was Stanisław Wyspiański, an eminent impressionist painter, as well as a poet and playwright, whose visionary works once again brought the national question to the forefront as had occurred under the romantics. Wyspiański's plays fascinated an entire generation by their break with the doctrine of conciliation and loyalism put forward by the "Stańczyks". They fought also against the mysticism of the Romantic epoch and once more called upon the nation to perform concrete deeds. His *Wesele* (The Wedding) of 1901 and *Wyzwolenie* (The Deliverance) of 1903 expressed both contemporary national ideals and acute social criticism. Wyspiański's great stagecraft, moreover, enhanced the suggestive power of his works.

Another spokesman, alongside Wyspiański, of new national and social

L. Wyczółkowski, *Digging Beetroot*, 1892

ideas, and the spiritual mentor of his generation was Stefan Żeromski. His novels dealt with troublesome and painful subjects, uncovering the wounds of society, scourging the selfishness of the upper classes and demanding from intellectuals sacrifices for the good of the cause, even of their personal happiness in his *Ludzie bezdomni* (The Homeless) of 1900. Żeromski also revived the cult of armed struggle for independence. His novel *Popioły* (Ashes) of 1904 deals with the Napoleonic epoch, as does his play *Sułkowski*. The January Insurrection is touched upon in many of his other works. Władysław Reymont is famous, above all, as the author of *Chłopi* (The Peasants) written in 1904–1909, an extensive novel about the life of a Polish village, for which the author received the Nobel Prize in 1924. The novel of manners with topical and journalistic undertones, was represented by Wacław Sieroszewski and Józef Weyssenhoff. Wacław Berent's works like *Żywe kamienie* (The Living Stones) presented a particular version of Nietzsche's ideas. Drama was represented, apart from Wyspiański and Kasprowicz, by Tadeusz Rittner, Jan August Kisielewski and Karol Hubert Rostworowski.

Olga Boznańska

The theatre played a tremendous role as a centre of national culture. In Warsaw the stage was the only place where Polish could be used publicly. While bowing to the taste of its bourgeois audience, the theatre cultivated also, thanks to a group of excellent actors the traditions of the Polish comedy of manners and founded the cult of Shakespeare. The Cracow theatre, with Kazimierz Kamiński and Ludwik Solski as its principal actors, working in more liberal conditions, appealed to the national spirit from the stage, boldly presenting a contemporary, serious repertoire of Henrik Ibsen, Maurice Maeterlinck, Stanisław Przybyszewski. The experimental theatre was represented by Tadeusz Pawlikowski, who began the staging of plays in a naturalistic and symbolic way, while Wyspiański, as author, stage designer and director, fought against the limitations of the traditional "box" theatres.

The "Young Poland" period brought also increased activity in the field of music. Numerous symphonic works were composed by Mieczysław Karłowicz, Ludomir Różycki and Karol Szymanowski and virtuoso performers were prominent like Ignacy Paderewski and Aleksander Michałowski.

In the arts, modern Polish painting began to take shape from the interplay of various trends: impressionism, postimpressionism, symbolism and "secession". Colouristic painting, especially landscapes, was represented by Jan Stanisławski, Józef Pankiewcz and Leon Wyczółkowski who was also an excellent graphic artist. Symbolism had an exponent in Jacek Malczewski, who used concrete forms and sharp lines in his work, thus combining the fantastic with the realistic. Portrait painting was done by Olga Boznańska and Teodor Axentowicz. The Cracow "secession" which sought to create a uniform style for all fields of visual art, tried to employ elements of Polish folk art and in this Wyspiański played a vital role.

In architecture, after a long period of bad taste and shoddy building, when speculative house building in the rapidly growing towns ignored the best principles of town planning and when public buildings, erected by a foreign administration purposely gave the cities a foreign look, like the Prusso-Nuremberg style in Poznań and the pseudo-Byzantine in the Kingdom, there appeared at the beginning of the twentieth century, especially among the Warsaw architects, Jan Heurich, Czesław Przybylski and others, a tendency anticipating functionalism, aimed at freeing the façade from heavy decoration.

The clientele of the artists also changed in this period. Alongside rich merchants and industrialists, there were now prosperous representatives of the urban intelligentsia, lawyers, doctors and professors.

All this showed that the Polish nation had broken with the moods emanating from the downfall of the Insurrection of 1863–1864 and that in the new era, which the twentieth century was ushering in, it was preparing to play a role corresponding, at least to some degree, to its historical tradition.

At the end of the nineteenth century, historical writing, breaking away from the influence of the Cracow school, appealed to these traditions. The majority of historians in Warsaw writing about modern times, like Tadeusz Korzon and Władysław Smoleński, represented an optimistic view of the national past, especially of the country's economic and cultural resurgence in the eighteenth century. In Lwów Szymon Askenazy, an excellent historian, wrote on the diplomatic history of the eighteenth and nineteenth centuries and on the Polish insurgent movement, in a spirit of independence and heroism, thus exerting a strong influence on many Polish intellectuals.

Chapter XX

THE PERIOD OF REVOLUTION AND THE APPROACHING EUROPEAN WAR (1904–1914)

CHANGES IN RUSSIAN ECONOMIC POLICY TOWARDS POLAND

The revolution, which as a result of defeat in the Japanese war of 1904–1905 spread over the Tsarist Empire, took on somewhat different aspects in the Congress Kingdom. The Polish lands under Tsarist rule were, as regards economic and social conditions, more advanced than Russia and the national question was closely connected with the social and political demands of the bourgeoisie, workers and peasants. The Russian Revolution was prepared by a rapid process of industrialization which was begun by the economic policy of Witte, who first took office as minister of finance in 1892. At that time the State itself directly financed the creation of great industrial concerns, primarily to achieve the expansion of the railway network. This became possible owing to the shift in Tsarist foreign policy. Russia concluded an alliance with France in 1891–1894 which made it possible to obtain immense French loans. Although Witte supported the development of industry in ethnically Russian lands, he took a different attitude towards the border regions, especially towards the Kingdom.

This was revealed in his tariff policy. The government placed customs duties on raw materials required for the industry in the Kingdom and in this way supported production in the interior of Russia. Russian industry found itself close to the source of raw materials and, as a result of differential railway rates, freight charges were markedly more expensive in the Kingdom than in Russia. For political and economic reasons foreign capitalists, who until that time had preferred to invest in the Kingdom, now transferred their capital to the interior of Russia.

The industrial relationship between the Kingdom and the Empire was reversed. From the end of the nineteenth century Russian industry developed more rapidly than that of the Kingdom, while in relation to the whole of the Empire, the percentage of the Kingdom's industrial production began to drop. In some fields Russian industry not only began to drive out Polish products from the Empire's markets, but also became competitive in the Kingdom itself.

Thus, if the Kingdom, in the thirty years after the Insurrection of 1863–1864 was in a favourable position by comparison with the rest of the Empire, at least economically, from the end of the century it experienced discrimination in this field as well. These changes took place slowly and unevenly in the various sectors of the economy.

The years preceding the outbreak of the Russo-Japanese war reveal economic difficulties all over Europe. The Kingdom felt this more acutely on account of the hostile economic policy of the Russian government. A spontaneous resistance of the Polish working class developed as the crisis progressed. Strikes occurred more frequently and were accompanied by violence. The Kindom experienced the revolutionary ferment even more than the rest of the Empire, and this was still further increased by the outbreak of the war with Japan.

This situation compelled the large industrialists and great landowners to organize themselves and seek a rapprochement with the government, which appeared to be the only power capable of maintaining social order. Such is the background to the founding in 1904 of the Conservative Party, or so-called "Realists".

On the other hand, in the summer of 1904 both Piłsudski and Dmowski arrived in Tokyo, independently of each other to confer there with the Japanese general staff. Piłsudski wanted to obtain assistance for his plans for an insurrection, to which Dmowski was opposed. The Japanese, however, gave up the idea of a Polish diversion, which was by then unnecessary in view of their decisive victories in Manchuria.

THE 1905 REVOLUTION IN THE RUSSIAN EMPIRE AND POLAND

When the liberally-inclined Prince Sviatopelk-Mirski formed his government in Russia, a memorandum was presented to him by the National League. It demanded the introduction of Polish into the schools and the administration of the Kingdom, together with municipal and rural local government. The Polish Socialist Party, on the other hand, organized its first armed demonstration in Warsaw on 13 October, 1904. Shots were fired for the first time at the Russian police in Grzybowski Square by armed groups of the Polish Socialist Party. A similar armed movement embraced Russia. The sign for a general revolutionary movement in the whole Monarchy was "Bloody Sunday", 22 January, 1905, when the priest Gapon set out for the Winter Palace, leading thousands of Petersburg workers, to present a loyal address to the Tsar. A massacre was the answer, and it provided the spark for the powder barrel.

In Warsaw the SDKPiL and the PPS proclaimed a general strike. This moment may be regarded as the beginning of the Revolution in the Kingdom.

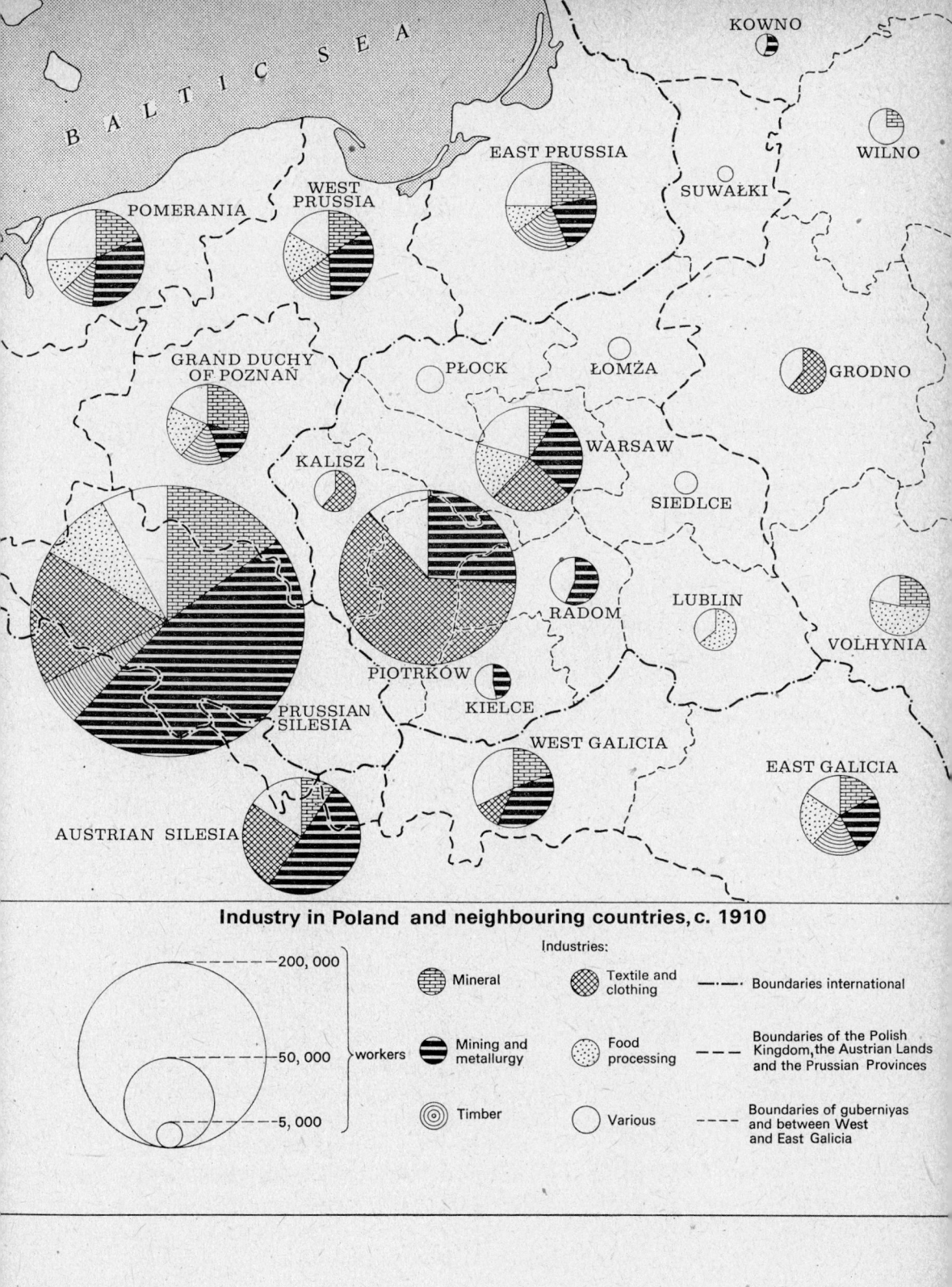

The strike lasted almost a month and took on, from the outset, a stormy character. Violent demonstrations took place, resisted by the Tsarist army and gendarmerie. Dozens of people were killed and hundreds wounded. The strike spread to other towns and factory settlements, resulting everywhere in bloody clashes with the army. About 400,000 workers went on strike during January and February. The wave of strikes, mostly successful, continued in the following months.

Because of the revolution, which embraced the entire Empire, the proletariat of the Kingdom obtained important concessions from the employers. Average wages increased by 50 per cent and the hours of work were reduced.

Already in the early spring the strike movement spread to the countryside. At first these were strikes of agricultural workers, but soon the struggle of the villages for pastures and woods began, leading to disturbances and the unauthorized cutting of the landowners' timber by the peasants. Finally, the movement took on the shape of a struggle for national rights, for introducing Polish into the villages administration, which was conducted in full solidarity by all peasants, rich peasants, small-holders and landless labourers.

At the same time as the general strike in Warsaw a school boycott was organized at the end of January, which was to exert a profound influence on that generation of the young intelligentsia. It was called on the initiative of the Union of Socialist Youth, which was under the influence of both the SDKPiL and PPS, as well as the Jewish Socialist Party, the Bund, but from the outset it was joined by organizations under the influence of the National League, like the unions created in the secondary schools by "Zet", such as "The Red Rose" and "The Future". The National League was not eager to support the school boycott, but Dmowski understood that, with tempers at such a revolutionary pitch, it was necessary to go along with the general movement in order not to lose control over the events. This showed his superiority over the "Realists", who opposed the revolutionary movement in principle, and thus were in a worse position than the League. In the field of education this became quite clear. During 1905 the government made minor concessions with regard to the use of Polish in schools, but the boycott of the Russian schools continued. Finally, in October, an ukase permitted the establishment of schools with Polish as the language of instruction.

The boycott of the Russian schools went on with undiminished force until 1908, when the National Democrats began to withdraw from this campaign. In 1911 the National League announced its opposition, after overcoming strong internal resistance, which led to a split. At that time, the SDKPiL also ceased to support the campaign, but in spite of this, the boycott lasted until 1914, supported by a fraction of the National League and the Polish Socialist Party.

The school strike was of great significance for the awakening of national

S. Lentz, *The Strike*, 1910

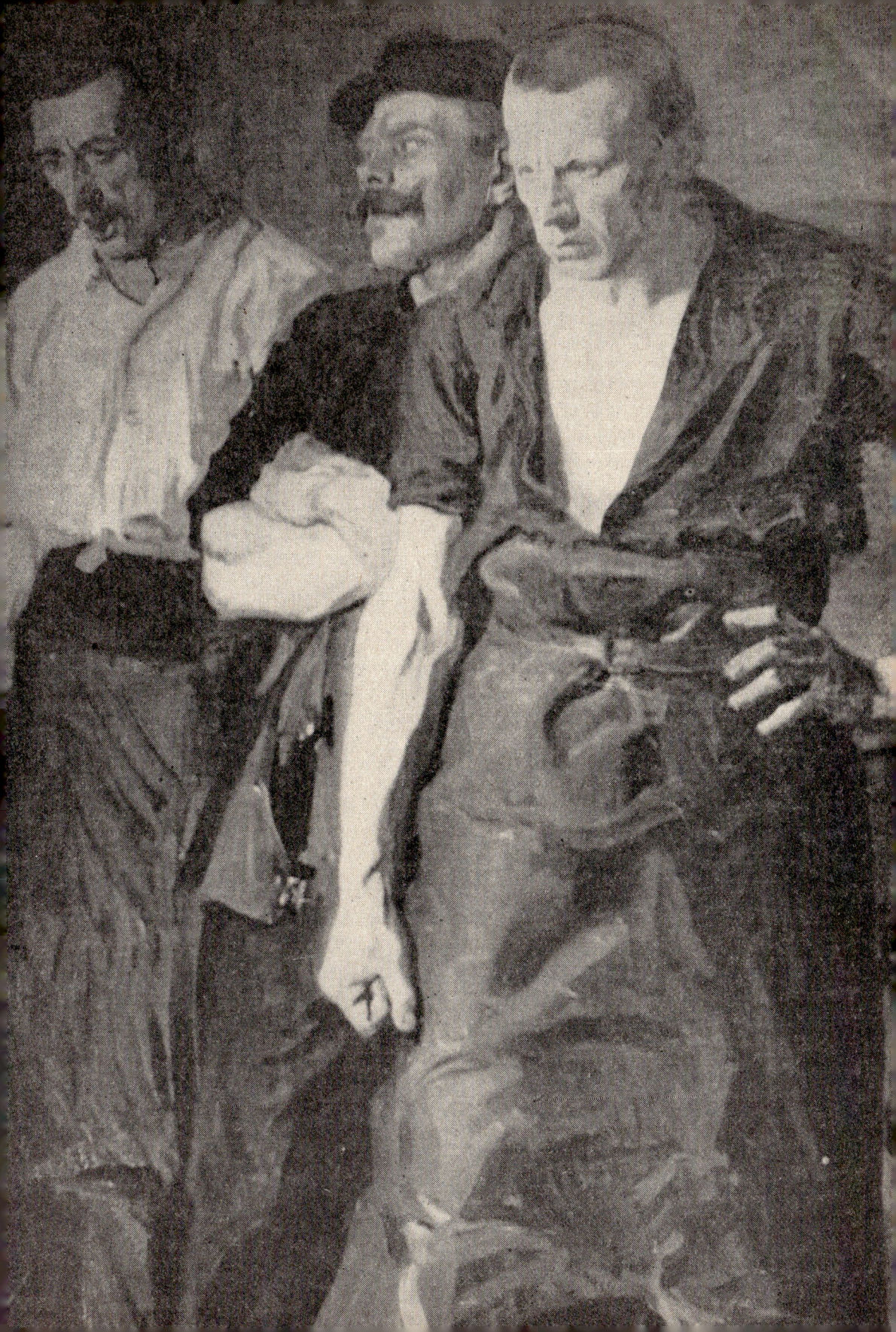

feeling among the youth. Moreover, the necessity, caused by the boycott, of leaving the Kingdom to study in Galicia and abroad not only raised the professional qualifications of the young people, but also drew them closer to their compatriots in the other parts of Poland. Young people were also more inclined to left-wing views, a fact which was of significance for the future development of the nation, because it was this generation which was soon to rebuild the Polish State.

While the strike action was waged in the secondary schools and the university was boycotted, attempts were also made to Polonize the primary schools. In October 1905 the Union of Primary School Teachers was founded, under the influence of progressives, while the National League called into being the Society of Primary School Teachers of the Polish Kingdom, which then had the same aim of Polonizing education. This campaign met with active support from the entire peasantry. It proved that the policy of the Tsarist régime, which had sought since the January Insurrection to base itself on the Polish peasantry as the social foundation of its rule, was a total failure. Similarly, as a result of the ukase of April 1905 with regard to religious tolerance, the Uniates in Podlasie, recently forcibly converted to Orthodoxy, returned to Catholicism *en masse*.

It could be said, in general, that the concessions made by the government up to the middle of 1905 signified the attainment of equal rights by the Kingdom, thus satisfying the aspirations of the "Realists", but public opinion did not want to stop at this, seeing the possibility of obtaining, thanks to the revolution, much greater national gains.

Throughout 1905 the Kingdom witnessed a growing revolutionary ferment, in which a leading part was played by the proletariat. May Day in 1905 led to bloody demonstrations. In June 1905 a strike in Łódź resulted in a fierce struggle between the workers and the Tsarist troops. Here, for the first time in the Empire, barricades were erected and the Łódź workers offered armed resistance to the Russian troops for three days.

The SDKPiL and PPS members conduced considerable revolutionary agitation at this time in many of the military garrisons in the Kingdom and organized the Warsaw Committee of the Military-Revolutionary Organization.

In the cities, towns, factory settlements and villages, the factory owners and the large landowners sometimes turned for assistance to the gendarmerie and Tsarist army. This helped the peasantry in no small degree to realize that the Tsarist government was not its friend, but its most bitter enemy, the mainstay of social and national oppression.

At this time armed groups of the PPS had driven the gendarmerie from the streets of the towns and compelled the government to introduce in the struggle against the revolution its ultimate argument of force, the army. The reprisals against the revolutionaries became ever more severe and many

S. Masłowski, *Spring of 1905*, 1906

armed fighters were sent to the gallows. In July 1905 an outstanding member of the PPS Fighting Organization, Stefan Okrzeja, was executed.

The domestic forces of reaction, moreover, engaged in armed struggle. In the middle of 1905 Dmowski set up the National Workers Union, subordinated to the National League. The Union also formed armed groups, but they fought not with the gendarmerie, but with the socialists. For many months fratricidal combat took place among the workers, especially in Łódź, for which Dmowski openly assumed responsibility. This coincided with his foundamental conception which was he must become the real representative of the Polish propertied classes and approach the Tsarist government with an offer to defeat the revolution in the Kingdom with local forces, in exchange for political concessions, by which he understood sharing power with the Poles.

The high tide of the revolution was the general strike in October 1905, which forced the Tsar to issue, on Witte's advice, his Manifesto of 30 October, promising a constitution. This Manifesto was regarded in Poland as ushering in an era of freedom. Tremendous and unprecedented demonstrations took place in Warsaw, to which the authorities replied with a massacre and on 11 November a state of siege was declared. It was precisely at this time, that Dmowski made his basic proposal to Witte, calling for autonomy for the Kingdom, with the guarantee that the Poles would themselves suppress the revolution in Poland, but Witte was in a much better position than Gorchakov and Alexander II in 1861, when the Margrave Wielopolski made similar proposals. In 1905 the Poles could find no support abroad for their aspirations. Even more important, the Tsarist régime could count on an awakened Russian nationalism and see in the struggle with the foreigner a very powerful anti-revolutionary force. Persecution of, rather than reconciliation with the Poles strengthened the régime's hand in this game and Dmowski's offer was rejected.

A general crisis of the revolution soon occurred. In December 1905 the workers' uprising in Moscow began, and upon the news of the struggle of the Moscow workers with the army, the PPS proclaimed on 22 December a similar uprising in the Kingdom. The attempt to seize power by the PPS, which had a temporary success only in Ostrowiec, ended, like the bloody struggle in Moscow, with the victory of the Tsarist troops. Thereafter, the revolution started to decline.

In this period the internal split in the Polish Socialist Party began to widen. The working class rank and file considered the activity of the Fighting Organization to be a weakening of the basic trends of class struggle. This organization was controlled by a group of "old" members headed by Piłsudski, Bolesław Jędrzejowski, Leon Wasilewski and Witold Jodko-Narkiewicz. The "old" members were opposed by a "young" group including M. Koszutska, J. F. Ciszewski, M. Horwitz-Walecki and M. Bielecki, which desired cooperation with the Russian Revolution and denounced the traditional insurrectionary ideas. From the outset, both sides sought to avoid an open break, especially when it seemed that the revolution would triumph, but towards the end of 1906, when it became obvious that disaster was imminent, a split took place at a meeting in Vienna, with the majority following the "young" group. The latter set themselves up separately as PPS Left Wing, while the minority asumed the name of the PPS Revolutionary Wing and continued its armed action. These came to an end ultimately in 1908, resulting in many casualties, though without, of course, changing the actual situation.

From the middle of 1906 the revolutionary spirit had collapsed both in the Kingdom and in Russia and the strike movement died down. In the final result it undoubtedly brought about a rise in the Polish workers' standard of living and their economic position did not revert to the pre-1905 conditions. What was more important, the revolutionary movement deepened fundamentally the political, social and national consciousness of the Polish masses.

THE REORIENTATION OF THE POLICY OF THE NATIONAL DEMOCRATS

National Democracy made progress in Russian Poland in the years following the defeat of the revolution. This was shown in the elections to the Duma, which were boycotted by the socialist parties. Out of the 36 deputies elected to the First Duma, on the basis of a curial voting system which favoured the propertied classes, 25 were National Democrats. There were also 25 Poles in the Duma elected from the western provinces of the Empire. In the Duma itself the Poles did not play a particularly significant part. But this was still a period of relative liberalism in the whole Monarchy, which made it possible to obtain legal sanction in the Kingdom for many social and national organizations, such as for example, the hitherto illegal "Macierz Szkolna" (School Union), which up to the end of 1906 had been able to set up 141 schools with 63,000 pupils. Other educational, scientific and cultural organizations were established. The cooperative movement, a permanent gain of the revolution, developed very rapidly. Its pioneers included individuals who had recently taken part in conspiratorial action, but now adopted legal methods, like Edward Abramowski, who had been active in the labour movement but later became an anarchist; and Stanisław Wojciechowski, a co-founder of the Polish Socialist Party, who became one of the chief organizers of cooperatives. In practice, this movement, as well as all open social activity, was taken over by the National Democrats. They were to maintain the same number of deputies elected to the Second Duma. The elections strengthened both the extreme wings of the parliament. The Polish Club put forth a project for autonomy for the Kingdom, but it was not even considered because the Second Duma was quickly dissolved and the electoral law amended in such a way that the Kingdom lost more than half of its seats.

Though the concept of a legal struggle for autonomy had collapsed, Dmowski did not, however, relinquish the policy to which the propertied classes had been driven by the revolution. Therefore in 1908, a year which became a turning point in many fields, Dmowski supported the policy of the Russian government not only in the domestic but also in the international fields.

This was shown, in the first place, in the support given to the Neo-Slav movement, which called for solidarity with the Slav peoples, oppressed by Austro-Hungary and Turkey. This was contrary to Polish tradition in the period after the partitions and Dmowski had to overcome strong opposition to this policy within the National League. Nevertheless, Polish politicians took part in the Slav Congress in Prague in 1908 on the recommendation of the League. Dmowski believed that in this way the Russian nationalists, who were the sponsors of this movement, would be more likely to offer concessions to the Poles, but these hopes also proved in vain. The next Congress in Petersburg in 1909 revealed a Russo-Polish conflict, so that the Poles did not attend the subsequent Congress in Sofia in 1910. The Poles had become indignant at the separation of the Chełm district from the Kingdom and its establishment as a separate province, which was finally carried out in 1912, with the new provinces placed under the administration of the governor-general of Kiev.

An even more important event in 1908 was the publication of Dmowski's book *Niemcy, Rosja i kwestia polska* (Germany, Russia and the Polish Question), which was immediately translated into other languages. It became the manifesto of a new Polish policy. In it Dmowski proclaimed the principle that Germany was Poland's main and most dangerous enemy, for which reason in the approaching European conflict Poland must side with Germany's opponents, Russia and her allies.

The solution of the Polish question lay, according to him, not in independence, but in the basic concept of integration. This could take place only in the event of a Russian victory, because a victory of her enemies would lead inevitably to a new partition. This line of reasoning was contrary to the whole tradition of the Polish insurrectionary struggle, and to Polish history since the partitions when the most important aim was always the regaining, even if only partial, of independence. Because Dmowski's conception expressed the real interests of the propertied classes, it gained considerable popularity among many of the bourgeoisie and the intelligentsia. Seeking to enhance the appeal of his policy, Dmowski attempted to give it chauvinist content for which reason his adherents in Galicia waged a bitter struggle with the Ukrainians and indulged increasingly in violent anti-Semitic agitation. In 1912 Dmowski proclaimed an economic and cultural boycott of the Jews.

Just as the founding of the Polish League had its roots in both the local and international situation, Dmowski's new policy also had a twin aspect. 1908 witnessed the aggravation of the situation in Europe, as a result of the annexation of Bosnia and Herzegovina by Austro-Hungary. Russia, defeated in the Far East, resumed its expansionist policy in the Balkans. From the moment when the Entente between Great Britain, France and Russia had been achieved, the Polish people were faced with the approach of a world war.

THE EXPROPRIATION DECREE
IN PRUSSIAN POLAND AND THE NATIONAL LEAGUE

The general situation in Poland influenced Dmowski more than the international scene. The attention of all the Polish parties was drawn to the intensified pressure on the Poles by the Prussian government in the last years of Bülow's chancellorship. At the end of 1907 the Prussian Landtag began to debate a project for the forcible expropriation of Polish landed estates, while, in the following year, the Reichstag discussed a special bill relating to the use of the Polish language. The expropriation law came into force in 1908; the government could, on this basis, purchase estates compulsorily from Polish landowners and colonize them with German settlers. This decree was contrary to the principle of the inviolability of property and therefore its passage was opposed by conservatives, but in an atmosphere of fervent nationalism sacred and established principles could be infringed. The Poles were faced with the fact that the struggle for ownership of the soil in which they had fought the Germans so effectively, was entering a new and extremely dangerous phase. It appeared that the existence of Poles in the Prussian area was in mortal peril. The idea still prevailed that the landholdings of the Polish gentry were synonymous with the Polish nation as such. It was not appreciated as yet that Polish nationality was deeply grounded in the peasantry of Poznań and Pomerania and in the working class of Upper Silesia. Undoubtedly, after the destruction of the Polish landowners, these social groups would be the next object of attack and the Germans, meeting increasing resistance, would use still more ruthless measures, but this was outside the comprehension of contemporaries.

The process of integrating the Polish nation progressed steadily, especially as a result of the development of education and national consciousness. The working-class movement was the first real manifestation of this trend in the social and political field. The nationalist movement also emphasized this unity of the three areas, seeing in this slogan an effective propaganda weapon. The National League conducted its activity under the guise of All-Polish slogans and its first legal organ was called "Przegląd Wszechpolski" (All-Polish Review). The politicians of the League employed this name as well, imitating in this, by the way, the name of the "Alldeutscher Verband" (Pan-German Union).

Therefore, the 1905 Revolution in the Congress Kingdom had its impact also on the two other areas. The school strike spread swiftly to the Poznań province, where in 1906 a general boycott by school children took place, with a refusal to attend religious instruction given in German. While the strike was suppressed after a year, it helped considerably in arousing a marked solidarity of the Polish people against the Prussian authorities. It showed that the national movement had embraced all elements of the nation and even the conservative Poznań press affirmed that this strike had been initiated by the masses and supported, above all, by them, and that the upper classes joined it only later.

It was at the time of the 1905 Revolution that the All-Polish movement began also to penetrate the Prussian area. "Zet" organizations had been active there from the end of the nineteenth century, conducting agitation among Poles in Wrocław and Berlin. The first paper under the League's influence, the "Dziennik Berliński" (Berlin Daily), edited by Marian Seyda, appeared there. It attacked the loyalism of the landowner politicians towards Germany. Seyda moved soon afterwards to Poznań and with the help of Bernard Chrzanowski began to spread the League's views among the gentry. In 1904 a clandestine National Democratic Party was founded, with a programme including more democratic slogans now that the earlier preponderance of clergy and aristocrats was no longer a factor. Since 1905 the All-Polish group was in control of the "Kurier Poznański" (The Poznań Courier) and for a short while also of the "Orędownik" (The Messenger), an old and well-established paper of the petty-bourgeoisie. In 1907 a legal Polish Democratic Society was set up, with members among both the petty-bourgeois and gentry.

One of the results of the 1905 Revolution was the organization of a peasant political movement in the Congress Kingdom. As early as 1904 a secret organization, the Polish Peasant Union, was established, under the influence at the outset of the Polish Socialist Party. This was the first peasant political organization in the Kingdom which supported the struggle for Poland's independence and the social liberation of the village. The Polish Peasant Union lasted up to 1907, when it was destroyed by the Tsarist gendarmerie. During the revolution itself the National League tried also to organize its own adherents among the peasants, creating the National Peasant Union. Soon both the National Peasant Union and the earlier National Workers Union broke with the League, because of its pro-Russian policy and the adoption of reactionary social policies. From the end of 1907 the radical peasant groups had their own publication "Zaranie" (The Dawn), which called for the emancipation of the village from the influence of the Church and manor and also for a partition of the landowners' estates. In spite of everything, however, the peasant movement in the Kingdom did not create a mass political party before the First World War.

On the other hand, it was in the years of the revolution that the peasant movement developed on a very large scale in the Austrian area.

POLITICAL CHANGES IN GALICIA

The 1905 Revolution had vitally affected the situation in the Austrian area. Democratic forces grew stronger, under the influence of the Russian Revolution, in the entire monarchy, especially in its western and more industrialized area. This compelled the government to introduce in Austria in 1907 universal, secret, equal and direct suffrage in elections for the Reichsrat in Vienna, but Galicia itself, which benefited from this, had also undergone distinct changes in its economic, social and political life from the end of the century. Mention has already been made of the large-scale emigration from Western Galicia. With the help of this movement, the purchase of estates of the gentry increased, thus enlarging the property of the village and raising both its standard of living and culture. This was reflected in the political field by the progressive weakening of the position of the Galician landowners.

The Galician working class likewise strengthened its position. The process of rapid industrialization reached this province also, though to a lesser degree than elsewhere. Considerable expansion of the oil industry took place. While in 1895 Galician oil production amounted to not quite 2 million quintals, by 1908 it reached 18 million or 5 per cent of world production. The mining of coal also increased. The more up-to-date among the propertied classes broke with the conservative "Stańczyk" tradition, according to which economic backwardness constituted a guarantee of social order.

The new electoral law changed the relative positions of the political forces in Galicia. The position of the conservatives collapsed. In 1907 the National Democrats, led by Stanisław Głąbiński, a Lwów University professor, won 16 seats in Parliament, while the Peasant Party, led by Stapiński, gained 17. From the outset, the Peasant Party deputies refused to join the Polish Parliamentary Club, with the result that the chairmanship went to Głąbiński, who therefore became the representative of Polish policy in Vienna. Through the intermediary of Bobrzyński, who was now appointed Viceroy in Galicia, the conservatives induced the peasant deputies to join the Polish Club in exchange for a number of concessions mostly of a personal nature. This gave rise to the beginning of demoralization in the peasant movement, which began to be infiltrated by various careerists.

In 1913 a split in the Peasant Party took place. The victor was the talented Wincenty Witos, who now became the leader of the newly formed Polish Peasant Party—"Piast". Stapiński's authority was undermined and he was left at the head of only the radical minority of the Left Wing of the Polish Peasant Party. The Peasant Party, though divided into two factions, remained an important political force in Galicia, but it should be noted that the Polish Social-Democratic Party, though having a much narrower social basis in this unindustrialized area, played a relatively greater role.

In effect, its influence was not limited to the working class. It reached the landless peasants and had a following among the intelligentsia. It became in practice the leading force in the struggle for democratizing conditions in Galicia. This was borne out especially in the struggle for a reform of the electoral law to the Galician Seym, where the curial system was still in force, making it impossible to elect representatives of the working class.

The struggle for electoral rights was closely associated in Galicia with the Ukrainian question. Just as towards the end of the century the Polish peasantry had formed its own political representation, creating its own organizations independent of sponsorship by intellectuals, so the national consciousness of the Ukrainian peasants also took shape only at this time. Different Ukrainian parties arose representing the various social sections of the newly awakened nation; an Ukrainian Social-Democratic Party, a Peasant Radical Party, and the Ukrainian National Democracy, the latter just as chauvinistic as the Polish National Democrats, came into being.

The Polish National Democrats after 1905 gained the support of Polish middle-class in Eastern Galicia, who felt their position to be threatened by the rapidly growing Ukrainian intelligentsia, still stronger because of its peasant origin and thus closely linked with its own predominantly peasant community. At the beginning of the twentieth century the social problem in the eastern Galician countryside manifested itself in tremendous peasant strikes. Directed against the Polish landowners and suppressed by an administration which was Polish, the strikes, though of an economic character, took on, as a matter of course, a national aspect.

Simultaneously the Jewish problem in Galicia became more acute and from the end of the century zionist tendencies developed, first among part of the intellectuals and then among broader masses of the Jewish population.

The main Ukrainian demands before 1914 were for proportional representation in the Seym and for proper rights in primary and secondary education, together with—and this was most annoying to Polish nationalists—the creation of a Ukrainian University in Lwów. These just demands were rejected by Polish public opinion in Eastern Galicia, dominated, as it was, by the nationalists.

THE DEBATE ON POLITICAL ATTITUDES ON THE EVE OF THE WORLD WAR

The political tension in Galicia was revealed by the unexpected assassination in 1908 of the Viceroy, Andrzej Potocki, by a young Ukrainian nationalist. The most eminent conservative politician in Galicia, Bobrzyński, took over the post. During his term of office, the 1911 elections to Parliament brought, as a result of administrative pressure, a decisive defeat of the National Democrats and, once more, a conservative, Leon Biliński, professor at Lwów University and previously many times a minister, became the chairman of the Polish Parliamentary Club. Bobrzyński fought against the All-Polish group among the National Democrats for reasons of general Austrian policy, because they would be pro-Russian in the event of an outbreak of an European war. The electoral reform became the crux of the political battle. The draft of the new electoral law, which was extremely complicated and gave very slight concessions to the Ukrainians and democratic forces, was passed during the 1913 session of the Seym. It met with the decided resistance of the All-Polish group and of the die-hard Eastern Galician landowners, aided by the bishops. This was the reason why Bobrzyński was compelled to resign the office of Viceroy and his place taken by Witold Korytowski, a politician of lesser calibre, with whom it was easier for the National Democrats and the "die-hards" to come to terms. In the following year an electoral law was finally passed, which did not differ markedly from the previous year's draft. It did not, however, go into effect before the outbreak of the war and Bobrzyński's resignation destroyed his efforts to reach some kind of Ukrainian-Polish agreement. This problem remained unsolved when the First World War broke out.

Since 1908 Galicia had been a base for those members of the Polish Socialist Party who, after the defeat of the revolution sought in the Austrian area possibilities of putting into effect a new conception, conceived by the Right Wing of the party. In view of the approaching conflict between the partitioning Powers, this group resolved to make preparations for insurrectionary action. The "Związek Walki Czynnej" (Union of Active Struggle) was formed, embracing the most active members of the PPS Fighting Organization and some of the Galician youth, an organization only formally subordinated to the PPS Revolutionary Wing. The Union was a kind of secret military school, which was to produce future officers for the insurrection. Its founders were Kazimierz Sosnkowski, Marian Kukiel and Władysław Sikorski. Piłsudski took over the command of the Union having closed down the activity of the Fighting Organization with a successful raid on a railway mail coach in Bezdany near Wilno. The Union sponsored the establishment of riflemen's unions in various Galician towns, taking advantage of an Austrian law which permitted the formation of para-military societies. In connexion with this, Piłsudski came into contact with the Austrian military authorities, who assisted him, hoping to create an anti-Russian diversion if war were to break out. Soon, an analogous secret organization, under the leadership of a section of the National League, called the "Polish Army" was formed, which set up its own "Riflemen's sections".

In 1912 the outbreak of the First Balkan War brought about new tension in Europe. It was then decided to give both secret organizations a legal political form. At the end of 1912 a Provisional Commission of Confederated Independence Parties was established, composed of representatives of the Polish Socialist Party, the Polish Social-Democratic Party, the National Workers Union, the National Peasant Union and several smaller political organizations from Galicia and the Kingdom. Sikorski, who was then beginning his political and military career, joined the Commission as the representative of one of these small groups, the Polish Progressive Party. A Polish Military Fund was established earlier, which collected money to prepare an insurrection. Anti-Russian sentiments fell on fertile ground in Galicia, where the insurrectionary traditions were openly encouraged. The German peril was more obvious to the other two areas, for which reason an anti-Tsarist attitude could spread only to relatively few social groups. In the Kingdom the propertied classes and the intelligentsia linked with them, had been inclined to adopt, after the defeat of the 1905 Revolution, Pan-Polish ideas, which, as is known, were pro-Russian.

In the Kingdom, only the PPS Revolutionary Wing and a few small groups of intellectuals were in favour of insurrection, but all the socialist organizations were extremely weak after the defeat of the revolution. Only after 1912 did they regain slowly, as a result of the rising tide of revolution in the Empire as a whole, the possibility of action. The PPS Revolutionary Wing, moreover, paid relatively little attention to the struggle for workers' rights, expending almost all its energy in preparing the insurrection. On the other hand, SDKPiL and PPS Left Wing, by rebuilding their organizations among the workers of the Kingdom, regarded the problem of war in a totally different light and considered it to be an imperialist conflict. Their programme called for a struggle against all the forces striving towards war, and, in the event of its outbreak, for opposition to the governments conducting this war. In this fashion these parties strove towards their fundamental aim, the preparation of a social revolution.

Thus, Polish society was divided, in face of the approaching war, between three points of view : the first and traditional one, represented by Piłsudski, the PPS Revolutionary Wing and all those who eagerly awaited the outbreak of the European war in order to launch an insurrection against the Tsarist régime ; the second, led by Dmowski, did not favour a war, but, if it were to occur, considered Russia's victory as the best result, because it would bring about an integration of all the Polish territories under one rule, which, as a consequence, would give the Poles such weight that they would have to obtain considerable autonomy, and according to this concept unification would preserve and strengthen Polish nationality and, in addition, a victorious Russian Empire would be a safeguard against the possibility of a social revolution ; finally, the third orientation was that of the socialist parties which wished to oppose the war, and, in event of its outbreak, prepare a social revolution.

If the first two concepts, which had been current for a few years before the war, appealed to the national interests, conceived in a nationalist spirit or moulded by slogans of solidarity for independence, the internationalist and revolutionary concept placed social aims in the forefront. The SDKPiL had even adopted a negative attitude to the slogan of Polish independence. This limited considerably the influence of this party within the Polish community.

Chapter XXI
THE FIRST WORLD WAR AND THE REBUILDING OF THE POLISH STATE (1914–1918)

PIŁSUDSKI AND THE LEGIONS

The outbreak of the war did not find the various Polish social groups and parties unprepared. Already on 2 August Piłsudski received permission from the Austrian government to march into the Kingdom. This took place only after the outbreak of the Russian-Austrian war on 6 August, a few days after the beginning of the Russo-German conflict. This difference in dates was not advantageous to Piłsudski. His plans depended on a march to the Dąbrowa Basin, where the Polish Socialist Party had some influence among the workers. In the meantime the region had already been occupied by the German armies. Piłsudski had to march towards Kielce where no particularly favourable conditions existed, to begin agitation for an uprising. Nevertheless, he was convinced that the appearance of Polish uniforms would fascinate Polish youth, which would join the insurgent army in large numbers. Such a military response was necessary for his political reckogning which he based on the experience of the January Insurrection. Just as the National Central Committee which began the uprising in 1863 proclaimed itself the Temporary National Government, but simultaneously established a dictatorship, so Piłsudski wished in 1914 to realize both these aims immediately. He surprised the politicians of the Commission of Confederated Independence Parties by announcing that a secret national government had been created in Warsaw which had appointed him commander of the armed forces and that "all must adhere to its orders". Actually all this was fiction. The march of Piłsudski's units led to the capture of Kielce, but it did not provoke an uprising in even a small part of the Kingdom. The inhabitants of this area did not see the Tsarist régime as the sole enemy, because for forty years the Germans had conducted a most vehement campaign of extermination against the Poles. In addition, on 7 August the Germans bombarded Kalisz, a town already behind the German front lines, and almost completely destroyed it which had a strong influence on the feelings of Polish people in the Kingdom. Besides, the German and Austrian armies invading Russian territories, moreover, addressed the inhabitants with proclamations so formulated that they could only confirm the Poles' convictions that nothing could be expected from the Central Powers. Austria disappointed them completely. It is true that in the first days of the war the Emperor Franz Joseph, taking the advice of leading Polish politicians, principally Bobrzyński, had the idea of issuing a manifesto which would declare the creation of Poland as a third member of the dual monarchy, but German diplomacy and the Hungarian political leaders determinedly opposed this idea.

Piłsudski's rash venture ended in failure. He was left alone in the Kingdom with a handful of soldiers against a passive, if not hostile, population. In Galicia, on the contrary, his actions were popular, but influential politicians were decidedly opposed to Piłsudski, seeing in his men the nucleus of a social revolution. Thus both the conservative politicians and the National Democrats wished, for various reasons, to paralyse Piłsudski's independent action. The disposition of Polish youth, especially in Lwów and Eastern Galicia, was so militant that the National Democrats could not openly voice their pro-Russian programme, which was equally unsafe, for fear of police action. They therefore had to pretend loyalty to the Austrian monarchy while waiting for further developments.

This led to the creation on 16 August 1914 of the Supreme National Committee (Naczelny Komitet Narodowy, abbreviated as NKN) in Cracow, which was to unite all Polish parties in the Austrian area. It was to look after military action which was to be put under the control of the Austrian command. The Polish Legions were created as an unit associated with the Austro-Hungarian army and Piłsudski was compelled to let his units become the nucleus of this formation. From then onwards the concept of an insurrection and an independent national government was doomed to failure. Undoubtedly, this was a victory for the Cracow Conservatives and a tactical success for the National Democrats, who became part of the Supreme National Committee and promised to organize in Eastern Galicia another unit, called the Eastern Legion. In practice, they employed delaying tactics until the retreat of the Austrian armies enabled them to withdraw from the whole affair. The Eastern Legion was moved from Lwów to the west and disbanded at Mszana in Western Galicia. Such a gesture was made possible for the politicians of Dmowski's party, because Russian propaganda proved much more effective than anything which the Central Powers could put out on the Polish problem.

On 14 August 1914 the Russian Commander-in-chief, the Grand Duke Nikolai Nikolayevich, issued a manifesto to the Polish people. In it he proclaimed the unity of all Polish lands under the sceptre of the Tsar and in a rather ambiguous way promised autonomy to these territories. Not only was the manifesto remarkably well written, but what is most important, is that it was the only document which set out a concrete programme for possible implementation in the event of victory. This excited an enthusiastic response in the Kingdom on the part of a large section of public opinion, prepared for years, by National Democratic propaganda, to accept this conception. The burgeois-gentry elements especially saw in their support of the Tsarist régime security against the spectre of revolution.

Hence, the Polish question depended upon the development of military events, in the first place, on Polish territory. The first weeks of the war showed the weakness of the Austro-Hungarian army. Galicia to a large extent was occupied by the Russians, with the Austrians holding only Cracow and a portion of the Kingdom of Poland, but Prussia held on to all her territory. Until spring 1915 Russia remained a formidable force, especially when on the French front the German war plans were halted by the battle of the Marne and nothing foretold a swift defeat of the Anglo-French armies. The prolongation of war, moreover, made the British blockade a particularly effective weapon. In these circumstances the superiority of the views favouring the Allies in 1914-1915 was decisive. Piłsudski, however, held in check by the political control of Galician politicians and the Austrian high command, attempted to create for himself some sort of independent force. Towards the autumn of 1914 he organized the Polish Military Organization (Polska Organizacja Wojskowa, abbreviated as POW) which, under his command, was to act in the rear of the Russian front as an intelligence unit and a subversive force. In fact, this organization was weak, but in Piłsudski's game it gave him some trump cards, which later, as the military situation developed, he was able to use cleverly. He was also clever enough to embellish his own military activities with legends. At the head of the Legions' First Brigade he played a useful part in the retreat of the Austrian army from the Vistula to Cracow and later took part in the winter counter-offensive, in which he fought victorious encounters near Łowczówek and Limanowa.

Piłsudski gathered in his headquarters devoted politicians and writers over whom he was able to obtain a personal influence. It was among these young people that the cult of the "Commander" was begun, which lasted to the end of his days. The legend of a man, who first worked in the underground, and then began a soldier's career fascinated wide and diverse elements in the Polish population who longed for their own army and were prepared to serve in it in the last years before the outbreak, when historical writing encouraged the cult of the Polish soldier, especially in the Napoleonic period and during the Polish insurrections.

At the turn of 1914 and 1915 the Second Brigade of the Legions fought in the eastern Carpathians. The majority of the officers were Galicians, socially inclined to be conservative. The most popular officer in the brigade was Colonel Józef Haller. Both brigades were controlled from the point of view of organization by the War Department of the Supreme National

Committee, headed by Colonel Władysław Sikorski in cooperation with Professor Stanisław Kot and Marian Kukiel. Soon the War Department came into conflict with the First Brigade and thus began a vehement struggle, both personal and political, symbolized by the antagonism between Piłsudski and Sikorski which lasted until the Second World War. Piłsudski adopted a flexible attitude and sought to free himself from the control of the headquarters of the Legions, which itself was controlled by an Austrian general, and from the Supreme National Committee which adhered to a pro-Austrian policy. This antipathy between Piłsudski and Sikorski depended rather on tactics than basic differences of opinion. But, when personal animosity was added, together with Piłsudski's tendency to invest himself with a cult of hero-worship, the matter in fact became one of the important factors of Polish political life during the course of the next generation, even when the earlier differences had long lost their meaning.

Even though in the winter of 1914-1915 a pro-Russian attitude in the Kingdom prevailed, the military operations of the Legions exerted an influence on the imagination of a large part of the Polish intelligentsia. Opponents of the Legions came forward, at the same time, with the idea of creating legions on the Russian side also. This idea met with great opposition. Attempts to organize in Puławy a Polish Legion, begun with the support of the Russian general staff without the approval of the government, produced meagre results and did not achieve any political significance.

The struggle between the various points of view transferred itself abroad and especially to the United States. The position of the American Poles could be of help for one side or the other. They could supply volunteers and money, they could also influence, to a certain degree, the American government and public opinion. In the autumn of 1915 the Supreme National Committee sent its representatives to America. Under their influence a Committee of National Defense was set up, an organization which sympathized with Piłsudski, but shortly afterwards Ignacy Paderewski arrived in the United States, a man who enjoyed tremendous popularity with public opinion as well as in government circles and among the Poles in the U.S.A. He came out on the side of the Allies and was decidedly against the propaganda of the NKN. He found support in the Polish national organizations influenced by the clergy, while the NKN found its followers in more progressive or socialist organizations.

Attempts to carry on propaganda in Europe were made from Switzerland. There a philanthropic organization was set up under Sienkiewicz and Paderewski with headquarters in Vevey, whose purpose was to give material aid to the Polish population who had suffered as a result of hostilities. At the end of 1915 a secret Political Circle was organized in Lausanne in support of Dmowski's views which acted as an intermediary between the Poznań politicians and the Polish National Committee active at this time in St. Petersburg.

THE AUSTRO-GERMAN OCCUPATION OF THE KINGDOM

In May 1915, after a break-through on the Russian front near Gorlice, the German and Austrian armies moved to the east. The Polish lands came under the rule of the Central Powers. Thus, the Polish question took on a new aspect. The Congress Kingdom was divided into two occupation zones, with Warsaw and a larger part of the territory under the German General Governor, General Beseler, and the smaller part with its seat in Lublin as an Austrian General Government.

In retreating from the Kingdom the Russians forced the population to abandon their homes and to move east. For this reason the armies of the Central Powers were, at first, greeted with relief, but soon the mood changed when it was realized that an occupation which began with the division of the Kingdom brought no solution to the Polish problem. In effect, the governments of the Central Powers did not wish to consider it. On the contrary, the occupation of large territories in the east was for them a bargaining point for the peace settlement. The tradition of alliance between the three Emperors still had significance as an alliance which could guarantee the permanence of monarchies in this part of Europe. This was especially true at the Tsar's court, where ultrareactionary circles were always pro-German, and it was understood that Tsarism was in a position of peril and only an understanding with Berlin could maintain the existing social order. The prolongation of the war, in fact, forced the leaders of the Central Powers to seek new political and military advantages in a war which was growing harder and exhausting economic and human resources.

The overall situation was not understood by the Poles, who wanted to conduct a political game with the Central Powers. The Supreme National Committee considered that once the Kingdom was freed from Tsarist rule it would be necessary to mobilize the total resources of the country for the Legions. Piłsudski, on the other hand, felt that procrastination would produce greater benefits for the Poles. For this reason he enlarged only the Polish Military Organization, which became a semi-secret organization and refused to submit to the control of foreign political or military agencies. As a result of the opposition of his followers, as well of all those, of course, who counted on a German defeat, recruitment to the Legions organized by the War Department of the NKN yielded very poor results. Enlarged to three brigades, the Legions found themselves on the Volhynian front, where they fought brave but bloody battles on the Styr and Stochód. In the eyes of the German units they won themselves a fine reputation. In short, this was to influence political decisions, over which the German military were gaining an ever greater authority.

The Kingdom was treated by the occupying Powers as a conquered territory. Food and all manner of raw materials were removed to their countries. Industry was systematically destroyed, factory installations were dismantled and valuable machines earmarked for scrap in order to obtain non-ferrous metals, the lack of which was felt more and more acutely in Germany. When there arose a shortage of manpower in Germany, Polish workers were encouraged to take work there, and, when voluntary recruiting did not yield sufficient results, compulsion was used.

These actions made closer contact between the Central Powers and Poland difficult. This fact was not ignored by the Warsaw General Governor, Gen. Beseler. For this reason, in spite of the war, the Kingdom had opportunities of much greater freedom in its political life than it had under the Russian government. Various parties began to carry on legal activities. It was precisely in this period that the peasant movement in the Kingdom reached its final organization. The Independent Peasant Union developed its Right Wing organization, while the Left Wing concentrated around M. Malinowski, editor of "Zaranie" and was to form later the Polish Peasant Party "Wyzwolenie" (Liberation). Parties of socialist leanings, like the Polish Socialist Party, the PPS Left Wing and the SDKPiL, began to issue their own publications. In this way the Austro-German occupation zone of the Kingdom became a school of fresh political life.

THE DECLARATION OF 5 NOVEMBER, 1916

The year 1916 clearly showed that the war would not be decided by swift military operations, but that it was a war depending on supplies of arms, food and men. The battle of Verdun, a German attempt to force France to make peace, resulted in an enormous loss of human life. The Germans began to understand that they also lacked the human resources to provide fresh reinforcements at the front. In those circumstances attention was drawn to the Kingdom of Poland which was a reservoir of recruits as yet not fully exhausted. To get these recruits it was necessary to create a Polish administration which would be able to obtain recruits in the name of Poland. This was the origin of the Proclamation of the Two Emperors on 5 November, 1916.

This declaration was preceded by long negotiations between both Powers and the Polish politicians in the Kingdom. Some Polish leaders did not wish to become involved at all in cooperation with the Central Powers. They were called "Passivists" in opposition to the "Activists" who wished to take advantage of the favourable situation. A part of the "Activists" wished to bring about an agreement with the Austrian government only. This conception, in view of the development of events, became less and less realistic when the Austro-Hungary position became weaker. Already in 1915 Austria needed help from Germany in order to subdue Serbia. From May 1915 Austro-Hungary had to fight on the Italian front. Finally, and this was most important, Brusilov's offensive in the summer of 1916 smashed the Austrian front on a broad sector in Volhynia, in view of which the Germans had to bring to the eastern front considerable forces from Verdun. As a result, the entire Russian front found itself under German command. This weakened Austria's political prestige considerably, giving the Germans the upper hand in dealing with the Polish question. That is why another section of the "Activists" considered that Poland's future should be linked with Germany. These politicians acted in isolation and never gained wide support. Finally, the third splinter group of the "Activists" were those, who in collaboration with the governments of the Central Powers saw other possibilities. They did not wish to prejudice any solution, but only to take advantage of temporary opportunities to create Polish institutions in education, administration and, above all, the army. This last conception was represented by Piłsudski. At this time he was quite clearly removing himself from the Polish Socialist Party and from socialism in general, seeking already to enlarge the area of his political influence, appealing to a section of the Polish propertied classes.

On 5 November, 1916, a declaration of William II and Franz Joseph promising the creation of a Polish State as a hereditary constitutional monarchy was proclaimed simultaneously in Warsaw and Lublin. It did not arouse enthusiasm in the Kingdom, but was on the whole favourably received in Galicia, though that area was not embraced by it. At the same time, a separate rescript of the Emperor Franz Joseph was issued in which Galicia was granted a separate status, thus giving effect to the resolution of 1868, but no one attached any importance to this rescript, because it was obvious that the Polish question, having been once raised, could not thereafter be disregarded. For this reason partial solutions of the problem were without significance.

The Declaration of 5 November became the starting point for arguments between Polish politicians in the Kingdom and the Central Powers, which had not been foreseen by the German politicians. The occupying Powers had all the material arguments on their side and the Poles could offer only passive resistance.

The clumsiness of German propaganda worked to the advantage of the Poles. Beseler's proclamation of 9 November in which he announced recruitment to a Polish army, made the worst possible impression. While it was to have Polish uniforms and standards, it was "temporarily attached to the German army, in the sence of its being subordinate to the German High Command and of military law". Thus instead of the expected formation of a Polish government and administration, the occupying Powers demanded only the donation of blood. The Polish answer was, of course, decidedly hostile. Demonstrations took place in the streets of Warsaw, organized by the Left, demanding the calling of a Polish government and Seym. Simultaneously, the Polish Military Organization announced a recruiting campaign of its own and though the Germans saw in this organization a kind of military training, which could be utilized in the formation of regular army units, it was, in fact, the nucleus of an armed force independent of the occupying Powers.

For this reason Beseler had the Polish Legions transferred from the Volhynian front to the Kingdom and the German occupation zone. They were to became the cadres for a future Polish army, dependent of the Germany military authorities. Simultaneously, on 6 December a Provisional Council of State was established which was "empowered to cooperate in the creation of further state institutions in the Kingdom of Poland". It was composed of fifteen members nominated by the German authorities and ten by the Austrian. It was to be a consultative body and not representative of the country as a whole. Nevertheless, prominent politicians of all shades of opinion agreed to accept the nomination. The opening of the Council took place on 14 January, 1917.

THE DOWNFALL OF THE TSARIST RÉGIME, 1917

In international politics the Polish question was regarded, in the first years of the war, as an internal Russian problem and therefore neither France nor Great Britain wished to raise this touchy issue, but soon Russia's attitude began to change. After the fall of the pro-German government of Stürmer, his successor, Trepov, proclaimed in the Duma the concept of "creating anew a free Poland in her ethnographical boundaries, indissolubly connected with Russia". This was a step further than the manifesto of the Grand Duke Nikolai, which spoke only of autonomy. On 25 December, 1916 the Tsar issued an order to the army and navy in which mention was made of "creating a free Poland out of all its three areas". All this showed that the declaration of 5 November was not without influence on the development of the Polish question in the international field. Shortly, President Wilson also, whose country was preparing to enter the war on the side of the Allies spoke in his message to the Senate on 22 January, 1917 about a free and united Poland with access to the sea. All these by no means specific or binding declarations showed, however, that the Polish problem had become a vital issue, in spite of the wishes of the political and military authorities of all the belligerent powers.

In such a situation the fall of the Tsarist régime in March 1917 became a turning point in the history of the Polish question in international relations and, at the same time, changed fundamentally the situation in the Polish territories. One partitioning Power ceased to exist and only Germany could be the real enemy of the revival of the Polish State. Austria, on the eve of internal disintegration and dependent on German military aid, could think only of her own salvation. With the fall of the Tsarist régime it might have appeared that now Germany would become the master of central and eastern Europe, and thus would decide the fate of Poland. This situation strengthened the position of the "Activists" in Warsaw, especially when the social implications were to their advantage. With the Tsarist régime there disappeared not only one of the partitioning Powers, but also one of the guarantors of the existing social order. Ultra-reactionary, monarchist circles now had to seek support from the German Empire.

For the Polish Left Wing the situation was likewise becoming completely different. Up to this time the Russian government was, in its opinion, the principal bastion of reaction in Poland, and the struggle against it was a struggle not only for national, but also for social freedom. With the fall of Tsardom Imperial Germany became the chief enemy, both in a national and a social sense. Declarations which were coming in from Russia on the Polish question made this matter ever more obvious. Already on 28 March, 1917 the Petrograd Soviet of Workers and Soldiers Deputies issued an appeal to the Polish nation, accepting Polish independence as its basis. Two days later the Provisional Government, as a result of this appeal, expressed its agreement to the creation of an independent Polish State remaining in a free military union with Russia. In this way Polish sovereignty was given international recognition by both sets of belligerents. Both Russia and the Central Powers recognized, at least in theory, the principle of Polish independence. This increased the freedom of movement of those Polish politicians, who had up to now sided with the Entente. Dmowski had been in the West since the end of 1915, attempting, within the limits of loyalty of a Russian subject, to conduct discreet propaganda in French and British government circles in favour of the Polish cause. His arguments were for a long time without avail, because the western Powers wanted, at all costs, to keep the Tsarist government in the Allied camp, and their raising of the Polish question would be precisely the strongest argument for the pro-German forces in Russia, which were advocating a separate peace with Germany.

Simultaneously with Dmowski's activity, Paderewski agitated in favour of Poland in American government circles, which resulted in the message of Wilson on 22 January, 1917. After the new Russian declaration on the Polish question, France took the initiative into her hands. Already on 5 June, 1917, a decree of President Poincaré was issued regarding the formation in France of a Polish army. The Polish National Committee, established in Lausanne by Dmowski, moved to Paris and was shortly afterwards recognized by the Allied governments as the official body to represent Poland. At the same time a Polish army was being formed in Russia. Already on the basis of the Emperor Nicholas's order of December 1916, the creation had been started of a volunteer division of Polish riflemen, recruited from Polish soldiers in the Tsarist army. After the revolution the movement for setting up separate Polish units proceeded apace. The rank and file hurried to the Polish flag in the hope of returning home. According to the intention of Polish conservative gentry circles these units were to isolate the Polish soldiers from the influence of the Russian revolutionaries.

A Supreme Polish Military Committee, presided over by Władysław Raczkiewicz, was created at a meeting of Polish military figures held in Petrograd in June 1917. On the initiative of this Committee, the Russian High Command nominated General Józef Dowbór-Muśnicki Commander of the First Polish Corps which began to be formed in the area of Mińsk. In this way, while in the country the occupation government could not recruit an army for itself, the organization of Polish armed forces, against Germany, had begun in its rear.

THE REGENCY COUNCIL

The politicians, who in the Kingdom collaborated with the occupying Powers, tried to draw advantage from this state of affairs. At meetings of the Provisional Council of State there were arguments about the organization of the army and its legal relationship to the Central Powers. Beseler considered himself the commander of the future Polish army. The military oath, which insisted on the soldiers' obedience to the German command, gave cause for a breakdown of negotiations. Piłsudski and his followers left the Provisional Council of State and that part of the legionaries which sympathized with him refused to take the oath. In consequence those legionaries who were Russian subjects, mostly from the First Brigade, partly from the Third, were interned in camps. A very small unit, called the "Polnische Wehrmacht", under Beseler's command was formed from the small group of legionaries who took the oath. Legionaries who were Austrian subjects were sent back to Galicia and those, who sympathized with Piłsudski, drafted in the Austrian army. A Polish auxiliary corps was formed from the remainder, its most outstanding officer being Colonel Józef Haller. This move showed the rivalry between the governments of Vienna and Berlin in the Polish question, which Austrian diplomacy did not wish to abandon. The Germans took less account of the Poles and this explains why they arrested Piłsudski and imprisoned him in Magdeburg which helped immensely in increasing his popularity. The arrest of Piłsudski meant that the independence movement passed decidedly over to the side of Germany's enemies. Shortly afterwards the rest of the members of the Provisional Council of State resigned. Thus in the summer of 1917 pro-German feeling in Poland had for practical purposes disappeared.

It was in such a climate that the Polish parliamentarians from Galicia passed an important Resolution on 28 May, 1917, in which they called for the reunion of all the Polish lands in an independent State with access to the sea. This was a break with the pro-Austrian orientation and showed that even such moderate politicians, like the majority of this group, did not consider Russia after the fall of the Tsarist régime to be an enemy of Poland.

While the Western governments were ever more involved in the Polish question, Great Britain was fighting the mortal danger of submarine warfare and the Russian army was evidently falling into disintegration. For Polish conservative circles it became obvious that, although Germany would not gain a victory in the west after the entry of the United States into the war, a compromise might be arrived at in which Germany would retain the possibility of deciding the fate of eastern Europe. This was understood by leading persons in Imperial Germany and therefore a new attempt to gain advantages for Germany in the Polish question was in the interest of both sides. In September 1917 a Regency Council was formed in Warsaw, which was nominally to exercise power in the Kingdom until the proclamation of a king. The regents were to call into being a Polish government, with a new Council of State filled partly by nomination and partly by election. The range of activity of these authorities was subject to the control of the governor-general and, what is most important, the Regency Council was not allowed to have diplomatic relations with foreign countries. In October the regents were appointed from persons of known conservative views, Monsignor Kakowski, the Archbishop of Warsaw, Prince Zdzisław Lubomirski and Józef Ostrowski.

At the outset the regents were inclined to an Austro-Polish solution, because at that moment in the light of the relations between the two Central Powers this was the most likely solution, though Germany demanded as the price of giving the Kingdom to Austria a reduction of its size and the incorporation of certain frontier districts to Prussia in return for compensation to Poland in the east. The question of these border adjustments dragged on until the end of the war, as did the problem of possible compensation which Poland would receive for this in the east, but in this question the German occupation authorities supported Lithuanian as well as Ukrainian nationalism as a safeguard against revolutionary movements coming from Russia. At the end of 1917 an independent Lithuanian State, with its capital in Wilno was established under German protection. Thus, both the German plans of annexation in the west and the Reich's policy in the east created considerable obstacles to an understanding with Imperial Germany, even for reactionary Polish politicians.

THE OCTOBER REVOLUTION AND THE PEACE TREATY OF BRZEŚĆ LITEWSKI (BREST LITOVSK)

After the outbreak of the Socialist Revolution in October 1917 few people in Poland were aware of the fact that a new epoch in history had begun. What was primarily seen was the immediate effect of the revolution, in which

Russia definitely withdrew from the war. For Polish socialists prospects of a Socialists Revolution now opened, while for reactionary politicians it became still more obvious that collaboration with Germany was necessary at any price, inasmuch as she was the only power in this part of Europe which could defend the existing social order. The leaders of the German Empire understood only the immediate consequences of this great upheaval. They saw that at this moment their military and political position had been strengthened. In opening peace negotiations in Brześć (Brest Litovsk) at the end of 1917 they considered the Polish question could not be used to advantage and was in fact rather inconvenient. Jan Kucharzewski, the Prime Minister nominated by the Regency Council, was not allowed to be present at the negotiations.

The Poles were shocked by the separate peace treaty between the Ukrainian Central Council and the Central Powers. This treaty was to give the Central Powers access to Ukrainian grain, without which the German and especially the Austrian population was threatened by famine and revolution. This is why far-reaching concessions were granted to the Ukrainians. The Chełm district was handed over to them as well as part of Podlasie and, in addition, they were promised Eastern Galicia. The news of this gave rise in Poland and, especially in Galicia, to violent demonstrations, strikes and disorders of almost revolutionary proportions. Even the officers of the Polish Auxiliary Corps, loyal to Austria, could not resist this pressure. On 15 February practically the entire corps under the command of Haller crossed the lines of the Austrian front, arms in hand, to join the Polish units formed out of the disintegrating Russian army. The corps had to continue its march farther to the east to avoid the Austrian and German units which were then occupying the Ukraine. Finally, on 11 May at the battle of Kaniów on the Dnieper Haller's troops were surrounded by German units. They fought bravely, but owing to the supremacy of the enemy they were forced to capitulate. Nevertheless, a large part of them, together with Haller, managed to fight its way into the interior of revolutionary Russia. Haller himself hastened through Murmansk to Paris, where he was placed in command of the Polish army being created there. This was under the political guidance of the Polish National Committee and was being recruited from Polish war prisoners from the German and Austrian armies, who had been stationed in the west, in considerable numbers, especially in Italy.

After the treaty of Brześć, which was concluded with Soviet Russia in March 1918, the situation for the Poles once more became complicated. Not only the "Passivists", but Piłsudski's followers also now regarded Germany as Poland's principal enemy and considered that a defeat of Germany could be inflicted solely by the Western Allies. For all those, who strove for an independent Poland and rejected the idea of a social upheaval, Bolshevik Russia did not seem to be a suitable ally, but one which rather began to appear increasingly dangerous. The Polish propertied classes had a completely negative attitude to the new Russia. The Polish units created by former Tsarist officers in the area embraced by the revolution now became a defence force for the Polish landowners against the Byelorussian or Ukrainian peasantry. Thus it was easy for them to reach an understanding with the Germans who were entering into these territories. General Dowbór-Muśnicki, who had already engaged in a struggle with Bolshevik troops, immediately after the Brześć treaty reached an agreement with the Council of Regency. Ultimately, after long negotiations and vacillations, in spite of the obstacles put forth by the Polish Military Organization, Muśnicki's corps surrendered to the Germans and was demobilized, with the disarmed soldiers returning to Poland.

GERMANY'S DEFEAT. THE DECLARATION OF THE POWERS ON THE POLISH QUESTION, 1918

In March 1918 the Germans undertook a final offensive on the Western front aimed at forcing France to conclude at least a compromise peace. The "Activist" group in Poland, already quite small, still calculated that, if Germany were to be successful in this offensive, she would maintain her hegemony in the East. The German political and military authorities also did not wish to declare themselves on the Polish question until the issue on the Western front had been decided. In such a situation even the National Democrats participated in the elections to the Council of State, which were boycotted only by the left-wing parties. It became obvious that questions of foreign policy no longer divided the Polish community, but rather internal social issues. The SDKPiL and the PPS Left Wing strove for a social upheaval on the model of the Russian revolution. The rest of the Polish Left, however, linked the slogan of independence with social reform rather than with a social upheaval. Its various groups were organized in a secret Convention directed by Piłsudski's men, who in addition had under their control the Polish Military Organization, which did not limit its now secret activity only to the Kingdom, but sent out emissaries to wherever Polish groups might be found. The Polish Socialist Party renewed in the autumn the activities of the Fighting Organization. Its most outstanding feat was the assassination of the German chief of the political police in Warsaw in October 1918. The main slogan became the struggle with the occupying Power. Thus when Germany suffered defeat and the occupation régime collapsed of its own accord Piłsudski's men had gathered all the trump cards in their hands.

In the summer it became clear that Germany would not be able to obtain even a compromise peace. The offensive on the Western front broke down and from July 1918 the military defeat of Germany was already inevitable.

Feverish diplomatic talks now began between Germany and Austria, because both Powers understood the value of the Polish question when the expected peace negotiations began.

At this moment a fact of considerable importance for the Polish question occurred. On 29 August, 1918 the Soviet government annulled all the partition treaties. The partitions of Poland were thus cancelled *de jure* and this gave rise to the necessity of a new settlement in this part of Europe. From this time onwards none of the European powers could deny the international character of the Polish question and the possibility of a return to the *status quo* of 1914 in the Polish territories, disappeared. The ultimate solution depended on whether it would be decided solely by foreign governments, or whether the Poles would find sufficient strength to influence the construction of their own national State.

In the meantime the revolutionary mood was spreading to every major section of the Polish population, especially in the Kingdom, where owing to the disorganization of the factories the workers were suffering hunger and unemployment. This was not without influence on the views of Polish politicians, even those who were conciliatory towards the Central Powers. While in March 1918, Prince Ferdynand Radziwiłł, the president of the Polish Parliamentary Club in Berlin, might still issue a conciliatory declaration and the Polish deputies voted for the war credits, already in June the Club selected a new president, Władysław Seyda, a National Democrat, and adopted a more hostile stand. In Vienna, as long as Count Czernin, one of the authors of the treaty of Brześć, was in control of foreign policy, the relations between the Polish Club and the government were for practical purposes severed. After Czernin's fall from office, Burian became Minister of Foreign Affairs and returned to the plan of an Austrian solution of the Polish question. The effective result was the abandonment of the trial of those legionaries of the Polish Auxiliary Corps, imprisoned in Marmaros Sziget in Hungary, who had not succeeded in crossing the front lines in February, and who were facing severe sentences. Their release without sentence was, in fact, a capitulation of the Austrian government, because the trial had aroused considerable interest and highly patriotic speeches have been made in the courtroom.

The fate of Poland at this time depended, on the one hand, on the Entente governments which soon, having gained a military victory over Germany, would dictate conditions to her, and, on the other hand, on the situation in Poland.

Already, during the negotiations at Brześć, President Wilson had proclaimed, on 8 January, 1918, his programme for a general peace in his famous Fourteen Points, of which the thirteenth related to Poland. Although it sounded very fine and could seem to be a fulfilment of all the aspirations of the Poles for their own independent State, it was formulated so obscurely that it made possible an interpretation, according to which the Prussian area would for the most part remain within the German State. Wilson had emphasized that the independent Polish State "should include territories inhabited by an indubitably Polish population", and, as was known, almost every part of the Prussian area could be the subject of dispute, because it was not ethnically homogeneous. Similarly the phrase dealing with Polish access to the sea did not simultaneously provide for the incorporation of Pomerania and Gdańsk into Poland. Later the British and French declarations on the Polish question went further in an anti-German spirit and the Polish National Committee gained an increasingly strong position when the Western Powers granted it large credits and the possibility of conducting consular activity as the representative of the future Polish State. On 3 June, 1918 the governments of Great Britain, France and Italy stated that "the creation of a united and independent Polish State with free access to the sea constitutes one of the premises of a lasting ... peace".

THE LIBERATION OF THE AUSTRIAN AREA

In face of the collapse of the Central Powers, ruling circles in Austria attempted at the last moment to reshape the monarchy into a federal State. But this half-century old conception now came too late. On 15 October the Polish deputies in Vienna declared to Emperor Charles that they ceased to consider themselves his subjects.

The legal liquidation of the multi-national monarchy had begun. The Emperor Charles' manifesto proclaimed not only the transformation of the monarchy into a federal State, but also promised the unification of the Austrian Polish territories with the rest of Poland. This was a result of the request for peace, which the Austrian government had sent to Wilson. The American answer, however, ruled out this conception. Wilson declared that the Fourteen Points he had issued were already partially out of date because the Allied governments had recognized the Czechoslovak National Council as a *de facto* government. This statement was tantamount to the end of the Hapsburg State. On 19 October, 1918 a Polish National Council was formed in Cieszyn which declared the adherence of the Cieszyn area to Poland. Simultaneously, the Czechs in this area set up their own "Narodni Vybor" (National Council) and on 5 November both committees concluded an agreement dividing Cieszyn-Silesia into a Polish and Czech area on an ethnic basis. The Poles did not know, however, that earlier on 28 September Masaryk, the chairman of the Czech National Council, had concluded a secret treaty with the French government which provided for the incorporation of Cieszyn-Silesia in the future Czech State. The agreement of 5 November was only a tactical move for the Czechs and it was shortly broken.

On 29 October, 1918 a Polish Liquidation Commission was set up in

Cracow which assumed power over all of Galicia without regard to Ukrainian demands in relation to the eastern part of the province. This Commission did not consider itself any longer an organ of the Austrian authorities and, therefore, it can be regarded as the first fully independent governing body in the Polish territories.

THE ŚWIEŻYŃSKI GOVERNMENT

The Regency Council, nominated by the occupying Powers, also sought to become such an independent Polish authority. When on 4 October Prince Max of Baden, the new German Chancellor, sent a request for peace to President Wilson, the Regency Council, understanding that it could not persist in the idea of creating a State at the side of the Central Powers, issued a proclamation dissolving the Council of State and promised the creation of a government composed of representatives of all political groups. This government was to establish the franchise for election to the future Seym, which would decide upon the Constitution, but contact with the Left was impossible for the Council of Regency. The growing pressure of the masses, which were becoming increasingly revolutionary, forced all the parties which did not want to lose their support in the community to take a more radical stand. In the first place, the Polish Socialist Party broke with the directives of the Convention of Piłsudski's followers, and on the contrary, imposed its leadership on the Left Wing. In these conditions neither Daszyński, the leader of the Polish Social-Democratic Party in Galicia, nor Witos, the leader of the right-wing Galician Peasant Party, agreed to enter the coalition government proposed by the Regency Council.

There were vacillations as well within the Polish Socialist Party. This party rejected in September 1918 the idea of carrying out a revolution similar to the one that had taken place in Russia, with the establishment of the dictatorship of the proletariat, but the plan of Jędrzej Moraczewski, one of the leaders of the Convention, who in understanding with the National Democrats proposed a coalition of all Polish parties in favour of independence, was also discarded. The formation of a united front between the PPS and the extreme Left was frustrated on the one hand by the influence of the Convention, and on the other, by the SDKPiL. This explains why the PPS Party Conference passed a resolution in October, from which it followed that the Party was prepared to cooperate with radical-democratic elements, even though non-socialist, if it could also carry out its programme of social reform.

In fact, the socialist parties had no mass organization at this moment, but only cadres which could follow public opinion and even influence it, but which did not have an adequate executive machinery. This was a consequence of the general situation in the country. Industry was destroyed and the working class impoverished and dispersed. In 1918 only 14 per cent of the total labour force employed in 1914 was at work in the Kingdom. The entire community regarded the enemy and the occupation governments as the cause of its misery and, therefore, the regaining of independence was a universal demand. Wide hopes were placed on the revival of Poland, with each social group seeing in it what it wanted to. This desire for independence was a most powerful factor which was to decide the future fate of the nation.

While for the parties of the Left cooperation with the Regency Council was impossible and equivalent to political suicide, the National Democrats accepted the proposal of the Regency Council. On 23 October the National Democrat government of J. Świeżyński was established. This government could not, however, assume real power, which remained in the hands of the Germans, nor gain the support of the Left. It was dismissed on 4 November, having discredited both the Regency Council and the National Democrats.

THE LUBLIN GOVERNMENT

As a result of the dissolution of Austrian authority in the Kingdom a Provisional Government of the Polish Republic was established on 7 November 1918 in Lublin. Daszyński became Prime Minister and the government was composed of representatives of the Polish Socialist Party, the Peasant Party "Wyzwolenie" and radical democratic intellectuals. Witos hesitated: though he signed the manifesto, he later withdrew, realizing that the composition of the government was too left-wing for his liking. The Lublin Government lasted, in fact, only five days, but the very fact of its creation and, above all, the programme outlined in its manifesto played a crucial role in crystallizing the political situation in these days, in a sense which was decisive for the future. The manifesto put forward a programme of radical social transformation. It introduced immediately the eight-hour working day, proclaimed the nationalization of forests, while referring more important issues to the decision of the Seym, which was to be elected on the basis of general, equal, secret and proportional ballot, giving both passive and active electoral rights to all adult men and women. Equal political rights for women, a fact of immense significance, can be considered the result of social development in Poland during the previous two generations.

The programme of the November Manifesto, had it been put into effect, would have brought Poland closer to socialism. The next few weeks were to decide whether these words would remain only a programme or be put into practice. The immediate political effects of the proclamation became obvious immediately. The Council of Regency understood that it had to disappear. The only way out was to surrender authority but in such a way as to save as much as possible of the social position represented by the Regents. Piłsudski's return from prison now appeared to be a way out of the situation. Świeżyński's government had already nominated him Minister of War and requested the German chancellor to set him free. Shortly afterwards revolution broke out in Germany. The monarchy fell and Piłsudski was released and arrived in Warsaw on 10 November. The next day the Regency Council gave him command over the army by which were meant the few units of the "Polnische Wehrmacht". The command of the Polish Military Organization which began to disarm the Germans, was his in any case. Upon hearing that the Republic had been declared the German troops began to set up Soldier's Council in solidarity with the revolutionary movement in Germany, and, for this reason, they were ready to give up their arms in order to speed their return home. Piłsudski reached an agreement with the Warsaw Soldiers' Council on the basis of which the peaceful evacuation of German troops from the Kingdom took place. Piłsudski aimed at the creation of a coalition government, but when the socialists began to organize demonstrations in Warsaw against the Regency Council, in order to keep a left-wing government in power, he decided, when the Regency Council transferred civil authority to him as well, to entrust Daszyński, as the Premier of the Lublin Government, with the task of forming a cabinet.

Eventually, Moraczewski became Prime Minister on 18 November. He was more subservient to Piłsudski and continued to have contacts with the National Democrats, because Piłsudski did not abandon the idea of creating a government on a broader political basis. For the time being Moraczewski's government was, in principle, the continuation of the Lublin Government and it protested that it wished to carry out the Lublin Manifesto. On 2 November a decree was published on the basis of which Piłsudski took over the office of provisional head of State until the Seym could be convened. He also kept for himself the supreme command of the army. In this way the reconstituted Polish State was formally established.

LIBERATED POLAND

More than two years were to pass before the situation in Poland was finally stabilized, her borders determined and her political and social order consolidated. Nevertheless, it is appropriate to consider the factors which had brought about the fact that the Polish people which for over a century had been without their own State now regained it, finding themselves once more among the free nations and able to shape their political life in independence.

The fundamental force, which was present during the whole period of subjection with greater or lesser intensity but never dead, was the determination of the Poles themselves, because they had never been reconciled to the partitions or to the loss of their independence. The proof of this lies in the history of the years after the partition, a history marked by the frequency of insurrection and constant efforts to rebuild an independent State. That Poland regained her independence in the second decade of the twentieth century must be explained by an additional factor. It was of fundamental importance that, if the Polish desire for independence immediately after the partitions embraced only a fraction of the nation, by the beginning of the twentieth century it had spread to the entire community. Certainly this desire was not equally strong in all sections of the community or in all parts of the country, but the effect was no longer that of a small élite. At the beginning of the nineteenth century those who fought for Poland's freedom were mainly the middle or *déclassé* gentry: the officers in Dąbrowski's Legions or the conspirators of the November Insurrection in 1830. From the middle of the century it was the intellectuals of gentry and later of bourgeois or peasant origin who founded the Red organization in 1862–1863 and later organized workers' and peasants' associations. It was they who carried education to the lower classes. Though the Polish intelligentsia might provide the nucleus for the National League, the "Związek Walki Czynnej" and the socialist movement, they were powerless until they began to express the needs of the masses. All the Polish insurrections failed, in some measure because the participation of the masses was insufficient, but when the thrones of the three partitioning Powers had tottered, there existed in Poland an active working class, peasantry and petty-bourgeoisie and a talented intelligentsia. This, probably, should be regarded as the major reason why Poland regained its independence.

The will of the nation would not have been sufficient by itself. A necessary condition was an international situation which made possible the fulfilment of these aims. War between the partitioning Powers, the military defeat of the Central Powers, the Russian October Revolution, the November Revolution in Germany and the disappearance of the Hapsburg monarchy, all these historical events, occurring independently of the Polish will, made possible the realization of Polish aspirations.

POLAND 1918-1939

by Henryk Wereszycki

Chapter XXII

THE DEMARCATION OF THE FRONTIERS AND THE ENACTMENT OF THE CONSTITUTION (1918–1921)

THE FIRST MOMENTS OF INDEPENDENCE

When in November 1918 the first government of independent Poland began to operate in Warsaw the sovereignty of the State and the authority of the government did not in the least extend to all the Polish territories. In signing on 11 November an armistice with the Allies the Germans did not give up the occupation of the territory they held in the east. The Allies did not require this, because they did not wish to deprive western Europe of the cordon which the German armies were to create against the danger of a socialist revolution. The fate of the German armies in the east and that of the countries occupied by them was to be decided later. By this action the Allies, without realizing it, placed the destiny of these territories into the hands of the indigenous peoples. These countries were in many cases, however, not homogeneous with regard to nationality. In this part of Europe there were rarely well-defined frontiers dividing one nationality from another.

On 1 November Lwów was occupied by the Ukrainians. At this time the majority of the city's inhabitants were Poles and there were numerous Polish enclaves in the Ukrainian territories throughout Eastern Galicia. The Polish population of Lwów offered an armed resistance and a Polish-Ukrainian war began. The Polish nationalists realized that the Ukrainian conflict was an excellent means of drawing the attention of the radical Polish masses away from burning social problems. This is why a bitter agitation in the name of bringing aid to struggling Lwów was launched against the Moraczewski government especially by Piłsudski, whom the propertied classes and the right-wing parties considered the standard bearer of the Left.

A second cause for dispute was Poland's attitude towards Germany. The Moraczewski government had established diplomatic relations with the newly-formed German Republic and accepted a German envoy to Warsaw. Piłsudski was anxious that the armies retreating from the Ukraine and Byelorussia should march to German through East Prussia, without crossing Polish territory, because they were still such a powerful force that there

Poland, 1918/1919

- —·—·— Frontiers of the Partitioning Powers, 1914
- — — — Boundaries of countries and provinces
- ·········· Boundaries of the Austrian and Prussian occupation zones in the Kingdom of Poland and of the territories under the administration of the "Ober-Ost" Command, October 1918
- Areas liberated 31 October and 1 November, 1918
- Areas liberated 10–19 November, 1918
- Areas liberated by the insurgents of the Poznań Area 17 December 1918–10 January 1919

could be no effective defence against them, if they had wished to reoccupy the Kingdom. An agreement was reached according to which the retreating German armies avoided Poland. Only then could diplomatic relations with Germany be broken off and adherence to the group of countries at war with

Germany effected, which was, of course, of great importance in view of the Peace Conference assembling in Paris.

The Polish National Committee, with its seat in Paris, had in its hands the possibility of becoming the sole representative of Poland accredited to the governments of the victorious coalition, but it had little authority in the country and was compelled to agree to a compromise. Professor Stanisław Grabski, a former socialist, who was now a National Democratic leader and a member of the Paris Committee, was entrusted with the mission to Warsaw, but he succeeded only in as far as Piłsudski sent his own delegates to Paris to join the National Committee. Grabski's efforts to bring about the formation of a coalition government at the time yielded no results. For this reason a plan was conceived by right-wing groups to overthrow the government by force.

On the night of 4 January, 1919 an attempt at a *coup d'état* in Warsaw ended in failure. Its authors did not, however, suffer personal consequences, because Piłsudski in fact sympathized with the idea of disposing of the socialist-peasant government and replacing it with a more right-wing administration, which he considered necessary in view of relations with the Entente and Poland's immense economic difficulties. In effect, the Moraczewski government was denied the cooperation of the propertied classes, while itself it rejected a revolutionary solution of the economic difficulties.

As in neighbouring countries, swept by revolution, Councils of Workers Delegates began to be formed in the industrial centres of Poland. In practice, they developed only in the Kingdom, where the working class had the strongest traditions.

In December 1918 the two extreme left-wing parties, the SDKPiL and the PPS Left Wing joined together to form the Communist Workers's Party of Poland, from 1924 KPP, or the Communist Party of Poland. The Communist Workers's Party wished to adopt the policy of the Bolsheviks and through the Councils of Workers' Delegates to get the working class to take power in the country. At the same time the PPS acted in the Councils with a completely different aim of depriving them of their revolutionary character. The PPS won a small majority in the Councils. Only in the Dąbrowa Basin did the Communists, with support of the Councils, take power into their hands for a short while and create a Red Guard.

At this critical moment the existence of a government with a socialist reputation was of immense significance. Moraczewski's cabinet had recourse to the army to put down Communist action in the Dąbrowa Basin and in Warsaw. It also expelled from Warsaw the Soviet Red Cross mission, which had proposed the establishment of diplomatic relations with Russia. On its return journey the members of the mission were murdered near the frontier. With the help of the PPS Moraczewski was able to paralyse and eliminate the Workers' Council movement. Simultaneously, in order to weaken the revolutionary pressure of the working class, the Moraczewski government hastily put into effect its programme of social reform.

A series of decrees instituted social insurance for the workers, established factory inspectors, introduced the eight-hour day and, above all, announced a very democratic franchise which gave women the right to vote. Women's suffrage did not assist the Left, because women, especially in the countryside, were prone to clerical influence and the majority of them voted for right-wing candidates. Nevertheless, these were achievements designed to forestall revolutionary action which the Right afterwards could not easily abolish. Moraczewski's decrees were, however, a step backward by comparison with the Lublin Manifesto. The nationalization of the forests, for example, had now been abandoned.

THE LEGISLATIVE SEYM

Ten days after the unsuccessful right-wing *coup* the government resigned at Piłsudski's request. The new cabinet under Paderewski was purely bourgois in character. The coming to power of the Right removed the possibility of far reaching legal and social changes. There remained a revolutionary way of satisfying the needs of the working classes. Not only the propertied classes, but also the well-to-do peasantry were strongly attached to the principle of private property and feared the revolutionary terror which they observed in Russia. The left-wing intelligentsia, reared in the tradition of struggle for social and national liberation, had high hopes that the desired Polish State would be based on social justice and carry out a revolution "in full majesty of the law", with the progressive forces winning a legal majority in the Seym.

The Paderewski government assumed office on 16 January, 1919 and the elections to the legislative Seym were held ten days later. For the time being they were conducted only in certain areas of the Kingdom, because some regions were still occupied by German armies, and in Western Galicia. Eastern Galicia, on the other hand, was to be represented in the Seym by deputies who had been elected to the Austrian Parliament, before the war, and similarly, the Prussian area by the Polish deputies elected to the German Parliament. No elections took place in the Cieszyn area where fighting between the Poles and Czechs broke out 23 January, ended only by the intervention of the allied governments.

An exceptional situation existed in the Prussian area. Immediately after the November Revolution power was assumed by Polish-German Councils of Workers and Soldiers Delegates, but side by side with them were created purely Polish People's Councils, which established a People's Supreme Council claiming authority over the country. The right-wing politicians of the Prussian area were in a majority everywhere and worked on the assumption that the Polish-German frontier would be defined by the peace treaty, for which reason Prussian sovereignty should be recognized up to that moment. Despite the right-wing leadership's views fighting broke out in Poznań with the German troops on 27 December, 1918, an event which quickly led to the liberation of the entire Poznań province. As a result the Allied Powers forced both sides to conclude a cease-fire. The liberated districts retained to some extent a distinction between themselves and the government in Warsaw and even set up a tariff barrier against the Kingdom in order to maintain their higher standard of living, especially in foodstuffs and to safeguard themselves against revolutionary upheavals. It should be noted that this area was not devastated by war at all, and that during the war and blockade its agriculture had flourished. For this reason, the Poznań province was in a much more advantageous situation after the armistice than the ruined Kingdom or even Western Galicia.

The Right Wing triumphed in the elections to the Seym. It did not gain an outright majority, but did obtain 35 per cent of the seats, while the Left gained 26 per cent and the Centre 35 per cent; the Communists boycotted the election. In this way the Centre had the decisive voice on the resolutions of the Seym, because it could support the proposals either of the Right or the Left according on the situation and the issues at stake. Together with other peasant groups, a vital part in the Centre was played by the "Piast" Peasant Party, led by Wincenty Witos. Thus the representatives of the prosperous peasants were in control of developments in Poland and this in a period when her Constitution was being drawn up. This had an unfavourable effect for the future fate of the State.

The Seym constituted itself on 14 February by electing its Marshal; the candidate of the Right, Wojciech Trąmpczyński, was elected with a small majority.

Piłsudski formally resigned his provisional power as head of State. On 20 February the Seym enacted the "Little Constitution". It resolved that the Seym should exercise sovereign and legislative power, and that the head of State should be the supreme executor of the Seym's resolutions. In collaboration with the Seym, he was entrusted with the formation of governments, which, like himself, were to be responsible to the Seym. The Seym then unanimously appointed Piłsudski head of State, and he now resumed office with its approval. This resolution made Poland a Republic with the balance of power weighted in favour of the legislature.

The main task of the Seym was to enact a permanent Constitution, but more urgent matters arose in the meantime and the work on the Constitution dragged on until 1921. In this period a war was being waged on almost all the borders. The defence of Poland herself was confused with the desire to expand beyond the ethnographic frontiers to the eastern borders of the former Commonwealth, inhabited in the main by Ukrainians, Byelorussians and Lithuanians.

In the early months the hardest battle was fought with the Ukrainians. Lwów was isolated and, for a certain period, cut off. It was only in the spring that the Ukrainians had been forced behind the Zbruch river as a result of fierce fighting, after the arrival of General Haller's army from France. The Polish National Committee had delayed sending this army to Poland in the belief that while it had it at its disposal it could be used as an instrument to gain power in Poland. After Paderewski's appointment as Prime Minister and the creation of a government of right-wing complexion, though nominally non-party in outlook, the struggle for power was shelved, especially when extremely urgent problems at home and abroad, had to be solved.

The chaos caused by the policy of devastation adopted by the occupying Powers did not cease with the moment of liberation. It was slow to disappear and in this connexion a more significant part was played by the voluntary effort of the population than by the official authorities who were inefficient in the early days of their formation. The currency question was the most difficult, a general feature in this part of Europe where a galloping inflation occurred, which was not as severe in Poland as in some other countries. Stabilization of the Polish mark established under German occupation was quite impossible as long as war lasted. The propertied classes could overcome the revolutionary situation only by requisite reforms and the organization of an efficient administration. Though the Councils of Workers' Deputies and the militias, created during the period of driving out the occupation authorities, had been abolished within a few months, the question of social reform demanded by the mass of the population, called for action. The problem of a land reform and the compulsory division of large estates was desired by the landless and small peasants.

In the summer of 1919 this issue was the main subject of discussion in the Seym. Every one agreed to the principle of agrarian reform, but a conflict arose over the size of estates not liable for division and over the possibility of dividing Church lands. The initial principles of the reform were agreed on 10 July, with the stipulation that areas of less than 80 or 180 hectares, according to the quality of soil and their location, should not be subject to division. On 22 July a bill was passed establishing the Central Land Office, which was to carry out the reform. Shortly afterwards the Seym passed a number of laws affecting the workers; introducing an 8-hour day, compulsory insurance and the rights of persons renting houses. Housing was of great importance because there had been virtually no new building since the beginning of the war. Almost all these laws, though they were later modified, survived the twenty years between the two world wars and made Poland one of the most progressive countries in the field of social legislation in the capitalist world.

THE PEACE TREATIES

The Paderewski government attained one undoubted success. During its tenure of office the Versailles Treaty was concluded in June 1919 which, while it did not fully satisfy Polish aspirations, gave international standing to a part of the Polish western frontier. The peace negotiations took place in a situation unfavourable for Poland. Great Britain supported the claims of Germany, wishing to preserve her power on the continent as a counterweight to the French hegemony and to Soviet Russia. Because Poland was considered a French field of influence, Germany was strengthened at Poland's expense. Upper Silesia, therefore, was not given to Poland; it was decided instead to conduct a plebiscite there as well as in Mazuria and Warmia in East Prussia. Gdańsk also was not incorporated in Poland, but made a Free City over which Poland did obtain suzerain rights. Supervision of the Free City was entrusted to the League of Nations. For the moment, therefore, Poland had regained the Poznań area, with some diminution in its western districts, and only a part of Gdańsk-Pomerania, reaching the sea by a thin strip of territory barely 70 kms wide. At Versailles the treaty on the protection of national minorities was imposed on Poland, but Poland obtained no reciprocal advantage. In this way the German minority in Poland had international protection, but the Polish minority in Germany was deprived of its rigths. In spite of everything, the Versailles Treaty was of fundamental significance to Poland, because it restored her existence as a sovereign independent State, thus legalizing in international law what had already taken place in fact.

The peace treaty concluded shortly afterwards with Austria did not settle the problem of Poland's right to certain territories formerly ruled by Austria. It was left to the great Powers to decide such problems as the question of Cieszyn and Eastern Galicia. In September 1919 the Allied Supreme Council decided to hold a plebiscite in the disputed Polish-Czech area. In November the Supreme Council granted Eastern Galicia to Poland for 25 years, with the provision that a plebiscite should be then held. The Polish Seym, however, rejected this decision. On the question of Poland's eastern frontier the Supreme Council at first forbade Polish military action in Lithuania but afterwards granted Poland the eastern frontier of the Congress Kingdom, with the addition of the district of Białystok, but without the Suwałki district. Possession of lands farther to the east was not resolved. The Western Powers still counted on the rebuilding of Tsarist Russia and did not intend to question her rights to these territories.

Against the background of the struggle for the agrarian reform, a rapprochement took place between the various peasant parties, for which reason these parties, who had at the end of 1919 a majority in the Seym, could form a Centre government. This government of L. Skulski lasted for a half a year. It did not settle two basic problems: to begin the implementation of the agrarian reform and to stabilize the currency. It fell during the difficult war situation which arose in the middle of 1920.

THE WAR WITH SOVIET RUSSIA

While on the western borders a solution was awaited from the peace conference, fresh fighting broke out in the east at the beginning of 1919 with the Red Army.

Piłsudski organized an expedition against Wilno and occupied it in April. Fighting became general on the whole eastern front and resulted in the occupation by Polish troops of Byelorussian ond Ukrainian territory up to the line of the Berezina, Sluch and Zbruch. Secret Polish-Soviet negotiations in the autumn of 1919 led to a *de facto* armistice of a few months.

Piłsudski's idea was to create between Poland and Russia a barrier of States in some measure dependent on Poland. This was the so-called "federal idea". An attempt to put this concept into practice was the alliance with the Hetman Petlura, whom Polish troops were to assist in regaining power in the Ukraine in the struggle against the Bolsheviks.

In exchange for this, Petlura surrendered Eastern Galicia to Poland. The Ukraine created by him would have really found herself in the Polish field of influence and, in this way, Poland might have decided the fate of eastern Europe. The Ukrainian masses did not support this policy, while in Poland the plan met with opposition from the National Democrats who wanted to create a national State in which the Polish element would be the largest section of the population and remaining nationalities would be Polonized. In this connexion, there was a conflict of views within the PPS; the Communist Workers' Party of Poland opposed these schemes vigorously.

The Soviet government, aware of Poland's internal situation, proposed peace negotiations at the end of December 1919. Patek, the Minister of Foreign Affairs, acting on Piłsudski's instructions, first tried to keep these proposals secret, and when they became known, he sabotaged them.

He succeeded in breaking off talks on the pretext of a dispute on the place of negotiations. Immediately afterwards, in April 1920, a Polish offensive, which had long been in preparation, was launched, leading to the capture of Kiev on 8 May, but only a few days later the Soviet counteroffensive began. Budënny's cavalry appeared in the Ukraine and it forced the Polish army to retreat as far as the Bug and the Dniester. In July large Soviet forces attacked on the northern front, effecting a breakthrough, and advanced with tremendous speed up to the outskirts of Warsaw, reaching Płock in the north. The defeat came as a shock to Poland. Skulski's government fell. In July a nonparliamentary government headed by Władysław Grabski was formed and, in addition, a State Defence Council was created, which was to have the decisive voice in the conduct of the war and the conclusion of peace.

A volunteer army was organized. The government and the parties and social organizations supporting it mobilized Polish resources to repel the Red Army. A Land Reform Law was hastily passed which went further, in many respects, than the initial principles accepted a year earlier. The Prime Minister went to Spa, where a conference of the Prime Ministers of France, Great Britain and Belgium was being held. The Powers made the grant of assistance to Poland dependent on the acceptance of a number of conditions. Grabski had to agree to submit the Cieszyn issue, the borders with Lithuania, the Gdańsk-Polish treaty and Eastern Galicia to the decision of the Supreme Council. In exchange the British government promised to propose to the Soviet government the conclusion of an armistice, with the demarcation line running along the Bug and east of Białystok as proposed in December 1919 by Lord Curzon, the British Foreign Secretary. In addition, the Western governments promised Poland material aid and an Allied military mission, led by General Weygand, went to Warsaw. The British government proposed mediation, but the Soviet government rejected it, agreeing only to direct Polish-Soviet negotiations for an armistice and peace. In this situation the Grabski government fell and the State Defence Council called into being a coalition government under Witos, the leader of the "Piast" Peasant Party, and Daszyński, the leader of the PPS. This government declared itself a "Government of National Defence" and appealed directly to the Soviet government for an armistice. The Soviet authorities replied that they were prepared to negotiate both an armistice and peace simultaneously and proposed Mińsk as the place for negotiations. At the same time a Provisional Revolutionary Committee of Poland was established on 2 August, 1920 in Białystok under Julian Marchlewski. This Committee started to organize a revolutionary authority in this area.

At this juncture the Polish army could draw upon the material aid promised by the Western Powers only with difficulty. The shipments of ammunition and arms sent to Poland from France and Great Britain were held up on the way by transport workers, dockers and railway men in various countries. Nevertheless, some supplies did arrive and helped to strengthen the main sector of Polish defence before Warsaw, which General Tukhachevsky's armies approached in the middle of August.

The Polish government, mobilizing all its resources in order to strengthen its defences, agreed at the same time to direct negotiations with the Soviet government, and a Polish delegation was sent to Mińsk on 14 August. At the precise moment when it crossed the front, a large scale operation, prepared by the Polish High Command since the beginning of August, was launched. The general plan of operations was to disengage from the enemy, who had already broken through the Bug defences and to concentrate a striking force on the Wieprz, on the left wing of Tukhachevsky's advancing armies. This force was to attack in a northerly direction, turn the Soviet left wing and roll up the front attacking Warsaw. Piłsudski himself took command of this group. The operation was completely successful. In a few days the Polish troops occupied Brześć and then Łomża, thus cutting off considerable Red Army forces and compelling them to cross the German border into East Prussia.

At the same time Budënny's cavalry army was repelled near Hrubieszów and a counter offensive was launched on the entire front.

Peace negotiations were being conducted in Mińsk during these battles and the Polish side would not accept the Soviet conditions. When the situation on the front changed, both sides agreed on 2 September to transfer the peace negotiations to neutral Riga, where they were continued from 21 September. The Polish delegation was headed by the Deputy Minister of Foreign Affairs, Jan Dąbski, and the Soviet by an outstanding diplomat, A. Joffe. During these talks large military operations continued, which ended in October with the success of the Polish troops in the battle on the Neman. Preliminaries of peace were signed in Riga on 12 October and ratified on 2 November. Thus the war was concluded, though the final peace treaty was signed only on 18 March, 1921. The frontier thus established between Poland and the Soviet Republics of Byelorussia and the Ukraine ran to the east of the Lwów–Wilno railway line and further to the north it separated Lithuania from Soviet Byelorussia with a strip of territory linking the Wilno area with Latvia near Daugavpils (Dyneburg). In the south the Zbruch river was the border, but further to the north the frontier moved eastwards in Volhynia and Polesie. In this way Poland received large territories inhabited by Byelorussians and Ukrainians.

During the Riga negotiations Polish troops under General Żeligowski occupied Wilno with the area of "Central Lithuania", allegedly on their own account but in reality on Piłsudski's orders. The Soviet troops had turned over Wilno to the Lithuanians during their retreat. This territory was soon afterwards in 1922 formally annexed to Poland.

THE DEMARCATION OF THE WESTERN FRONTIERS

The retreat of the Polish army in the summer of 1920 had a prejudicial effect on the fate of the western frontiers. On 28 July the Council of Ambassadors hastily marked out the Polish-Czech border line leaving within Czech territory a large amount of Polish population. At the same time, a plebiscite was held in Mazuria and Warmia with the Prussian administration and police present and many brutal acts of violence were committed by Prussian officials. Moreover, 150,000 German citizens brought in from the Reich were permitted to vote. Polish efforts to have the plebiscite postponed

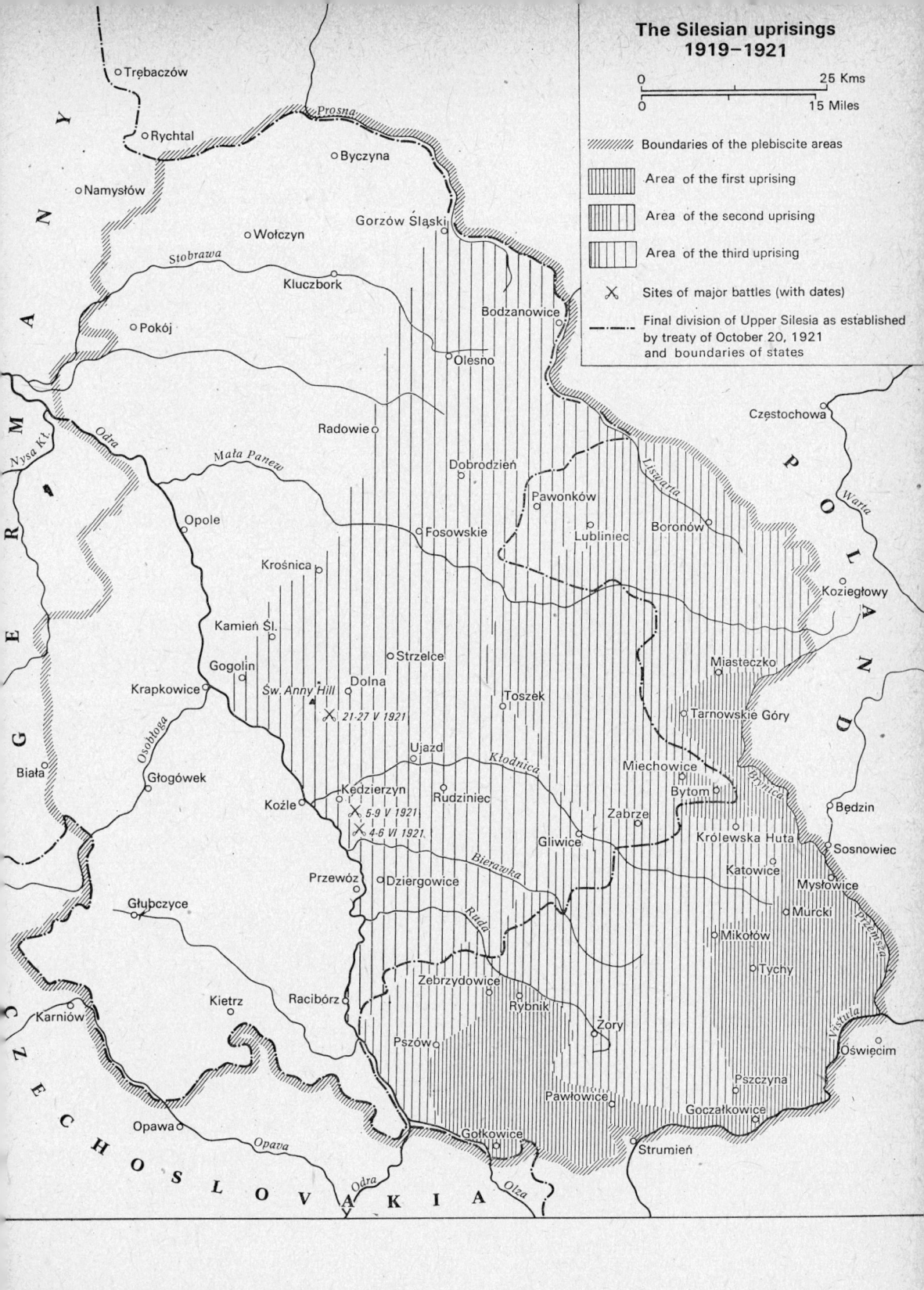

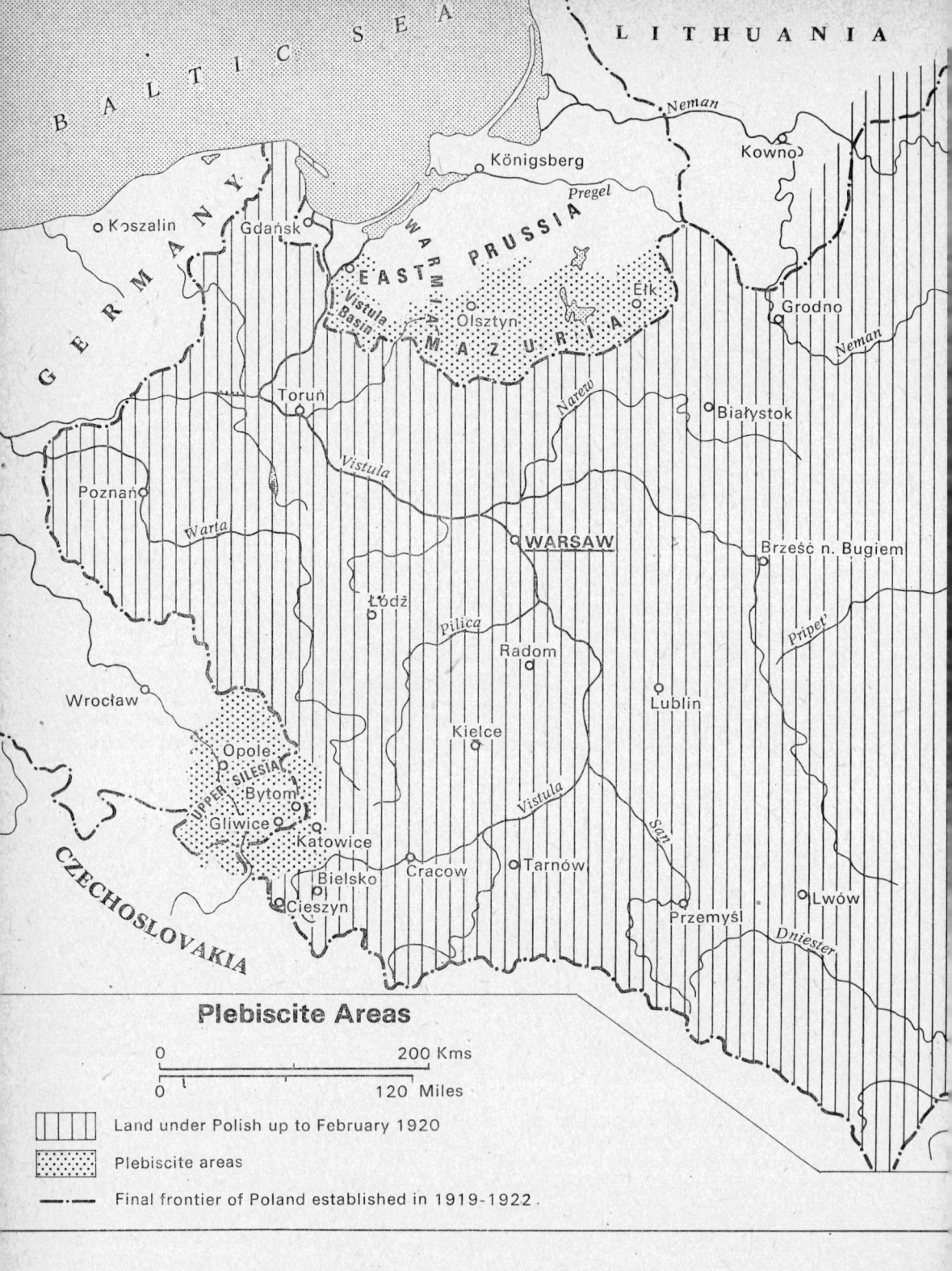

were of no avail, because the Western Powers were aware of the fact that the date appointed by them considerably improved German chances. The Poles suffered a defeat and already in August a territorial settlement, on the basis of this plebiscite, took place with the result that Poland obtained only a few villages in the plebiscite area.

A plebiscite also took place in Upper Silesia on 20 March, 1921. The Allied authorities, who controlled the plebiscite area, were in practice unfavourably disposed to the Polish cause. They condoned German terror and allowed 200,000 people to vote, who, though born in Silesia, had not lived there for a long time. Ultimately 500,000 voted for Poland, 700,000 for Germany. The Supreme Council was to carry out a division of the area on the basis of this result. Great Britain and Italy were not favourably inclined towards Poland and only France supported the Polish point of view, though not very determinedly.

In May 1921, fearing an unfavourable decision by the Allies the Polish population of Upper Silesia took up arms. This was already the third Polish rising in Silesia; the risings of August 1919 and August 1920 had ended in failure. This time the insurrectionary forces took control of the industrial district after fierce fighting. An intervention by the Allied Powers led to an armistice and after long negotiations the decision was reached to grant Poland the south-eastern part of Upper Silesia, including about half of the industrial area.

Thus the frontiers of the Polish State were determined and they were to last until the Second World War. Poland extended over 388,634 sq.km and was divided into 16 voivodships. It was a state with a large number of national minorities amounting to 31 per cent of the population in 1921. All Poles, moreover, did not find themselves within the borders of the reconstituted State. In particular, the Opole area, Warmia and Mazuria together with the area west of Poznań and western portions of Gdańsk-Pomerania remained under German rule.

THE MARCH CONSTITUTION, 1921

The Seym enacted the Constitution on 17 March, 1921. This was a democratic parliamentary Constitution. The head of State was to be a president, with limited powers and elected by a National Assembly, consisting of both Chambers of Parliament in joint session. The president was invested with the right to appoint the government which was, however, responsible to the Seym. The president did not have the right to dissolve the Seym, unless he had the approval of a three-fifths majority of the Senate to this effect. Parliament was composed of two chambers: the Seym and the Senate. The Senate had no initiative in legislation and could postpone a bill passed by the Seym for only sixty days. The March Constitution guaranteed civic rights, the freedom of education and association. It also guaranteed property rights, with such modifications as might be in the public interest. It provided for the possibility of compulsory purchase of land and the regulation of its sale. Fundamentally, this Constitution was modelled on European systems and in particular on the French, and similar, systems.

Thus at the beginning of 1921 the Polish State had fixed frontiers and had achieved its internal consolidation. It was, however, only experience of public life which could mould the true social and political nature of the new State.

Economic issues were to be decisive. Poland emerged from the wars with her economy in ruins. The devastation caused by military operations, and, above all, by devastation by the occupying Powers were estimated at from 30 to 70 thousand million pre-war francs, which was an immense part of the national wealth. Industry had suffered, especially in the Kingdom and there was far-reaching destruction and diminution of capital. In agriculture, buildings and stocks were destroyed and livestock depleted. Trade was disorganized and the railway and road network destroyed to a large degree, and poorly adapted to the needs of the new State. The war had consumed eighty to ninety per cent of the community's savings. Under these circumstances, total production in 1919 reached only 30 per cent and in 1920 40 per cent of the pre-war level. Moreover Poland entered the new stage in her life with immense debts, resulting from being forced to pay a part of the debts of the partitioning Powers, mainly of Austro-Hungary, without being granted reparations for the damage consciously perpetrated by the Germans. The maintenance costs of Polish troops in France and expenses incurred for the war materials furnished by the Allies also had to be paid for. These obligations amounted to about three thousand million zlotys, payable in gold. They burdened the budget right up to 1939, when they still amounted to 78 per cent of the State's foreign debts.

In these circumstances the easiest immediate solution of administrative and economic problems seemed, at first, to be inflation, which was equivalent to burdening the working people with the expenses of the recovery. The standard of living of the mass of the people fell, while the owners of factories, especially in big industry, were given tremendous bonuses. The capitalists received credits and advances for deliveries to the State, which they later repaid in depreciated currency. In effect, this was subsidizing capitalists at the expense of the workers. As a result of this policy economic reconstruction was fairly rapid, but the poverty of the population increased and social tension grew. Inflation lasted in Poland until the end of 1923. It then became socially dangerous to the propertied classes themselves, and, by turning into a superinflation, it ceased to bring any economic advantages at all.

At the outset, however, it enabled industry to compete in the international markets on the basis of its falling labour costs, but the main difficulties of industry were not removed. From the mid-nineteenth century Polish production was designed for foreign markets, in the Kingdom for eastern markets, and in Upper Silesia for Germany and Austro-Hungary. The domestic market could not fully replace the export market not only because its capacity was small in view of the low standard of living in the country, but also because production was not suited to its needs. In time Polish industry was to readjust to the changed conditions, but this involved an immense outlay. There arose, moreover, the question of who was to pay. Not only the urban workers and the capitalists were in dispute over this, but agriculture and industry also. The big estates in a predominantly peasant country were stronger politically and imposed an economic policy on the country at variance with the needs of industrialization, which was the direction in which Poland could develop economically. These contradictions between social and economic interests explain the constant political tension and the wavering political equilibrium in the first period of independence. Soon other contradictions were to appear as a result of the multinational structure of Poland's population.

Chapter XXIII
PARLIAMENTARY GOVERNMENT (1922–1926)

THE 1922 ELECTIONS

After enacting the Constitution the Seym still did not dissolve, prolonging its own existence until the passing of the electoral law which only took place in July 1922. The period of a year and a half between the enactment of the Constitution and the elections in 1922 was marked by a fierce political struggle on the question of who was to bear the burden of stabilizing the country's finances and of economic reconstruction. During this period of over twelve months cabinet crises were frequent, but in general the Centre groups controlled the government and a decisive role was played, in particular, by the "Piast" and its leader, Witos.

In such a political situation it was, of course, impossible to stabilize the budget or to curb the mounting inflation.

The new Seym differed from the first one with the appearance of a strong group representing national minorities who gained one fifth of the seats. The largest minority group were the Jewish deputies, with the Ukrainians slightly fewer, because in Eastern Galicia they had boycotted the elections not wishing to recognize the annexation of this territory by Poland. For this reason only Ukrainian deputies from Volhynia and the Chełm district entered the Seym. For the first time the communists, who gained two seats, appeared in the Seym. The position of the Centre was weakened, but nevertheless it remained the strongest group, having obtained 30 per cent of the seats. It was not, however, internally united, because apart from the "Piast", which had 70 seats, it also included some smaller groups. The Right Wing, or Bloc of Christian National Unity, gained 28 per cent of the seats and was a more coherent force. The left-wing parties were somewhat weaker, having just over one fifth of the seats and were even more divided. The "Wyzwolenie" Party had 48 seats, while the PPS had 41. In such a situation a parliamentary government could be carried on only by a coalition of the Centre with the Right or with the Left Wing. A government exclusively of the Left or of the Right was impossible. The Senate, whose political role remained limited, did not differ basically in composition from that of the Seym, with the difference that the Right Wing was slightly stronger, owing to the higher age qualification for election to the upper chamber.

From the beginning of the second Seym an alliance of the Centre and the Right Wing seemed likely and as a result Maciej Rataj of the "Piast" Party was elected Marshal of the Seym, while Trąmpczyński, a National Democrat, was chosen Marshal of the Senate. On the other hand, the question of electing a president had not been settled beforehand. On the fifth ballot the choice lay between Count Maurycy Zamoyski and Gabriel Narutowicz, an eminent professor of the Zurich Polytechnic, who had only returned to Poland in 1920 and had recently been Minister of Foreign Affairs. He was supported by the Left Wing, the national minorities and part of the Centre, and thus obtained a small majority over Zamoyski.

The Right Wing viewed this as a disaster and launched an unusually bitter agitation against his election, employing the argument that the national minorities could not decide the election of a head of State. Violent street demonstrations occurred in Warsaw, while the President was taking the oath of office.

On 14 December, 1922 the President became head of State. Two days later during the opening of an exhibition of paintings he was shot by the painter, Eligiusz Niewiadomski, a fanatic acting under the influence of the agitation conducted by the National Democratic press against the President.

The murder of the first President of independent Poland made a tremendous impression in the country and abroad. In conformity with rules of the Constitution the Marshal of the Seym temporarily took over the office of President and appointed a new government headed by General Sikorski as Prime Minister. Piłsudski became Chief of General Staff and W. Grabski, Minister of the Treasury. On 20 December the National Assembly chose Stanisław Wojciechowski as President with the same majority of votes of the Centre, Left Wing and national minorities and confirmed the Sikorski government in office. The events connected with Narutowicz's election and death made impossible, for the time being, an understanding between the "Piast" and the Right Wing. When this did occur later, Sikorski had to resign. During his government Poland obtained on 15 March, 1923 a decision of the Conference of Ambassadors, which recognized the eastern frontier of Poland as determined by the Riga Treaty, which also meant the final assignment of Eastern Galicia to Poland. Thanks to Grabski's action the devaluation of the mark was stopped, though only for a short time.

The negotiations between the "Piast" and the Right Wing dragged on owing to the difference of opinions regarding the implementation of the land reform. Ultimately a compromise was reached and on 15 May an agreement was signed, with a part of the "Piast" members, headed by J. Dąbski, dissenting. As a consequence the coalition which formed a new government was very weak in the Seym. On 28 May a cabinet led by Witos was formed. On the next day Piłsudski resigned as Chief of Staff and also from all his military functions.

The most important issue with which the new government was faced was the stabilization of the currency, but the parties representing the propertied classes did not agree to the demands of Grabski, who remained in this cabinet as Minister of the Treasury. As a result, Grabski resigned after a few weeks and the devaluation began to gather a catastrophic impetus. This was a consequence of the hyperinflation which had overcome Germany, with which the Polish economy was still strongly connected. While during Sikorski's government in the spring of 1923 the dollar was worth 50,000 Polish marks, by the autumn of the same year its value had risen to 200,000 marks in November and to 5 million in December. Inflation resulted in the fall of real wages and a bitter strike movement began as a result of the rise in prices. In October 1923 a strike of railway workers occurred which the government replied by the conscription of the railway workers. In November the PPS declared a general strike. The government replied by introducing the state of siege. Bloody disturbances took place on 6 November in Cracow. The army took part in this action and some of the units joined the workers. Both the army and the workers suffered casualties. The government now granted some partial concessions. These events, which had repercussions in Tarnów and Borysław, undermined the authority of the government. It was not these events, however, which caused its downfall in the Seym, but the question of the land reform which was torpedoed by the Right Wing. This caused a small group of deputies to leave the "Piast", thus depriving the government of its majority. The government resigned on 15 December.

WŁADYSŁAW GRABSKI AND THE STABILIZATION OF THE CURRENCY

The fall of the right-wing Centre government with a parliamentary majority showed that the composition of the Seym elected in 1922 did not favour this kind of system. The President appointed an extra-parliamentary government headed by Grabski, whose main task was to put the economy in order. Grabski's cabinet, though subject to many changes, remained in power for two years. He obtained powers which made it possible by means of presidential decrees to change tax legislation, contract loans, introduce a new monetary system and set up a bank to issue notes. By these means, Grabski was able in a few months to balance the budget, introduce a new currency, the zloty, and establish a Bank of Poland whose capital, amounting to 100 million zlotys (20 million dollars), was obtained from shares

issued on the domestic market. The part played by the working class in buying these shares was considerable, but the participation of the large landowners and farmers in general was relatively small. The important result, however, was that the currency was stabilized, though on a level which, as it was proved later, was too high, with the zloty being equal to one gold franc.

The immediate result of the stabilization of currency was a fresh economic crisis. Industry lost the export bonuses which inflation had given it and immediately showed itself to be technically backward by comparison with Western countries and unable to compete on the world markets. This gave rise to a renewed fall of industrial production and a consequent fall in employment. The number of spindles used in production in the cotton industry in 1923 amounted to 97 per cent of the 1913 total, but in the next year fell to 76 per cent of the pre-war figure. This tendency continued up to 1926. Economists had hoped that once the currency had been stabilized foreign capital would flow into Poland, where it would find profitable investment. These hopes were disappointed. American capital, which began to play a dominant role in war-devastated Europe, considered Poland, to a large extent under the influence of German propaganda, which called Poland "ein Saisonstaat", a country unworthy of confidence. The Germans had an important voice in these affairs because the German banks acted as intermediaries in the investment of American and British capital in central and eastern Europe. As a result an immense flow of American and British capital to Germany took place, while Poland was ignored. From the point of view of international finance Poland was merely a source of raw materials and semi-manufactured goods, an attitude which did not assist the backward economy of Poland. During the inter-war period Poland exported primarily coal, timber, sugar, agricultural produce and livestock. For this reason Poland's balance of payments was now determined by earnings from the export of raw materials rather than by the export of finished goods. In these circumstances the Polish economy could be transformed only by a revolutionary change of the entire system, but there were no social forces in the country strong enough to make such a revolution possible.

The influence of international capital on the Polish economy was felt all the more because concentration of industry was far advanced and kept increasing. Towards the end of the 1930's 69 per cent of the workers were employed in 4 per cent of enterprises. In general, Polish industry in the twenty years after the First World War consisted of relatively few large plants accompanied by an immense number of small and weak workshops.

In 1925 the economic situation was worsened temporarily by a bad harvest, the fall of world prices for coal, timber and sugar, and chiefly by the hostile commercial policy of Germany. The Polish-German commercial convention, concluded after the division of Silesia, expired in June 1925. It had obliged Germany to buy a specified amount of coal in Poland. The

Germans now ceased to make these purchases, which caused the Polish government to ban the import of a large number of German commodities. A customs war was begun which Poland won in the end, but the immediate effects of this war were considerable losses, which undermined the newly established Polish currency. This took place in July 1925. Expected foreign aid did not arrive. It is true that Poland was granted an American loan of 60 million dollars in June 1925, but she obtained in fact only 25 million, having been refused the second instalment in the autumn of 1925.

These events shook the position of Grabski's government. The Seym became once more an arena of struggle over the land reform. The radical law of 1920 had not been carried into effect, because the government deferred it to the time when the currency problem could be settled. Now the land reform was restricted to favour the landowners and the rich peasantry. A new law enacted in November 1925 after prolonged and tempestuous debates provided for the division of estates of over 180 hectares. In Poland's eastern territories the area not subject to division was raised to 300 hectares, because it was considered that large landed properties there were the mainstay of the Polish element. The ceiling for industrial estates was raised to as much as 700 hectares in order to encourage farming. According to the new law the State was to provide credits for the division of land in order to help, in the first place, the agricultural labourers and small peasants. This was the theory, but the law itself was not as decisive in practice. As a result there was a fierce struggle for power and upon it depended the determination of social conditions in the Polish countryside.

Grabski's government fell in the middle of November 1925 owing to the position adopted by the Polish Bank which refused to provide more foreign currency to prop up the rate of exchange. After a short crisis a coalition government took office on 29 November, led by A. Skrzyński, up to that time Minister of Foreign Affairs. The coalition embraced parties from the National Democrats to the PPS, but the "Wyzwolenie" peasants remained in opposition. The new cabinet had to struggle, in the first place, with the problem of a new devaluation. Grabski had set the rate of the zloty at 5.98 to the dollar, but in December it had already fallen to 9.10. The number of registered unemployed grew to 300,000, which did not take into account disguised unemployment, both rural and urban. Thanks to economies, a balanced budget was soon achieved, which was an essential condition for overcoming the financial crisis. In the spring the value of the zloty actually began to rise, but unemployment continued to increase. Violent demonstrations took place throughout the country. In this situation the PPS was tired of measures which continued to place the burdens of economic recovery on the shoulders of the working classes. The socialists left the coalition in April 1926 and this led shortly afterwards to the resignation of the cabinet. On 10 May, 1926 a right-wing Centre government was formed by Witos. After a few days it was overthrown by Piłsudski.

THE UKRAINIAN AND BYELORUSSIAN QUESTIONS

One of the essential causes of the weakness of parliamentary government in Poland was the problem of the national minorities amounting to one third of the population who either of their own volition took no part in the constitutional system, or were not induced to do so. Most acute was the Ukrainian problem, especially in Eastern Galicia, or as their territory was called after incorporation to Poland, Eastern Little Poland. This area had witnessed in 1918-1919 a war which deepened the existing difficulties. There were, moreover, in this agricultural area no strong working class parties which could oppose the nationalists. The Ukrainian Nationalist Party remained in contact with the former West Ukrainian dictator, Petrushevich, an émigré living in Vienna. He also found support from the Czech government and later in Germany. In 1921 a Ukrainian Military Organization was created, under the leadership of Colonel Konovalets; it engaged in armed raids and acts of terror. In the summer of 1922 buildings and crops on Polish estates were set on fire. In 1921 a Ukrainian nationalist attempted unsuccessfully to assassinate Piłsudski, then head of State, in Lwów. The Ukrainian Military Organization recruited its cadres from young people who were unable to find jobs in the civil service, because these remained exclusively in Polish hands. In this respect the situation of the Ukrainians grew worse than it had been under Austrian rule. The Ukrainians also failed to obtain a university. Eventually, on the one hand a secret Ukrainian University was established in Lwów, while on the other, many young people left to study in foreign schools, first of all in Prague. After returning home this new intelligentsia joined the rapidly developing Ukrainian cooperative movement which soon became not only an economic, but also a political power. The Ukrainian press developed and scientific institutions were set up, but the Ukrainian school system was discriminated again and its position worsened by comparison with that prevailing in Austrian Galicia. A law was passed in 1924, which defined the use of Ukrainian in the schools, courts and civil service. It provided, among other things, in the elementary and secondary schools for the equality of both tongues, Polish and Ukrainian. The Ukrainians, however, considered this provision harmful to them, because they had had purely Ukrainian secondary schools under Austrian rule.

The Ukrainian problem in Volhynia was somewhat different since the Ukrainian national movement in this province was of more recent origin and less developed. On the other hand, there were no compact Polish ethnographic islands in Volhynia, so that the position of the Volhynian Poles was still weaker than in Eastern Little Poland, where the Polish population amounted to one-third of the total. The Polish administration in the eastern areas harassed the population and often was a discredit to the Polish State. In this respect the three voivodships of Volhynia, Polesie and Nowogródek were the most discriminated, because these regions had been ruined by war and remained economically backward. In the Byelorussian area the political situation was not much better, though here a local Polish element existed and some of the Byelorussian politicians were initially inclined to cooperation with Poland. The general poverty, however, which was particularly acute in Polesie, created conditions for a national independence movement, to some extent connected with the communists. An additional subject of irritation in the eastern borders was the problem of reclaiming the Orthodox Churches which had been compulsorily taken from catholics in Tsarist times. Thus side by side with nationalist antagonism a factor of religious discontent appeared, which could become especially dangerous among the rural population of these backward areas.

Taking advantage of the general dissatisfaction numerous armed detachments were formed in the eastern borderlands and engaged in subversion and sabotage. The attack in August 1924 on a train carrying the Voivode Downarowicz was especially noteworthy. As a result, a special Frontier Defence Corps was then established.

THE COMMUNIST MOVEMENT

The influence of the communists increased not only in the east, but also in the central voivodships as a result of the worsening of the workers' position and the growth of unemployment. Changes within the Communist Party of Poland favoured the strengthening and broadening of its activities. In 1923 the Party's Second Congress reconsidered its attitude to the peasant question. In consequence it was possible to state a few years later that "the growth of the peasant section of the Party is progressing faster than that of the workers". Nevertheless, the Party as a progressive though illegal organization remained relatively small. In 1922 it had 5000 members, in 1923 6000 and in 1924 7000. The influence of the Party was, of course, much more extensive as was shown during the elections to the Seym when, for example, in 1922 132,000 votes were cast for the communist candidates, while in the next election of 1928 it obtained almost a million. In 1924 the communists gained a majority in the elections to the social security boards in the Dąbrowa Basin. Alongside the KPP the Communist Union of Youth was established in Poland in 1922. The Communist Parties of the Western Ukraine and Western Byelorussia, both of which were active within the Polish State, cooperated with the KPP. While in 1931 the KPP had 6800 members, the Communist Party of Western Ukraine and that of Western Byelorussia had only 2600 each. The Communist Union of Youth had 9400 members and there were 6000 communists in jail. Thus altogether the number of organized communists in Poland in that year amounted to 27,000.

The Party was weakened, however, by factional struggles which frequently led to the removal from leading positions of such outstanding members as Horwitz-Walecki, Warski and Maria Koszutska, known under the pseudonym of Wera Kostrzewa.

In the 1920's the KPP showed considerable activity. In contrast with communist parties in many European countries it was illegal; membership of it was itself punishable and sentences in such cases became increasingly severe.

POLISH FOREIGN POLICY AND LOCARNO

In Europe after Versailles the Polish State, reborn after Germany's defeat and opposed to Soviet Russia, could seek support only of France and the French system of alliances directed both against Germany and Soviet Russia. The peace negotiations in Riga were still dragging on when Piłsudski went to Paris in order to sign the Franco-Polish alliance on 19 February, 1921. This treaty, formulated on somewhat general lines, was supplemented on 22 February by a military convention which enumerated their mutual obligations in greater detail. Poland obtained the pledge of French support in the event of an attack by Germany or war with Russia. A commercial treaty was linked with this alliance which was clearly unfavourable to Poland. Nevertheless, the alliance with France gave Poland, who up to this time had been isolated, its first support in international politics.

It assisted the conclusion of an alliance with Rumania on 3 March, 1921, directed against Soviet Russia. On the other hand, the attempts of Polish diplomacy, then and later on to bring about such an alliance with the newly established Baltic States did not yield results. The attitude of the Soviet government in the light of the Polish-Rumanian alliance, which guaranteed to Rumania the possession of Bessarabia, which was not recognized by the Soviet Union, prevented closer contact between the Baltic States and Poland. The alliance with France and the search for contact with the Baltic States were the guiding lines of Poland's foreign policy in the subsequent years. Poland did not enjoy good relations with any of her remaining neighbours. Germany did not wish to observe the provisions of the Versailles Treaty, seeking constantly to achieve its revision and regarding its decision relating to Poland as the easiest field for attacking the treaty. Her task was facilitated by the fact that Great Britain from the outset, in spite of having signed the treaty, did not wish to involve herself in guaranteeing the state of affairs on Germany's eastern frontiers. Polish-Soviet relations did not develop favourably after the treaty of Riga. The Soviet government saw in Poland, not without cause, an area for assembling forces aimed at overthrowing the new social order in Russia. The Soviet-German Treaty concluded in Rapallo in 1922 was interpreted in Poland as signifying that both the neighbouring Powers aimed at revising the Versailles and Riga Treaties at the expense of Poland.

Anti-Czech attitudes stimulated by the Cieszyn affair prevented a Czechoslovak-Polish agreement. The agreement concluded with Beneš on 6 November, 1921 during the visit of the Polish Foreign Minister Skirmunt to Prague was not ratified by Poland.

Relations with Lithuania were in a bad state. The Lithuanians did not recognize the possession of Wilno by Poland and rejected all the federalist plans put forward by Warsaw, though they had the partial support of the Western Powers. Up to 1938 there were no diplomatic relations between Warsaw and Kaunas in spite of all the negotiations throughout these years whether direct or at the League of Nations. The Polish-Lithuanian frontier, however, was recognized by the League of Nations Council on 3 February, 1923. All these international instruments were to the advantage of Poland, as a recognition of Polish sovereignty and confirmation of her internal stability.

In the following years the League of Nations became a centre of international politics, in which Poland began to play a more important role, especially when Skrzyński, who had considerable international repute, became Foreign Minister. Proof of the improvement of Poland's situation was the visit to Warsaw on 27 September, 1925, of Chicherin, the Soviet Foreign Minister, who in view of the approaching entry of Germany into the League of Nations wished to have Berlin understand that Polish-Soviet relations need not always be unfriendly. This was connected also with the final recognition of the Soviet government by Great Britain and France, who wished to deprive Germany of its monopoly of good relations with the Soviet Union.

All of this did not safeguard Poland from the revisionist aims of Germany, who was rebuilding herself after the defeat. German propaganda concentrated its attack on the question of Gdańsk and the issue of the "Corridor" as the Germans called it, or Polish Pomerania. The Germans sought to convince world opinion that the "Corridor" was cutting through the German nation and that this injustice called for a remedy. The disputes between the Free City and Poland before the League of Nations were instigated by the Germans to show that Poland was a threat to peace and that her very existence was a germ of the future war which all nations justifiably feared. Thus, a small dispute about the placing of Polish post-office boxes in the area of the Free City in 1925 became, thanks to this anti-Polish propaganda, a great international issue. Poland won this dispute, but it was one of the reasons for the withdrawal of some American finance corporations from investing in Poland, because it was considered an unsafe area, exposed to war.

In these circumstances Poland had to reconcile herself with the new European situation with regard to the German question, as a result of the Locarno Treaty signed on October, 1925. In these agreements the inviolability of the new frontiers between Germany, France and Belgium was recognized and the signatories were obliged to defend them. In relation to Czechoslovakia and Poland, Germany promised only to conclude arbitration treaties, in other words she promised not to seek alteration of these frontiers by force. On the other hand, Poland and Czechoslovakia obtained a French guarantee for their frontiers, but within the framework of the Covenant of the League of Nations. This deprived the existing French alliances of immediate implementation because their application now became dependent upon a slow and complicated League procedure. This was an obvious weakening of the French alliance and, what was more important, the different treatment of Germany's frontier in the west from the frontier in the east meant that the atmosphere for German plans of revision in the east became more favourable, although for the time being Germany did not yet have sufficient military power to carry out such a change.

At the moment of the collapse of Poland's parliamentary system in May, 1926, her internal economic and political situation, like her position in foreign affairs, was unfavourable. The new Poland found herself among independent nations in a historical moment, when Europe had been devastated by war and had lost her primacy in the world. The first years of independence after a century and a half of foreign rule brought no solution of either her economic, social or national problems.

EDUCATION, SCIENCE AND CULTURE

The tasks facing the Polish State in the field of education were exceptionally difficult. It was necessary to unify an educational system based on the legislation of the three partitioning Powers, to expand and adapt it to the needs of the State and open the possibility of education to the mass of the people. Free primary education for a compulsory period of seven years was organized, but the authorities succeeded in keeping at school all the children of school age for only a short time. There was a lack of educational facilities and provision of teachers. Secondary education, which was on a high level, embraced mainly young people from the more prosperous social groups. Extramural education was organized primarily by social organizations like the Workers University Society and the Peasant Universities.

The Polish Teachers' Union played a considerable part in shaping a system of progressive instruction and in democratizing the schools.

Higher education was soon reconstructed. A Polish university was established in Warsaw during the time of the German occupation. Universities in Cracow and Lwów existed already. New universities were founded in Poznań and Lublin and a university was re-established in Wilno. A number of higher technical schools were also set up. In 1937–1938 there were 27 institutions of higher education in Poland, including 6 universities and 3 technological universities, with 48,000 students including 13,000 women.

The institutions of higher education were accessible primarily to children of the more prosperous social groups. High fees and the small number of scholarships made it difficult for children of working class or peasant origin to attend and still more to complete higher education. The level of lecturers and the standard of examinations were generally quite high and in this respect Poland was among the leading countries of the world, in spite of the fact that in many fields only the first steps in the organization of learning were being taken.

After the regaining of independence new prospects of development opened before Polish science and learning. Scientific research was undertaken by specialists already appointed to posts, reinforced by Polish scholars returning from abroad. While the State was not able to furnish proper patronage for science and learning, an essential part was played in this respect by scientific societies and organizations like the Polish Academy of Sciences and Letters in Cracow, the Mianowski Foundation in Warsaw, and the Warsaw Scientific Society.

Generally speaking, in the humanities during the years 1918–1938 there was proliferation of disciplines. The fields which were considerably expanded included Polish linguistics, classical philology, comparative linguistics, modern philology and Oriental languages.

Archaeologists, anthropologists and historians undertook research on the origins of the Polish State of whom J. Kostrzewski, J. Czekanowski, and Z. Wojciechowski were the most distinguished.

Polish historical writing was marked by a predominance of interest in political history. The foundations of economic history were laid by F. Bujak, J. Rutkowski and N. Gąsiorowska. Polish sociology had considerable achievements and it was represented in this period by F. Znaniecki, famous for his "analytical trend", L. Krzywicki, a many sided investigator of social life, and S. Czarnowski, the historian of culture and religion. B. Malinowski, the creator of the functional method of ethnographic sociological research did his work in London.

In philosophical studies the Lwów-Warsaw school of logic was outstanding for the work in formal logic and semantics of K. Twardowski.

Two schools of mathematics arose during this period and they rapidly gained a leading position in the world. The Warsaw school gathered around the "Fundamenta Mathematica", under Z. Janiszewski, W. Sierpiński, S. Mazurkiewicz and K. Kuratowski, and the Lwów school around the "Studia Mathematica" of H. Steinhaus and S. Banach.

Important physical and chemical research in the field of inter-phase balance were also conducted in Poland by W. Świętosławski.

Medical science developed rapidly headed by microbiology under L. Hirszfeld and R. Weigl and biochemistry in which J. K. Parnas was famous for his research into muscular metabolism.

Polish literature in the first years of independence deliberately wished to

Stefan Żeromski

depart from national didacticism and consciously strived for contact, above all, in poetry with the artistic trends in Europe, seeking a subjective expression for an individual "spiritual adventure", regarding with optimism transformations of society and civilization. Later, this individualism was to give place to an attitude of involvement in political and social problems and optimism was to be replaced by revolt against social injustice and by disquiet in the face of fascism and the danger of war.

Żeromski was still writing in the first years after the war and gave expression in his novel *Przedwiośnie* (Before the Spring) in 1924 to anxiety regarding the future of the nation because of the unsolved social problems. He was also the first to understand the significance of the problem of the sea for the new state, *Wiatr od morza* (Wind from the Sea) written in 1922.

A. Strug, a political writer and leader, dealt with the problems of the past war and of contemporary life in Poland and the world in many of his novels.

Among the writers, who were then beginning their literary career, J. Kaden-Bandrowski, Z. Nałkowska and M. Dąbrowska come to the fore. Kaden-Bandrowski, as a follower of Piłsudski, combined political passion with expressionist anti-aestheticism. In his cycle of contemporary novels he showed a considerable satirical talent. Z. Nałkowska presented a subtle psychology in her novels like *Romans Teresy Hennert* (The Love of Teresa Hennert) in 1923, and at the same time the ability of combining psychological with social poblems as in *Granica* (Boundary Line). M. Dąbrowska's works are marked by a classical narrative style which links up with the traditions of the nineteenth century. Her novel *Noce i dnie* (Nights and Days) presents an epic picture of life among the Polish intelligentsia of gentry origin in the years 1863–1914, a family saga similar to that of Mann's *Buddenbrooks*.

The next generation of writers included J. Iwaszkiewicz, who revealed talents as a poet and, above all, as a short story writer.

L. Kruczkowski, a writer connected with the revolutionary movement, revised the traditional view of the role of the peasantry in the national liberation struggles of the nineteenth and twentieth centuries in his novels *Kordian i Cham* (Kordian and the Churl) in 1932 and *Pawie pióra* (Peacock's Feathers) in 1935.

In the 1930's there was an increase in the works showing clear revolutionary and democratic tendencies. Among these were the novels of W. Wasilewska, *Oblicze dnia* (The Face of the Day), P. Gojawiczyńska's *Dziewczęta z Nowolipek* (Girls of Nowolipki), Z. Uniłowski's *Wspólny pokój* (Sharing a Room), G. Morcinek's *Wyrąbany chodnik* (Story of a Mining Gallery) and J. Kurek's *Grypa szaleje w Naprawie* (Flu Epidemic in Naprawa).

A different trend in prose was represented by those writers who sought new path in psychological fantasies like B. Schulz in his *Sklepy cynamonowe* (Cinnamon Shops) and *Sanatorium pod Klepsydrą* (Hour-Glass Sanatorium) or in social criticism like W. Gombrowicz in his *Ferdydurke*.

The inter-war period witnessed a particularly lively phase in the development of poetry. The poets of the "Young Poland" period were still writing and reaching the heights of their creativeness as, for example, B. Leśmian, in whose verses symbolism assumed a most fantastic, disturbing and visionary shape, and L. Staff whose work was marked by a Parnassus-like cult of beautiful form, classical order and affirmation of life.

The new generation of poets who grouped themselves around the monthly "Skamander" in the years 1922–1928 included J. Tuwim, J. Lechoń, A. Słonimski, K. Wierzyński and J. Iwaszkiewicz. These were virtuosos in their use of words which proclaimed the principle of spontaneity and of a "golden mean" between tradition and innovation. In subsequent years they developed into very different but outstanding individuals. The revolutionary poet W. Broniewski was close to the "Skamander" group, but only in respect of form, as were the poetesses K. Iłłakowicz and M. Pawlikowska-Jasnorzewska.

The "traditional" lyrics of the "Skamander" groups were opposed by the avant-garde, after a short period of experimentation in futurism. This school included B. Jasieński in the poem *Słowo o Jakubie Szeli* (Song on Jakub Szela) in 1926, T. Czyżewski and A. Stern. The Cracow "Zwrotnica" became the centre of the avant-garde with T. Peiper, J. Przyboś, A. Ważyk and, somewhat later J. Czechowicz. On the eve of the Second World War a "catastrophic" tone was to be noted on an increasing scale in the poetry of M. Jastrun, J. Zagórski and C. Miłosz.

In drama, the first years of independence were marked by the plays of Żeromski like *Uciekła mi przepióreczka* (Quail Escaped Me). K. H. Rostworowski, at the outset, wrote dramas about classical antiquity in the style of "Young Poland" like *Caligula* and *Judas*, using at the same time modern means of group staging. After a time he returned to the style of bourgeois naturalism in *Niespodzianka* (Surprise). The plays of J. Szaniawski, filled with the spirit of psychological symbolism, were particularly popular. Plays by Nałkowska and Iwaszkiewicz were also performed. The very eminent expressionist playwright, S. I. Witkiewicz, however, was not performed or known to a large audience.

Contact with the masterpieces of modern and past world literature was maintained by numerous translations which were in many cases as brilliant as the originals. T. Boy-Żeleński was a phenomenal translator who rendered into Polish several hundred works of French literature ranging from *The Song of Roland* to Proust, but with particular emphasis on the classical period. Boy-Żeleński was at the same time an able theatre and literary critic, a satirical writer and journalist who fought against ignorance, backwardness and clericalism. K. Irzykowski was also an eminent critic whose theories were derived from Croce.

During the inter-war period dramatic art in Poland was presented in many permanent theatres in Warsaw and each of the larger cities had a few theatres. High standards of performance and staging were set by excellent actors. One of the Polish theatre managers was L. Schiller, a pupil of E. C. Craig, himself a stage designer of remarkable temperament and culture, and J. Osterwa, a superb actor and producer, who founded the theatre "Reduta" as a workshop for new artistic forms. S. Jaracz was an excellent actor who was the first to take his theatre to the working class. The repertory was very large. It ranged from Shakespeare and Molière through the Polish

Tadeusz Żeleński (Boy)

Xawery Dunikowski, *Bolesław the Bold*. Tombstone, 1916–1917

romantics and "Young Poland" to Tretyakov's *Shout, China*. The theatre was faced with financial difficulties and it was often forced to produce light comedies appealing to the tastes of the petty-bourgeois public.

As in the entire world the cinema had become the basic form of entertainment of the urban population. Polish film production in the first period concentrated mainly on the adaptation of well-known works of

H. Kuna, *Christ*, 1926

literature, but subsequently on comedies and melodrama. In the 1930's an avant-garde group of film makers including A. Ford, W. Jakubowska, S. Wohl and J. Toeplitz introduced the idea of the "socially useful" film like *Legion ulicy* (Legion of the Street) and *Strachy* (Ghosts).

After the regaining of independence, orchestras, operas and musical publications flourished. The younger generation of Polish composers, A. Ma-

W. Skoczylas, *Stone Stairs*, c. 1930

lawski and T. Szeligowski, educated mostly in the Warsaw Conservatory by K. Sikorski and in Paris by Nadia Boulanger, P. Ducas and A. Roussel, under the influence of K. Szymanowski's works continued and developed Polish musical composition.

Painting during this period did not follow a single trend. About thirty groups of painters existed of which the "Formists", A. and Z. Pronaszko, T. Czyżewski, L. Chwistek, S. I. Witkiewicz and A. Zamoyski were of national importance. The works of the "Formists" showed along impressionist lines the influence of cubism and futurism, as well as appealing to Polish folk art. An important role was played by a group of painters living in Paris, the "Cercle des Artistes Polonais à Paris" founded in 1928, including L. Gottlieb, G. Gwozdecki and E. Zak. Polish painters like Tadeusz Makowski and Alicja Halicka played an important role in forming the École de Paris. In particular Makowski's works dealing with his beloved world of children were an important element linking Polish and French art.

The "Block" group of W. Strzemiński, the sculptors K. Kobro, M. Szczuka and H. Berlewi represented abstract art. In 1925 a branch of the Cracow Academy of Fine Arts was established in Paris headed by J. Pankiewicz. The group of painters associated with it, Jan Cybis, J. Czapski, J. Jarema, T. Potworowski and Z. Waliszewski, was especially close to the painting of P. Bonnard and exerted a great influence on Polish painting evident up to the present time. In the 1930's a group of "revolutionary artists" collected around W. Strzemiński and K. Kobro. At the same time painters and graphic artists like W. Borowski, W. Skoczylas and Z. Stryjeńska and the sculptors, T. Breyer, H. Kuna, E. Wittig, established the group "Rhytm"; their painting tended to be stylized and frequently dealt with folk motifs, while sculpture was marked by neoclassical tendencies. X. Dunikowski created his own individual style both in minor works and in his immense statues. The functioning of the Institute for the Popularization of Art in Warsaw was of considerable significance for artistic development.

Political independence marked a turning point in town planning. Polish architecture entered more and more into the general trend of contemporary European art. The dominant trait was the simplification of the façade of buildings, an example of which in Warsaw was the Ministry of Education by Z. Mączeński completed in 1927 and the National Museum by T. Tołwiński in 1927. An eminent role was played in the years 1925–1930 by the Architectural Department of the Warsaw Polytechnic under R. Miller and R. Gutt and the "Praesens" group of B. Lachert, J. Szanajca and H. and S. Syrkus. This group dealt with the problem of national housing construction and the contemporary town planning of residential districts as could be seen in the Warsaw Housing Cooperative and the Żoliborz Housing Estate. The work of B. Pniewski, E. Norwerth and C. Przybylski were an original contribution to Polish architecture.

Chapter XXIV

PROSPERITY AND THE CRISIS: THE STRUGGLE TO LEGALIZE PIŁSUDSKI'S DICTATORSHIP (1926–1931)

THE MAY *COUP D'ETAT*

After the creation of a Centre-Right Wing government in 1923 Piłsudski withdrew from the army and political life. He settled in Sulejówek near Warsaw, where he devoted himself to writing. The rank of Marshal had been confered on him in 1920, when he still held the post of Head of the State. Piłsudski was resentful that the nation accepted this self-imposed isolation, because he himself and his followers from the Legions believed that the attainment of independence was the personal and almost exclusive achievement of the "Commander". Piłsudski continued to enjoy a great personal authority in the PPS and the "Wyzwolenie" Peasant Party included people blindly obedient to him who actively built up a myth around him. The right-wing parties saw in him a dangerous enemy and cast aspersions against him. He resented most of all the assertion that the operational plan of August 1920 was not his, but that of either the French General Weygand, which was certainly not true or, to some extent more accurately, of Gen. T. Rozwadowski, the then Chief of General Staff. A new law defining the position of the military high command gave Piłsudski the greatest offence. When still Head of the State he had settled the relations of the Minister of War, the Chief of General Staff and the Commander-in-Chief in such a way that the two principal military offices were subordinated to the general designated as Commander-in-Chief. In 1923, during Witos's government, the Minister of War, Gen. Szeptycki, tabled a bill in the Seym absolutely contrary to Piłsudski's conception. Piłsudski criticized this draft, maintaining that the inner life of the army would become dependent on party manoeuvres through the intermediary of a Minister of Military Affairs, politically responsible to the Seym. He indulged in violent polemics on this subject and his adherents demanded Piłsudski's return to active service. The situation became acute, when in 1924 the Ministry of War was taken over by General Sikorski who, even in the time of the Legions, was considered Piłsudski's rival. A vehement campaign launched by Piłsudski against Sikorski aggravated the relations among the senior officers, among whom the supporters of Piłsudski constituted an unusually close-knit group amounting to a military conspiracy. After W. Grabski's fall Piłsudski would not permit Sikorski to remain in the government, with the result that in Skrzyński's coalition cabinet Gen. L. Żeligowski, Piłsudski's trusted friend, took over the War Ministry. Żeligowski made a number of changes of personnel and in the location of army units, which later made possible Piłsudski's *military coup*.

News about the appointment of Witos as Prime Minister on 10 May, 1926 was understood in left-wing circles and among the workers as paving the way for a right-wing dictatorship. Piłsudski gave a press interview derogatory to the new government and demonstrations were begun on the streets of Warsaw by Piłsudski's supporters. On 12 May Piłsudski at the head of army units loyal to him moved from Sulejówek to Warsaw to induce Witos to resign and convince President Wojciechowski of the necessity of changing the government. At the news of Piłsudski's approach Witos actually did announce his resignation, but Wojciechowski, who previously had not been enthusiastic about appointing Witos as Prime Minister, did not wish to succumb to military pressure and prevented him from resigning. Wojciechowski himself went to the Poniatowski Bridge joining Warsaw with its right bank suburb Praga, which had already been taken over by Piłsudski's detachments. A famous encounter took place there, during which Piłsudski demanded the dismissal of Witos from Wojciechowski, while the President required Piłsudski to yield to the legal government. After this conversation Wojciechowski issued an order to the army units loyal to the government to open fire on the rebellious troops. The President's attitude took Piłsudski by surprise. His officers understood that there could be no turning back and continued the attack on their own, by evening capturing the northern districts of Warsaw. The government withdrew to the Belvedere Palace, the President's residence, and there waited for reinforcements from the provinces. In fact, the military situation was resolved by the attitude of the railway men who supported Piłsudski by hampering the movement of the government units and facilitating the transport of Piłsudski's troops. During the fierce battles of 13–14 May, talks were conducted through intermediaries which were designed to find a peaceful solution to the conflict. When on the afternoon of 14 May the situation began to favour Piłsudski, the President and the government left the Belvedere for the Wilanów Palace on the outskirts of the city. There, at a cabinet meeting, in spite of the opposition of the generals, it was decided to call off the struggle. The government submitted its resignation and the President decided to gave up his office. According to the Constitution the President's successor was the Marshal of the Seym, a "Piast" Party representative, Rataj, who on 15 May in understanding with Piłsudski, appointed as Premier K. Bartel, professor of the Lwów Technical University and a close associate of Piłsudski. In the cabinet Piłsudski became Minister of War, a post he retained until his death in 1935. A. Zaleski, who during the First

World War had been the unofficial representative of the NKN in England, took over the Foreign Affairs. On 16 May the arrest occurred of several generals who had been on the side of the fallen government. It was later sought to accuse some of them of offences of a criminal nature to justify the slogan of "moral rehabilitation" ("sanacja"). For this reason the government of the Piłsudski régime was commonly called "Sanacja".

THE SOCIAL ASPECT OF PIŁSUDSKI'S DICTATORSHIP

Immediately after his victory, Piłsudski stated in press interviews that the *coup* would not have revolutionary consequences either in the political or social sense. This meant that there would be no changes in the social structure and, more important, that the *coup*, contrary to the convictions of those left-wing circles which supported it, would not bring any changes to the benefit of the working classes. Big business realized this immediately and that is why it was not inclined to regard the *coup* with hostility. It was understood that power over the army had definitely passed into the hands of Piłsudski and his followers and that foreign policy would assume an increasingly marked anti-Soviet character.

On 31 May the National Assembly elected Piłsudski President by a large majority. Only the Right Wing voted for its own candidate. Much to everyone's amazement Piłsudski did not accept the post. It is true that he regarded the Assembly's vote as a legalization of his *coup d'état*, but he considered that the Constitution gave too few prerogatives to a President for him to assume this function. Thus, on the next day, upon Piłsudski's proposal, Ignacy Mościcki, professor of the Lwów Technical University and a world famous chemist, in 1912 a professor of the Fribourg Polytechnic in Switzerland, was elected President. Not only the Right Wing, but also the PPS nominated their candidates against him. It was only in further voting that Mościcki gained an absolute majority. Bartel again became Premier and the composition of the new government was practically unchanged. As early as 16 June the government presented to the Seym a proposal for changing the Constitution which would give the President the right to dissolve the legislative bodies and the right to issue decrees with the force of law during the recess period, subject, however, to parliamentary approval at the next session of the Seym. These constitutional changes were passed on 2 August by a large majority of votes, but on this occasion the PPS was in opposition. The left-wing parties expected an immediate dissolution of the Seym which was accused of responsibility for the catastrophic state of affairs, above all, in the field of finance, but it was more convenient for Piłsudski to keep this compromised Seym than to call new elections, which would have more than likely strengthened the Left Wing. Piłsudski wanted to rule above the parties, seeing in his own person and in a strong administration, a guarantee of government independent of sectional interests. In reality this conception suited the interests of the upper ruling classes. As a result, the opposition to Piłsudski, which at first was conducted by the Right Wing, now took on a left-wing character and in the Seym was conducted by the PPS.

THE STRUGGLE BETWEEN THE GOVERNMENT AND THE SEYM

Disputes between the Seym and the government had begun already by the end of 1926. The government formally followed a legal path, but it actually attacked and discredited not only the Seym but the Constitution itself. In connexion with one such incident, Piłsudski took over the office of Premier himself. In order to get the large landowners to withdraw their support from the Right Wing he began to woo the conservatives, giving them two cabinet posts, and in the autumn of 1926 he paid a visit to Nieśwież, the residence of Prince Radziwiłł. Anxious to find a broader political backing in the country, Piłsudski assigned to his closest collaborator, W. Sławek, a former member of the PPS fighting squads and then an intelligence officer in the General Staff, the task of creating an organization called the Non-Party Bloc for Cooperation with the Government, under the slogan "moral rehabilitation". An attempt was made to secure wider support for the new régime, above all, among the intelligentsia. Into the ranks of the Non-Party Bloc soon came numerous careerists and opportunist politicians from various sides who understood that the old parties had lost their influence and would not secure the appointment of their followers to important posts. In the autumn of 1927 Sławek met in Dzików at Count Tarnowski's house a group of conservatives whom he wished to draw into cooperation with the government. Shortly afterwards two aristocrats were appointed as voivodes. These efforts, however, were of little avail. It turned out that the Polish aristocracy lacked suitably qualified persons to take advantage of the opportunity offered them. Only Prince J. Radziwiłł played a prominent political role after May 1926. No other aristocrat was any longer equal to this. Few diplomatic posts, the traditional realm of nobility, were held by representatives of the aristocracy.

After taking over the government Piłsudski gained control of the army where he appointed to key positions only officers loyal to himself. Changes in the civil administration were less radical, but there too, at first gradually, but afterwards more rapidly, the rule was followed that key positions could be held only by the "Marshal's men". As the opposition increased, the criminal courts, formally independent, were brought under control and the press was more and more severely restricted. All this occurred gradually and the general public did not become aware at the beginning that the country was

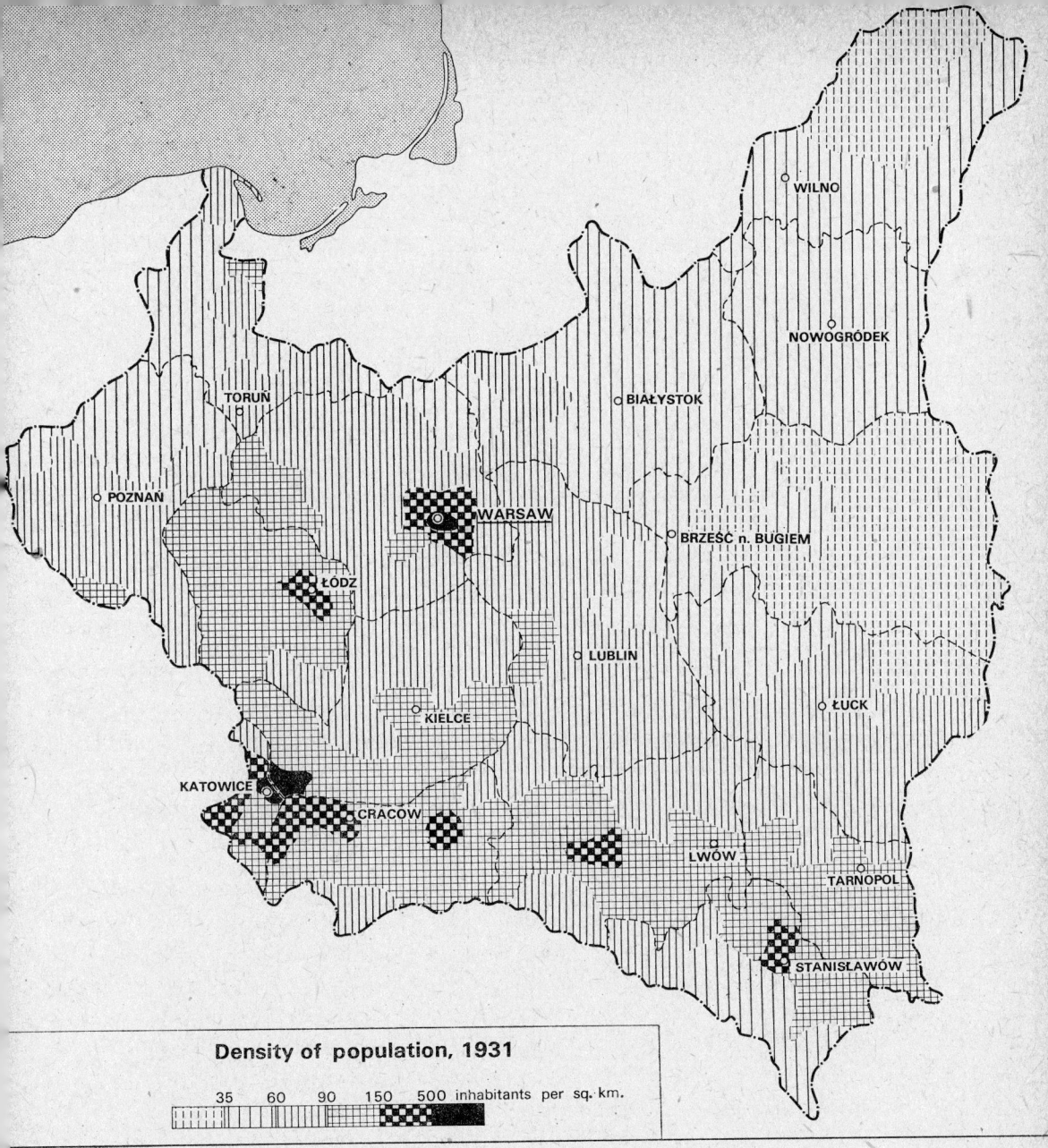

Density of population, 1931

35 60 90 150 500 inhabitants per sq. km.

under a military dictatorship. The growing role of the political police was likewise not realized at first. The persons who during Piłsudski's time took over the most important positions in the State, came primarily from the ranks of officers in the Legions or the Polish Military Organization, who during 1919–1920 had served in the 2nd Bureau of the General Staff, responsible for intelligence and counter-intelligence. Now they applied the same methods to ruling the State. Personnel departments in civil service as well as in state enterprises were controlled by officials connected with military intelligence, who in this way held in their hands the threads of the entire machinery of State. The only savage reprisal against enemies of the *coup d'état* was the disappearance of General Zagórski. He was Piłsudski's personal opponent from the days of the war as Chief of Staff to the Legions and later Chief of the Air Force. He was arrested after the May *coup* and undoubtedly murdered by Piłsudski's followers. There were moreover incidents of assault on well-known opposition politicians and journalists by "persons unknown".

GDYNIA AND MOŚCICE

The first years of Piłsudski's government coincided with economic prosperity. The British coal strike in 1926 opened possibilities of export for Polish coal. This immediately balanced the losses which coal exports had suffered after the lapse of the Upper Silesian Convention and as a result of the tariff war with Germany. Foreign currency came into Poland in sufficient quantities to stabilize the zloty and Polish coal won new foreign markets, so that Britain was forced after the end of the strike to conclude an agreement with Poland about the limitation of markets. Public opinion, influenced by the government press, might have assumed that a "strong-arm" government, independent of the Seym, had led to the currency stabilization. The years 1926–1929, moreover, were prosperous on the whole in the capitalist world which helped to strengthen the régime in Poland and make pro-government propaganda easier.

Benefiting from a budget surplus and receiving an American loan in the autumn of 1927 for the purpose of increasing the established capital of the Bank of Poland and stabilizing the currency, the government undertook investment. In the first place, at the instance of the Minister of Trade and Industry, E. Kwiatkowski, who formerly worked with Professor Mościcki in administering a fertilizer plant in Chorzów, the building of a port was begun in Gdynia, a small fishing village on the coast north of Gdańsk. In this way Poland sought to free herself from dependence on the Free City of Gdańsk, which to the detriment of its own interests supported the German anti-Polish policy. Within a few years, as a result of the devoted efforts of the whole nation not only was a modern port built, but also a modern city. Another major investment was the construction, on the initiative of President Mościcki, of a factory of nitrogeneous fertilizers near Tarnów, which was to supply the farmers and, in case of war, could become a base for the armament industry. Public opinion was proud of these achievements, without realizing that in the existing situation in the world and Europe all these efforts could not create for Poland an economic potential capable of satisfying the re-

Gdynia. Harbour

quirements of a modern society or sustaining the great historical traditions which the people did not wish to forget. It must be taken into consideration that only in about 1929, the last year of prosperity, did the Polish economy manage to achieve the level of 1914. War damage was repaired only after ten years. It must be remembered also that the destruction was not only the result of war activities alone but was primarily brought about by the occupying Powers with the deliberate aim of weakening the Polish nation. On the other hand, post-war reconstruction was accomplished by the national effort alone, without decisive help from outside and without the payment of adequate reparations by the former enemy countries.

In general it may be said, that in the first decade of independence the necessary conditions for the overall requirements of the country's economy were created. Economic and financial legislation was brought into uniformity and a unified administrative machinery was created. The transport network was expanded, joining up the districts which were formerly kept divided by the very fact of partition. A uniform system of social insurance and labour laws was introduced at a relatively high level by comparison with other capitalist countries.

THE CENTRE-LEFT AND THE BRZEŚĆ AFFAIR

During the period of prosperity the government was biding its time with regard to the opposition. The administration remained in the hands of Piłsudski's group and the majority in the Seym, ever more discredited, did not dare to begin a battle with the government.

New elections took place only in 1928. By this time the government had to its credit the stabilization of the economic situation, controlled a well-organized propaganda machine and had at its command a subservient civil service, but even though authorities officially engaged in the elections in support of their own candidates and committed many abuses, the Non-Party Bloc list obtained less than 30 per cent of the seats. The Left Wing was victorious. It was astonishing that the communists, even though the KPP was illegal, obtained around a million votes and won seven seats in the Seym. The Centre and Right Wing experienced a disaster. It was impossible however to form a majority in the Seym made up of the Non-Party Bloc, the PPS and the peasants. The government was decidedly opposed to the parliamentary system. In this situation the legal opposition parties, considering the demand for parliamentary government futile and pointless, conducted in 1928–1930 a rather hesitant and cautious struggle against the stranglehold of an ever more anti-democratic dictatorship. These years were characterized by a reluctance on both sides to seek a trial of strength. Piłsudski wished, for as long as possible, to maintain the appearance of legality. The opposition knew its own weakness, though undoubtedly it overestimated it. The Seym was able to pass budgets owing to the fact that the opposition often refrained from voting. Besides, two points of view existed in ruling circles. One was represented by the former Prime Minister Bartel who did not want an open conflict with the Left and was anxious to retain a maximum of formal liberalism within the framework of Piłsudski's régime. The second view was represented by the "colonels group" with W. Sławek as its leader, who wished as soon as possible to get rid of all restraints of legality and to move perceptibly towards an open dictatorship.

The first major parliamentary clash was the indictment of the Minister of Finance, Czechowicz, before the State Tribunal for floating large loans for investment without the approval of the Seym. This involved the Seym's right of scrutinizing the budget, which was a fundamental constitutional right. Piłsudski took the responsibility upon himself before the State Tribunal for Czechowicz's infringement of the budget. The Tribunal did not pass a verdict, but remitted the case to the Seym to assess the case on its merits. Piłsudski exacerbated the situation with press interviews, in which he abused the Seym and its representatives in most caustic terms. At the opening of the autumn session in 1929 a large group of armed officers appeared in the hall of the Seym, for which reason Daszyński as Marshal of the Seym refused to open the debate. The session was postponed for a month. After the reopening of the Seym a vote of no confidence was passed against the government at the head of which stood one of the "colonels' group", Major K. Świtalski. The President again appointed Bartel Prime Minister, a man likely to follow a milder course, hoping in this way to gain the Seym's support for the budget. After the passing of the budget Bartel provoked the Seym into passing a vote of no confidence in one of the ministers. This resulted in the resignation of the cabinet and a long government crisis which was a comedy from the point of view of Piłsudski and allowed him to wait until the constitutional end of the debates on the budget.

Sławek then became Prime Minister. In answer to this the left-wing parties and the Centre, who came closer together in opposition to the government, organized a Centre-Left ("Centrolew" in Polish) Congress in Cracow where decidedly hostile resolutions were passed. On this occasion the Premiership was taken over by Piłsudski and the Seym was dissolved. On 10 September, 1930, Witos, Lieberman and several other opposition politicians were arrested. They were imprisoned contrary to the law in a military prison in the fortress at Brześć, where they were maltreated. Shortly after the elections they were released on bail. A trial was then held of the "Centrolew" politicians and they were sentenced to several years imprisonment. Some of them served their term while some, including Witos and Lieberman, went abroad. The demand for an amnesty became one of the main slogans of the opposition, especially the peasant party members.

The 1930 elections, called the "Brześć elections", were speeded up and took place under strong administrative pressure which on this occasion gave rise to many more abuses than occurred two years before. The campaign, conducted under the slogan of amendments to the Constitution, was to be, like the Brześć incident, a trial of strength to show everyone that the government was strong, while the opposition could only have recourse to weak demonstrations, because the masses, in whose name it spoke, did not give it real support. In this way the government waged battle with its own people as well as with the strongest national minority group, the Ukrainians in the south-eastern voivodships. The communist movement there combined the social struggle with a fight for national independence. At the same time Ukrainian nationalists engaged in vigorous activity. In 1929 Konovalets set up abroad a new terroristic organization, the OUN (Ukrainian Nationalist Organization) with a definite fascist or rather national-socialist character. It worked in understanding with Hitler and renewed armed subversive and terrorist action. This action assumed large proportions in 1930 and the "Sanacja" government began brutal repressions. In the autumn the famous "pacification" began in Eastern Little Poland. The rural population was terrorized by the army by billeting and investigations. It is true that bloodshed was avoided, but many acts of violence took place. This considerably discredited the Polish State abroad, especially in the Anglo-Saxon countries, even though the League of Nations in its answer to the protest brought by the Ukrainians, stated that they had provoked these repressions on the part of the Polish government by their own activities. The "pacification" for the moment achieved its purpose of stifling the subversive activity of the Ukrainians, but in reality it was a severe blow to the Polish State both at home and abroad. It was denounced in Poland by the communists and socialists. Other parties, especially the right-wing, sided with the government, alluding to the anti-Polish character of the Ukrainian nationalists' actions, which were in fact directed from Berlin and served German purposes. They sought to present the Ukrainian's national struggle as only a terrorist campaign.

The 1930 elections brought victory for the Non-Party Bloc in the sense, that it obtained an absolute majority, even though it did not have two-thirds majority needed to amend the Constitution. Nevertheless, the internal situation underwent a fundamental change, because the government now no longer needed take into consideration the parliamentary opposition and had obtained freedom of action. Not only electoral manipulation brought the government victory. Quite a broad section of the electorate, discouraged by the parliamentary struggle, saw no possibility of changing the system by parliamentary elections. In the eastern regions, moreover, making use of their low level of education and high percentage of illiteracy, the administration could influence the elections much more easily, so that in the final analysis the largest number of pro-government representatives came from areas inhabited by Byelorussians and Ukrainians in Polesie and Volhynia.

THE GREAT ECONOMIC CRISIS OF 1929–1931

At the time when this new political system was being established, the country experienced the disaster of the world-wide economic crisis. Poland, as a primarily agricultural country, was especially hard hit, because prices of farm produce dropped disproportionately to prices of industrial goods. In addition, the government, which held in its hands all the instruments for influencing the economy, kept rigidly to one principle, the maintenance of the rate of exchange, by the sole means of deflation. This rigid currency policy only intensified the ruinous effects of the depression. Civil service salaries were cut and State investment reduced to a minimum in the name of deflation. The final result was that Poland emerged from the crisis with a stabilized currency, but with a ruined economy, a vastly lowered standard of living for the mass of the people, and large permanent body of unemployed, irreducible even in prosperity, which particularly affected the countryside. Only after the world crisis had passed, in the last years before the outbreak of war in 1939 was investment begun again by the State and thoughts turned to changing the agricultural system. But it was already too late not only to offset the losses suffered by the whole national economy during the crisis, but also to direct further development onto the proper paths.

The lowest point of the crisis in Poland was in 1932, when the index of general production fell to 54 per cent of the 1929 level. It began to rise slowly but up to 1939 it never reached the level pertaining before the crisis.

Chapter XXV
TOWARDS TOTAL DICTATORSHIP (1931–1939)

THE FOREIGN POLICY OF PIŁSUDSKI

The year 1930 was also a turning point in Polish foreign policy. This was brought about by the appointment of Colonel Józef Beck as Deputy Minister of Foreign Affairs. From 1926 he had been Piłsudski's *Chef de Cabinet* when the latter was Minister of War. He became Deputy Prime Minister in the Piłsudski's government of 1930 and was responsible, among other things, for the Brześć affair. When he went to the Foreign Ministry, which he took over as its head in 1932, he became Piłsudski's trusted agent in this department, which was by now the only sphere of the Marshal's interest, apart from military affairs. Piłsudski had ceased to concern himself with domestic and economic issues. Neither was he interested in the amendments to the Constitution, handing this matter over to Sławek. In these years Poland had to conduct a more elastic foreign policy because Germany's revisionist tendencies were growing stronger every year. The Western Powers were inclined to direct German expansion to the East and had no intention of defending Poland's territorial integrity.

In 1932 the Soviet Union signed pacts with Finland, Latvia and Estonia. Eventually a three year Polish-Soviet non-agression pact was concluded on 25 July, 1932. Poland had made the signature of such an agreement dependent on the conclusion by the Soviet Union of similar pacts with Finland, Latvia and Estonia. There followed shortly afterwards an exchange of visits by politicians and journalists which led to a distinct improvement of Polish-Soviet relations.

Taking advantage of this relaxation, Polish diplomacy was determined to demonstrate Polish rights in Gdańsk, where the Senate of the Free City was constantly conducting a policy hostile to Poland, supported not only by Berlin but also by British diplomacy. Gdańsk complained, amongst other things, that Poland was aiming at the ruin of the Free City by the building of Gdynia. This allegation was obviously groundless. On the contrary, Gdańsk benefited tremendously from the fact that it was the main harbour of the Polish customs area. Its turnover had increased many times after the war, from 187,000 tons in 1913 to 8,290,000 tons in 1930.

An occasion for such a demonstration of Polish rights was provided by the sending of the Polish destroyer "Wicher" to Gdańsk in July, 1932 during the visit of a British squadron. But it was only Hitler's coming to power which led to a crisis that was to initiate a new phase of diplomatic relations between Warsaw and Berlin.

On 16 February, 1933 the Senate of the Free City unilaterally denounced the agreement with Poland regarding the administration of the port. Subsequently, on 6 March, a battalion of Polish infantry was disembarked on the Westerplatte in the harbour area where Poland had an ammunition depot, in order to strengthen the Polish garrison there. The chanceries of the Western Powers reacted in an unfriendly manner, while Berlin behaved with reserve, being aware of the military weakness of the Reich at the time. Poland agreed to a compromise solution of the dispute, which had been brought before the League of Nations. The battalion was withdrawn and the port police were restored. Nevertheless, there was a conviction in Berlin that the aim of the Polish government was to provoke a preventive war. In reality the situation was different. Piłsudski and Beck felt themselves threatened by the suggested plan of a pact of the four great Powers, Great Britain, France, Germany and Italy, which would override the views of smaller States. This was a plan Mussolini put forward in March 1933, and Poland would undoubtedly have had to pay the price for such an agreement. The "Four Powers' Pact", however, did not come to fruition, in part because of Poland's opposition. Beck countered it with an attempt to reach an agreement with Germany by himself. The Polish offer at this juncture was advantageous to Hitler, who felt himself isolated internationally and for this reason agreed to a temporary relaxation of German policy with regard to Poland. The first sign of this new move was a press communiqué issued after the conversation of the Polish Ambassador, Lipski, with the Chancellor on 2 May. Shortly afterwards, an improvement of Polish-Gdańsk relations followed; the Nazi Senate of the Free City undertook, on orders from Berlin, direct negotiations with Warsaw without recourse to the normal intermediary of the League of Nations.

Negotiations between Warsaw and Berlin had been in progress since the autumn of 1933. At that time Germany had left the League of Nations. This was held to justify the Polish government in its attempt to seek an arrangement with Germany, which up to now depended in many respects upon the League. A non-aggression pact for ten years was signed on 26 January, 1934. It was advantageous for Hitler, because it safeguarded him from the danger of Poland launching a preventive war, which was still feared in Berlin. Polish government circles maintained that for Poland it was an assurance that Germany would abandon her revisionist propaganda for some time and, in addition, that other Powers would not be able to settle their differences with Germany at the expense of Poland's western frontier. On the other hand, Polish and European public opinion, as well as European diplomatic circles, took a decidedly unfavourable view of the pact with Hitler, because they saw in it a loosening of the Franco-Polish alliance and Poland's adoption of a policy of cooperation with Hitler against the Soviet Union, thus, in effect strengthening fascism. It was also assumed that the pact contained unpublished secret clauses, which actually did not exist. Polish diplomacy wanted, however, to continue the policy of holding the balance between Berlin and Moscow. Therefore when Georing visited Poland and made allusions to a joint march against Russia Piłsudski gave a negative reply. Immediately after the conclusion of the pact with Germany Beck executed a tactical manoeuvre. He went on a visit to Moscow giving an assurance to the Soviet Union that Poland had no thought of hostile action against the Soviet Union in collaboration with Germany. This visit proved to be effective; in May 1934 the non-aggression pact with the U.S.S.R. was extended for a further ten years and thus it was to last longer than the similar pact with Germany.

Consequently Poland did not oppose the entry of the Soviet Union into the League of Nations but, not wishing to risk the possibility that the U.S.S.R. would utilize the minorities treaty in the League, she declared on 13 September, 1934, that she would not cooperate in matters arising out of this treaty with international organizations, as long as the treaty was not binding on all interested countries. This unilateral denunciation of treaty obligations was, of course, received very unfavourably by European public opinion, because it placed Poland among the States violating international agreements.

Polish diplomacy was rendered still more unpopular by its position with regard to the Eastern Pact conceived by Louis Barthou, the French Foreign Minister. This pact was to include the Soviet Union and to guarantee the *status quo* in eastern Europe. It was known, of course, that Germany would not want to join this pact and thereby it would be aimed precisely against her. Polish diplomacy was the first to oppose the pact, objecting openly to the participation of Czechoslovakia. This was interpreted as a desire to direct German revisionism against the Czechs, with whom Poland's relations now again began to deteriorate. In addition, Beck's opposition to the Eastern Pact was derived from the hostility which Piłsudski felt towards the Soviet Union and from his unwillingness to have closer contact with Poland's eastern neighbour. This led to a worsening of Polish-Soviet relations which had recently shown a definite improvement.

THE DEATH OF PIŁSUDSKI. THE CONFLICT IN THE RULING PARTY

A change in the Constitution was carried out while Piłsudski was still alive. The Non-Party Bloc, taking advantage of the momentary absence of the

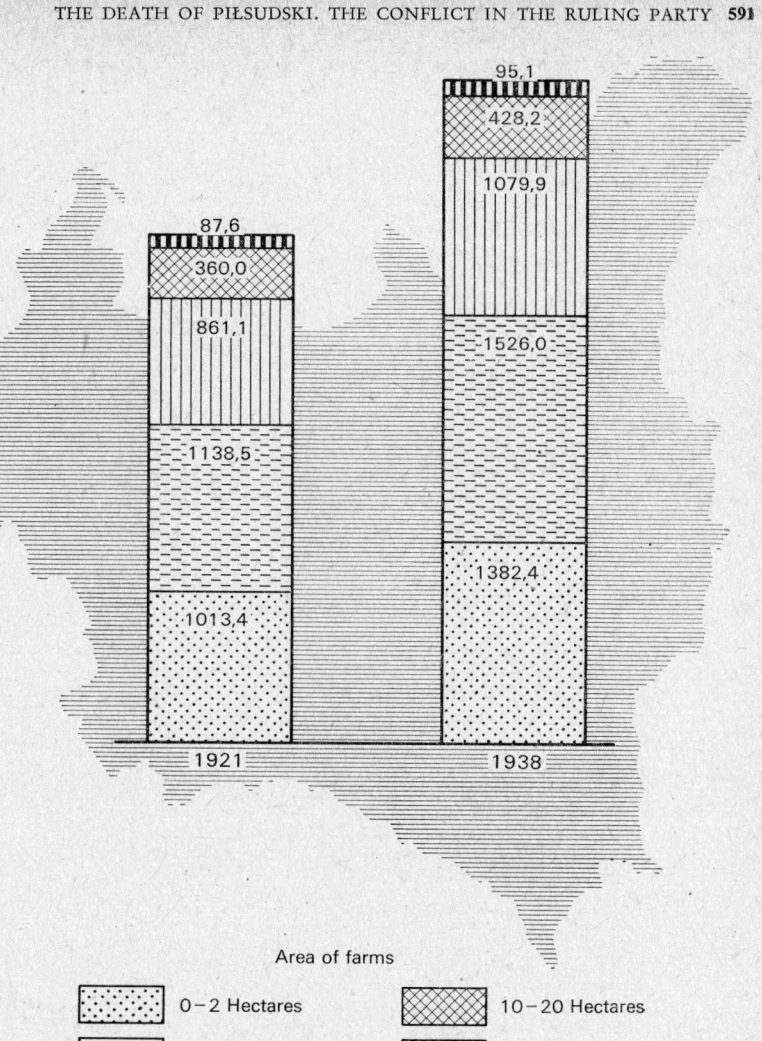

Area of farms

- 0–2 Hectares
- 2–5 „
- 5–10 „
- 10–20 Hectares
- 20–50

V. Structure of small holdings in Poland
(Number of farms in thousands)

opposition deputies in the Seym, who did not wish to cooperate in the revision of the Constitution, passed a bill for a reform of the Constitution on 26 January, 1934. The rules of procedure were broken, it is true, but because the Non-Party Bloc had the necessary majority in the Senate the new Constitution was ultimately enacted and proclaimed in April, 1935. It invested the President with extensive powers by limiting the role of Parliament and, what is most important, made possible the introduction of a franchise which contradicted every principle of a democratic State. Those who drafted the Constitution thought of Piłsudski as the one who would take over the

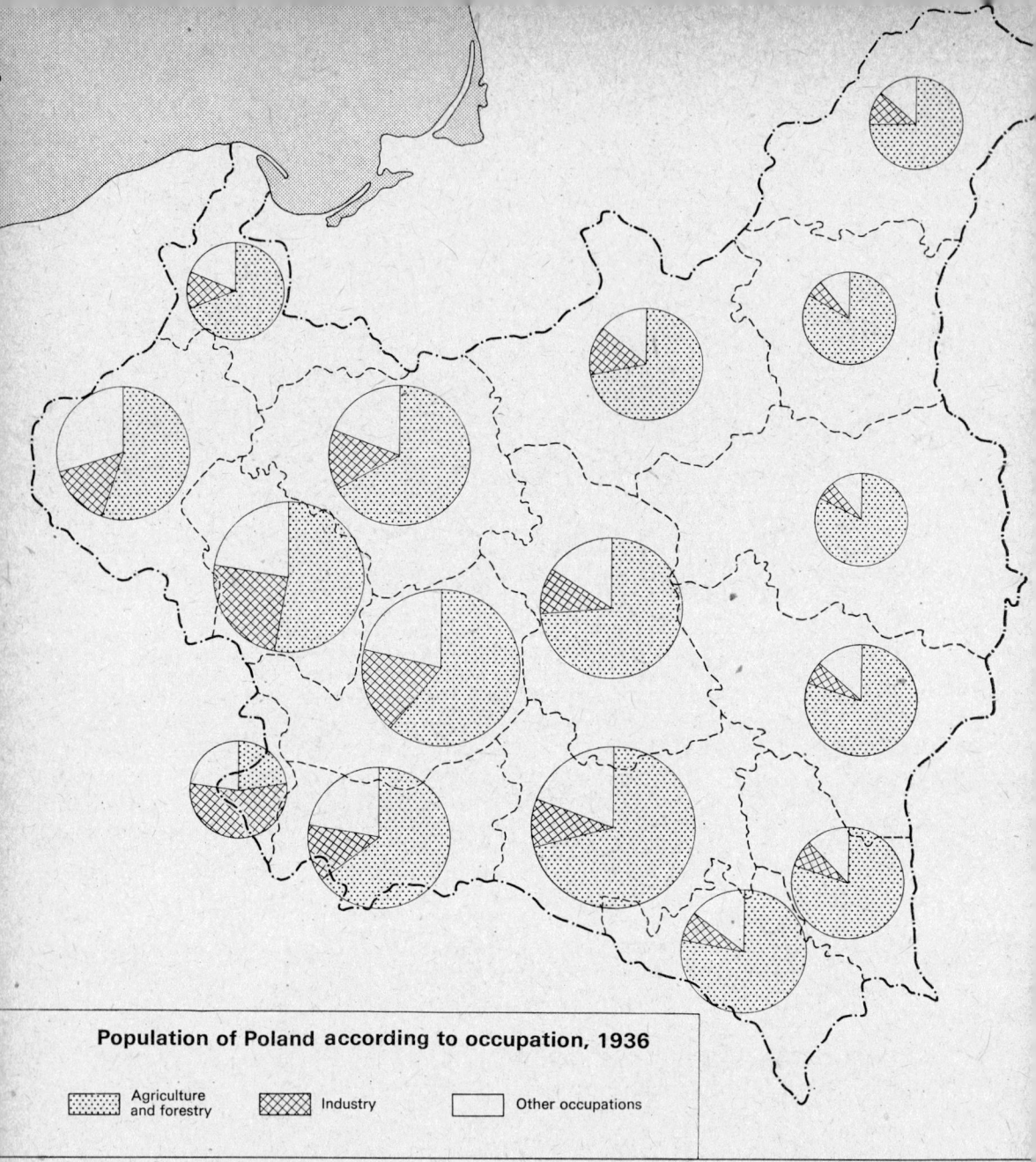

Population of Poland according to occupation, 1936

Agriculture and forestry — Industry — Other occupations

President's power, but Piłsudski was already mortally ill at the moment when the Constitution was approved.

From 1930 when the Seym had been reduced to subservience the growth of the dictatorship manifested itself in the ever greater use of coercive methods of government. Their organizer, one of the ablest members of the "colonels' group", B. Pieracki, was killed in 1934 by an Ukrainian nationalist in circumstances which are still far from clear. Pieracki's death was used as a pretext for establishing an "isolation camp" in Bereza Kartuska in the Polesie region. This camp, modelled on the Nazi concentration camps, was a sign of the progressive growth of fascism. Persons sent there were mostly communists and members of the Ukrainian and Byelorussian opposition.

It was not only the efficiency of the police machinery which helped to maintain the Piłsudski régime. An attempt was made to popularize Piłsudski by encouraging the mystique surrounding his person through all the media of mass communication, the government press, radio and schools. Many eminent writers agreed to serve the régime which, desirous also of gaining popularity among literary circles, set up the Polish Academy of Literature. It was to be in its way a counterpoise to the Polish Academy of Sciences and Letters in Cracow, still controlled by liberally minded professors hostile to the régime. The people were told about the "ideas of Marshal Piłsudski", but these were not elaborated in detail. A cult of the State was encouraged in distinction to the National Democratic cult of the nation. Actually, the cult of Piłsudski signified the dominance of the State machinery. This served the interests of the propertied classes, and, to an even greater degree, that of the large landowners rather than of big business.

The State tried in some sectors of the economy to oppose the malpractices of foreign capital, a struggle more for show than effect. This was the case in the conflict over the Żyrardów Textile Mill and the Warsaw Electric Power Plant, in which French capital behaved in a manner too obviously contrary to the interests of the country. In fact, however, the position of international capital became still stronger in Poland. The economic crisis was an opportunity for foreign capital to proceed to further concentration and to encourage the growth of monopolies. While German capital in Poland avoided proclaiming itself as such, it often penetrated under the guise of American companies, and no one dared to offer resistance.

Piłsudski died on 12 May, 1935 and was buried beside the Polish kings in the Wawel Cathedral in Cracow. The ruling group now faced the difficult task of carrying on the dictatorship without the authority of Piłsudski among those social classes who either actively supported the dictatorship, though these were very few indeed, or, what is most important, who supported it passively. Dissension within the ruling party began at once. A section, harking back to earlier left-wing traditions, desired liberalization. This group largely included former members of the Polish Military Organization and among them the most prominent part was played by M. Zyndram-Kościałkowski; another section, grouped around Sławek, aimed, on the contrary, at a stronger dictatorship. One of the immediate issues to settle was the succession to Piłsudski in the army. General Rydz-Śmigły became the Inspector General of the Armed Forces and thus was the presumptive Commander-in-Chief. President Mościcki thought that in his relations with Rydz-Śmigły, whom he appointed, it would be easy to maintain his own position. Mościcki was soon able to render Sławek politically harmless and in the

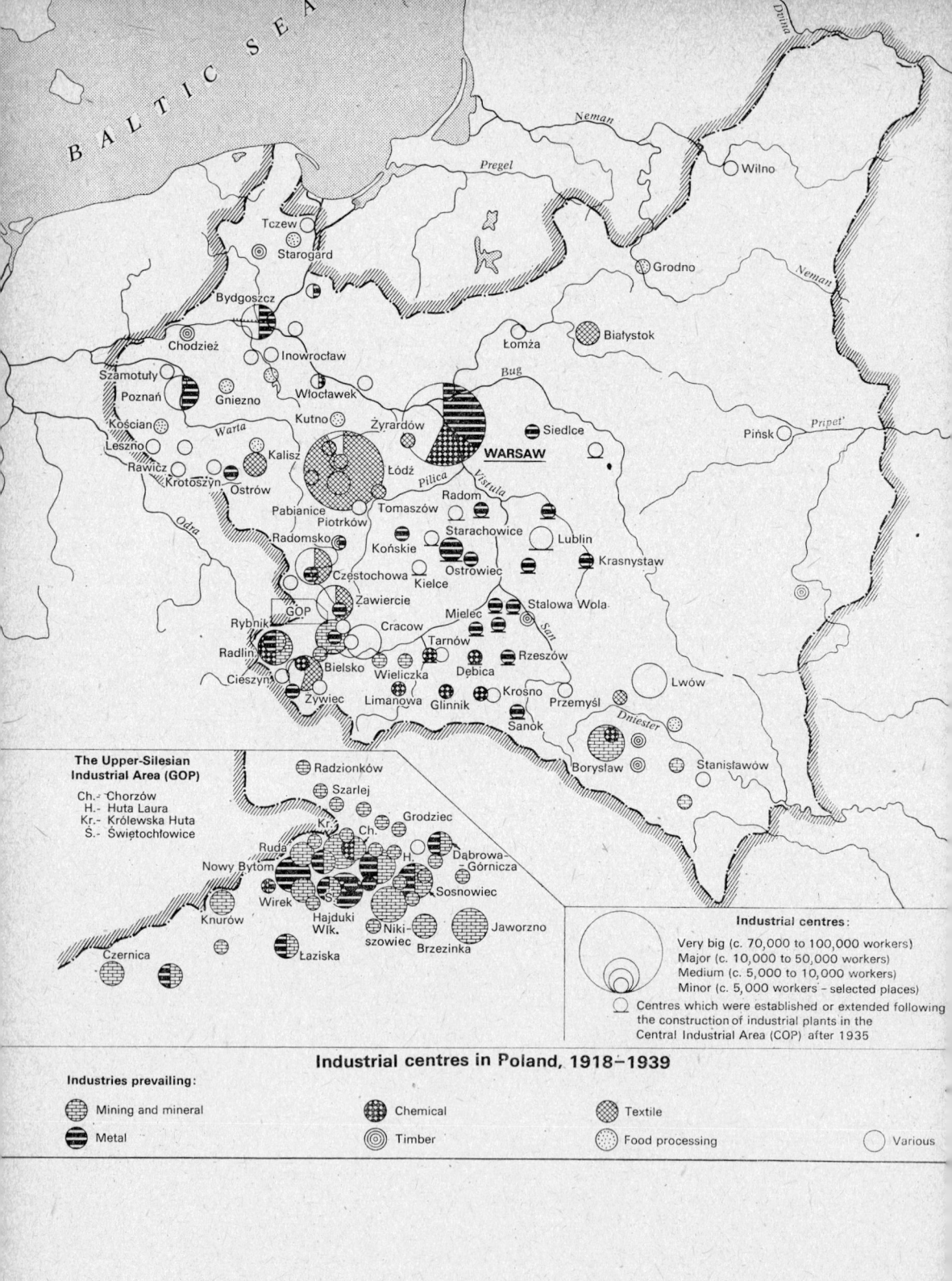

autumn of 1935 Kościałkowski was made Premier. The decisive role in this cabinet was played by the Vice-Premier, Kwiatkowski, who now became in effect the director of the government's economic policy. An end was at last put to rigid principles of deflation; it was easier to do so now, because the world crisis was over. On Kwiatkowski's initiative the construction of the Central Industrial Area in the triangle of Tarnów–Skarżysko–Przemyśl was begun. A base for the armament industry was to be laid here at a distance from the exposed frontiers.

The Kościałkowski government met with underhand opposition within the ruling group itself. An agreement between Rydz-Śmigły and Mościcki was reached. In this fashion the head of the army was drawn into political intrigues and brought to the front as the apparent leader of the nation.

THE GROWTH OF OPPOSITION

In the early period after Piłsudski's death the legal opposition parties of the Left were, in effect, impotent. They were even ready to reach a compromise with the Kościałkowski government, building their hopes for an agreement of this type on the person of Rydz-Śmigły.

The National Party, the former National Democrats, had broken up. Some of its members, in view of the hopelessness of opposition, went over to the government side, while its younger members in imitation of fascism which was gaining ground in Europe, established the National Radical Camp with a pronounced nationalist character. Breaking with the remaining liberal traditions of the former National Democrats they adopted a clearly fascist tone. From the National Radical Camp there emerged the "Falanga" group which openly imitated the Nazis. The Right Wing, both the National Party and the National Radical Camp, now primarily gave voice to anti-Semitic slogans.

Changes in the peasant movement occurred still earlier. The various groups united into one Peasant Party under Rataj. Although the Peasant Party placed the name of Witos, who was in emigration, on its banners, the party in effect took on a much more radical appearance. This was due to the activity of its younger members, organized in the Union of Rural Youth "Wici" (The Messengers).

The authority of the PPS declined at this juncture, when death had removed its most popular leaders like Daszyński, Perl and Diamand. At the same time revolutionary tendencies among the working class increased, thus strengthening the position of the communists.

Under the influence of the threatening danger of Nazism the KPP issued the slogan of a United Front which met with considerable response in the left-wing circles among the socialists. The Fourth Plenary Session of the KPP in 1936 advocated a rapprochement with the PPS for the defence of Poland's independence threatened by the Third Reich.

The United Front policy had a considerable influence on the strike movement which grew in these years, on account of the economic oppression of the working class and the system of police government which was becoming more and more discredited. The years 1936 and 1937 witnessed the largest strikes during the entire inter-war period. In 1936 strikes in industry embraced 22,000 plants and involved 4 million working days. These strikes were often victorious and in many of them, though they were begun for economic reasons, political demands were later voiced.

In the period of the United Front the working-class movement was weakened, however, by the fear of right-wing leaders of the PPS of starting a bitter domestic struggle when the external dangers threatened the State. On the other hand, the KPP was dissolved in 1938 by the Comintern as a result of unproved charges.

All these political changes resulted from a fundamental transformation in political thinking. The coming of the great economic crisis immediately after a period of prosperity first gave rise to a feeling of political depression and general apathy. This was intensified by unemployment which could not be shown in figures, because only these were registered, who drew unemployment allowances. These being available only for a short time caused the unemployed on their expiry, if possible, to return to the villages where they still had families. There they gave vent to revolutionary feeling. As a result the peasant masses, above all, became more radical in the years immediately following the climax of the crisis. One should remember that it affected agriculture to a very considerable degree. The big landowners, more sensitive to international market conditions, struggled to maintain the profits of their estates by lowering the wages of their agricultural workers. The resulting strikes were brutally suppressed by the police. Thus, the radicalization of the masses in these years progressed from the countryside to the city and then returned once more, still stronger, to the countryside.

In the spring of 1936 there occurred in Cracow, Lwów and Częstochowa violent working class demonstrations of an almost revolutionary character. There were numerous killed and wounded. The movement soon passed on to the villages. In the summer, southern Poland as well as the Lublin area witnessed a new kind of strike. The peasants stopped all food deliveries to the towns. These strikes ended in disturbance and bloodshed. In 1937 the peasant strike was repeated in southern Poland with still greater effect. It was a clear political demonstration and a challenge to the dictatorship.

THE NATIONAL UNITY CAMP

Because the opposition parties had not participated in the 1935 elections, the Seym and Senate were composed entirely of supporters of the ruling party with the addition of a small fraction of moderate Ukrainian nationalists.

Ruling circles were bound to feel isolated from the people. They therefore sought a new source of authority and a new basis for support in the country. Thus General Rydz-Śmigły was advanced as the leading figure. On his initiative General Sławoj-Składkowski was appointed Prime Minister in May, 1936. In this cabinet Kwiatkowski remained Deputy Premier for Economic Affairs, just as Beck remained in charge of foreign affairs and J. Poniatowski retained the Ministry of Agriculture, seeking some solution of the hopeless situation in the countryside where the number of "redundant persons" was estimated at around five million. The new cabinet was the result of a compromise between Mościcki and Rydz-Śmigły. Shortly afterwards the Premier sent a famous instruction to all officials on 15 July, 1936, in which he stated that, after the President, Śmigły was the second person in the State, to whom everyone, including the Prime Minister, should "pay due honour and obedience". This was not in accord with the Constitution but it represented the facts of the situation, because the régime, being a military dictatorship, needed a real dictator.

In the autumn of 1936 the President appointed Śmigły a Marshal and thus he was to be the successor of Piłsudski, but if Piłsudski, especially in the last years of his life, concerned himself exclusively with the army and foreign affairs, the new Marshal was not to obtain any great influence on foreign affairs, because their management lay solely in Beck's hands.

Beck's policy was unpopular in the country, because he was regarded as an ally of Nazi Germany. Śmigły attempted to play on these sentiments by demonstrating sympathy for France. The visit he paid to Paris in 1936 was interpreted by Polish opinion as a return to the French alliance and it was thought that Śmigły would become a counterweight to the excessive inclination of Polish diplomacy towards the Fascist powers. Although, in effect, the personal relations between these two were never close, Beck did not relinquish the conduct of foreign policy until the very end.

The hopes placed by the left-wing opposition on Śmigły were rapidly dispersed. A confrontation took place during the festivities in honour of Pyrz, a peasant from the village of Nowosielce who perished in the struggle against the Tartars in the seventeenth century. The Peasant Party assembled about 200,000 of its followers who paraded before Śmigły when he decorated Pyrz's monument with the Cross of *Virtuti Militari*. The organizers of this immense manifestation did not achieve the political results they had sought. The crowd loudly demanded an amnesty for Witos and Śmigły felt offended. For the same reason talks conducted by government politicians and Peasant Party leaders also failed to yield results. Much more profound causes were involved. The military dictatorship could look for cooperation only to the Right. Already, while Piłsudski lived, the government's agrarian policy favoured the large landowners. The land reform was not carried out, although it was indispensable in view of the overpopulation of the countryside which was felt even more, when after the foundation of the Polish State the possibility for emigration had been stopped. During the great world crisis some States, like France, in fighting against unemployment forced Polish workers, who in times of prosperity were employed in French coal mining and industry, to return to their homes.

In order to reach an agreement with the Peasant Party it was necessary to carry out a land reform. The government group, linked with the large landowners, was not inclined to do this. In 1929, 164,000 hectares were made available, a relatively small amount, but by 1934 this figure had declined to 56,000 hectares. On the other hand, fascist and anti-Semitic slogans could easily be used for an understanding with the Right. Therefore, when it was decided to formulate some sort of government programme to obtain the support of public opinion, Śmigły decided that this programme should have a right-wing, clerical and anti-Semitic character. This led to the formation of the National Unity Camp which was to become the new government party. As a result, part of the National Radical Camp went over to the government's side. The country soon became the scene of anti-Semitic outrages, especially in the universities, with the police openly tolerating them. The government press increasingly had recourse to the necessity of combatting the Jews.

The ruling camp likewise used the tense Ukrainian question to gain support from the Right Wing. While a part of the Ukrainian nationalists of Eastern Little Poland participated in the 1935 election, the rest supported the irreconcilable activity of the underground opposition. It was thus easy for the government to exploit the reaction of Polish nationalism in the borderlands for its own benefit. This was shown in relation to the policies of H. Józewski, the Voivode of Volhynia, who for many years had tried to put into effect the conception of an anti-Soviet Polish-Ukrainian agreement. With this in view he supported the former followers of Petlura. After Śmigły had taken charge of political affairs, the military started to sabotage Józewski's policy, and, finally, in 1938 he was removed from office. In the Chełm district sporadic attempts were made at forcibly converting Orthodox to Catholicism. Moreover, a number of abandoned Orthodox churches were blown up. In the south-eastern voivodships a campaign to win over the so-called village gentry was launched. Descendants of the former petty gentry were sought for among the population and attempts were made to establish this group as a type of privileged élite, which was to be the mainstay of the Polish element in the borderlands. This odious policy led to a still greater exacerbation of mutual hatred. It followed from the basic tendency of anchoring social support for the dictatorship of the ruling party by means of a nationalist-fascist campaign.

BECK AND THE CIESZYN QUESTION

In such internal conditions Poland had to face the great international crisis which was to lead to the outbreak of the Second World War and to the destruction of the Polish Republic.

The key to the situation in these years lay in Germany. In 1935 immediately after Piłsudski's death Beck paid a visit to Berlin, where he gave assurances that Polish policy towards Germany would remain unchanged. On this occasion, however, after the visit in Berlin Beck did not make a trip to Moscow. The possibilities of manoeuvre had become limited. From 1935 onwards friction between Prague and Warsaw grew and relations with Paris weakened still further. Poland refused to participate in the Franco-Soviet and Soviet-Czech alliances. She took an ambiguous position with regard to Italy's aggression in Abyssinia and observed the League of Nations resolutions calling for economic sanctions against Italy only formally. Poland was also the first to abandon the sanctions and recognize the conquest of Abyssinia, before the League of Nation had passed a vote on this issue. By these moves Beck's policy showed his sympathy with the Fascist powers.

When on 7 March, 1936, the German armies marched into the demilitarized Rhineland, Beck immediately notified the French ambassador that he would adhere to the conditions of the Franco-Polish alliance, but neither France or Great Britain wished to take military action against Hitler, although it was known that he did not as yet have adequate forces to begin a war with the Western Powers. The passivity of the Western Powers towards Nazism gave Beck arguments for leaning towards Germany, especially when Mussolini became Hitler's ally. Poland continued to maintain an irreconcilable position on the question of Gdańsk as far as her own rights were concerned. Meanwhile, she tacitly reconciled herself to the Nazis assuming control of the Free City. In reality both France and Great Britain had ceased to concern themselves with this issue. The post of the League of Nations' High Commissioner in Gdańsk, generally held by Englishmen, was given at the beginning of 1937 to a Swiss who did not exercise much influence on events during the remaining years of the Free City's existence. On the other hand, Hitler's diplomacy sought to appease the Poles during these years with constant assurances that a war would not be started over Gdańsk and that in general Germany did not have any territorial claims on Poland.

Nevertheless, Poland did continue to feel concern over her relations with the Western Powers. As a result of Śmigły's visit to France in 1936, Poland obtained a loan to build the Silesia–Gdynia railway and, in addition, a promise of assistance for rearmament. While in Piłsudski's time the Polish army had remained backward, clinging to outmoded techniques and military tactics, maintaining, for example, numerous regiments of cavalry instead of converting to motorized units, after his death the new Inspector General sought to modernize armaments and to adapt training to new requirements.

Poland lacked, of course, the industrial resources for putting her forces on a modern footing, especially with regard to the air force and armoured units.

In these years Beck sought a rapprochement with Great Britain in which he was successful insofar as Britain also conducted an undecided policy and was anxious to reach a compromise both with Hitler and Mussolini. For Poland the basic aim of a rapprochement with Great Britain was to strengthen the military alliance with France. Since from the time of Locarno the implementation of this alliance depended on the League of Nations, it was clear that the behaviour of the French government would be determined by the position of British diplomacy should the *casus foederis* arise. While courting France and Britain, both of whom followed a vacillating course in respect of the Fascist powers and the Berlin–Rome Axis, Beck continued to seek the sympathies of the latter. Thus, during the Spanish Civil War, the law forbidding Polish citizens to serve in foreign armies was applied to the Polish volunteers fighting in Spain against the Fascists, for which they were deprived of citizenship. Similarly the Polish government recognized the newly established empire of Manchukuo, which was an acceptance of the partition of China by Japan.

Beck's policy was put to severe tests in 1938. When the annexation of Austria by the Reich took place in March, Beck, to save his prestige, sent an ultimatum to Kaunas demanding that Lithuania immediately establish normal diplomatic relations with Poland. The very coincidence of these facts shows that Beck had nothing left but gestures designed to mask the worsening of Poland's situation. In fact, the establishment of relations with Lithuania was advantageous for both sides, but it was, of course, no compensation for Poland's weakness in the face of the considerable increase of German power.

The inequality of forces appeared still more vividly in the case of Czechoslovakia. After 1935 Poland's relations with this country had been tense. The theme of anti-Czech propaganda was the ill-treatment of the Polish population in the western part of Cieszyn-Silesia belonging to Czechoslovakia, called the Zaolzie district in Polish. The real reason for attacks on Prague was the Czech-Soviet alliance of May 1935, which was an integral part of the Franco-Soviet alliance. When, after the Anschluss of Austria, the question of the Sudeten Germans arose, Polish diplomacy sought to connect the Sudeten question with Zaolzie and demanded that both the Western Powers and the Czech government should accord the same treatment to the Polish minority as to the other minorities of the country. In May, during the first Czech-German crisis, Beck obtained this promise both from the Czech government and, less specifically, from Great Britain and France. When it became clear in September that the Western Powers had decided to sacrifice the Sudeten area for the purpose of "saving peace", Beck resolutely demanded the incorporation into Poland of areas inhabited by Poles. Germany obtained the Sudetenland at Munich, but the Zaolzie question was referred to the Powers for a future decision. Beck saw in such a settlement of the question a double danger in that either promises would not be kept, or Germany would make their fulfilment dependent on territorial concessions by Poland, for example, in Gdańsk or Pomerania. For this reason a 24-hour ultimatum was sent to Prague on 30 September, which the Czechs were forced to accept, and subsequently the Polish armies occupied Zaolzie up to the frontier set by the Polish-Czech treaty of 5 November, 1918. Small adjustments of the border were demanded at the expense of Slovakia in the Tatra and Pieniny areas. This change of frontiers, accomplished by Poland by means of the threat to use force at the moment of Hitler's rape of Czechoslovakia, placed Poland among the aggressors, breaking international law and violating principles of justice. The indignation and shame of the Poles in opposition to the régime was immense. It was also understood that Poland's situation had deteriorated disastrously, while Germany's power had increased immensely as a result of the fall of Czechoslovakia.

FACING GERMAN AGGRESSION (1938–1939)

It soon became obvious that the danger of German aggression, which, according to expectations immediately after Munich, was to be postponed for a long time, had on the contrary increased. For the moment, however, only Polish diplomacy was aware of this in the autumn of 1938. Already in October Germany presented her proposals for a "final" settlement of Polish-German affairs, clearly demanding the annexation of Gdańsk and of a strip of territory to join East Prussia with the rest of Germany. In this situation Beck was still able to improve the tense relations with the Soviet Union, which had threatened Poland during the Czech crisis with the denunciation of the non-aggression pact. In November a Polish-Soviet communiqué was published, which was supposed to testify to a return to normal good-neighbourly relations between the two States.

Beck acted as if he were not aware of the seriousness of the situation. He not only concealed German demands from the Polish public, but also from Poland's ally, France. He concentrated his efforts instead on obtaining a common frontier with Hungary by having Hungary annex the Subcarpatho-Ukraine. As an argument he used the Ukrainian danger, lest this area, which after Munich was governed by Hitler's agent, Father Voloshyn, might become a springboard for German plans with regard to the Ukraine as a whole. The attempts to win over the Rumanian government for this concept with the offer of a part of Subcarpatho-Ukraine, were of no avail. Beck also failed to draw the correct conclusions from the fact that the German demands had been renewed during his visit in Berchtesgaden in January, 1939 and during Ribbentrop's visit to Warsaw in the same month. The Germans were now pressing their demands more firmly and openly proposed Poland cooperation in aggression against the Soviet Union. Polish diplomacy rejected all these proposals outright, probably in the belief that Hitler would not decide to break the understanding with Poland.

The annexation of Bohemia and Moravia in March, 1939 and the proclamation of the protectorate over Slovakia finally clarified the situation. While at that moment Poland was able to obtain a common frontier with Hungary, this fact did not in any way compensate for a new strategic situation in which Poland found herself threatened on three sides by German military bases. At this juncture Ribbentrop set out once more, this time in the form of an ultimatum in his conversation with Ambassador Lipski on 22 March, the German demands upon Poland. The Polish government replied by a partial mobilization and concentration of troops on the German frontier and on 26 March formally and categorically rejected the German demands. Now the tension between Poland and Germany could no longer be concealed and not only European diplomacy became aware of it, but the Polish people also.

British intervention followed. On 31 March Neville Chamberlain, the British Prime Minister, declared in the House of Commons that Poland would receive a guarantee in the event of agression and her armed opposition to it. In consequence Beck went to London at the beginning of April and a Polish-British declaration on mutual assistance was made public. In reply Hitler denounced on 28 April the pact of non-aggression with Poland and the treaties with Great Britain. In turn Beck made a speech in the Seym on 5 May, in which he rejected the German demands, but left the door open to further negotiations with Germany. In Poland the danger of war was understood and the whole country showed a determination to oppose the threatened attack. An optimistic attitude was prevalent, deriving from the conviction that the Polish army was properly prepared and that the power of the Western Allies guaranteed an ultimate victory. In addition, it was thought that Hitler's successes had resulted from a lack of resistance on the part of his opponents and had been based on bluff, and that Hitler, therefore, this time would not dare to launch a war which had to end in his inevitable defeat.

Such was also the opinion of the Polish ruling circles, which did not wish to agree to the Soviet Union joining the defensive alliance. Beck considered that the moment he signed an alliance with Moscow he would eliminate finally the possibility of an understanding with Berlin, which he was still seeking by indirect means. German diplomacy, however, refused to resume fundamental talks with Warsaw.

In May a Polish-French military agreement was concluded, which guaranteed French assistance to Poland in case of German attack and promised to launch an offensive on the western front on the seventeenth day after mobilization, but this agreement was dependent on the conclusion of a political treaty which, in effect, was signed only after the outbreak of the war, on 4 September. In this way the French government retained the possibility of not fulfilling its obligations as an ally of Poland.

In connexion with the German-Polish tension the German press began atrocity propaganda about the alleged persecution of Germans in Poland. The situation in Gdańsk also became acute. Hitler aimed at convincing Western opinion that the Polish-German dispute was caused by the issue of Gdańsk, a city with a German population which wished to join the united German State. German propaganda sought to present the situation to the French in such a way as to give the impression that they would "die for Gdańsk" (*mourir pour Danzig*). In effect, Hitler had already decided to begin the war in order to destroy the Polish State and incorporate the greater part of it into Germany.

Meanwhile in Moscow, in August negotiations were taking place between a British and French military mission and the Soviet Military Staff. The negotiations did not yield any results. The Polish government would not agree to the Soviet proposals for mutual defence. On 21 August the signing of the non-aggression pact between Ribbentrop and Molotov took place, which, as later emerged, only temporarily put off the outbreak of the German-Soviet war. On 26 August Hitler decided to launch military operations. European diplomacy still thought that Hitler was engaged in bluff, but he for his part did not believe in Anglo-French assistance to Poland.

In effect, after the conclusion of the pact with Moscow, Hitler was convinced that the Western Powers had given up the idea of concerning themselves with east European affairs. In view of this the British government concluded the alliance with Poland on 25 August to make it quite clear that an attack on Poland would lead to a European war. In reply Hitler began negotiations with Great Britain to make it possible for her to withdraw and for this reason cancelled the order for opening the military operations. At the last moment German diplomacy played its game in such a way as to give proof of its desire for an understanding with Poland. Ribbentrop demanded the despatch to Berlin of a plenipotentiary of the Polish government to conclude a final settlement with Germany, but, at the same time, Germany did not desire such a direct agreement, because it would be shown then that the German demands could not be reconciled not only with Poland's territorial integrity, but even with her independence. On the evening of 31 August the final German conditions, contained in 16 points, were announced. They called for the immediate incorporation of Gdańsk into Germany and a plebiscite in Pomerania, which was to be evacuated immediately by the Polish administration and army. The plebiscite was to take place a year later, but these conditions, which were completely unacceptable to the Polish government, were considered by the German government to be of no account even at the moment of their publication, on the grounds that Warsaw had not sent a plenipotentiary to Berlin in time. The publication of these 16 points was designed to convince not European opinion but the German people, to whom they were presented as proof of Hitler's unlimited willingness to reach a compromise with Poland.

The German attack on Poland began at dawn on 1 September. Within a few weeks the Polish army, in spite of its heroic struggle, was defeated. The Polish nation underwent for almost six years a system of oppression and destruction which in its frightfulness surpassed anything that the history of Poland, so full of tragedy, had up to that time experienced.

CONCLUSION

The "Second Republic of Poland", which emerged after the First World War in the aftermath of the collapse of the three partitioning Powers, took shape under difficult conditions which did not carry the promise of a long life. Without defensible frontiers in the east and in the west and weakened by the discontent of national minorities which constituted thirty per cent of her population, Poland was a small and impoverished bourgeois State, a creation of the Versailles system standing against Bolshevism on the one hand and against the German policy of revenge on the other. Poland had no means of conducting an independent foreign policy, except for the brief periods of tension between Berlin and Moscow. Furthermore, Poland could not count on the effective assistance of her powerful supporters in Paris and London.

Poland's achievements during the twenty years between the two wars, however, should not be underrated. The scars of war were healed and the three zones of partition were welded together again. The State was restored and a new generation of young citizens grew up in conditions of independence. The government failed in two major tasks. It was unable either to raise the country out of the economic slump or to ensure its external security.

In the final years of this period before the Second World War Poland's industrial production did not succeed in reaching the level for the period before 1914. Primarily, this was a consequence of the subordination of the Polish economy to foreign capital, which drew excessive profits from its old investments without making new ones. This situation reduced to a mere illusion the cherished concept of the Piłsudski faction, the idea of Poland's participation in power politics independent both of Germany and of the Soviet Union.

Even the foreign minister, Beck, had to realize that Poland's cooperation with Germany against the U.S.S.R. was impossible in view of Hitler's unconcealed desire to dismember the Polish State. Cooperation with the U.S.S.R. against Hitlerism was not acceptable to the powerful supporters of the

Polish bourgeoisie and landowners, because it carried with it a threat of social revolution and the loss of the eastern provinces, where the major part of the population was not Polish. In conflict with her neighbours, weakened by unemployment, incapable for economic reason of putting a modern army in the field, unsure of one-third of her population, Poland was completely defenceless in September, 1939.

The Second World War and over five years of Nazi occupation were perhaps the most dramatic episode of Poland's entire history. Nazism made its bid for world domination. The Poles were not assigned a place in this world. The extent of the plans laid down by the invaders is more than well known from secret documents which were made public after 1945. They called for the extermination of the entire Polish intelligentsia, for the Germanization of the few elements that could be persuaded that they belonged to the German race, for the gradual destruction of the mass of the Poles, pressed into forced labour for the *Herrenvolk*. This programme was put into effect with merciless consistency. It was slowed down to an insignificant degree by the necessity of conducting a war. The means employed were mass expulsions and deportation of Poles to forced labour in the Reich, anti-Polish property laws, kidnapping in the streets and public executions, the cruelty of the Gestapo and the camps of mass extermination of the Polish people. Millions of Poles were killed by the Nazis; the overwhelming part of Polish Jews fell victim to this policy of extermination. The levelling to the ground of the Jewish district of Warsaw after the rising in the Warsaw Ghetto in the spring of 1943 and of the entire capital after the Warsaw rising at the end of 1944 revealed the fate which was in store for the Poles and the Polish cities in the event of Hitler's victory.

The nation was fully aware of this formidable danger. There were no Quislings in Poland during the Second World War, not because the Germans did not seek to employ them, but rather because they would have found no faction or social group willing to support them. The Poles unanimously rejected Hitler's ultimatum and were the first in Europe to offer him armed resistance. In this manner the people exerted pressure on the British and French politicians who in September, 1939 were still thinking of a fresh Munich. Defeated in the military campaign, the nation did not for a moment acknowledge defeat. Through the next five years Polish soldiers, pilots and seamen fought the enemy on all war fronts, from Narvik to Tobruk and from London to the Oka river. In the occupied country the activity of Polish partisans grew more powerful year by year and the entire population participated in all manner of sabotage and passive resistance. The Polish underground countered the sentence of extermination passed on Polish culture by secret secondary schools and universities, clandestine lectures, art exhibitions and secret artistic publications. The people tried to survive and despite everything dealt the enemy many a painful blow.

The outcome of the war was sealed when Hitler's first Soviet offensive broke down and more especially after the battle of Stalingrad. From then on the struggle on all fronts was accompanied by a political struggle for the future order of the world, in which the Anglo-Saxon Powers treated with suspicion their ally, the Soviet Union.

From the beginning of 1943 an analysis of the situation on the war fronts made it clear that the liberation of Poland from Nazi annihilation could come only from the East and that the Soviet Union would obtain a predominant influence in the settlement of this part of Europe. The lesson drawn from the experience of the inter-war years and from the recent struggle against Fascism was that Poland could expect support against the Germans from her neighbour to the east and that she should adopt social reforms that would revive her sluggish economy. Polish communists, assembled since 1942 in the Polish Workers' Party, proclaimed this programme, which found a growing response among the masses and broader understanding among the progressive intelligentsia. Polish property owners could not give their support to this programme for the same reason that they rejected cooperation with the U.S.S.R. before the outbreak of the war. The central issue was the future social system of the country and its eastern frontiers. The Polish government-in-exile, transferred in 1940 from France to London, put all its hope into the restoration, with the support of Britain and the U.S.A., of the Polish State as it had been before the war or with slightly altered boundaries, a State which would be ruled by the bourgeoisie.

The two programmes and the two points of view produced in occupied Poland two competing political centres and two partisan armies. As might be expected, formations of the Soviet Army together with the First Polish Army, organized in Russia, crossed the line of the Bug in July, 1944. At this time, Polish military units of the Polish government-in-exile were fighting far from Poland, in Italy and on the Rhine. At this precise moment the headquarters of the underground Home Army, owing allegiance to London, precipitated the outbreak of an armed rising in Warsaw. The Warsaw uprising, directed in the military sense against the Germans, was in the political sense a demonstration against the Soviet Union. It was to provide proof that the London government was entitled to assume power in the country. The heroic fighting lasting over two months ended with capitulation. Almost 200,000 persons died under the rubble of their capital.

Meanwhile, in the liberated areas east of the Vistula, the Polish Committee of National Liberation announced land reform, the nationalization of industry and the transfer of authority into the hands of the working masses. A few months later, in 1945, Polish soldiers together with the Soviet armies liberated the western part of the country, crossed the Odra and placed their standards on the Brandenburg Gate in Berlin. The Western Powers accepted the existing state of affairs and recognized the Government of National Unity set up in Warsaw. The point of view represented by the government-in-exile in London was rejected.

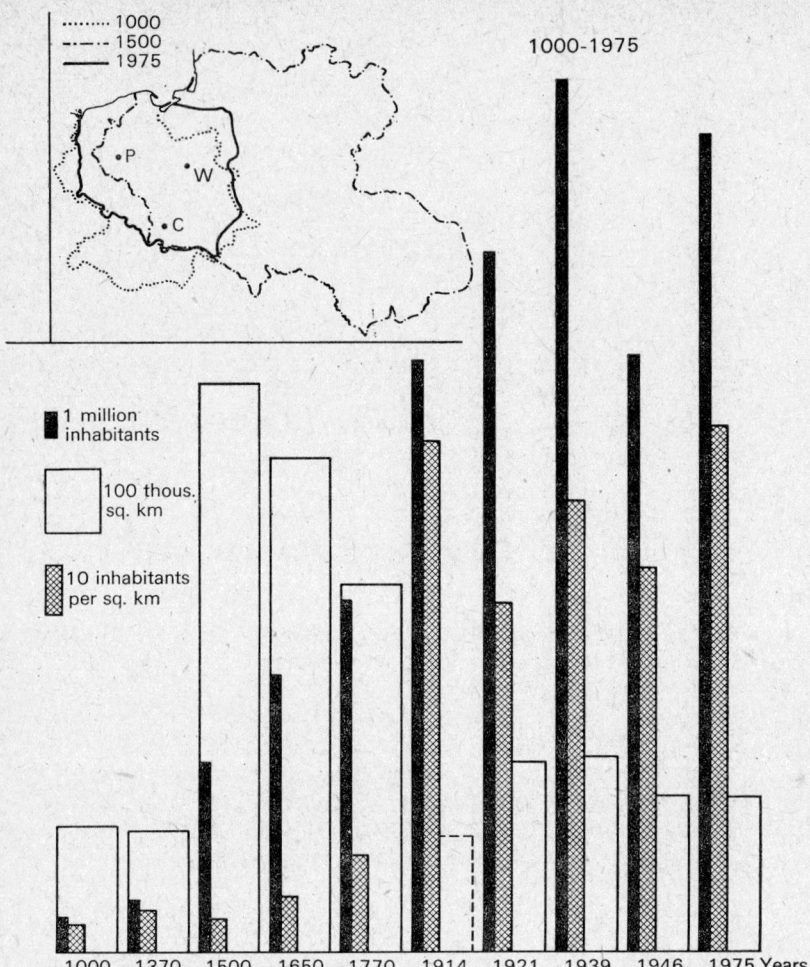

VI. Growth of population in Poland
The Data for 1914 relate to the three partition areas

Post-war Poland recognized the new frontiers in the east and gave up the regions inhabited by Ukrainian, Byelorussian and Lithuanian majorities. At the Potsdam Conference Poland recovered the whole of Silesia, Pomerania, Mazuria and Warmia, provinces which in ages past had been conquered by the Germans. Poland's present boundaries are roughly coextensive with those at the dawn of her history under Mieszko I and Bolesław the Brave. The population within these boundaries consists of 98 per cent native Polish nationals.

Diagram VI illustrates clearly the oscillation in Polish population figures from the early tenth century to the present day. It brings out forcibly the high price Poland paid in the two world wars. Desiring to avoid a fresh catastrophe, Poland wishes to become a protagonist of peace in Europe and

in the world. At home Poland is building socialism ; in her external relations Poland has an alliance with the Soviet Union and with the neighbouring States of People's Democracy. She does not, however, abandon her friendship and cooperation with the nations of the West.

Poland has repaired the enormous devastation of war, she has raised her capital out of the rubble, wiped out illiteracy and laid the foundations of modern industry. Poland now occupies the fourth place in world coal extraction, the second in sulphur extraction, the ninth in the output of refined copper and the eleventh in building ocean-going ships (as regards high-sea fishing vessels Poland competes with Japan and the GDR for the first place in the world). Industrial growth has provided employment for every citizen, has raised the standard of living and opened doors to social advancement. Working to make up for centuries of economic and social neglect, the Polish people wish to insure for themselves a free, secure and prosperous future in a world free from the horrors of war.

CHRONOLOGICAL TABLES

POLISH HISTORY

4th–6th cent.	Slavonic migrations westwards of the Odra (Oder) and southwards of the Carpathians
Beginning of 7th cent.	Formation of political organization of the Slavs south of the Baltic
Middle of 9th cent.	Foundation of small regional Slavonic States in the Odra and Vistula basin
2nd half of 9th cent.	Expansion of the Great-Moravian State into the area of southern Poland; foundation of the State of the Polanie (the Piast dynasty) in Great Poland
1st half of 10th cent.	Conquest of Mazovia by the Piasts
Before 963 to 992	Reign of Mieszko I
966	The Polish Court adopts Christianity
972	Conquest of Western Pomerania by Mieszko I
992–1025	Reign of Bolesław the Brave
1000	Emperor Otto III recognizes Poland's independence; foundation of the archbishopric in Gniezno
1004–1018	Bolesław the Brave's war against the Germans
1018	Peace of Bautzen (Budišyn); Bolesław the Brave's expedition against Kiev and the incorporation of the Czerwień Castles into Poland

GENERAL HISTORY

4th–7th cent.	The great migration of people
5th–7th cent.	The Merovingian State
800	Charlemagne's Imperial coronation
c. 830	Foundation of the Great-Moravian State
843	Treaty of Verdun
9th cent.	Foundation of the Bohemian State
End of 9th cent.	Foundation of the State of Kiev
906	Fall of the Great-Moravian State
950	Bohemia recognizes the suzerainty of the Empire
962	Otto I crowned Emperor
987	Beginnings of the Capetian dynasty in France
988–989	Duke Vladimir of Ruthenia adopts Christianity

		1024	Beginning of the Salic dynasty of the Franks in Germany
1025	Bolesław I the Brave crowned King of Poland		
1025–1034	Reign of Mieszko II		
1033	Mieszko II renounces the royal crown		
1034–1058	Reign of Casimir I the Restorer		
1037	Casimir I the Restorer expelled from Poland; anti-feudal and anti-Christian rising of the people		
1038 or 1039	The Bohemian Duke Břetislav invades Poland		
1039	Casimir I the Restorer returns to Poland; reconstruction of the State begins		
		1054	Beginning of the Eastern schism
1058–1079	Reign of Bolesław II the Bold		
		1066	The Norman conquest of England
1076	Bolesław II the Bold crowned King of Poland		
		1077	Henry IV in Canossa
1079	Revolt of the nobles and expulsion of Bolesław II the Bold		
1079–1102	Reign of Władysław Herman	1096–1099	First Crusade
1102–1138	Reign of Bolesław III the Wrymouth		
1109	Invasion of Poland by Emperor Henry V		
1121–1122	Western Pomerania reincorporated into Poland		
		1122	Concordat of Worms
1124–1128	Christianization of Western Pomerania		
1138	Death of Bolesław III the Wrymouth; beginning of Poland's territorial division with a Grand Duke as senior among the provincial rulers		
1138–1146	Reign of Władysław II as Grand Duke of Poland		
1146–1173	Reign of Bolesław IV the Curly as Grand Duke		
		1147–1149	Second Crusade
		1152–1190	Reign of Emperor Frederick I Barbarossa
		1154	Beginning of the Plantagenets' rule in England (Henry II)
1173–1177	Reign of Mieszko III the Old as Grand Duke	1171	Conquest of Egypt by the Seljuks
1177–1194	Rule of Casimir II the Just as Grand Duke		
1180	Congress of Łęczyca, concessions by Casimir II the Just in favour of the clergy		
1181	Western Pomerania made dependent on the Empire		
		c. 1200	Foundation of the University of Paris
1202–1227	Reign of Leszek the White as Grand Duke	1202	Establishment of the Order of Knights of the Sword in Livonia
		1204	The Crusaders capture Byzantium
		1206	Establishment of the Mongolian State and beginnings of Mongolian expansion
		1215	*Magna Charta Libertatum* in England

1226	Conrad of Mazovia brings the Teutonic Knights into Poland		
1227	Death of Leszek the White, decline of the institution of Senior Duke		
		1228–1229	Sixth Crusade
1232–1234	Conquest of Little Poland and a part of Great Poland by the Silesian Duke Henry the Bearded		
		1240	Tartars capture Kiev and conquer Ruthenia
1241	First Mongol invasion of Poland; battle of Legnica, death of Henry the Pious	c. 1241	Establishment of the Hansa
1249–1252	Conquest of the Lubusz Land by the Margraves of Brandenburg	Middle 13th cent.	Foundation of parliaments in France and England
		1254–1273	The Long Interregnum in Germany
1291–1292	Conquest of Little Poland by King Wacław II of Bohemia		
1295	Coronation of Przemysł II as King of Poland		
1296	Death of Przemysł II		
1300–1305	Reign of Wacław II as King of Poland		
		1302	The States-General constituted in France
1306	Władysław I the Short conquers Little Poland		
1308–1309	The Teutonic Knights capture Gdańsk and Eastern Pomerania		
		1309–1377	The "Avignon captivity" of the Popes
1314	Władysław I the Short conquers Great Poland		
		1316–1341	Reign of Giedymin and unification of the Lithuanian State
1320–1333	Reign of Władysław the Short as King of Poland; end of territorial division		
1325	Polish-Lithuanian alliance against the Teutonic Knights		
		1328	Ivan Kalita gains the title of Grand Duke of Muscovy
1331	Battle of Płowce, victory of Władysław the Short over the Teutonic Knights		
1333–1370	Reign of Casimir III the Great, the last king of the Piast dynasty		
1335	Congress of Vyšehrad: John of Luxemburg renounces his claims to the Polish throne and Casimir III the Great—his rights to Silesia		
		1337	Outbreak of the Hundred Years' War
1340–1349	Poland occupies the greater part of Vladimir and Halicz Ruthenia		
		1342–1382	Reign of Louis d'Anjou as King of Hungary
		1346	Battle of Crécy
		1348	Foundation of the University of Prague
Middle of 14th cent.	The Statutes of Great Poland and Little Poland—first codification of the common law		
1355	Privileges for the gentry granted by Louis d'Anjou in Buda in return for the recognition of his succession in Poland		
1364	Foundation of the University of Cracow		
1370–1382	Reign of Louis d'Anjou		

		1371	Beginning of the reign of the Stuarts in Scotland
		1377–1417	Western schism
		1380	Battle of Kulikovo Pole, victory of Demetrius Donskoi over the Tartars
1384	Jadwiga, daughter of Louis d'Anjou, becomes Queen of Poland		
1385	Polish-Lithuanian Union at Krewa		
1386	Baptism of the Lithuanian Grand Duke Jagiełło and his marriage to Jadwiga		
1386–1434	Reign of Władysław Jagiełło; beginning of the Jagiellonian dynasty		
		1397	Union of Denmark, Norway and Sweden at Kalmar
1399	The Lithuanian Grand Duke Witold in the battle with Tartars on the Vorskla river		
1400	Restoration of the Cracow University		
		1409	Theses of Ian Hus
1410	Battle of Grunwald		
		1414–1418	Council of Constance
		1419–1434	Hussite wars
1420	Władysław Jagiełło rejects the Bohemian crown offered to him by the Hussites		
1422–1433	The gentry obtain the charter *Neminem captivabimus nisi iure victum*		
		1429	Joan of Arc in Orléans
1434–1444	Reign of Władysław III		
1440	Władysław III ascends to the Hungarian throne; Casimir IV—to the Lithuanian throne; the Prussian Union formed		
1444	Battle of Varna and death of Władysław III		
1447–1492	Reign of Casimir IV in Poland		
		c. 1450	Discovery of print by Johannes Gutenberg
		1453	Constantinople captured by the Turks; end of the Hundred Years' War
1454	Incorporation of Prussia into Poland		
1454–1466	Thirteen Years' War with the Teutonic Knights		
		1455–1485	War of the Roses in England
		1462–1505	Reign of Ivan III and liberation of Russia from Tartar dependence
1466	Peace of Toruń with Teutonic Knights		
1473	First printing shop in Cracow		
		1481	Inquisition established in Spain
1492–1501	Reign of John Albert	1492	Discovery of America; conquest of Granada—the end of Spain's *reconquistà*
1492–1506	Reign of Alexander in the Grand Duchy of Lithuania		
1496	Statutes of Piotrków: the rights of peasants and burghers abridged		
1497	John Albert's defeat in Moldavia	1497–1498	Discovery of the sea-route to India (Vasco da Gama)
1501–1506	Reign of Alexander	1503–1513	Pope Julius II
1505	*Nihil Novi* Constitution		
1506–1548	Reign of Sigismund I the Old		
1514	Muscovite troops take Smoleńsk; Polish-		

1515	Lithuanian victory at Orsza Meeting in Vienna of Sigismund I the Old, Władysław Jagiełło (son of Casimir IV) and Emperor Maximilian Hapsburg: the Hapsburgs receive the guarantee to succeed to the Bohemian and Hungarian throne in case of extinction of the Jagiellonian dynasty		
1518	Arrival to Poland of Bona Sforza, wife of Sigismund I the Old	1517	Theses of Martin Luther
		1519	Charles V becomes Emperor
		1519–1521	Conquest of Mexico by Hernán Cortès
		1519–1522	Ferdinand Magellan's expedition round the world
1520	First royal edicts against dissenters	1521	The Edict of Worms outlaws Martin Luther as heretic
		1524–1525	Peasant war in Germany
1525	Secularization of the Teutonic Order in Prussia; the Prussian Prince Albrecht pays homage to Sigismund I the Old		
1526	Extinction of the Mazovian line of Piasts; incorporation of Mazovia to the Crown	1526	The succession of the Hapsburgs in Bohemia and Hungary
		1527	"Sacco di Roma"
1529	Sigismund II Augustus ascends to the throne of Lithuania		
		1531–1536	Conquest of Peru by Francisco Pizarro
		1534	Establishment of the Jesuit Order; separation of the English Church from Rome
1543	Nicolaus Copernicus *De revolutionibus orbium coelestium*		
		1545–1563	Council of Trent
		1547–1584	Reign of Ivan the Terrible in Russia
1548–1572	Reign of Sigismund II Augustus	1556–1598	Reign of Philip II as King of Spain
		1558–1603	Reign of Queen Elisabeth in England
1561	Secularization of the Livonian Order; incorporation of Livonia and establishment of the Duchy of Courland		
1563–1570	The Seven Years Northern War		
1564	Jesuits brought into Poland		
1569	The Union of Lublin		
1570	Compact of Sandomierz—agreement of the Protestant denominations for the defense of religious freedom		
		1572	St. Bartholomew's Night in France
1573	The principle of the free election of kings adopted; religious peace guaranteed		
1573–1574	Reign of Henry de Valois		
		1574–1589	Reign of Henry III de Valois as King of France
1576–1586	Reign of Stephen Batory	1576	Outbreak of rising the in the Netherlands
1577	War with Gdańsk		
1577–1582	War with the Grand Duchy of Muscovy for Livonia		
1578	Foundation of the Wilno Academy		

1587–1632	Reign of Sigismund III Vasa		
		1579	Establishment of the Republic of United Provinces in the Netherlands
		1588	Victory of the English Navy over Spain's Great Armada
		1589–1610	Reign of King Henry IV in France
1594–1596	Cossack uprising under Severin Nalevaiko		
1595	Foundation of the Zamość Academy		
1595–1596	Union of Brześć		
1600	Outbreak of the war with Sweden	1600	Establishment of the East India Company in England
		1603	Death of Elisabeth Tudor, beginning of the Stuart dynasty in England
1604–1606	Polish participation in the action of the False Demetrius		
1605	Victory over the Swedes at Kirchholm		
1606–1607	Rebellion of Mikołaj Zebrzydowski		
1609–1619	War with Russia		
1610	Stanisław Żółkiewski's victory over the Russian army at Kłuszyn		
		1611–1632	Reign of Gustavus Adolphus in Sweden
		1613	Beginning of the rule of the Romanovs in Russia
		1618	Beginning of the Thirty Years' War
1620	Defeat of the Polish army in the battle with the Turks at Cecora	1620	Defeat of the Bohemians at Bilá Hora
1621	Defense of Chocim and peace with Turkey		
1627	Battle of the Polish and Swedish navies at Oliwa		
1629	Victory over the Swedes at Trzciana; truce with Sweden		
1632–1634	War with Russia	1632	Battle of Lützen and death of Gustavus Adolphus
1632–1648	Reign of Władysław IV Vasa		
		1642	Beginning of Revolution in England, the Long Parliament
1648	Outbreak of the rising under Bohdan Chmielnicki in the Ukraine	1648	Peace of Westphalia
1648–1668	Reign of John Casimir		
		1649	Execution of Charles I Stuart
1651	Victory over Bohdan Chmielnicki's army at Beresteczko		
1652	Seym broken up by the first *Liberum veto*		
		1653–1658	Protectorate of Oliver Cromwell
1654–1667	Polish-Russian war	1654	Compact of Perejasław between Ukraine and Russia
1655–1660	Polish-Swedish war		
1657	Treaties of Wehlau and Bydgoszcz; Poland renounces the Prussian fief		
1658	Arians (Antitrinitarians) expelled from Poland; compact of Hadziacz		
1660	Peace with Sweden at Oliwa		
		1661–1715	Reign of Louis XIV
1665–1666	Rebellion of Jerzy Lubomirski		
1667	Truce of Andruszów		
1669–1673	Reign of Michael Korybut-Wiśniowiecki		
1672	Turkish invasion of Poland		
1673	Victory over the Turks at Chocim		

1674–1696	Reign of John III Sobieski	1682–1725	Reign of Peter the Great in Russia
1683	Siege of Vienna by the Turks and the Polish relief		
		1684	Creation of the first anti-Turkish League
1686	Peace with Russia (the Grzymułtowski treaty)		
1697–1733	Reign of Augustus II the Strong		
1699	Peace with Turkey at Karlovci	1699	The Hapsburgs complete the conquest of Hungary
		1700–1721	The Northern War
		1701	Proclamation of the Kingdom of Prussia
		1701–1714	The Spanish war of succession
1702	Swedish invasion of Poland		
1704	The opponents of Augustus II proclaim an interregnum; election of Stanisław Leszczyński		
1709	Augustus II again recognized as King		
		1714	George I ascends to throne in England, beginning of the Hanover dynasty
1715–1716	The Confederation of Tarnogród	1716–1720	The affair of John Law in France
1717	The "Mute Seym"		
1733	Double election of Augustus III and Stanisław Leszczyński		
1733–1735	The struggle of Stanisław Leszczyński against Augustus III for the Polish throne		
1734–1763	Reign of Augustus III		
1740	The Collegium Nobilium established by Stanisław Konarski	1740–1748	The war of Austrian succession and the Silesian Wars
		1740–1786	Reign of Frederick II in Prussia and of Maria Theresa in Austria
		1742	Frederick II occupies Silesia
		1751	Volume I of the Encyclopaedia published in France
		1756–1763	The Seven Years' War
		1762–1796	Reign of Catherine II in Russia
1764–1795	Reign of Stanisław Augustus Poniatowski		
1764–1766	Constitutional reforms carried out by the "Convocation Confederation"		
1766–1768	Russian intervention on the side of reactionary opposition		
1767	The Confederation of the Dissenters and the Confederation of Radom	1767	James Watt's steam engine
1768–1772	The Confederation of Bar		
1772	First partition of Poland		
1773	Establishment of the Commission for National Education	1773	The Jesuit Order dissolved
1775	Establishment of the Permanent Council		
		1776	First Workers' Union organized in England
		1776–1782	The American War of Independence
		1787	Proclamation of the Constitution of the United States of America
1788–1792	The Four Years' Seym		
1789	"The Black Procession" of burghers in Warsaw	1789	Outbreak of the Great Revolution
1790	"Warnings for Poland" by Stanisław Staszic		

1791	Constitution of the 3rd May		
1792	The Confederation of Targowica and war with Russia	1792	Overthrow of the monarchy in France
1793	Second partition of Poland		
1794	The Kościuszko Insurrection		
1795	Third partition of Poland	1795–1799	The Directory in France
1797–1803	Polish Legions at the side of the French army		
		1799	The *coup d'état* of the 18th Brumaire
1800	The Society of Friends of Sciences established in Warsaw; reorganization of the University in Wilno		
		1804	Napoleon Bonaparte Emperor of the French
1806	Napoleon's Prussian campaign; rising in Great Poland; Warsaw occupied by the French	1806	End of the Roman Empire of the German Nation
1807	Establishment of the Duchy of Warsaw; its Constitution	1807	Peace of Tilsit
1808	Introduction of the Code of Napoleon		
1809	Polish-Austrian war; the territory of the Duchy of Warsaw extended	1809	French-Austrian war
1811–1823	Enfranchisement of peasants in Polish provinces under Prussian rule		
1812	The army of the Duchy of Warsaw participates in Napoleon's Russian campaign	1812	Napoleon's campaign in Russia
		1814	Napoleon abdicates; George Stephenson's first locomotive
		1814–1815	Congress of Vienna
1815	Foundation of the Kingdom of Poland and of the Free State of Cracow	1815	The "Holy Alliance" formed
1816	Foundation of the University of Warsaw		
1817–1823	Activities of the Philarets and Philomaths in Wilno		
1819–1825	Activities of the National Freemasonry and of the Patriotic Society	1820–1823	Liberation of the Latin American countries; revolutionary movements in Spain and Italy; liberation of Greece
1823–1825	Contacts of the Patriotic Society with the Decembrists in Russia	1825	The Decembrists' rising in St. Petersburg
1828	Establishment of the Bank Polski		
		1830	The July Revolution in France
1830–1831	The November Insurrection	1830–1832	Revolution in Belgium
1831	Beginning of the Great Emigration		
1832	The autonomy of the Kingdom of Poland abridged; the Polish Democratic Society formed in France	1832	Electoral reform in England
1833	Józef Zaliwski's expedition	1833	Abolition of slavery in the English colonies
1834–1836	Activities of the secret independence organization "Young Poland"	1834	Giuseppe Mazzini forms "Young Europe"
1834–1840	Conctruction of the "Huta Bankowa" ironworks		
1835	The association "Lud Polski" (Polish People) formed (The Grudziąż Commune)		
1835–1838	Szymon Konarski's activities in Podolia, Ukraine and Lithuania		
		1837–1901	Reign of Queen Victoria in England
		1839–1842	Opium War in China
1840–1844	Father Piotr Ściegienny's activities in the Kielce region		
1842–1845	Activities of the "Plebeian Union" in Poznań		

1846	Cracow revolution; peasant rising in Galicia; the Free State of Cracow abolished			
		1847	The Workers' Union formed in London	
1848	Uprising in Great Poland; revolutionary ferment in Galicia and Silesia; Warsaw-Vienna railway inaugurated; enfranchisement of peasants in Galicia			
1848–1849	Polish participation in the revolutionary events in Europe	1848–1849	Revolution in France, Austria Germany, Italy, Hungary; the Communist Manifesto of Karl Marx and Friedrich Engels	
		1850–1864	Taiping rebellion in China	
1851	Customs union of the Kingdom of Poland and the Russian Empire			
		1852–1871	The Second Empire in France	
		1853–1856	The Crimean War	
1853	Ignacy Łukasiewicz discovers the kerosene lamp	1857	Uprising in India	
		1859–1860	Struggle for the unification of Italy	
1860–1862	Patriotic manifestations in the Kingdom of Poland			
		1861	Enfranchisement of peasants in Russia; Abraham Lincoln inaugurated as U.S. President; American Civil War (1861–1865)	
1862	Central Committee of the Reds established in Warsaw; Aleksander Wielopolski becomes chief of the civilian government in the Kingdom of Poland; inauguration of the Main School (University) in Warsaw			
1863–1864	The January Insurrection			
1863	Manifesto on the enfranchisement of peasants issued by the leadership of the Insurrection			
		1864	The First International formed	
1866–1885	Gradual elimination of the Polish language from the schools in the Kingdom of Poland	1866	Prussian-Austrian war, battle of Sadova	
1867	Autonomy of Galicia	1867	The Austrian State transformed into a Dual Monarchy	
		1869	Opening of the Suez Canal; establishment of the Workers' Social-Democratic Party in Germany	
		1870–1871	Franco-Prussian War	
		1871	Proclamation of the German Reich; the Paris Commune	
		1871–1886	The *Kulturkampf*	
1873	The Academy of Sciences and Letters established in Cracow			
1876	Abolition of the separate judiciary in the Kingdom of Poland and introduction of the Russian language into courts			
1878	First socialist organizations formed in Poland	1878	The Congress of Berlin	
1880	Trial of Ludwik Waryński and his associates in Cracow			
1882	The "Proletariat" formed	1882	The Triple Alliance formed	
1885–1886	Trial of the "Proletariat" leaders			
1886	The Colonization Commission in Great Poland established by the Prussian authorities; foundation of the Polish League			
1889	Polish Workers' Union formed	1889	The Second International formed	

1890	The First Workers' May Day in Poland	1890	The First Workers' May Day celebrations in London
1892	Foundation of the Polish Socialist Party		
1893	Foundation of the Social-Democratic Party of the Kingdom of Poland (since 1900: Social-Democratic Party of the Kingdom of Poland and Lithuania) and of the Polish Social-Democratic Party of Galicia and Silesia; foundation of the National League		
1894	The "Hakata" formed in the Prussian-annexed part of Poland	1894	The Russo-French Alliance
1895	Foundation of the Peasant Party in Galicia (from 1893—Polish Peasant Party)		
1897	Foundation of the National Democratic Party		
1898	Anti-Polish emergency laws in the Prussian-annexed part of Poland	1898	Discovery of radium by Pierre Curie and Maria Skłodowska-Curie
		1900	Establishment of the Labour Party
1901	Strike of school children in Września against the Germanization of schools	1903	The Nobel Prize awarded to Antoine Henri Becquerel, Pierre Curie and Maria Skłodowska-Curie
		1904–1905	Russia-Japan War
1905–1907	Revolution in the Kingdom of Poland	1905–1907	Revolution in Russia
1906	The Polish Socialist Party (PPS) split into the PPS Left and the PPS Revolutionary Wing		
1906–1907	School strike in the Prussian-annexed part of Poland		
		1907	The Triple Entente formed
		1911–1912	Revolution in China and proclamation of the Republic
		1912–1913	The Balkan wars
1914	Supreme National Committee in Galicia; formation of the Polish Legions at the side of the Austrian army	1914	Outbreak of World War I
1915	The Kingdom of Poland occupied by the German and Austrian armies		
1916	Act of the German and Austrian governments on the Polish question (5 Nov.)	1916	Battle of Verdun
1917	The Legions dissolved; establishment of the Polish National Committee in Lausanne (it later functioned in Paris); establishment of the Regency Council	1917	February Revolution in Russia, Tsardom overthrown; U.S.A. enters war; victory of the Great Socialist October Revolution in Petrograd; the Petrograd Workers' Soviet recognizes Poland's right to independence
1918	Ignacy Daszyński forms a government in Lublin; Józef Piłsudski becomes chief of the independent Polish State on 11th November; establishment of the Polish Communist Workers' Party (since 1925: Communist Party of Poland—KPP)	1918	Woodrow Wilson's 14 Points of Peace; declaration of the Soviet government on the annulment of treaties on the partitions of Poland; outbreak of revolution in Germany; surrender of Austria and Germany
1918–1919	Uprising in Great Poland; Councils of Workers' Delegates in Poland		
		1919	Peace treaty signed in Versailles; establishment of the League of Nations; the Third International formed
1919–1920	Polish-Soviet war		
1919–1921	Silesian uprisings		

1920	Plebiscites in Warmia, Mazuria and Powiśle		
1921	The Constitution of March voted; peace treaty of Riga; plebiscite in Silesia		
1922	Assassination of President Gabriel Narutowicz; Stanisław Wojciechowski elected President	1922	Benito Mussolini's *coup d'état*
1923	Second Congress of the KPP; workers' rising in Cracow		
1924	Financial reforms of Władysław Grabski; establishment of the Bank Polski; construction of the port of Gdynia launched		
		1925	Treaties of Locarno
1926	Józef Piłsudski's May *coup d'état*		
1929	The "Centrolew" (Centre-Left) formed	1929–1933	The great depression
1931	The trial of Brześć		
1932	Non-aggression pact with the U.S.S.R.		
		1933	Hitler assumes power; the Reichstag fire trial
1934	Non-aggression pact with Germany		
1935	The Constitution of April passed	1935	Remilitarization of Germany; Italian aggression in Abyssinia
1936	Strikes in Cracow and Lwów; peasant strikes in Little Poland	1936	The Berlin–Rome Axis formed
		1936–1939	Fascist *coup* and civil war in Spain
1937	National Unity Camp formed	1937	Japanese aggression in China; Italy joins the German–Japanese pact
1938	The Communist Party of Poland dissolved by the Communist International; annexation of the Zaolzie region (part of Cieszyn Silesia) by Poland	1938	Annexation of Austria by Germany; Germany occupies the Sudetenland; the Munich agreements
1939	Nazi Germany attacks Poland (1 Sep.); the September campaign (1 Sep.–5 Oct.); the Soviet army enters West Ukraine and West Byelorussia (17 Sep.); Gen. Władysław Sikorski forms the Polish Government-in-exile in France; establishment of the General-Gouvernment by the Nazi occupying power	1939	Annexation of Czechoslovakia by Germany; Soviet-German non-aggression pact; outbreak of World War II

BIBLIOGRAPHICAL NOTES

A. BIBLIOGRAPHICAL WORKS

Bibliografia historii Polski (Bibliography of Polish History), ed. by H. Madurowicz-Urbańska Vol. I–III, Warszawa 1965–1974 et sqq.
Bibliografia historii polskiej (yearly Bibliography of Polish History—contains current bibliography), ed. by J. Baumgart and co-workers, Wrocław-Warszawa-Kraków 1952 et sqq.
L. Finkel, *Bibliografia historii polskiej* (Bibliography of Polish History). Vol. I–III with supplement. Lwów-Kraków 1891–1914. Anastatic reprint, Warszawa 1955.
S. Skwirowska, *Bibliographie des travaux des historiens polonais en langues étrangères parus dans les années 1945–1968*, Wrocław 1971.

B. MORE IMPORTANT TEXT-BOOKS AND SYNTHETICAL WORKS

Atlas Historyczny Polski (Historical Atlas of Poland), 3rd ed., Warszawa 1973.
J. Bardach, B. Leśnodorski, M. Pietrzak, *Historia państwa i prawa polskiego* (History of the Polish State and Legislation), Warszawa 1976.
A. Brückner, *Dzieje kultury polskiej* (History of Polish Culture), 3rd ed. Vol. I–III, Warszawa 1958; vol. IV, Kraków-Warszawa 1946.
The Cambridge History of Poland, Cambridge 1950–1951.
Dzieje Polski (History of Poland), ed. by J. Topolski, Warszawa 1975.
Dzieje Uniwersytetu Jagiellońskiego (History of the Jagiellonian University), ed. by K. Lepszy. Vol. I, II, Kraków 1964–1965 et sqq.
Historia chłopów polskich (History of the Polish Peasants), ed. by S. Inglot. Vol. I–II, Warszawa 1970–1972.
Historia nauki polskiej (History of Polish Science), ed. by B. Suchodolski. Vol. I–VII, Wrocław 1970–1975.
Historia państwa i prawa Polski (Constitutional and Legal History of Poland), ed. by J. Bardach. 2nd ed. Vol. I, II, Warszawa 1964–1966.
Historia Polski (History of Poland), ed. by the Institute of History of the Polish Academy of Sciences. Vol. I (parts 1–3), vol. II (parts 1–4), vol. III (parts 1–3), vol. IV (part 1). Warszawa 1955–1974 et sqq.
Historia sztuki polskiej w zarysie (History of Polish Art, An Outline), ed. by T. Dobrowolski, W. Tatarkiewicz. Vol. I–III, Kraków 1962, 2nd ed. 1965.

Kościół w Polsce (The Church in Poland), ed. by J. Kłoczowski. Vol. I : *Średniowiecze* (Medieval Poland), Kraków 1966 ; vol. II : *wiek XVI–XVIII* (16th–18th Centuries), Kraków 1969.
Miasta polskie w tysiącleciu (Polish Towns in Millennium). Vol. I, II, Wrocław–Warszawa–Kraków 1965–1967.
La Pologne au Xe Congrès International des Sciences Historiques à Rome, Warszawa 1955.
Poland at the 11th International Congress of Historical Sciences in Stockholm, Warszawa 1968.
La Pologne au XIIe Congrès International des Sciences Historiques à Vienne, Warszawa 1965.
La Pologne au XIIIe Congrès International des Sciences Historiques à Moscou, Warszawa 1970.
Poland to the 14th International Congress of Historical Sciences, San Francisco, Warszawa 1975.
Polski Słownik Biograficzny (Polish Biographical Dictionary), ed. by W. Konopczyński, K. Lepszy, E. Rostworowski. Vol. I–XX, Kraków–Wrocław 1935–1977 et sqq.
J. Rutkowski, *Historia gospodarcza Polski* (Economic History of Poland). Vol. I, II, Poznań 1946–1950.
Słownik Historii Polski (Lexicon of Polish History), VI ed., Warszawa 1973.
Zarys historii gospodarstwa wiejskiego w Polsce (An Outline of the History of Polish Agriculture). Vol. I, II, Warszawa 1964.
Zarys dziejów wojskowości polskiej do roku 1864 (An Outline of Polish Military History up to 1864), Warszawa 1965–1966.

C. TEXT-BOOKS COVERING LONGER PERIODS

R. Grodecki, S. Zachorowski, J. Dąbrowski, *Dzieje Polski średniowiecznej* (History of Medieval Poland). Vol. I, II, Kraków 1926.
W. Konopczyński, *Dzieje Polski nowożytnej* (History of Modern Poland), 2nd ed. Vol. I, II, London 1958–1959.
M. Kukiel, *Dzieje Polski porozbiorowej 1795–1921* (History of Poland after the Partitions), London 1961.

D. HISTORY OF VARIOUS REGIONS AND TOWNS

M. M. Drozdowski, A. Zahorski, *Historia Warszawy* (History of Warsaw), 2nd ed., Warszawa 1974.
Dzieje Szczecina (History of Szczecin), ed. by G. Labuda. Vol. II (up to 1805), Warszawa 1963.
Dzieje Wielkopolski (The History of Great Poland), ed. by J. Topolski, W. Jakóbczyk. Vol. I–II, Poznań 1965–1973.
Dzieje Wrocławia (History of Wrocław), ed. by K. Maleczyński. Vol. I, Warszawa 1958.
Dziesięć wieków Poznania (Poznań's Ten Centuries), ed. by K. Malinowski. Vol. I–III, Poznań–Warszawa 1956.
I. Gieysztorowa, A. Zahorski, J. Łukasiewicz, *Cztery wieki Mazowsza. Szkice z dziejów 1526–1914* (Four Centuries of the History of Mazovia. Sketches from the History 1526–1914), Warszawa 1968.
Historia Pomorza (The History of Pomerania), ed. G. Labuda. Vol. I–II, Poznań 1971–1976.

Historia Śląska (History of Silesia), ed. by K. Maleczyński. Vol. I, Wrocław 1960–1961.
Kraków. Studia nad rozwojem miasta (Cracow. Studies on the Development of the City), ed. by J. Dąbrowski, Kraków 1957.
G. Labuda, *Polska granica zachodnia. Tysiąc lat dziejów politycznych* (Poland's Western Frontier. A Thousand Years of Political History), 2nd ed., Poznań 1974.
Osiemnaście wieków Kalisza (Kalisz and Its Eighteen Centuries), ed. by A. Gieysztor and K. Dąbrowski. Vol. I–III, Kalisz 1960–1962.
Szkice z dziejów Pomorza (Sketches from the History of Pomerania), ed. by G. Labuda and S. Hoszowski. Vol. I, II, Warszawa 1958–1959.

MEDIEVAL POLAND
(Up to the End of the fifteenth Century)

A. MAIN PUBLICATIONS OF SOURCES

Monumenta Poloniae Historica. Vol. I–VI Anastatic reprint, Warszawa 1960–1961.
Monumenta Poloniae Historica. Nova Series. Vol. I–III, IV, VI, VII, VIII, IX, X, Kraków–Warszawa 1946–1976 et sqq.

B. MAIN REFERENCE BOOKS

P. David, *Les sources de l'histoire de Pologne à l'époque des Piasts*, Paris 1934.
J. Dąbrowski, *Dawne dziejopisarstwo polskie (do roku 1480)* (Ancient Polish Historiography till 1480), Wrocław–Warszawa–Kraków 1964.
Dzieje sztuki polskiej (The History of Polish Art). Vol. I : *Sztuka polska przedromańska i romańska do schyłku XIII w.* (Pre-Romanesque and Romanesque Art in the Late 13th Century), ed. by M. Walicki, Warszawa 1971.
Z. Kozłowska-Budkowa, *Repertorium polskich dokumentów doby piastowskiej* (Register of Polish Documents of the Piast Era). Vol. I, Kraków 1947. (In the introduction major publications of collections of medieval documents are also recorded).
Słownik starożytności słowiańskich (Lexicon Antiquitatum Slavicarum). Vol. I (A–E); vol. II (F–K); vol. III (L–M); vol. IV (P–R); vol. V (S–Ś), Wrocław 1961–1975 et sqq.

C. MORE IMPORTANT AND RECENT WORKS RELATED TO VARIOUS PERIODS AND PROBLEMS

1. SLAVONIC ANTIQUITY

W. Hensel, *Ziemie polskie w pradziejach* (Ancient Polish Territories), Warszawa 1969.
K. Jażdżewski, *Ancient Peoples and Places of Poland*, London 1965.
H. Łowmiański, *Początki Polski* (The Rise of Poland). Vol. I–V, Warszawa 1963–1973.
K. Tymieniecki, *Ziemie polskie w starożytności. Ludy i kultury najdawniejsze* (Polish Lands in Ancient Times. Peoples and Culture), Poznań 1951.

2. THE ORIGINS OF THE POLISH STATE

J. Kostrzewski, *Kultura prapolska* (Ancient Polish Culture), 3rd ed., Warszawa 1962. French translation of the 2nd ed. : *Les Origines de la civilisation polonaise. Préhistoire—protohistoire*, Paris 1949.
Początki państwa polskiego. Księga Tysiąclecia (The Beginning of the Polish State. Book of the Millenium). Vol. I, II, Poznań 1962.
Z. Podwińska, *Zmiany form osadnictwa wiejskiego na ziemiach polskich we wczesnym średniowieczu* (Changes in Rural Settlement on Polish Lands in the Early Middle Ages), Wrocław 1971.
Polska pierwszych Piastów. Państwo, społeczeństwo, kultura (Poland of the First Piasts. State, Society, Culture), 2nd ed., ed. by T. Manteuffel, Warszawa 1973.
S. Trawkowski, *Jak powstała Polska* (The Foundation of Poland), 4th ed., Warszawa 1968.
A. Żaki, *Archeologia Małopolski wczesnośredniowiecznej* (Archaeology of Early Medieval Little Poland), Wrocław 1974.

3. THE YOUTH OF THE POLISH STATE

K. Buczek, *Ziemie polskie przed tysiącem lat. Zarys geograficzno-historyczny* (Polish Lands Thousand Years Ago. A Geographical and Historical Outline), Wrocław 1960.
S. Kętrzyński, *Polska X–XI wieku* (Poland in the 10th and 11th Centuries), Warszawa 1961.
L'Europe aux IXe–XIe siècles. Aux origines des Etats nationaux, ed. by T. Manteuffel and A. Gieysztor, Varsovie 1968.
K. Maleczyński, *Bolesław III Krzywousty* (Bolesław III the Wrymouth), Wrocław 1975.

4. THE AGE OF MATURITY

Mistrza Wincentego kronika polska (Polish Chronicle by Master Wincenty), ed. K. Abgarowicz, B. Kürbis, Warszawa 1974.
Les Origines des villes polonaises, ed. by P. Francastel, Paris 1960.
S. Smolka, *Mieszko Stary i jego wiek* (Mieszko the Old and His Age), 2nd ed., Warszawa 1959.
T. Wojciechowski, *Szkice historyczne jedenastego wieku* (Historical Sketches of the 11th Century), 3rd ed., Warszawa 1951.

5. THE AGE OF ECONOMIC PROGRESS AND THE CHANGING SOCIETY

J. Baszkiewicz, *Powstanie zjednoczonego państwa polskiego na przełomie XIII i XIV w.* (The Rise of a United Polish State at the Turn of the 13th Century), Warszawa 1954.
H. Dąbrowski, *Rozwój gospodarki rolnej w Polsce od XII do połowy XIV wieku*, in : *Studia z dziejów gospodarstwa wiejskiego* (The Development of Agriculture in Poland from the 12th till the Mid–14th Century in : Essays on the History of Rural Economy). Vol. I, Warszawa 1962.
Polska dzielnicowa i zjednoczona. Państwo, społeczeństwo, kultura (Poland of the Ducal Provinces and United Poland. State, Society, Culture), ed. by A. Gieysztor, Warszawa 1972.
Z. Świechowski, *Budownictwo romańskie w Polsce. Katalog zabytków* (Romanesque Architecture in Poland. A Catalogue of Monuments of Art), Wrocław 1963.
B. Zientara, *Henryk Brodaty i jego czasy* (Henry I the Bearded and His Time), Warszawa 1975.

6. CORONA REGNI POLONIAE AT THE PEAK OF ITS POWER

M. Biskup, *Trzynastoletnia wojna z Zakonem Krzyżackim 1454–1466* (The Thirteen Years' War with Teutonic Knights 1454–1466), Warszawa 1967.

J. Dąbrowski, *Korona Królestwa Polskiego w XIV wieku* (The Polish Crown in the 14th Century), Wrocław 1955.

Z. Kaczmarczyk, *Monarchia Kazimierza Wielkiego* (The Kingdom of Casimir the Great). Vol. I, II, Poznań 1939–1946.

P. W. Knoll, *The Rise of the Polish Monarchy, Piast Poland in East Central Europe, 1320–1370*, Chicago 1972.

S. Kuczyński, *Wielka wojna z Zakonem Krzyżackim w latach 1409–1411* (The Great War with the Teutonic Knights 1409–1411), 3rd ed., Warszawa 1966.

H. Samsonowicz, *Złota jesień polskiego średniowiecza* (The Golden Autumn of Medieval Poland), Warszawa 1971.

Sztuka i ideologia XIV wieku (Art and Ideology of the 14th Century), ed. by P. Skubiszewski, Warszawa 1975.

M. Walicki, *Malarstwo Polskie. Gotyk, renesans, wczesny manieryzm* (Polish Painting. Gothic, Renaissance and Early Manierism), Warszawa 1961.

THE COMMONWEALTH OF THE GENTRY

(From the sixteenth to the eighteenth Century)

A. MAIN PUBLICATIONS OF SOURCES

Akty powstania Kościuszki (Acts of the Kościuszko Insurrection). Vol. I–III, Kraków–Wrocław 1918–1955.

Materiały do dziejów Sejmu Czteroletniego (Source Material for the History of the Four Years' Seym), compiled by J. Woliński, J. Michalski, E. Rostworowski. Vol. I–V, Wrocław 1955–1964 et sqq.

(Volumina legum). Prawa, konstytucye y przywileie Królestwa Polskiego y Wielkiego Xięstwa Litewskiego y wszystkich Prowincyi należących... uchwalone (The Laws, Constitutions and Privileges of the Kingdom of Poland and the Grand Duchy of Lithuania). Vol. I–VIII, Warszawa 1733–1782; vol. IX, Kraków 1889; vol. X, Poznań 1952.

B. MORE IMPORTANT AND RECENT WORKS RELATED TO VARIOUS PERIODS AND PROBLEMS

B. Baranowski, *Kultura ludowa w XVII i XVIII w. na ziemiach polskich* (Folk Culture in the 17th and 18th Centuries on Polish Territories), Łódź 1971.

J. S. Bystroń, *Dzieje obyczajów w dawnej Polsce, wiek XVI–XVIII* (The History of Customs in the Past in Poland, 16th–18th Centuries), 3rd ed. Vol. I–II, Warszawa 1976.

W. Konopczyński, *Dzieje Polski nowożytnej* (History of Modern Poland), 2nd ed. Vol. 1 *(1506–1648)*; vol. 2 *(1648–1795)*, London 1958.

W. Konopczyński, *Le liberum veto. Étude sur le développement du principe majoritaire*, Paris 1930.

Kościół w Polsce (The Church in Poland), ed. J. Kłoczowski. Vol. 2: wieki XVI–XVIII (16th–18th Centuries), Kraków 1969.

Errata

Page	Line	For	Read
118	9	Victory	Viceroy
149	34	of voivodship	or voivodship
245	23	Augustus II	Augustus III
275	38	clumsy alliance	a clumsy alliance
309	10	Russia	Russian

History of Poland

S. Kot, *Rzeczpospolita Polska w literaturze politycznej Zachodu* (The Polish Commonwealth in Western Political Literature), Kraków 1919.
W. Kula, *Teoria ekonomiczna ustroju feudalnego* (The Economic Theory of the Feudal System), Warszawa 1962.
J. Maciszewski, *Szlachta polska i jej państwo* (The Polish Gentry and Their State), Warszawa 1969.
H. Olszewski, *Sejm Rzeczypospolitej epoki oligarchii 1652-1763* (The Seym of the Commonwealth in the Age of Oligarchy 1652-1763), Poznań 1966.
A. Wyczański, *Polska Rzecząpospolitą szlachecką 1454-1764* (Poland the Commonwealth of the Gentry), Warszawa 1965.

1. THE SIXTEENTH CENTURY. SOCIAL AND ECONOMIC QUESTIONS

M. Bogucka, *Gdańsk jako ośrodek produkcyjny w XIV-XVIII w.* (Gdańsk as a Production Centre), Warszawa 1962.
H. Łowmiański, *Uwagi w sprawie podłoża społecznego i gospodarczego unii jagiellońskiej* (Remarks on the Social and Economic Background of the Jagiellonian Union), Wilno 1935.
S. Mielczarski, *Rynek zbożowy na ziemiach polskich w drugiej połowie XVI i pierwszej XVII wieku* (The Grain Market on Polish Territories in the Late 16th and Early 17th Centuries), Gdańsk 1962.
R. Rybarski, *Handel i polityka handlowa Polski w XVI stuleciu* (Poland's Trade and Her Commercial Policy in the 16th Century), 2nd ed. Vol. I, II, Warszawa 1958.
A. Tarnawski, *Działalność gospodarcza Jana Zamoyskiego kanclerza i hetmana w. kor. (1572-1605)* (The Economic Activity of Jan Zamoyski), Lwów 1935.
A. Wyczański, *Studia nad folwarkiem szlacheckim w Polsce w latach 1500-1580* (Studies on the Gentry's Manor Farm in Poland 1500-1580), Warszawa 1960.
L. Żytkowicz, *Studia nad gospodarstwem wiejskim w dobrach kościelnych XVI w.* (Studies on Agriculture of Church Estates in the 16th Century), Warszawa 1962.

2. LEGAL AND CONSTITUTIONAL PROBLEMS

K. Grzybowski, *Teoria reprezentacji w Polsce epoki Odrodzenia* (The Theory of Representation in Poland at the Renaissance Period), Warszawa 1959.
I. Kaniewska, *Małopolska reprezentacja stanowa za czasów Zygmunta Augusta, 1548-1572* (Little Poland Class Representation During the Reign of Sigismund Augustus), Kraków 1974.
A. Sucheni-Grabowska, *Monarchia dwu ostatnich Jagiellonów a ruch egzekucyjny* (The Monarchy during the Reign of the Last Two Jagiellons and the "execution movement"). Part 1: *Geneza egzekucji dóbr* (Genesis of the Movement to Bring about Legislation for the Restitution of the Royal Gifts to the Magnates in the Form of Landed Estates), Wrocław 1974.

3. GENERAL PROBLEMS OF THE RENAISSANCE PERIOD

Odrodzenie w Polsce. Księga zbiorowa (The Renaissance in Poland. Collective Work). Vol. I—History, Warszawa 1955.
Polska w epoce Odrodzenia. Państwo-społeczeństwo-kultura (Poland during the Epoch of the Renaissance. State-Society-Culture), ed. by A. Wyczański, Warszawa 1970.
Społeczeństwo staropolskie. Studia i szkice (Society in Ancient Poland. Studies and Sketches), ed. by A. Wyczański, Warszawa 1976.

Swojskość i cudzoziemszczyzna w dziejach kultury polskiej (Polish and Foreign Influence in the History of Polish Culture), ed. by Z. Stefanowska, Warszawa 1973.

Tradycje szlacheckie w kulturze polskiej (Gentry Traditions in Polish Culture), ed. by Z. Stefanowska, Warszawa 1976.

4. POLITICAL HISTORY

A. Dembińska, *Polityczna walka o egzekucję dóbr królewskich w latach 1559–1564* (The Political Struggle for Treasury Contributions from Royal Estates in 1559–1564), Warszawa 1935.

L. Kolankowski, *Zygmunt August wielki książę Litwy do roku 1548* (Sigismund Augustus Grand Duke of Lithuania up to 1548), Lwów 1913.

W. Pociecha, *Królowa Bona (1494–1557)* (The Queen Bona, 1494–1557). Vol. I–IV, Poznań 1949–1958.

Z. Wojciechowski, *Zygmunt Stary (1506–1548)* (Sigismundus the Old, 1506–1548), Warszawa 1946.

5. THE REFORMATION AND THE COUNTER-REFORMATION

A. Brückner, *Różnowiercy polscy* (The Polish Dissidents), 2nd ed., Warszawa 1962.

L. Chmaj, *Bracia polscy. Ludzie, idee, wpływy* (The Polish Brethren. People, Ideas and Influence), Warszawa 1957.

A. Jobert, *De Luther à Mohila. La Pologne dans la crise de la Chrétienté 1517–1648*, Paris 1974.

K. E. Jordt Jorgensen, *Ökumenische Bestrebungen unter den polnischen Protestanten bis zum Jahre 1645*, Kobenhavn 1942.

S. Kot, *Socinianism in Poland. The Social and Political Ideal of the Polish Antitrinitarians in Sixteenth and Seventeenth Centuries*, Boston 1957.

S. Kot, *Andrzej Frycz Modrzewski. Studium z dziejów kultury polskiej XVI w.* (Andrzej Frycz Modrzewski. A Study on the History of Polish Sixteenth Century Culture), 2nd ed., Kraków 1923.

G. Schramm, *Der polnische Adel und die Reformation, 1548–1607*, Wiesbaden 1965.

Studia nad arianizmem (Studies on Arianism), ed. by L. Chmaj, Warszawa 1959.

L. Szczucki, *W kręgu myślicieli heretyckich* (In the Milieu of Heretic Philosophers), Wrocław 1972.

J. Tazbir, *A State without Stakes. Polish Religious Toleration in the Sixteenth and Seventeenth Centuries*, New York–Warszawa 1973.

6. SCIENCE AND CULTURE

Andrzej Frycz Modrzewski i problemy kultury polskiego Odrodzenia (Andrzej Frycz Modrzewski and Cultural Problems of the Polish Renaissance), ed. by R. Bieńkowski, Wrocław 1974.

C. Backwis, *Szkice o kulturze staropolskiej* (Sketches on Ancient Polish Culture), Warszawa 1975.

H. Barycz, *Dzieje nauki w Polsce w epoce Odrodzenia* (The History of Science and Learning in Poland at the Renaissance Period), Warszawa 1957.

L. A. Birkenmajer, *Mikołaj Kopernik* (Nicolaus Copernicus). Part 1, Kraków 1900.

Kultura staropolska (Ancient Polish Culture), Kraków 1932.

T. Mańkowski, *Genealogia sarmatyzmu polskiego* (The Genealogy of Sarmatism), Warszawa 1946.
Renesans. Sztuka i ideologia (Renaissance. Art and Ideology), Warszawa 1974.
P. Rybicki, *Odrodzenie* (Renaissance), in: *Historia nauki polskiej* (History of Polish Science). Vol. 1, ed. by B. Suchodolski, Wrocław 1970.
T. Ulewicz, *Sarmacja. Studium z problematyki słowiańskiej XV i XVI w.* (Sarmatia. A Study on Slavonic Problems 15th and 16th cent.), Kraków 1950.

7. THE SEVENTEENTH CENTURY

E. Angyal, *Die slawische Barockwelt*, Leipzig 1961.
H. Barycz, *Barok* (Baroque), in: *Historia nauki polskiej* (History of Polish Science). Vol. II, Wrocław 1970.
W. Czapliński, *O Polsce siedemnastowiecznej* (Seventeenth-Century Poland), Warszawa 1966.
W. Czapliński, *Władysław IV i jego czasy* (Władysław IV and His Time), 2nd ed., Warszawa 1976.
A. Kersten, *Stefan Czarniecki (1599–1665)*, Warszawa 1963.
J. Maciszewski, *Wojna domowa w Polsce (1606–1609)* (The Civil War in Poland 1606–1609). Part 1, Wrocław 1960.
O naprawę Rzeczypospolitej XVII–XVIII w. (For the Improvement of the Commonwealth, 17th–18th Centuries), ed. by J. Gierowski, Warszawa 1965.
Z. Ogonowski, *Socynianizm a Oświecenie. Studia nad myślą filozoficzno-religijną arian w Polsce XVII w.* (Arianism and the Enlightenment. Studies on the Philosophical and Religious Thought of the Arians in 17th-century Poland), Warszawa 1966.
Polska XVII wieku. Państwo–społeczeństwo–kultura (Seventeenth-Century Poland. State–Society–Culture), ed. by J. Tazbir, 2nd ed., Warszawa 1974.
Polska w okresie drugiej wojny północnej 1655–1660 (Poland During the Second Northern War 1655–1660), ed. by K. Lepszy. Vol. I–III, Warszawa 1957.
J. Tazbir, *Rzeczpospolita a świat. Studia z dziejów kultury XVII wieku* (The Commonwealth and the World. Studies on the History of 17th-century Culture), Wrocław 1971.
M. Wajsblum, *Ex regestro arianismi. Szkice z dziejów upadku protestantyzmu w Polsce* (Essays on the History of the Downfall of Protestantism in Poland), Warszawa 1947.
Wiek XVII–Kontrreformacja–Barok. Prace z historii kultury (Seventeenth-Century-Counter-Reformation. Work on the History of Culture), ed. by J. Pelc, Wrocław 1970.
Z. Wójcik, *Traktat andruszowski i jego geneza* (The Truce of Andruszów and Its Genesis), Warszawa 1959.

8. THE EIGHTEENTH CENTURY

W. Borowy, *O poezji polskiej w wieku XVIII* (On Polish Poetry in the 18th century), Kraków 1948.
W. Konopczyński, *Fryderyk Wielki a Polska* (Frederic the Great and Poland), Poznań 1947.
W. Konopczyński, *Polscy pisarze polityczni XVIII w.* (Eighteenth-Century Polish Political Writers), Warszawa 1966.
J. Rutkowski, *Poddaństwo włościan w XVIII w. w Polsce i niektórych innych krajach Europy* (The Serfdom of the Peasantry in 18th Century Poland and in some other European Countries), Poznań 1921.

9. THE SAXON TIMES

S. Bednarski, *Upadek i odrodzenie szkół jezuickich w Polsce* (Downfall and Revival of Jesuit Colleges in Poland), Kraków 1933.

J. Feldman, *Stanisław Leszczyński*, 2nd ed., Warszawa 1959.

J. Gierowski, *Między saskim absolutyzmem a złotą wolnością. Z dziejów wewnętrznych Rzeczypospolitej w latach 1712–1715* (Between Saxon Absolute Rule and the Golden Freedom. Internal Problems of the Polish Commonwealth in 1712–1715), Wrocław 1953.

W. Konopczyński, *Polska w dobie wojny siedmioletniej* (Poland During the Seven Years' War). Part I, II, Warszawa 1909–1911.

E. Rostworowski, *O polską koronę. Polityka Francji w latach 1725–1733* (For the Polish Crown. Policy of France in 1725–1733), Wrocław 1958.

Um die Polnische Krone. Sachsen und Polen während des Nordischen Krieges, 1700–1721 (Collective work of Polish and German scholars), Berlin 1962.

10. THE ENLIGHTENMENT PERIOD. SOCIAL AND ECONOMIC PROBLEMS

W. Kula, *Szkice o manufakturach w Polsce XVIII wieku* (Studies on Manufactures in 18th-Century Poland), Warszawa 1956.

R. Rybarski, *Skarbowość Polski w dobie rozbiorów* (Finances of Poland in the Period of Partitions), Kraków 1937.

11. POLITICAL HISTORY

B. Dembiński, *Polska na przełomie* (Poland at Cross-Roads), Lwów–Warszawa–Poznań [1913].

O. Forst-Battaglia, *Stanisław August Poniatowski und der Ausgang des alten Polenstaates*, Berlin 1927.

W. Kalinka, *Der vierjährige Polnische Reichstag 1788–1791 (Aus dem polnischen übersetzte deutsche Originalausgabe)*. Vol. I, II, Berlin 1896–1898.

H. H. Kaplan, *The First Partition of Poland*, New York–London 1962.

W. Konopczyński, *Konfederacja Barska* (Bar Confederation). Vol. I, II, Warszawa 1936–1938.

W. Konopczyński, *Geneza i ustanowienie Rady Nieustającej* (The Origins and the Establishment of the Permanent Council), Kraków 1917.

B. Leśnodorski, *Polscy jakobini* (The Polish Jacobins), Warszawa 1960. French edition: *Les jacobins polonais*, Paris 1965.

R. H. Lord, *The Second Partition of Poland*, Cambridge 1915.

E. Rostworowski, *Ostatni król Rzeczypospolitej—geneza i upadek Konstytucji 3 maja* (The Last King of Commonwealth. The Origin and the End of the Constitution of 3rd May), Warszawa 1966.

W. Tokarz, *Insurekcja warszawska* (The Warsaw Insurrection), 2nd ed., Warszawa 1950.

12. CULTURE IN THE AGE OF REASON

M. Chamcówna, *Uniwersytet Jagielloński w dobie Komisji Edukacji Narodowej* (The Jagiellonian University at the Time of the Commission for National Education). Vol. I, II, Wrocław 1957–1959.

J. Fabre, *Stanislas-Auguste Poniatowski et l'Europe des Lumières*, Paris 1952.
A. Jobert, *La Commission d'Education Nationale en Pologne (1773–1794), son œuvre d'instruction civique*, Paris 1941.
W. Smoleński, *Przewrót umysłowy w Polsce wieku XVIII* (The Intellectual Revolution in Eighteenth Century Poland), 3rd ed., Warszawa 1949.

POLAND UNDER FOREIGN RULE
(1795–1918)

A. MAIN PUBLICATIONS OF SOURCES

Dyaryusz sejmu z r. 1830–1831 (Minutes of the Seym Proceedings in 1830–1831), ed. by M. Rostworowski. Vol. I–VI, Kraków 1907–1912.
Galicyjska działalność wojskowa Piłsudskiego 1906–1914 (Piłsudski's Military Activity in Galicia), ed. by S. Arski, J. Chudek, Warszawa 1967.
Polskie programy socjalistyczne 1878–1918 (Polish Socialist Programmes). Selection and commentary by F. Tych, Warszawa 1975.
PPS-Lewica. Materiały i dokumenty 1906–1918 (The PPS Left Wing. Materials and Documents, 1906–1918), ed. by F. Tych, J. Kancewicz, J. Kasprzakowa. Vol. I, II, Warszawa 1961–1962.
Socjaldemokracja Królestwa Polskiego i Litwy. Materiały i dokumenty (The Social-democracy of the Kingdom of Poland and Lithuania. Materials and Documents), ed. by H. Buczek, F. Tych. Vol. I, II, Warszawa 1957–1963.
Ustawodawstwo Księstwa Warszawskiego (The Legislation of the Duchy of Warsaw), ed. by W. Bartel, J. Kosim, W. Rostocki. Vol. I–III, Warszawa 1964–1967.
Walki chłopów Królestwa Polskiego w rewolucji 1905–1907 (The Fighting of the Peasantry of the Kingdom of Poland in the 1905–1907 Revolution), ed. by S. Kalabiński, F. Tych. Vol. I–III, Warszawa 1958–1961.
Vosstanie 1863 goda. Materiały i dokumenty. Powstanie styczniowe. Materiały i dokumenty (The January Insurrection. Materials and Documents), ed. by E. Halicz, L. Jakovlev, S. Kieniewicz, V. Koroluk, I. Miller, F. Ramotowska, Moskva–Warszawa 1961 et sqq.
Źródła do dziejów klasy robotniczej na ziemiach polskich (Sources for the History of the Working Class on Polish Territory). Vol. I (part 1, 2), II, ed. by N. Gąsiorowska-Grabowska, Warszawa 1962; vol. III (part 1), ed. by S. Kalabiński, Warszawa 1968.

B. MORE IMPORTANT AND RECENT WORKS RELATED TO VARIOUS PERIODS AND PROBLEMS

B. Bajer, *Przemysł włókienniczy na ziemiach polskich od początku XIX wieku do 1939 roku* (The Textile Industry in Polish Territory from the Early 19th Century till 1939), Łódź 1958.
Ekonomika górnictwa i hutnictwa w Królestwie Polskim 1840–1910 (The Economics of Mining and of the Iron and Steel Industry in the Kingdom of Poland 1840–1910), ed. by W. Kula. Vol. I, II, Warszawa 1959–1961.
K. Grzybowski, *Galicja 1848–1914. Historia ustroju politycznego na tle historii ustroju Austrii* (Galicia 1848–1914. Constitutional History against the Background of the Austrian Constitutional History), Wrocław 1959.

W. Jakóbczyk, *Studia nad dziejami Wielkopolski w XIX w. Dzieje pracy organicznej* (Studies on the History of Great Poland in the 19th Century. The History of "Organic Work"). Vol. I, II, Poznań 1951–1959.

A. Jezierski, *Handel zagraniczny Królestwa Polskiego 1815–1914* (The Foreign Trade of the Kingdom of Poland, 1815–1914), Warszawa 1967.

S. Kieniewicz, *The Emancipation of Polish Peasantry*. The University of Chicago Press, 1969.

S. Kowalczyk, J. Kowal, W. Stankiewicz, M. Stański, *Zarys historii polskiego ruchu ludowego* (Outline of the History of the Polish Peasant Movement). Vol. I (1864–1918), Warszawa 1963; vol. II (J. Borkowski, J. Kowal, S. Lato, W. Stankiewicz), Warszawa 1970.

W. Kula, *Historia gospodarcza Polski w dobie popowstaniowej 1864–1918* (Economic History of Poland after the Insurrection, 1864–1918), Warszawa 1947.

W. Kula, *Kształtowanie się kapitalizmu w Polsce* (The Shaping of Capitalism in Poland), Warszawa 1955.

T. Łepkowski, *Początki klasy robotniczej Warszawy* (The Origins of Warsaw's Working Class), Warszawa 1956.

J. Łukasiewicz, *Przewrót techniczny w przemyśle Królestwa Polskiego 1852–1886* (The Technical Revolution in the Industry of the Congress Kingdom of Poland, 1852–1886), Warszawa 1963.

K. Orzechowski, *Chłopskie posiadanie ziemi na Górnym Śląsku u schyłku epoki feudalnej* (Peasant Land-Holdings in Upper Silesia during the Decline of Feudalism), Opole 1959.

I. Pietrzak-Pawłowska, *Królestwo Polskie w początkach imperializmu 1900–1905* (The Kingdom of Poland at the Beginning of Imperialism, 1900–1905), Warszawa 1955.

W. Pobóg-Malinowski, *Najnowsza historia polityczna Polski* (The Newest Political History of Poland). Vol. I–III, Paris 1953–1960.

R. Rozdolski, *Stosunki poddańcze w dawnej Galicji* (Serfdom Relations in Former Galicia). Vol. I, II, Warszawa 1962.

J. Wąsicki, *Ziemie polskie pod zaborem pruskim* (Polish Lands under Prussian Rule). Vol. I. (South Prussia 1793–1806); vol. II (New Eastern Prussia 1795–1806), Wrocław 1957–1963.

H. Wereszycki, *Historia polityczna Polski w dobie popowstaniowej 1864–1918* (Political History of Poland after the Insurrection, 1864–1918), Warszawa 1948.

1. THE NAPOLEONIC ERA

S. Askenazy, *Napoleon a Polska* (Napoleon and Poland). Vol. I–III, Warszawa 1918–1919.

E. Halicz, *Geneza Księstwa Warszawskiego. Studia* (The Origin of the Duchy of Warsaw. Essays), Warszawa 1962.

M. Handelsman, *Napoléon et la Pologne (1806–1807)*, Paris 1909.

M. Kukiel, *Czartoryski and European Unity 1770–1861*, Princeton 1955.

G. Zych, *Armia Księstwa Warszawskiego 1807–1812* (The Army of the Duchy of Warsaw, 1807–1812), Warszawa 1961.

2. THE CONGRESS KINGDOM OF POLAND AND THE NOVEMBER INSURRECTION

S. Askenazy, *Łukasiński*. Vol. I, II, 2nd ed., Warszawa 1929.

J. Dutkiewicz, *Francja a Polska w 1831 r.* (France and Poland in 1831), Łódź 1950.

R. F. Leslie, *Polish Politics and the Revolution of November 1830*, London 1956.

M. Meloch, *Sprawa włościańska w powstaniu listopadowym* (The Peasant Question during the November Insurrection), 2nd ed., Warszawa 1948.

W. Tokarz, *Wojna polsko-rosyjska 1830–1831* (The Polish-Russian War of 1830–1831), Warszawa 1930.

S. Wachholz, *Rzeczpospolita Krakowska. Okres 1815–1830* (The Free State of Cracow. Period from 1815 to 1830), Warszawa 1957.

W. Zajewski, *Walki wewnętrzne ugrupowań politycznych w powstaniu listopadowym* (Internal Political Struggle in the November Uprising), Gdańsk 1967.

3. THE GREAT EMIGRATION AND THE EUROPEAN REVOLUTION 1848

M. Handelsman, *Czartoryski, Nicolas I et la question du Proche Orient,* Paris 1934.

M. Handelsman, *Adam Czartoryski.* Vol. I–III, Warszawa 1948–1950.

S. Kieniewicz, *Ruch chłopski w Galicji* (The Peasant Movement in Galicia), Wrocław 1951.

S. Kieniewicz, *Społeczeństwo polskie w powstaniu poznańskim 1848* (The Polish People in the Poznań Uprising 1848), Warszawa 1960.

E. Kozłowski, *Generał Józef Bem* (General Józef Bem), Warszawa 1958.

4. THE JANUARY INSURRECTION

S. Bóbr-Tylingo, *Napoléon III, l'Europe et la Pologne en 1863–1864,* in : *Antemurale.* Vol. VII, VIII, Roma 1963.

J. Feldman, *Bismarck a Polska* (Bismarck and Poland), 3rd ed., Warszawa 1966.

F. H. Gentzen, *Grosspolen im Januaraufstand. Das Grossherzogtum Posen 1858–1864,* Berlin 1958.

S. Kalembka, *Towarzystwo Demokratyczne Polskie w latach 1832–1846* (The Polish Democratic Society in 1832–1846), Toruń 1966.

S. Kieniewicz, *Powstanie styczniowe* (The January Uprising), Warszawa 1972.

I. Koberdowa, *Wielki Książę Konstanty w Warszawie 1862–1863* (The Grand Duke Constantine in Warsaw 1862–1863), Warszawa 1962.

R. F. Leslie, *Reform and Insurrection in Russian Poland 1856–1865,* London 1963.

H. Wereszycki, *Anglia a Polska w latach 1860–1865* (England and Poland in 1860–1865), Lwów 1934.

S. Zieliński. *Bitwy i potyczki 1863–1864* (Battles and Skirmishes 1863–1864), Rapperswil 1913.

5. THE BEGINNING OF THE WORKERS MOVEMENT

L. Baumgarten, *Dzieje Wielkiego Proletariatu* (History of the Great Proletariat), Warszawa 1965.

Historia polskiego ruchu robotniczego (History of the Polish Labour Movement). Vol. I : *1864–1939,* ed. by T. Daniszewski, Warszawa 1967.

S. Kalabiński, F. Tych, *Czwarte powstanie czy pierwsza rewolucja. Lata 1905–1907 na ziemiach polskich* (The Fourth Uprising or the First Revolution. The years 1905–1907 on Polish Territories), Warszawa 1969.

P. Korzec, *Walka rewolucyjna w Łodzi i okręgu łódzkim w latach 1905–1907* (Revolutionary Struggle in Łódź and the Łódź Area, 1905–1907), Warszawa 1956.

F. Tych, *Związek Robotników Polskich 1889–1892. Anatomia wczesnej organizacji robotniczej* (Union of Polish Workers 1889–1892. The Anatomy of Early Working-Class Organizations), Warszawa 1974.

A. Żarnowska, *Klasa robotnicza Królestwa Polskiego 1870–1914* (The Working Class in the Polish Kingdom 1870–1914), Warszawa 1974.

6. WORLD WAR I

L. Grosfeld, *Polityka państw centralnych wobec sprawy polskiej w latach 1914–1918* (The Policy of the Central Powers Regarding the Polish Question in 1914–1918), Warszawa 1962.
J. Holzer, *Polska Partia Socjalistyczna w latach 1917–1919* (The Polish Socialist Party in 1917–1919), Warszawa 1962.
J. Holzer, J. Molenda, *Polska w czasie I wojny światowej* (Poland during World War I), Warszawa 1963.
H. Jabłoński, *Polska Partia Socjalistyczna w czasie wojny 1914–1918* (The Polish Socialist Party during the 1914–1918 War), Warszawa 1962.
T. Komarnicki, *Rebirth of the Polish Republic. A Study in the Diplomatic History of Europe, 1914–1920*, London 1957.
M. Leczyk, *Komitet Narodowy Polski a Ententa i Stany Zjednoczone 1917–1919* (Poland's National Committee, the Entente and the United States 1917–1919), Warszawa 1966.

POLAND
(1918–1939)

A. MAIN PUBLICATIONS OF SOURCES

Dokumenty i materiały do historii stosunków polsko-radzieckich (Documents and Materials for the History of Polish-Soviet Relations). Vol. I–V, Warszawa 1962–1966.
K. W. Kumaniecki, *Odbudowa państwowości polskiej. Najważniejsze dokumenty 1912–styczeń 1924* (The Rebirth of the Polish State. Most Important Documents 1912–January 1924), Kraków 1924.
Materiały archiwalne do historii stosunków polsko-radzieckich (Archival Materials for the History of Polish-Soviet Relations). Vol. I, Warszawa 1957.

B. MORE IMPORTANT AND RECENT WORKS RELATED TO VARIOUS PROBLEMS

M. Drozdowski, *Polityka gospodarcza rządu polskiego 1936–1939* (The Economic Policy of the Polish Government 1936–1939), Warszawa 1963.
H. Jabłoński, *Narodziny Drugiej Rzeczypospolitej 1918–1919* (The Birth of the Second Republic 1918–1919), Warszawa 1962.
H. and T. Jędruszczak, *Ostatnie lata II Rzeczypospolitej* (The Last Years of the Second Republic of Poland), Warszawa 1970.
J. Kowalski, *Trudne lata. Problemy rozwoju polskiego ruchu robotniczego 1929–1935* (Difficult Years. Problems of the Development of the Polish Workers' Movement, 1929–1935), Warszawa 1966.
J. Krasuski, *Stosunki polsko-niemieckie 1919–1925* (The Polish-German Relations 1919–1925). Part 1, Poznań 1962.
J. Krasuski, *Stosunki polsko-niemieckie 1926–1932* (The Polish-German Relations 1926–1932). Part 2, Poznań 1964.
Z. Landau, J. Tomaszewski, *Zarys historii gospodarczej Polski 1918–1939* (Outline of Polish Economic History 1918–1939), 3rd ed., Warszawa 1971.
C. Madajczyk, *Burżuazyjno-obszarnicza reforma rolna w Polsce 1918–1939* (The Agrarian Reform of the Bourgeoisie and Landlords in Poland 1918–1939), Warszawa 1956.

K. Ostrowski, *Polityka finansowa Polski przedwrześniowej* (The Treasury Policy of Poland before September 1939), Warszawa 1958.

J. Popkiewicz, F. Ryszka, *Przemysł ciężki Górnego Śląska w gospodarce Polski międzywojennej 1922–1939* (The Upper Silesian Heavy Industry and the Economic Policy of Poland between the Two World Wars 1922–1939), Opole 1959.

A. Próchnik, *Pierwsze piętnastolecie Polski niepodległej* (The First Fifteen Years of Independent Poland), 2nd ed., Warszawa 1957.

P. Wandycz, *France and her Eastern Allies 1919–1925. French-Czechoslovak-Polish Relations from the Paris Peace Conference to Locarno*, Minneapolis 1962.

M. Wojciechowski, *Stosunki polsko-niemieckie 1933–1938* (The Polish-German Relations 1933–1938). Part 3, Warszawa 1965.

J. Żarnowski, *Społeczeństwo II Rzeczypospolitej, 1918–1939* (Society in the Second Republic of Poland, 1918–1939), Warszawa 1973.

J. Żarnowski, *Struktura społeczna inteligencji w Polsce w latach 1918–1939* (Social Structure of the Intelligentsia in Poland in 1918–1939), Warszawa 1964.

INDEX

Abramowski Edward (1868–1918) 513
Abyssinia 599
Academy of Science and Letters 463, 468, 568, 593
"Activists" 526, 528, 533
St. Adalbert, Wojciech (c. 955–997), Bishop of Prague 44, 48, 52, 56, 64, 106
Adamski Stanisław (1875–1967) 489
Administrative Council 367, 382, 391, 437, 454
Adriatic 122
Agency (Paris, 1795) 342
Agricultural Society in Warsaw 433, 436, 437, 439
Aigner Piotr (1756–1841) 299
Aiguillon Emmanuel-Armand, duc de (1720–1782) 280
Akkerman 112, 122, 148
Albert (–c. 1377) magistrate in Cracow 85, 101
Albert, Albrecht, II of Hapsburg (1397–1439), King of Germany, Hungary and Bohemia 119
Albrecht Frederick (1553–1618), Duke of Prussia 168
Albrecht I of Hapsburg (1255–1308), German King 99
Albrecht of Hohenzollern (1490–1568), Duke of Prussia 147, 157
Alexander (–1156), Bishop of Płock 78
Alexander (1461–1506), King of Poland 146, 148, 150
Alexander I (1777–1825), Emperor of Russia, King of Poland 345, 346, 347, 356–358, 363, 364, 373, 374, 377, 392

Alexander II (1818–1881), Emperor of Russia 431, 435, 439, 441, 512
Alexander III (1845–1894), Emperor of Russia 491
Aleksandrów 369
Alexis (1629–1676), Tsar of Russia 214
Alfred of Wessex (c. 848–899), King of England 37
"Alldeutscher Verband" (Pan-German Union) 490, 515
"Allgemeiner Deutscher Verband" (General German Union) 490
Allied Supreme Council 549
Allies, Allied Powers 523, 528, 532, 543, 547, 548, 555, 556, see Entente
All-Polish groups 516, 518, 520
Alps 29, 173
Alsace 243
Altmark (truce of, 1629) 190
Alvensleben Gustav (1803–1881) 441
America 170, 471, 499
Amsterdam 233
Andrusikiewicz Jan (1815–1850) 411
Andruszów (truce of, 1667) 217, 222, 223
Andrzej (–c. 1317), Bishop of Poznań 99
Andrzej Gałka of Dobczyn (c. 1400–c. 1450), professor 133
Andrzej Łaskarz of Gosławice (1362–1426), Bishop of Poznań 117
Angevins 107, 114
Ankwicz Józef (c. 1750–1794) 327
Anna (1693–1740), Tsarina of Russia 244
Anna (1795–1865), Grand Duchess of Russia 357

Anna (1476–1503), Duchess of Western Pomerania 125
Anna Jagiellonka (1523–1596), Queen of Poland 167
Apukhtin Alexandr (1822–1903) 491
Aquileia 29
Arab East 50
Archetti Giovanni Andrea (1731–1805) 284
Arcole (battle of, 1796) 343
Arians 155, 160, 161, 169, 191, 197, 200, 217, 225, 229, 231, 233
Armenians 131, 132, 136, 293
Arnholdt Jan (1841–1862) 439
d'Arquien de la Grange Marquis (1613–1707) 220
Arrovaise 78
Askenazy Szymon (1867–1935) 504
Asnyk Adam (1838–1897) 472
Asow 238
Association of the Polish Nation 407
Association of the Polish People 405, 406
Atlantic 225
Attila (–453), Chief of the Huns 33
Auerstädt (battle of, 1806) 346
Augsburg 50, 62
Augusta, Maria Augusta (1782–1863), Princess of Saxony 317
Augustus II (1670–1733), King of Poland 235–243, 246, 247, 250
Augustus III (1696–1763), King of Poland 236, 244, 245, 247, 248, 253, 256, 264, 266, 268, 270
Aukštote 115
Austerlitz (battle of, 1805) 346
Austria 21, 77, 192, 198, 216, 219–222, 235, 239, 242, 244, 245, 247, 251, 268, 271, 275, 280, 281, 305, 306, 309, 320, 322, 339, 341–344, 346, 355, 358, 363, 364, 380, 389, 410–422, 435, 443, 450, 456, 459, 460, 475, 480, 492, 494, 516, 522, 526, 528, 531, 534, 535, 549, 600
Austro-Hungary 483, 513, 514, 556, 557
Avars 33, 45
Axentowicz Teodor (1859–1938) 504

Bacciarelli Marcello (1731–1818) 299
Baden (insurrection of, 1849) 421
Badeni Kazimierz (1846–1909) 494
Balicki Zygmunt (1858–1916) 484, 492, 493
Balkans 21, 32, 33, 208, 280, 281, 341, 346, 404, 447, 484, 514
Baltic 17, 19, 28, 36, 45, 48, 50, 51, 56, 59, 62, 75, 85, 87, 93, 107, 117, 122, 126, 147, 156, 190, 204, 215, 228, 239, 244, 288, people 34, 36, 40, 46, 91, 93
Balts 37, 38, 40
Bar see Confederation of Bar
Baranów 174, 179
Bardowski Piotr (1846–1886) 477
Barnim I (c. 1209–1278), Duke of Western Pomerania 85, 92
Baroque 202, 226, 227, 230, 253, 257, 259, 297
Barss Franciszek (1760–1812) 315, 342
Bartel Kazimierz (1882–1941) 578, 579, 584, 585
Barthou Jean Louis (1862–1934) 590
Basel 333, 343
Bathsheba 106
Baudouin de Courtenay Jan (–1822) 315
Baudouin de Courtenay Jan (1845–1929) 466
Bautzen (Budišyn) 53
Bavaria 37, 49, 50, 228, 305, 322
Bavarian Geographer (9th cent.) 39
Bayle Pierre (1647–1706) 233
Bayonne (treaty of, 1808) 351
Bebel August (1840–1913) 474, 489
Beck Józef (1894–1944) 588–590, 597, 599–603, 605
Beghards 104
Beguines 104
Belcredi Richard (1823–1902) 459
Belgium 77, 380, 551, 566
Bem Józef (1794–1850) 421, 422
Benedek Ludwig (1804–1881) 411
Benedict XIV, Pope (1740–1758) 263
Benedictus Polonus (13th cent.) 104
Benedictines 77, 78, 102, 105
Beneš Eduard (1884–1948) 566
Berchtesgaden 601
Berek Joselewicz (1764–1809) 353
Berent Wacław (1873–1941) 502
Bereza Kartuska 593
Berezina (battle of, 1812) 358, 550
Berg 68
Berg Fiodor (1790–1874) 445, 454
Beresteczko (battle of, 1651) 214
Berlewi Henri (1894) 576
Berlin 267, 268, 275, 306, 309, 346, 394, 414, 417, 433, 453, 456, 489, 490, 500, 516, 525, 530, 534, 566, 586, 589, 590, 599, 600, 603, 605, 607
Bernard (Spanish missionary) 67
Bernardines 131

Berrecci Bartolommeo (c. 1480–1537) 174
Berwiński Ryszard (1819–1879) 426
Besançon 399
Beseler Hans (1850–1921) 525, 526, 527, 528, 530
Bessarabia 565
Bestuzhev-Riumin Alexis (1693–1766) 246
Bethlen Gabor (1580–1629), Duke of Transylvania 189
Beust Friedrich Ferdinand von (1809–1886) 459
Bezdany (raid of, 1908) 519
Bezprym (986–1031), Duke of Poland 55
Biała Cerkiew (Byelaya Tserkov) 214
Białobrzeski Marcin (c. 1530–1586) 201
Białystok 258, 347, 384, 394, 476, 549, 551, 557
Biecz 174
Bielecki Marian (1876–1912) 512
Bielski Marcin (c. 1495–1575) 173
Biernat of Lublin (c. 1465–c. 1529) 171, 173
Biliński Leon (1846–1923) 518
Biłgoraj 196
Biron Ernst Johann (1690–1772) 244, 268
Biskupin 27
Bismarck Otto (1815–1898) 441, 456, 458, 483, 490
Black Death 127
Black Sea 19, 29, 87, 107, 112, 115, 120, 122, 126, 127, 148, 188, 190, 281, 288, 289, 305, 320, 340
Block of Christian National Unity 558
"Block" (group of artists) 576
Blocke Abraham van den (1572–1628) 230
Blocke Wilhelm van den (c. 1550–1628) 230
Bobola Andrzej (1540–1616) 185
Bobrowski Stefan (1841–1863) 443
Bobrzanie 40
Bobrzyński Michał (1849–1935) 470, 517, 518, 522
Bochnia 292
Bochum Polish Workers' Union 489
Bodin Jean (1530–1596) 146
Bogumił (–1092), Archbishop of Gniezno 65
Bogusław I (–1187), Duke of Western Pomerania 92
Bogusław X (1454–1523), Duke of Western Pomerania 125
Bogusław XIV (1625–1637), Duke of Western Pomerania 206
Bogusławski Wojciech (1757–1829) 300
Bogusza (–1320), judge of Gdańsk-Pomerania 101
Bogusz family 411
Bohemia 28, 31, 37, 41, 47, 49, 50, 51, 52, 53, 65, 66, 67, 77, 87, 99, 101, 107, 108, 118, 119, 121, 126, 148, 168, 187, 189, 190, 252, 422
Bohemian Brethren 159, 160, 161, 199
Bohomolec Franciszek (1720–1784) 259, 300
Bohuszewicz Maria (1865–1887) 478
Bolesław I the Brave (966–1025), King of Poland 52, 55–57, 59, 62, 65, 73, 75, 608
Bolesław II the Bold (1039–1081), King of Poland 65, 72, 77
Bolesław III the Wrymouth (1086–1138) Duke of Poland 66–68, 71, 76, 78, 89
Bolesław II the Curly (1125–1173), Grand Duke of Poland 68, 69, 90
Bolesław the Pious (1221–1279), Duke of Great Poland 91, 131
Bolesław the Chaste (1226–1279), Duke of Cracow-Sandomierz 86, 89, 90
Bolesław George of Mazovia (–1340), Prince of Vladimir-Halicz 112
Bolestraszycki Samuel (17th cent.) 200
Bolko II (1312–1368), Duke of Świdnica 126
Bologna 104
Bolsheviks 545, 550, 605
Bona Sforza (1494–1557), wife of Sigismund I 150, 171, 179
Bonaparte Jerôme (1784–1860) 347
Bonaparte Napoleon Joseph (1822–1891) 435
Boner family 174
Boniface VIII Pope (1294–1303) 99
Boris (1112–1155), Prince of Hungary 67
Bornholm 29
Borodino (battle of, 1812) 357
Borowski Wacław (1885–1954) 576
Borysław 487, 560
Borzykowa 91
Bosnia 514
Bosphorus 208
Bossuta-Bożęta (–1028), Archbishop of Gniezno 64
Boulanger Nadia (1887) 576
Bonnard Pierre (1867–1947) 576

Bourbons 243
Boznańska Olga (1865-1940) 504
Bracław 217, 220, 222
Brandenburg, Brandenburges 91, 92, 95, 99, 101, 111, 125, 211, 216-218, 200, 222, 228, 235
Brandenburg-Prussian State 251, 253
Branicki Jan Klemens (1689-1771) 258, 265, 269-271
Branicki Ksawery (1730-1819) 277, 283, 284, 286, 287, 306, 308, 309, 315, 320, 322
Brasil 498
Breinl Joseph 410
Bretislav I (c. 1012-1055), Duke of Bohemia 56
Breyer Tadeusz (1874-1952) 576
Brodnia 368
Brodnica 390
Brodowski Antoni (1784-1832) 379
Brody 196
Broniewski Władysław (1897-1962) 571
Brożek Jan (1585-1652) 175, 232
Brühl Heinrich von (1700-1763) 245, 246, 250, 251, 266
Bruno of Querfurt (c. 974-1009), Archbishop *gentium* 48, 64
Brusilov Alexiej (1853-1926) 526
Brussels 401, 413, 425, 474
Bryansk 115
Brzeg 126, 204
Brześć (Brest Litovsk) 118, 173, 552, 584, 585
— privilege of (1425) see Law
— treaty of (1917-1918) 531, 532, 534
— union of (1595/1596) 183, 189
Brzeziński Mieczysław (1858-1911) 466
Brzostowski Paweł (1739-1827) 290
Budny Szymon (c. 1530-1593) 160
Budënny Semion (1883) 550, 552
Bug 55, 64, 117, 288, 333, 406, 450, 550, 551, 607
Bujak Franciszek (1875-1953) 568
Bulgaria, Bulgars 47, 120, 465
Bülov Bernhard (1849-1929) 515
Bund, Jewish Socialist Party 508
Buonarotti Filippo Michele (1761-1837) 399
Burgundy 29, 52, 104, 105
Burian Stephen (1851-1922) 534
Burschenschaften 373
Burski Adam (c. 1560-1611) 232
Byczyna 181, 233
Bydgoszcz 27, 153, 196, 331, 350

Byelorussia, Byelorussians 115, 169, 214, 223, 234, 246, 255, 278, 293, 345, 357, 371, 376, 339, 345, 357, 373, 378, 384, 391, 431, 444, 453, 543, 548, 552, 564, 586
Bytom 93
Bytów 206, 216
Byzantium 19, 34, 55, 63, 120

Calatrava Order 94
Calvinists 155, 159, 161, 163, 169, 174, 199, 200
Campo Formio (treaty of, 1797) 343
Canaletto (Bernardo Belotto) (1720-1780) 299
Canons of the Holy Sepulchre 77
Canons Regular 105
Canute the Great (c. 995-1035), King of England, Norway and Danemark 51
capitaneus 108 *see starosta*
Caprivi Leo (1831-1899) 490, 491, 495, 496
Carbonarism 375, 399-401, 405
Carnuntum 29
Carolingian Empire 39
Carpathians, Carpathian Mountains 17, 25, 28, 30, 33, 50, 421, 523
Casimir I the Restorer (1016-1058), Duke of Poland 55, 56, 57, 64, 65, 77
Casimir II the Just (1138-1194), Duke of Cracow-Sandomierz 68, 71, 89, 93
Casimir III the Great (1310-1370), King of Poland 108, 111-114, 119, 124, 126, 127, 131-135
Casimir IV (1427-1492), King of Poland 120, 122, 125, 131, 134, 136, 146, 170
Casimir I (c. 1211-1267), Duke of Kujawy 91
Casimir (1351-1377), Duke of Słupsk 112, 113
castellans 58, 68, 75, 76, 94, 108, 111, 149
Castlereagh Henry Robert Stewart (1769-1822) 363
cathedral chapters 77
Catherine II (1729-1796), Tsarina of Russia 235, 267, 269, 270, 271, 272, 275, 276, 277, 305, 320, 322, 332, 334, 340
Catholic League 189
Caulaincourt Armand de (1773-1827) 357
Cavour Camillo (1810-1861) 435
Cecilia Renata (1611-1644), Queen of Poland 204
Cecora (battle of, 1620) 189
Cedynia (battle of, 972) 51

Celts 28, 29, 30
Celtis Conrad (1459–1508) 134
Central Board, "Centralizacja" see Polish Democratic Society
Central Industrial Area 595
Central Land Office 548
Central Powers 522, 525–527, 529–536, 539
"Centralizacja" (of Lwów, 1796) 341
Centre 547, 558–560, 577
Centre-Left, "Centrolew" 584, 585
"Cercle des Artistes Polonais à Paris" (1928) 576
Chałubiński Tytus (1820–1889) 430
Chamber of Deputies see Parliament
Chamberlain Neville (1869–1940) 602
chancellor's office 108
Charlemagne (742–814), Emperor of the West 36
Charles (1733–1796), Duke of Courland 266, 268, 270
Charles IV (1316–1378), Emperor, King of Bohemia 113
Charles VI (1685–1740), Emperor 242, 243, 244, 252
Charles X Gustavus (1622–1660), King of Sweden 211, 214, 215, 216
Charles XII (1682–1718), King of Sweden 237, 239
Charles IX (1550–1574), King of France 167
Charles I Robert d'Anjou (1289–1342), King of Hungary 99
Charles I (1887–1922), Emperor of Austria, King of Hungary 535
Chartres 106
Chassidic movement see Jews
Chełm 455, 514, 532, 558, 588
Chełmno 37, 43, 85, 94, 95, 174
— law of, 1235 see Law
Chełmoński Józef (1849–1914) 473
Chernishev Zachar (1722–1784) 280
Chicherin Georgij (1872–1936) 566
China 369, 600
Chłopicki Józef (1771–1854) 382–384
Chmieleński Ignacy (1837–c. 1865) 438, 439
Chmielnicki Bohdan (c. 1595–1657), 208, 210, 212–214, 217, 400
Chmielów 174
Chochołów (insurrection of, 1846) 411
Chocim (battle of, 1673) 189, 190, 220
Chodkiewicz Jan Karol (1560–1621) 183
Choiseul Étienne François, duc de (1719–1785) 277, 280

Chomentowski Michał (–1794) 329
Chopin Fryderyk (1810–1849) 17, 380, 426
Chortyca 188
Chorzów 582
Chościszko (9th cent.), Duke of Polanes 42
Chreptowicz Joachim (1729–1812) 284, 285, 290, 302, 317
Christana (1626–1689), Queen of Sweden 213
Christian (–1245), Bishop of Prussia 94
Chrzanowski Wojciech (1793–1861) 421
Chrzanowski Bernard (1865–1944) 516
Chwistek Leon (1884–1944) 576
Cienia (privilege of, 1228) see Law
Cieszkowski August (1814–1894) 425
Cieszyn 79, 320, 535, 546, 549, 566
circumequitatio, circuitio (custom) 82
Cisalpine Republic 343
Ciszewski Józef Feliks (1877–1937) 612
Citeaux 104
Cistercians 77, 83, 92, 94, 102, 104, 106
City Committee (1861) see Reds
cives, burgenses, hospites 83
civitas 60
Classical School 378, 379
Clement XIV, Pope (1769–1774) 283
Collegium Maius (Cracow) 136
Collin Ludwig (1781–) 410
colloquia (assemblies of the lords and the gentry) see Parliament
Cologne 57, 78, 79, 422
Colonization Commission 482–484, 491, 495
Comintern see International Third
Commission of Confederated Independence Parties 521
Commission of Justice 454
Commission of National Education 283, 298, 302–304, 307, 310, 316, 345
Committee of National Defense 524
Commune Paris (1871) 451
Communist Party of Poland (KPP) 545, 550, 564, 584, 586, 595, 596
Communist Party of Western Byelorussia 564
Communist Party of Western Ukraine 564
Communist Union 413
Communist Union of Youth 564
Communists 558, 564, 584, 593, 595
Condé Louis de ("The Great Condé") (1621–1686) 219
Condillac Étienne Bonnot de (1715–1780) 299, 303

"confederation" (1439) 119
Confederation of Warsaw (1573) 161, 164, 183, 200
— of Sandomierz (1702–1716) 237
— of Środa (1703–1704) 237
— of Warsaw (1704–1709) 237
— of Tarnogród (1715–1717) 240, 241
— of Dzików (1734–1735) 244
— of Radom (1767) 275, 279, 285, 321
— of Bar (1768–1772) 277, 279, 289, 296–298, 306
— of Targowica (1792–1793) 321–324, 327, 328, 332, 337
Confederation (1796) 341
— (1812) 357
Conrad III (c. 1093–1152), German King 68
Conrad I (c. 1187–1247), Duke of Mazovia 91, 94, 95, 104
Conservatives 522, 531, 580
Constance (Council of, 1414–1418) 117
Constantine (1779–1831), Grand Duke of Russia 321, 332, 367, 373, 382, 383, 388
Constantine (1827–1892), Grand Duke of Russia 439, 440, 445
Constantinople 113, 280
Constitution of
— Nihil Novi (1505) 150
— 3rd May (1791) 294, 304, 315–321, 323, 324, 330, 357
— the Duchy of Warsaw (1807) 348, 350, 353, 354, 364
— the Kingdom of Poland (1815) 364, 373–375, 380, 389, 391
— Organic Statute (1832) 391
— "Little" (1919) 547
— March (1921) 547, 555, 556, 558, 559, 578–580, 588
— April (1935) 591, 597
Conti François Louis, Prince de (1664–1709) 235
Conti Louis François, Prince de (1717–1776) 245
Convention 533, 536
Copernicus Nicolaus (1473–1543) 17, 134, 146, 175, 176, 179
Corazzi Antonio (1792–1877) 379
Corneille Pierre (1606–1684) 230
Cossacks 184, 188–191, 195, 206–208, 210–215, 217, 220, 223, 238, 239, 246, 248, 277
Council of Ambassadors 552
Council of Regency 533, 536–538

Council of State 454, 528, 531, 533, 536
Councils of Workers and Soldiers Delegates 545, 548
Counter-Reformation 176, 180, 189, 191, 197–199, 202, 215, 216, 226, 227, 229, 230, 232, 252, 255
coup d'état (of May 1926) 577–579, 582
see Piłsudski Józef
Courland 157, 236, 237, 242, 244, 246, 266, 268, 293
Cracow 30, 31, 33, 36, 37, 41, 45, 49, 51, 52, 60, 62–65, 68, 71, 75–79, 83, 85–91, 93, 95, 98, 101, 105, 106, 111–114, 120, 122, 126, 127, 129, 131–133, 135, 150, 153, 158, 167, 173, 175, 178, 196, 199, 215, 223, 225, 230, 235, 237, 252, 261, 308, 324, 325, 331, 333, 341, 355, 358, 363, 379, 392, 394, 397, 398, 405, 410–412, 418, 423, 443, 463, 472, 475, 479, 487, 493, 500–504, 522, 523, 536, 560, 567, 568, 571, 585, 593, 596
— Academy *see* University of Cracow
— Academy of Fine Arts 576
— Duchy of 364
— Free City of 411, 460
— Republic of 392
— Scientific Society 430
"Cracow lords" 111, 112, 114
Cracow-Sandomierz duchy 89
Craig Eduard Gordon (1872–1966) 571
Crell Jan (1590–1633) 233
Crimea 208
Croats, Khorvats 32, 421
Croce Benedetto (1866–1952) 571
Crusading movement 77
cubism 576
Curzon George Nathaniel (1859–1925) 551
Cybis Jan (1897) 573
Cyprus 113
Czacki Tadeusz (1765–1813) 345
Czapliński Daniel (17th cent.) 208
Czapski Józef (1896) 576
Czarniecki Stefan (1599–1665) 215, 216, 218
Czarnkowski Stanisław (1526–1602) 169
Czarnowski Stefan (1879–1937) 568
Czartoryska Izabella (1746–1835) 345
Czartoryska Zofia (1699–1771) 250
Czartoryski Adam Jerzy (1770–1861) 346, 357, 358, 363, 367, 377, 382, 383, 388, 389, 399, 404, 420, 422
Czartoryski Adam Kazimierz (1734–1823)

41 History of Poland

269, 270, 283, 287, 294, 302, 304, 306, 309
Czartoryski August (1697–1782) 250, 268, 272, 275
Czartoryski Michał (1696–1775) 250, 268
Czartoryski Władysław (1828–1894) 541
Czartoryskis 227, 243, 248, 250, 251, 265, 266, 269, 270, 271, 275, 278, 282, 287, 300, 355, 404 see "The Family"
Czech styles 257
Czechoslovak National Council 535
Czechoslovakia, Czechs 21, 33, 421, 462, 535, 555, 566, 567, 590, 599, 601
Czechowic Marcin (1532–1613) 160
Czechowicz Gabriel (1876–1938) 584
Czechowicz Józef (1903–1939) 571
Czechowicz Szymon (1689–1775) 258
Czekanowski Aleksander (1833–1876) 471
Czekanowski Jan (1882–1965) 568
Czernihów 187, 217
Czernin Ottokar (1872–1932) 534
Czerski Jan (1845–1892) 471
Czerwień 55
Czerwieński Bolesław (1851–1888) 475
Czerwińsk 105
Częstochowa 216, 255, 278, 596
Czorsztyn 213
Czyński Jan (1801–1867) 387, 399
Czyżewski Tytus (1880–1945) 571, 579

Danes 92
Danube 28, 29, 148, 188, 236, 355
Darasz Wojciech Władysław (1808–1852) 402
Daszyński Ignacy (1866–1936) 487, 494, 536–538, 551, 584, 595
Davout Louis Nicolas (1770–1823) 350
Dąbrowa Basin 370, 394, 469, 521, 545, 564
Dąbrowska Maria (1889–1965) 570
Dąbrowski Jan Henryk (1755–1818) 331, 343, 344, 346, 347, 348
— Legions 406–408, 342–344, 539
Dąbrowski Jarosław (1836–1871) 438, 439, 440, 444, 451
Dąbrówka Jan (15th cent.), professor 134
Dąbski Jan (1880–1931) 552, 559
decadentism 501
Decembrists 373, 377, 388
decree of December (1807) see Peasants
Deczyński Kazimierz (1800–1838) 369
Dekert Jan (1738–1790) 315
Delegation Municipal (1861) 436

Dembiński Henryk (1791–1864) 387, 422
Dembowski Edward (1822–1846) 407, 408, 411, 420, 426
Demetrius Donskoi (1362–1389), Grand Duke of Moscow 115
Denisko Joachim Mokosiej (1756–c. 1812) 341
Denmark 51, 67, 77, 92, 101, 111, 113, 125, 157, 216, 237, 275
"Deutscher Ostmarkenverein" (The German Union of the Eastern Marches) 496
Deputation (Paris, 1795) 343, 344
Déroulède Paul (1846–1914) 492
Deulino (truce of, 1618) 187, 188
Dębe Wielkie (battle of, 1831) 384
Dęblin 464
Dębno 136
Diamand Herman (1860–1931) 595
Diebitsch Ivan (1785–1831) 384, 385
Dietl Józef (1804–1878) 430
Dietrich 52
Directory (1861) see Whites
dissenters 155, 169, 179, 183, 185, 199, 202, 203, 215, 227, 231, 233, 254, 275, 276, 277
Długosz Jan (1415–1480), historian 134
Dłuski Kazimierz (1855–1930) 475
Dmochowski Franciszek (1762–1808) 302, 313, 323, 328, 329, 342
Dmowski Roman (1864–1939) 492, 493, 506, 508, 511–514, 520, 522, 524, 529
Dnieper 19, 25, 28, 31, 148, 156, 188, 207, 217, 220, 226, 237, 238, 268, 357, 450, 461, 532
Dniester 31, 190, 268, 290, 550
Dobrava, Dubravka (–977), Duchess of Poland 49, 64
Dobrolyubov Nicolaus (1836–1861) 434
Dobronega Maria (c. 1012–1087), Duchess of Poland 57
Dobrzyń Land 112
Dogiel Maciej (1715–1760) 264
Dolabella Tommaso (c. 1570–1650) 230
Dolgoruki Grigory (1656–1723) 241
Dołęga-Chodakowski Zorian (Czarnocki Adam) (1784–1825) 378
Dominicans 93, 104
Doroshenko Piotr (1627–1698) 220
Dowbór-Muśnicki Józef (1867–1937) 530, 533
Downarowicz Medard (1878–1934) 564
Dreikaiserbund 483

Dresden 236, 257, 263, 270, 277, 297, 349, 350, 421
Drohobycz 487
drużyna 38, 47
Drzymała Michał (1857–1937) 495
Dubienka (battle of, 1792) 321, 323
Dukas Paul (1865–1935) 576
Dukla Pass 62
Duma 513, 528
Dumouriez Charles François (1739–1823) 278
Dunajec 62, 88
Dunikowski Xawery (1875–1964) 576
Dupont de Nemours Pierre Samuel (1739–1817) 298
Dutch art 230
Dvina 156, 168, 169, 190, 217, 357
Dybowski Benedykt (1833–1930) 471
Dygasiński Adolf (1839–1902) 467, 472
Dyneburg, Daugavpils 169, 552
Dziadoszanie, Dadodesani 40
Dzierżyński Feliks (1877–1926) 488
Dzików (agreement of, 1927) 580

Ehrenberg Gustaw (1818–1895) 406
Elba 363, 364
Elbe river 31–33, 36, 363
Elbląg 37, 87, 95, 101, 121, 133, 167, 174, 228, 282, 289
Eleanor of Hapsburg (1653–1697), Queen of Poland 219
Elector of Brandenburg see Frederick William, "Great Elector"
Elisabeth of Hapsburg (1436–1505), Queen of Poland 121
Elisabeth of Poland (1305–1380), Queen of Hungary 114
Elisabeth (1709–1762), Tsarina of Russia 266–268
Elster 357
emancipation of women 426, 453
emigration 450, 452, 484, 498, 499, 500, 517, 597
Emigration Great 399, 450
Emperor 204 (Ferdinand III, 1608–1657); 219, 221 (Leopold I, 1640–1705); 411, 418, 420 (Ferdinand I, 1793–1875)
Enfranchisement see Parliament see also Peasants
franchise see Parliament
Engels Friedrich (1820–1895) 390, 413, 447
England 19, 179, 233, 235, 242, 244, 254, 263, 272, 275, 281, 306, 363, 443, 493, 578 see Great Britain
Enlightenment 22, 234, 235, 287, 288, 294, 296–300, 302, 306, 309, 354, 373, 377
Entente 514, 529, 534, 545
Enthusiast Circle 426 see emancipation of women
Erfurt (programme of, 1891) 488
Eric Segersäller (–c. 995), King of Sweden 51
Eric I (1382–1459), Duke of Słupsk, King of Danemark, Norway and Sweden 125
Ernest of Hapsburg (1553–1595), Archduke 183
Estonia 157, 183, 588
Eugene III, Pope (1145–1153) 69
Eugene IV, Pope (1431–1437) 120
Evans Brothers 370
Executive Committee (1864) 452
expressionism 473
"execution-of-the-law" 169
Eylau, Iławka (battle of, 1807) 348
Ezzon Herenfried (10th/11th cent.), Palatine of Lorraine 53

"Falanga" see National Radical Camp
False Demetrius, first (Gregory Otrepiev) (–1606) 184, 186
False Demetrius, second (–1610) 186
"The Family" 250, 251, 265, 266, 269–272, 274, 288, 309 see Czartoryskis see also Poniatowskis
Far East 490, 514
fascism 591, 597, 599, 600, 607
Feliński Alojzy (1771–1820) 378
Ferdinand d'Este (1781–1850), Archduke of Austria 354, 355
Finland 588
Firlej Jan (c. 1521–1574) 163
Five Brothers Eremits (c. 1003) 64
Flanders 87
Flemings 84
Flemming Jakob Heinrich (1667–1728) 240, 250
Florence 421
Florentine della Lora Francis (–1516) 174
Fontana Jakub (1710–1773) 299
Ford Aleksander (1908) 575
"Formists" 576
forum liberum see Law
Fouché Joseph (1757–1820) 345
France, Frenchmen 103, 104, 134, 168, 179,

189, 193, 204, 217–221, 233, 235, 237, 239, 241–244, 247, 248, 251, 255, 257, 263, 268, 275, 278, 281, 282, 297, 299, 322–324, 333, 339, 342–344, 346, 351, 354, 355, 357, 361, 363, 380, 388, 389, 399, 400–404, 412, 420, 456, 460, 465, 493, 514, 525, 528, 535, 548, 551, 555, 556, 565, 566, 598–601, 607

Franciscans 102, 104, 131, 135
Franco de Polonia (13th cent.), astronomer 103
Frank Jakub (1726–1791) 294
Frankfurt on the Odra 126
Frankists 294
Frankowski brothers 438
Franz Joseph I (1830–1916) Emperor 435, 459, 522, 527
Frączkiewicz Antoni (1st half of the 18th cent.) 258
Frederick Augustus I, Elector of Saxony *see* Augustus II, King of Poland
Frederick Augustus (1750–1827), Elector, King of Saxony, Grand Duke of Warsaw 317, 348, 350
Frederick Barbarossa (c. 1122–1190), Emperor 69, 92
Frederick Christian (1722–1763), Elector of Saxony 270
Frederick I (1657–1713), King of Prussia 238
Frederick II (1712–1786), King of Prussia 246, 252, 253, 266–268, 270, 273, 275, 276, 278, 280–282, 288, 305, 320, 334, 360
Frederick William "Great Elector" (1620–1688) 204, 219, 233, 238
Frederick William I (1688–1740), King of Prussia 242, 244
Frederick William II (1744–1797), King of Prussia 306
Frederick William III (1770–1840), King of Prussia 346
Fredro Aleksander (1793–1876) 378, 426
Fredro Andrzej Maksymilian (c. 1620–1679) 230
freeholds *see* Peasants
free-masonry 263, 298, 341, 376, 400, 484 *see* carbonarism
Freytag Adam (1608–1650) 230
Fribourg 579
Friedland (battle of, 1807) 348
Frontier Defence Corps 564

Frycz-Modrzewski Andrzej (c. 1503–1572) 146, 155, 161, 171, 174, 175, 176, 178
functionalism 504
futurism 571, 576
Galicia 306, 308, 339, 340, 342, 343, 355, 383, 393, 396, 405–407, 409–413, 415, 416, 418, 419, 420, 427, 444, 446, 455, 459–463, 466, 468, 475, 479–481, 493, 494, 498, 510, 514, 517–519, 522, 523, 527, 530, 532, 536, 543, 546, 547, 549–551, 558, 563

Gallus Anonymus (11th/12th cent.), chronicler 78
Gapon Gieorgij (1870–1906) 506
Garczyński Stefan (c. 1690–1755) 264
Garibaldi Giuseppe (1807–1882) 435
Gaul 29, 36
Gąsiorowska Natalia (1881–1964) 568
Gdacius Adam (c. 1610–1688) 233
Gdańsk 28, 43, 60, 74, 75, 83–85, 87, 89, 91, 101, 121, 126, 129, 133, 136, 151, 153, 158, 167, 168, 174, 190, 196, 204, 225, 228, 235, 244, 257, 261, 264, 274, 280–282, 288, 289, 305, 306, 308, 348, 363, 535, 588, 599–601, 603
— Free City 549, 566, 582, 599
Gdów 411
Gdynia 582, 588, 599
Gembicki Piotr (1585–1657), Bishop of Cracow 213, 230
"Generality" (1769) 278
Geneva 474, 475
Genoa 421
— colonies 112, 122
George of Podiebrad (1420–1471), King of Bohemia 121
George Frederick of Hohenzollern (1539–1603), Duke of Prussia 168
George II Rakoczy (1621–1660), Duke of Transylvania 213, 216,
Gepidae 29
German Law *see* Law
German Order of St. Mary (Knights of the Cross) 95
German Social-Democratic Party 488, 489
Germany, Germans 17, 28–30, 33, 36, 49, 52, 53, 55, 56, 64, 65, 69, 84, 87, 97, 99, 107, 121, 125, 126, 131, 134, 136, 158, 179, 229, 231, 233, 241, 252, 257, 310, 337, 350, 360, 370, 380, 395, 400, 412, 413, 417, 420, 422, 447, 456, 457, 459,

462, 465, 474, 475, 480, 483, 484, 488–491, 496–498, 514, 515, 517, 521, 525–535, 537, 538, 543, 544, 546, 547, 549, 550, 555, 556, 557, 560, 561, 565–567, 582, 588, 590, 596, 597, 599–604, 606, 607

Gerson Wojciech (1831–1901) 430
Gertrude of Poland (c. 1025–1108), Grand Duchess of Kiev 77
Geyer Ludwik (1805–1869) 394
Giecz 60, 63
Giedymin (c. 1275–1341), Grand Duke of Lithuania 107
Gierymski Aleksander (1850–1901), 473
Gierymski Maksymilian (1846–1874) 473
Giller Agaton (1831–1887) 440, 443
St. Gilles en Provence 77, 79
Girey dynasty 122
Gizewiusz Gustaw (1810–1848) 398
Glayre Maurice (1744–1819) 298
Gliński Michał (c. 1470–1534) 148
Głąbiński Stanisław (1862–1943) 517
Głogów 60, 66, 85, 88
Głowacki Bartosz (c. 1758–1794) 327
Gniezno 41, 44, 51, 52, 56, 62–65, 67, 68, 71, 74, 76–78, 88, 92, 98, 99, 104, 106, 117, 126, 136, 457, 489
Gobi 104
Godunov Boris (c. 1551–1605), Tsar of Russia 183, 184
Goering Hermann (1893–1946) 590
Gojawiczyńska Pola (1896–1963) 568
Golęszyce, Golensizi 40
Gołuchowski Agenor (1812–1875) 459, 462
Gombrowicz Witold (1904–1969) 570
Gonta Ivan (–1768) 278, 400
Gopło 60
Gorajski family 196
Gorchakov Michaił (1793–1861) 436
Gorchakov Alexandr (1798–1883) 512
Gorczycki Grzegorz (c. 1665–1734) 258
Gorlice 525
Gorzkowski Franciszek (1760–1830) 342, 356
Gorzkowski Ludwik (1811–c. 1857) 410
Gorzów, Landsberg 95
Goslar Julian (1820–1852) 420
Goszczyński Seweryn (1801–1876) 379
Gothic 106, 136, 173, 174, 379
Goths 28, 29
Gottlieb Leopold (1883–1934) 576
Government of National Unity 607

Górnicki Łukasz (1527–1603) 172
Górsk 88
Górzno 190
Grabowski Stanisław (1780–1845) 373
Grabowski family 373
Grabski Stanisław (1871–1949) 545
Grabski Władysław (1874–1938) 550, 559, 560, 562, 578
Great Britain 281, 346, 368, 404, 492, 514, 528, 531, 535, 549, 551, 555, 565, 566, 582, 589, 599, 600, 602, 603, 607 see England
Great Poland 36, 38, 43, 50, 56, 63, 66, 68, 73, 77, 80, 84, 86, 89, 90–93, 95, 98, 99, 101, 105, 108, 111, 120, 124, 126, 127, 131, 133, 156, 158, 215, 216, 227, 246, 263, 278, 290, 306, 321, 331, 352, 355, 417
Greece 465
Gregory VII, Pope (1073–1085) 65
Gregory XVI, Pope (1831–1846) 407
Gregory Tsamblak (15th cent.), Greek Metropolitan 117
Grochów (battle of, 1831) 384, 436
Grodno 322, 324, 332
Grotniki (battle of, 1439) 119
gród (castle-town) 38, 58, 60, 72, 75
Grudziądz 402
"Grudziąż Commune of the Polish People" 402
Grunwald (battle of, 1410) 116, 135, 137
Grzegorz Paweł of Brzeziny (c. 1525–1591) 160
Grzegorz of Sanok (c. 1407–1477), Archbishop of Lwów 134
Grzegorzewski Aleksander (1806–1855) 410
Grzybowski Piotr (–1651) 213
Grzymułtowski Krzysztof (1620–1687) 219
Guibert de Gembloux (12th cent.), scholar 105
guilds 131, 135, 371
Gurowski Adam (1805–1866) 387
Gutakowski family 373
Gutt Romuald (1888) 576
Guzów 185
Gwozdecki Gustaw (1886–1935) 576

Habich Edward (1835–1909) 471
Hapsburgs 107, 119, 122, 147–149, 168, 181, 183, 184, 187, 189, 198, 204, 221, 226, 239, 242, 244, 252, 337, 412, 418, 422, 452, 459, 461–463, 535, 539

Hadziacz (compact of, 1658) 217
Haithabu, Hedeby 37
Halicka Alicja (1894) 576
Halicz 104, 112, 113
Haller Józef (1873–1960) 523, 530, 532, 548
Hansa 85, 95, 125
Hansemann Ferdinand (1861–1900) 496
Hauke-Bosak Józef (1834–1871) 445
Hedwig, Jadwiga, Duchess of Silesia see Jadwiga, Hedwig
Hegel Georg Wilhelm Friedrich (1770–1831) 425
St. Hélier 402
Heltman Wiktor (1796–1878) 375, 401, 402
Hennin Pierre Michel (1728–1807) 265
Henrician Articles see Law
Henry I (–1309), Duke of Głogów 99, 101
Henry (–1166), Duke of Sandomierz 68, 69
Henry of Valois (1573–1574), King of Poland 163, 164, 167, 179
Henry I the Bearded (c. 1163–1238), Duke of Silesia 85, 89, 90, 98
Henry II the Pious (c. 1191–1241), Duke of Silesia 89, 90, 93, 98
Henry II (973–1024), German King and Emperor 52, 53
Henry IV (1050–1106), German King and Emperor 65, 66, 90
Henry IV Probus (c. 1258–1290), Duke of Wrocław 90, 98, 103
Henry V (1081–1125), German King 66
Henryk Kietlicz (c. 1150–1219), Archbishop of Gniezno 91
Henryków 82
Herodotus (5th cent. BC) 28
Hertzberg Ewald Friedrich (1725–1795) 306, 320
Hertzen Alexandr (1812–1870) 434, 440
Herzegovina 514
Hetmen 167, 239–242, 246, 247, 250, 269, 284, 287, 309, 310, 316, 324
Heurich Jan (1873–1925) 504
Highlanders (in the Tatra) 462
"Hirsch-Duncker Unions" 474
Hirszfeld Ludwik (1884–1954) 568
Hitler Adolf (1889–1945) 585, 589, 590, 599–603, 606
H.K.T. (Hakata) 496
Hodo (–993), German Margrave 51
Hohenlinden (battle of, 1800) 344
Hohenstaufens 93

Hohenwart Karl Siegmund (1824–1899) 463
Hohenzollerns 157, 251, 252
Holland 235, 263, 306, see Netherlands
Holstein 267
Holy Alliance 21, 373, 380, 388, 392, 404, 409–413, 447
Holy Land 77
"Holy League" 221
Holy Roman Empire 49, 50, 51, 52, 53, 55, 93
Holy See 169, 171, 175, 198, 221, 226, 263, 266, 389 see Papacy
Horodło (union of, 1412) 117
Horwitz-Walecki Maksymilian (1877–1937) 512, 565
Hosius Stanislaus (1504–1579) 179, 201
Hospitallers 126 see Templars
hospites 85
Hospodar of Moldavia 149 (Peter IV Rareš, –1538)
Hôtel Lambert 404, 422, 435, 443 see Czartoryskis
Hoyer Henryk sr (1834–1907) 466
Hubertsburg (treaty of, 1763) 267
Huczwa 55
Huguenots 163
L'Huillier Simon (1750–1840) 303
Humanism 146, 170, 171
Humań (masacre of, 1768) 278
"Humań Commune of the Polish People" 402
Hungary, Hungarians 21, 42, 46, 48, 51, 52, 55, 62, 66, 93, 95, 101, 107, 111–114, 120, 121, 148, 171, 179, 187, 188, 221, 222, 271, 280, 412, 420, 421, 422, 462, 463, 534, 601, 602
Huns 33
Hurko Osip (1828–1901) 491
Huss John (c. 1369–1415), Czech Reformer 117
Hussitism 104, 118, 131, 133

Iaxa (12th cent.), Polish lord 77
Ibrahim ibn-Yaqub (10th cent.), Jewish merchant 47, 62
Ibsen Henrik (1826–1906) 504
al Idrisi (12th cent.), Arabian geographer 76
Iganie (battle of, 1831) 384
Iłłakowicz Kazimiera (1892) 571
Imeretinsky Alexandr (1837–1900) 492
immunities 84, 108
impressionism 504

incompatibilitas (principle of) *see* Law
Independent Peasant Union 526
Innocent III, Pope (1198–1216) 93
Institute of the Popularization of Art in Warsaw 576
interdictio, inhibitio, hereditatis see Law
International First 448, 541
International Third 595
Irzykowski Karol (1873–1944) 571
Isaac of Troki (1533–1594) 229
St. Isidore Labourer (c. 1070–1130) 202
Israel ben Eliezer (Beszt) (c. 1700–1761) 294
Italy 36, 49, 62, 63, 103, 104, 107, 131, 134, 231, 241, 244, 257, 258, 263, 299, 342–344, 350, 380, 400, 420, 435, 459, 532, 535, 555, 599, 607
Italian style 174
ius civile see Law
ius Culmense see Law
ius municipale see Law
ius Novi Fori Sredense see Law
ius stapulae, depositorii see Law
ius terrestre, iudicia terrestria see Law
ius Teutonicum see Law
Ivan IV the Terrible (1530–1584), Tsar of Russia 157, 184
Iwaszkiewicz Jarosław (1894) 568, 570
Izaslav (c. 1024–1078), Grand Duke of Kiev 65, 77

Jabłonowski Antoni (1793–1855) 376
Jackowski Maksymilian (1816–1905) 478
Jacobinism 310, 323, 328–332, 339, 341, 342, 344, 347, 354, 356
Jadwiga, Hedwig (c. 1174–1243), Duchess of Silesia 104
Jadwiga, Hedwig of Anjou (1374–1399), Queen of Poland 114, 115, 116, 135
Jagiellons 19, 107, 120, 122, 136, 145, 148, 149, 163, 175, 187, 190, 236
Jagiełło, Iogailas *see* Władysław II Jagiełło
Jakub of Paradyż (–1464), theologian 134
Jakub Świnka (–1314), Archbishop of Gniezno 98
Jakub (James) (–c. 1148), Archbishop of Gniezno 68
Jakubowska Wanda (1907) 575
Jakuszowice 33
Jan of Głogów (1445–1507), professor 134
Jan of Ludzisko (c. 1400–c. 1450) 134

Jan Muskata (–1320), Bishop of Cracow 101
Jandołowicz Marek (1713–1799) 277
Janicki Klemens (1516–1543) 174
Janiszewski Zygmunt (1888–1920) 568
Janko of Czarnków (c. 1320–c. 1387), historian 113, 134
Jankowo 44
Janocki-Jänisch Jan Daniel (1720–1786) 263
Janowicz Ludwik (1858–1902) 476
Janowski Jan Nepomucen (1803–1888) 399
Jansenism 255
Janusz (13th cent.), Palatine of Cracow 90
Janusz Suchywilk (c. 1310–1382), Chancellor, Archbishop of Gniezno 113
Japan 490, 506, 600
Jaracz Stefan (1883–1945) 571
Jarema Józef (1900) 576
Jarosław Bogoria (–1376), Archbishop of Gniezno 136
Jarosławiec (negotiations of, 1848) 416
Jasieński Bruno (1901–1939) 571
Jasiński Jakub (1759–1794) 327, 329, 331, 332
Jasło 487
Jassy (peace of, 1792) 320
Jastrun Mieczysław (1903) 571
Jaśkiewicz Jan (1749–1809) 302
Jaworów (alliance of, 1675) 220
Jazdów 93, 94
Jedlnia 118
Jelski Florian (2nd half of the 18th cent.) 329
Jena (battle of, 1806) 346
Jersey Island 402
Jesuits 169, 184–186, 197, 198, 200–202, 230, 252, 254, 259, 264, 265, 283, 269, 302, 303
— Academy 231
Jews 36, 76, 84, 131, 132, 136, 229, 257, 278, 285–296, 312, 319, 339, 352, 433, 437, 439, 453, 472, 598, 606
Jewish Enlightenment (Haskala) 294 *see* Enlightenment
Jezierski Franciszek (1740–1791) 302, 313
Jeżowski Józef (1798–1855) 375
Jędrzejowski Bolesław Antoni (1867–1914) 512
Jędrzejów 101, 185
Joachim Frederick of Hohenzollern (1546–1608), Duke of Prussia 187
Joannites 93

Jodko-Narkiewicz Witold (1864–1924) 512
Joffe Adolf (1883–1927) 552
John Albert (1459–1501), King of Poland 122, 125, 126, 146, 147, 148, 150
John Casimir Vasa (1609–1672), King of Poland 211, 213–217, 219
John III Sobieski (1629–1696), King of Poland 180, 183, 218, 220–223, 225, 226, 235, 238, 252
John Christian (1591–1638), Duke of Brzeg and Legnica 204
John of Luxemburg (1296–1346), King of Bohemia 99, 101, 111, 112
Jordan (–984), Bishop of Poland 49
Joseph II (1741–1790), Emperor, 280, 305, 339, 340, 409
Józefowicz Herszel (2nd half of the 18th cent.) 315
Józewski Henryk (1892) 598
Judith-Maria of Salic Dynasty (1047–c. 1105), Duchess of Poland 66
Jurgens Edward (1823–1863) 433
Jurkowski Jan (17th cent.) 232
Jutland 37

Kaden-Bandrowski Juliusz (1885–1944) 570
Kaffa 112, 122
Kakowski Aleksander (1862–1938) 531
Kalinka Walerian (1826–1886) 470
Kalisz, Kalisia 30, 41, 60, 86, 88, 112, 131, 350, 368, 369, 379, 393, 521
Kallimachus-Buonaccorsi Filippo (1437–1496), humanist 134
Kaluga 276
Kamieniec Podolski 220, 222
Kamienna 370
Kamień 59, 66, 67, 92, 106
Kamieński Henryk (1813–1865) 408, 426
Kamieński Mikołaj (1799–1873) 421
Kamiński Kazimierz (1865–1928) 503
Kaniów, Kaniov (battle of, 1918) 306, 532
Karłowice (treaty of, 1699) 222, 237, 238, 248
Karłowicz Mieczysław (1876–1909) 504
Karpiński Franciszek (1741–1825) 300
Kartuzy 498
Karwicki Dunin Stanisław (1640–1724) 240
Kashuby, Kashubians 253, 462, 498
Kasprowicz Jan (1860–1926) 501, 502
Katowice 489
Kazimirski Mikołaj (–1598) 169
Kazimierz 132

Kazimierz Dolny 153, 196, 214, 230
Kennemann Hermann (1815–1910) 496
Kettler Gotthard von (1517–1587), Duke of Courland 157
Kiejstut, Kestutis (–1382), Duke of Lithuania 115, 119
Kielce 230, 292, 370, 393, 407, 441, 521
Kiev 19, 37, 48, 55, 57, 62, 77, 117, 158, 217, 220, 222, 305, 375, 376, 464, 514, 550
Kilia 112, 122, 148
Kiliński Jan (1760–1819) 327, 493
King of Prussia 464 see Frederick William III
Kirchholm (battle of, 1605) 183
Kisiel Adam (–1653) 212
Kisielewski Jan August (1876–1918) 502
Kherson 290
Kleck 148
Klemensów 395
Kliszów (battle of, 1702) 237
Klonowic Sebastian (c. 1545–1602) 229
Kluczbork 233
Kluk Krzysztof (1739–1796) 302
Kłodzko Pass 28
Kłuszyn (battle of, 1610) 186
Kmita family 174
Knapius Grzegorz (c. 1565–1639) 230, 232
Kniaziewicz Karol (1762–1842) 344
Kniaźnin Franciszek Dioniszy (1750–1807) 300
Knights of Christ, Dobrzyń friars 94
Kober Marcin (c. 1580–c. 1609) 230
Kobro Katarzyna (1898–1950) 576
Kochanowski Jan (1530–1584) 146, 161, 173–176, 178, 233
Kochowski Wespazjan (1633–1700) 232
Kolberg Oskar (1814–1890) 468
Kołakowski Wojciech (–1651) 213
Kołbacz 92, 106
Kołłątaj Hugo (1750–1812) 298, 302, 304, 310, 311, 312, 313, 315, 317, 318, 319, 321, 323, 328, 330, 332, 342, 346, 354, 356
"Kołłątaj's Forge" 313, 324
Koło 124
Kołobrzeg 36, 52, 59, 66, 75, 92, 125
Kołomyja 149
Komarzewski Jan (1744–1810) 286
Komenský Jan Ámos (1592–1670) 231
Konarski Adam (1518–1574) 163

Konarski Stanisław (1700–1773) 264, 265, 269, 298, 302, 309
Konarski Szymon (1808–1839) 405
Konaszewicz-Sahajdaczny Piotr (–1622) 189
Konicz Tadeusz (1733–1793) 258
Koniecpolski Aleksander (1620–1659) 208, 227
Koniecpolski Stanisław (c. 1590–1646) 208
Koniecpolski family 192
Königsberg 121, 190, 233, 289
Konopnicka Maria (1842–1910) 472
Konovalets Evhen (1891–1938), 563, 585
Konstantynów 369
Kopczyński Onufry (1735–1817) 302
Köprülü Ahmed (1635–1676), Visir 220
Koprzywnica 106
Korfanty Wojciech (1873–1939) 497
Kornecki Piotr (1st half of the 18th cent.) 258
Korsuń (battle of, 1648) 208
Korytowski Witold (1850–1923) 519
Korzeniowski Apollo (1820–1869) 438
Korzeniowski Józef (1797–1863) 426, 430
Korzon Tadeusz (1839–1918) 504
Košice (privilege of, 1372) see Law
Kosiński Krishtof (–1593) 189
Kossakowski Józef (1738–1794) 327
Kossakowski Szymon (1740–1794) 327
Kostka Napierski Aleksander (c. 1620–1651) 213
Kostrzewski Franciszek (1826–1911) 430
Kostrzewski Józef (1885) 568
Koszutska Maria (Kostrzewa, Wera) (1876–1939) 512, 565
Kościelski Józef (1845–1911) 490, 494
Kościuszko Tadeusz (1746–1817) 294, 321, 324, 325, 327, 330–332, 334, 337, 339, 341, 342, 344
Kot Stanisław (1885) 523
Kowno, Kaunas 566, 600
Koźmian Kajetan (1771–1856) 378
Koźminek (union of, 1555) 160
Krakus (tumulus of) 45
Krasicki Ignacy (1735–1801) 300
Krasiński Adam (1714–1800) 277
Krasiński Michał (1712–1784) 277
Krasiński Zygmunt (1812–1859) 425, 426, 430
Kraszewski Józef Ignacy (1812–1887) 426, 430
Kraziewicz Julian (1829–1895) 478
Kremlin 184, 187

Kretchetnikov Piotr (1727–1800) 278
Krewo (union of, 1385) 116
Krępowiecki Tadeusz (1798–1847) 375, 387, 388, 399, 400, 402
Kromer Marcin (1512–1589) 173, 179
Kronenberg Leopold (1812–1878) 439, 443
Krotowski Jakub (Krauthofer) (1806–1853) 416
Krowicki Marcin (c. 1500–1583) 160
Kruczkowski Leon (1900–1962) 570
Krukowiecki Jan (1770–1850) 389
Kruszwica 31, 41, 60, 79
Krużlowa 136
Kryński Adam Antoni (1844–1932) 466
Krzemieniec 345
Krzeszów 106
Krzycki Andrzej (1482–1537) 175
Krzywicki Ludwik (1859–1941) 468, 568
Krzyżanowski Seweryn (1787–c. 1839) 376
Krzyżtopór 230 see Ossoliński family
Kubicki Jakub (1758–1833) 299
Kucharski Aleksander (1741–1819) 299
Kudak 207
Kufstein 406
Kujawy 36, 68, 75, 77, 89–91, 99, 101, 105, 108, 112, 114, 158
Kukiel Marian (1885) 519, 523
Kulturkampf 456–458, 483, 489, 496
Kuna Henryk (1885–1945) 576
Kunicki Stanisław (1861–1886) 476, 477
Kuratowski Kazimierz (1896) 568
Kurek Jalu (1904) 570
Kurozwęki 112 see Poraj family
Kurpie 223
Kwiatkowski Eugeniusz (1888) 582, 595, 597
Kwidzyn (customs of, 1765) 274

labour dues, labour services see Peasants
Lachert Bogdan (1900) 576
Lachy 40
Ląd 41
Lambert (10th/11th cent.) son of Mieszko I 49
Lambert II (Suła) (–1071), Bishop of Cracow 64
Lanckorona (battle of, 1770) 279
Land Credit Society 368
land diets see Parliament
land reform (1919–1925) 548, 549, 551, 562 see Peasants
Langiewicz Marian (1827–1887) 443
Laon 77

Latvia 552, 588
Lausanne 524, 529
Law
  mos liberorum hospitum (12th cent.) 80
  interdictio, inhibitio hereditatis (12th cent.) 82
  of Magdeburg (1188) 85
  forum liberum (12th/13th cent.) 83
  ius stapulae, depositorii (12th/13th cent.) 87
  ius municipale (12th/13th cent.) 111
  ius Teutonicum, German law, *ius civile* (13th cent.) 84–87, 95, 111, 127
  locatio civitatis (13th cent.) 85, 86
  of Lübeck (13th cent.) 85
  Polish law (13th cent.) 86, 111, 127
  of Środa, *Novum Forum ducis Henrici, Novi Fori Sredense* (1221) 85
  privilege of Cienia (1228) 89
  of Chełmno, *ius Culmense* (1235) 85, 95, 155
  ius terrestre, iudicia terrestria (13th/14th cent.) 111
  privilege of Košice (1372) 114
  privilege of Brześć (1425), *Neminem captivabimus nisi iure victum* 118, 185
  Nieszawa Statutes (1454) 121, 125, 131
  incompatibilitas (16th cent.) 150
  pacta conventa 163, 183
  Henrician Articles (1573) 163, 164, 170
  Napoleonic Civil Code (1807) 350, 353, 355, 359, 453
League of Nations 549, 566, 586, 589, 599
Le Brun André (1737–1811) 299
Lechoń Jan (Serafinowicz Leszek) (1899–1956) 571
Lednica 63
Ledóchowski Mieczysław (1822–1902) 457
Ledóchowski Stanisław (–1725) 240
Legnica 60, 93, 126, 133, 168, 204
Leipzig (battle of, 1813) 358
Leitha 462
Lelewel Joachim (1786–1861) 380, 381, 384, 387, 389, 390, 400, 401, 404, 405, 425
Leliwa family 112
Lenartowicz Teofil (1822–1893) 428
Lengnich Gotfryd (1689–1774) 264
Lengyel 40
Lenin Vladimir (1870–1924) 362
Lenkai 40
Leo XIII, Pope (1878–1903) 489

Leoben (armistice of, 1797) 343
Leszczyński Jan (–1678) 219
Leszczyński Rafał (c. 1526–1592) 155
Leszczyński Rafał (1579–1636) 199
Leszczyński Stanisław *see* Stanisław Leszczyński
Leszczyński family 230
Leszek, Lestek, Lestko (9th/10th cent.), Duke of Polanie 42
Leszek the Black (c. 1241–1288), Duke of Cracow–Sandomierz 91, 98, 104
Leszek the White (c. 1186–1227), Duke of Cracow–Sandomierz 86, 89, 91, 104
Leszno 199, 230, 233
— Academy of 231
Leśmian Bolesław (1878–1937) 570
Lewin Mendel Satanower (1741–1819) 294
letters patent of Joseph II (1780–1790) *see* Peasants
Leżajsk 230
Leźno 44
Lębork 206, 216
Lędzice, Lendizi 40
Libelt Karol (1807–1875) 406, 407, 417, 425
liberum veto see Parliament
Lieberman Herman (1870–1941) 585
Liebknecht Wilhelm (1826–1900) 474, 489
Liège 49, 50, 78
Limanowa 523
Limanowski Bolesław (1835–1935) 474, 475, 488
Linde Samuel Bogumił (1771–1847) 345
Lipski Józef (1894–1958) 602
Liske Ksawery (1838–1891) 470
Lisowski Aleksander (–1616) 189
Lithuania, Lithuanians 21, 28, 37, 84, 93, 95, 101, 104, 107, 111, 113, 115, 116, 118, 120, 121, 122, 128, 133, 136, 148, 150, 156–158, 163, 164, 173, 211, 214, 215, 217, 223, 229, 238, 253, 254, 275, 278, 279, 280, 293, 302, 331, 339, 342, 345, 357, 373, 376, 384, 385, 387, 437, 440, 444, 445, 453, 475, 531, 548, 549, 551, 552, 566, 600
Little Poland 36, 38, 43, 50, 68, 73, 76, 80, 83, 84, 89, 90, 98, 99, 101, 104, 111, 112, 114, 119, 124, 126, 127, 131, 132, 135, 136, 156, 158, 159, 227, 239, 240, 563, 598
Livonia 156–158, 168, 169, 183, 190, 217, 236, 237, 242

Livonian Order of the Knights of the Sword 95, 156
Livy (59 BC-17 AD) 134
local diets see Parliament
Locarno (treaty of, 1925) 566, 600
locatio civitatis see Law
Locke John (1632-1704) 233
Loga 329
Lombardy 79, 105, 343, 412, 421
Lompa Józef (1797-1863) 398, 417
London 281, 388, 401, 413, 440, 444, 447, 568, 602, 605, 606, 607
Lorraine 49, 55, 77, 244
Lothair III (1075-1137), German King and Emperor 67
Louis d'Anjou (1326-1382), King of Hungary and Poland 113, 114
Louis I (c. 1311-1398), Duke of Brzeg 126
Louis Henri de Bourbon, duc (1692-1740) 243
Louis XIV (1638-1715), King of France 219, 220, 235, 239
Louis XV (1710-1774), King of France 239, 243, 245, 266
Louis (Dauphin) (1729-1765), son of Louis XV 266
Louis-Philippe (1773-1850), King of the French 413
Low Countries see Netherlands
Lübeck 85, 87, 91
— law see Law
Lubecki-Drucki Ksawery (1778-1846) 368, 369, 373, 374, 377, 382, 394, 463
Lubiąż 106
Lubieniecki Stanisław (1623-1675) 232
Lublin 60, 77, 93, 98, 136, 153, 158, 179, 185, 199, 214, 264, 355, 356, 384, 393, 407, 469, 525, 527, 537, 596
— Provisional Government of the Polish Republic 537, 538
— Union of (1569) 158, 164, 168, 192
Lubliński Julian (1799-1872) 375
Lubomirski Jerzy (1616-1667) 211, 216, 218, 219
Lubomirski Stanisław (1719-1783) 283, 284, 286
Lubomirski Stanisław Herakliusz (1642-1702) 230
Lubomirski Zdzisław (1865-1941) 531
Lubomirski family 227, 230, 300
Lubrański Jan (-1520) 175
Lubusz, Lebus 67, 68, 91, 95, 98, 111, 126, 154, 263
Lucchesini Girolamo (1751-1825) 308
Ludgarda of Mecklemburg (c. 1261-1283), Duchess of Great Poland 104
Lugii 28, 29
Lunéville (treaty of, 1801) 263, 344
Lusatia, Łużyce 25, 27, 33, 53, 55, 85, 122, 148
Lusławice 173
Luther Martin (1483-1546) 148, 158
Lutheranism 148, 159, 174, 199, 254, 257
Lutomyśl 98
Lützen (battle of, 1813) 357
Luxemburg dynasty 101, 107
Luxemburg Rosa (1871-1919) 488, 489
Lwów 112, 113, 122, 126, 131, 136, 153, 196, 214, 216, 220, 226, 257, 264, 341, 392, 405, 418, 461, 463, 475, 487, 493, 504, 518, 522, 543, 552, 563, 568, 578, 579, 595

Łańcut 230, 300 see Lubomirski family
Łaski Jan, John a Lasco (1499-1560) 160
Łaski Jan (c. 1455-1531), Archbishop 148, 160, 163
Łaszcz Samuel (c. 1590-1649) 201
Łęczyca 31, 43, 60, 63, 68, 88, 89, 101, 102, 105
Łomża 348, 552
Łowczówek 523
Łódź 369, 370, 394, 433, 435, 464, 476, 487, 510, 511
Łubieński Feliks (1758-1848) 350, 354, 356
Łubieński Henryk (1793-1883) 394
Łubieński Tomasz (1784-1870) 394
Łuck 226
Łukasiński Walerian (1786-1868) 376
Łuków 93
Łysiec Mount see Świętokrzyskie Mountains
Łyszczyński Kazimierz (c. 1634-1689) 225

Mably Gabriel, Bonnot de (1709-1785) 279, 298
Maciej Kolbe of Świebodzin (15th cent.) professor 133
Maciejowice (battle of, 1794) 332
"Macierz Szkolna" (School Union) 513
Madaliński Antoni (1739-1805) 325
Maeterlinck Maurice (1862-1949) 504
Magdeburg 36, 62, 85, 155, 530
— law see Law

652 INDEX

Magnus of Denmark ("King of Livonia") (1540–1583) 157, 169
Magyars *see* Hungarians
Main School *see* University of Warsaw
Mainz 36
Majer Józef (1808–1899) 430
Makowski Tadeusz (1882–1932) 576
Malawski Artur (1904–1957) 576
Malbork 121, 136
Malczewski Antoni (1793–1826) 379
Malczewski Jacek (1854–1929) 504
Malinowski Bronisław (1884–1942) 568
Malinowski Marian (1876–1948) 526
Malinowski Tomasz (1802–1880) 402
Malonne 78
Małachowski Stanisław (1736–1809) 307, 309, 310, 317, 321, 347
Małachowski family 263
Manchuria 506
Manchukuo empire 600
Mann Thomas (1875–1955) 570
mansus 127
Mantua (capitulation of, 1799) 431
manufactory 143, 197, 262, 263, 288, 292, 461
Marcin Król of Żurawica (c. 1422–1460) professor 134
Marcinkowski Karol (1800–1846) 395, 413
Marconi Henryk (1792–1863) 430
Marie-Casimira (1641–1716), Queen of Poland 220, 235
Marie d'Anjou (1371–1395), Queen of Hungary 114
Marie-Josephine (1699–1757), Queen of Poland 242
Maria Leszczyńska (1703–1768), Queen of France 243, 244
Marie-Louise de Gonzague (1611–1667), Queen of Poland 208, 213
Maria Theresa (1717–1780), Empress 280
Markomanns 29
Marmaros Sziget 534
Marne (battle of, 1914) 523
Martin the Pole (–1279), Archbishop of Gniezno 104
Maruszewski Tomasz (1769–c. 1834) 329
Marx Karl (1818–1883) 413, 447
Masaryk Tomaš Garrigue (1850–1937) 535
Massalski Ignacy (1725–1794) 298
Matejko Jan (1838–1893) 472
Mateusz of Cracow (c. 1330–1410), professor 134

Matthias Corvinus (c. 1443–1490), King of Hungary and Bohemia 121, 122, 126
Matuszewicz Marcin (1714–1773) 256
Matuszewicz Tadeusz (c. 1765–1819) 356
Mauersberger Ludwik (1796–1823) 375
Max von Baden (1867–1929) 536
Maximilian I (1459–1519), Emperor 148
Maxilimian II (1527–1576), Emperor 167
Maximilian of Hapsburg (1558–1618) 181
Mazepa Ivan (1644–1709) 238
Mazovia, Mazovians 36, 38, 44, 50, 56, 57, 60, 62, 66, 68, 73, 83, 84, 85, 89, 91, 93, 94, 108, 127, 128, 133, 135, 156, 158, 163, 369
Mazuria, Mazurians 127, 253, 397, 398, 457, 498, 549, 552, 555, 607
Mazurkiewicz Stefan (1888–1945) 568
Mazzini Giuseppe (1805–1872) 400, 401
Mączeński Zdzisław (1878–1961) 576
Mączyński Jan (c. 1520–c. 1584) 172
Mątwy (battle of, 1666) 219
Medical Academy 433, 434 *see* Warsaw
Mecklenburg 47, 101
Mediterranean basin 28
Meissen 62, 99
Mejer Józef (–1825) 329
Melsztyn *see* Leliwa family 112
Memel 320
Mendelson Stanisław (1858–1913) 474, 475, 488
Mendelssohn Moses (1729–1786) 294
Merlini Dominik (1730–1797) 299
Merovingian Kingdom 33
Messianism 425
Mestvin II, Mściwój (–1294), Duke of Gdańsk-Pomerania 91, 92
Methodius (–885), Apostle to the Slavs 41, 50
Metternich Klemens (1773–1859) 363, 412
Meuse 77, 106
Mędrzecki Adam (1762–1832) 315
Miarka Karol (1824–1882) 458
Michael Romanov (1595–1645) 187
Michał Korybut Wiśniowiecki (1640–1673), King of Poland 219, 220
Michałowski Aleksander (1851–1938) 504
Michałowski Piotr (1801–1855) 427
Mickiewicz Adam (1798–1855) 17, 359, 375, 376, 379, 380, 421, 424–426, 492, 500
Miechowita Maciej (c. 1457–1523), professor 173, 176, 179

Miechów 77
Miecław, Mojsław, Masław (–1047), Duke of Mazovia 56, 57
Mielnik (act of unia, 1501) 150, 157
Mielno 117
Mielżyński Maciej (1790–1870) 413
Mierosławski Ludwik (1814–1878) 409, 415, 416, 421, 434, 435, 438, 443
Mieszko I (–992), Duke of Poland 34, 42, 47, 48, 49, 50, 51, 52, 53, 56, 57, 59, 62, 64, 93
Mieszko II Lambert (990–1034), King of Poland 50, 55, 57, 60, 64, 77
Mieszko III the Old (c. 1126/7–1202), Duke of Great Poland 68, 69, 89, 90, 92
Mikołaj of Radom (15th cent.), composer 135
Mikołaj Trąba (c. 1358–1422), Archbishop 117
Milan 421
"Millenaries" 433, 435, 438
Milsko, Milzenland 53
Milyutin Nicholas (1818–1872) 445
Miłkowski Zygmunt (1824–1915) 484
Miłosław (battle of, 1848) 416
Miłosz Czesław (1911) 571
Minin Kuzma (–1616) 187
Mińsk 530, 551
Misiowski A. (mid–18th cent.) 258
Mitzler de Kolof Wawrzyniec (1711–1778) 263
Mława 464
Młodzianowski Tomasz (1622–1686) 226
Mniszech Jerzy (–1613) 184
Mniszech Jerzy August (1715–1778) 251, 269
Mniszech Maryna (–1614) 184
Mochnacki Maurycy (c. 1804–1834) 375, 379, 381, 387, 390
Modlin 389
modernism 499
Mogilno 77, 79
Mohammed IV (1641–1692), Sultan 220
Mohylów 255 see Orthodox Church
Mokronowski Andrzej (1713–1784) 298, 302
Moldavia 116, 122, 148, 188, 222, 232, 238, 271, 281, 290, 341
Molière Jean Baptiste (1622–1673) 259
Molotov Viacheslav (1890) 603
Mongol Empire, Mongols 86, 93, 98, 104
Moniuszko Stanisław (1819–1872) 430

Montesquieu Charles Louis (1689–1755) 312, 313, 315
Monti Antoine (1684–1738) 243
Montpellier 104
Moraczewski Jędrzej (1870–1944) 536, 538, 543, 545, 546
Moravia 31, 41, 44, 45, 50, 53, 55, 122, 148, 252
Moravian Gate 28, 62
Morcinek Gustaw (1891–1963) 570
Morsztyn Jan Andrzej (c. 1613–1693) 229
Morsztyn Zbigniew (c. 1628–1689) 229, 233
mos liberorum hospitum see Law
Moscow 157, 212, 357, 464, 512, 550, 590, 603, 605
Mościce 582
Mościcki Ignacy (1867–1946) 579, 582, 593, 595, 597
Moulin Pierre de (–1658) 200
Muraviev Michail (1796–1866) 445, 450, 453
Mszana 522
Münchengrätz (treaty of, 1833) 392
Munich 600, 601, 606
Murmańsk 532
Muscovy 115, 146, 147, 148, 149, 156, 157, 168, 169, 184, 186, 187, 198, 214, 219, 222, 227 see Moscow
Mussolini Benito (1883–1945) 589, 599, 600
Myszkowski Zygmunt (1562–1615) 185
Myszkowski family 175

Nalevaiko Semen (–1597) 189
Nałkowska Zofia (1884–1954) 570, 571
Nałkowski Wacław (1851–1911) 468
Namysłów 112
Nancy 263
Naples 343
Napoleon Bonaparte (1769–1821), Emperor of the French 341, 343–349, 351–353, 354–360, 363, 364, 367, 377, 502, 523
— Civil Code see Law
Napoleon III (1808–1873), Emperor of the French 431, 435, 441, 444
Narew 37
"Narodnaya Volya", Narodniks 476, 485
"Narodni Vybor" (National Council) 535 see Czechoslovakia
Naruszewicz Adam (1733–1796) 302
Narutowicz Gabriel (1865–1922) 559
Narva (treaty of, 1704) 237
Narvik (battle of, 1940) 606

42 History of Poland

Natanson Jakub (1832–1884) 464
National Central Committee (1863) 440–443, 521 see Reds
National Committee (Poznań uprising, 1848) 414, 415
National Committee (Cracow, 1848) 418
National Council (Lwów, 1848) 418, 419
National Democratic Party, National Democrats 492, 493, 494, 508, 513, 516, 517–519, 522, 523, 533, 534, 536–538, 545, 550, 559, 562, 593, 595
National Party 516
National Government (Cracow, 1846) 410
National Government 443, 444–446 see National Central Committee
National League 492, 493, 497, 506–511, 513, 514–516, 519, 539
National Liberals 483
National Peasant Union 516, 519
National Radical Camp 595, 598
National Unity Camp 598
National Workers Union 511, 516, 519
nationalism 482, 483, 486, 492, 513, 515, 518, 520, 531, 598
nazism 589, 595, 599, 606
Nax Ferdynand (1736–1810) 302
Near East 50, 404
Neman 288, 348, 552
Neminem captivabimus nisi iure victum see Law
Neo-classicism 377
Neo-slav movement 513
Nero 29
Nertchinsk 407
Netherlands 189, 229, 231
Newton Isaac (1642–1727) 233
Nicholas I (1796–1855), Emperor of Russia, King of Poland 377, 380, 383, 387, 391, 407, 414, 422, 431
Nicholas II (1864–1918), Emperor of Russia 491, 529
Nicolaus of Poland (13th cent.), physician 104
Niemcewicz Julian Ursyn (1758–1841) 377, 464
Niemcza 64
Nida 119
Niemirich Jurij (c. 1612–1659) 217
Niemojewski Jakub (c. 1532–1584) 169
Niemojowski Bonawentura (1787–1835) 374
Niemojowski Wincenty (1784–1834) 374
Niepołomice 174

Niesiecki Kasper (1682–1744) 264
Nieszawa 385
— Statutes see Law
Nieśwież 173, 258, 580 see Radziwiłł family
Nietzsche Friedrich Wilhelm (1844–1900) 502
Niewiadomski Eligiusz (1869–1923) 559
Nikolai Nikolayevich (1856–1929), Grand Duke of Russia, 522, 528
Nisztad, Neustadt 280
Nobel Prize 471, 502
nomads 34
Non-Party Block for Cooperation with the Government 580, 584, 586, 591
Norbert of Magdeburg (c. 1080–1134), Archbishop 67
Norblin Jean Pierre (1745–1830) 299
North March 52
Norway 101
Norwerth Edgar Aleksander (1884–1950) 576
Norwid Cyprian Kamil (1821–1883) 428
Noskowski Andrzej (1492–1567) 174
Novara (battle of, 1849) 421
Novosiltzov Nikolai (1762–1838) 367, 374, 375
Nowa Huta 30
Nowe Miasto Korczyn 119, 142
Nowogródek 563
Nowosielce 597
Nowogród Siewierski 217
Nowy Sącz 88, 216
Nowy Targ 191
Nuremberg 87, 136
Nysa river 85
Nysa 280

Obertyn 149
Obodrits 32, 47
Oda (19th/11th cent.), Margravine of North March, Mieszko's I second wife 52
Odessa 340, 375
Odra 17, 19, 25, 29, 31, 32, 33, 43, 45, 48, 49, 50, 51, 52, 59, 60, 62, 64, 67, 92, 95, 126, 252
Odrowąż family 79
Ogariev Nicholas (1813–1877) 440
Ogiński Michał (1728–1800) 279, 280, 288, 299, 306
Ogiński family 300
Ogrodzieniec 174 see Boner family
Oka 606
Okół 88

Okrzeja Stefan (1886–1905) 511
Olgierd, Algirdas (c. 1296–1377), Grand Duke of Lithuania 115
Oleśnica 126
Oliwa (peace of, 1660) 106, 190, 217
Olkusz 127
Olsztyn 176
Olszewski Karol (1846–1915) 470
Ołbin 79
Opaliński Krzysztof (1600–1655) 215, 227
Opaliński Łukasz (1581–1654) 195
Opaliński family 230
Opava 104
Opitz Martin (1597–1639) 233
Opolanie, Opolini 40
Opole 60, 74, 204, 233, 397, 555
Orchowski Jan Alojzy (1767–1832) 329
Order of the Knights of the Sword see Livonian Knights
Order of the Teutonic Knights see Teutonic Knights
Organic Statue see Constitution
"Organic work" 395–397, 407, 426, 433, 435, 438, 465, 466, 482
Orléans 243
Orlik Filip (Fyłyp Orłyk) (1673–1742) 238
Orłowski Łukasz (–1765) 258
Orsza (battle of, 1514) 148
Orthodox Church 173, 183, 185, 186, 187, 189, 192, 200, 206, 225, 254, 255, 271, 391, 455, 494, 564, 598
Orthodox Empress 277 see Catherina II
Orzelski Świętosław (1549–1598) 161
Orzeszkowa Eliza (1841–1910) 472
Osiński Antoni (mid–18th cent.) 258
Osiński Józef (1738–1802) 302
Osman II (1604–1622), Sultan 189
Ossoliński Hieronim (–1576) 155
Ossoliński Józef Maksymilian (1748–1825) 345, 392
Ossoliński Jerzy (1595–1650) 212, 213
Ossoliński family 230
Ossowski Michał (1743–) 319
Ossowski Michał (1863–1886) 477
Osterwa Juliusz (1885–1947) 571
Ostroróg Jan (c. 1436–1501), political writer 134
Ostrowiec 512
Ostróda 398
Ostróg 264
Ostrogski Konstanty (1527–1608) 183
Ostrogski Vasilii (1526–1608) 192
Ostrogski family 192

Ostrołęka (battle of, 1831) 385, 387
Ostrowski Józef (1850–1924) 531
Ostrowski Teodor (1750–1802) 302
Ostrów Tumski 88
Oświęcim (Duchy of) 120
Otto (c. 1060–1139), Bishop of Bamberg 67
Otto I (912–973), German King and Emperor 42, 49
Otto II (955–983), German King and Emperor 51
Otto III (980–1002), German King and Emperor 52, 62
Ottoman Empire 169, 188, 189, 220 see Turkey
— Sublime Porte 221, 222
Ożarowski Piotr (–1794) 327

Pabianice 369
pacta conventa see Law
Paderewski Ignacy (1860–1941) 504, 524, 529, 546, 548
Padlewski Zygmunt (1835–1863) 441, 444
Padniewski Filip (–1572) 175
Palij Semen (–1710) 239
Palmerston Henry (1784–1865) 431
Pan-Germanism 492
Panin Nikita (1718–1783) 275, 280, 281, 284, 305
Pankiewicz Józef (1866–1940) 504, 576
Panslavism 421
"Panta Koina" ("Everything in Common") 375
Papacy 51, 65, 93, 148, 154, 167, 176, 183, 221, 226, 255, 284, 455
Parliament see Constitution
  Chamber of Deputies 149, 164, 185, 284, 316, 318, 350, 354, 364
  colloquia, assemblies of the lords and the gentry 124
  land diets (*conventiones particulares*) 122, 125, 149, 150
  land diets (*sejmiki*) 121
  liberum veto 218, 272, 275, 276, 281, 285, 310
  local diets 184, 185, 192, 224, 232, 239, 241, 253, 269, 285, 308, 309, 311, 312, 315, 316, 317, 350
  Polish Parliamentary Club (in the Austrian Parliament) 494, 517, 518
  Polish Parliamentary Club (in the Prussian Area) 534
  Privy Council 149

Senate 149, 150, 161, 164, 168, 203, 217, 234, 278, 350, 364, 377, 392, 528, 555, 559, 591, 596
Senate of the Free City Gdańsk 588, 589
Seym 125, 149, 150, 153, 155, 156, 157, 160, 161, 163, 164, 167, 170, 172, 185, 192, 195, 200, 203, 206, 217, 218, 219, 224, 232, 235, 239, 240, 241, 242, 265, 269, 271, 272, 274, 275, 276, 281, 284, 289, 292, 294, 298, 302, 303, 306, 308, 309, 310, 311, 312, 315, 316, 318, 319, 320, 321, 322, 323, 324, 325, 328, 330, 334, 339, 348–350, 354, 357, 364, 374, 377, 381, 384, 385–388, 391, 392, 396, 459, 462, 463, 479, 517, 519, 527, 536, 537, 538, 547–549, 555, 558–560, 562, 577, 578, 580, 584, 591, 596, 602
viritim (principle of election) 170
voting system 513
Paris 77, 97, 104, 133, 163, 167, 219, 263, 281, 310, 323, 328, 341, 343, 352, 357, 363, 388, 404, 405, 413, 418, 421, 426, 430, 434, 435, 443, 444, 471, 473, 529, 532, 545, 565, 576, 597, 605
Parnas Jakub Karol (1884–1949) 568
Parkany (battle of, 1683) 221
Partynice 30
Pasek Jan Chryzostom (c. 1636–c. 1701) 239, 256
Paskevich Ivan (1782–1856) 385, 389, 391, 394, 395, 416, 422
"Passivists" 526, 532
Pastorius Joachim (1611–1681) 233
Patek Stanisław (1866–1945) 550
Patriotic Society 376, 383, 387, 388, 399
Paul I (1754–1801), Tsar of Russia 340
Paul IV, Pope (1555–1559) 160
Paul V, Pope (1605–1621) 186, 189
Paulines 216
Paulus Vladimiri of Brudzeń (1370/3–c. 1434), professor 117, 134
Paweł of Przemankowo (–1296), Bishop of Cracow 90
Pawlikowska-Jasnorzewska Maria (1894–1945) 571
Pawlikowski Józef (c. 1770–1829) 310, 311, 312, 313, 329, 344
Pawlikowski Tadeusz (1862–1915) 504
Peasant Association 407 *see* Ściegienny
Peasant Party (in Galicia) 494, 517, 536 *see* Polish Peasant Party "Piast"

Peasant Radical Party 518
Peasant Party 597, 598
— Universities 567
Peasants
  decree of December (1807) 367
  enfranchisement 337, 338, 350
  woods and pastures question 419, 420, 451, 452, 460, 479, 481, 508, 537
  freeholds 441, 444, 445
  labour dues, labour services, serfdom, serf labour 151, 153, 191, 196, 197, 198, 223, 225, 261, 262, 277, 284, 289, 293, 312, 318, 327, 328, 337, 340, 341, 350, 351, 358–361, 364–368, 383, 385, 387, 392, 393, 401, 404, 409, 411, 412, 418, 419, 431, 433, 435, 437, 441, 444, 452, 460
  land reform (1919–1925) 548, 549, 551, 562
  letters patent of Joseph II (1780–1790) 339, 340
  Manifesto of Połaniec (1794) 325
  Manifesto of the Temporary National Government (1863) 441
  movement 479, 493, 494, 516, 526, 535
  "Regulation Reform" (in the Prussian area, 1848–1850) 450 serf fight 324
  "Settlement Decree" (in the Prussian area, 1807–1811) 361, 362
  ukase of the Tsar (1864) 445
Peiper Tadeusz (1891) 571
Pelplin 106
People's Supreme Council (Prussian area) 546 *see* Polish People's Council
Perejasław (compact of, 1654) 214
Perl Feliks (1871–1927) 595
Permanent Council (1775–1788) 283, 284–287, 295, 302, 303, 305–309; (1793–1794) 322, 325, 327
Persia 186, 243
Petcheneguians 52
Peter I (1672–1725), Emperor of Rusia 235, 238, 241, 242, 243, 245, 247, 254, 255
Peter III (1728–1762), Emperor of Russia 267
St. Peter's Pence 41, 93, 101, 102 *see* Papacy
Peter of Lusignan (14th cent.), King of Cyprus 113
St. Petersburg 268, 269, 270, 272, 274, 280, 281, 284, 285, 305, 307, 320, 322, 332, 333, 355, 357, 377, 383, 392, 433, 434, 437, 438, 439, 441, 455, 461, 473, 474, 491, 492, 493, 506, 514, 524

Petlura Semen (1877–1926) 550, 598
Petrograd 530 see St. Petersburg
— Soviet of Workers and Soldiers Deputies 529
Petrushevich Eugen (1863–) 563
Petrycy Sebastian of Pilzno (c. 1554–1624) 229, 232
Philippe d'Orléans (1674–1723) 243
Philomats 375, 379
physiocracy 262, 298, 299, 319
Piarists 259, 264
Piast, mythical founder of the dynasty 42
Piast (dynasty) 19, 42, 51, 58, 60, 62, 89, 107, 108, 118, 126, 168
— of Kujawy 114
— of Silesia 126, 206, 252
Piattoli Scipione (1749–1809) 298, 316, 317, 319
Pieniny 601
Pieracki Bronisław (1895–1934) 592
Pieskowa Skała 174
Pietrusiński Jan (1864–1886) 477
Pilica 333
Piła 310
Piławce (battle of, 1648) 212
Piłsudski Józef (1867–1935) 488, 492, 506, 512, 519, 520, 521–524, 525, 527, 530, 532, 533, 536, 537, 538, 543, 545, 546, 547, 550, 552, 559, 560, 562, 563, 565, 570, 577–582, 584, 585, 588–595, 597, 599, 605
Pińczów 173, 174, 179
— Academy of 174 see Calvinists
Piotr of Byczyna (14th cent.), historian 134
Piotr of Silesia, son of Włost (–1153), Silesian lord 68, 78, 79
Piotrków 122, 156, 310
Piramowicz Grzegorz (1735–1801) 302
Pisecki Tomasz (c. 1578–c. 1648) 233
Pistorius Szymon (17th cent.) 233
Pius VII, Pope (1800–1823) 353
Pius IX, Pope (1846–1878) 420
Plautus (c. 250 BC–180 BC) 186
Pliny the Elder (23–79), Roman naturalist 29
Płock 37, 60, 65, 68, 78, 79, 196, 348, 393, 550
Płowce (battle of, 1331) 141
Pniewski Bogdan (1897–1965) 576
Poczobut Marcin (1728–1809) 302
Podgórze see Cracow
Podhajce (battle of, 1667) 220

Podhorce 304 see Rzewuski Wacław
Podhale 191, 213, 223
Podlasie 84, 127, 158, 223, 258, 342, 441, 510, 532
Podolia 113, 220, 222, 223
Poincaré Raymond (1860–1934) 529
Poitiers 401 see Polish Democratic Society
— Manifesto 401, 406, 408, 409, 411
Pokucie 149
Pol Wincenty (1807–1872) 426
Polanie, Polani, Polanes 40, 41, 42, 47, 64
Polanowo (peace treaty of, 1643) 180, 188, 204
Polesie 552, 563, 564, 586
Polish Academy of Literature 593
Polish Auxiliary Corps 534
Polish Brethern see Arians
Polish Committee of National Liberation 607
Polish Democratic Society 399–404, 406, 408, 421
Polish Democratic Society (Prussian area, 1907) 516
Polish law see Law
Polish League (Poznań, 1848) 417
Polish League 484, 485, 492, 514 see National League
Polish Liquidation Commission 535
Polish Military Organization (POW) 523, 525, 527, 533, 537, 538, 581, 593
Polish National Committee (1831) 399, 400
Polish National Committee (1917) 524, 529, 532, 535, 545, 548
Polish National Council 535
"Polish National Venta" 400 see freemasonry
Polish Parliamentary Club see Parliament
Polish Peasant Party (PSL) "Piast" 517, 547, 551, 558–560
Polish Peasant Party (PSL) "Wyzwolenie" 526, 537, 577
Polish Peasant Union (Congress Kingdom, 1904–1907) 516
Polish People's Councils 546
Polish Progressive Party 519
Polish Social-Democratic Party of Galicia and Cieszyn-Silesia (PPSD) 487, 518, 519, 536
Polish Socialist Party (PPS) 488, 489, 506–513, 516, 519, 520, 521, 526, 527, 533, 536, 550, 551, 577, 580, 595, 596

Polish Socialist Party (PPS) of the Prussian area 489, 497
Polish Teachers' Union 567
Polish Technical University 378
Polish Workers' Party (PPR) 607
Political Circle in Lausanne see Polish National Committee
Polock 169
Połaniec (Manifesto of, 1794) 325 see Peasants
Połtawa (battle of, 1709) 238
Pomerania, Pomeranians 21, 28, 31, 35, 37, 43, 48, 50, 52, 59, 60, 66, 73, 75, 77, 91, 92, 97, 116, 121, 127, 180, 206, 245, 257, 289, 331, 362, 397, 398, 405, 407, 417, 456, 462, 480, 484, 495, 515, 535, 566, 601, 608
— Gdańsk 28, 43, 44, 57, 62, 66, 84, 86, 89, 91, 94, 95, 98, 99, 106, 111, 112, 121, 397, 494, 549, 555
— Eastern 60
— Western 36, 43, 50, 57, 60, 66, 67, 68, 73, 84, 85, 89, 91, 92, 95, 101, 106, 111, 112, 125, 126, 168, 179, 206, 216, 238, 251, 397, 498
Poniatowski Józef (1763–1813) 321, 330, 348, 354, 355, 357, 358
Poniatowski Juliusz (1886) 699
Poniatowski Michał (1736–1794) 285, 292, 302, 304
Poniatowski Stanisław (1676–1762) 250, 264, 268–272
Poniatowski Stanisław (1732–1798) see Stanisław Augustus
Poniatowski family 250, 265, 266, 312, 316
Poniński Adam (1732–1798) 281, 308
Pope 186, 189 (see Paul V); 353 (see Pius VII)
Popiel, mythical dynast 42
Popiel Michał 455
Popławski Antoni (1739–1799) 302
Popławski Jan Ludwik (1854–1908) 485, 492, 493
Poprad 52, 88
Poraj family 112
Portsmouth 402
positivism 430, 449, 465, 466, 472, 482, 500
postimpressionism 504
Potemkin Grigorij (1739–1791) 284, 285, 305, 309

Potocki Alfred (1817–1889) 463
Potocki Andrzej (1861–1908) 518
Potocki Antoni (–1766) 265
Potocki Franciszek Salezy (–1772) 269
Potocki Ignacy (1750–1809) 309, 310, 311, 315, 316, 317, 318, 321, 323, 330, 332
Potocki Jan (1761–1815) 300
Potocki Prot (–1801) 290, 319
Potocki Stanisław (1755–1821) 287, 302, 323, 345, 348, 354, 373, 378
Potocki Szczęsny (1751–1805) 306, 315, 320, 322
Potocki Wacław (1621–1696) 229
Potocki family 227, 243, 247, 248, 250, 251, 265, 283
Potsdam (treaty of friendship, 1805) 346
Potworowski Gustaw (1800–1860) 413
Potworowski Tadeusz Piotr (1898–1952) 576
Powodowski Hieronim (c. 1547–1613) 201
Pozharski Dimitrii (1578–c. 1642) 187
Poznań 31, 41, 60, 62, 65, 68, 79, 85, 86, 87, 88, 89, 117, 129, 133, 153, 196, 199, 225, 264, 347, 348, 361, 362, 363, 369, 383, 392, 393, 395, 397, 398, 406, 407, 409, 410, 414, 415, 416, 417, 420, 422, 426, 446, 456, 457, 478, 480, 481, 491, 495, 496, 504, 515, 524, 547, 549, 555
— Society of the Friends of the Sciences 430
PPS Fighting Organization see Polish Socialist Party
PPS Left Wing 512, 520, 526, 533, 545 see Polish Socialist Party
PPS Revolutionary Wing see Polish Socialist Party
"Praesens" (group of architects) 576
Praga (masacre of, 1794) 332
Prague 50, 56, 62, 133, 461, 514, 563, 566, 599, 601
Prandocin 79
Prażmowski Mikołaj (1617–1673) 18
Prądzyński Ignacy (1792–1850) 384
Premonstratensians 105
Premyslids dynasty 49
Prešov 278
Pripet' 288
Privy Council see Parliament
"Proletariat Great" 476, 478, 488
"Proletariat Second" ("Little") 478
Pronaszko Andrzej (1888–1961) 576
Pronaszko Zbigniew (1885–1958) 576

Prószyński Konrad (Promyk) (1851–1908) 466
Prosna 30
Prośnica 59
Protestants 159, 172, 174, 180, 189, 198, 200, 202, 204, 226, 227, 232, 254 see dissenters
Proust Marcel (1872–1922) 571
Provincial School Council (Galicia) 479, 494
Provisional Commission of Confederated Independence Parties 519
Provisional Council of State 530
Provisional Revolutionary Committee of Poland (Białystok, 1920) 551
Provisional Substitutional Council (1794) 327
Prus Bolesław (Głowacki Aleksander) (1847–1912) 467, 472
Prussia, Prussians 21, 95, 127, 131, 133, 135, 137, 148, 156, 157, 158, 159, 168, 170, 175, 187, 190, 200, 204, 211, 216, 220, 223, 228, 233, 239, 242, 244–248, 251–254, 266–268, 270, 271, 275, 277, 280–282, 289, 305, 306, 307, 309, 316, 320, 321, 322, 323, 331–334, 338–341, 346, 351, 352, 354, 360–364, 370, 380, 389, 392, 397, 398, 402, 408, 410, 411, 414–417, 419, 422, 435, 441, 450, 456–459, 474, 475, 478, 480, 482, 483, 489–491, 495, 498, 515, 516, 523, 531, 533, 535, 543, 547, 549, 552, 601
"Prussian Alliance" 121
Prusso-Nuremberg style 504
Prut (treaty of, 1711) 238
Pruthenia, Prussia, Prussians 31, 37, 50, 52, 56, 62, 69, 77, 84, 85, 88, 93, 95, 121
Przedbórz 369
Przemysł I (1220/1–1257), Duke of Great Poland 91
Przemysł II (1257–1296), Duke of Great Poland, King of Poland 90, 91, 92, 98, 99, 104
Przemyśl 55, 60, 62, 226, 595
Przesmycki-Miriam Zenon (1861–1944) 500
Przeworsk 230
Przyboś Julian (1901–1970) 571
Przybylski Czesław (1880–1936) 504, 576
Przybyszewski Stanisław (1868–1927) 500, 504
Przyłuski Jakub (–1554) 155, 175
Przypkowski Samuel (c. 1592–1670) 233
pseudo-Byzantine style 504
Pskov (battle of, 1581) 136, 169

Pszczyna 253
Ptolemy Claudius (2nd cent.), geographer 30
Pudłowski Stanisław (1597–1645) 232
Puck 190, 498
Pułaski Aleksander Kazimierz (1800–1838) 387, 399, 402
Pułaski Józef (1704–1769) 277
Pułaski Kazimierz (1747–1779) 279
Puławy 214, 287, 300, 345, 346, 356, 524
Pułtusk 79, 174, 385
Pyrz Michał (–1624) 597
Pyrzyczanie, Prisani 40

Quisling Vidkun (1887–1945) 606

Racibórz 206
Racławice (battle of, 1794) 327
Raczkiewicz Władysław (1885–1947) 530
Radom 88, 276, 355, 379
Radziejowski Hieronim (1622–1667) 215
Radziwiłł Antoni Henryk (1775–1833) 392
Radziwiłł Bogusław (1620–1669) 211, 215
Radziwiłł Ferdynand (1834–1926) 534
Radziwiłł Janusz (1612–1655) 215
Radziwiłł Janusz (1880–1967) 580
Radziwiłł Karol (1734–1790) 269, 271, 276, 306
Radziwiłł Michał (1778–1850) 384
Radziwiłł Urszula (1705–1753) 258
Radziwiłł family 211, 227
railways 394, 464, 551, 599
Rakoczy, Duke of Transylvania see George II Rakoczy
Raków 179, 231, 233
— Academy of 200
Ramorino Girolamo (1792–1849) 389
Rapallo (treaty of, 1922) 565
Raszyn (battle of, 1809) 354
Rataj Maciej (1884–1940) 559, 578, 595
Ratisbona, Regensburg 37, 50
"Realists" 506, 508, 510 see Conservatives
Red organization, Reds 438–440, 443, 444, 459, 517–520, 522–524, 540, 632
Red Guard 545 see Communists
Reformation 154, 158–163, 168, 172, 173, 183, 189, 197, 198
"Regulation Reform" see Peasants
Reichenbach (convention of, 1790) 316
Rej Mikołaj (1505–1569) 155, 173, 174, 179
Renaissance 19, 21, 117, 146, 149, 153, 161,

170, 171, 172, 173, 174, 175, 176, 178, 180, 227, 228, 229, 231, 233, 299, 430
Repnin Nikołaj (1734–1801) 276, 277
Reszel 88
retrait lignager (custom) 72
Revel 157, 168
Reymont Władysław (1867–1925) 502
Reytan Tadeusz (1742–1780) 282
Rhine 244, 322, 607
Rhineland 29, 45, 105, 480, 599
"Rhytm" (group of artists) 576
Richeza (–1063), Queen of Poland 55
Richeza, Ryksa, of Poland (1288–1335), Queen of Bohemia 99
Ribbentrop Joachim (1893–1946) 601–603
Riga 167, 168 ; (peace of, 1921), 552, 559, 565
Rittner Tadeusz (1873–1921) 502
Rococo 257
Rojecki F. (mid–18th cent.) 358
Romanesque art 63, 78, 105, 106
Roman Empire 29, 32, 33
Romanticism 300, 377–380, 422, 424, 472, 500, 573
Romanowski Mieczysław (1834–1863) 428
Rome 19, 77, 92, 198, 203, 222, 226, 256, 263, 407, 455
Rome 48, 208, 298, 343, 421, 473, 600
St. Romuald (956–1027), hermit 64
Ronsard Pierre (1524–1585) 146
Rostkowski Franciszek (–1862) 439
Rostock (land peace, 1283) 92
Rostworowski Karol Hubert (1877–1938) 502, 571
Rousseau Jean Jacques (1712–1778) 279, 298, 310, 315
Roussel Albert (1869–1937) 576
Rozwadowski Tadeusz (1866–1928) 577
Rożdzieński Walenty (c. 1560–c. 1622) 233
Różycki Ludomir (1884–1953) 504
Rudawski Jan (1617–c. 1690) 232
Rudolf I of Hapsburg (1218–1291), German King 99
Rügen 67
Rulhière Claude Carloman de (1735–1791) 279
Rumania, Rumanians 232, 404, 412, 421, 565
Ruric dynasty 112
Russia, Russians 17, 21, 37, 45, 46, 51, 55, 57, 62–65, 66, 75, 77, 87, 93, 113, 116, 136, 148, 157, 163, 168, 169, 183, 184, 186–189, 197, 204, 211, 214, 216, 218, 222, 234, 235, 237–239, 241–244, 251, 254, 266, 267, 268, 270–282, 285, 305–307, 309, 316, 321, 322, 323, 324, 327, 331–333, 337, 338, 339–341, 345, 346–348, 354–358, 363, 364, 369, 373, 376, 377, 380, 383, 384, 388, 391, 392, 394, 395, 408, 411, 412, 421, 422, 431, 433, 434–436, 438–440, 444, 445, 447, 449, 451–454, 455, 460, 461, 463–465, 474, 476, 480, 483, 488, 491, 493, 500, 505, 506, 512, 514, 520, 522, 523, 525, 528–532, 536, 539, 545, 546, 549, 550, 565, 590, 607
"Russians Little" 461 *see* Ukrainians
Russophils, Old Ruthenians 461
rustici ducis 71
Ruthenia 37, 45, 51, 55, 57, 62, 63, 65, 66, 75, 77, 84, 87, 93, 104, 107, 113, 116, 124, 127, 129, 158, 173, 217, 227, 440, 519 *see* Ukraine
Rutkowski Jan (1885–1949) 567
Rybiński Maciej (1784–1874) 389, 397, 399
Rydz-Śmigły Edward (1886–1941) 537, 593, 595, 597, 598, 599
Rytwiany 230 *see* Opaliński family
Rzewuski Henryk (1791–1866) 426
Rzewuski Seweryn (1743–1811) 276, 284, 287, 306, 309, 315, 320, 321, 322, 332
Rzewuski Wacław (1706–1779) 258, 276

Sadova (battle of, 1866) 460
Sala Sebastian (17th cent.) 230
"Salamander Society" 121
Saldern Kaspar von (1711–1786) 275, 280
Salomea (c. 1101–1144) 68
Salomon Polonus (2nd half of the 18th cent.) 315
Sambia 37
Samogitia, Żmudź, Samogitians 115, 116, 117
Samuś (Samijło Iwanowicz) (2nd half of the 18th cent.) 239
San 55
San Domingo (Haiti) 344
Sandomierz 31, 40, 60, 62, 68, 88, 89, 90, 93, 98, 106, 129, 136, 153, 174, 185, 196, 355, 441
Sapieha Kazimierz Nestor (1754–1798) 284, 298, 307, 355, 441
Sapieha Leon (1802–1878) 396
Sapieha family 227, 238

Sarbiewski Maciej (1595–1640) 229
Sardinia (Savoy-Sardinia) 244
"sarmatism" 173, 228, 230, 232, 253, 256, 257, 272, 297–300, 377
Satanów 295 see Levin Mendel
Sava 32
Savannah (battle of, 1779) 279
Savoy 400 see Sardinia
Saxon times 235, 249, 251, 257, 258, 261, 262, 276, 285, 292, 300
Saxony, Saxons 235, 237, 240–247, 248, 250, 252, 254, 261, 263, 265, 266, 268, 270, 276, 277, 278, 285, 292, 300, 317, 322, 348, 357, 358, 362, 364, 368, 369
Sącz Nowy see Nowy Sącz
Sącz Stary 88
Scandinavia, Scandinavians 28, 29, 45, 48, 49, 51, 63, 77
Scheibler Karl Wilhelm (1820–1881) 433
Schiller Leon (1887–1954) 571
Schlüsselburg 376
Schlichting Jonasz (1592–1661) 233
Schmerling Anton (1805–1893) 459
Schönbrunn (peace treaty of, 1809) 355
Schulz Bruno (1892–1942) 570
Scott Walter (1771–1832) 378
scultetus 83, 86, 127
"secession" 504
secular canons 77
Semigalia 157 see Livonia
Senate see Parliament
Senate of the Free City Gdańsk see Gdańsk see also Parliament
Serbia 31, 525
serfdom, serf labour see Peasants
serf fight see Peasants
"Šettlement Decree" see Peasants
Seyda Marian (1879–1967) 516
Seyda Władysław (1863–1939) 534
Seym see Parliament
— Galician see Galicia
Sęp-Szarzyński Mikołaj (1550–1581) 175
Shakespeare William (1564–1616) 571
Shein Michał (–1634) 187
Shuiski Vasili (1552–1613), Tsar of Russia 184, 186
Shuvalov Paul (1830–1918) 491
Siberia 168, 279, 391, 406, 407, 453, 455, 472, 475, 488, 500
Sicily 421
Siciński Władysław (–1664) 218

Sicz 188, 208
Sieciech, Sethec (11th/12th cent.), Palatine of Poland 66
Siedlce 355
Siemomysł (10th cent.), Duke of Polanie 35, 42
Siemowit (9th cent.), Duke of Polanie 42
Siemowit I (1224–1262), Duke of Mazovia 91
Siemowit IV (c. 1352–1426), Duke of Mazovia 114
Sieniawska Zofia see Czartoryska Zofia
Sienicki Mikołaj (c. 1521–1582) 155, 161
Sienkiewicz Henryk (1846–1916) 466, 472, 482, 524
Sieradz 43, 60, 68, 76, 101, 124, 369
Sierakowski Zygmunt (1827–1863) 434, 438, 439, 444
Sieroszewski Wacław (1858–1945) 502
Sierpiński Wacław (1882) 568
Siewierz 120, 187
Sigismund, son of Korybut (–1435), Lithuanian Prince 118
Sigismund, son of Kiejstut (–1440), Lithuanian Prince 119
Sigismund I (1467–1548), King of Poland 126, 132, 146, 148, 150, 155, 466
Sigismund Augustus (1520–1572), King of Poland 145, 155, 156, 159–161, 167, 173, 175, 181, 188
Sigismund III Vasa (1566–1632), King of Poland 158, 181, 183, 184, 185, 186, 187, 189, 196, 198, 200, 203, 218
Sigismund of Luxemburg (1368–1437), King of Hungary and Bohemia, German King, Emperor 114, 119
Sigrid Storrada, Świętosława, of Poland (c. 970–c. 1014), Queen of Sweden and Denmark 51
Sikorski Władysław (1881–1943) 519, 523, 524, 560, 577
Sikorski Kazimierz (–1895) 576
Silesia, Silesians 28, 36, 40, 43, 48, 51, 53, 56, 57, 60, 66, 68, 73, 80, 84, 85, 90, 93, 97, 98, 102, 103, 104, 106, 118, 119, 121, 122, 126, 127, 129, 131, 133, 135, 136, 148, 153, 158, 168, 180, 187, 199, 204, 215, 216, 219, 233, 236, 242, 360–362, 369, 397–398, 407, 417, 449, 456, 457, 458, 473, 474, 555, 561, 599, 607
— Cieszyn 535, 600

— Lower 38, 44, 62, 82, 84, 89, 90, 93, 263, 397
— Upper 21, 28, 84, 89, 97, 361, 362, 393, 394, 396–398, 417, 457, 458, 474, 480, 489, 496, 497, 515, 555, 557
Simokattes Teophylaktos (6th/7th cent.), Byzantine historian 33
"Skamander" (group of poets) 571
Skarbek Fryderyk (1792–1866) 378
Skarbimir (c. 1117), Palatine of Poland 67
Skarga Piotr (1536–1612) 185, 186, 201, 226
Skarżysko 595 see Central Industrial Area
Skirmunt Konstanty (1866–1951) 566
Składkowski Felicjan Sławoj (1885–1962) 597
Skłodowska-Curie Maria (1867–1934) 17, 471
Skoczylas Władysław (1883–1934) 576
Skrzetuski Wincenty (1745–1791) 302
Skrzynecki Jan (1787–1860) 385–387
Skrzyński Aleksander (1882–1931) 562, 566, 578
Skulski Leopold (1878–c. 1942) 549, 550
Slovakia, Slovaks 31, 33, 278, 421, 601, 602
Sluch 550
Sławek Walery (1879–1939) 580, 584, 588
Sławno 92
Słomniki 159
Słonim see Ogiński family 300
Słonimski Antoni (1895–1976) 568
Słowacki Juliusz (1809–1849) 425, 426, 500
Słuck 275
Słupie 47
Słupsk 92, 112, 113, 206
Smarzowa 411 see Szela Jakub
Smith Adam (1723–1790) 319
Smoleńsk 115, 156, 186, 187, 217, 357, 464
Smoleński Władysław (1851–1926) 486, 504
Smolka Franciszek (1810–1899) 405, 418
Smuglewicz Franciszek (1745–1807) 299
Sobieski Jan see John III
Sobieski Jakub (1667–1737), son of John III 222, 234
Sobieski family 196
Sobiesław (–1178), Viceroy of Gdańsk-Pomerania 89
Sobolewski family 373
Social Democracy of the Kingdom of Poland and Lithuania (SDKPiL) 488, 506–510, 520, 526, 533, 536, 545

socialism 457, 474–476, 482, 483, 486, 487, 488–491, 492, 494, 532
Society of the Friends of Sciences 378, 379, 391
Society of Philomats see Philomats
"Societies of Polish Workers" 489
Society of Polish Republicans 342
Society of Primary School Teachers of the Polish Kingdom 510
"Sodalitas Litteraria Vistulana" 134
Sofia 514
Sokołowo (battle of, 1848) 416
Solski Ludwik (1855–1954) 503
Solski Stanisław (1622–1701) 230
Soldiers' Councils 538
Sołtyk Kajetan (1715–1788) 276
Sołtyk Stanisław (1753–1831) 340
Sophia of Holszany (c. 1405–1461), Queen of Poland 118, 119, 135
Sosnkowski Kazimierz (1885) 519
"Southern Society" 376
Soviet Union 17, 532, 552, 565, 566, 588, 590, 601–603, 605, 607, 609
Sowiński Józef (1777–1831) 389, 435
Spa (conference of, 1920) 551
Spain, Spanish people 36, 47, 198, 204, 244, 268, 282, 351, 354, 600
Spasowicz Włodzimierz (1829–1906) 492
Spielberg 406
Spiritual College in St. Petersburg 455
Spisz 280
Spytek of Melsztyn (–1431), Hussite Chief, Castellan of Biecz 119
Spytko of Melsztyn (–1352), Castellan of Cracow 113
Stablewski Florian (1841–1906), Archbishop 489
Stackelberg Otto Magnus von (1736–1800) 283, 284, 285, 306, 307
Stadion Franz (1803–1853) 418, 419
Stadnicki Stanisław (c. 1551–1610) 195
Staff Leopold (1878–1957) 501, 568
Stalingrad (battle of, 1942/3) 607
Stalmach Paweł (1824–1891) 458
St. Stanisław (–1079), Bishop of Cracow 65, 101, 104
Stanisław of Skalbmierz (–1431), professor 134
Stanisław I Leszczyński (1677–1766), King of Poland 199, 237, 238, 239, 243, 244, 250, 263, 264
Stanisław Augustus Poniatowski (1732–

1798), King of Poland 234, 269–277, 279, 282, 284, 285, 286, 288, 290, 292, 297, 298–300, 302, 303, 305, 306, 307, 309, 310, 316, 317, 318, 319, 321–324, 332, 333, 334
Stanisławski Jan (1860–1907) 504
Stańczyk 464, 517
"Stańczyk" group 470, 494, 501
Stapiński Jan (1867–1946) 494, 517
starosta, starostwa 86, 92, 108, 126, 132, 154, 159, 167, 191, 195, 197, 269, 308, 319, 339
Starowolski Szymon (1588–1656) 198, 231
Starża (Polish noble clan) 90
Staszic Stanisław (1755–1826) 310, 311, 312, 345, 354, 370
State Council 348, 353, 437
State Defence Council 551
State Tribunal 584
Statorius Piotr (–1591) 172
Stefanowicz (17th cent.) 230
Stein Heinrich Karl (1757–1831) 361
Stefański Walenty (1813–1877) 407, 409, 415
Steinhaus Hugo (1887) 568
Steinkeller Piotr (1799–1854) 394
Stempkowski Józef (–1790) 278
Stephen Batory (1533–1586), King of Poland 156, 167, 169, 170, 179, 181, 187, 188, 195, 236
Stephen III (–1504), Great Prince of Moldavia 122, 148
Stern Anatol (1899) 571
Sterne Laurence (1713–1768) 378
Stochód 525
Stockholm 212, 215
Stojałowski Stanisław (1845–1911) 479, 493
Stolzman Karol (1793–1854) 401
Stołowicze (battle of, 1771) 279
Stralsund 125
Strojnowski Hieronim (1752–1815) 302
Strug Andrzej (Gałecki Tadeusz) (1871–1937) 570
Stryjeńska Zofia (1894–) 576
Strzelno 105
Strzemiński Władysław (1893–1952) 576
Stürmer Borys (1848–1917) 528
Styr 525
suburbia 60, 72, 85, 87, 88
Suchorzewski Jan (2nd half of the 18th cent.) 315

Sudeten 25, 28, 33, 361, 393, 600
Sudetenland 600
Sudovia, Jaćwież, Sudovians 31, 37, 48, 56, 93, 94
Sulejów 106
Sulejówek 577, 578
Suła see Lambert II
Sułkowski Józef (1768–1798) 344
Supreme Council 551, 555 see Council of Ambassadors
Supreme Council of Wilno (1794) 327
Supreme National Committee (Naczelny Komitet Narodowy, NKN, 1914) 522–525, 579
Supreme National Council (1794) 325, 327, 332
Supreme Polish Military Committee (1917) 530
Suvorov Alexandr (1729–1800) 278, 331, 332
Suwałki 379, 549
Svatopolk (978/9–1019), Grand Duke of Kiev 55
Svatopolk-Mirski Petr (1857–1914) 510
Swabia 77
Swarog-Swarożyc 43
Sweden, Swedes 51, 77, 101, 157, 183, 184, 186, 190, 200, 204, 206, 211, 214, 215, 216, 217, 218, 222, 224, 236, 237, 238, 239, 242, 243, 244, 275, 306, 316
Sweyn Forkbeard (964/5–1014), King of Denmark 51
Switzerland, Swiss 107, 263, 400, 491, 524, 599
symbolism 504
Syrkus Helena (1900) 576
Syrkus Szymon (1893–1964) 576
Syrokomla Władysław (Kondratowicz Ludwik) (1823–1862) 428
Szachowski Stanisław (1843–1906) 438
Szafranek Józef (1804–1874) 417
Szafraniec Stanisław (–1598) 161
Szanajca Józef (1902–1939) 576
Szaniawski Jerzy (1886–1970) 571
Szaniawski Józef Kalasanty (1765–1843) 329, 342, 356
Szaniecki Jan Olrych (1783–1840) 387
Szarffenberg Maciej (–1547) 173
Szarffenberg Marek (–1545) 173
Szczebrzeszyn 230
Szczecin 50, 59, 66, 76, 85, 87, 92, 125, 157, 217, 252

Szczekociny (battle of, 1794) 330
Szczuka Mieczysław (1898–1927) 576
Szela Jakub (1787–1866) 412
Szeligowski Tadeusz (1896–1963) 575
Szeptycki Stanisław (1867–1956) 577
Szermentowski Józef (1833–1876) 430
Szreder Jakub (–1853) 376
Sztumska Wieś, Stumsdorf (truce of, 1636) 204, 215
Szujski Józef (1835–1883) 470
Szydłowiec 174
Szydłowiecki family 174
Szymanowski Karol (1882–1937) 504, 576
Szymonowic Szymon (1558–1629) 175, 229

Ściegienny Piotr (1800–1890) 407
Ślęzanie, Sleenzani 40
Ślęża — Sobótka 28, 44, 78
Śliwicki Piotr (–1862) 439
Śmiglecki Marcin (1564–1618) 198
Śniadecki Jan (1756–1830) 302, 345
Śniadecki Jędrzej (1768–1838) 345
Śniatyń 149
Środa 85, 124, 417 see Law
Świdnica 126
Świdrygiełło, Svitrigailas (–1452), Grand Duke of Lithuania 119
Święca (Polish noble clan) 101
Świeżyński Józef (1868–1948) 536, 537, 538
Świętochowski Aleksander (1849–1938) 466, 471
Świętokrzyskie Mountains 30, 72, 263
Świętosława see Sigrid Storrada
Świętosławski Wojciech (1881–1968) 568
Święty Krzyż (Holy Cross) see Świętokrzyskie Mountains
Świniarski Michał (1740–1793) 315
Świtalski Kazimierz (1886–1962) 585

Taborites 118
Talleyrand Périgord Charles Maurice (1754–1838) 364
Tamerlane (c. 1336–1405), Mongol Conqueror 116
Targowica see Confederation of Targowica
Tarnogród see Confederation of Tarnogród
Tarnopol 355
Tarnowski Jan (1488–1561) 149
Tarnowski family 174
Tarnowski Zdzisław (1862–1937) 580
Tarnów 112, 136, 174 see Leliwa family
Tartars 19, 113, 116, 122, 148, 157, 167, 206, 208, 211, 214, 221, 227, 238, 248, 293, 411
Taszycki Gabriel (1755–1809) 329
Tatra 280
Tchernyshewski Nicolas (1828–1889) 434
Tczew 86
Templars 93, 126
Temporary National Government (1863) 441 (see Peasants) 443, 521
Teodor (12th/13th cent.), Palatine of Cracow 90
Terespol 464
Tetmajer-Przerwa Kazimierz (1865–1940) 501
Teutonic Knights 85, 88, 93, 94, 95, 101, 108, 111, 116, 121, 146, 147, 156, 176, 253
Teutonic Prussia see Mazuria
Tęczyn 112, 174 see Topors
Tęczyński family 174
Thietmar (975–1018), Bishop of Merseburg 44
Thomas II (–1292), Bishop of Wrocław 90
Tiedemann-Seeheim Heinrich (1843–1927) 496
Tilsit (secret parleys of, 1807) 348, 356
Tobruk (battle of, 1940–1942) 606
Tochtamish (14th cent.), Tartar Khan 116
Toeplitz Jerzy (1909) 575
Tokyo 506
Tołwiński Tadeusz (1888–1951) 576
Tomaszów 369
Tomicki Jan (c. 1510–1575) 163
Topors (Polish noble clan) 112
Toruń 84, 87, 88, 95, 106, 121, 133, 135, 136, 153, 174, 196, 228, 233, 254, 275, 306, 308, 321, 364, 478
Towiański Andrzej (1799–1898) 425
Transylvania 190, 200, 211, 213, 216, 236
Traugutt Romuald (1826–1864) 445
Trąmpczyński Wojciech (1860–1953) 547, 559
Trebbia (battle of, 1799) 344
Trembecki Stanisław (c. 1740–1812) 300
Trent (Council of, 1545–1563) 197
Trentowski Bronisław (1808–1869) 425
Trepov Alexandr (1862–1928) 528
Tretyakov Siergiej (1892–1939) 573
Trębicki Antoni (1764–1834) 313
Troki 115 see Kiejstut
Truso–Drużno 37
Trzebnica 88, 106
Trzecieski Andrzej (16th cent.) 172

Trzemeszno 63, 77, 79
Tukhachevsky Michail (1893–1937) 551
Turkey, Turks 107, 120, 122, 132, 148, 149, 169, 175, 181, 183, 188, 189, 190, 197, 206, 214, 220, 221, 222, 223, 224, 227, 237, 238, 242, 243, 244–247, 251, 257, 268, 271, 277, 278, 289, 305, 306, 323, 331, 337, 341, 404, 422, 465, 513
Tuwim Julian (1894–1953) 571
Twardowski Kazimierz (1866–1938) 568
Twardowski Samuel (–1661) 229
Tylkowski Wojciech (c. 1629–1695) 232
Tylman de Gameren (c. 1632–1706) 231
Tymawa 94 see Calatrava Order
Tyniec 77, 79
Tyssowski Jan (1817–1857) 410, 411
Tyszowce 216
Tyzenhaus Antoni (1733–1785) 289

St. Udalrich (10th cent.), Bishop of Augsburg 50
Ujejski Kornel (1823–1897) 428
ukase of the Tsar (1864) see Peasants
Ukraine, Ukrainians 19, 21, 115, 188, 191, 192, 195, 200, 206, 208, 213, 214, 217, 223, 232, 234, 238, 246, 248, 255, 277, 278, 289, 290, 293, 294, 306, 308, 331, 339, 340, 357, 373, 377, 378, 385, 391, 402, 405, 419, 437, 451, 454, 461, 462, 548, 550, 558, 563, 564, 585, 586, 592, 596, 598, 601
Ukrainian Military Organization 563
Ukrainian National Democracy 518
Ukrainian Nationalist Organization (OUN) 585
Ukrainian Nationalist Party 563
Ukrainian Social-Democratic Party 518
Ungler Florian (–1543) 173, 174
Uniates 254, 255, 391, 455, 510
Uniłowski Zbigniew (1909–1937) 570
Union of Free Poles (1820) 375
Union of the Plebeians, "Plebeians" 407, 409, 413
Union of Polish Cooperatives 490
Union of Polish Socialists Abroad 488
Union of Polish Youth ("Zet") 508, 516
Union of Primary School Teachers 510
Union of Rural Youth "Wici" (The Messengers) 595
Union of Socialist Youth 508
United Front 595, 596
United Provinces see Netherlands

United Slavs Society 377
United States of America 279, 315, 323, 324, 498, 524, 531, 607
University of
  Cracow 117, 133, 136, 172, 174, 175, 231, 252, 264, 265, 302, 310, 378, 405, 567
  Greifswald 125
  Lublin 567
  Lwów 470, 517, 567
  Paris 117, 133
  Poznań 567
  Prague 133, 563
  Warsaw, Main School 375, 378, 439, 454, 463, 466, 467
  Wilno 231, 302, 345, 375, 378, 379, 567
U.S.S.R. see Russia
Uznam, Usedom 66, 67

Valachia 116, 188, 232, 280
Valdensians 104
Varangians 56
Varna (battle of, 1444) 120, 189
Vasas 180, 215, 231, 236
Vatican see Papacy
Veleti 31, 49, 50, 51, 52, 64
Velikye Luki 169
Venice 208, 221
Venceslaus see Wacław II
Verdun (battle of, 1916) 527
Versailles 258, 272, 402, 406, 408
— treaty of (1919) 549, 565, 605
Vevey 524
Vienna 29, 149, 189, 212, 219, 221, 242, 280, 364, 369, 373, 377, 380, 388, 392, 394, 396, 413, 418, 419, 421, 433, 444, 460–463, 464, 473, 479, 512, 517, 530, 534, 553, 563,
— Congress of (1815) 362, 363, 380
viritim (principle of election) see Parliament
Vislanes, Wiślanie 40, 50
Vistula 17, 28, 29, 31, 32, 37, 40, 43, 45, 48, 60, 62, 87, 88, 91, 93, 101, 153, 190, 214, 244, 288, 322, 332, 333, 346, 354, 358, 363, 368, 381, 384, 385, 388, 397, 450, 464, 523, 607
Vitelo (13th cent.), astronomer 103
Volhynia 112, 113, 158, 191, 345, 464, 527, 552, 558, 563, 586, 599
Voloshyn August (1874) 601
Voltaire François-Marie Arouet (1694–1778) 373

Vorskla (defeat of, 1399) 116
Vota Maurizio Carlo (1629–1715) 226
voting system *see* Parliament

Wacław, Venceslaus, II (1271–1305), King of Bohemia, Poland and Hungary 98, 99, 108
Wacław III (1289–1306), King of Bohemia, Poland and Hungary 99
Wagram (battle of, 1809) 355
Waliszewski Zygmunt (1897–1936) 576
Walloons 79, 83, 84
Walter (–1169), Bishop of Wrocław 78
Wapowski Bernard (c. 1450–1535) 173, 176
Warcisław I (c. 1147), Duke of Western Pomerania 67, 89
Wargocki Andrzej (16th/17th cent.) 201
Warmia 121, 158, 216, 397, 457, 498, 552, 555, 608
Warsaw 94, 132, 153, 157, 158, 161, 196, 206, 215, 216, 225, 230, 231, 235, 236, 237, 241, 256, 257, 263, 264, 271, 275, 276, 278, 280, 287, 289, 292, 295, 297, 300, 305, 307, 308, 309, 310, 315, 318, 323, 324, 327, 328, 331, 332, 333, 347–350, 352–355, 357, 358, 363, 364, 369–372, 374, 375, 377–387, 389, 391–394, 397, 398, 406, 407, 415, 416, 426–430, 433–440, 443, 445, 464, 466, 468, 474, 475, 476, 484–487, 492, 493, 500–504, 506, 508, 521, 525, 527, 528, 531, 533, 538, 543, 545, 547, 550–552, 566, 568, 576–578, 589, 593, 599, 601, 602, 606, 607
— Duchy of 338, 344, 348, 350, 351–356, 361, 362, 364, 446
— Conservatory 576
— Hausing Cooperative 576
— Society of the Friends of Science 345
— Soldiers' Council 538
Warski Adolf (1868–1937) 564
Warszewicki Krzysztof (1543–1603) 185
Warta 41, 44, 51, 60, 95, 126, 322, 348
Waryński Ludwik (1856–1889) 474–478
Wasilewska Wanda (1905–1964) 570
Wasilewski Leon (1870–1936) 512
Wasilewski Gustaw (1839–1863) 438
Wawel 60, 64, 78, 106, 136, 174, 175, 258, 593
Wawer (battle of, 1831) 384
Wawrzecki Tomasz (1753–1816) 332
Ważyk Adam (1905) 571

Wąchock 106
Weigl Rudolf (1883–1957) 568
Wejherowo 498
Welawa 216, 220
Wends, Veneti 25, 28, 29
Western Powers 535, 549, 555, 566, 588, 589, 599, 602, 603
Westerplatte 589
Westphalia 217, 489
Wettins 236, 237, 242, 266, 268, 270
Weygand Maxime (1867–1967) 551, 577
Weyssenhoff Józef (1860–1932) 502
Węgierski Kajetan (1775–1787) 300
Węgrów 179
White Party, Whites 438, 439, 441–444, 459
Widukind (–1004) Saxon chronicler 50
wiec 38
Wielhorski Michał (–1790) 298
Wieliczka 127, 197
Wielopolski Aleksander (1803–1887) 412, 437, 439, 440, 445, 491, 512
Wielopolski Jan (–1688) 218
Wielopolski Zygmunt (1833–1902) 491
Więckowski Aleksander (1854–1920) 474
Wieluń 118
Wieprz 48, 55, 551
Wierzyński Kazimierz (1894–1969) 571
Wietor Hieronim (–1536) 173
Wilanów 578
Wild Plains 188, 248
Wilhelm (1370–1406) Prince of Austria 114
William of Holland (c. 1227–1256) King of Germany 93
William I (1797–1888), King of Prussia, German Emperor 435, 483
William II (1859–1941), King of Prussia, German Emperor 527
Willisen Wilhelm (1790–1879) 415
Wilno 119, 136, 150, 230, 324, 327, 331, 345, 357, 375, 378, 391, 406, 453, 488, 519, 531, 550, 552, 566
— Academy *see* University of Wilno
— Jesuit Academy *see* Jesuits
Wilson Thomas Woodrow (1856–1924) 528, 529, 534–536
Wincenty Kadłubek (c. 1160–1223), Bishop of Cracow 102
Wincenty of Kielce (13th cent.), hagiographer 102
Wiszowaty Andrzej (1608–1678) 233
Wiślica 60, 69, 124, 136, 185

Wiśnicz 174
Wiśniowiecki Jarema (1612–1651) 192, 212, 213, 220
Wiśniowiecki family 184, 192
Wit Stosz, Stwosz (c. 1445–1533), sculptor 136
Witkiewicz Stanisław Ignacy (Witkacy) (1885–1939) 570
Witold, Vytautas (1350–1430), Grand Duke of Lithuania 116, 117, 118
Witos Wincenty (1874–1945) 517, 536, 537, 547, 551, 558, 560, 577, 585, 595, 597
Witte Serghei (1849–1915) 505, 512
Wittig Edward (1879–1941) 576
Władysław I Herman (1040–1102), Duke of Poland 65, 66
Władysław II the Exile (1105–1159), Grand Duke of Poland 68, 69, 77, 90
Władysław I the Short (c. 1260–1333), King of Poland 91, 98, 99, 101, 108, 111, 112, 114, 124
Władysław II Jagiełło (c. 1351–1434), Grand Duke of Lithuania, King of Poland 115, 116, 117, 118, 119, 135, 136
Władysław III (1424–1444), King of Poland and Hungary 119, 120
Władysław IV Vasa (1595–1648), King of Poland 180, 186, 188, 200, 203, 204, 206, 208, 213
Władysław Spindleshanks (c. 1165–1231), Duke of Great Poland 89, 90, 91
Władysław, son of Odo (c. 1190–1239), Duke of Great Poland 90
Władysław the White (–1388), Duke of Kujawy 114
Władysław (–1401), Duke of Opole 114
Władysław II (1456–1516), King of Bohemia and Hungary 119, 122, 126, 148
Władysławowo 204
Włocławek, Włodzisław 60, 68, 79
Włodzimierz, Vladimir 112, 113
Wohl Stanisław (1913) 575
Wojciech of Brudzewo (1446–1495), professor 134
Wojciechowski Stanisław (1869–1953) 513, 559, 578
Wojciechowski Zygmunt (1900–1955) 568
Wojniakowski Kazimierz (1772–1812) 299
Wolborz 91
Wolfowicz Szymel (2nd half of the 18th cent.) 315
Wolin 50, 59, 66, 67

Wolinianie, Velunzani 40
Wołczyn 232
Wołogoszcz, Wolgast 92
Worcell Stanisław (1799–1857) 403, 434
Workers University Society 567
working-class movement 449, 473, 476, 478, 482, 487, 488, 500, 515
— eight-hour day 546, 548
Wrocław 30, 31, 52, 60, 62, 65, 66, 68, 76, 78, 79, 83, 85, 86, 87, 88, 89, 90, 98, 99, 102, 104, 105, 106, 126, 129, 131, 135, 168, 252, 360, 393, 394, 417, 474, 516
Wróblewski Walery (1836–1908) 451
Wróblewski Zygmunt (1845–1888) 470
Września (affair of, 1901) 495
Wschowa 253
Wszebor, Palatine 68
Wulfstan (9th cent.), traveller 37
Wybicki Józef (1747–1822) 284, 343, 346
Wyczółkowski Leon (1852–1936) 504
Wyhowski Jan (–1664) 217
Wysłouch Bolesław (1855–1937) 493
Wysocki Józef (1809–1873) 421
Wysocki Piotr (1799–1875) 380
Wyspiański Stanisław (1869–1907) 501–504

Xavier, son of Augustus III (1730–1806) 270

Yam Zapolsky 169
Yaroslav (c. 980–1054), Grand Duke of Kiev 57
Yermak (–1585) 168
"Young Germany" 400
"Young Italy" 400
"Young Poland" 401, 405
"Young Poland" 500–504, 570, 571

Zabiełło Józef (–1794) 327
Zabłocki Franciszek (1750–1821) 300, 315
Zagórski Jerzy (1907) 571
Zagórski Włodzimierz (1882–1926) 582
Zahorowski Hieronim (1582–1634) 202
Zajączek Józef (1752–1826) 329, 332, 347, 356, 367
Zalewski August (1883) 578
Zaliwski Józef (1797–1855) 400, 405
Załuski Andrzej Stanisław (1695–1758) 263–265
Załuski Józef Andrzej (1701–1774) 264, 276
Załuski family 263

Zambocki Jan (-1529) 175
Zamość 196, 261
— Academy of 231
Zamoyski Andrzej (1716-1792) 274, 284, 289, 290, 302, 310
Zamoyski Andrzej (1800-1874) 395, 433, 436, 437, 440
Zamoyski August (1893) 576
Zamoyski Jan (1542-1605) 163, 167, 169, 170, 181, 188, 231
Zamoyski Maurycy (1871-1939) 559
Zamoyski Stanisław (1775-1856) 355
Zamoyski Family 196, 355, 393
Zan Tomasz (1796-1855) 375
Zaolzie 601
Zapolska Gabriela (1860-1921) 472
Zaporozhe 188, 207, 208
Zasławski Dominik (c. 1618-1656) 192
Zator 120
Zawady 47
Zawadzki Stanisław (1743-1806) 299
Zawichost 104, 106
Zawisza Czarny of Garbowo (-1424), Polish knight 117
Zawisza of Kurozwęki (-1382), Bishop of Cracow 114
Zbaraż 213
Zbigniew (-1112), Duke of Poland 66, 77
Zbigniew of Oleśnica (1389-1455), Bishop of Cracow 118, 119, 120
Zborowski Jan (-1605) 163
Zborowski Samuel (-1584) 169, 181
Zborów 196, 213

Zbruch 548, 550, 552
Zduńska Wola 369
Zebrzydowski Mikołaj (1553-1620) 181, 185, 186, 198
Zejssner Ludwik (1807-1871) 430
"Zemlya i Volya" (Land and Liberty) 439, 440
"Zentrum" 457, 458, 483, 496, 497
Zgierz 369, 476
Zhelezniak Maxim mid-18th cent.) 278
Zieleńce (battle of, 1792) 321
Ziembice 126
Złotoryja (in Auro) 85
Znaniecki Florian (1882-1958) 568
Zurich 559
"Związek Walki Czynnej" (Union of Active Struggle) 519, 539
Zwoleń 175
Zyndram-Kościałkowski Marian (1892-1946) 593, 595

Żak Eugeniusz (1884-1926) 576
Żeleński-Boy Tadeusz (1874-1941) 570, 571
Żeligowski Lucjan (1865-1946) 552, 578
Żeromski Stefan (1864-1925) 571
Żolibórz Housing Estate 576
Żółkiew 196
Żółkiewski Stanisław (1547-1620) 186, 189. 196
Żółte Wody (battle of, 1648) 208
Żórawno 220
Żyrardów 476, 593